A LIBRARY OF LITERARY CRITICISM

A LIBRARY

Frederick Ungar Publishing Co., New York

OF LITERARY CRITICISM

Modern Romance Literatures

Compiled and edited by

DOROTHY NYREN CURLEY

Chief Librarian, Northbrook Public Library
Northbrook, Illinois

ARTHUR CURLEY

Director, Palatine Public Library
Palatine, Illinois

FOREWORD

Readers in America today have manifested a considerable amount of interest in modern writers of France and Italy and to a lesser extent in those of Spain, Portugal and the other countries which speak in whole or in part a Romance dialect, Switzerland, Belgium, and Rumania.

This interest became especially noticeable after World War II when French Existentialism caught the attention of the younger generation everywhere and Italian Neo-Realism, as exported through the cinema, became a dominant world mood.

Dada, Surrealism, the New Novel, the philosophy of the absurd have all come from the Romance countries. Their influence is felt in America through the translations of Romance writings and through the works Americans themselves have subsequently produced.

This book is intended as a reference guide to the criticism of the more important European Romance writers whose works have become known in the United States and have become a part of our cultural life.

The authors have been chosen for inclusion both because of their intrinsic merit and because of the extent of American interest in them, the degree to which their work has been translated, and their presence in such general sources as *Twentieth Century Authors, The Concise Encyclopedia of Modern World Literature,* and *Reader's Advisor* as well as in more specialized critical compilations.

This volume treats of writers of the twentieth century and of a few who lived at the turn of the century and whose influence was more important after 1900 than before. There are, of course, authors who have only recently come to prominence in their own countries and who have had to be excluded from this reference source—intended for an English-speaking audience—because of the unavailability of their works in translation and the absence of a sufficient amount of critical commentary.

Critical materials excerpted in this guide come from both books and periodicals, chiefly from American and British sources, though occasionally from continental publications. All quotations have an exact citation which makes it possible for the reader to go to the original source and read more there, which the reader is urged to do.

A very selective list of works is appended to each section as suggested first readings and as a beginning list of acquisitions for libraries.

We wish to thank the many publishers who have been so generous and helpful in granting permission to use excerpts from their publications.

D.N.C.

A.C.

AUTHORS INCLUDED

Adamov, Arthur
Alain-Fournier
Alberti, Rafael
Alvarez Quintero, Joaquín
Alvarez Quintero, Serafín
Alvaro, Corrado
Anouilh, Jean
Apollinaire, Guillaume
Aragon, Louis
Artaud, Antonin
Aymé, Marcel
Azorín
Bacchelli, Riccardo
Baroja, Pío
Bassani, Giorgio
Beauvoir, Simone de
Beckett, Samuel
Benavente, Jacinto
Bernanos, Georges
Berto, Giuseppe
Betti, Ugo
Blasco-Ibáñez, Vicente
Brancati, Vitaliano
Breton, André
Butor, Michel
Calvino, Italo
Campana, Dino
Camus, Albert
Cassola, Carlo
Cayrol, Jean
Cela, Camilo José
Céline, Louis-Ferdinand
Cespedes, Alba de
Char, René
Claudel, Paul
Còccioli, Carlo
Cocteau, Jean
Colette
D'Annunzio, Gabriele
Del Castillo, Michel

Deledda, Grazia
Desnos, Robert
Duhamel, Georges
Dumitriu, Petru
Duras, Marguerite
Dutourd, Jean
Echegaray, José
Eluard, Paul
Espina de Serna, Concha
Ferreira de Castro, José Maria
Fogazzaro, Antonio
France, Anatole
Gadda, Carlo Emilio
García Lorca, Federico
Gary, Romain
Gascar, Pierre
Genet, Jean
Ghelderode, Michel de
Gide, André
Ginzburg, Natalia
Giono, Jean
Giraudoux, Jean
Gironella, José María
Gómez de la Serna, Ramón
Gourmont, Rémy de
Goytisolo, Juan
Gracq, Julien
Green, Julian
Guareschi, Giovanni
Guillén, Jorge
Huysmans, Joris-Karl
Ionesco, Eugène
Jacob, Max
Jammes, Francis
Jarry, Alfred
Jiménez, Juan Ramón
Lampedusa, Giuseppe di
Landolfi, Tommaso
Levi, Carlo
Machado, Antonio

Maeterlinck, Maurice
Malaparte, Curzio
Mallarmé, Stéphane
Mallet-Joris, Françoise
Malraux, André
Maraini, Dacia
Martin du Gard, Roger
Martínez Sierra, Gregorio
Matute, Ana María
Mauriac, Claude
Mauriac, François
Michaux, Henri
Miró, Gabriel
Mistral, Frédéric
Montale, Eugenio
Montherlant, Henry de
Morante, Elsa
Moravia, Alberto
Ortega y Gasset, José
Otero, Blas de
Palacio Valdés, Armando
Palazzeschi, Aldo
Pardo Bazán, Emilia
Pasinetti, Pier Maria
Pavese, Cesare
Péguy, Charles Pierre
Pérez de Ayala, Ramón
Pérez Galdós, Benito
Perse, St.-John
Pirandello, Luigi
Ponge, Francis
Pratolini, Vasco
Proust, Marcel
Quasimodo, Salvatore

Queneau, Raymond
Radiguet, Raymond
Ramuz, Charles Ferdinand
Reverdy, Pierre
Ribeiro, Aquilino
Rimbaud, Arthur
Robbe-Grillet, Alain
Rolland, Romain
Romains, Jules
Rostand, Edmond
Saba, Umberto
Sagan, Françoise
Saint Exupéry, Antoine de
Salinas, Pedro
Sarraute, Nathalie
Sartre, Jean-Paul
Sender, Ramón
Silone, Ignazio
Simenon, Georges
Simon, Claude
Soldati, Mario
Soupault, Philippe
Svevo, Italo
Unamuno, Miguel de
Ungaretti, Giuseppe
Valéry, Paul
Valle-Inclán, Ramón del
Vercors
Verga, Giovanni
Verhaeren, Emile
Verlaine, Paul
Vittorini, Elio
Volponi, Paolo
Weil, Simone

PERIODICALS REPRESENTED

Where no abbreviation is indicated, the magazine references are listed in full.

	Accent	*HorizonL*	Horizon (London)
Ams	Américas	*HR*	Hopkins Review
AS	American Scholar	*Hsp*	Hispania
At	Atlantic	*HspR*	Hispanic Review
BA	Books Abroad	*Ind*	Independent
BHS	Bulletin of Hispanic	*IQ*	Italian Quarterly
	Studies	*Ital*	Italica
Bkm	Bookman	*KR*	Kenyon Review
BkmL	Bookman (London)	*LA*	Living Age
CC	Christian Century	*LJ*	Library Journal
ChR	Chicago Review	*LLT*	Life and Letters Today
CL	Comparative Literature	*LM*	London Mercury
CM	Carleton Miscellany	*LMg*	London Magazine
Cmty	Commentary	*MD*	Modern Drama
Com	Commonweal	*MF*	Mercure de France
Corn	Cornhill Magazine	*MG*	Manchester Guardian
Cq	Critique	*Mjn*	Meanjin Quarterly
	Critic	*MLJ*	Modern Language Journal
CR	Contemporary Review	*MLN*	Modern Language Notes
CSM	Christian Science Monitor	*MLQ*	Modern Language
Csmp	Cosmopolitan		Quarterly
CT	Chicago Tribune Book	*MLR*	Modern Language Review
	Section	*MR*	Massachusetts Review
	Dial	*NAR*	North American Review
DR	Dublin Review	*NaRL*	National Review of
DS	Drama Survey		Literature
EdR	Edinburgh Review		Nation
EM	English Miscellany		
Enc	Encounter	*NationL*	Nation (London)
Eng	English Review	*NC*	Nineteenth Century
FR	French Review	*NL*	New Leader
FS	French Studies	*NMQ*	New Mexico Quarterly
Ftn	Fortnightly Review	*NO*	New Outlook
FW	Free World	*NR*	New Republic
	Harper	*NRF*	Nouvelle Revue Française
HdR	Hudson Review	*NSN*	New Statesman and Nation
	Horizon	*NY*	New Yorker

NYEP	New York Evening Post Book Section	*RR*	Romanic Review
NYHT	New York Herald Tribune Book Section	*SAQ*	South Atlantic Quarterly
		SoR	Southern Review
NYR	New York Review of Books	*Spec*	Spectator
NYT	New York Times Book Section	*SR*	Saturday Review
		SSR	Sociology and Social Research
NYTd	New York Times (daily)	*SwR*	Sewanee Review
NWW	New World Writing	*Sym*	Symposium
O	Outlook	*TA*	Theatre Arts
PMLA	Publications of the Modern Language Association	*TC*	Twentieth Century
		TDR	Tulane Drama Review
	Poetry	*TT*	Time and Tide
PR	Partisan Review	*UNM*	University of New Mexico Bulletin
QRL	Quarterly Review of Literature	*UTB*	University of Texas Bulletin
	Reporter		Voices
RGB	Revue Generale Belge	*WHR*	Western Humanities Review
RLM	Revue des Lettres Modernes	*WR*	Western Review
RMS	Renaissance and Modern Studies	*YFS*	Yale French Studies
		YR	Yale Review

ADAMOV, ARTHUR (1908–   )

All of Adamov's plays to date rest upon the author's poignant apprehension of man's solitude and on his deep-seated feeling that "whatever he undertakes, man runs head on into the impossible," that "there is . . . no remedy for anything except for bagatelles." But the *word* "solitude" is never spoken in the plays, there are no disquisitions on metaphysics, no discursive conclusions. Everything is directly rendered in movement, gesture, sounds, objects, and in words which, as in our own lives, are but imperfect vehicles for communication. These things fill the physical space of the theatre and are grasped by the spectator through his "histrionic sensibility" and his imagination; they operate simultaneously to produce an autonomous *"univers crée"* which has the immediacy of plastic forms or of music.

Carlos Lynes, Jr. YFS. Winter, 1954–5. pp. 54–5

Arthur Adamov's plotless theater presents an appearance similar to that of Ionesco. However, his theater is more successful than Ionesco's to the extent that the latter's anger—what Saurel calls his "guilt"—is replaced in Adamov by anxiety. . . . The meaningless puns and nonsense that absurdly reflect the absurd in Ionesco, the systematic debasing of the individual, all this is generally absent from Adamov's plays. These undertake the more difficult task of rendering that absurd through the substance rather than through the form of the play, or, more precisely (for this disciple of Artaud), in rendering the dream that informs an idea of cruelty and of fright.

David I. Grossvogel. The Self-Conscious Stage in
Modern French Drama (Columbia). 1958. pp. 318–9

His twelve or so plays, published in France by Gallimard, but not yet in English translations, toy with techniques and dramatic progressions that yield all kinds of fruitful developments and promise even more for the future. His dialogue is not a split-up monologue, as it is in the bulk of modern naturalistic plays, not a "message" propounded by one wise and insufferable character and pushed forward by prompt lines from others. Adamov's characters lead their own lives, talk their own thoughts. Their speeches impinge on each other and glance away. Usually it is hard to detect a central theme; the scenes hop about in suddenly different directions, throwing off many ideas. Later in the play each idea is subtly recaptured and made to work for the overall impact—a welcome change from the "planted" line and heavy-handed cross-reference of today's "well-fashioned" drama.

Albert Bermel. *TDR*. Sept., 1959. p. 105

Adamov builds his theater around personal dreams. . . . But Adamov's dreams can be termed realistic, for the framework, objects, and characters belong to the writer's everyday universe. His dreams are merely rearrangements of the elements, a new logic imposed on the relations of people among themselves, an order and a causality sometimes normal and sometimes absurd in the eyes of someone awake. The nonsense appears only in the sequence of events. Beyond the impression of nightmare, yet because of it, the spectator—who has not been enchanted by any great display of fantasy—meets with an impression which reflects on the normal world: that of the instability of the real, the possibility of ordinary things taking unforeseeable directions with the same apparent necessity as that we generally accord them—and the resulting terror.

Jacques Guicharnaud. *Modern French Theatre* (Yale).
1961. p. 172

Slight, dark, with piercing, probing eyes in a saturnine face, no longer a ragged figure roaming Paris in abject poverty but still preferring to live in a small Left Bank hotel and holding court in his favorite *tabac* on the Boulevard Saint-Germain, Adamov has become the main spokesman of the committed, political theatre in France. At the same time, he is regarded as one of the masters of a noncommitted, anti-political theatre of the soul. Like one of his characters, he is the embodiment of two conflicting tendencies coexisting within the same person.

Martin Esslin. *The Theatre of the Absurd* (Doubleday).
1961. pp. 77–8

A play of Adamov must be seen to be appreciated, for the text is only a scenario, describing in rather great detail the physical movement that is to take place, and will constitute the major impact and the principal means of communicating with the audience. Dialogue has been reduced to dry and frequently dull platitudes without any of the humor or verve of Ionesco, or the naked, suggestive poetry of Beckett. The characters are often ciphers, represented by letters . . . or by generic names. . . . It is only with difficulty that we become involved in their plight, for they are rarely alive enough to elicit pity or sympathy.

The treatment is episodic rather than linear, and we must sometimes follow many characters with various symbolic values through a series of short tableaux with little apparent connection.

Leonard Cabell Pronko. Avant-Garde (California).
1962. p. 133

His sickness is related to the "mystery of sex." Specifically, Adamov, in "*L'Aveu*," feels a need to be humiliated by women who represent "the Other," the contrary of himself. . . . In Adamov's self-exorcism he must plumb his own depths in order to find the meaning or the sense of his separation. . . . In this process woman becomes the agent of self-investigation, and, as such, woman symbolizes both the attraction of death (with attendant fears of castration) and the possibilities of renewal.

Richard E. Sherrell. MD. Feb., 1965. pp. 400–401

See *Ping-Pong* (play).

ALAIN-FOURNIER (1886–1914)

Now and again—it is not often—a book appears which has about it a quality of magic. *The Golden Age* and *Green Mansions* are examples. They are fairy tales in the truest sense. And though their people are ghosts, and we do not believe in them, they speak with authority to whatever of our childhood still remains in our educated bosoms, so that to read them is both a pain and a delight. *The Wanderer* is of that same quality. . . . It comes dangerously near the life of common day at times, and at others trails more than a suggestion of the dark romantic gloom which covers *Wuthering Heights*. But on the whole it must be admitted to that jealously guarded land of the fairy tale for grown-ups: and where is the blackguard who will criticize it?

T. S. Matthews. NR. Feb. 13, 1929. p. 357

Fournier does not give a dazzling vision of the world; he does not describe it; he does not transcend it from such a height that he seems to create it entirely himself. He gives us a sense of it. He has a feeling for, a comprehension of it, and carries in himself a sense of the earth, its forms, its colors and its sounds. He recreates them, not in an immediate and clearly defined way, but as they are after being a long time in him, with their legends, their relationships, and the appearance that they have slowly assumed, shrouded, cooled, elaborated, born from the intimate union of things and the soul.

Marcel Arland. NRF. Nov. 1, 1938. p. 824.
Tr. by Dorothy Nyren Curley

Fournier's predicament was to be peculiarly susceptible to the dynamic and disruptive element in any human enterprise or relationship. Departure is the essence of his novel. . . . What gives Fournier's predicament its poignancy is that though he felt departure to be his destiny, he was so aware of all he was leaving. . . . It was at a harrowing price to himself that he played his part: of asserting, not that human happiness is illusory, but that it only lasts in so far as it is more than pleasure or content; that it is not only a refuge, but also a point of departure; that even the unbelievably happy ending must always be a new beginning.

Janet Adam Smith. NSN. June 27, 1953. pp. 780–1

Thought, for Fournier, is not limited to the faculty which permits man to attain scientific or pseudoscientific truth. It is the total psychological activity which permits him to progress toward a personal truth, that is, an adequate interpretation of his experience. Dream enters into this definition of thought, especially since Fournier has taken care to define it as a "vision of the past." He is always afraid of losing the substance of his experience through an abstract interpretation.

Robert Champigny. Portrait of a Symbolist Hero
(Indiana). 1954. p. 11

The first fact to note . . . is the strong link which binds Le Grand Meaulnes to his own interior drama, or, if one prefers, the importance of his work—which is not just a semblance or echo of his personal drama—is related to the depths of this drama by right of its being a component part, a source, and a resolution. Far from being only a game for which he made the prizes and rules, it is the stuff and plan of his existence. His life follows his work, as much as and perhaps more than his work follows this inner life. One could not conceive of one independent of the other. They are indeed two forms of one reality.

Clément Borgal. Alain-Fournier (Editions Universitaires).
1955. p. 109. Tr. by Dorothy Nyren Curley

Le Grand Meaulnes is an exploration of that fleeting period of life, perhaps unsensed by many, between the end of youth and the beginning of full manhood, when life itself is a mingling of dream and reality, love, adventure and chivalry. It is a time radiant with the promise of supreme earthly happiness, when youth still seeks a shrine at which to worship, or a cause for which to die, and it is fired with the longing for perfection and the Absolute. At no other period in life is love so non-possessive, belief in happiness so powerful, purity for its own sake so precious, faith in one's ideals so deep and strong. For a bitter-sweet while, the vision lasts and then, either because of the betrayal of one's ideals, or simply because the problems of Life are replaced by the problems of living, the spell is broken, and only regrets remain.

It was this cherished vision of youth, this intangible sense of exceptional powers that Alain-Fournier struggled to retain, and the loss of which he feared so much.

Robert Gibson. *The Quest of Alain-Fournier*
(Hamish Hamilton). 1953. p. 271

What he has done is to write perhaps the last novel of idyllic love which is likely to have universal appeal. Within a few years of its publication the terms of romance were already different. . . . No doubt the concepts of peasant life in the Sologne, of lost domains, and impossibly tormented lovers, are by now too far from experience ever to be revived. The motor-car and the telephone, *Paris-Match* and the television screen have so buried a not-so-distant past that the symbols of *Le Grand Meaulnes* seem much cruder than they were even a generation ago. But the aspirations of the lover change only on the surface. And so, while we may laugh a little at the elucidation of all that so puzzled Meaulnes at first, we can still easily share in his enchantment.

Alan Pryce-Jones. Introduction to *The Lost Domain*
(Oxford). 1959. pp. xvii–xviii

To characterize the language of Alain-Fournier, let us make a comparison which he himself risked: one with Debussy. . . . What he loves are harmonies which begin to dissolve: sorts of half-hearings, of attempted arpeggios, of vague polyphonies. And these harmonies create the tonality of chapters. No novelist possessed to this degree the gift of opening a story as a musician introduces a harmony of tonality. The wind, the rain, warmth, the sun make up his scale in a minor key.

Fernand Desonay. *Le Grand Meaulnes d'Alain-Fournier*
(A.-G. Nizet). 1963. pp. 199–200.
Tr. by Dorothy Nyren Curley

Henri Alain-Fournier not only accounted the world well lost for love (his youth is a chronicle of failed examinations) but considered love well lost for art. He stumbled on the same vision of the lost paradise as Proust but while Proust devoted his imagination and intelligence over many years to digesting the honey-dew through Bergsonian philosophy, Alain-Fournier was more robust and at the same time more mystical. He was determined to create a magical world that was only just around the corner, plausible in space and time. His world . . . is a world of symbolism suddenly immersed under a cold douche of reality and emerging strengthened, as in the work of his two contemporaries, Eliot and Kafka, a closed ingrowing vision.

Cyril Connolly. *Previous Convictions*
(Hamish Hamilton). 1963. p. 214

See *The Wanderer* (novel).

ALBERTI, RAFAEL (1902–   )

Rafael Alberti is a great poet. He represents the sincere effort, quite successful in his case, of a bourgeois writer who has identified himself with the class struggle and who is enthusiastically helping the workers in their courageous fight. . . . [These poems] show the application of a highly sophisticated virtuosity (rich metaphors and images, complex vision, juxtaposition of lyrical planes) to present revolutionary conditions—a T. S. Eliot or a Hart Crane who had read with understanding the *Communist Manifesto*. . . . We find, above all, a keen satirist—the bourgeois poet evoking his bourgeois background and exposing its deadly elements and corruption. . . . Alberti has swayed the working class with poems in the traditional vein, reminiscent of popular ballads and folkpoems . . . and, then again, with poems in free verse, easy to grasp, convincing, robust. The toiling masses . . . have rightly appropriated them and recite or sing them throughout Spain. Alberti has become *the* Revolutionary Poet of Spain.

Angel Flores. Introduction to *A Spectre Is Haunting
Europe: Poems of Revolutionary Spain*
(Critics Group). 1936. pp. 10–11

With *Sobre los Angeles,* we reach the peak of Alberti's production, and enter into a new world. These poems are no more than earlier ones of a Surrealist nature the result of psychic dictation, although many of the images are automatic. Surrealism is utilized for artistic purposes. Alberti is incoherent only when it is logical to be incoherent. He does not delude himself as to the possibility of attaining to pure psychic dictation, and therefore rises above his medium. In the first half of *Sobre los Angeles,* the uncertain images, the volatile essence, and general vagueness belong to a tradition which goes back through Juan Ramón Jiménez to Bécquer. The realm is one half-way between the real and the unreal, recalling certain aspects of Cubism. Form is no longer of interest, and adapts itself to the inner rhythm of the poem. Sometimes it is regular; more usually it is irregular, with short lines in the aery first part of the book, and with long lines in the more dynamic second half. It is in *Sobre los*

Angeles that Alberti approaches nearest to pure poetry, and it is significant that he dedicates the book to Jorge Guillén.

Eric Proll. *BHS*. April, 1941. pp. 76–7

With *Marinero en tierra,* written in 1925, Rafael Alberti became the most accurate and most beloved disciple of Juan Ramón Jiménez. The Jiménez of *Piedra y cielo* felt himself rejuvenated and extended in the work of this young compatriot who had captured the popular feelings of both the Western and coastal regions of Andalusia, who gave them a new life in vigorous and icy expression. And it is curious to note here how this word "icy," as well as all others which express the idea of cold, may be found continually in Alberti's poetry. His poems seem to climb upwards until they become luminous and frozen, only to descend once more searching for the heat of a suffering blood-swept earth.

Alfredo de la Guardia. Introduction to *Selected Poems of Raphael Alberti* (New Directions). 1944. pp. 4–5

Through all the phases of his career, from early mariner songs, surrealism and satire to the mystically sentient elegies and war poems of his maturity, Alberti is an eclectic who stands solidly in a sphere of his own. He is the contemplative classic, the surveyor of the modern metaphysical. To say, however, that he is classic is not to imply that he is traditional or conservative. On the contrary, he seems to be experimenting continually. It is the purity of his approach to whatever he attempts that gives his poetry the sense of the classic. . . . It is inevitable to make some sort of comparison with García Lorca. . . . Alberti is more controlled, yet more individual, in his technique. His thought is rounded to include the entire poem. No one phrase or section is a key to its meaning. The poem itself is the image. Those who know Spain say these two poets, one impulsive and sensuous, the other subjectively wise, are complementary components of the Spanish character.

Ruth Stephan. *Poetry*. Dec., 1945. pp. 166–8

Just as Eliot in "The Waste Land" depicts the crisis of the modern spirit which has lost the dignity and style of the past, so Alberti is above all the poet of those who have been forced to recognize the imperfections of existence, but, instead of complaining about it, have decided to face it with courage and candour.

In *Sobre los Angeles* Alberti shows how an experience which might seem to be depressing and devitalising can be turned into the highest poetry. . . . Intellectual passion and passionate desire for the truth . . .

both makes his poetry relevant to the experience of other men and gives to it a strength which nothing can shake. In every poem we feel this solid foundation of fact, this determination to portray experience as it really is, and not to make any concessions to any romantic or sentimental outlooks. In this Alberti takes his place with the best poets of his time.

C. M. Bowra. *The Creative Experiment* (Macmillan).
1949. pp. 251–3

About the year 1929, Rafael Alberti was generally considered by Spanish critics to be the most promising poet of his generation . . . yet today there still exists no book of criticism dedicated to Alberti's work . . . and it is impossible to buy, officially, any of Alberti's post-1930 poetry in Spain. . . . Rather than to any influence of the censorship, however, the neglect of Alberti's later work by the Spanish critics seems to be due to a change in sensibility which dates from the end of the Civil War. . . . A new group arose, consisting mainly of poets writing on religious themes and in many cases returning to the Spanish Renaissance for their models. To those sympathetic towards the ideas of this group, Alberti's later poems would not appeal. The main accusations levelled against Alberti by the critics of the post-war period are that there is no real development or continuity in his work, that he is an expert imitator of the styles of earlier poets but has no real style of his own, and that whilst he can appear to show emotion in his poems, really he is a superficial, cold-blooded man who can imitate emotion without ever experiencing it.

G. W. Connell. *RMS*. 1959. pp. 95–6

No young poet of the Spanish Twenties exemplified the experimental, joyful quality of those years more than Rafael Alberti. He combined with rare skill the refinement of his elders (Juan Ramón Jiménez, for instance) and the simplicity of the traditional rhythms and themes. His direct, candid songs, set against a background of Spanish land and sea, couple with his glittering, Góngora-sounding sonnets to give Alberti's poetic voice an echo-like quality; but one feels an authenticity of emotion entirely his own. . . . Alberti's power of stylization, and hence of universalization, was the result of his fusion of the popular forms . . . with the *ultraístas'* method of unexpected juxtapositions. The *ultraísmo* current was at that time emphasizing the freedom of the poet as regards words and images, going against, in a sense, the deep-rooted Spanish feeling of the immutability of verbal entities and patterns. That Alberti should have been at the same time an obvious traditionalist (with his mastery of folk-song metrics) and a striking innovator is a clear indication of his originality.

S. S. Marichal. *The Poem Itself,* ed. by
Stanley Burnshaw (Holt). 1960. pp. 252–3
See *Selected Poems* and *A Spectre Is Haunting Europe: Poems of Revolutionary Spain.*

ÁLVAREZ QUINTERO, SERAFÍN (1871–1938)
ÁLVAREZ QUINTERO, JOAQUÍN (1873–1944)

Sane optimism and realism suffused with poetry are the inspiring forces of the brothers Quintero. They have no thesis to prove, except that life is sweet and worth living; no didactic aim, except to show that human nature is still sound in the main. . . . In the later plays of the Quinteros one notices an increasing eagerness to impress the beauty of vigorous, right-minded living upon the audience. One must be frank, and say that the most successful plays are those in which the moral is best concealed. They do not always escape the pitfall of bourgeois sentimentality.

S. Griswold Morley. Introduction to *Doña Clarines*
(Heath). 1915. pp. xii–xiii

The Brothers Quintero are modernists by temperament and by artistic affiliation. The interest of a play, in their conception, does not lie in what is about to happen, but in what is happening at the moment, of which the future promise is but a phase. Art cannot subsist upon mere illusion, it derives its strength from observation, from its closeness to life. It remained for the Quinteros to take an insignificant subject, present it simply through a succession of commonplace events of which the protagonists were neither persons of remarkable originality nor of intellectual power, were torn by no heroic passions nor involved in any enterprise at all spectacular, abnormal, bizarre, or strange, and yet in so doing to produce a series of plays of universal appeal.

John Garrett Underhill. Introduction to *Malvaloca*
(Doubleday). 1916. p. viii

According to Azorín . . . the originality of the Quintero brothers consists in showing perfect equilibrium between individual emotion and the collective emotion. . . . Azorín traces an unbroken development from Lope de Vega . . . to the Quintero brothers. The latter, according to Azorín, have attained perfect equilibrium between the individual and society with the result that the question is constantly being asked:

Which is right, the individual or society? And in the conflict, the Quintero brothers find nobody utterly to be abhorred and condemned.

Lula Giralda Adams. Introduction to *Puebla de las Mujeres* (Appleton). 1926. pp. xi–xii

A light hearted, poetic and probably gently sceptical pair, they are, it would appear, frankly bored by that grim Logician . . . called Causality . . . and put out of countenance (and possibly a little scandalized) by the eruptive Strong Man . . . called Destiny. . . . In none of [their plays] . . . does anything much *happen* . . . the people simply *are*. . . . Because in their quiet way the dramatists enjoy and make us feel their enjoyment so much—life becomes its own justification.

Robert Nichols. *NSN*. Feb. 11, 1928. p. 564

When one has said of the play [*A Hundred Years Old*] that a certain delicacy in the writing does as much as could possibly be done to make tolerable its unrelieved sweetness, one has said about all that can be said in its favor. There is no surprise, no conflict, no movement, and no ideas—unless a few sentimental platitudes may be defined by the name of the latter. . . . The appearance of such a play is always the occasion for various people to ask why, after all, there isn't a legitimate place for what they call "wholesome sentiment"; but the answer is not so difficult as they seem to imply. Sentimentality has been well defined as the attitude which arises in those who are so anxious to believe things what they ought to be that they pay no attention at all to what they are. It means the end not only of drama but of every vestige of the critical attitude toward persons and events. There are only two ways of dealing with life—the way of passion and the way of intellect. Either one can accept reality and master it after a fashion, but sentiment refuses to play the game at all unless it can do so with loaded dice.

Joseph Wood Krutch. *Nation*. Oct. 23, 1929. p. 474

The best genre of the modern Spanish drama [is] that of the farce-comedy, at which the Quinteros excel. . . . As Andalusians they are sensitively aware . . . of the immense variety and colour of Southern Spain. . . . The Quinteros, with their immense knowledge of and love for the south of Spain, were the perfect dramatists to carry on the native farcical tradition, and they have neglected few opportunities to convey with the keenest realism the life, manners, mannerisms, customs, and speech of the inhabitants of Andalusia.

Hamilton Eames. *BkmL*. Sept., 1931. p. 319

What quality is dominant with the Quinteros? Their humanity, we have said. On the more technical side, one hazards, the perfect ease of the action and dialogue. . . . This is not profound drama, but it is alive. It is . . . like a stream in its middle course, done with the hills and the rapids, not yet come to the deeps of the river or the sea. It flows swiftly and diversedly, sunshine glints back from it, now it is one colour, now another, it eddies and ripples and sings. If there is nothing profound in it, it is irresistibly alive.

> Helen and Harley Granville-Barker. Introduction to
> *Four Comedies* by Serafín and Joaquín Álvarez Quintero
> (Samuel French). 1932. pp. xviii–xxi

See *Four Comedies, Malvaloca,* and *The Fountain of Youth* (plays).

ALVARO, CORRADO (1895–1956)

This strange dream novel, *Man Is Strong* . . . is without form, fluid, surrealist impressions dissolving one into another. . . . Fear, corrosive and degrading to man's dignity, is the single dominant motif of this book, determining both its mood and style. The mood is muted, an atmosphere bathed in sepia tones and misty shadows. For here is no study of terror which sharpens the senses, but rather of constant, gnawing, ever-present fear which blunts them. Mr. Alvaro explores that curse of our age, mass fear, as it lurks in the subconscious and distorts all conscious experience. His characters are obsessed with it and the symbols it evokes, to a point where they become themselves imaginary symbols of anxiety, fugue, deception, corruption. Participants in a national danse macabre, they glide in and out of the hero's path, mere silhouettes, each manifesting a different phase of the disease. . . . This novel is an imaginative analysis, unique and certainly sincere, of man's soul and spirit in modern bondage.

> Jerome D. Ross. *NYHT*. Aug. 29, 1948. p. 3

Man Is Strong . . . is a symbolical protest against cruelty and corruption. The author, since he was an Italian journalist living in Italy, had to cloak his denunciation of fascism in sufficient obscurity so that his book could be published, so that it could be considered an attack on Russia instead of on all totalitarianism. The result is artificial, cloudy, and dull. The two central characters have no personality at all—they are only sensitive victims of the fear, suspicion, and arbitrarily induced sense of sin and guilt which are part and parcel of a police state.

To make matters even more unreal and dreamlike, Mr. Alvaro has let his minor characters remain nameless and faceless symbols, and has wrapped his whole story in a cocoon of pretentious, precious, and peculiar prose. His protest against fascism while he was living under it does Mr. Alvaro great credit. But, unfortunately, it is a dull and life-less protest.

Orville Prescott. *YR.* Autumn, 1948. pp. 189–90

[Even] the Fascist censors . . . were affected by the pall of fear which he builds up [in *Man Is Strong*] into a mood of positively, or one might better say, negatively Kafkan effect. For the result of living under totali-tarian supervision is shown in the disintegration of all of Alvaro's char-acters with the exception of the investigator, symbol of all secret police. . . . Like both Waugh and Koestler, Alvaro is . . . a man of much greater intellectual force than we are accustomed to find among our native novelists. If he lacks the compassion which, without losing his artistic integrity, Koestler achieved only in *Darkness at Noon*; if he fails to show the clear purpose of Waugh's mature irony, it may be that as a realistic Latin he discerns more grays than blacks and whites in the complex relation of modern man to society.

Harry Bull. *SR.* Sept. 4, 1948. p. 11

Scourges as immense as fascism and war present the novelist with a knotty problem of ways and means. A Frenchman has aptly remarked that "a single man killed is a misfortune, a million is a statistic." How to encompass the emotional reality of that aggregate of horrors which so easily becomes "a statistic" or a remote abstraction—"war dead," "purge," "pogrom"? Camus's answer in *The Plague* was vivid realistic allegory. Alvaro's is the symbolism and super-realism of Kafka, with its dreamlike intensity. Many of his devices have their exact parallel in *The Trial*—the mysterious circumstance left unexplained, the sinister coincidence, the felt presence of unseen, omnipotent powers, and so on. . . . What he is so successful in achieving is the anguished climate of nightmare and baleful unreason.

Charles J. Rolo. *At.* Oct., 1948. pp. 106–7

There seems to be a notion of Italian local color which is restricted to a rural, picturesque and poverty-ridden south. This notion is of course warranted by one literary tradition. . . . But one sees no reason why Rome should not be "local." . . . Local color can be made also of gardens behind walls, long bureaucratic corridors, and dim *pensioni.*

Besides, Italian writers seem to possess, to a higher degree than the average, the capacity to take their locale as an "occasion" and to turn it into some sort of personal myth. . . . Corrado Alvaro's Calabria, as he presents it in the short novel [*Revolt in Aspromonte*] . . . and in some of his short stories, would be an outstanding illustration of the "myth-making" trend.

P. M. Pasinetti. *KR*. Autumn, 1950. p. 679

There are two Italys. There is the prosperous, elegant, buoyant Italy of "the Italian miracle" that one hears about so much today in press and films. Then there is the other—the painful, bitter, eternal Italy of the peasants, particularly of the Southern peasants, as different from the first as day is from night. No Italian writer has more succinctly expressed the elemental anguish and frustrations of that second Italy than Corrado Alvaro. . . . Alvaro . . . is considered in contemporary Italian letters as the voice of Calabria, that dramatically beautiful but poverty-stricken land which lies at the tip of the Italian boot. . . . [*Revolt in Aspromonte* is] swift, powerful and compassionate. . . . Its characters, for all their simplicity, are not inarticulate primitives. . . . Transcending time and space as they move against the somber, poetic grandeur of their forbidding mountains, they take on an almost legendary stature and become symbols of the age-old struggle that has kept Italy cleft in twain and all the poorer for it.

Helene Cantarella. *NYT*. June 17, 1962. p. 5

When Corrado Alvaro died in 1956 it is probably no exaggeration to say that he was the most respected man of letters in Italy. His life, no less than his works, had reflected qualities of integrity and dedication which had brought him the affection and admiration of his fellow writers and intellectuals—a group not given normally to charitable judgments. Yet the feeling was also widespread that, viewed simply as a creative artist, Alvaro had done his best work in his early years. . . . [In *Revolt in Aspromonte,* a] sample of Alvaro's early work . . . a whole primitive world is deftly and sympathetically reconstructed. The original title was "Folk in Aspromonte," which gives a better idea of the author's approach, for . . . it is the people rather than the revolt that we remember. . . . Necessity is the law in these hills and forgotten villages, but the people . . . cling to their dreams and their hope of ultimate justice. *Revolt in Aspromonte* is a little masterpiece.

Thomas G. Bergin. *NYHT*. June 17, 1962. p. 8

See *Man Is Strong* and *Revolt in Aspromonte* (novels).

ANNUNZIO, GABRIELE D'

See D'Annunzio, Gabriele

ANOUILH, JEAN (1910–   )

Anouilh . . . writes comedies . . . [which] go back . . . to the style of Marivaux, who himself stemmed from the *commedia dell'arte*. To the comic intrigue of the *commedia* Marivaux added grace, wit, sentiment, almost a Watteau-like quality. . . . And now . . . Anouilh writes *"L'Invitation au Chateau,"* translated into "Ring Round the Moon," which is obviously filled with the comic intrigue of the *commedia* (so much so that some find it a bit bewildering), and like the *commedia* with individual scenes or set pieces for the actors. But all this is garnished with wit, with a wry and mocking sentiment, and with a verbal dexterity which is a constant delight.

Walter Prichard Eaton. NYHT. Dec. 24, 1950. p. 4

European visitors have been known to complain that we Americans do not spend enough time talking about love. In my country, they sometimes explain happily, a mixed company will often spend a whole evening discussing only one fine point in the casuistry of that infinite subject. At such a symposium Jean Anouilh must be a star performer who can talk all fellow aficionados under the table before he even reaches the ultimate subtleties.

Joseph Wood Krutch. Nation. Jan. 12, 1952. p. 44

By his ideas Anouilh is related to the existentialists, but perhaps the most important affiliation here is not Sartre (whom Anouilh antedates) but that Italian existentialist, Luigi Pirandello. . . . To join yourself to Pirandello is, luckily, to join yourself not only to his ideas, but to the great tradition of comic Latin theatre which reaches back to the *commedia*. Anouilh will stand or fall in the degree to which he belongs to this tradition. I would not say his ideas are uninteresting—as yet. I would only record the impression that his special gift is an imagination that is histrionic, scenic, and musical. In a word, Anouilh is theatrical.

Eric Bentley. NR. Dec. 22, 1952. pp. 22–3

Whereas a French audience sits enthralled when Anouilh's lovers and their various assistant philosophers engage in a non-stop discourse on the tortures and agonies of amour, pausing only now and then to bestow paradoxical, passionate kisses upon one another, an American audience remains passive nigh to the border of coma. . . . That Anouilh, many of whose plays bear a basic resemblance to one another, has a definite talent somewhere in his makeup is nevertheless plain to anyone familiar with the bulk of his work. It is a pity, however, that . . . he cannot resist burying it out of notice by heaping upon it clods of pretentiousness and the ashes of long overused sexual animadversions.

George Jean Nathan. *The Theatre in the Fifties*
(Knopf). 1953. pp. 161–3

Hidden in the disturbing violence that has distressed so many people and turned them away from Anouilh's work is the expression of a deep and unremitting poetic anguish. He has grown more tolerant, more ready with pity, though still basically resentful—for the source of his pity is still a passionate feeling of disgust at the wretchedness of human destiny. He seems to have grown to an ever more terrible understanding of the way in which petty defects and concessions, small meannesses and betrayals can turn life into a vile, festering sore. This genuine sense of pity and distress that is never lacking in Anouilh is a compensation for the harshness that his resentment against fate drives him to show.

Edward Owen Marsh. *Jean Anouilh* (W. H. Allen).
1953. p. 179

Anouilh is not the only dramatist who has used the theatre to expose what may be unreal and inauthentic in life. The characters of Sartre, for example, also try to escape the possession which is their lot. . . . Yet, his criticism of theatrical bad faith is not so far-reaching as Anouilh's, even though it is more deliberate. For the authenticity which Sartre sets up as an ideal is not the poetic "purity" of Anouilh. Sartre's morals are ethical, not poetic. . . . The romantic purity to which Anouilh alludes is more exacting. It can perhaps be found in man's relation to the world, not in man's relation to man. It is the purity of the physicist, of the craftsman, of the artist (but not of the dramatist). It requires the elimination of the other as such. In Anouilh's theatre, the theatre aspires to commit suicide.

Robert Champigny. *YFS*. Winter, 1954–5. p. 63

Rather than black and rose, Anouilh's theater is frequently just black and white. Black and white are the terms of the conflict, black and white is the hero's elementary complexity, both terms being derived from the same harsh reality and the splendid illusion which it enfolds.

Face to face with these white and sinful heroes are the black and not-so-condemned non-heroes. Their constitution is as simple as that of the heroes, of whose same cloth they are cut. More than a physical affinity, theirs is in nearly every case a veritable kinship to the hero which is meant to signify emphatically the hero's effort to get away from himself.

David I. Grossvogel. *The Self-Conscious Stage in Modern French Drama* (Columbia). 1958. p. 173

The pessimism of Anouilh is no put-up romantic attitude of wearing one's heart on one's sleeve, or of crying to the waves and to the winds wondering why one cries or why one feels miserable; it is the revolt of a sensitive being appalled and wounded by the cruelty of life and expressing man's despair at never being able to know his true self or to meet another self in a state of purity. It is the regret of the lost Eden, but it is something taking place in a man who is obviously endowed with a capacity for poetry, which manages to flower at times on the very ruins of destroyed hearts or in the grey dawns of hopeless morning.

> Joseph Chiari. *The Contemporary French Theatre*
> (Macmillan). 1959. pp. 176–7

Anouilh's comic art has not yet, I think, been fully realized. One is aware of it too often at moments in his plays when he uses it as a device to effect some relaxation, some respite from the problem at hand at a point when the problem reaches a moment of tension and anguish. Anouilh's complexity comes from the conflict in himself between a fundamental pessimistic outlook and a theatrical presentation that is as basically comic as it was in Molière. If this conflict is ever resolved so that the dramaturgy of the idea, of the philosophic concept, will be totally focused on the comic, Anouilh may well become a major writer in the history of the French theatre. He is certainly of his time, fully aware of the manias and the problems of his age. But in order that the public in France today may laugh with him, without shame, and for future publics in France and elsewhere to continue to laugh without shame, he will have to effect a more drastic aesthetic transposition than he has yet achieved.

> Wallace Fowlie. *Dionysius in Paris* (Meridian).
> 1960. pp. 122–3

Anouilh first came to attention in America falsely labeled as a playwright of the French Resistance; he has lately become a playwright resisting modern France. Always disposed towards traditionalism in his forms and techniques, Anouilh is now trying to dramatize the anachronistic quality of his own position—based on the conflict between the past and the present, his recent plays are about the importance and futility of maintaining traditional values in a world which no longer cares.

> Robert Brustein. *NR*. Jan. 4, 1960. p. 21

When Anouilh was younger . . . he saw life intensely, brilliantly: it was all black and pink or both. The world was a sweet pill coated with a thick layer of wormwood, and somewhere in the middle of one's choking on the bitterness there would be one fleeting, unforgettable soupçon of sweetness. Out of such black and rose matter are fairy tales made—made, surely, by very young people who remember their childhood, or very old ones who have regained it. But there is no such thing as middle-aged bitterness or mellow pink-and-blackness. In . . . his middle-aged phase, Anouilh resorts to the paradox. . . . "Becket" is full of witty, epigrammatic paradoxes: blacknesses that are really pink, rosinesses that are actually black. The only trouble with whirling these parti-colored globes around with prestidigitator's speed is that what then meets the eye is merely grey.

John Simon. HdR. Winter, 1960. pp. 588–9

The classical spirit is evidenced in the simplicity of action, the unity of plot, a harmony in the ideas expressed and their means of expression, and the use of myth. . . . Each play presents implicitly the ideas of the author, not simply expressed through rational argumentation, but embodied in the entire complex of the piece. And these ideas, by their very nature, are of universal interest. They are also particularly dramatic, for they reveal life in terms of a fundamental and insoluble conflict, and they are translated with consummate skill into theatrical terms. Anouilh is undoubtedly one of the most finished craftsmen writing for the theater today.

Leonard Cabell Pronko. The World of Jean Anouilh
(California). 1961. pp. 213–4

In the last analysis Anouilh's theatre is ambiguous: man's defeat in face of life, but his victory as a total actor, on whom neither Creons nor Inquisitors nor passionate kings can have any real hold.

The consequences of such an attitude are dual. On the one hand, it is the source of multiple theatrical effects, either original or borrowed from all that is obviously theatrical in the Commedia dell'Arte, Shakespeare, Molière, or Beaumarchais. On the other hand, it gives enormous rights to the theatre, since it is not only a metaphor of life but also a solution.

Jacques Guicharnaud. Modern French Theatre
(Yale). 1961. p. 128

After some years of educative theatergoing, I have learned to trust Jean Anouilh. This is not to say that M. Anouilh can be trusted to produce a perfect play every time out. What can be looked for each time, though, is a defined intention, a deliberate style, a particular shape—and sometimes a very odd shape indeed—for highly particular materials. What M. Anouilh does most often, it seems to me, is construct from crepe paper and other party materials an engaging little child's house, inside which adult things may happen.

Walter Kerr. *The Theater in Spite of Itself* (Simon).
1963. p. 148

See *Antigone, Becket, Poor Bitos,* and *Ring Round the Moon* (plays).

APOLLINAIRE, GUILLAUME (1880–1918)

There is, about the figure of Guillaume Apollinaire, an irresistible atmosphere of ribald exuberance, genial madness, grotesque inspiration, and pure impudence. . . . He entered Montmartre like a happy goldfish restored to its natal bowl. Darting, with incomparable energy, hither and there, he maneuvered his way to the fore of every artistic battle line. Whatever the cause—what cared he for the cause, save that it be audacious?—his metaphorical bugle was ever the first sounded, his taunts the most insolent, his accents the most shrill. Apollinaire's capacity for the enjoyment of simple living was prodigious. His derisive skepticism was a likewise absolute quantity, equaled only by the exuberance of his animal spirits. To those who could endure the strenuosity of his gross wit, his impiety, and his complete lack of any reticence or tact, he was one of the most attractive personalities of his time.

William A. Drake. *Contemporary European Writers*
(John Day). 1928. pp. 124–5

It is possible that Apollinaire, thirsting for escape, suffered from a certain poverty of imagination. Clearly, he was preoccupied by a small number of themes, and he returns again and again to the same images. At the same time, his poetics of the arbitrary and the surprise, his eagerness to tempt chance by throwing his dice at every opportunity, after having destroyed all possibility of a regulated game, requires the constant presence of a teeming and subtle imagination, close to external objects but capable of freeing itself from them, and capable of metamorphosing them into all sorts of monsters and chimeras. Ultimately, it is difficult to say—and this is not one of the least attractive aspects of the enigma he represents—whether Apollinaire might have been that great poet of whom he makes us think, or whether his poems with their equivocal, suggestive charm show him in a flattering light.

Marcel Raymond. *From Baudelaire to Surrealism*
(Wittenborn). 1949. p. 238

Poetry, to Apollinaire, was not a compensation for life; it accompanied and heightened every moment of his existence. It could be written on postcards and sent to friends, flower out of casual conversation, or be composed under fire in the trenches. . . . Continually filled with curiosity and always ingenious, Apollinaire was never trapped by his methods or his material. He exposed his conscious and unconscious nature with a perfect willingness to push frankness to the point of absurdity.

Louise Bogan. NY. Oct. 28, 1950. p. 129

The charge that Apollinaire merely played with conceptions which he did not fully grasp, much less execute, is unavoidable. . . . I suggest that we should take the label "modernist" and give it a special meaning virtually confined to Apollinaire. It would certainly not mean contemporary with Gide, Proust, or the rising Picasso, or even with the first aeroplanes. It could be with the discovery of Montparnasse. It corresponds to a cry of "Life! Life!" raised by a young man in a city to which he does not possess the clue. . . . The cultural centre of Paris eludes him. It changes cafés. The coteries shuffle or meet. But an undiminished appetite for life keeps him going. He will use it all, unorganized as it comes. So if his "modernism" and his cosmopolitanism now resemble a St. Vitus's Dance, they at least represent an authentic human attitude. It is not much. But it is neither Bohemianism nor nostalgia nor irony nor revolt. It exists separately and should be expressed.

Geoffrey Brereton. NSN. Oct. 9, 1954. pp. 444–5

Reacting against the "clean sheet" system advocated by the *avant-garde* movements, he declared his faith in France's admirable literary past; affirmed that art has a country, that a new lyricism can be born from mechanism without entirely excluding the classics. . . . The past, the present and even the future were his domain. He was the brilliant and noisy synthesis of a period, whose riches have still not been exhausted, and which the 1914 war struck, like him, on the head.

There was not a field which he did not enter with varying success. He tried everything, was the prophet of every novelty, the defender of every audacity, full of a prodigious love of life in all its most brilliant and most repellent aspects and of a tireless benevolence, a perpetual goodness.

Marcel Adéma. Apollinaire (Heinemann). 1954.
pp. 266, 272

Poetry like Apollinaire's does not try to fathom the supernatural or the miraculous, but simply to state the incomprehensibleness of the ordinary and the commonplace. Every human expression Apollinaire saw became sphinx-like for him, and every word he overheard resembled a sibyl's utterance. His language has a baptismal gravity about it. Nascent language it would seem to be, rediscovering its virginity, as the poet, performing his earliest role of demiurge, calls the world to be born again by naming it.

Wallace Fowlie. *Com.* July 1, 1955. p. 333

Alcools . . . has become for the modern world one of the best known and most appealing volumes of French verse of any century. Why?

The essential answer and the obvious one lies in the quality of individual freshness—a freshness that characterized each poem when it was written and that for reasons varying with each continues to infuse most of them with life today. Some of the poems continue fresh because they continue to sing; in others the freshness seems to spring from surprising images, or from downright bizarreness, or from mystery, or from classic form, finish, and perfection. The poems or parts of poems . . . are all very different, and the life of each springs from no common characteristic except their writer's genius.

Francis Steegmuller. *Apollinaire* (Farrar). 1963. p. 244

Apollinaire's poetics may be situated by a series of projects that he either did not care to define, or was unable to formulate with precision. The creator is not necessarily an effective theoretician, and a doctrine may have a wide influence entirely through imaginative texts. Apollinaire wrote down his experiments with word and image as they seemed to him to attain maturity, only to realize before long that he could do better; then, having done his best, he abandoned the project for something new. There is, then, no continuity, but rather a series of experiments, and each major attainment is a decisive step forward.

Francis J. Carmody. *The Evolution of Apollinaire's Poetics 1901–1914* (California). 1963. pp. 122–3

"Who is he?" they used to ask on the terrace of the *Closerie des Lilas,* and even those who were closest to him admit that they still do not really know. . . . Perhaps he himself has provided an answer, better than anyone else has been able to do. *Je suis ivre d'avoir bu tout l'univers.* . . . Perhaps we should see Apollinaire as a vast sponge, assimilating, soaking up his times; responding to every trend, to every personality; and by some alchemical process transforming everything into living Myth, restoring to all what he has taken from each one. He was as multiple as Cubism, a personification of the Cubist age. And just as in the Cubist vision of life no one angle is more "real" or more "true" than another, so every aspect of Apollinaire was at once true because it was a part of the whole and false because it was not the Whole. The essence of his genius lies, perhaps, in the fact that he was never wholly himself. Perhaps the true answer to the question that was so often whispered as he passed should have been: Everyone and No one.

Cecily Mackworth. Guillaume Apollinaire and the
Cubist Life (Horizon). 1963. pp. 236–7

In fact Apollinaire's governing principle was neither new nor unknown. This quality which he himself had christened "Orphism," and which later he re-baptised as "sur-naturalisme" and then eventually "sur-réalisme," was what he had always aimed at capturing, life at its most intense pulsation, the life-force naked, bereft of the cluttering trammels of everyday existence. It was this mysterious quality which came to him at moments either through the weaving patterns of his own fantasy or through an ecstatic, visionary enthusiasm by which he felt united with all other manifestations of life in the cosmos. There were even times when if he simply looked at the world around him with enough loving intensity "the most curious and moving things" would be washed up by the sea of life at his feet.

Margaret Davies. Apollinaire (St. Martin's). 1964. p.234

His lyricism of immediate reality, outer and inner, burst forth in all directions and passes through an endlessly renewed cycle of enthusiasm and despair. His own terminology seems a little grandiose: poet of Order and Adventure. It is simpler and truer to say that in his village there is always a sunny and a shady side of the street. He keeps crossing and recrossing like a restless child until he finally disappears, or multiplies to fill the whole street with his alternate selves, or turns up again as a forlorn wanderer weary with wisdom.

Roger Shattuck. NYR. May 14, 1964. p. 5

See *Alcools* (poetry).

ARAGON, LOUIS (1897–   )

Louis Aragon is the prophet of a black, furious crepuscular storm. With vociferous wrath, he denounces the crimes of our society and gloatingly visualizes its catastrophic collapse in a near future. In *Fin du Jour, Mouvement Perpétuel, La Grande Gaieté,* and *Persécuté Persécuteur,* a mass of gross invectives, cynical jests, and foul blasphemies gathers and rumbles ominously, ready to crush under its sheer irresistible weight a world conceived by him as a crazy jumble of tottering absurdities.

> Georges Lemaitre. *From Cubism to Surrealism in French Literature* (Harvard). 1941. p. 312

Blessed by the elder French writers as a young lord of language, applauded by his contemporaries as a champion of youthful experiment, he was recognized everywhere for . . . boundless, already mature talent. . . . There would be long walks through the darkened streets of Paris, with Aragon talking, talking about every conceivable problem of life or literature. This gift of his for speech he carried over directly into his writing. The French are naturally articulate, but the ability to reproduce in the written word the very tone and accent of common speech belongs particularly to Louis Aragon among his generation.

> Hannah Josephson. *SR*. Sept. 6, 1941. p. 10

He writes easily with apparently endless powers of invention. . . . For the poetry he wrote during the war, his special gift was necessary. There was no time for self-questioning, for writhing in the pains of composition; there was not much time to write at all, except for a man like Aragon who could do his work in barracks, in trains, in waiting rooms, and on the beach at Dunkerque. Unlike less naturally gifted poets, he was able to set down his impressions and emotions as they came, so that his six volumes of wartime poetry became a month-by-month record of the struggle: the boredom and loneliness of the "phony war"; the grotesque horrors of the German invasion, like Breughel's conception of hell; the utter weight of defeat, under which Aragon was among the first to stand erect; . . . and at last the frantic joy of "Paris, Paris, of herself liberated"—all of it is there, in Aragon's verse.

> Malcolm Cowley. *Aragon: Poet of the French Resistance,* ed. by Hannah Josephson and M. Cowley (Duell). 1945. pp. 7–8

The war poetry of Aragon is not uniformly good, and toward the end it lost some of its purity and force. At its best it is at once strong and limpid. Its strength lies in its essential simplicity. Aragon does not refract his emotions. They are stark, and they are those which the clean heart must feel in moments of disaster. I do not mean to say that as verse or as a body of allusion his work is simple. Technically the verse structure is exact and individual, and is designed to provide, as it were, a gravely lyrical "music" that shall never obscure the "words."

> Ralph Bates. *NR*. Dec. 17, 1945. p. 843

He is no simple singer, no matter how keen an ear he may have for the songs of the people. He is a tireless technician, experimenter, innovator —even juggler. His habit of prosodic calculation is such that studied effects seem always to be at the service of his most spontaneous, most deeply felt emotions. Particularly in the field of rhyme is he original, ingenious, and successful: here he has won new freedom for French poetry, and staked out claims to supplement those established by his acknowledged master, Guillaume Apollinaire.

Ben Ray Redman. SR. Jan. 19, 1946. p. 21

Aragon's general position is an odd one. Like two finer artists in his own time, Gide and Valéry, he has been conspicuous less for concrete, enumerable achievements than for attitudes sketched out and examples set to the young. At a low estimate, his genius has been that of a cultural organizer.

Rayner Heppenstall. NSN. Aug. 24, 1946. p. 138

It was ravishing—and I use this violent adjective with intent—to realize at a time when duty and austerity were like DDT powder in the air we breathed, that a man doing his duty to society, in the greatest danger, felt no puritanical impulse to deny the importance of love in its most individualistic form. I could not realize then, as I was to do later, that few of the conscious services Louis Aragon and Elsa Triolet performed for the Resistance were more useful than their unconscious service of providing it with a legend: the legend of a long-married couple whose love was wilder than had it been illicit and who had shared their public as well as their private lives.

Monica Stirling. At. Sept., 1949. pp. 76–7

We may well wonder whether Aragon, a thinker, an inexorable logician, has ever been a surrealist except occasionally and out of curiosity. What he prizes above everything is revolt; he joined the revolt of the dadaists, of the surrealists, and of the communists. . . . For a long time, his fear of being snugly placed somewhere in a world irretrievably given over to stupidity, more or less close to those whom he abhors, as well as his love for disorder and his refusal to be interested in anything except his revulsions and hatreds, imprisoned him within a circle of blasphemies and monotonous vociferations. . . . But once Aragon became a communist, it was the poet in him that he assassinated, and this without leaving a trace.

Marcel Raymond. From Baudelaire to Surrealism
(Wittenborn). 1949. pp. 301–2

Aragon's finest novels are directed to the bourgeoisie—his readers—more than to the proletariat. In *Les Communistes* he is addressing the proletariat, to whose existing legend he is adding a new page. The fictional chronicle he writes is shamelessly partial and its fictional value is almost nil. And yet . . . Aragon is a born novelist. He knows how to tell an ample, living story, full of color and movement; he is able to sustain unusual and strongly differentiated characterizations; his satire is often pungent. In addition, a holdover perhaps from his surrealist years, he has a fertile imagination that often carries him into the realm of pure fantasy. One can detect in Aragon a poet whose senses are alive to form and color, in particular to the charm of feminine beauty and fashion. One can detect the romantic writer of melodrama.

Germaine Brée and Margaret Guiton. *An Age of Fiction*
(Rutgers). 1957. pp. 87–8

It is the naivety of the feelings behind the sometimes hair-raising virtuosity of the form that brings a smile to our contemporaries, more used to seeing complication of thought combined with awkwardness of expression. Obviously all these old-fashioned dresses taken out of some antique wardrobe have been done over in his own style by a Christian Dior, half demon, half urchin, and our grandmothers would not recognize them at first glance. But when the first surprise is over, we know where we are. Even this approach to communism under the inspiration of a Beatrice is more like a conversion in the style of Verlaine than a conviction formed by assiduous study of Marx. It is not a meditative poetry, a poetry of reflection, but of immediate reaction to beings and events, a poetry of the nerves.

Auguste Anglès. *YFS*. Spring-Summer, 1958. pp. 93–4

Out of the disaster [the fall of France in World War II], poetry surges with an urgent mission which Aragon is not abashed to call "noble"; for poetry seems to him the last foothold on dignity left in his moment of abject humiliation. . . . But when pictures of heroism, devastation, treason, assassination, pillage, murder, human separations invaded the works of Aragon did they indicate a return to narrative verse, a recapture of classical eloquence?

Quite the contrary. The surrealist state of mind prevails in the majority of these writings. . . . In these series of poems he raises the incidents to a plane of universality by using one of the basic techniques of surrealism: the exploration of the myth which replaces the circumstantial reality of history with the metaphysical reality of the legend.

Anna Balakian. *Surrealism* (Noonday). 1959.
pp. 168–71

Throughout Aragon's work, Elsa's name recurs much like a leitmotif.
. . . Elsa Triolet, the woman, and Elsa Triolet, the writer, are completely intertwined in the skein of Aragon's veneration. . . . Her name
is never absent from his writings—each article, each lecture, each interview that bears his name also evokes hers. . . . Elsa Triolet caused
Aragon to abandon surrealism, offering him instead a vision of a world
where the hope of building a new society was possible. . . . Since the
books and characters Elsa Triolet has created have become an integral
part of Aragon's experience, the frequency with which he speaks of her
becomes something more than a simple question of poetic interest; it is
rather a necessity.

> Marie-Monique Pflaum-Vallin. *YFS.* Spring-Summer,
> 1961. pp. 87–9

Aragon is unquestionably a gifted story teller, and he has solidly
grounded his novel [*Holy Week*] on a selected number of facts and gone
into painstaking research to insure the physical accuracy of his various
settings. But he has also used an episode of French history as other
writers might have used a Greek myth, thus making characters and
events unmistakably his own. *Holy Week,* the impression of somewhat
naïve commentators notwithstanding, is *engagé* in the fullest sense of the
term: a philosophy of history, a social ethic, and a political ideology
inform its entire structure.

> Leon S. Roudiez. *SR.* Oct. 7, 1961. p. 40

And so it was that I succumbed to the charm of Aragon, a man assuredly
endowed with the qualities needed for an idol, even to the terror-fascination which he exerted. He was handsome, legendary, the very epitome
of courage. He was elegant, in a precise and almost austere fashion,
somewhat in the manner of Saint-Just; and simple to so perfectly contrived a degree and with so rigorous an eye to effect that, in remaining
true to oneself, one felt guilty of playing a false role.

> Pierre Emmanuel. *NR.* Dec. 25, 1961. p. 18

See *Aragon: Poet of the French Resistance* (poetry and prose); also *Aurelien*
and *Holy Week* (novels).

ARTAUD, ANTONIN (1896–1948)

Everywhere Artaud betrays the attitudes and prejudices of a puritan,
self-depriving and with a nausea for ordinary food. I should guess that
he clung precariously to his sanity by warding off fantasies of cannibal-

ism and other things he thought depraved. When the theatre broke
through this shell and provided him a real excitement, he inevitably
thought of it as totally destructive and hellish; it had raped him. . . .
He is wearing blinders. He does not seem to conceive of the more ordinary neurotic or simply unhappy man to whom the magic of a work of
art is its impossible perfection, its promise of paradise.

Paul Goodman. *Nation.* Nov. 29, 1958. p. 412

The principal tenet of Artaud's essay, *Le Théâtre et son Double,* is that
reform in the modern theatre must begin in the production itself, with
the *mise-en-scène.* Artaud looks upon it as far more than a mere spectacle. It is a power able to move the spectator closer to the absolute.
The theatre is not a direct copy of reality, it is another kind of dangerous
reality where the principles of life are always just disappearing from
beyond our vision, like dolphins who, as soon as they show their heads
above the surface of the water, plunge down into the depths. . . . A play
which contains the repressed forces of man will liberate him from them.

Wallace Fowlie. *SwR.* Fall, 1959. pp. 647–8

Actuality is not in the theater. Dangerous reality is not in the theater.
The two are identical. Actuality and the theater are identical. They are
Antonin Artaud between 1946 and 1948. What I mean to say is that
after he left the Rodez asylum, although only two years of life were left
to him, Antonin Artaud integrated in poetry, in poetic reality the totality
of his experience. There is no longer conceptual, rational investigation;
there is no longer reasoning, litigation, doctrinal elaboration, work that
is critical or polemical. There is only Antonin Artaud who speaks and
who poetically organizes all his constituent elements. There is only
Antonin Artaud who builds again his body. The Mexican experience,
the Mexican quest, the coming back, the tables of law given to the theater, the body which lived from asylum to asylum, each takes its place in
the body of Antonin Artaud who creates himself for himself again. The
last words say all that.

Georges Charbonnier. *Essai sur Antonin Artaud*
(Editions Pierre Seghers). 1959. pp. 191–2.
Tr. by Dorothy Nyren Curley

Artaud tried to totally redefine theatre. By using the now well-known
metaphor of *Le Théâtre et la peste,* he claimed that theatre is very much
the same as the plague in that both provoke liberating and revealing
"frenzies." During the plagues of the Western world, men were rid of
their Western character (order, reason, morality) and restored to their

true powers. Great theatre not only presents the spectacle of individuals restored to power, but reveals those powers within the spectator.

> Jacques Guicharnaud. *Modern French Theatre*
> (Yale). 1961. p. 225

Antonin Artaud directed Vitrac's Surrealist plays and is the author of one or two dramatic sketches, but his real importance for the theatre of the Absurd lies in his theoretical writings and in his practical experiments as a producer. . . . Under the influence of the powerful impression made on him by the subtle and magical poetry of the Balinese dancers, Artaud wanted to restore the language of gesture and movement, to make inanimate things play their part in the action, and to relegate dialogue . . . to the background. Quoting the music hall and the Marx Brothers as well as the Balinese dancers, he called for a true language of shapes, light, movement, and gesture.

> Martin Esslin. *The Theatre of the Absurd* (Doubleday).
> 1961. pp. 277–8

In *The Theatre and Its Double* Artaud placed the blame for the imaginative poverty of the conventional French theatre as squarely as possible on "culture." By culture, Artaud meant the patterns of artificiality which civilization—especially Western civilization—had imposed upon human nature; and, indeed, Artaud's concept of the theatre obviously stems from an intense desire to do justice to what he considered the essentials of the human personality, as much as from purely artistic considerations. Artaud's yearning for theatrical innocence, which hauntingly recalls Rousseau's belief that the human soul is crushed by the restraints imposed upon it by a corrupting civilization, had predictably revolutionary ramifications.

> Michael Benedikt. Introduction to *Modern French
> Theatre* (Dutton). 1964. p. xxvi

Though he was of medium stature, his bearing was imposing because of the way he turned his head as he thrust back his rather long hair, the brilliance of his gaze, the bright blue of his eyes. There was something "regal" about him in spite of his excessive thinness and his ravaged face, the result of ten years of privation (he did not have any teeth). . . . Artaud had achieved something very rare: he had succeeded in giving a meaning to *his* life and, by the same token, to *life*. One could not remain insensitive to this. Everything he said seemed, at the moment he said it, so evident and so true. He was this truth to such a degree that one accepted him, totally.

> Paule Thévenin. *TDR*. Spring, 1965. pp. 101, 103–4

Artaud, unlike Brecht, the other towering theoretician of twentieth-century theater, did not create a body of work to illustrate his theory and sensibility.

Often, the sensibility (the theory, at a certain level of discourse) which governs certain works of art is formulated before there exist substantial works to embody that sensibility. Or, the theory may apply to works other than those for which they are developed. . . . It seems doubtful that the only production which Artaud ever supervised, Shelley's "The Cenci," came close to following the brilliant recipes for the theater in his writings, any more than did his public readings of Seneca's tragedies. We have up to now lacked a full-fledged example of Artaud's category, "the theater of cruelty." . . . Hence the great interest of "Marat/Sade" [by Peter Weiss], for it, more than any modern theater work I know of, comes near the scope, as well as the intent, of Artaud's theater.

Susan Sontag. PR. Spring, 1965. pp. 217–8

See <i>The Theatre and Its Double</i> (essays).

AYALA, RAMÓN PÉREZ DE
See Pérez de Ayala, Ramón

AYMÉ, MARCEL (1902–   )

He is a seeker, a worshipper, a contemplative, for whom love is the mainspring of the universe; whose song is a prayer, a hymn of creation, an alleluia to the creator, an <i>hommage</i> to the dignity of humanity, a care for the vocation of man on earth, a lamentation, a eulogy, a sigh, a cry of joy, the spirit of childhood reborn, a dream realized when wide awake, a marvel, a mystery, an incantation to life; . . . whose aim is a search for human contact, a conscious collaboration with the great realities of life.

Georges Robert and André Lioret. Marcel Aymé insolite
(La Revue Indépendante). 1955. p. 101.
Tr. by Dorothy Nyren Curley

His work owes its brilliance and freshness to an original blend of truth and daydream.

Dichtung und Wahrheit* at best achieve an unstable combination. But it is from this effervescent mixture that genuine human experience

---

*A reference to the title of Goethe's autobiography, literally "poetry and truth," here has the meaning "imagination (or fantasy) and truth."

springs. Marcel Aymé's writings depend upon a strange, uneasy tension of opposites. The souls of his shabby characters are crushed by acceptance of frustration, ennui, the endless flow of empty years, and lifted by the wildest leaps toward freedom, bliss, paradise. Their moods vary from resigned indifference to things to outbursts of maniacal passion. The drabness of daily living on archaic forms or in modern cities merges with the universe of wish-fulfillment through magic, crime, and madness. . . . It is not the least among our writer's achievements that his semifantastic, seminaturalistic tales almost inadvertently turn into parables of the reader's secret life and longings.

Claude Vigée. *SR*. Jan. 24, 1959. p. 18

Some of the same poker-faced fantasy is present in Thurber—in a story like "The Unicorn in the Garden," for instance—but there the whole cloth is fable. In Aymé, the fantasy is embedded in a traditional naturalism. . . . Aymé's chief fault is a tendency to let his fantasy just ramble on, "agreeable nonchalance," leading his story nowhere in particular and failing to impart any significance. But at the same time there is a wholesome giddiness in his best work which offers an enormous relief to the dead-earnestness that holds so many novelists in its strait-jacket today. He is like a man who quite naturally walks about three inches above the ground.

Roger Becket. *NYHT*. Jan. 25, 1959. p. 8

In these tales Aymé combines an unerring sense of the ridiculous with a quite humane delight in the quirks of human beings manifest in the most ordinary circumstances—their cruelties, perversities and infinite capacity for self-justification included. . . . Beneath the unexpected twists and satiric audacity of these tales we sense what gives Aymé's writing its real dimensions: his relentless attack upon our incapacity to see things as they are, the hypocritical blindness with which we consider our enterprises, and the basic ferocity at work in our society. Though Aymé is a moralist with a highly individual and somewhat controversial point of view, the moral of his tales appears only obliquely. As a storyteller he delights and shocks, but he never allows us to sink into boredom or complacency. Without doubt, he is a master in the art of the short story.

Germaine Brée. *NYT*. April 30, 1961. p. 22

Aymé has never become involved in literary and ideological cults; he is an old-fashioned individualist, more interested in people than in ideas. He is, moreover, a born storyteller, one of the best practicing in any language. . . . He distrusts or finds ridiculous high-minded idealists, revolutionary middle-class intellectuals—in fact, people of all kinds who want to remake the human animal or bowdlerize the truth about his nature. For Aymé, hypocrisy is more vicious than the natural vices of man, and one senses in his work a strong affection for life as it is. Within this framework, his range is wide. In addition to being consistently amusing, he can be gay, tender, cruel, horrifying, or sardonic.

Charles J. Rolo. *At.* June, 1961. p. 102

Marcel Aymé . . . brought to French literature an earthy sense of the life of the peasantry, a robust attachment to the concrete, a vigorous hatred of all escapisms, be they philosophical, esthetic, or political, and an admirably pungent gift of style. . . . The butts of Marcel Aymé's satire are the savagery of human beings when their welfare is at stake, as was the case during the years of rationing and of starvation; the selfishness of the middle class and its lack of idealism and of charity; the pomposity of the intellectuals and of the politicians, who disguise their greed for power or for importance under fake and pretentious posturing; the injustice of much French, or human, justice.

Henri Peyre. *SR.* July 22, 1961. p. 25

See *The Barkeep of Blémont, The Conscience of Love,* and *The Green Mare* (novels); also *Across Paris and Other Stories, The Proverb and Other Stories* and "Clérambard" in *Four French Comedies* (Putnam).

AZORÍN (1873–   )

Señor Ruiz, better known by his pseudonym of Azorín, . . . whose chief sources of inspiration seem to have been Flaubert and the Spanish classics, has developed a style of his own, which at its best has a charm of a highly finished and subtle kind. In his use of Arabic terms and revival of fine old words he has enlarged the vocabulary and given a new harmony to modern Spanish, though some may feel that his short sentences, his avoidance of the beautiful Spanish diminutives, and other peculiarities of style are not in accordance with the genius of the language.

Ida Farnell. *Spanish Prose and Poetry* (Oxford).
1920. p. 174

Azorín has arrived at [a] unique method of criticism. . . . This method of, so to speak, literary assaying by the reconstruction of dust-laden masterpieces for the modern reader, gives all that is truly fine in literature a life, beneath his subtle touch, beyond the death which pedantry and the ages have set upon it. Azorín, although his scholarship stands unquestioned, has little use for dates, for bibliography, philology, and the lichen-grown accouterments of scientific classical criticism. He probes for two things alone: for the spirit which inspires and the spirit which is contained in a work of art. His essays, from the first of what we may term his mature spirit . . . whether their subjects chance to be modern or classical, are all in this manner, all seeking in the end this precious and elusive substance.

William Drake. *Contemporary European Writers*
(John Day). 1927. pp. 241–2

It is a self-denying and exacting art, even more so than that exquisite mastery over words and silences which made Anatole France famous. For the Frenchman's reticence was one of style and form. He left many things unsaid but not unmeant, not unachieved, not unobserved. Azorín's reticence is one of fact. He turns away before the end. He leaves the theatre in the middle of the second act—or even earlier. Or he turns in at any inconspicuous moment of the play and watches one and a half scenes and lets the rest—beginning and end—to be imagined in freedom or left in the vague world of the unimagined, thus tasting a mere side-light, as if it was the texture of life that mattered and not the full, somewhat square and matter-of-fact shape of it.

Salvador de Madariaga. Introduction to Azorín's
An Hour of Spain (Routledge). 1930. pp. xi–xii

Azorín has put himself at the head of a stylistic revolution, and has replaced the sonorous and rolling periods of his predecessors with short, clear-cut luminous sentences, that go to form these brilliant historical sketches where, whatever may be the period of their action, the reader is made one with the living present.

This revolution in style, for which Azorín is in the main responsible, formed part of the artistic programme of . . . the "Generation of 1898." . . . It is this love for the present, by which the past is made to live again, coupled with the most original of methods in literary and historical research, that has established Azorín's chief claim to greatness—that of throwing light on the dark periods of his country's history, and of rescuing the mystic or the poet from an unjust oblivion, of making the decayed provincial city live again the age of its power and its prosperity.

Charles K. Colhoun. *BkmL.* Sept., 1931. p. 294

Inquiry into the birth of the literary personality, Azorín [is] to a great extent, . . . a study in ideals. The *colegial* who dreamed of a distin-

guished public career, the ardent republican, . . . the literary anarchist
and the militant journalist were idealists, each in his own way. . . . The
religious environment of the early years, the long hours spent absorbed
in books, established a firm foundation for the creative achievement of
the future *aristocrata espiritual*. . . . As a law student, indulging avidly
freedom of thought in the works of poetry and philosophy, psychology
and sociology that replaced the Spanish classics of his earlier days,
respect for authority and traditional institutions yielded to the ironic
mask of Cándido and Ahrimán. Admiration for the principles of the
French Enlightenment . . . led to political idealism and a passionate zeal
for social reform. The fruits of this utopianism, for the scholar unprac-
ticed in the ways of men and the world was . . . misunderstanding on
the part of that very humanity that he hoped to lead to better ways.

Anna Krause. *Azorín, the Little Philosopher*
(California). 1948. p. 274

Azorín's plays . . . are mainly a continuation of the themes presented
by the author early in his career. With the exception of *"La Fuerza del
Amor"* every Azorínian play sets forth the themes of time and space,
repetition in time, *paisaje, ensueño,* and love as a force which solves
the most difficult problems. . . . Every one of the author's plays, like
his essays and novels, is subjective and autobiographical. . . . Azorín
has closely followed his credo on the theatre in writing his plays. . . .
Almost without exception he has made the dialogue the most essential
part of his plays, and . . . he has purposely suppressed stage directions.
. . . Azorín also followed his credo by attempting to renovate the Spanish
theatre in the introduction of surrealism. . . . Azorín's theatre is largely
an escape theatre. The author's use of surrealist techniques, such as
illusion, fantasy, *lo maravilloso,* the dream, the subconscious, a reality
above reality, etc., is his method of creating the theatre-spectacle form
advocated in his dramatic credo.

Lawrence Anthony LaJohn. *Azorín and the Spanish Stage*
(Hispanic Institute). 1958. pp. 197–8

While Valle-Inclán achieves illusory effects by the application of visual
perspectives, his contemporary, Azorín, applies the concept of interior
duplication temporally instead of spatially and by so doing imparts to it
a cosmic significance: the plot-within-a-plot now assumes the force of
existence-within-existence. This grandiose concept is a direct adaptation
of Nietzsche's "Eternal Return," to which the time-obsessed Azorín has
constant recourse in his work and which is the theme of an entire novel,
Doña Inés. The concept of the inevitable repetition of the relentless cycle

of the universe thus confers on the technique of interior duplication the dignity and consequence of a universal law.

Leon Livingstone. *PMLA*. April, 1958. p. 403

As a critic Azorín records the sensations produced in him by works of literature, as a creator he interprets objective reality through his sensibility. . . . Sensibility for him is not . . . the mere receptive capacity for sensations. . . . The sensation produced by the work (literary criticism) or by objective reality (creative writing) is adapted in a certain way by the sensibility. . . . Azorín uses insignificant authors and works to define the Spanish literary spirit. He does the same thing in his novels and vignettes. In order to represent reality he chooses a detail—usually an unimportant one—and, disdaining form and color, he tries to evoke the hidden eternal rhythm. . . . This personal reaction to objects and events of daily life is the root of all the art of [the Generation of] 1898. Objective reality loses its real contours and is transformed into symbols. . . . *Sinfronismo* is the key to Azorín's creative work as well as to his literary criticism.

Edward Inman Fox. *Azorín as a Literary Critic*
(Hispanic Institute). 1960. pp. 153–4
See *The Sirens and Other Stories*; also *An Hour of Spain* (essay).

BACCHELLI, RICCARDO (1891–   )

Bacchelli's style is very rhythmic with an easy musical cadence and long periods; *legato* one might almost say in contrast to the *staccato* of Papini. It is perhaps more poetic than forceful; more suited to description than to narration, but it is certainly both very beautiful and highly individual. . . . But more than a stylist Bacchelli is a philologist, more precisely a philologue. He is a lover of words, not in the sense that D'Annunzio and his followers were, but a lover of exact words, words that have accurate concrete meaning, *"mots justes."* One can trace to this love of words some of the more important aspects of his art.

T. G. Bergin. *Ital.* June, 1940. pp. 64–5

Bacchelli is the most impressive and complex Italian literary personality of the day. He is a humanist who possesses the penetration and finished training of a great historian. Some of his most remarkable novels are in fact on historical themes; notably *The Devil at the Longbridge* . . . and *The Mill on the Po.* . . . In both these novels—and this is Bacchelli's basic characteristic—poetry and history are interwoven without being merged, and because they are not merged they nourish each other. . . . Most of this author's work [is] distinguished from other contemporary writing by the somewhat remote and regal style, and by his attitude of subtly reactionary individualism.

Elena Craveri Croce. *NR.* May 10, 1948. pp. 25–6

What is it . . . that gives history its continuous flow, what is it that preserves what might be called the personality of a country? The answer is to be found in *The Mill on the Po*: it is the people, the little people. . . . There are two distinct story elements in *The Mill on the Po,* yet the author has blended them into one artistic whole, creating an epic novel on the largest and most satisfying scale, crowded with dramatic incident and superb character-portrayal. . . . On the one hand, there is the story of these little people . . . and on the other, there is the genesis of modern Italy as a unified and independent country. . . . In many ways much of its contents transcends the story of Italy, for it leaves one with the feeling that no one in this world is so small or unimportant that he does not in some manner or other, by his actions, contribute to or influence the destiny of others.

Robert Knittel. *NYT.* Sept. 17, 1950. p. 5

If the novel is the epic of the common man, then the common man, as the novel's hero, should be worthy of an epic. . . . Should he display, instead of . . . nobility, the less spiritual but more human qualities of self-aggrandizement, fear of the law and of other people's opinions, and indifference to the progress of political liberty, he is back where he started—a minor character in the perpetual drama . . . unworthy of being tested and therefore employed as clown, emissary, and fool. In *The Mill on the Po* . . . the common man who is given the role of hero fails to demonstrate nobility; . . . he never cares about what is happening to fortunes other than his own, and he never realizes what is happening to his country, his church, or to Europe and Western Civilization in general. . . . The long book . . . is therefore more like a peasant's journal than an epic; it gives a village view of history, but even the village is without dignity or importance in the lives of its inhabitants.

Thomas Sugrue. *SR*. Sept. 30, 1950. p. 19

The Mill on the Po, massive as it was, represented only the first two volumes of a trilogy. . . . *Nothing New Under the Sun* is the final section of the total work.

In its entirety, the trilogy is immense. There can be no doubt that it is an Italian literary landmark and that it takes a secure place in that gallery of European peasant epics which includes the work of such men as Manzoni, Reymont, Nexo, Hamsun, and others. . . . In its full sweep it is a majestic, tragic human chronicle. Its panorama of Italian history is enlarged by the universal elements of its conflicts between man and nature and between man and man.

Bacchelli is preoccupied, as was Tolstoy, with the impact of vast historical movements upon human lives. His theme, therefore, is change, and time.

Edmund Fuller. *CT*. Sept. 11, 1955. p. 4

The French have coined an apt word, *roman-fleuve*—literally, "a river-like novel"—to define certain works of fiction which are peculiarly rich in subject-matter and long-stretched in time. To no other Italian novel of our age could the term be applied more fittingly than to Riccardo Bacchelli's *The Mill on the Po.* . . . Mr. Bacchelli is a traditional writer; that is, one who feels that "the old world is always new." He also feels that nothing is more patent than a nation's character, nor firmer than its destiny. In other words, he is a novelist who has chosen *not* to be modern, and therefore prefers to relate rather than to explore. He is nostalgic about the past, yet sure that the future will, substantially, resemble it. His narrative gifts are outstanding, and his fresco of Italian life is a memorable period-piece.

Paolo Milano. *NYT*. Sept. 11, 1955. p. 5

So removed is he from his contemporaries that within a hundred years or so . . . it might be possible for some perceptive Italian graduate student to establish irrefutably that Riccardo Bacchelli could not possibly have written when it is claimed that he did; that it is difficult to see how he could have been the contemporary of Moravia, Pavese, Ginsberg; that his style is unmistakably that of the last half of the nineteenth century; that his outlook on life, art, politics, and religion is a skillful, frequently successful attempt to perpetuate the legacy of Manzoni. . . . There is a place for neither smugness nor despair in Bacchelli. Only a sense of life, which is not a violent outburst or a quiet oozing away, but a purposeful movement, although not necessarily seen as such by men. Life is often dark, but there are slits in the curtain.

Serge Hughes. *SR*. Oct. 8, 1955. p. 16

See *The Devil at the Longbridge, The Mill on the Po,* and *Nothing New under the Sun* (novels).

BAROJA, PÍO (1872–1956)

Pío Baroja is sincere and ingenuous to the point of cynicism, as spontaneous and natural as if there had never been literature before him. . . . These novels are always personal expressions of the author; the world seen through eyes that are at once childlike and skeptical, sad and humorous. . . . Baroja has demonstrated throughout his work a profound sympathy with those beings that show an exaggerated or abnormal development of personality, incapable of associating themselves with others . . . and the reader of Baroja sees through these erratic, illogical beings an illogical world, a world in which things happen and pass as incessantly as in life itself.

It is therefore idle to seek in his novels a harmonious structure, orderly, rounded, and complete. For the spirit of Baroja is as errant as that of his characters; he dearly loves digressions, he delights in details. And in this very fact lies his originality and charm.

Federico de Onís. *NYT*. May 4, 1919. p. 257

[An] anarchical strain in his character manifests itself in his work, in which there is a marked predilection for rebels and adventurers and outcasts, for those who live on the margin of society. . . . But the career of a vagabond nowadays has little of the light-hearted freedom of olden times; his revolt is sombre and tinged with a philosophy undreamed of by Gil Blas and his companions. And the writer's attitude is modified accordingly. Baroja paints the scenes in vivid colors but with absolute detachment, offering no comment and drawing no moral. His power resides in this impassive clarity, this reflection of life in cold sharp strokes like the lines of an etcher bitten with acid—the acid of an ironical and pessimistic humor. The logical end of the lawless world surveyed by Baroja is anarchy.

Ernest Boyd. *Nation.* Dec. 27, 1922. p. 720

His style is as uncompromising as his matter, and words and sentences are served raw, with a "take it or leave it" gesture full of an independence bordering on ill temper which is, on the whole, amusing and does no harm to his books. Nor is it possible to pass by this feature of Baroja's work without connecting his contempt for form with that monkish contempt for the world which is so deeply ingrained in the Basque mind. Thus Baroja's style is but the twentieth-century manifestation of a tendency which, in the sixteenth century, would have made him wear a hair shirt and eat stale bread and spinach boiled in water without salt. . . . In renouncing most of the attractive methods of literary art, he has gained a freer scope for the intensity and power of his vision. The result is a writing which for directness and simplicity has no rival in Spain.

Salvador de Madariaga. *The Genius of Spain* (Oxford). 1923. pp. 114–5

Weeds and *The Quest* . . . are a genuine and non-literary account of an almost extinguished flare of revolt against the great machine. These humble people, . . . fitfully and helplessly as they stray along their appointed paths, are none of them mob minded; . . . they are unwillingly driven to the treadmill. Their children, the inhabitants of the new white stone Madrid that has sprouted in five years, go consentingly. Business and sport, industry and prosperity are undisputed gods. . . . As a record these books are immensely valuable, and perhaps there is more than that to them. There is a dignity and restraint in the writing, and quietly distilled poetic energy that is very hard to describe. Baroja is a great novelist, not only in his time, on railway bookstalls and in editorial offices, but in that vigorous emanation of life and events that . . . people . . . call literature.

John Dos Passos. *Nation.* Jan. 19, 1924. p. 37

As a novelist, he derives from Dickens, Dostoevsky, Stendhal, Turgenev, and Balzac, rather than (as all good Spaniards should) from Pérez Galdós and Pereda. A Basque, he writes Castilian as if it were his native dialect; his style is acrid, economical to rigidity, almost brusquely direct, and innocent of the rhetorical subtleties and the finished periods hallowed by his forebears and assiduously cultivated by most of his contemporaries. His concern is for the idiom, never the phrase; and to the cultivated and orthodox Castilian ear, his style is crude and ungrammatical in structure. In this connection, a happy comparison has been suggested between Baroja's style and Dreiser's, which aims at the same idiomatic emphasis and, in an identical way, at first gives the impression of diffuseness and crudity, yet, upon closer scrutiny, is found to be so exactly suited to the subject that no word of it could be altered or cut.

William A. Drake. *Contemporary European Writers*
(John Day). 1928. p. 115

Baroja is above all a fighter. . . . Priests, established morality and religion, marriage; all these and other corner-stones of our society are fiercely assailed. . . . Baroja's materialism—he is or was a doctor by profession—has about it much that was characteristic of self-righteous nineteenth century atheists. He revels in "anarchistic" iconoclasm, the angularity of his style being well suited to the angularity of his opinions.

Peter Trentham. *BkmL*. Sept., 1931. p. 292

The accent on heroism places Baroja squarely among the romantics, both as regards his use of heroic characters and as regards his sources. . . . Had Baroja kept to the romantic school, his protagonists might all have been of the heroic type. But when he attempts to plant his man of action in the middle of modern society . . . out of this conflict is born the semi-hero, merging, at the other extreme, with the botched hero, or Hamlet. . . . The three steps . . . are roughly parallel to three stages in Baroja's career: At the first, enthusiasm for action, and heroes who sweep all opposition before them; then doubt, and semi-heroes who start well but end in failure; and at the last disillusionment, and men who are endowed like heroes but see the futility of heroics, and do not even make a beginning in action.

Dwight L. Bolinger. *Hsp*. Feb., 1941. pp. 93–4

His aversion for the *americano* is based, first, upon a defensive attempt to restore his faith in Spain by depreciating the materialistic outgrowth of Latin American culture. Secondly, it is related to a feeling of self-hatred on the part of the author, who feels that these people whom he finds both obnoxious and opposed to his values, serve to lower his nation and his race in the eyes of the world. Finally, it is the logical result of a feeling of guilt, whereby the author rationalizes his nation's responsibility for the American dilemma by shifting it to the Americans themselves.

Walter Borenstein. *Sym.* Spring, 1957. p. 59

Simple and direct, his novels are like collections of long telephone messages or telegrams, punctuated by character sketches. . . . The spell which Baroja imposed at his best was unmistakable. All nations are liable to self-falsification and for Spaniards, rhetoric was certainly their downfall at the turn of the century. A famous generation of intellectuals recognized the fact and Baroja cut through it, simply, as a story-teller, and without intellectualizing. He set down his "brief lives" of people and families, recording their hopes, errors, pretences and fates, with sardonic precision. It was like reading the newspaper, for his novels have no plots. No idea forces daily life into some pattern of value or moral struggle, unless it is pity for illusion. Disbeliever, pessimist, anthropologist collecting data in which gossip has its place, Baroja breaks off abruptly. He is an anarchist. Society is disagreeable. He looks for the inexplicable outbreak in human character. . . . For Baroja, the core of difference in us is the very source of life. He is interested in what is unanswerably ourselves.

V. S. Pritchett. *NSN.* Sept. 26, 1959. p. 396

The Restlessness of Shanti Andía, . . . in its account of coastal Basques in the last century and of the coming to old age of a typical seaman like its protagonist, . . . is a quintessence of Spanish nature in a given epoch, and its linear figures moving realistically through their experiences set it in the great tradition of the picaresque initiated by Alemán and Cervantes.

But it is not a work apart from its author. Throughout it bears evidence of his spirit—his pessimism, his belief in action, his inveighing against injustice, his awareness of human motive, his bristling against environment. . . . What is ultimately significant about Señor Baroja, however, is . . . something that is archetypal in him as it is in Thoreau and Shaw.

Like the former he represents the individual against the arrogations of society; like the latter he stands for the free mind against the equivocation, the speciousness, the fraud endemic in mass thought.

Max Cosman. *Com.* Sept. 25, 1959. p. 544

The most interesting thing in this author's books is the personality of the novelist himself, elusive and, nevertheless, ever present. A fugitive man, voluntarily withdrawn from the social current and from the interests of his time. And of all times. He seemed to have come to this planet by mistake. And to write only to make his own idleness tolerable. . . . In all his vast work there is not a single rhetorical phrase. He wrote in an oral, careless and direct manner and said lively, original and deep things with frequent errors in syntax. . . . He was the least brilliant man of his time and maybe of all times. He fled from brilliance the way some animals flee from light. In his moral character and in his sense of beauty there was a difficult originality and delicacy, which saved him and which save his work from triviality. Not only is he a novelist of real distinction, but he is the most important novelist in the Spanish language since Pérez Galdós.

Ramón Sender. *NMQ*. Spring, 1960. pp. 7–9

Among the novelists of the generation of 1898, Pío Baroja is the one most likely to be honored in future histories of literature. Satirist, philosospher, and dreamer, he is a spokesman of his age and as such a very subjective writer who reveals his intense loneliness. A reader on first becoming acquainted with Baroja's work, and following him on his wandering, restless journey over Spanish and European soil, is probably impressed most of all by the author's dissatisfaction with human society, particularly as found in Spain. But scarcely less evident is the more significant note of troubled reflection on man's place in the cosmos. The novelist's outlook, in fact, appears to be an all-inclusive pessimism impregnated with a paralyzing doubt growing out of the scientific and philosophical literature of the nineteenth century.

Sherman H. Eoff. *The Modern Spanish Novel* (N.Y.U.).
1961. p. 165

In the sense of an elaboration, there is no "style" in Baroja, his style being an attempt to bypass rhetoric in a driving attempt to get at the things described. . . . It is with the element of style which is selectivity that Baroja is most sensitive and most decisive. His dramatic end he achieves by understatement. What he chooses to say is a résumé of the unsaid, and his characters are sketched with the rapidity of a sharp-eyed draftsman. His visual approach is that of an artist filling his sketchbook. The Madrid books are triumphs of a black and white technique; the Basque books have pages of subtle watercolor and occasionally the larger composition of a colorist working in oils.

The poetry of his prose is quickened by his pantheistic feeling for nature; there is a Celtic peopling of the forests and water-courses, a Druidical awe before trees and rocks.

Anthony Kerrigan. Foreword to *The Restlessness of Shanti Andía and Selected Stories* (New American Library). 1962. p. xxix

See *Weeds* and *The Quest* (novels); also *The Restlessness of Shanti Andía and Selected Stories.*

BASSANI, GIORGIO (1916–   )

[*The Gold-Rimmed Spectacles*] by Giorgio Bassani loosely links the fate of a middle-aged doctor in Ferrara, who invites catastrophe by liking the sort of young man who wants to kick him, and a student who has to face persecution in Mussolini's Italy because he is a Jew. Which is the more tragic case? The man who reaps what he has sown, or the one who is exploited as a scape-goat? The question is not resolved, but remains to trouble us because the Italian scene is so clearly conjured that one feels the shadows dragging behind one with sharper remorselessness.

Oswell Blakeston. *TT*. Feb. 6, 1960. p. 148

Bassani belongs to the small élite of Jewish intellectuals (among whom are Natalia Ginsburg, Carlo Levi, Franco Fortini, and the critic Debenedetti) who by choice and inclination are in the avant-garde of creative critical writing in Italy today. Both Bassani's religious inheritance and his experience as a member of the underground during the last war have sharpened his sensitivity to bigotry and social cruelty; both have similarly proved to be a rich source from which he has drawn the material for his stories.

Sergio Pacifici. *SR*. Aug. 27, 1960. p. 16

The prevailing impulse of the "serious" English and American novel, and to a degree of the French, is toward richness and audacity: toward Byzantine elaboration of form, toward proliferate theme and grotesque comedy, and toward language of pyrotechnic inventiveness. . . . In this atmosphere the conventional quiet realist is scorned or dismissed, and very often with justice. Thus the wry precise Flaubertian notation and wise irony of Lampedusa's *The Leopard* (and its well-deserved success) came as a considerable surprise. And now *The Gold-Rimmed Spectacles* introduces in Giorgio Bassani another distinguished and subtle Italian consciousness, and a voice even quieter than Lampedusa's. It is rare to encounter a novel so self-denying and so free of meretricious appeal.

This very short novel is a small triumph of controlled perspective, and develops with minute care its counterpointed stories of sexual and political exile. . . . Giorgio Bassani's mind does indeed refuse to let itself be violated, even by intelligently perceived theme. This is a writer to be reckoned with, if only because of his refusal to exploit.

Albert J. Guerard. *NYHT*. Aug. 28, 1960. p. 4

[In the] masterful novel, *The Garden of the Finzi-Continis,* by Giorgio Bassani, . . . there is a telling awareness . . . of the same stylists, Stendhal and Proust, who influenced Lampedusa. . . . He pulls the reader into the vortex of a small world within a small city, becoming a character himself. . . . Seldom have the yearnings and sighings, the disappointments and palpitations of youthful life been conveyed so faithfully. . . . *The Garden of the Finzi-Continis*—lacking the universality of *The Leopard* and its great central character—is more a novel about the demise of a small dynasty than a love story. . . . The plot of the book is its mood rather than its events, but that mood is unforgettable.

Herbert Mitgang. *NYT*. Aug. 1, 1965. pp. 4–5

The Second World War remains the overwhelming event of our time. It is possible that even now we have not yet really begun to face it. It is certain that we have not begun to overcome it. It is a trauma in the collective mind of Western society. So much was brought to an end by it; so much can never exist again as a result of it. And so much happened in it for the first time. . . . [*The Garden of the Finzi-Continis*] undertake[s] to deal with that cataclysm and certain of its implications. . . . It . . . is an exercise in nostalgia, but of a direct and unironic kind. It celebrates and memorializes the small community of Ferrarese Jews, a large number of whom were wiped out during the War. It brings at once to mind Sybille Bedford's *A Legacy,* but Bassani's work is smaller in scope and gentler in tone. . . . We soon come to see that in his eyes the garden of the Finzi-Continis is an enchanted garden, that its walls enclosed and protected a whole culture. This was the culture of nineteenth-century liberal European society, a way of life that continued to exist until the second War. . . . No such existence is possible today, and Bassani's work is a graceful and charming elegy upon this vanished life.

Steven Marcus. *NYR*. Aug. 5, 1965. pp. 20–1

Mr. Bassani is a man of proven political courage (a founder of the Action party in 1942) and courageous taste (he was an editor of *Botteghe Oscure,* as many of us remember gratefully). [If] *The Garden of the Finzi-Continis* . . . is a book about the debility of a generation or a class, then I follow. But must the telling of it be so dutifully genteel, so chic? The first kiss in this novel, so long put off, seems an obscene solecism, and an eventual visit to a brothel is no more exciting or vivid than Charlus eyeing a slice of cucumber. *The Garden* strikes me as evasive and precious, confirming a suspicion that such power and weight as there is in current Italian fiction is in the work of such as Pratolini, Pasolini and Vittorini. The rough boys. . . . Bassani's prize-winning novel typif[ies] a well-bred, over-cultivated school given to a kind of anemic arabesque: a true automatism indeed, caging something that is visibly tame.

Paul West. *NYHT*. Aug. 8, 1965. p. 8

The Italians have a tendency to soften asperities. The Italian novel, from Manzoni onwards, has been a thoroughly comfortable product; the golden haze of idyll and euphoria has hung about it. One notices something similar in the Italian films; they get the best of two worlds. . . . If one thinks of Fellini and Antonioni as *attacking* idleness, then one has to say that they are hedging their bets.

Something similar is true of Giorgio Bassani. The theme of his earlier, and brilliant, *The Gold-Rimmed Spectacles* was the nemesis attending moral inertia, of pretending till too late that unpleasant things are simply not happening. In *The Garden of the Finzi-Continis* . . . it has been [the] strength [of the Finzi-Continis] to pretend that unpleasant things are simply not happening. . . . But it is also their most fatal vanity and weakness.

Bassani's judgment on the Finzi-Continis is clear, but it hasn't stopped him, I feel, from writing a novel in which their values carry too much weight. . . . He handles it all with high conventional competence and in delicious detail. . . . All the same, to make so comfortable a novel out of so grim a theme! It is characteristic of something equivocating and Arcadian in the whole Italian conception of fiction. Bassani has located the enemy accurately, but he judges it with . . . leniency.

P. N. Furbank. *Enc.* Oct., 1965. pp. 83–4

The Finzi-Continis of Mr. Bassani's novel are . . . aristocrats. But they are not imitators or even spiritual heirs of the Italian aristocracy; what they uphold is the Jewish tradition of "separation from the nations" which in Western Europe, when joined to wealth and refinement, sometimes produced genuine aristocrats. Though the old religious vigor of this tradition has considerably weakened in the Finzi-Continis, it is still observed by them in a style of life that insists on keeping a certain distance between them and the world. And the tradition prepares them morally for the fate that strikes their co-religionists down completely unawares. . . . The theme of separation, of the outsider, indeed of the outsider as Jew, is a familiar one in modern literature. Mr. Bassani deliberately embraces this theme. But it changes its meaning under his hand. His outsiders are those who turn away from the flat, untransfigured present to immerse themselves in the past which alone is full of feeling and goodness and mystery. . . . This describes a kind of radical nostalgia; the penetrating vision *into* modern life of the great modern literature here turns into a nostalgic looking backwards. . . . I . . . praise this novel, which, with its elaborate sentences and careful art, is literary in a good, old-fashioned way. Above all it has sweetness, a genuine, unsentimental, clear-eyed sweetness. . . . The novel is a work of genuine piety.

Martin Greenberg. *Reporter*. Nov. 18, 1965. pp. 51, 53

See *The Gold-Rimmed Spectacles* and *The Garden of the Finzi-Continis* (novels).

BAZÁN, EMILIA PARDO
See Pardo Bazán, Emilia

BEAUVOIR, SIMONE DE (1908–   )

In the novels of Jean-Paul Sartre . . . it is the individual who receives the chief emphasis. . . . But in the novels of Simone de Beauvoir the focus is kept chiefly upon a conflict of free beings and the problems which they encounter as they struggle to achieve an authentic co-existence. The problem raised in *L'Invitée* is how one can preserve his uniqueness as an individual while participating in collective relationships. . . . In *Le Sang des autres* the problem is whether an individual has the right to involve anyone in a conflict or cause which may or may not succeed and which may cost the one involved his life. . . . For her characters, liberty is not a pursuit but a state of living . . . ; it is not an abstraction, but is realized by the individual only as he participates with others in the affairs of their common existence.

Gwendolyn Bays. *YFS*. Spring-Summer, 1948.
pp. 106–7, 111

Simone de Beauvoir's characters [in *The Blood of Others*] are practicing existentialists, literally mouthpieces for the basic tenets of the philosophy. It would seem that she has succeeded where Sartre has failed. She violates some of our conceptions of good narrative writing, true; but she has written the real thesis novel in an economical, sometimes flat style which conceals a remarkably sustained note of suspense and mounting excitement due to the sheer vitality and force of her ideas. This is perhaps the way a novel of ideas should be presented, not loosely sprawled all over the place, trying to appeal to three or four levels at the same time.

Richard McLaughlin. SR. July 17, 1948. p. 13

The Second Sex, by Simone de Beauvoir, is one of the few great books of our era. It flows from a quality men often deny to women: genius— at least by my definition of that lofty capacity. Genius, I think, is the ability to discover or to create a new *category* or a new *dimension* of human knowledge, human understanding, or human experience. Simone de Beauvoir has finally succeeded in adding that much insight to the subject of woman and the twice-larger subject of human sexuality. That is why I feel no one can leave her book unread and still be considered intellectually up-to-date. It makes a fresh contribution to awareness that cannot be missed any more than the contribution of Freud, say, or Einstein or Darwin—without the onset of a private cultural lag.

Philip Wylie. SR. Feb. 21, 1953. p. 28

Miss Beauvoir is an odd mixture of naïveté and sophistication; she goes wrong usually when she applies existentialism as a solution for human situations that are, as she knows in her deeper self, insoluble.

Yet there is something heroic, if also inadequate, in the post-war European attempt to glorify the frustration that is at the core of the existentialist view. If the heroine of *She Came to Stay* seeks deliberately to encompass her own destruction, it is only, we realize, to sound the limits of her own endurance, and during this process the novel has the merit of being thoughtful and honest about rather exotic emotions.

Maxwell Geismar. Nation. April 24, 1954. p. 368

By writing [in *The Mandarins*] about men corroded by their inner life, perpetually busy reconciling irreconcilables—their ideals, their private lives, and political reality—she has written the most humane novel that has appeared in France in recent years.

Humane, for there can be no more representative description of man than one that presents intellectuals forced by their very craft to harmonize the happenings of their lives and the dictates of consciences. It is also a novel that is true in the purest sense of the term, for Simone de Beauvoir, a philosopher, cannot handle fiction otherwise than by describing step by step things she has experienced.

Madeleine Chapsal. *Reporter*. Jan. 27, 1955. p. 16

Is accuracy enough? For literature to bear witness, there must be not only brilliant observation and analysis, but also deep imaginative transformation and structure. What is in question here is the meaning of "bearing witness." The lack of imaginative grasp in a novel is the more acutely felt if the ordinary social world of customs and virtues is also absent. *The Mandarins* is a novel about loss of faith, about the contradictions of freedom, about the possibility of despair. The author is disillusioned, exceedingly intelligent, and anxious also to be positive and hopeful. But in the denuded atmosphere which her very honesty has created we are starved for power of the imagination.

Iris Murdoch. *Nation*. June 9, 1956. p. 494

She has a lyricism which well conveys her interior warmth, a love of life which gives its own expression to the work of Simone de Beauvoir. . . . Whether it be in fiction, dialectics, polemics or a report, something human and, one must say, feminine comes through between the lines. It is striking to see the deep swells of existential pessimism break against the fundamental optimism of a vigorous nature, a taste for the concrete coloring and animating abstract lines of thought and to come across everywhere, through and against everything, the will to hope that men are advancing towards some purposefulness, that will to hope which is expressed by the celebrated phrase of Camus, quoted somewhere by Simone de Beauvoir: the future is the perfection of men without God.

Genevieve Gennari. *Simone de Beauvoir* (Editions Universitaires). 1958. p. 120.
Tr. by Dorothy Nyren Curley

She recalls herself as a noble, serious-minded, introspective, anxious little girl whose imago struggled for years towards its final bursting into the freedom of existentialism. In the end, despite her tentative excursion into a Rimbaudesque "systematic derangement of the senses," she remains a noble, serious-minded, introspective, anxious intellectual. Although her spirited break from the stiff pattern laid down for her at birth has been complete, in her literary style she remains *rangée,* or conventional. The secular and bourgeois disciplines in which she was formed have, up to this point at least, determined and limited the spread of her wings.

Dilys Laing. *Nation*. June 27, 1959. p. 579

Two themes may be distinguished in Simone de Beauvoir's writings, that receive particular attention and to some extent account for the specific quality of her work. These are *womanhood* and *the role of the intellectual*. . . . Simone de Beauvoir is indeed speaking of herself, when she offers us the example of a woman who has rejected the conventional paths trodden by womanhood, but this individual example may acquire the force of a principle. It is a principle which she submits to ceaseless examination. Not only in her life but in her books also. And when she defends the "second sex," she speaks of all women to all women. She speaks to them of a woman's rights, of her right to choose her own life, to assume responsibility for her own destiny and to refuse what society would thrust upon her.

And a like responsibility is involved—this time on the political plane —when she portrays the French "mandarins" of the post-war years. Just as a woman can no longer be satisfied to be attractive and nothing more, similarly the intellectual cannot continue to play the seer, enveloping himself in a timeless purity and timeless responsibility.

Jacques Ehrmann. *YFS*. Spring-Summer, 1961.
pp. 26, 32

Mme. de Beauvoir's existence has always been governed not by Heideggerian *angst,* as orthodoxy demands and as earlier writings seemed to indicate, but by a relentless drive to *happiness*. . . . Her capacity for absorbing what she calls "happiness" is truly frightening. And the salvation she pursues is typical of our age, insofar as it is a strictly individual one; she must build her happiness all alone, *toute seule, sans secours*. . . . How can we save ourselves, concretely, in the absence of God, if not by surpassing our fellow human beings in all sorts of worldly endeavors? . . . Mme. de Beauvoir is the voice of all the other feminine first-prize winners. She reinterprets the traditional culture of France from the perspective of the career woman; she expresses a viewpoint entirely novel to the French social set-up in a language worthy of a long intellectual past.

René Girard. *YFS*. Spring-Summer, 1961. pp. 41–3

Simone de Beauvoir is without doubt the most original figure in contemporary feminine literature. . . . Simone de Beauvoir is a lively personage, tenacious, spirited, spontaneous, proud, demanding, gifted with a magnificent mind, nourished by a violent and passionate sensibility. She is a strong woman but she tries to rule no one but herself. . . . She is of the line inexhaustibly voluble and intellectually powerful in which belong Mme. de Sévigné, Mme. de Staël, George Sand, of whom she reminds us, assuring for herself a permanent place. She is all that and at the same time the companion of J.-P. Sartre, with whom she shares the glory, a glory open to discussion and yet in some way definite, of having established in France atheistic existentialism.

Georges Hourdin. *Simone de Beauvoir et la Liberté*
(Editions du Cerf). 1962. pp. 181–2.
Tr. by Dorothy Nyren Curley

No chronicler of our lives since Theodore Dreiser has combined so steadfast a passion for human justice with a dullness so asphyxiating as Mme. de Beauvoir. While other writers reproach the reader gently, she flattens his nose against the blackboard, gooses him with a twelve-inch ruler, and warns him if he doesn't start acting grown-up she's going to hold her breath till he does. . . . No other modern writer has moved millions of women, leading submerged lives, towards lives of their own while leading her own vicariously. No other writer has exposed the myths of femininity so lucidly while guarding her own so jealously. Her humanitarianism would be irrefutable if it weren't for men and women getting in the way.

Nelson Algren. *Harper.* May, 1965. p. 134

Madame de Beauvoir has in practice followed Sartre in rejecting the pursuit of a phantom precision, and in assuming the duty of prompt and copious utterance. . . . Madame de Beauvoir's words can be respected for many qualities: integrity, courage, decency, pertinacity, a certain shrewdness, a flair for intellectual and moral dilemmas, an explicit and anguished sharing in the conscience and consciousness of our time. These qualities make many of her books important and interesting, but I doubt if anyone will ever wish to remember a line she wrote.

Conor Cruise O'Brien. *NYR.* May 20, 1965. p. 5

See *The Mandarins* and *She Came to Stay* (novels); also *Memoirs of a Dutiful Daughter, Prime of Life,* and *Force of Circumstance* (autobiography) and *The Second Sex* (social comment).

BECKETT, SAMUEL (1906–   )

It is easy to "refute" Beckett, to reassure oneself (thank God) that this isn't the way things are at all. But Beckett happens to be a master stylist, whose words are assigned their values with almost mathematical precision, and whose total meaning is something far more complex than simply a statement of deep negation shot through (perhaps because it is beyond despair) with a wild Irish humor. Sometimes as we watch his characters wandering through the vivid darkness, their brains clicking like Geiger counters, yet lost even among the simplest categories of space and time, we catch some fragment of ourselves in a gesture of shivering acquiescence. It is then that we slam the book shut in half-fearful impatience and disgust, which is exactly what Mr. Beckett wants us to do.

Jerome Stone. *SR*. Oct. 27, 1956. p. 25

Reading Beckett is an enigmatic experience and often an unpleasant one, but it is an experience. Those of us who do not take a wholly pessimistic view of life cannot help believing that anyone who feels as deeply as Beckett does and writes as passionately automatically refutes his own pessimism: the very existence of these books, with their originality and their beauty, seems to demonstrate that the world is larger and richer than he makes it appear to be. But whether this is sound or not, there is no doubting the authenticity of his voice. He is not paralyzed, as perhaps in all logic he ought to be, by the bleakness of his philosophy; he is diverse, unpredictable, sometimes funny, sometimes disgusting, always impressive. He is one of the true innovators of our period, and it is easy to guess that he will have a large influence.

Granville Hicks. *SR*. Oct. 4, 1958. p. 14

[*Waiting for Godot*] is a poetic harlequinade—tragicomic as the traditional *commedia dell'arte* usually was: full of horseplay, high spirits, cruelty and a great wistfulness. Though the content is intellectual to a degree, the surface, which is at once terse, rapid and prolix in dialogue, is very much like a minstrel show or vaudeville turn.

The form is exactly right for what Beckett wishes to convey. Complete disenchantment is at the heart of the play, but Beckett refuses to honor this disenchantment by a serious demeanor. Since life is an incomprehensible nullity enveloped by colorful patterns of fundamentally absurd and futile activities (like a clown's habit clothing a corpse), it is proper that we pass our time laughing at the spectacle.

Harold Clurman. *Lies Like Truth* (Macmillan). 1958.
pp. 220–1

Perhaps the most interesting feature of Beckett's work is the emergence of a new literary type. His characters are in a more advanced state of despair than Camus's "absurd" men or *révoltés,* than Colin Wilson's "outsiders." They are physically maimed as well as psychologically at disproportion with their society. We might refer to this new literary creature by the letter M, probably suggesting *mort* (death). Beckett goes to startling lengths, particularly in his novels, to have the names of his characters begin with M: Murphy, Molloy, Moran, Malone, Macmann, Mahood. . . . Perhaps the closest counterpart to Beckett's "M" man is that other creature who is identified by a letter of the alphabet, Kafka's K. . . . They have in common an acute lack of awareness, an inability to cope with the exterior world. Their only concrete wrong, in the moral sense, seems to be that they exist.

Melvin J. Friedman. BA. Summer, 1959. p. 281

Each of Beckett's works reflects the same dilemma—one of waiting. Only the form, the outward manifestation varies. All the characters— in the plays as well as in the novels—are one, a fact that deepens their loneliness and desolation. . . . For Beckett the curse and marvel of human existence are its tenacity. Characters run through a gamut of moods and attitudes toward their individual plights, but they assert themselves vigorously to the end. Even then, they are removed from our sight by the exigencies of literary or dramatic composition; in effect, they exist beyond the arbitrary conclusion of any single work. How should Beckett falsify this theme which haunts him by contriving novels in the ordinary sense, novels that probe the psychologies of contrived personages, novels that raise and resolve unreal conflicts? Such devices mean little to him. There is one story; it is his own and perhaps ours.

Ralph J. Mills, Jr. CC. Dec. 30, 1959. p. 1525

Like Joyce, Beckett has reached a kind of outer limit, beyond which reading and perhaps writing itself, already arduous enough, is no longer conceivable. It is a question of letting language speak in order to see whether or not it is adequate for the expression of the reality that it claims to describe. A set purpose of admirable precision that ends by destroying not only the fictional value (it has passed beyond the novel) but the aesthetic and even the expressive values of these books. Samuel Beckett gladly gets along without the aesthetic value. But what about style? . . . By means of a literature that, by negating all literature, annihilates itself in the catastrophe it has created, Samuel Beckett, an exemplary *alittérateur,* opens a door in us which, even after Joyce and Kafka, might perhaps have remained closed. . . . One cannot deny . . . the extraordinary impression, I dare not say of enrichment, since it concerns awareness of an absolute poverty, that Samuel Beckett creates. Poverty that is our only wealth. Inexhaustible, fascinating poverty.

Claude Mauriac. The New Literature (Braziller). 1959.
pp. 81–2

In all Beckett's later works, there is no way of distinguishing fact from fiction. Their inseparability and irreconcilability is a recurrent theme of his trilogy of novels. In each successive novel, the hero-narrator undergoes further physical degeneration. Ironically, composition takes place during decomposition. Just as dying had a specifically sexual connotation for the Elizabethans, so it seems to have a specifically creative one for Beckett—artistically creative.

Ruby Cohn. *Accent*. Autumn, 1960. p. 233

A special virtue attaches to plays which remind the drama of how much it can do without and still exist. By all the known criteria, Samuel Beckett's "Waiting for Godot" is a dramatic vacuum. Pity the critic who seeks a chink in its armour, for it is all chink. It has no plot, no climax, no *dénouement*; no beginning, no middle, and no end. Unavoidably, it has a situation, and it might be accused of having suspense, since it deals with the impatience of two tramps, waiting beneath a tree, waiting for a cryptic Mr. Godot to keep his appointment with them; but the situation is never developed, and a glance at the programme shows that Mr. Godot is not going to arrive. "Waiting for Godot" frankly jettisons everything by which we recognize theatre. It arrives at the customhouse, as it were, with no luggage, no passport, and nothing to declare; yet it goes through, as might a pilgrim from Mars. It does this, I believe, by appealing to a definition of drama much more fundamental than any in the books. A play, it asserts, is basically a means of spending two hours in the dark without being bored.

Kenneth Tynan. *Curtains* (Atheneum). 1961. p.101

Beckett's entire work can be seen as a search for the reality that lies behind mere reasoning in conceptual terms. He may have devaluated language as an instrument for the communication of ultimate truths, but he has shown himself a great master of language as an artistic medium. *"Que voulez-vous, Monsieur? C'est les mots; on n'a rien d'autre."* For want of better raw material, he has molded words into a superb instrument for his purpose. In the theatre he has been able to add a new dimension to language—the counterpoint of action, concrete, many-faceted, not to be explained away, but making a direct impact on an audience. In the theatre, or at least in Beckett's theatre, it is possible to bypass the stage of conceptual thinking altogether, as an abstract painting bypasses the stage of the recognition of natural objects. In "Waiting for Godot" and "Endgame," plays drained of character, plot, and meaningful dialogue, Beckett has shown that such a seemingly impossible tour de force can in fact be accomplished.

Martin Esslin. *The Theatre of the Absurd*
(Doubleday). 1961. p. 46

Mr. Beckett's patient concern with bicycles, amputees, battered hats, and the letter M; his connoisseurship of the immobilized hero; his pre-occupation with footling questions which there isn't sufficient evidence to resolve; his humor of the short sentence; his Houdini-like virtuosity (by preference chained hand and foot, deprived of story, dialogue, locale): these constitute a unique comic repertoire, like a European clown's. The antecedents of his plays are not in literature but—to take a rare American example—in Emmett Kelly's solemn determination to sweep a circle of light into a dustpan: a haunted man whose fidelity to an impossible task—quite as if someone he desired to oblige had exacted it of him—illuminates the dynamics of a tragic sense of duty. . . . The milieu of his novels bears a moral resemblance to that of the circus, where virtuosity—to no end—is the principle of life, where a thousand variations of three simple movements fill up the time between train and train, and the animals have merely to pace their cages to draw cries of admiring sympathy that are withheld, whatever his risks, from the high-wire acrobat: the spectators settled numbly in the ritual of waiting, the normal emotions of human solidarity not perverted but anesthetized.

Hugh Kenner. Samuel Beckett (Grove). 1961. pp. 13–14

The actions of these Chaplinesque clowns [in *Waiting for Godot*] are but parodies of action. Taking up one sentiment of endeavor and then quickly abandoning it for another, which is just as summarily developed, they are like those circus clowns who turn from trying to put out a bon-fire with an atomizer to falling off a horse in an attempt to emulate the bareback rider to playing a miniature violin—all within the space of a few minutes. . . . Their actions have a clownish lack of dignity, even when they are supposed to be noble ones: witness the burlesque falling down of Vladimir and then Estragon when they attempt to help their fellow humans to get up. Verbal activity too is parodied: the formulae of friendship, of meeting and parting, of politeness, of humanitarianism and religion, of argument and oration, of logic, are delivered with a cool automatism often similar to the patter of the "straight-man" comic and interlocutor couples of the vaudeville variety act.

Judith J. Radke. YFS. Spring-Summer, 1962. pp. 60–1

Beckett has reconciled the atheist and antitheist positions by making God a figment of the misanthropic and masochistic side of our nature, in whose service is perfect misery. . . . Starting with the undeniable fact of human suffering, he concludes that not all is right with the world and asks what kind of God could have created it or even permitted it.

To this old question he offers two different answers: in the plays God is if not all-powerful at least all-stupid, which for purposes of domination is perhaps even better, and infinitely malicious—nothing is too low or mean for him to do, no practical joke is too banal; but in the novels God becomes man repeatedly, incarnating himself in a series of weary neurotics whom he delights in frustrating, tormenting, mutilating and driving mad. Only when he speaks in his own proper Neo-Platonic person—an absurd contradiction for which he says he is not responsible —do we realize that his creatures have created him—or are creating him—and that he is merely carrying out the assignment they have given him—or are in process of giving him.

J. Mitchell Morse. HdR. Winter, 1962–3. pp. 512-4

The basic materials of Beckett's work are selves as inquiring selves, selves as objects, other objects, and the degrees and forms of distance between one of these and another. There are no clear lines of differentiation: both inanimate objects and distances have universal properties, or rather residual properties left over from the Cartesian universe. Beckett's heroes describe lines and curves of relationship. They are first of all disturbed over the matter of creation (cannot determine if they or a "something other" is a creator); secondly are puzzled over the question of the identity of created things (if the original creative source is not clearly known, it follows that creatures will be confused with one another); finally are engaged in the bewildering process of defining objects, as individually and separately objects or as extensions of the self.

All of these facts about Beckett's world set it off from that of his contemporaries. Both illogicality and absurdity have already been assumed; Beckett is not concerned to prove either one. Instead, his writings are attenuations of meaning: a ceaseless and noisy and repetitious echoing of logical questions and near-definitions.

Frederick J. Hoffman. Samuel Beckett (Southern Illinois).
1962. pp. 80–1

A Beckett hero is always in conflict with objects around him, for only he himself has reality. Just as Descartes separated mind and body and then tried to re-integrate them, Beckett divorces people from objects and then attempts to find some relationship between them. The recent French novel typified by the work of Alain Robbe-Grillet, Michel Butor, and Nathalie Sarraute is, in one way, a footnote to Beckett's output of the last two decades. . . . A Beckett protagonist, be he Murphy, Watt, Molloy, or Malone, has long ago refused complicity with objects. Or else, objects have remained outside his attainment. In every instance, he is divided from the rest of the world, a stranger to its desires and needs. The dichotomy between his own mind and body finds an analogy in the outside world in the dichotomy between people and objects. Thus, Beckett's world operates in halves, and the dialectic of any given novel occurs when these halves conflict, when tension is created between mind and body, on one hand, and people and objects, on the other.

Frederick R. Karl. *The Contemporary English Novel*
(Farrar). 1962. p. 21

Beckett's nihilism is a last phase of anti-literature, and *The Unnamable* brings up to date a tradition that began in the eighteenth century with *Rameau's Nephew,* then went on through Dostoevsky and Gide and Kafka. Beckett's wish to extinguish the self is not the romantic nihilism of Nietzsche or the terrorists or other nineteenth-century heroes for whom suicide was an ultimate affirmation of the self. Paradoxically enough, the romantic nihilist made the self an absolute by destroying the self. With Beckett the affirmation is gone; but the paradox remains, for after the self has shriveled, the human remains—in some unlocalized area of perception or response. To repeat: we have an existence, however unwillingly, after we have lost an identity; and we do not seem able to diminish this existence below a certain point. Beckett's hero has no voice, but he must speak. Or as the Unnamable says, nothing troubles him; yet he is troubled.

Wylie Sypher. *Loss of the Self* (Random). 1962. p. 154

As a novelist, Beckett stands as a living link between the young French authors and the foreign master James Joyce, whom they all revere. Beckett's ghostly and grisly fictions, which parody the world and man's lot, derive quite clearly from Joyce and anticipate the sort of writing the new generation advocates. Whether the name is Murphy, Molloy, Moran, or Malone, the protagonist is always Everyman recounting the human adventure on earth. Depending on which name he goes by, he is closer or farther away from the term of life; but for him, existence has been a quest ending in nothing. Like the outsider-heroes of the new novel, he is—by circumstances or by his own volition—isolated from his fellow men, free in his solitude to record his sensations and to ruminate endlessly upon the suffering of mortals. The work of Beckett is one long cry of metaphysical despair, and in its utterance nothing is left of the novel we refer to as conventional.

Laurent Le Sage. *The French New Novel*
(Pennsylvania State). 1962. p. 47

The delights offered by Beckett are of an old and tried variety. He has re-invented philosophical and theological allegory, and as surely as Spenser he needs the right to sound sub-rational, to conceal intention under an appearance of dreamlike fortuity, to obscure the literal sense. The only difference is that his predecessors were sure there was such a sense, and on this bitch of a planet he can no longer have such certainties. This difference does not affect the proposition that Beckett's flirtations with reality are carried on in a dialect which derives from the traditional language of learning and poetry. It is nevertheless true that the more accustomed we become to his formal ambiguity, the more outrageously he can test us with inexplicitness, with apparently closed systems of meaning.

Frank Kermode. *NYR*. March 19, 1964. p. 11

See *Malone Dies, Molloy, Murphy, Watt,* and *The Unnamable* (novels); also *Waiting for Godot, Endgame, Happy Days* and *Krapp's Last Tape* (plays).

BENAVENTE, JACINTO (1866–1954)

The theatre of Benavente is dynamic, because it deals with thought in the process of crystallization. Hence the secret of its power. It anticipates appearances, and makes short work of artificialities. Although all classes of men and women are reproduced in his work, there are no types. Through all his scenes, one will search in vain for one hero, and one will search in vain for one villain. The machinery of life plays small part in his analyses, which delve beneath occupation. The human terms of problems engage him, the postulates which inhere in their solution, the working out of these in feeling and ways of thought, and in acts afterward of human and irremediable import. His drama . . . lives with a strange, vivifying power, which . . . makes his work in its totality one of the most human documents that literature has known. Benavente's is the most sophisticated of arts, because it is the flower of an old, anciently corrupt, disillusioned civilization, which has at length awakened spiritually and searched itself, taking account of the evil with what there is of good, and set itself again to become strong.

John Garrett Underhill. Introduction to Benavente's
Plays (Scribner). 1919. v. 2, pp. xiv-xv

In his dramas he is never a propagandist and but rarely a partisan. On the contrary, he is a dilettante, and, like Anatole France, interested in everything and disturbed at nothing. He has no thesis to prove, no problem to solve, and no remedy to offer. The feminine heart, the frivolous philanderer, royalty and the moneyed class, misjudged charity and *bourgeois* morality, and a hundred and one comedies and tragedies of daily life, are just spoils for the author's keenness of observation and his genius for irony. A true pedagogue, he teaches by laughter.

Alexander Green. *Outlook*. Dec. 31, 1919. p. 594

It is said of the Spanish playwright, as it has been said of Bernard Shaw, that he has no higher aim than to be the super-clever popular playwright of his day; that he is utterly frivolous; that he lacks that stability which belief in any carefully thought out and firmly held philosophy would give him. . . . He does not exhort, he does not preach, he does not advise. He is content to show us some particular phase of life as he himself sees it, and then leaves us to draw our own conclusions. He does this deliberately, not as a refuge for mediocrity, but because he is convinced that the true function of the drama is to picture life on the stage, and he accomplishes his purpose so well that he wins at once extravagant blame and praise. He is blamed unjustly for a lack of serious purpose, and so lifelike are his portraits that he has been overpraised as a student of character. . . . The best of Benavente's claims as a depicter of character rests upon his capability as a revealer of motives through speeches. Literally his people are convicted out of their own mouths, and this is surely one of the rare gifts of the dramatic genius.

William Haynes. *Dial*. Jan., 1920. pp. 116–7

In the essence of his personality one finds the characteristic traits of the *señorito* of Madrid: refinement and gentility, keen intuition, a biting malicious humor, cynical indifference where moral issues are involved, genial skepticism. . . . Benavente was, however, more than just a satirist . . . his works took on a moral and human significance. They contain not merely amusing jesting at the world we live in, but an ideal for a better humanity. A poet full of compassion for the weak and the suffering is revealed in the stinging satirist. . . . Benavente's philosophy of life . . . is based on a belief in the virtues of self sacrifice, resignation and forgiveness, which qualities he assigns his feminine characters. Strangely, Benavente almost always sees the nobler side of life through his women. The perspicacity of his analysis of the feminine soul, and his entire freedom from sex prejudice, constitute one of the innovations of his art.

Federico de Onís. *NAR*. March, 1923. pp. 359–62

The revolution introduced by Benavente into Spanish drama was part of a new movement which was taking place throughout Western Europe.

... Just as Shaw by his ridicule destroyed bombastic unreality on the English stage, so Benavente in Spain led his public gradually away from "Sardoodledom" (to use a coin of Mr. Shaw) on which they had been sunk. . . . He destroyed the aside and the soliloquy, introducing in their stead the quick, jerky dialogue of ordinary speech. But Benavente's mission was a deeper one; he wanted to get away from the old romatic love story and draw nearer to the presentation of modern life as it is. . . . In examining Benavente's crowded stage we shall see pass before our eyes all the types of modern life, and we shall watch the struggle between the new growth of modern twentieth century civilization superimposed on top of a layer of old traditions that never died out and that give a characteristic flavor to the Spanish character.

Walter Starkie. *Jacinto Benavente* (Oxford). 1924. pp. 20–1

His initial success was based upon a definite break with the Echegaray tradition, and although it is hardly likely that the Sardoodledum of that dramatic platitudinarian can be restored, Benavente has resuscitated some of his peculiarities; notably, the use of a desolating and far-fetched philosophy expressed in hollow symbols. . . . He is not a writer with fundamental ideas, with a definite philosophy, like Shaw . . . whose aim has been to create a public for the drama of ideas, the play with a criticism of social and economic conditions. Benavente's lack of equipment for such a rôle is evident. . . . His real function is that of a genial and sceptical satirist of manners, who deftly and discreetly strips the gilt off the surface of society and reveals the eternal imbecilities and hypocrisies of the conventional world. His art is that of the miniaturist; and he often lacks the broad strokes which are effective across the footlights.

Ernest Boyd. *Studies from Ten Literatures* (Scribner). 1925. pp. 101–3

The significance of Benavente's plays, apart from their intrinsic merit as drama, lies, indeed, in the bridge which they offer between the new intellectualism and the old romanticism. In him the conflict between the two is never fully resolved, and his work thus reflects the doubts and uncertainties that perplex civilization today. . . . He sees all points of view; he explodes human foibles, conventions and conceits with the innumerable pinpricks of his satire: but he remains a destroyer. He has no solution to offer for the problems which he is so skillful in revealing. Pessimism is, indeed, one of the two prevailing characteristics of his work—a pessimism that is not so much cynicism as that "sad irony which cannot weep and so smiles." It is, in a word, a pessimism redeemed by pity—an overmastering sense of pity which alone gives some unity of outlook to Benavente's otherwise complicated and vacillating vision.

> Gilbert Thomas. *Spec.* April 25, 1925. pp. 661–2

It was Benavente who caught the essence of the Ibsenian drama. . . . Benavente followed Ibsen into the inner sanctum of the human soul, where man struggles with himself. He became, in other words, the leading exponent in Spain of the modern psychological drama of which Ibsen was the father. . . . What were some of the Ibsenian elements . . . [in] Benavente's works? . . . It is not in the technique of his plays, but in the ideas with which they deal that we must look for the important parallels. And here we meet first of all the favorite theme of so many of the dramatists who followed in the wake of Ibsen: namely, the past acting as a dead weight upon the present; . . . [then] the theme of feminine revolt . . . the heredity motif . . . the self-sacrificing type . . . the thread which is, perhaps, the most characteristic of Benavente's entire dramatic web: the spirit of renunciation, of resignation to one's fate . . . [and finally] the philosophy of individualism.

> Halfdan Gregersen. *Ibsen and Spain* (Harvard).
> 1936. pp. 139–52

Benavente's work marks both the rise and fall of the well-made play in the twentieth century Spanish theatre. . . . James Graham Luján . . . insists that Benavente is to the Spanish theatre what Edna Ferber is to the American novel—a rapid, able workman, possessed of a formula that has been highly successful, popular and witty, turning out a great deal of popular work, but not to be considered a great artist. The comparison is provocative. It does not, however, take account of Benavente's service in bringing to the Spanish stage all the currents that were blowing across the European stage in his half century of play writing. Pirandello, Giraudoux, Jean Cocteau, George Bernard Shaw, Synge, and Molnár are only a few of the playwrights whose ideas have been transmogrified in terms of the Spanish theatre by the versatile and indefatigable Don Jacinto.

> Mildred Adams. *A History of Modern Drama*, ed. by
> Barrett H. Clark and George Freedley (Appleton).
> 1947. pp. 567–8

The very variety of Benavente's contributions to the stage indicates that he is no faithful follower of the realistic tradition. Rather it might be said that on the stock of the traditional vigorous Spanish poetic drama he grafts the twig of Ibsen and his followers. His quality, therefore, depends less on his pursuit of the realistic problem play in itself than upon the strength that comes to him from outside that particular sphere.

Allardyce Nicoll. *World Drama* (Harcourt). 1950. p. 676

There are abstruse or philosophical overtones in many of his plays. . . . Benavente appends a philosophy of society and sentiment to a *commedia dell'arte* plot . . . [in] "The Bonds of Interest" [which] is a brilliant trifle about matters that are not trifles.

The same symbolization appeared in some of the author's weightier plays and with greater straining for profundity. . . . But profundity gained at the expense of a rationality or credibility of dramatic plot is normally not worth the effort. . . . In another age like seventeenth century France, when he would have operated within a convention of poetic artifice, Benavente might have become a comic poet like Moliére; in their modern investiture Benavente's realistic satires are clever but mild.

John Gassner. *Masters of the Drama* (Dover). 1954.
pp. 429–30

Benavente has been called "the Bernard Shaw of Spain." There is no doubt that he would have liked to live up to the title, but Spain, even the Spain of that earlier era, offered no climate for Shaws. The Spanish dramatist wrote to the day of his death . . . at the age of 84 . . . but unlike Shaw he had his say, if he had anything really worth saying, by 1900. In short, Benavente was no thinker. . . . He was a sensitive man of the theater and a magnificent craftsman. It was he who brought to the Spanish stage all the currents of the European theater of that first quarter of the century. In most of his works (he wrote around 200) he may have practiced a quick formula, as many claim, but he is the author of three unquestionably fine plays; "Señora Ama". . ."The Bonds of Interest" . . . [and] "The Passion Flower." . . . If most of Benavente's theater is frail as literature, it is rich as a mirror of a particular spiritual and social confusion. . . . The Spain of Benavente's plays offers a fascinating picture of a society lost between faith and nihilism.

Roberto G. Sánchez. *BA*. Winter, 1955. pp. 41–3
See *Plays* (4 vols.).

BERNANOS, GEORGES (1888–1948)

Let us be quite frank and admit that an element of Bernanos's appeal to his reader is pornographic. Flagellation, transvestism, the seduction of fourteen-year-olds by middle-aged rakes, the sadistic murder of pure girls of good family by proletarian debauchees who are foreigners and peeping Toms into the bargain . . . these are the familiar ingredients of rubber-shop literature, with or without the shutters of the confessional, the priestly robe, the candle-lit study and the clouds of incense. Yet Bernanos is a serious and at times an exquisite artist. He is a suberb rhetorician, a profound judge of motive, a man tender and generous (as only a Latin seems able to be) in his attitude to public affairs and a considerable scholar. His narrative technique is possibly unequalled in our time.

Rayner Heppenstall. *The Double Image* (Secker and Warburg). 1947. pp. 34–5

What sort of a novelist is it that seems to know none of the tricks of novel-writing, whose plots are almost unintelligible, whose themes erupt rather than develop and whose dining rooms are as devoid of furniture and food as they are filled with violent talk? What sort of thinker is it that hates the brain and all its works and pomps?

Plato . . . could have supplied the answer. Bernanos on his highest level is a poet; not a verse-writer but a special kind of being, like William Blake, who tries to use words to communicate a vision, or rather to infect others with the possibility of seeing a vision. . . . Words are instruments of emotion and extralogical revelation.

Donat O'Donnell. *KR*. Summer, 1949. p. 422

Bernanos was transparent, luminous with truth. Even his adversaries bowed instinctively in the presence of that amazing probity. He forced respect, even admiration. The essential qualities of his work, charity and necessary nobility, were written in his face. His glacier-blue eyes spoke entire loyalty, limitless kindness and courage. He was a knight of the spirit—*sans peur et sans reproche*. . . . Bernanos was the most indulgent of fathers, the most obliging of neighbors and the kindest of friends; but he had in him something of the warrior. He proclaimed again and again his love for the company of monks and soldiers. . . . He was a man whose Yes and No were categorical and unqualified.

Ernst Erich Noth. *BA*. Winter, 1949. pp. 21–3

It will seem perhaps quixotic that the violent one, the fighter of this time, Georges Bernanos, should be preaching neither science nor vice nor even the "natural man," but traditionalism in every sense. Should be royalist and Catholic and a believer in knights: should passionately advocate continuity, that sense of the past which in England, he remarks, is so often confused with the sense of humor. . . . It is an indication of the quality of Bernanos that although utterly dedicated to the Christian Heritage, he will not accept the dotage of the Catholic myth, but prefers to howl against the storm like Lear, without even a fool beside him. . . . He is devoured by a sense of right, not only of Godly right but of a most human justice, and he is not stupid.

> Eleanor Clark. *The Kenyon Critics,* ed. by
> John Crowe Ransom (World). 1951. p. 260

Bernanos comes close to Dostoievsky, who creates his own mental universe and fills it with creatures to his own image and likeness; not to Tolstoi, who rebuilds and brings back to life a world familiar to all of us. It is remarkable that even Bernanos's priests, despite their dazzling reality, resemble no living priest. . . . Indeed, their disturbing presence is the presence of Bernanos himself, that priestly soul condemned to wander among us under the guise of a man of letters; for thirty years we have admired and loved from a distance that wild bird that hurled itself against the bars of a materialistic cage in which we all settled down as best we could, with the least inconvenience, and with that desire for comfort which no apocalyptic vision could discourage.

> François Mauriac. *Letters on Art and Literature*
> (Philosophical Library). 1953. pp. 12–13

Bernanos's stylistic greatness is of the same kind as that of Dante or Pascal. He explains the supernatural with everyday analogues as though he had experienced it himself. He even harmonizes these analogues with the mentality of the heroes so that the symbols perfectly fit the characters. Moreover, he challenges the real mystics who invented the most subtle comparision for their experiences, and, finally, he discovers poetical analogies that are true symbols, the kind called by Flaubert *rapports fatals* and by Baudelaire *correspondances.*

> Helmut Hatzfeld. *Trends and Styles in Twentieth
> Century French Literature* (Catholic U.). 1957. p. 180

Perhaps Bernanos's vision of reality and the astonishing gallery of demons that torment him are too highly individual, too violently imposed upon his fictional world to take on universal significance. What remains is the powerful, exasperated and exasperating individual whose own daily life took place on just such a heroic and tempestuous plane. Through the few characters who really live in our imagination, through the tormented atmospheres of the novels themselves, we can make our way toward so genuinely individual a vision of our world, so sincere a cry of distress on its behalf, that we feel we have touched something essential, something that is of greater significance than anything encountered in the polished and more traditional novels of Green, Bosco, Giono, or Mauriac.

Germaine Brée and Margaret Guiton. *An Age of Fiction*
(Rutgers). 1957. p. 130

The anguish of Bernanos may indeed be the anguish caused by sin, the sin of the whole cosmos, but it is also anguish caused by the abyss within oneself, the spectacle of frightening potentialities in the darker depths. The element of self-pursuit, or self-flagellation, which there undoubtedly is in his imaginative work . . . could be profitably investigated. However, it is a measure of the effectiveness of Bernanos that he could disturb us sufficiently to make us seek arms to use against him, which we may use only half-heartedly, entertaining a secret conviction, fear even, perhaps, that that ruthless vision of his, with its nightmarish quality, approximates nearer than most to the plight in which we should be seen, or in which at least we should see ourselves.

Ernest Beaumont. *DR.* Summer, 1957. p. 155

The word "prophet" comes involuntarily to one's mind when speaking of Bernanos—for several reasons: his *indignation* before the spiritual state of the modern world, his loud and eloquent *denunciation* of certain people and classes and his readiness to show the rood of a radical regeneration, that is his *forgiveness*. These are, however, the qualities of a prophet, and are not, on every point, reconcilable with those of the polemicist. As a result, we find Bernanos often guilty of remaining within the sphere of generalities, neglecting the duty of illustrating the problems he raises, as if the fire of the truth he proclaims—and with which we agree—were sufficient to illuminate the unelaborated details of his subject. At other times, however, the image he uses is so expressive that it replaces, by itself, a painstaking documentation, and gives us the supreme satisfaction of seeing, in a flash, from within.

Thomas Molnar. *Bernanos: His Political Thought and
Prophecy* (Sheed). 1960. p. 196

The immense drama of salvation which unfolds throughout Georges Bernanos's works, from the early *Dialogue d'ombres,* through the novelist's last and most complex novel, *Monsieur Ouine,* is conceived poetically as a contest between two elements, water and earth. . . . In veritable biblical floods, we see the precious living forms of creation swallowed up by the vengeful water and creation itself returning to nothingness. But above all, the Bernanosian shipwrecks testify to the human spirit's deep vulnerability to the infinitude of the sea—realm of the fallen Angel —and, on the psychological level, to the vertiginous dream of death through which Satan lures the weary quester of Paradise back into the abyss of unconsciousness.

Gerda Blumenthal. *The Poetic Imagination of Georges Bernanos* (Johns Hopkins). 1965. p. 7

See *Diary of a Country Priest* (novel).

BERTO, GIUSEPPE (1914–   )

As the phoenix is said to rise from the smoke and ashes of past civilizations, so does the creative spirit reassert itself after chaos, violence, and despair.

From Italy now comes a novel that is a most poignant expression of life in the rubble-ruin of the late World War. . . . *The Sky is Red* is one of the few current documents which take their strength from poetic insight rather than from reportorial accuracies. . . . Much of Berto's success derives from the rhythm of his words, the happy and easy way his language moves from the general to the particular; above all from his deep feeling for his characters and their tragic plight in the face of a war the reasons for which are beyond their immature understanding.

John Gross. *CSM*. Sept. 30, 1948. p. 11

The Sky is Red . . . is so characteristic and moving a response to the despair felt by millions of ordinary, non-political Italian victims of the war that it will be read as a document of the times. Yet I must add that despite its truth and power of sympathy, its literary distinction is slight. In the current Italian situation it is reminiscent of the proletarian novels we had in the thirties—statistics of degradation, inviting the total disgust that is presumably the prelude to revolution. In Europe today, such novels are fundamentally testimony to the disintegration of order. . . . The book hangs not on its story, but on an environment of mood. This Berto tries to convey in a prose . . . [that is] deliberately colorless. . . . With his carefully toneless air of disillusionment, it is as if he were trying to pin his story onto the long weariness of Italy with a strong suggestion of some very old Italian submission to life, by writing with as little personal force as possible.

The influence of Hemingway is enormous . . . [but] Berto . . . lacks Hemingway's secret lyricism and above all Hemingway's insistence on the ultimate dignity of man. With one word following stolidly after an-

other, Berto's simplicity seems not so much a way of reaching for essential things as a reaction against centuries of the national rhetoric.

Alfred Kazin. *NYHT*. Oct. 10, 1948. p. 14

We have all read of a new Italian renaissance in art and letters. Returning visitors tell [of] . . . a strange stirring and vibrancy as if some
new energy were germinating from out of the decay. The Italian movies
are soft, dejected, full of a pain and despair that hardly raise their
voices. Yet they strike us as if with a powerful ray of life-giving force.

All this tallies with the impression one gets on reading Giuseppe
Berto's *The Sky is Red* . . . the story of Italy's "lost generation." . . . The
hope is in the writing, in the fact that it was written at all, in the resolute confrontation of tragedy. The hope is in its tenderness, its
eloquence through quiet, its warmth without bathos. Its sentiment is
simply truth unashamed. It has a reality that stands out clearly in the
glow of a stately, subdued light. . . . There is in it a shade of human
completeness. Entirely of our day, *The Sky is Red* exemplifies the great
tradition of classic Italian art.

Harold Clurman. *NR*. Oct. 25, 1948. p. 24

Signor Berto is far more in control of his material than most novelists
of World War Two. There is no cardboard about his characters, no
exploitation of a tragic situation for its fictional possibilities. But his
book *The Sky is Red* is entirely predictable. Good-will leads him straight
into an over-simplified allegory. The lesson of the horrors of war, especially as they fall on the poor, must be taught. And so the typical in
the four main characters, the fact that they behave exactly as one
would expect, finally blurs the individual. . . . The illusion of free will
evaporates not because of any views the author may hold but because
of the necessities of the fictional pattern. It is a fault radical to this
novel and to many of the most seriously intentioned novels of our time.

Ernest Jones. *Nation*. Jan. 1, 1949. p. 23

[A] curious lack of guilt pervades all Berto's work. The people are innocent, the soldiers not unkind, perhaps history is to blame—but what
is history? An event one got in the way of. In such a landscape all
that one can be sure of is that the children are most completely the
victims and most nearly the absolute blameless. Pity flows toward them
unimpeded, with no qualifications, no doubts. They are, in a measure,
outside history. This gives them the central pivoting place they occupy
in Berto's and in other contemporary writers' stories. They are ideologi-
cally spotless, and what else is anywhere in a world in which guilt and
innocence are so terribly interlocked?

Alfred Hayes. *NYHT*. June 18, 1950. p. 8

The Brigand . . . communicates a vivid sense of familiar moral anxieties and a sincere and undemonstrative compassion, and yet . . . brings too little of the authority of mind and feeling which is the better part of talent to the treatment of material which has been genuinely experienced. . . . *The Brigand* . . . just misses a real effect of tragedy through ignoring until it is virtually too late the psychological, as distinct from the social, determinants of a tragic situation. . . . This second novel shows a truthful and humane mind contemplating the after-war peasant scene of poverty and land hunger in Southern Italy. . . . The lively humanity of the story and an all but innocent note of satire occasionally bring to mind the film "Bicycle Thieves."

R. D. Charques. *Spec.* June 1, 1951. p. 730

The Brigand is not Berto's best book (for one thing it lacks the emotional force of *The Sky is Red*), but it is his most professional. . . . The book's setting recalls recent Italian films, and the reader will find here the same honesty and passion, the same faithful descriptions made memorable by such films as "Tragic Hunt" and "Open City." This passionate honesty of Berto's rings through all the social "message" of the book, though at times the expression of that message may seem a little ingenuous. It is impossible to write about southern Italy without becoming involved in sociology, and Berto at least has avoided the pitfalls of false sophistication.

William Fense Weaver. *NYT.* Dec. 9, 1951. p. 28

Although Guiseppe Berto's *The Brigand* ends in the annihilation of most of the characters, it, like his earlier *The Sky is Red,* convincingly dramatizes the efforts of the Italian people to escape the Fascist "law of life." Until he goes berserk at the end, the brigand . . . is both a symbol of opposition to tyranny and a fully realized human being. . . . Much of the virtue of the novel is in the description of the villagers, of the confusing ignorance they inherit and of their dubiously optimistic assertions of the right to live as human beings. *The Brigand* is neither a people, yes, nor a people, no; it is a more compressed and restrained Italian *Grapes of Wrath*, an eloquent tract for our times.

Harvey Curtis Webster. *NR.* Dec. 10, 1951. pp. 26–7

One of the most obvious signs of American influence on Berto is . . . the abundance and character of the dialogues. It would naturally be preposterous to ascribe every occurrence of dialogue to Hemingway's example. But whenever you come across what purports to be a faithful reproduction of conversation, with all its repetitions and apparently meaningless expletives, with its short sentences falling like drops in a vacuum, creating an atmosphere almost by the significance of the pauses, by barely hinted gestures and actions—whenever you come across this, you may depend on it that an American influence is at hand.... The bare word is occasionally used in incantation, as if, by sheer repetition, it could take on all the life of the thing itself.... The repetitions, the short sentences, give in the long run the impression of simplicity, of elementariness, of closeness to nature, which we associate with American novels, in particular Hemingway's.

> Mario Praz. *The Literary Reputation of Hemingway*
> *in Europe,* ed. by Roger Asselineau
> (Lettres Modernes). 1965. pp. 118–9

In [Berto's] previous work nothing exists to prepare the reader for what occurs in [*Incubus*]. The author, in the late forties and early fifties, of a handful of novels that lay well within the main conventions of postwar Italian fiction—on the one hand naturalistic and rooted in social phenomena, and on the other vaguely psychological and still more vaguely metaphysical—he has, after a long creative silence . . . , suddenly produced a work of fiction which has all the earmarks of a revolutionary act of the imagination. . . . What is of considerable importance . . . is Berto's technical intention and partial achievement. His novel proceeds from the widely shared (if seldom daringly acted upon) notion that ordinary forms of narrative are exhausted, unconvincing, that in order to exist at the present moment fiction has to present itself in new guises. Berto's mask is that of a man who in giving an account of his psychic history is seemingly bent on establishing the truths of that history, but who is actually engaged in quite a different enterprise: the presentation of a way of apprehending reality so that it takes on the non-factual, non-verifiable, totally self-contained and extraordinary nature of esthetic truth. . . . Like the writers he most resembles—Carlo Emilio Gadda and the French anti-novelist Claude Simon—Berto is not writing "about" life but about the means we have to speak about life.

> Richard Gilman. *NYT.* Feb. 20, 1966. p. 5

See *The Sky Is Red, The Brigand,* and *Incubus* (novels); also *The Work of God and Other Stories.*

BETTI, UGO (1892–1953)

[In *Uomo e Donna*] Betti is trying to put on paper philosophical reflections on the origins and destinies of the human race. He is on the whole successful, and his compact verses have a solemnity and depth of feeling that are rare in modern Italian verse. Since he is dealing with universals most of the poems are impressive rather than moving, but there are a few which are more personal and more in line with his prose personality. . . . For clarity of thought and depth of emotion, as well as for willingness to deal in universals, this volume of poems stands out prominently among all the modern verse of the last ten or twenty years.

Thomas G. Bergin. *BA*. Autumn, 1939. p. 501

Our author's dramas are a mass of words, at times leavened by vague ideas, but dehumanized, abstracted from life, food only for the intellectual elite of a too-sophisticated and moribund culture. They are fit for armchair perusal by a person with a strong stomach for pessimism, not fit fort he stage. . . . Years ago George Meredith criticized the naturalist Zola who "seeing the hog in nature, took nature for the hog." With slightly different emphasis one might say the same of Betti whose black pessimism is a defect of his art because it leaves no place, as the French say, for *"un certain contraire."* The later plays reflect, perhaps, the psychic condition of the modern world with its lack of faith and its scorn for the ideals which have always activated humanity, its consequent pessimism, general abasement and mortification of spiritual forces; but they fail to give the very thing Betti says he is aiming for, esthetic and poetic truth, the idea of the reality of moral good.

Lander MacClintock. *MLJ*. April, 1951. p. 257

"The Gambler" . . . is another in the lengthy line of plays concerning themselves with the protagonist's defeated attempt to make logic triumph over emotion, but in the process so runs up and down the side-alleys of metaphysics, theology, ethics, morals, mysticism, Freudianism and other topics and accompanies the running with such ceaseless, lofty rhetoric that any drama that might conceivably be in the materials is completely talked out of them. . . . Where a Shaw in "Don Juan in Hell" dealt with some of the items in Betti's philosophical catalogue not only with a likelier intelligence but with simplicity, compulsion and wit, the Italian author, a jurist by profession, brings to them a solemnity, portentousness and depressive fog. . . . The so-called play . . . resolves itself finally and only into a watery chowder of the thought of Pirandello, Strindberg, Dostoievski, Anouilh, Sartre, and the kind of minor playwright esteemed by the late Brander Matthews as a colossus.

George Jean Nathan. *The Theatre in the Fifties*
(Knopf). 1953. pp. 173–4

Pirandello's mantle has not fallen on Ugo Betti, for this is a dramatist with his own vision of a world on trial, a vision which avoids the innate pessimism of the great Italian master. Ugo Betti was a High Court Judge, and an acute observer of the reaction of those condemned. As a philosopher of man, Betti realises the transcending quality of human courage and the need for Christian charity in a world where social conditions and upheavals make us all in some degree condemned, and even the best of us incompetent to judge other men. His characters long for a reconciliation with God, so that they can reveal the nobility of their souls. Betti is not a dramatist of pessimism, far from it, but living through an era of Fascism and disaster for Italy, Betti could not help being a wiser and a sadder man than others.

> Frederick Lumley. *Trends in Twentieth Century Drama*
> (Rockliff). 1956. p. 246

Apart from a handful of comedies, his plays are tragic in cast, and often violent, frightening or bizarre. They are also—increasingly so in the later plays—austerely Christian in implication. His subject is wickedness; . . . he studies its preposterous growths with an habituated candour. . . . The series of thirteen plays which Betti produced between 1941 and his death in 1953 must be among the greatest creative outbursts in dramatic literature. In none of these is there what we are used to in England as "religious drama"; yet they are all concerned with one aspect or another of men's fatal disregard or defiance of God. . . . They confront us with a dramatist whose unusual maturity of vision gives us pity and terror, where we normally find only their modern substitutes, pathos and hysteria. . . . A sense of classical tragedy . . . persists in [his] plays . . . [even] when the structure is far from being classical.

> Henry Reed. Foreword to *Three Plays* by Ugo Betti
> (Grove). 1956. pp. 6, 8

"The Burnt Flower-Bed" might be classed, like Shakespeare's last play, "The Tempest," as a synthesis or summing up of a great dramatist's philosophy and view of life, with the mysticism of the humane writer moving towards death. It was a play packed with intellectual argument, a play of team-work with a fine but slightly diffused dramatic technique. "The Queen and the Rebels," on the other hand, takes the stage like an atomic explosion. It is far more melodramatic in theme; but the core of the same philosophy—the respect and dignity of the individual soul—flowers unscorched in a new setting. . . . [It is] a play which never releases its finely sprung tension (it is interesting to note that in both these plays Betti uses the technical device of bringing down his curtain on a point of suspense and commencing the next Act at exactly the same moment, so that the action is, in fact, continuous). . . . The impact of Betti on our theatre is almost certain, in time, to bear creative fruit, and his influence to be felt among our young dramatists as that of Ibsen and Chekhov continues to be felt.

Audrey Williamson. *Contemporary Theatre, 1953-1956* (Rockliff). 1956. pp. 65–7

Human actions have little immediate signficance for Betti's purpose. We understand and feel that the words and actions of the characters are brought into the play, primarily in order to afford the sonorous counterpart to the ineffable conversation that is carried on between the souls of the various protagonists, or between their individual souls and the Great Judge of whose presence they are so agonizingly aware. . . . From [an] examination of Betti's message, it is possible to understand his statement that our age is one that has a close affinity to the Middle Ages, and that its theatre must take up once more the bond that links it with the religious, spiritual life of the age, as it did in Ancient Greece and Medieval Europe. Indeed, its connection with Greek drama is obvious, if we compare Betti's dramatic theory and practice with the definition of Greek tragedy as "the story of human blindness and error leading to effects opposite from those intended, the truth of which is ironically revealed."

J. A. Scott. *Ital.* March, 1960. pp. 52, 55

One leaves a play by Ugo Betti . . . with a sense of the incomplete. His failure is not being great. He makes the demands of a champion playwright; he confronts his audience like Ibsen; he presumes like Strindberg. Betti has all the paraphernalia of strength, the terrible fundamental themes, the gift of the mighty gab, the pedestal gestures, but he entirely lacks the power to lift. He is the master builder who leaves flat land behind. . . . There's no denying that he deserves his international reputation, yet nobody knows what that reputation is. The lip service we pay to Betti is a mumble. . . . His mythical way of writing succeeds only if the force of the language can take the different levels of interpretation and reshape them into one piece. It is an expanding process that requires heat, the poet in his forge. Ugo Betti is not smith enough. His weights of legend, fact, psychological reality, fall separately and in succession upon the same point and wear it thin. He is a writer diminished by argument; he suffers from being pro and con. The great image makers are not so rational. . . . Is Betti, then, a hollow playwright? To say so would be shamefully unjust. . . . There is an intention of grandness in his work, a desire to ascend beyond the top of almost every other writer of his generation that must be respected.

H. A. L. Craig. *NSN.* Feb. 10, 1961. p. 228

The harsh reality of the courtroom colored Betti's view of life and his literary work is typical of his era in its lack of facile optimism if not in its catholic sorrow. Despair has been the burden of most playwrights of the past quarter century, and currently it is reaching a nervewracking pitch in the efforts of Ionesco, Genet, [Beckett], and Jack Gelber. . . . Behind the tortured masks of these and similar writers there is, of course, a dreadful uncertainty, but it is an uncertainty somehow not quite convincing, or at best a bit too strident, like the lament of a child, intense but not fully informed. . . . Perhaps it is not too much to say that the absence of an articulated moral or rational frame of reference results ultimately in our feeling tricked; we have been moved by an experience that we do not and cannot understand, except in terms of a limited view of human nature which even in these troubled times seems unnecessarily onesided. It is Ugo Betti's virtue that while he views life with the pessimism typical of the most sensitive writers of his era he never quite loses confidence in the essential dignity of mankind, a confidence unusual in a theatre inclined today to see man as an abomination.

Frank W. Wadsworth. *DS*. Fall, 1961. p. 167

Ugo Betti's "The Queen and the Rebels" is as serious as anything London has seen since Marie Corelli's "The Sorrows of Satan" in 1897. It is exactly what large numbers of people (most of them non-playgoers) expect a serious play to be. So was the same author's "The Burnt Flower-Bed." . . . It deals with the dilemma of the contemporary conscience, and with a crisis of self-determination in the individual soul. I know this because the author will not let me forget it; he rubs it in as often and as explicitly as his fondness for rhetoric will allow. . . . Betti was a pupil of Pirandello, as Pinero was a pupil of Ibsen, and for him implications are not enough. Heaven forbid that he should be caught forgetting to philosophise! Or that a moment should pass without some evidence of high seriousness! . . . When a playwright manages to create characters larger than life, nobody is happier than I. But this is just where Betti fails. He has taken the tritest figures of old-fashioned melodrama and inflated them, which is by no means the same thing.

Kenneth Tynan. *Curtains* (Atheneum). 1961. pp. 108–9

Betti assumes a very difficult task by making himself the spokesman for men and women whose desires and needs for compassion and love are eternally thwarted. There are no happy endings in Betti's plays. Yet he avoids the innate pessimism of his great predecessor Pirandello. . . . Betti's worth lies in his ability to identify himself with our times in terms of their negative aspects: anguish, moral decay, lack of communication, endless search, melancholy and suspicion. This suspicion is the fear of having been deceived, and the gap that exists for man between intention and realization had become the very form of his own drama. Throughout the plays certain themes recur: justice vs. pity, redemption through suffering, hope beyond death, and a powerful central irony: It is the function of the couple to make man become conscious of his loneliness. . . . Like Bertolt Brecht . . . Betti wrote dramas to teach us how to survive. Unlike Brecht, who looks down on humanity, Betti often casts a tender glance beyond to some undefinable cause.

Paul A. Mankin. *BA*. Spring, 1962. pp. 132–3

One experiences some hesitation about accepting [his characters] as creatures of flesh and blood unless one bears in mind that Betti's art, like Dante's, is allegorical, and that the stylization is as natural within its context as the stylization of medieval painting or sculpture. . . . [It is] Betti's view . . . that man's first disobedience is a present reality, and that we are all exiles from a primeval state of happiness and innocence, to which we instinctively long to return. . . . Betti has been called "the dramatist of Original Sin." . . . The symbolism of his plays is indeed directed at emphasizing man's loss of Eden.

G. H. McWilliam. Introduction to *Three Plays on Justice*
by Ugo Betti (Chandler). 1964. pp. xiii–xiv
See *Three Plays* and *Three Plays on Justice*; also *Crime on Goat Island* (play).

BLASCO-IBÁÑEZ, VICENTE (1867–1928)

Rough, vigorous, not always even grammatical, sometimes crudely naturalistic, sometimes breaking out into impassioned lyricism, always an uncompromising revolutionist, aggressive and combative, ardently concerned with social problems, and a faithful painter of the common people whose life he knows so well, Blasco-Ibáñez is a great force in literature. . . . In his life and in his works this son of indomitable Aragon has displayed all the typical Spanish virility, the free-ranging personal energy, the passion for independence which of old filled Saragossa with martyrs and heroes. . . . It has been by passion, by virility, by moral energy carried to the farthest point, that the firm-fibred soul of Spain has achieved its place in the world.

Havelock Ellis. *The Soul of Spain* (Houghton). 1908.
pp. 270–1, 413–4

There has come into prominence [in Spain] a new group of novelists, less competent as artists, to be sure, but inspired with a more virile craving for progress, a more violent spirit of protest against the torpor of Spain. This intense reaction against the Church, a priest-ridden royalty, and the general somnolence of the people, ignorant and indifferent, is the haunting characteristic of the apostle of this movement, Vicente Blasco-Ibáñez. . . . However little sympathy we may have with his materialism, however Utopian his dreams may be, we cannot but admire and respect him as a man. As an artist he is less deserving of praise. His enthusiastic devotion to Zola and naturalism . . . too often leads him into violation of the highest standards of art. He is carried away by his exuberant fancy. . . . Leaving aside the question of his Gallicisms and bad grammar, with which he is charged by his Spanish critics, his wonderful force and visualizing power cannot fail to make an impression. His riotous imagery, his lack of grace and elegance, may in part be ascribed to hasty production. . . . At least, in Sr. Ibáñez Spain has a leader whose courage is strong, an apostle whose faith in the future is firm.

R. H. Keniston. Nation. Dec. 24, 1908. pp. 622–3

One of the secrets of the immense power exercised by the novels of Vicente Blasco-Ibáñez is that they are literary projections of his dynamic personality. Not only the style, but the book, is here the man. This is especially true of those of his works in which the thesis element predominates, and in which . . . [he] appears as a novelist of ideas-in-action. . . . In the bulk of the noted Spaniard's books there is waged, on both a large scale and a small, the ceaseless, implacable struggle of the new against the old. . . . It is the clash of these ancient and modern forces that strike the spark which ignites the author's passion. . . . His dominant figures, chiefly men, are representative of the Spain of tomorrow . . . a tomorrow of rebirth, of rededication to lofty ideals and glowing realities. . . . The entire works of Blasco-Ibáñez attain an architectural unity in which not the least of the elements are a flaming nobility of purpose and a powerful directness of aim. . . . Not so very long ago, it was the fashion in certain quarters to regard Blasco-Ibáñez as impossible and utopian . . . [but] the Spain of tomorrow will be found to have moved more in the direction of Blasco-Ibáñez than in that of his detractors.

Isaac Goldberg. Introduction to Blood and Sand
(Dutton). 1919. pp. v, vii, xii

[Blasco-Ibáñez is] the most commanding among the contemporary Spanish novelists. . . . I do not mean that Vicente Blasco-Ibáñez is greater than Perez Galdós, or Armando Palacio Valdés or even the Countess Pardo-Bazan; but he belongs to their realistic order of imagination, and he is easily the first of living European novelists outside of Spain, with the advantage of superior youth, freshness of invention and force of characterization. . . . The author shares . . . hate or slight of ecclesiasticism with all the Spanish novelists, so far as I know them . . . but it may be said that while he does not go farther than Galdós, for instance, he is yet more intensively agnostic. He is the standard bearer of the scientific revolt in the terms of fiction which spares us no hope of relief in the religious notion of human life here or hereafter that the Hebraic or Christian theology has divined.

W. D. Howells. Introduction to The Shadow of the
Cathedral (Dutton). 1919. pp. v, xiii

There may be contemporary novelists of deeper philosophy, with a keener sense of beauty, finer in moral purpose, more richly dowered with the power to evoke laughter or tears, but Vicente Blasco-Ibáñez is the great storyteller of today. In sheer ability to narrate, to make even the minutest analyses of the thought process of his characters part of his action, he stands peerless.

T. R. Ybarra. NYT. April 18, 1920. p. 198

Why was . . . [<i>The Four Horsemen of the Apocalypse</i>] so successful? Fifty per cent of its success, perhaps more, was due to clever advertising; but the <i>Four Horsemen</i> also galloped up Fifth Avenue at the psychological moment. The war was at its height, the newspapers were crowded with bewildering details, . . . everybody was feverish for news, . . . and into this hubbub . . . rolled the big (I must use the word) crude canvas of <i>The Four Horsemen of the Apocalypse</i>. Obviously the author is a vital man, and man of parts and energy, who had seen the war, who had felt its horror and sorrow, who has a big (forgive me) surging imagination, so riotous that while he is composing he is quite unable to pause anywhere for art's sake. . . . He is a forge; he has gusto and vitality. . . . A vital, vigorous, fearless man . . . a man of imagination and dynamic driving power. My only objection to him is that he allows himself to be called "the greatest of living novelists."

C. Lewis Hind. More Authors and I (Dodd). 1922.
pp. 166–9

Blasco-Ibáñez excels in the portrayal of virile manhood. It seems, indeed, that by a projection of his own dynamic personality he creates the characters of iron will, his fighters who struggle against great odds.

That they must succumb in the end is a reflection of Blasco's own philosophy. Progress is slow and the efforts of one man are unavailing against age-old powers. Therefore the end of life should be action for its own sake and not for the work achieved. In contrast to these are weaklings . . . and the contrast and interplay of these two types heighten the effect of reality. Although Blasco, too, shows a simplicity in psychological motivation, he does not carry it to the point of making the physiological govern the psychological as Zola tried to do. There is great inequality in Blasco's character portrayal, but the characters of outstanding personality tend to overbalance the effect of the weak and colorless.

Katherine Reding. *Hsp.* Dec., 1923. p. 369

Señor Blasco-Ibáñez writes . . . with great attention to detail, careless of the structure of his novel and quite indifferent to the arts of economy and suggestion. He paints a full canvas, satisfying rather than inciting the imagination. His work strikes one, consequently . . . as a kind of vigorous and powerful journalism.

Louis Kronenberger. *NYT.* July 24, 1927. p. 13

Unfortunately for Spain, the novelist whose works are best known outside that self-contained country looks at life from the cosmopolitan angle. Perhaps in consequence of this quality, perhaps by reason of their meretricious glitter, Ibáñez's novels have obtained a best-seller popularity in Europe and America out of proportion to their real value. They lend themselves easily to the film producer. . . . Ibáñez writes vigoriously, painting his pictures of bullfights and Valencian peasant life in strong, attractive colours. It may be melodrama, but it is melodrama of the first rank. . . . As a writer and as a thinker he is on an altogether lower plane than either Ayala, Baroja or Azorín. Possibly he was too much of a politician to be a great writer, and his novels are often coloured with revolutionary theses or political beliefs. . . . Politics may possibly gain by the entrance of literary men into their ranks, but literature is more often the loser.

Peter Trentham. *BkmL.* Sept., 1931. p. 293

[In] a best-seller of twenty-five years ago . . . *Los Cuatro Jinetes del Apocalipsis* by Vicente Blasco-Ibáñez . . . a German professor of history, a certain Julius von Hartrott . . . proclaims the political ambitions of the German people—as I then thought—in a most exaggerated and even ridiculous manner. This champion of the wildest Pan-Germanism seemed to me unreal and I regarded his arrogant and arbitrary ideologies merely as malevolent exaggerations of the author.

Now as I re-read this book a quarter of a century later, I could not believe my own eyes . . . because, unfortunately, Hartrott's absurd theories have become through Hitler the official code of seventy million Germans. . . . Blasco-Ibáñez' fiction has shown again that it is the poet who understands his time and the future better than the professors of politics.

Stefan Zweig. *FW*. Dec., 1942. pp. 234–5

Juxtaposing Ibáñez with . . . twentieth century authors only points up how completely and exclusively nineteenth century Ibáñez is. Politically, his faith in the rights of man . . . goes back to the French Republic of 1792. His conception of the novel places him squarely among the positivistic realists and naturalists. His thesis novels, which now seem so vacuous and rhetorical, take him back even further to the Hugo of *Les Misérables*.

Edith F. Helman. *HspR*. April, 1950. p. 188

Blasco-Ibáñez is a writer who has too often been judged by his worst novels: these made him famous abroad and damaged his reputation in Spain. But even his best books have, I think, something that makes them antipathetic to the Castilian mind. There is a certain gulf of incomprehension between the peoples of the Mediterranean seaboard and those of the table-land, and in his coloured style, his lack of ironic comment, his pagan feeling for nature, Blasco-Ibáñez is a pure Levantino. There was also a crudeness and vulgarity in his nature that, when he lost touch with his native soil, allowed him to sink to the lowest depths of popular writing. Perhaps one can best sum him up in the language of painting as a *fauve* and point to Paul Gauguin as the artist who most nearly resembles him.

Gerald Brenan. *The Literature of the Spanish People*
(Cambridge). 1953. p. 414

See *The Shadow of the Cathedral*, *Blood and Sand*, and *The Four Horsemen of the Apocalypse* (novels).

BRANCATI, VITALIANO (1907–1954)

No reader disposed to relish Brancati's humor can possibly wish to quarrel with the logic or plausibility of characters that . . . are mere pretexts for conversation pieces to carry the author's Rabelaisian comicality. And just as Brancati's characters are mere interlocutors, even so his backdrop is a mere sounding-board. He is a master of racy dialogue.

S. E. Scalia. *BA*. Summer, 1950. p. 296

Signor Brancati's novel [*Antonio, the Great Lover*] is a Sicilian joke; in order to appreciate it, it is necessary (and, thanks to the author's shameless vigour, easy) temporarily to become a Sicilian. . . . [There is] an astonishing flow of language, as molten as lava, as harsh, heady and vulgar as wine drunk jetting from a goatskin. Antonio himself is, alas, impossible as well as powerless; but he is a folk-hero, a Till Eulenspiegel whose whole point lies in his inability to perform merry pranks; he is the nucleus of incredibility that is essential to a legend. . . . Sicily in verbal action is the overriding theme of this entertaining and highly finished folk-satire. Could Signor Brancati's work, if Antonio had been made a person rather than a comic myth, have gained as a novel without losing as a folk-tale? That, it must be confessed, is a question one feels absolutely impotent to determine.

George D. Painter. *NSN*. May 24, 1952. p. 625

If . . . the American reader enters with an open mind the burnished town of Catania [home of *Antonio, the Great Lover*] . . . he cannot fail to enjoy the author's wit, satire, and bursts of impassioned rhetoric, nor can he fail to find, beneath the farcical aspects of Antonio's misfortune, the elemental pathos of the lot of man. . . . Of all . . . [the] lively and persuasive characters, however, it is [one who is] . . . dying of the diseases of the flesh and spirit caught in the Spanish war, who steals the show. In his mouth, the author puts the words of anger, defiance, longing and ultimate faith in life which lift this tale of misadventure from the realm of pure farce to a plane where philosophy and emotion come together in a moving cry, no longer specifically Sicilian, but simply of any human heart.

Virgilia Peterson. *NYHT*. Aug. 31, 1952. p. 7

Vitaliano Brancati has not only written a humorous novel [*Antonio, the Great Lover*]. He has also composed an incisive satire, peopled with strong, wonderfully articulate characters. Antonio bears more than a coincidental resemblance to fascism. Mr. Brancati is unquestionably a writer and thinker of eloquence and integrity, whose language has the universality of the true humanist.

Robert Knittel. *NYT*. Sept. 28, 1952. p. 4

The theme of *gallismo,* of the excessive and exclusive interest in women, treated by Brancati in his previous novels, *Don Giovanni in Sicilia* and *Il bell' Antonio,* is here [in *Paolo il caldo*] developed and indeed deepened, achieving a dramatic and moralistic impact. Paolo . . . is a sinner with a Counter Reformation soul, racked by doubts and self revulsion

and an authentic yearning for good. . . . His character acquires in the
long run a symbolic value and his condemnation casts a light of desperate pessimism and sorrow over all humanity.

> Margherita M. Silvi. *BA*. Winter, 1956. p. 37

The most important representative of Sicilian provincialism in recent
Italian fiction is Vitaliano Brancati. . . . The salient aspect of his "Sicil-
ianity," his preoccupation with Sicilian eroticism, contributes to his
strength as a literary artist. . . . Brancati chose, however, to satirize erotic
excess . . . as part of a more general comic critique of bourgeois and
upper class culture. . . . He is engrossed with the manner and morals
of Sicilian classes which are out of the struggle for mere material existence . . . , choosing to satirize those in whom education and breeding
have driven a wedge between sentiments and sense. . . . The deeply rooted
moralistic strain in his fiction imbues the erotic themes with an undeniable fundamental seriousness, for, in spite of a somewhat differing
literary aesthetic, Brancati resembles Stendhal in his concern and curiosity about an important aspect of the human condition, *la recherche du
bonheur.* . . . Brancati illuminates the erotic aspects of the human
comedy with enlightened irony and compassionate humor.

> Louis Tenenbaum. *BA*. Summer, 1957. pp. 233–4, 236

See *Antonio, the Great Lover* (novel).

BRETON, ANDRÉ (1896–1966)

He excels in conjuring up a turbid atmosphere of instability and inco-
herency in which fragmentary images coalesce and dissolve according
to a law which does not belong to our tangible universe. In this dizzy
mirage, no violent catastrophe ever comes to disrupt the flowing development of vague forms which melt slowly, endlessly, into one another. Nevertheless, the haunting premonition of a secret, indefinite
menace seems to hover permanently about this alarming phantasmago-
ria. Here the plausible and the fabulous meet and unite monstrously
to beget weird and uncertain hybrids which simultaneously partake of
the forceful intensity of actual objects and of the disturbing incon-
sistency of chimerical nightmares.

> Georges Lemaitre. *From Cubism to Surrealism in French
> Literature* (Harvard). 1941. pp. 209–10

Breton entered the Surrealist movement from French Dadaism. He has
been its leader almost continuously, in spite of, or because of, his high

handed manner of leadership. The changes through which Surrealism has passed have Breton's intransigent nature behind them. Breton has, in fact, commited repeatedly what, according to early Surrealist doctrine, is one of the chief literary sins: he has taken himself too seriously. . . . He has multiplied his effects, rather than developed his gifts.

Louise Bogan. NY. Nov. 9, 1946. pp. 114–5

Like all the surrealists, Breton, their great Mage, repeats with variety to which there is no calculable limit, the sense impressions colliding in the private consciousness. His materials are selected according to a code in which a mystical preoccupation with assents and conflicts in sex represents reality. Poetry, reality, and freedom are recovered, according to Breton and his precursors and followers, through their basic and mystical formula.

Jeremy Ingalls. SR. Jan. 4, 1947. p. 24

In Breton's quest for the poetic absolute, in the practice of surrealism, his intransigence is as extreme as it is in theory. You cannot follow him unless you consent to give ground and abandon yourself without reservation to a prose which ambles along at a regular pace, fluid and smooth as a piece of pliable wood without knots. His domain is that of the marvelous. . . . It is inherent primarily in images, whence it spreads to the atmosphere which becomes lighter, transfigured, pervaded by an abnormal ultra-violet or infra-red light. A vague restlessness, which sometimes turns into anguish, hovers over it like a nocturnal demon.

Marcel Raymond. From Baudelaire to Surrealism
(Wittenborn). 1949. p. 302

Breton's vein of imagery is inexhaustible and would grant total escape from the miseries of the world if he so desired—and it actually does so in some of his love poems. But Breton refuses to be transported by the image. Rather, he puts it to work in dramatizing the need to change the world.

Breton's notion of the absolute is altered by the war years as was that of Aragon and Eluard. His preoccupation shifts from the spiritual and sensual to the moral field. . . . But unlike Aragon and Eluard, he keeps free of political involvements. . . . He has exemplified not the pure but the *total* poet, clarifying to a greater degree than anyone in our time, what the position of a poet can be in society: not to seek to please and be admired, but to know and to communicate knowledge.

Anna Balakian. Surrealism (Noonday). 1959. pp. 190–3

Breton's appearance was majestic and noble. It was very easy to credit him with the first rôle of leader and spokesman and theoretician of surrealism. He is a very large man with a handsome leonine head. His countenance bore an expression of solemnity which I don't remember his ever breaking with a smile. His gestures were sober and reduced. His voice had resonance and great beauty.

> Wallace Fowlie. *Age of Surrealism* (Indiana). 1960.
> p. 103

He had a huge head, like one of the old Jacobin leaders, a mass of wavy brown hair, pale blue eyes, regular—though heavy—features, and jaws of granite. Like the men of 1793, he had in him a combination of fanatical idealism and ruthlessness. Whereas his closest friends, Aragon and Philippe Soupault, were spontaneous in manner, he was deliberate, speaking in long periods like an old-style orator and in a voice of deep and musical timbre. More the scholar than the other men, he had absorbed much from the iconoclastic writings of Nietzsche. . . . Breton's medical experience in the treatment of mad soldiers had also turned his interests towards psychiatry. The relationships between the illusions of mad persons and the creative processes of art absorbed him.

> Matthew Josephson. *Life Among the Surrealists* (Holt).
> 1962. p. 117

See *Najda* (novel) and *Young Cherry Trees Secured Against Hares* (poetry).

BRULLER, JEAN
See Vercors

BUTOR, MICHEL (1926–   )

Although [*A Change of Heart*] tells a traditional story, it distinguishes itself by its original technique. Even in this regard there are elements we should recognize, such as Valéry Larbaud's subtle stream of consciousness flowing through an Italian railway compartment, Gide's forcing the reader to cooperate by reconstructing the truth, Proust's identification of the beloved with a landscape which we can possess only through possessing her.

There is also something Proustian in the final resolve, less motivated than in Proust, to make a novel of these ruminations over earlier trips, with all the violence they do to chronology, whose differences and similarities eventually fuse in a strangely insistent unity. But Butor has combined these elements with a new twist, and he has added the device of calling his protagonist "you."

Justin O'Brien. *NYT*. March 29, 1959. p. 33

The technique of [*A Change of Heart*] has been compared to that of Joyce's *Ulysses*. In one sense this is true, since most interior monologues remind us of Joyce. The total effect, however, is almost opposite. Joyce writes for the ear and Butor for the eye. The appeal of Joyce is the appeal of music; that of Butor is the appeal of painting or sculpture. No recent novel is more full of brilliant objective description. So brilliant, in fact, that, though the thoughts of the hero are painful, the reader is never completely depressed.

Vernon Hall, Jr. *NYHT*. April 5, 1959. p. 4

Like so many of the significant writers of our period, from Proust to Joyce, Butor is concerned with time. And while, like Proust and Joyce, he marks the succession of time's moments by descriptions . . . his intention, like theirs, is actually to create a timeless myth which fuses past and future in a meaningful, symbolic present. . . . He achieves it above all through the extraordinary device of writing in the second person, with "you," directly addressing the reader and drawing him in quite literally, where another writer would have simply described the situation from the outside. . . . By incorporating the reader ineluctably into his hero's drama, Butor has written a kind of modern Everyman.

Jerrold Lanes. *SR*. April 25, 1959. p. 18

Butor has read, and written interestingly about, Joyce, and though their methods are not alike, some of their interests are similar. Butor does not use a stream-of-consciousness notation, has not been tempted to break down syntactical or word structures. But the area of personality which interests him is the private one where the real life of the individual takes place. Much of what he does well seems less original to those who have grown up in the Joyce tradition than it may to French readers whose norms of rationality may make it seem somewhat alien. Butor's object is to forge in the smithy of his soul much less the uncreated conscience of his race than that of his self, but Joyce would have recognized, and Joyce's readers do recognize, what he is about.

W. M. Frohock. *YFS*. Summer, 1959. pp. 57–8

Michel Butor, in a work which is the most elaborated, the most studied, the most intellectual, indeed, of these years when intelligence has been yielding to instinct, wishes to preserve Genesis. He does not discuss

man at his birth, but at his rebirth. He is a humanist, who judges humanity as of chief importance and who does not consider wasting it, much
less of writing it off, but helps it to grow. . . . For Michel Butor the new
novel is the novel of newness, the novel of discovery—he makes advances in it, as Christopher Columbus towards America, across the
unexplored areas of Time and Space.

Philippe Sénart. *MF*. May, 1960. p. 103.
Tr. by Dorothy Nyren Curley

These novels resemble neither buildings nor cottages. Barely habitable,
without intellectual comforts—not easy to read—without traditional
trinkets. Neat. Everyone would be able to say in them anything he
had ever thought, even in desperation. Everyone could repeat himself
untiringly. Everyone could take turns being intelligent, foolish, affected,
frightened, absurd, loving, maladroit, calculating, etc. As in life.

Georges Perros. *NRF*. July, 1960. p. 163.
Tr. by Dorothy Nyren Curley

See *A Change of Heart, Degrees,* and *Passing Time* (novels).

CALVINO, ITALO (1923–   )

Italo Calvino is one of the younger writers of contemporary Italy who emerged from—and one might say is a product of—the resistance movement, and this, his first novel [*The Path to the Nest of Spiders*] . . . is a sympathetic and moving portrait of one small segment of that revolutionary period as seen through the eyes of a small boy. . . . As narrative, the tale moves on swiftly and is told with that elliptic economy with which readers of Vittorini and Pavese will be familiar. Yet the background is the author's own, as is the kind of ferocious, almost gay, irony which characterizes his treatment of a little boy lost in a world whose purpose eludes even his elders. An allegory of loneliness, the tale is also realistically placed.

Thomas G. Bergin. *NYHT*. Nov. 17, 1957. p. 6

The notion of such a Tarzan-like existence [as that of *The Baron in the Trees*], even in a powdered wig, makes a compelling myth—a dream of escape and superiority deeply dear to most children. While Cosimo [the Baron] remains a child, the myth holds: but later, it loses some of its force, as Cosimo achieves impossible feats and comforts, and his creator seeks fresh words and adventures new. The moral, I suppose, is that even campers need canned food and sleeping-bags: that in the modern world there's literally "no place to hide." *The Baron in the Trees* obscures that issue by dazzling technical trickery, somewhat reminiscent of the fantasies of Marcel Aymé. Nevertheless, . . . it remains a persuasive, sensitive, and very likeable experiment.

Richard Mayne. *NSN*. Aug. 8, 1959. p. 170

Eccentricity is growing more rare in contemporary fiction. Many a twentieth-century novelist, muscle-bound with too much sober craftsmanship and industrious subtlety, will not suffer a crotchet among his characters without analyzing it into a neurosis. *Don Quixote,* I fear, might emerge from today's electric typewriters not as the sad and hilarious story of a man, but as the earnestly documented biography of a maladjustment.

Italo Calvino has tackled a quixotic theme in the novel at hand, and I am happy to say that he has the narrative leisure to do it at least initial justice. . . . *The Baron in the Trees* tells of a time and a circle that encouraged the innocent flowering of the bizarre. . . . [The

Baron's] deportment is not meant as mere imaginative self-indulgence but as a superb, downright apocalyptic gesture. By eating, sleeping, loving on the bough, the Baron defies all the petty earth-bound conformities of man. By never obeying the thousands of commands to slide down, he upholds an uncompromising individual freedom. . . . Mr. Calvino, then, seems to have intended nothing less than the deliberate transmutation of fantastic notion into universal allegory.

Frederic Morton. *NYT*. Oct. 11, 1959. p. 35

[*The Baron in the Trees* is] a tour de force, . . . a stunning one, which consists in making us believe that life in the trees is as natural as life on earth. But Calvino's achievement must be measured against the pitfalls he has avoided: the superimposed symbolisms of Duerrenmatt, the ponderous allegories of Golding, the philosophical meanderings of Hesse, and the cuteness of Capote. Any one of these traps, in the hands of a lesser writer, could have spoiled the delights of this tale.

The secret of Calvino's success is to be found in his refusal to have a fixed moral point of view. . . . The elements of Calvino's style [are] the understatement, the wry turn, the careful, cadenced phrasing, . . . logic and force.

After all, "charming" was not always a word of depreciation. Calvino is knowing, uncluttered, warm, humorous, and exceedingly charming. What his publishers call "satire" is really fantasy: Cosimo [the Baron] attacks no one, nothing, and Calvino's detachment, sometimes carried to deliberately absurd lengths, underlines foolishness but does not castigate it. The stylization and artificiality into which his novel could have fallen are artfully avoided much as the Commedia dell' Arte avoids them: by being spry and self-amused as well as amusing. And the genre, the pastoral-picaresque, is one that Calvino has all to himself. It is a wonder and a delight.

Keith Botsford. *SR*. Nov. 7, 1959. pp. 21–2

Literary fantasy seldom exists for its own sake. Written by a classicist, it becomes "hard" satire, tough-minded, with a naive but educable protagonist—like Swift's Gulliver, who is a "gull," but who learns. Fantasy written by a romantic becomes "soft" satire, tender-minded, with a hero who is amorous, free-thinking, cynical—learning little, becoming more intensely himself—like Byron's Don Juan.

A prime example of soft satire [is] Italo Calvino's *The Baron in the Trees.* . . . The romantic paradox: by removing himself from his fellows and making himself the outcast, the eccentric, the outsider, [the Baron] is able to deal with mankind more wisely and more intimately that if he had remained below. An old riddle with a new twist, eternally interesting. . . .

[Calvino's] fantasy is entertaining not because it tells us of our world but because it refuses to look at it.

Frances Mayhew Rippy. *NMQ*. Winter, 1960. pp. 457–8

His three tales [*The Baron in the Trees, The Nonexistent Knight,* and *The Cloven Viscount*], as Calvino readily confesses, were written when he lost interest in depicting realistic situations. . . . Each of [them] tries to dramatize the situation of modern man who, after Marx and Freud, has become aware of his "alienation" and "'repressions." Each one of his novels enabled the author to answer for himself some of the problems which he had posed initially: thus, for example, his *Visconte dimezzato* ultimately symbolizes man whose humanity has been, so to speak, cut in half, while the *Baron rampante,* by choosing to live up on the trees where he creates a wonderful and rich life for himself, stands for man who, by choosing and acting an extraordinarily eccentric role, tries to fulfill a certain aspiration of diversity apparently denied to man in our age.

Sergio Pacifici. *BA*. Winter, 1962. pp. 67–8

Italo Calvino . . . is a very serious man. But, like many another serious writer before him, he is endowed with a sly and oblique second vision which permits him on occasion to indulge in whimsical fantasies which are more real, in their intrinsic truths, than reality itself. Like Voltaire, Swift, and others of this sophisticated fraternity of genuine wits and social critics, he can transcend the immediate and transmute it in terms of every man and every age. . . . Set in the brightly emblazoned Middle Ages of the *chansons de geste* and the romances of chivalry, *The Nonexistent Knight* is a mock epic rooted in concrete neorealism. . . . *The Cloven Viscount* is a dark-hued Gothic gem which transports us into the mysterious late medieval world of Altdorfer's teeming battle scenes and Bosch's hallucinating grotesques. . . . What lies at the core of these ingenious spoofs? Because Calvino is too sophisticated to be an obvious moralist, his parables are open to a number of political and psychological interpretations. To this reader they would seem to imply that in a world split, then as now, between good and bad, true believers and infidels, East and West—sanity and the future belong only to the wholly committed and not to the alienated or mutilated, however lofty their aims and ideals.

Helene Cantarella. *NYT*. Aug. 5, 1962

The protagonist [of *The Baron in the Trees*] was intended as a satiric portrait of a nineteeth-century militant liberal who longs to be *engagé* and detached at one and the same time. . . . But if you simply transpose the Baron's perplexities to modern life, where they presumably belong, what you are left with is a long-winded justification for an intellectual's endurance of all those ignoble, bloody deeds which Italian fellow-travelers tend, rather inappropriately, to call Socialist politics. At the moment, however, the Italians are calling these things by their rightful name—that is, Stalinism. So, overnight, *The Baron in the Trees* has become as quaint and remote as its elaborately archaic setting and machinery. An ironic fate, especially for a writer who thought himself the essence of contemporary pertinence. . . . One can view all of Italo Calvino's recent work as the shamefaced legerdemain of a half-baked Stalinist caught on untenable ground and trying rather lumpishly to veil his problems in allegory.

Raymond Rosenthal. *NL*. Feb. 4, 1963. p. 24

See *The Baron in the Trees* and *The Path to the Nest of Spiders* (novels), and *The Nonexistent Knight and The Cloven Viscount* (two novellas); also *Italian Fables* (traditional folk tales).

CAMPANA, DINO (1885–1932)

He would go from table to table, making the rounds of the best-known cafés, to sell his poems. And he would often make fun of those who bought them. He would look hard at their faces, making out their philistine natures; then, he would burst out laughing with that laugh of his that seemed to belong to some comely, bronzed faun (by the way, I have not yet mentioned the fact that Campana is a handsome youth), tearing out pages from the book he had just sold, upon the specious and hardly flattering pretext that the buyer would never have understood them. Many such amusing scenes took place at Paszkowski's in Florence.

Bino Binazzi. *IQ*. Summer, 1958. p. 5. Written in 1928

Campana was a personality in a way that later Italian poets—chiefly professorial and intellectual—have not been. Sbarbaro thus describes a visit: "My family barely tolerated him because of his lice. In the evening he had an almost maidenly modesty about taking off his clothes. Hospitality was quickly irksome to him, and by the third day he would have no more of it. I watched him go off, stubborn, with his vagabond's gait, toward Sottaripa. For his only baggage he had in his pocket *Leaves of Grass*." The circumstances of Campana's life (he died in an insane asylum and his years before confinement were passed in vagabondage), his frequent use of "poetic prose," and his striving for a poetry which would be a primary emotional experience shorn of intellectual categories and hence a first-hand contact with reality, have led most critics to compare him with Rimbaud, but the luminous landscapes which are glimpsed through the broken architecture of his verse are purely Italian: they are peaceful landscapes where archaic figures stand in attitudes of immemorial rite.

Edward Williamson. Poetry. Dec., 1951. pp. 167–8

Campana, who heard *all things* in the voice of the element, could not have done otherwise than wish to express all things. . . . Campana's world includes, without boundaries, both dreams and reality, so that his transports always appear boundless. The association of things and images, immobility and movement, segment and arabesque, proceeds spontaneously from his poetic fancy. It is a complex world, but one of substantial unity, which is revealed in the freedom with which the poet moves therein, and which is reflected in his language. This is essentially unitary, even in cases of interruption and repetition, and especially in its general categories. . . . But what really matters is the poet's sure ability in this world of his, composed of nature and dreams; his natural ability to dominate it, sweep through it and retain vast, serried sections of this in each image. . . . I think it is necessary to specify that the vehemence of Campana's poetic transports has nothing to do with the progress of madness or psychic hypertension. On the contrary, it represents an extreme concentration of the individual's powers, a considerable detachment from the chains of matter, and hence a capacity of the spirit, in its intensely free unity, to obey the slightest impulse with great impetus.

Fredi Chiappelli. IQ. Summer, 1958. pp. 6–9

High over the Futurist bandstands and across the wan sky of the Crepuscolari, the poetry of Dino Campana flashed in 1914 like the wildest of meteors. Driven since he was fifteen by a nervous compulsion, the bronze-haired blue-eyed roustabout had wandered over much of the world, *Leaves of Grass* in his pocket; he had been in and out of jail and of the asylum that finally claimed him, had himself peddled his crudely printed *Canti orfici*—whose very title, *Orphic Songs,* suggested mystery, magic, revelation. Campana lived for poetry; when close to him, said Cecchi, one could feel it like an electric shock or a high explosive. His own work, too idiosyncratic to be imitated, provided the young writers with a new sense both of the freedom poetry might enjoy and of its pictorial and musical possibilities.

John Frederick Nims. The Poem Itself, ed. by
Stanley Burnshaw (Holt). 1960. p. 298

The perplexity that followed the collapse of futurism was quickly over-come by the possibilities proclaimed by [the magazine] *La Voce,* and the response was general. . . . What united [the poets of *La Voce*] and gave their movement a certain cohesion was their common desire for a renewed awareness of social and spiritual questions and of moral responsibility. . . . The anguished need for moral self-justification reached a pitch of exasperation in the tragic personality of Dino Campana. None of the poets of *La Voce* achieved the lyric purity of Campana, but his recurring mental derangement, which became permanent in the last part of his short life, precluded any possibility of a personal solution of the problem. The tormented life of Campana found its only relief in out-bursts of lyricism, which, when they corresponded to moments of mental lucidity, have no equal in twentieth-century Italian poetry. But more often, his beclouded poetry is only a harmony of words and a race of images. It is nonetheless beautiful, even when it is marred by the obscurities of an infirm mind.

Carlo L. Golino. *Contemporary Italian Poetry*
(California). 1962. pp. xii–xiii

See poems in *Contemporary Italian Poetry,* ed. by Carlo L. Golino.

CAMUS, ALBERT (1913–1960)

How are we to classify this clear, dry work [*The Stranger*], so carefully composed beneath its seeming disorder, so "human," so open, too, once you have this key? It cannot be called a story, for a story explains and coordinates as it narrates. It substitutes the order of causality for chronological sequence. M. Camus calls it a "novel." The novel, how-ever, requires continuous duration, development, and the manifest presence of the irreversibility of time. I would hesitate somewhat to use the term "novel" for this succession of inert present moments which allow us to see, from underneath, the mechanical economy of something deliberately staged. Or, if it is a novel, it is so in the sense that *Zadig* and *Candide* are novels. It might be regarded as a moralist's short novel, one with a discreet touch of satire and a series of ironic portraits, a novel that, for all the influence of the German existentialists and the American novelists, remains, at bottom, very close to the tales of Voltaire.

Jean-Paul Sartre. *Literary and Philosophical Essays*
(Criterion). 1955. p. 41

One feels about Camus that, like Silone, he is a writer to be trusted to the very end. Because he is a man like all other men, he is also a writer who may mislead; but because he has looked at the face of power and turned away, he will not violate his readers with ideological or spiritual trickery. By the essential modesty of his manner, in which gravity and diffidence quietly blend, Camus validates the idea of friendship between the man who writes and the other man, unknown to the writer, who reads his work.

Irving Howe. NR. March 31, 1958. p. 17

M. Camus is notably more interested in the story's philosophical import than in its appeal as a narrative . . . He remains a little distant, offering a little self-consciously the abstract lucubrations of the rebuffed intellectual. . . . He puts political man first: he deals in terms of environment. He talks the politics of survival, not the aesthetics of resignation. He fits, in fact, Pater's idea of asceticism—"the sacrifice of one part of human nature to another, that it may live in what survives the more completely." His intellect has the ascendency over that rhapsodic side which tumultuously escaped in *Summer* in a *mystique* of the sea. Essentially a North African, M. Camus yet compels himself to maltreat his imagination because it impairs the vocation of seriousness.

Paul West. NWW. June, 1958. pp. 90–1

The "two or three ideas" which Camus has made his own are simple ideas and do not grow into a complex philosophical system. Despite the simplicity of his ideas, they become extraordinary when coupled with Camus's demand that they be lived to the limits of what human passion can reach. In Camus's thought, the truth value of an idea can never be rationally developed to a point of satisfaction; ideas are substantiated only in human experience and action. In Camus's philosophy, truth is revealed in what has been called a "dialectical-dramatic" form, in the ongoing tension of human ideas and human passion. Hence the developing thought of Albert Camus is not to be considered as a pilgrimage which drives relentlessly towards its goal; for there is no such goal. The value which man seeks is not in the future, nor is it beyond his ken; it is within man, part of his nature, and is to be found and incarnated only in the creative tension of the passionate life. The philosophical career of Albert Camus has been a running battle with life and with the ideas of his times, and this battle goes on within the limits which make up the human condition, within this proportion which rests in the nature common to all men.

Thomas Hanna. The Thought and Art of Albert Camus
(Regnery). 1958. pp. 249–50

What Camus has forced us to think about is the very warrant for continued human existence and the possible resources of the human spirit in a universe that appears no longer to make sense; a universe from which God has silently withdrawn; a universe in which, as Caligula says with bitter amazement, "men die and they are not happy"; a universe unspeakably indifferent to the natural aspirations of men. In his first few books, Camus used and abused the word "absurd" to identify such a universe (and also, confusingly, to identify the kind of person who learns how to get along with it, as well as the work of art that faithfully mirrors it). . . . As Camus has elaborated on the word, and made it more complex, it has drawn to itself suggestions from the Latin words to which it is related: *absurdus,* which means harsh or grating and the root word *surdus,* which means deaf. An absurd universe is a tuneless universe—a universe that is tone-deaf. . . . It is a universe crowned by a deaf heaven that the individual, like the lover in Shakespeare's sonnets, troubles with his bootless cries.

R. W. B. Lewis. *The Picaresque Saint* (Lippincott).
1959. pp. 60–1

He makes no metaphysical distinctions between organic and nonorganic existants save for the human, of course. The only rational result of man's attempt to make sense of the natural world is the concept of the absurd. Yet having once accepted the basic irrationality of things and man's consequent alienation from nature, Camus makes a partial return. He is a little like the existential lover, who after failing to become one with the beloved, learns to know the intense joy of recognizing and cherishing the other's separate being. The beauty of the world, the immediate sensuous enjoyment of what is simply there are for Camus absolute goods. The glory of the African sun and sea and mountains needs and allows no explanation. They provide no reason for living, but they make it possible for one to want to go on living.

Hazel E. Barnes. *The Literature of Possibility*
(Nebraska). 1959. p. 370

In the closing pages of *The Liberal Imagination,* Lionel Trilling points out that there exists a lack of sympathy between the "tradition of democratic liberalism as we know it" and the most significant of the modern European writers. . . . While the early Camus of *The Outsider* and *The Myth of Sisyphus* illustrates the dichotomy of which Lionel Trilling speaks, the later Camus of *The Plague* and *The Rebel* seems almost like an effort to refute him. On criticizing the tradition of revolt, Camus seems to bring a certain current of opinion back into the main stream of liberal thought. In insisting upon the value of the individual, on the value of empiricism and modesty in politics, on the need for moderation and comprehension, Camus is restating the basic principles of liberal democracy. The extent to which he manages convincingly to bridge the gap between liberal democratic society and the climate of opinion predominant in the literature of this society is the true criteria of his activity as *"l'écrivain de la révolte."* His achievement cannot be judged by comparison with that of any other contemporary writer for he has been alone, so far, in attempting it.

Philip Thody. Albert Camus (Grove). 1959. pp. 72–3

In the work which is now behind him, Camus grappled with the forces that reject and menace . . . freedom. He has called these forces of life, incarnated them, and mapped out their violently destructive career. For a young man brought up "in the sunlight, the delight in life, the freedom" of long Algerian summers, the task was hard. "To think," he writes, "is to learn how to see anew." The outer world thrust upon him a vision he abhorred. Camus recognized at the outset that the "tragic" element in our time was intellectual in character. To look unflinchingly at the world around him, "refusing to lie" to himself or others, was the task he set himself. From *L'Envers et l'endroit* to *La Chute* the existence of the "kingdom of man" that he had sought from the outset was more and more sharply challenged, and Camus felt that it was imperative to integrate into his vision his own violently disruptive experience. He thus delivered his world from the "phantoms" which invaded it, slowly establishing its fundamental unity and its limits in human terms.

Germaine Brée. Camus (Rutgers). 1959. p. 250

His concern for individuals, his hatred of cruelty, his fight against totalitarianism, his opposition to capital punishment—these are attitudes which he found natural, which he could hardly help. But they were attitudes to which he gave a strong intellectual bias as well because he found, as others have found, that we live in an age when even elementary goodness must often be justified and defended in the face of ideological attack. It is important, then, that we should see Camus under a double aspect—as a man of conscience and integrity, and also as an intellectual whose mind could be subtle, ironic, incisive, yet grounded in commonsense. To see him in this way is to understand both his direct descent from the great French *moralistes* and his importance for ourselves at the present time.

John Cruickshank. Albert Camus and the Literature
of Revolt (Oxford). 1960. p. viii

Camus is profoundly opposed to all Christianity stands for: first the notions of incarnation, of grace, of redemption, of repentance and of collective guilt for some sin committed, unbeknown to us. . . . But Camus's most original revolt is against hope, *"cette petite Espérance,"* with which Péguy was convinced that the French people had concluded a secret pact. Camus indicts hope as a form of resignation, robbing man of energies which he needs, in order to enrich a God who "hardly needs them," . . . Camus's world is one of universal condemnation to death, as Pascal's world was. But to the stranger, to the unfortunate man of good will in Oran harrassed by the plague, to his companions in the Resistance, to the unbelievers of today who spurn the use of those small screens which Camus declared he had seen in Italian museums, through which the scaffold was concealed from men sentenced to death, to the bitter characters sketched in *The Fall* and *Exile and the Kingdom,* the issue seems to require an anti-Pascalian answer: what are the positive values which persist in this world of mortals sentenced to death?

Henri Peyre. *YFS*. Spring, 1960. pp. 23–5

Camus . . . feels his way towards a philosophy of *indifference* in matters of religion. . . . Camus, like Valéry and the main line of modern French thought, is more concerned with the sins of the spirit against the flesh than with those of the flesh against spirit. The latter, touching a few persons, are venial compared to the racist appetite of the former. . . . Camus has written that man is sustained by the wine of absurdity and the bread of indifference. He means that, in this best communion, the bread is an antidote to the wine. For the latter, distilled in the vertigo of absurdity, becomes the spirit of nihilism, of a revolt inspired by a deep consciousness of the world's indifference to man. But from that same source comes a sober bread. Camus describes it as a "yes" within the "no," a yes to the no the human body offers to ultimate fictions. . . . His possession of a soul or other souls becomes to him a matter of indifference: the earth, the order of nature, is life-work enough.

Geoffrey H. Hartman. *YFS*. Spring, 1960. pp. 109–10

The essential thing, in Camus, is . . . consciousness eager for justice, in which a whole youthful generation saw mirrored its own anguish, discovered its own values and, like Sisyphus, learned to snatch joy from the core of the absurd—not an ingenuous and irresponsible joy but one that represented a victory over the forces of darkness, over the absurd itself. For Camus the absurd was named political crime, injustice, deceit, murder, the guillotine, colonialism, death; in a word, oppression in any garb. He has set himself the impossible task of endowing each and every one with the right to rejoice in his own *innocent* moiety. As a Mediterranean man Camus recognized that this did not exist, but he knew too that no one could revel in it uninhibitedly as long as innocent children continue to die.

Jacques Ehrmann. YFS. Spring, 1960. p. 96

It would be difficult to overestimate the influence of war and its aftermath upon the thought of Camus. For, if he was an avowed atheist, his revolt was not rooted in Prometheanism but rather sprung from the spectacle of the world as he beheld it in his day. He protested against whatever moved to snuff out the divine spark in man, and the world in his day seemed joined in a great conspiracy to snuff out whatever spark might still be left. It is this aspect of Camus's thought that has led critics and even Camus himself to insist that he is not an evangelist of the absurd.

It is strange indeed that Camus has been described as a "new" writer when so much in his manner and thought are not really very new at all. His manner of expression is direct and even chaste in its fashion; his use of the forms he selects is not marked by any of the experimentation that some authors think is required of them; his essential plea is for charity, justice, and truth. But perhaps, it is this simple presentation of the fundamental conflict between moderation and violence, stability and change, honesty and sham that constitutes the quality of what all admit to be the greatness of Camus.

Spire Pitou. BA. Spring, 1960. p. 125

Camus expressed feelings; this is something few contemporary writers do—or even want to do. Moreover, the kind of feelings he made vivid are those we ourselves have only felt incipiently, not fully, yet recognize that we should have felt more completely when we read their expression by him. He is the poet of what we ought to have felt in a given situation, but did not quite feel. Reading him, we wish we had.

He was a moralist, then, in his attentiveness to, and cult of, the better, the nobler feeling; he was not importantly the moralist of the better or more decisive act. However, action is modified by sensibility, and feeling what ought to be felt is a kind of doing. In striving to feel what ought to be felt, there is, of course, always the risk of being insincere, of falling into pose. Nowadays, people generally, and writers particularly, do not like such risk; Camus did; he has been accused of pose; and at times I myself thought the charge just. Yet for me, Camus's best quality is not diminished by the fact that it was not always with him. What you ought, you can, said Kant. He should have added:

not always. Besides, there are any number of occasions when it is easier
to do what you should than to feel as you ought.

Lionel Abel. Cmty. Feb., 1961. p. 172

If Camus's moral earnestness at times ceased to enthrall and began
to irritate, it's because there was a certain intellectual weakness in it.
One sensed in Camus, as one senses in James Baldwin, the presence of
an entirely genuine and historically relevant passion. But also, as with
Baldwin, that passion seemed to transmute itself too readily into stately
language, into an inexhaustible self-perpetuating oratory. The moral imperatives—love, moderation—offered to palliate intolerable historical
or metaphysical dilemmas were too general, too abstract, too rhetorical.
. . . Camus's problem in the last years of his life was not that he became
religious, or that he subsided into bourgeois humanitarian seriousness,
or that he lost his socialist nerve. It was, rather, that he had hoist himself on the petard of his own virtue. A writer who acts as public conscience needs extraordinary nerve and fine instincts, like a boxer. After
a time, these instincts inevitably falter. He also needs to be emotionally
tough. Camus was not that tough, not tough in the way that Sartre is. . . .
Camus's life and work are not so much about morality as they are
about the pathos of moral positions. This pathos is Camus's modernity.
And his ability to suffer this pathos in a dignified and virile way is what
made his readers love and admire him.

Susan Sontag. NYR. Sept. 26, 1963. pp. 2–3

See *Exile and the Kingdom, The Fall, The Plague,* and *The Stranger* (novels);
The Possessed and *Caligula and Three Other Plays*; and *Myth of Sisyphus,
The Rebel,* and *Resistance, Rebellion, and Death* (essays).

CASSOLA, CARLO (1917–   )

Carlo Cassola is recognized in Italy as the still, small voice of the
intellectually hostile generation that grew to manhood during fascism.
Like Vittorini and Pavese, his masters and seniors in the postwar neo-
realist movement, Cassola roots his work in understatement. He writes
a terse, dry prose, geared to sparse action conveyed through the medium
of an astringent, almost "hermetic" dialogue. Yet his style bears the
unmistakable personal stamp of a pervasive melancholy akin to that
evoked by the lunar-white chalk hills that surround the dreamlike
Etruscan town of Volterra, which serves as the backdrop for most of
his works.

Helene Cantarella. NYT. June 26, 1960. p. 4

Cassola's work has always been that of an accomplished, single-minded craftsman. . . . [*Bebo's Girl*] is a somber and yet hopeful novel, for . . . Cassola strikes a note of faith, if not in the perfectability of man, at least in his possibility to learn from experience, to become more human.

In his usual sparse and concrete manner, . . . it is the facts themselves that speak. . . . Noteworthy is Cassola's solution of the problem of language in the modern novel. In his portrayal of simple, untutored country people, firmly rooted in a given provincial milieu, he rejects the usual solution of allowing dialect forms to enter into his writing. Cassola is in every way a distinctive personality in contemporary Italian literature.

Olga Ragusa. BA. Spring, 1961. pp. 136–7

The Strega prize is a very fair assurance of quality in Italian literature. . . . Now a moving and deceptively simple story of love, immaturity and honour called *Bebo's Girl* by Carlo Cassola has won it. . . . Excluding Moravia there is no Italian novelist with an established international reputation. . . . Cassola could, I think, become an international writer. His particular qualities (honesty, simplicity and insight) remind one of a less intellectual Camus. . . . The whole novel has that quality of serenity and elation which is so moving in the acting of Vanessa Redgrave.

Julian Jebb. TT. Jan. 25, 1962. p. 31

Ever since that topheavy girl slopped through the paddy fields in *Bitter Rice,* the Italian film and novel have been stuck with her as the classical image of the Latin Woman. They may have shaded her down a little, even sophisticated her to some extent in the suburbs of Moravia, but she is still essentially the same. Her continual fascination for the Anglo-Saxon is, I think, due to the conflict of hot, Latin passion and an anti-sex morality that gives every bout of love-making with her (and after all, what else are Italian books about?) the added excitement of the classical rape.

In *Bebo's Girl* by Carlo Cassola, a fatuous love-story, she is the girl friend of a young trigger-happy partisan.

Frank McGuinness. LMg. March, 1962. p. 86

What makes Cassola's elegant prose . . . more than a specimen of Italian neo-realism is its wholeness and radiance, its singleness of breath. Of course he has read, as adverse critics never fail to stress, the Russians and the Americans, particularly Gorky, Chekhov and Hemingway; but his manner has its own terseness, poetic rhythm and deft use of understatement in climactic passages. There is no doubt that . . . [Cassola] is one of Italy's most interesting writers. . . . He belongs to the "second" generation of Italian novelists, those who grew up between fascism and war, who took part in the resistance movement in 1943-45 and were just involved and then disappointed in communism. . . . All the works of Cassola have a geographic and social unity, and he has been labeled "a regionalist with a conscience." . . . He always depicts the countryside around Volterra, the city of alabaster and Etruscan remains; his protagonists are local workmen and peasants who move within the orbit of the Communist party.

Marc Slonim. NYT. June 10, 1962. p. 6

Cassola has awakened widespread, if disparate, opinions. Of these, the ones which point out the real consistency of his development—his growing possession of human insights and of the means for their expression—are more convincing (Baldacci speaks of the change from biography to objectivity) than those who reduce Cassola's experience to a simple linguistic fact (Barberi Squarotti writes of "white" or "neutral" language). . . . Cassola feels, even in his least successful work, the necessity of telling purely and simply that which his imagination has intuited. Then the words come bare from his pen, because his style is born from the urgency of what must be said. His strength lies in this: there is no economy in writing, or technique which can be rationally explored and made artificially necessary. His stories have the urgency of the imagination, and it is for this reason that he is a poet, his pages are clean and dry like an ancient chronicler who never lets true human motives slip by. When he writes these actions contain in themselves the secret.

Riccardo Scrivano. IQ. Fall-Winter, 1962. pp. 61–2

The reader will find in this work of Cassola's youth [<i>La visita</i>] the key to a fuller understanding of his later and better known novels. . . . The sketches appear to be separate and independent details of a large canvas —life itself—not explicitly drawn by the author but dimly perceived in the background and animated by the events in the lives of common people. The sketches are not sharply defined and they bring to mind the apparent indefiniteness of the paintings of the Impressionist school.

Cassola believes that a tale is a recital of common life events and, as such, it must be written in simple and direct words. His tales show us that modest, squalid, provincial life is not unworthy of being lived. Rather, his characters are fully free and alive in their commonplace existence.

Alba della Fazia. BA. Summer, 1963. p. 326

See <i>Bebo's Girl</i> and <i>Fausto and Anna</i> (novels).

CASTILLO, MICHEL DEL
See Del Castillo, Michel

CASTRO, JOSÉ MARIA FERREIRA DE
See Ferreira de Castro, José Maria

CAYROL, JEAN (1911–   )

Jean Cayrol is one of the best endowed novelists of the younger generation and this story [*Le Déménagement*], moving and serious, seems
to me to be one of his best. The story of this couple who move from
one apartment to another during a Paris winter . . . has allowed Cayrol
to use again, with contemporary coloring, all his chosen themes. Themes
of which one must say that they constitute, above all, a world of his
own: a world of exodus, of wandering, of deprivation, of a shadowed
no-man's-land, of anonymous poverty, a world of Lazarus, of death
from which comes a hope for resurrection.

> Gaëton Picon. *MF*. July, 1956. p. 499.
> Tr. by Dorothy Nyren Curley

Beggars and proletarians are introduced not only from the sociological
viewpoint but also from the psychological and religious angle in the
novels of the Catholic poet from Bordeaux, Jean Cayrol. . . . Cayrol is
much closer to reality than the allegorical novels and dramas of the
bum by Samuel Beckett. . . . In Cayrol's work a delicate psychology
dignifies the suffering and erotic aberration of men who knew concentration camps, poverty, and dereliction. . . . Cayrol's main asset, comparable to that of the priest-workers, is the preservation of human dignity, even in a debased proletarian world.

> Helmut Hatzfeld. *Trends and Styles in Twentieth Century
> French Literature* (Catholic U.). 1957. pp. 188–9

The figures in Cayrol's fictional world . . . are in constant motion, walking endlessly, seemingly at random, in the real space of the world of
phenomena, which is both familiar and strange, disturbing and reassuring. This movement seems to spatialize man's loneliness, his vague
aspirations toward reconciliation and renewal; it also keeps him free
to follow paths where chance encounters may lead to recognition and
love—love which here is not the exalted passion of the Romantics, but

a humble, patient, human emotion which may, nevertheless, bring the modern Lazarus back to life.

Carlos Lynes, Jr. *YFS*. Summer, 1959. pp. 66–7

Foreign Bodies by Jean Cayrol poses some interesting paradoxes. It dilates on the sordid and despicable—and yet it is a powerful affirmation of life. Its framework is a sequence of the ambiguous reveries of a half-drunk murderer—and yet the picture it draws has dramatic lucidity. . . . M. Cayrol's novel surges with a virility that, come to think of it, the French have admired in some of our books. But the author's pungent lyricism is uniquely his own, as is his particular grasp of reality.

Martin Levin. *NYT*. March 20, 1960. p. 4

Jean Cayrol, like so many of his generation . . . was influenced by the Surrealists. We have the same virgorous style, the same insouciance with regard to a story line, the same indifference to "prettiness." Yet each section (I was going to say poem, but the form is prose) is a gem of beauty and clarity whose only resemblance to the results of automatic writing is the feeling of wonder and *dépaysement* you are left with after having read several pages.

Herbert S. Gershman. *BA*. Summer, 1961. p. 235

Appearing as a novelist in the immediate postwar world, Cayrol was already firmly established before the new novel became a literary issue. However, critics of the new school have considered him a kindred spirit, which he is indeed by aspects of his technique, theme, and concept of the novel. His writing stands quite apart from the French sociological or psychological tradition, belonging rather to that of the *Entwicklungsroman,* the "duration" novel which Sartre and the new novelists all advocate. His hero moves blindly along in the adventure of his life, neither knowing where he is going nor ever really arriving. He is seeking something, his salvation perhaps, but all we can be sure of is that he will discover the world.

Laurent Le Sage. *The French New Novel* (Pennsylvania State). 1962. p. 79

See *Foreign Bodies* (novel).

CELA, CAMILO JOSÉ (1916–   )

The history of the Spanish novel records few cases of such stern and merciless realism as Cela's. The young Galician has little to say in favor of mankind. Few if any rays of sunshine penetrate his pages, in which ugliness, brutality, selfishness and the principle of *homo homini lupus* predominate. Cogent reasons exist for classifying him as a full-fledged naturalistic writer. From the very beginning of his career, Don Camilo has exhibited a predilection and a genius for portraying life, man and society at their worst. . . . Much like Pío Baroja, he conceives of the novel as a malleable and flexible instrument for the mirroring of life's realities. The novelist is to him "the keeper of his times and his world" whose duty it is to lash out against deceit, dishonesty and sham.

Jacob Ornstein and James Y. Causey. *BA*. Spring, 1953.
pp. 136–7

It is not to be wondered that the Franco censorship disapproves of Cela's novels. Life in Madrid as he portrays it is brutal, hungry and senseless. Hyprocisy, fear and oppression are in command. Cela's political loyalties may be conservative or reactionary, but his literary affiliations are of the most radical; they are with Camus and Sartre, with Moravia, with Zola and French naturalism. Only Cela has very little of the theoretician about him and has no existential, sexual or political message to deliver. It is in his directness and lack of squeamishness that he resembles Sartre and Moravia.

Saul Bellow. *NYT*. Sept. 27, 1953. p. 5

A lover of crude realism, of the slice-of-life variety, Cela's eye is clinical and miry. In this respect and on his sexual insistence he is reminiscent of the Céline of *Journey to the End of the Night,* or, to think in Spanish terms, of the novel of roguery, especially of Quevedo's work. His is a Quevedan vitriolic moralism, a ferocious wrath against hypocrisy and conformism. But the extremes of anguish make one wonder whether he means that society perverts man or whether man is preverted *ab ovum.*

Angel Flores. *NYHT*. Sept. 27, 1953. p. 6

The Spanish novelist Camilo José Cela . . . is suffused with anger and bitterness at society in Madrid. "They lie," he says, "who want to disguise life with the crazy mask of literature. The evil that corrodes the soul, the evil that has as many names as we choose to give it, cannot be fought with the poultices of conformism or the plasters of rhetoric and poetics. My novel sets out to be no more—yet no less either—than a slice of life, told step by step, without reticence, without external tragedies, without charity, exactly as life itself rambles on."

Wonderful words—which we have not often heard in this country since the first generation of native realists in the 1900's. . . . And *The*

Hive itself, as a study of impoverished, frustrated lower-middle-class city people—less vicious, really, than ignoble and less ignoble maybe than starved—has undoubted power and a deliberately flat, acrid, angry style.

Cela's true position, however, is that of the aristocratic moralist who scourges the values of a corrupt and decaying urban society; the moments of warmth and affection in his narrative are few.

Maxwell Geismar. *Nation*. Nov. 14, 1953. p. 404

In *The Hive* Cela deliberately presents the inconsequential moments of his hundred and sixty characters in a disjointed and episodic manner which emphasizes the atomization of city living, the breakup of a cohesive pattern of society and social feeling. His people are tragic not because they are poor, but because they have no longer the resources that in the past made poverty something man could bear with dignity.

George Woodcock. *NR*. July 12, 1954. p. 16

If we add Unamuno's concern for the Nietzschean, the violent, even the demonic, to Baroja's rejection of systematic assembly, we have something close to the essence of Camilo José Cela. . . . Cela prefers the weird, the apparently meaningless and the amorphous. The world of his novels has been likened to that of Hieronimus Bosch and Brueghel; he sees man as a prisoner in a forbidding universe where chaos and imperfection always defeat the idealist. . . . With over a score of books to his name he still pursues the bizarre and the sordid grotesque, almost as if he thinks that a heightening of the everyday will amount to an opinion expressed. It does, provided we can attune ourselves to his stylish garbling of an already garbled society. Cela is the Goya of Franco's Spain.

Paul West. *The Modern Novel* (Hutchinson).
1963. pp. 419–21

On the whole there is a marked distinction between the acrimonious Cela of the nineteen forties and the ironical Cela of the nineteen fifties. . . . He does not relent in his criticism, but his mood becomes more temperate. Only hunger remains as his implacable enemy. He can ridicule most everything, even the absurd excesses of his government, but he cannot retain a sense of humor about starvation. In his writings, the ghost of Cela the man cries out for vengeance. There is no mercy for hunger. . . . Out of a degenerate society that groped for survival, Cela forged a new artistic reality. The intense reaction of Spanish life reaches aesthetic heights in the form of characters and situations that reflect the inner truth of man while perpetuating an era of Spanish existence. With intuitive genius Cela molds his art in the image of his society. The explosive shape of his composition conforms to the abortive nature of his times.

Robert Kirsner. *The Novels and Travels of Camilo José Cela* (N. Carolina). 1963. pp. 184–5

The Family of Pascual Duarte was published in the same year (1942) as Camus's *L'Etranger*. . . . Perhaps it is not inconsequential that both books revolve around meaningless murder. Both books, like two great tolling bells, resound with the sound of a spiritual void. The knells come across a sparse empty steppe of the soul. The sound is metallically rich—and roundly hollow. Emptiness resounds, for music's sake, even better than fullness. Emptiness of this sort, a rarefaction, is like the blackness in sunlight, as potent as a black sun. There is a purity in atheism, perhaps, as distinct as the mystic clarity of a St. Teresa or the quietest ardor of a Miguel de Molinos. Behind and below both books, there is the abyss of a War just passed into its climax, the encroaching desolation of the aftermath already foreseen, a lack of belief in anything not immediate, the myth unraveled, the absurdity of chance. . . . Either of these two heroes, these anti-heroes [Pascual Duarte and the Stranger], could have been preparing to be the century's great lone killer at Dallas.

Anthony Kerrigan. Introduction to *The Family of Pascual Duarte* (Little). 1964. pp. ix–x

Pascual Duarte speaks of suffering and ferocity so appalling as to be almost beyond the reach of our sympathy. They stun even more than they horrify—and that, incidentally, is the ground for differing with the common judgement that Camilo José Cela's novel is a literary classic. Powerful it is without a doubt. Archetypically portentous it seems to be, but what meaning can be attached to Pascual Duarte's mindless violence and mindless repentance eludes our power of conception. . . . One could offer sociological or psychological accounts of Pascual Duarte's life that would be adequate on their own terms, but those terms are not really relevant to the abasement and prostration he represents. As children of the Enlightenment, we are quite firm about wanting to change the conditions that produce a Pascual Duarte. But there is that in him that suggests a condition anterior to all "conditions," and evokes in us a superstitious terror that the humanization of man may be unrealizable.

Emile Capouya. *SR*. Nov. 28, 1964. p. 38

See *The Hive* and *The Family of Pascual Duarte* (novels).

CÉLINE, LOUIS-FERDINAND (1894–1961)

Journey to the End of Night is a powerful and memorable book. It is also a one-sided one, with much of its strength arising, like the strength of some of those post-war German caricatures, from its exaggerations; everything in it is a little out of focus. Many of the characters, fat, gross, belching monstrosities, remind one of those cartoons of profiteers of the post-war period; and M. Céline particularly concentrates on showing these creatures in their least dignified moments, when they are industriously scratching themselves, say, or digesting a big dinner or getting their heads blown off.

Robert Cantwell. *NO*. May, 1934. p. 53

The essential virtue of Céline's art lies in the extraordinary imagery, the inexhaustible flood of metaphor by which everything that it touches is recreated. With this goes a language more personal, rich, pungent, and brutal than anything that has come out of France, possibly, since the sixteenth century. It is the language that creates the effect of extraordinary scope, the mood of the endlessness of suffering and defeat.

Haakon M. Chevalier. *Nation*. May 2, 1934. p. 511

Journey to the End of Night is a masterpiece that has to be read, and one that holds its readers whether or not they like what they are reading. Essentially it belongs to the tradition perfected by Joyce and Proust, that of the "pure" novel, autobiographical in content, extreme in its subjectivism, tormented and bold in its psychology. But it breaks decisively with this tradition by making the theme of individual solitude, hitherto treated in an opaque fashion for a limited audience, clear and acceptable to the man in the street. No erudition comparable to that required to read *Ulysses* is necessary to understand and enjoy the *Journey* and to feel its frantic despair.

Norbert Guterman. *NR*. May 9, 1934. p. 368

To be readable is to be formidable, if one has anything of importance to say, and M. Céline is readable, and the sharpess of his conviction that what he has to say is important makes it important. His persistent self-pity is a social phenomenon with which society will have to reckon. ... M. Céline's fairy-tale is, broadly speaking, written all in one tone. It is an inversion of fairy-tale sentimentalism, and monotony remains monotony whether it be painted *couleur de rose* or the color of mud. This is a world of ordure, betrayal, surrender and despair. What one knows of the king's youngest son in this world is not that he will succeed where his elders have failed but that he will be either baser than his elders, or more unfortunate, and probably both.

Edward Shanks. *LM*. August, 1934. pp. 332, 336

He is a great talker—in both senses of the phrase. And a silent man. The paradox must be forgiven, for it aims to express the fact that he either talks a lot, and admirably, or not at all; and it attempts to suggest the great effect of his words after his long silences: large words, voluble, twirling, brilliantly descriptive, tumbling over each other, yet each precise, accurate, analytical. His talk is of real people and equally real ideas; seldom of things. . . . Nothing that is human fails to interest him. Nothing that you tell him lacks his attention.

John Marks. *BkmL*. Oct., 1934. p. 32

Céline has been frequently compared to Rabelais and James Joyce. To be sure he has in common with them lengthiness, a love of scatology, and a dissatisfaction with the current vocabulary, but he lacks their learning and careful composition. When Rabelais and Joyce enrich the language, for instance, they make subtle graftings and invent onomato-poetic images, while Céline simply scrambles common words as a strong man bends iron. He dominates language as he does the rest of his material, crushing it with a heavy hand. . . . In reality Céline belongs to the strictly contemporary school of hard-boiled writers, of which we know more here than they do in France.

Justin O'Brien. *Nation*. Aug. 27, 1938. p. 208

The new naturalism, which sprang up after the war as a consequence of the destruction of the old moral fabric, has given up the notion of struggle. The protagonist has become a propathetist; an island of feeling through whose sensory impressions the nature of the environment is simply reported. Thus the new naturalism has become overlaid with impressionism; its heroes are more acted upon than acting.

Of this tendency Céline is the predominant example in France, as James Farrell is in America. The mildest thing that can be said about his work is that it is unpleasant. He is a pessimist by temperament, and he hovers like a buzzard over the charnel houses of society. He hunts out every stench and cancer diligently and brings them richly to our nostrils or our eyes.

Harold Strauss. *NYT*. Sept. 4, 1938. p. 6

His second-raters appear on the scene beyond the point of failure and roll along from one humiliation to the next among the irredeemably defeated. The principle he seems to rely on is expressed in the old saying "The toad beneath the harrow knows where each point of the harrow goes"; the theory apparently is that the harder you have been hit by life and the social machine, the more you will know about life and how to live it. So, naturally, the ideal hero becomes a semi-criminal bum, and the man who writes about him assumes the stylistic equivalent of a three-day beard, a whiskey breath, and a well-slept-in suit.

Anthony West. *NY.* June 12, 1954. p. 104

He was the first to announce and depict that particular kind of human despair which has become an almost exclusive theme in contemporary literature: the absurdity of human life. We tend to forget how much writers like Sartre, for example, and Raymon Queneau, owe to Céline, who first established an agreement between the absurd in man's existence and the obscene in the expression he gives to daily existence. . . . The novels of Céline . . . have been compared to vast poems or to lyric structures because of the endless thematic repetitions which characterize his writing and because of the constant metamorphoses of reality into hallucination which convert each scene in the novel into a dark underground and each character into a monster. Not since Rabelais has the torrential flow of oral speech been so copied in a literary work. This style of oral popular speech has been taken over from Céline by Sartre and by a group of younger writers in France today. But Céline surpasses them all in richness.

Wallace Fowlie. *Com.* July 9, 1954. p. 346

Macabre comedy, brutal hilarity are in Céline's vein. Behind the self-pity and the cynicism is an admiration of power and violence, a belief in frenzy and excitement and the sentimental exaltation of the irrational. In practice this may mean no more than falling down stairs dead drunk into a pile of crockery or beating an old woman with an umbrella. He does penetrate the sullen, private world of the conceited outcast; what offends is that he wallows in it very self-consciously, whereas the underdogs themselves do not know they are wallowing. He puts a lurid spotlight on them and then winds the handle of his literary barrel organ.

V. S. Pritchett. *NSN.* Oct. 2, 1954. pp. 412–4

With the passage of time, *Voyage au bout de la nuit* has emerged as one of the most significant French novels of the inter-war years. . . . [It] sprawls over 400 pages and ends as abruptly as it begins. There is no *dénouement,* no conclusion in the usual sense of the word. A conclusion presupposes resolution of the central problems posed in a novel. It is

impossible here, where the basic problems admit of no solution. . . .
If [it] is a depressing book, it is because it is an honest book. . . . He
never suggests a possibility of release from Man's predicament. He states
a problem to which he cannot propose a solution.

J. H. Matthews. *CR*. March, 1957. pp. 158–61

The ultimate limitation in Céline's work is a limitation of intelligence.
He does not know what to do with his outpourings, except to multiply
them; he cannot surmount his brilliant monomania. He is unable to
distinguish among the kinds and degrees of loathsomeness, between a
speck of dust and a mound of filth. Irritation and outrage, triviality
and betrayal grate on his nerves almost equally. Except on grounds of
radical incompleteness, it would be difficult to quarrel with Céline's
description of twentieth century experience; but there is something
exasperating, at times even stupid, about a writer who roars with the
same passion against nuisance and disaster.

Irving Howe. *A World More Attractive* (Horizon).
1963. p. 204

See *Journey to the End of Night, Death on the Installment Plan,* and
Guignol's Band (novels).

CESPEDES, ALBA DE (1911–   )

Alba de Cespedes . . . is a kind of feminine knight-errant, tilting her
literary lance in behalf of women. But it is not against their economic,
political, or social plight that she tilts so much as against the plight of
their psyche, the anguish of their hearts. Yet in this novel, *The Best of
Husbands* . . . , the author reveals, almost unwittingly, that no bridge
crosses the psychological abyss between men and women. Her lance
breaks against the stubborn facts of human nature. . . . This tale of an
unresigned Cinderella . . . moves toward its climax of violence with
emotional power and a certain genuine sensitivity. But the climax itself
is somehow incredible. The lament for wives which underlies the story
and appears to justify it is somehow absurd and immature, when we all
know that the earth would cease to turn on its axis if men were to
stop adventuring and crusading and grow so concerned with domesticity
that they remained to coddle their wives at home.

Virgilia Peterson. *NYHT*. Nov. 2, 1952. p. 14

There are many good things in this book [*The Best of Husbands*]. . . .
But . . . other aspects of the work are dwarfed by the main theme which

can be stated simply as the tragic failure of men to understand women. The title in the original *(Dala parte di lei—Her Side of the Case)* brings out its feminism very clearly. . . . Alessandra . . . is not abnormal among sensitive and intelligent women of today in wanting from her husband not so much protection as comradeship, not so much privilege plus disregard as respect and interest. Tragedy comes about not because her best of husbands doesn't understand her but because he simply doesn't see that there is anything to understand.

Thomas G. Bergin. *SR*. Nov. 8, 1952. p. 52

[*The Secret*] is by far the most profound yet the simplest of her books, written with the powerful insight that only a sensitive, highly intelligent woman could bring to the basic problem of Western woman: how to use the freedoms she has won, how to play the manifold roles of wife, mother and professional woman, yet still retain the essential touchstone, the self.

Signora de Cespedes is one of the few distinguished women writers since Colette to grapple effectively with what it is to be a woman. Her brilliant handling of Valeria's moral hegira places her in the forefront of contemporary novelists.

Frances Keene. *NYT*. Sept. 28, 1958. p.5

Between Then and Now is a short novel written with a disciplined, restrained intensity that makes its effect in depth. It has a circular shape like a well-constructed play. . . . The way in which . . . a simple domestic incident is made to link present and past, and illustrate the speed of contemporary social flux is formally satisfying. The author has been compared with crashing ineptitude to Colette. Though her writing touch is light she is full of lofty ideals, like one of those noble souls that so delighted Stendhal when he first arrived in Italy.

Maurice Richardson. *NSN*. Sept. 2, 1959. p. 328

Between Then and Now . . . is a peculiarly feminine view of the dilemma of the "old-fashioned" liberal all at sea in contemporary society, and it has considerable documentary value. More important still, Miss de Cespedes combines the finest sort of purely feminine sensibility with a not so feminine, almost classical talent for organising her sensitive perceptions and reactions into a strong, complex, and wonderfully lucid novel.

W. L. Webb. *MG*. Sept. 18, 1959. p. 8

Alba de Cespedes, one of Italy's most popular woman journalists, writes well. It is not her style, but her subject matter that leaves one unimpressed. Writing in the first person, she tells of the main character's years of young womanhood, lived during a war, and in a country which not only was a main battlefield, but found itself simultaneously fighting on both sides; she speaks of at least two love affairs and one broken engagement, and one wonders that so many currents of history, drama, and mankind brought to bear on one person could have resulted in so little feeling, understanding, or compassion. In this, *Between Then and Now* has the aroma of the Deux Magots, the Paris school of this-is-how-we-are-how-did-we-get-this-way.

When the reader reflects that this novel was written in sunny Rome, city of immemorial life and loud and vigorous living, he cannot but conclude that it may have been written in the wrong place, at the wrong time, and in the wrong original language.

John H. Secondari. *SR*. March 26, 1960. p. 28

See *The Best of Husbands, Between Then and Now*, and *The Secret* (novels).

CHAR, RENÉ (1907–   )

As an alchemist works for queens, he has ceaselessly decanted river sand. People have been right to write that Char's poetry is a quintessence. It is almost impossible to go further in alchemy. He has scorned the easy methods of alchemy, rejected the help of facile religions, ignored convenient curses. What attracted him from the heroic period was the gold in all things. He knew how to love, to be loved, to fraternize with the forces of Light, hold his head high for the blessing of Motion, finally to TRANSMIT. . . .

Pierre Berger. *René Char* (Editions Pierre Seghers). 1951. pp. 74–5. Tr. by Dorothy Nyren Curley

The impression I get from the poems and fragments of poems of René Char is that they are all parts of something larger, from the same block. . . . Sometimes he catches no more than the tail of an idea as it were in passing. . . , once he gets the theme he follows it in example after example with telling effect until gradually it becomes clear by the sheer persistence of what he has to say. It is a perfectly legitimate device of the artist and increases the pleasure of the reader by piling up the emphasis with variations of detail until the total effect is overwhelming.

William Carlos Williams. *NR*. Sept. 17, 1956. p. 18

A poem of Char makes manifest a sum of individual energy grown to sovereign power over the domain of the inorganic, that prodigious fount of forces working and wrestling like fire on fire. It is a drastic formulation of a singular truth in the face of truths where power's self-conflict remains impersonal. Against this fatal and infallible world, the poet with his "bellicose fervour" maintains his images, his words of deliverance, the fragile human world with its chances, duties and burdens.

> Gabriel Bounoure. *René Char's Poetry* by Maurice Blanchot
> and others (Editions de Luca). 1956. p. 49

Ancient and new as it is, his poetry is both subtle and simple. It carries day-time and night on the same impulse. In the brilliant landscape where Char was born, the sun, as we know, is something dark. At two in the afternoon, when the land is fagged with heat, a black breath blows over it. And so, when Char's poetry appears to be obscure, it is because a furious condensation of imagery, an intensification of light removes it from that degree of abstract transparency which we all too often demand only because it makes no demand on us. But at the same time, that point of darkness, as in the sun-soaked landscape, creates around it vast reaches of light in which the human face is laid bare.

> Albert Camus. *René Char's Poetry* by Maurice Blanchot
> and others (Editions de Luca). 1956. p. 56

The verses of Char, the aphorisms which abound in his work, and the brief condensed tales which appear in company with the aphorisms, all speak of the nature of poetry. It is that which is lived, for Char, experienced with the penetrating realization of submitting to human destiny. It is a comparatively easy matter to describe a literary work which is about life. But such a definition would not apply to the poetry of Char. This poet looks upon his art as an assault on life. He answers, in the writing of his poems, not some outside command, but the uprising surge of his nature and his feelings. No cause which can be defined as such will move him as much as the proportions of his own human nature, with its contradictions and its puzzling enigmas.

> Wallace Fowlie. *YFS*. Spring-Summer, 1958. pp. 83–4

René Char, half a generation younger than André Breton, appears to carry on the tradition of surrealism better than anyone else, although he has supposedly gone through and beyond surrealism. Like Breton, simply and completely a poet, he has faced up to "this rebellious and solitary world of contradictions" as he terms it in *Le Poème pulverisé,* and has decided that it is impossible to live without having the image of the unknown ever before one's eyes. His universe built as Breton's, upon a structure of metaphysical metaphors, is a place of discovery, where even "the harvest of the abyss" is a possibility.

Anna Balakian. *Surrealism* (Noonday). 1959. pp. 193–4

We recognize the style—the series of lean flashes that are more brilliant for their leanness, and we see that the poet's treatment of his usual themes (the indistinct line between reality and unreality, love, and, above all, poetry itself) remains incisive, impersonal and frankly didactic. Indeed, at times Char is a kind of aesthetic La Rochefoucauld *"Dormez, deséspérés, c'est bientôt jour, un jour d'hiver."*

C. E. Nelson. *BA*. Autumn, 1962. p. 393

Char inaugurates a postsurrealist phase of intensified poetic communion with life and nature. Fundamental humanistic values (love, beauty, justice, fraternity, personal integrity, a sense of elevation and nobility) are reasserted here, in a mood of exasperated serenity. Like his friend Albert Camus, René Char recreates the ethics of modern man, but he grounds them on a deeper level of poetic mystery, where he is experiencing them as a sudden revelation of essences, as a manifestation of the sacred, as a strength of existence.

Alexander Aspel. *Contemporary French Poetry* (Michigan). 1965. p. 9

See *Hypnos Waking* (poetry).

CLAUDEL, PAUL (1868–1955)

There is in Claudel a natural genius that is robust and even somewhat heavy, complex and strongly sensuous; but there is also in him a logician enamoured of vast systems of thought, a theologian who has worked out finally his disciplines and his forms. He is, we might say, a romantic who has laid upon himself a classic discipline; and by this constant reaction of his "rational soul" on his "sensory soul" Claudel is indeed a Latin and a Roman. We may disagree as to the effect of his conversion and his long struggle on his art. But . . . there is a certain attraction and grandeur.

Pierre Chavannes. Introduction to *The Hostage* (Yale). 1917. p. 10

It is better to approach M. Claudel on his dramatic side, because the faults which do so obstinately beset him are less obvious in his plays than in his canticles. When he abandons himself to his strange infatuated rhapsodies, he is apt to lose the thread of his intention, and to wander about in a cloud of noble words, from the midst of which proceed magnificent flashes of imagery and eloquent detonations of thought. But his plays are most always clearer than his cantatas, more external, more vivid; there have to be characters in them who move and speak; there have to be localities which are made visual to us.

Edmund Gosse. *Books on the Table* (Heinemann). 1921. pp. 242–3

Once the first moment of surprise is overcome . . . the reader accustomed to the Elizabethan theatre easily enters the Claudelian stage. . . . This brutal strangeness, this epic savageness, in Claudel is the proof of a genius which cannot contain itself, but which suddenly overflows in waves so rapid that the stream arrives in jerks and frightens us. . . . Claudel, while seeking to give a character of eternity to his conception, wishing to embrace the whole universe, accumulates image, metaphor, and picture, uniting the four corners of the world in a few lines. He is a veritable Rubens in poetry.

G. Turquet-Milnes. *Some Modern French Writers* (McBride). 1921. p. 175

It was an art of bold rough strokes brought by Claudel. It was an art of large piercing human images drawn from daily life and ships and machinery, and of a violent and exalted style formed on the Greek and Hebrew poets and sown with foreign and technical terms which it had taken upon itself. It was an art all mouth, straining to hold the utterance close to the fluid form which it had taken when it left the burning fountain of the soul, and careless of accepted euphony and measure.

Paul Rosenfeld. *Men Seen* (Dial). 1925. pp. 303–4

As a rhythmician Claudel has disregarded the traditions of French verse and created his own, the "Claudelian verse," as it is called. Rhythm and not versification interests him and he set aside all hackneyed distinctions between verse and prose. There is no poetry outside the living speech as it comes out musically from the heart and the lungs, beating to and fro to the rhythm of things. . . . We need not look for models of Claudel's verse outside his inner sense of the motions and modulations of the living speech.

Régis Michaud. *Modern Thought and Literature in France* (Funk). 1934. p. 50

Finished *Le Soulier de Satin*. Staggering. It is hard to imagine that in another religion Claudel's shortcomings could have developed as unimpeded as in Catholicism. . . . Claudel has always treated Goethe with an easily sovereign scorn. Oh, how this scorn puts me at ease! So much voluntary (and instinctive) lack of intelligence, that set purpose to reject what cannot be annexed, gives extraordinary encouragement to my resistance, and I am more grateful to them than they could imagine (to Claudel, Massis, etc.) for their rejections.

André Gide. The Journals (Knopf). 1949.
v. 3, pp. 76, 133

Hope of eternal reunion with a beloved person is strong in the human race, and that hope inspires the great plays of Claudel. If we question the validity of converting the *feeling* of lovers into a *certainty,* we question one of the fundamental assumptions made by Claudel. . . . However, the reservations that may be made with regard to his basic assumptions need not blind us to the splendour of Claudel's attempt to solve one of the deepest human problems, recognising alike the frailties and potentialities of man, and having ever in mind the true end of love.

Ernest Beaumont. The Theme of Beatrice in the Plays
of Claudel (Rockliff). 1954. pp. 98-9

Claudel's poetic diction offers no middle course; his poetry lives only when it is in full flight. Then it can soar very high, perhaps higher than other verse of our time, but when the flight ceases we fall to the ground, half-dead, and then we spend long moments of boredom and drudgery preparing for the next flight. His poetry has no vertebrae to hold it erect, waiting for life to flow into it; either the spirit is there and raises it, or it is nothing. With him we never have the complex experience of watching a perfect instrument which, even in repose, can give us a hint of its tremendous possibilities; there is no repose, no slow motion, only fantastic gales which might blow one off the earth.

Joseph Chiari. The Poetic Drama of Paul Claudel
(Kenedy). 1954. p. 171

Claudel's is a difficult drama even for Catholics; his plays never allow departures from the terrible reality of punishment for those who break the rules, and there is the necessity to be superhuman not to yield to the forbidden. . . . Claudel's ambitions are vast. . . . He wishes to explore the whole range of human experience, and the only difficulty is to find the means of communicating our perception. He demands that an audience should complete what it sees by imagination. . . . For this reason naturalist critics with a strong anti-Catholic bias are not likely to accept the world which Claudel himself believes in and introduces into his plays, which explains the sudden leaps from the mystical and displays a revelation of the infinite as Claudel makes a transition from one plane to the other.

Frederick Lumley. *Trends in Twentieth Century Drama* (Essential Books). 1956. pp. 64–5

Claudel intends his poetry to be accessible to any reader who will take trouble over it. What he demands is spiritual insight—the approach through intuition and experience—rather than the approach through literature in its technical and "hermetic" aspects. He therefore takes the kind of language which comes first to hand and requires the least premeditation and blows into it with the full force of his eloquence to create now gorgeous, now monstrous, serpentine shapes. Occasionally the language collapses before him and the result is limp and ludicrous, but that risk has to be taken. In the last resort he does not care about language, or rather, he regards it as infinitely expendable.

Geoffrey Brereton. *An Introduction to the French Poets* (Essential Books). 1957. p. 244

His characters speak with the voices of real men and women who feel that humanity forms one body in that each man is responsible at every moment of his existence for all other men. In each scene of his many plays we have the impression of following some aspect or other of one of the most difficult and mystical dogmas of all, that of the communion of the saints. For Claudel the universe is total at every moment of every man's existence. Every story he undertakes to unravel he finds to be an anecdote or an element of the same drama of man which is continually unfolding in the world. Claudel has spoken of the "passion of the universe" which he feels, and of the exaltation he derives from contemplating the millions of things that exist at the same time.

Wallace Fowlie. *Dionysius in Paris* (Meridian). 1960. pp. 127–8

From the very beginning, from the minute the curtain goes up on a Claudel play, the poet's dogmatic and uncompromising position must be accepted, for to the merest detail it dominates his vision of man and history. . . . In Claudel, anecdote and drama are deliberate illustrations of a doctrine. His works are didactic—not demonstrations, but pure and simple affirmations, for faith does not allow of discussion.

Every one of Claudel's plays is a parable meant to illustrate concretely a lesson given in advance.

Jacques Guicharnaud. *Modern French Theatre* (Yale). 1961. pp. 70–1

I admired the poet's noble brow, rounded like a Romanesque arch, and his eyes, strangely motionless in the effort of concentration. I wondered at the curve of the mouth, quick to express disdain, greedy and sensuous perhaps, but appearing to scorn overdelicate savors. His opinions and assertions were phrased without grace or shading in an almost mechanical voice, strongly marked with the accent of his native Champagne. He literally chewed his words, biting and tasting them as though they were a food, extracting all their flavor and pungency.

Louis Chaigne. *Paul Claudel* (Appleton). 1961. p. 6
See *The Satin Slipper* and *The Tidings Brought to Mary* (plays); also *Three Poems of the War.*

CÒCCIOLI, CARLO (1920–   )

There are men who have a sun inside them. There is nothing cheerful about it. This sun is black. . . . Còccioli is the victim of an obsession. . . . Why give a name to an obsession? You know that Còccioli has been seized by one, you know he has reacted to it. . . . His work . . . is a solar system. It revolves about the sun inside him. . . . [The] leitmotif, underlying and transcending Còccioli's obsession, is a biting, painful constantly renewed localization of our human condition. . . . This realized, there is nothing more to explain. Everybody understands it, and the author's task recalls the parable of the Unjust Judge. He must insist to the point of exasperation, over and over like the widow, with tears, irony, prayers, threatening, each petitioner according to his individual nature, to obtain justice for man. He must recite with monotonous stubbornness the frightful condition to which he has been reduced. And above all, his loneliness. . . . Còccioli is a remarkable writer, but that is not important. The important thing is that he will not let us rest.

Yves Velan. *BA.* Summer, 1950. pp. 238–41

Còccioli is a writer . . . with cunning in his craftsmanship and an artistic eye able to follow reality in its progress not only from the physical to the mental but through that misty, confusing transition from the mental to the spiritual. In this latter practice he exceeds the skill of the English Catholic writers with whom he is compared, Graham Greene and

Evelyn Waugh, though as a technician he is outmatched by the former and, in the use of objective detail as a substitute for subjective judgment, the latter is his peer. As an Italian his awareness that good and evil are the arms, right and left, of every man dominates his understanding and his estimation of man.

Thomas Sugrue. *NYT*. July 13, 1952. p. 4

Còccioli can frame a story of spiritual malaise, can place a portion of today's struggle, as sharply, as fiercely, and as intemperately as does the priest about whom he writes [in *Heaven and Earth*]. . . . The author is moved, as is his protagonist, . . . by the basic problem of how to make peace between the conflicting selves of man, how to survive in a world rent by useless and evidently unjust, though not unjustified, conflict, and especially, I would say, by the reconciliation of man's "fall" with his "redemption" or, in lay terms, the tranquillization of his guilt by the freeing of his capacities for usefulness.

Còccioli seeks two frames of reference—the world of the militant Catholic Church, with which he seeks to identify himself, and the world of the beleaguered homosexual, which, but for the libel laws, I would guess he has held for years like thorns to his breast.

Frances Keene. *Nation*. July 26, 1952. p. 75

In most contemporary Catholic novels, the struggling Christian's spiritual progress is from man to God, from earth to heaven. This, of course, is as one would expect, but the complaint has been made that in some of the most distinguished of these works there lurks an essentially unhealthy hatred of the flesh which renders the elaborate tribute paid its charms ironic and void—a Jansenistic horror which extends beyond sin to make suspect all the works of man. . . . The spiritual pilgrimage of . . . the tortured hero of *Heaven and Earth* reverses the usual pattern. His progress is from God to *man*. Nor can Mr. Còccioli be accused of the Jansenism which some discern in other Catholic authors. On the contrary, the lesson he has his hero learn (and the learning of it is his hero's "salvation") is that it is not enough to love the sinner, one must also love the sin.

William P. Clancy. *Com*. Aug. 29, 1952. p. 513

There have been almost no good novels written about Mexico—even by Mexicans. . . . It has proved a pitfall for the greatest artists—from D. H. Lawrence to Graham Greene. It has been a fatal trap for writers of the second rank like Steinbeck. And the "big" Mexican novels of the past twenty years share the same faults; wordiness, tub-thumping, sentimentality about the Noble Indian, and carelessness in construction haunt Azuela, Guzmán, Vasconcelos, and Yañez, just as they betray the tourist bards. [*Manuel the Mexican*] is a theme novel too. At times it tacks dangerously between the dark blood mysticism of *The Plumed Serpent* and the Redemption through Sin and Pity of *The Power and the Glory,* between the lisping bucolic lyricism of *The Pearl* and the brutal nihilism of *The Underdogs.* The fact that it does tack is enough to make it unique. Its very formlessness—its constant shifts in point of narrative and from allegory to the picaresque to private journal— provides the framework for some remarkable insights into the essential ambiguity of Mexico. . . . *Manuel the Mexican* for all its prolixity is an absorbing and challenging work. It may stand for some time as the definitive fictional statement of the Meaning of Mexico.

Donald Demarest. *SR*. Dec. 20, 1958. p. 24

What gives [*The White Stone*] its curious impact is the form its takes. A narrator provides the link that binds into an organic whole the intricate sheaf of letters, journals, diaries, eye-witness and second-hand reports through which we follow [a] suffering, agnostic priest. Despite their surface dislocations, these disassembled parts succeed in conveying not only an image of the protagonist but that of all the other priests whom he perceives in fleeting but dramatic moments of spiritual crisis. By juxtaposing and superimposing these fragments in a manner not un- mindful of the way Picasso decomposes and analyzes disparate elements to recreate a new synthesis, Còccioli presents us with a startling portrait of the modern priest at grips with the agonizing doubts and temptations of our godless, mechanized world.

Helene Cantarella. *NYT*. Nov. 27, 1960. p. 6

The White Stone is the story of a man's struggle to convince himself that he has lost faith in God, and to replace that faith with something else. It is a fantastic and persuasive novel—and an exciting mystery as well. . . . This is a resonant novel. Its parts echo and amplify each other. Its episodes . . . suggest that [the hero's] conflict defines the whole state of Christ's Church and possibly of the world. Together these episodes dramatize an idea. Like the author of the Acts of the Apostles, who represented the Holy Ghost as the real hero of his saga, Còccioli perceives a greater presence dwelling in his own reluctant apostle. . . . But the knack of this novel lies not in the fact of revelation; it lies rather in the circumstantial evidence which gradually reveals the mystery.

Albert Van Nostrand. *SR*. Dec. 10, 1960. p. 25

The White Stone is immense, a kind of spiritual who-done-it—the answer, presumably, being God. . . . There is a deeply significant and deeply symbolic confusion between Satan (who actually appears, at one point, in the guise of a Mr. Page. Anglo-Saxon?) and homosexuality.˙. . . There is a great deal of solid prose. . . [but] it is as though Mr. Graham Greene had reported a minor vision after an over-dose of benzedrine.

Penelope Mortimer. TT. Aug. 31, 1961. pp. 1442–3

See *Heaven and Earth, Manuel the Mexican,* and *The White Stone* (novels).

COCTEAU, JEAN (1889–1963)

He is a leader by virtue of his aristocratic coolness and personal magnetism. He is not greatly concerned with *variable* aspects of life and art; he believes that the *convergences* are more important than the *divergences*. He himself can be taken as an axis around which not only a personal school but most of the moderns of France, with their various conceptions, systems, techniques are grouped as a composite whole. . . . Cocteau is horrified at the idea of eclecticism. He has no desire to be classified.

Clifford Bower-Shore. BkmL. July, 1933. pp. 195–6

His theory of the drama solves many problems that had proved too much for the fancy-dress tragedians and the poetic dramatists. First, he clarifies . . . the nature of theatrical as opposed to lyric poetry. His watchword is not poetry *in* the theater but the proper poetry *of* the theater. Second, he calls for a "cooling off" of the drama, which had indeed reached rare temperatures in the nineteenth century—not excluding the New Theater movement of the eighties and nineties. This cooling is most triumphantly manifested in "The Infernal Machine," where Cocteau minimizes suspense by having a chorus tell the whole story beforehand. He amply makes up for sweaty excitement and cheap thrills by richness of texture. Thirdly, Cocteau follows Apollinaire (instead of the symbolists and neo-romanticists) in requiring gayety, fancy, and extravagance in the theater.

Eric Bentley. The Playwright as Thinker (Reynal and
Hitchcock). 1946. pp. 229–30

His art was the most important thing to Cocteau, and he was simple enough to think, for that reason, that God would feel the same way about it. Art would be very dear to God, the language of God, say.

Cocteau would have the artist, with the saint, unlike the rest of men, an intimate of God. For if the artist, in a sense, spoke the word of God, would he not have known it from God? "Art for God" was Cocteau's big idea of the time. Not art for art's sake, which was just silly, or art for the people. Art was too good for itself and too good for the people. Art was only fit for God.

J. F. Powers. *Com.* May 14, 1948. p. 104

Cocteau . . . was not an idiot or *naif* when he wrote any of the plays he based on myth. He was a clever Frenchman and theatrician, perhaps slightly deluded by his own cleverness but able to shift his ground quickly. And he does shift it by constantly reminding us in his nimble playwriting that he stands outside his play as an artificer detached alike from the myth and the characters. . . . The historical role of Jean Cocteau has been to give sanction with his unquestionable talent and intelligence to prestidigitational playwriting. Modernism has become more and more identified with it. And I, for one, would have no objection to it if it were not presented as a profound or important contribution to dramatic art and were simply considered showmanship. My only other reservation would then be that although showmanship is very much a desideratum in the theater, drama is, if not something *else,* something *more* than that. I find myself, then, willing to accept "theatricalism" as almost anything except a formula for creating dramatic masterpieces.

John Gassner. *The Theatre in Our Times* (Crown).
1954. p. 193

The impact of his work is theatrical and its buoyancy, grace, and fluidity are perpetually close to dancing. Yet all the time an extraordinary discipline is at work, balancing and welding the different elements. Cocteau believes that an artist's discipline of mind and spirit should be achieved in the same way as an athlete, an acrobat, or a dancer acquires his physical skill. The result is an unending, compelling, closely disciplined dance, as insistently hypnotic as the music of Bach.

Margaret Crosland. *Jean Cocteau* (Knopf). 1956. p. 20

The precision of a magician—the very French word *prestidigitateur* suggests euphoniously the lightness of touch that is required—is Cocteau's secret. But it is not the old professional magician who produces rabbits from top hats as if from slot machines, it is rather like an earnest young magician who is producing the rabbit for the first time in his professional career: since Cocteau is only interested in performing the trick once, he does it creatively. With the irresponsible ambition of youth he has ransacked the history of the theatre, and given his version to the major periods; the ancient Greek legends, the folklore of the Middle Ages, Elizabethan passion, classical tragedy and romantic drama are not forgotten in his own *théâtre*.

Frederick Lumley. *Trends in Twentieth Century Drama* (Essential Books). 1956. p. 115

Some men's names—Churchill, Einstein, Sartre—evoke empires, eras, movements. Jean Cocteau, for many of his contemporaries, evokes a subtle, pervasive, vital condition of being, reached and re-created at continuous high cost—*la difficulté d'être,* as he has described it. Cocteau renews, for himself and for other artists, especially those preoccupied with the visual arts, the essential "life" of the creative life, that concentrated other-world oxygen the creative artist must find in the atmosphere about him, must breathe freely, if he is to quicken the work it is his duty to undertake and, having undertaken, to carry to its conclusion "at the extremity of himself."

Evelyn Eaton. *SR.* Sept. 22, 1956. p. 18

Cocteau himself is the perfect exemplar of, not French, but Frenchy-International Set culture. He early found the right people and has long stuck close to them. He cultivated, with secret circumspection, an elaborately gaudy career, a glittering "personality." His poetry is not just brittle, it is glassy and transparent. Within the conventions of the cubist generation it is thoroughly conventional. The dissociation of Apollinaire, the imagism of Reverdy, the metaphysical clownery of Jacob, the a-logical dialectic of Salmon, Cocteau combined them all in a *chic* collage. Now the *avant garde* of Caracas and Des Moines are saying, "One of ours has been made a member of the French Academy!" Let the *fumistes* of the outlands rest easy in their fuming. The Academy still knows its own.

Kenneth Rexroth. *Nation.* Dec. 8, 1956. p. 504

It is impossible not to be impressed by the brilliance of Cocteau's . . . performance. The image of the marksman is curiously appropriate. Every time Cocteau fires, down come the clay pipes, paper flowers and dolls which seem to adorn every shooting gallery at every fair in France. It is when we come to examine the results of the performance that doubts arise. We begin to wonder whether the prizes were really worth all the skill that he used to win them, whether the glittering imagery is not after all an alibi which conceals an absence of vision, whether in short he is not a victim of precisely the same weakness that he detects in Flaubert—the disparity between the extraordinary technical accomplishment and the relative poverty of experience which emerges.

Martin Turnell. *Com.* Dec. 21, 1956. p. 309

In the course of his long career, Cocteau has brought his own special vision to many aspects of life and art, enriching them and ennobling them in the effort to make life worthy to be lived. He has played a major part in the creation of a theatrical tradition equalled nowhere else in the world. He has tried to express the ethics and emotions of heroism in a world without values. His partial failure is worth many victories. It is a victory of failure, the only kind worth having. It has been earned. Cocteau saw so deeply into history that no one believed him. Perhaps he has even ceased to believe himself. But another prophet of pure poetry understood the depth and significance of Cocteau's hermetic communications. Rainer Maria Rilke commented on Cocteau's casual familiarity with the secret of history in these words: "Tell Cocteau that I love him, for he is the only one who returns bronzed from the world of myth as from the shores of the sea."

Neal Oxenhandler. *Scandal and Parade* (Rutgers). 1957. p. 259

Now, traditionally, a poet is the watcher and commemorator of others. It is the passion of Paris, or the wrath of Achilles, from which he makes his song. In Cocteau, we have Orpheus on Orpheus. His personal history as a Parisian Pied Piper and Jack-of-all-arts has been the raw material for a nimble and sagacious myth about all poets—even better, about any creature whose awareness and daylight self are at the service of an inner vision, a dark angel, that sovereign source which Cocteau calls simply *poésie,* but which might also be called the Kingdom of Heaven. His Orpheus can therefore enlighten not only other poets, but any innerly dedicated man.

Robert Phelps. *SR.* July 4, 1959. p. 14

Angelism, as Cocteau seems to understand it, is a system of contradictions, because it is essentially an explosion of the divine in the human. The supernatural is found to be everywhere, in the most commonplace and ordinary objects. This discovery is not unrelated to Cocteau's fundamental aesthetic. As an artist his goal is perfection found in simplicity. On every occasion when he has defined his integrity, he has stated his distrust of the artificially beautiful and ornamental. Such doctrine seemed an innovation when Cocteau first defined it. But it is always difficult to assess the innovator. During the forty years of Cocteau's career, he has moved from innovator and experimentalist to a classic figure, to the stature of a stylist who represented his age because now his age copies him. Only during the process of development did he seem to be defiant and shocking.

Wallace Fowlie. Dionysius in Paris (Meridian).
1960. p. 88

Cocteau has a love of the theatre which is evident from his general declarations, but which can also be found in the conception of his plays themselves. A metaphor of illusion, theatre should be presented with all the signs of illusion. . . . A Protean theatre, it is the faithful image of a Protean universe. The number of forms that the traps of the universe can take is infinite; so are the forms taken by man's illusory defenses. The meaning of reality is finally lost in the game of lies and counter lies. Through an intransigence recalling the Baudelairian dandy, Cocteau, as the only possible affirmation of his identity, succeeds in immobilizing two elements of the confusion: theatre and the emotion of fear. His double game is tragic even when individually his plays are not. It is a recognition, a voluntary act. For Cocteau, writing a play is taking man's part—but he takes it in all lucidity, for by resorting to devices and descriptive illusion, he affirms that he defends a lost cause.

Jacques Guicharnaud. Modern French Theatre
(Yale). 1961. pp. 67–8

Slow-reflecting minds, like Gide, accused him of "leaping over steps." He merely climbs them more quickly than others. The proof of this is that whenever he completes an exploit, he returns to tell us precisely, patiently, where we must place each foot to catch up with him, for he has a horror of solitude. But once we have come shoulder to shoulder with him again, we do not cease to dispute his right to the title of "pioneer," of advance scout. This misadventure occurs so often, it is so "human," that one is surprised to see Cocteau astonished by it and suffering from it as though it had happened for the first time. But his periods of hopelessness (during which he vows he will never do anything again) are succeeded by a new drive for work.

André Fraigneau. Cocteau (Grove). 1961. p. 128

There was a winged intelligence in everything he did and said. He appreciated Picasso, Stravinsky, Diaghilev from the first. He hailed the advent of the post Debussy-Ravel composers: Milhaud, Poulenc, Honegger, Auric. He brought the boy genius, Raymond Radiguet, to the world's attention. He celebrated Josephine Baker. He sought (and won) freedom from life imprisonment for Jean Genet. He was everywhere by the side of original talent and fixed its image in the public consciousness by the point of his epigrams.

His large jet black eyes radiated a constant sense of surprised glee at the pleasures of existence, joy of the senses, smiling ecstasies of the mind. . . . He struck me as a French eighteenth-century sprite in the guise of a twentieth-century intellectual sport embodying the Spirit of Perennial Awareness.

Harold Clurman. *Nation*. Nov. 2, 1963. p. 282

See *The Infernal Machine and Other Plays* and *Holy Terrors* (novel).

COLETTE (1873–1954)

Reading Colette, it is not difficult to understand why nature, especially human nature, can be seen as a skein of the animal senses. The opposing concept, the classic view of life, seeks to establish nature as a pattern of reason, whether mathematical or organic. Colette's invariable theme is: nature, man, and animal are identical. She is primarily the artist of profound and subtle sensations translated into a medium that is a strict expression of what the eye beholds and the hand touches. Even her landscapes are animal in the sense that they are reflected in her style as sensory and ever in motion. Always in her work there is a longing, as she says somewhere, "to possess the wonders of the earth with my eye." Her women and her cats are interchangeable; her men can be scarcely told apart except for their oddities of physical make-up. And yet, although she is outstandingly a poet of voluptuousness, she uses no vulgar tricks to bring off her effects.

Pierre Loving. *Nation*. Aug. 23, 1933. p. 222

We are formed in the hours when we hardly know we are being formed. In Colette's warm but discreetly limited mind the flower, the animal, the human being live together in sensuous design. The observation of diurnal happening is extraordinary and marvellously conveys the strange hold that the tedium of life has on us. We feel the hours are our true "familiar spirit," the indissoluble intimate. But the marking of lost hours is not an occasion for the imaginative sensibility such as one sees in another very feminine writer like Virginia Woolf. Colette's pagan mind never leaves the surface of life, never ceases as it were to touch the skin;

yet the effect is not trite nor arid. It is moving. She has the direct eye of an older civilisation.

V. S. Pritchett. *NSN*. Aug. 11, 1951. p. 160

Colette invested from the beginning in small and slow but lasting virtues. Without imagination, she has cultivated her acuity and richness of sensuous perception; without ideas, she has cultivated common sense and at least three kinds of Wisdom: female, village, and worldly; without the strength for large, new, or dramatic forms, she has evolved a wonderful skill in the texture and transitions of the anecdotal prose-poem; without power or passion, she has cultivated verve and tenderness, and above all her own strong, specific, mainly Burgundian *saveur*, which has made her irresistible.

Within her deliberate limitations she has the irreducible authenticity and natural body which more enterprising writers must risk and often lose.

Donald Sutherland. *NR*. Nov. 23, 1953. pp. 17–18

Having no knowledge of psychology, which had not been popularized when she began to write and has never been taken seriously in France, Colette never learned how a novelist was expected to build up her characters. She merely put them together as a painter composes a still life from objects lying about in his studio. She could not invent characters, she could only describe herself and the people she knew or heard about, adding a few extra traits here and there. This is the weakness, and at the same time, the strength of her work. It is weakness because a novelist is expected to be inventive, and Colette is not. It is strength because the people she produces are real people, and fiction should presumably have a link with life in one way or another if only because it is intended to be read.

Margaret Crosland. *Colette* (British Book Centre). 1954. pp. 229–30

In the first half of the twentieth century, Colette became an institution for many literary connoisseurs. That she was the finest French prose writer alive was an unchallenged opinion. Expert as she is as a stylist, exquisite as her chiseling of words and images can be at times, we believe that her prose is too ornate and too remote from the naturalness and simplicity of the very great works of art for her to rank with the truly eminent masters of French prose. Her mannerisms soon pall on the fastidious reader. Her characters are too monotonous and they wander complacently in an atmosphere of venal loves, carnal concerns, and gigolos, without rising to the stature of Proustian lovers or Toulouse-Lautrec's mournful seekers of joy.

Henri Peyre. *The Contemporary French Novel*
(Oxford). 1955. p. 282

Born with talent, she achieved style. . . . She was at her most gifted in her descriptions of what she noted through any of her five senses, all abnormally alert—through her large gold-flecked, feral eyes; through her flaring nostrils; through her ears which heard small, far-off, distinguishing sounds; through her palate which held intact its own memories and judgments of ruddy wines, pink flesh or fine fruits eaten only in season since, being a gourmet, she disapproved of edibles falsely matured at the wrong time of year; and through her strong hands which in touching objects or bodies sent a series of tactile images and news rushing to her writer's brain. All she wrote in these realms read like precise, sensual, human records such as had not been seen in French literature. Only a woman could have compassed them for they were physically female, as different as a woman's voice is from a man's.

Janet Flanner. Introduction to *Seven by Colette*
(Farrar). 1955. pp. vi–vii

Few writers have ever been less engaged. This does not mean merely that she has no political or social ideas and no ethical convictions beyond those which an unthinking generosity and kindliness suggest. It means also an introversion so complete that she is a prisoner of herself and unaware of things outside herself except in so far as she can make them part of that self. As blind as a child to everything not part of her own experience she is also childishly alert to and absorbed in everything which is. . . . She is so intelligent and so shrewd while remaining so completely unintellectual that inevitably she suggests the gamin—one would even be tempted to say the guttersnipe if the connotations were not so unfavorable and, what is more important, if her passionate interest in country life did not carry a constant reminder that an important part of the child she remained was the child who had grown up in a provincial garden.

Joseph Wood Krutch. *Nation*. March 26, 1955. p. 268

She absolutely had to know the name of anything she was contemplating, whether animate or inanimate, and if this name was unfamiliar to her, or escaped her, she never could rest until she had found it. This was not so much to store it in her memory, but because the name completed the identity of the thing in question, and was inseparable from it. . . . She even loved certain words for themselves, quite apart from the idea which they represent. She loved them for their music, but still more for their graphic aspect, their design. Had she not spoken somewhere of the letter S "standing on end like a protecting serpent"? During periods of intense work she would dream of words. "I've had a typographical dream," she sometimes said to me in the morning.

Maurice Goudeket. *Close to Colette* (Farrar).
1957. p. 20

Colette has been accused of not dealing, in her works, with the important political and human problems of her time, and of concentrating too much on her own small and particular domain of love and lovers, of nature and its manifestations. And to this accusation is always appended the reproach that Colette is indifferent to questions of morality, that she is incapable, perhaps, of dealing with them. But in her aimless "promenade," and "meditations," her constant evocations of the past, are the evidences of Colette's long dialogue with the real, with those things—love, a flower, an animal—which held her attention as intensely as her mother's was held by the rose cactus. Nothing is more "real" or more important to Colette than this contemplation of the actual, than this relationship which the human being establishes in solitude, with the world of living things. The implicit moral imperative is again, *"Regarde,"* and the accompanying aesthetic imperative and the key to her style is also *"Regarde"*; "Look"—and, prepared to struggle with words, faithfully reproduce the object, the sensation.

Elaine Marks. *Colette* (Rutgers). 1960. p. 224

Certainly nothing ever replaced love for her as a subject for fiction. What other subject possibly could in her particular conception of the novel as a poetic condensation of emotional crisis in the life of ordinary people? Power, ambition, greed? She, like many other women, was just not interested. . . . But in her nonfictional work it was a different matter. Here there was no need to choose a subject which would engender the drama of emotional conflict, or charge a tightly-knit plot with the explosive qualities of suspense and irony and shock, no need even to create characters outside herself. She could, with her charmed pen, explore herself, and what she knew about life, write of all the myriad things that absorbed and delighted her—love, of course, among them, but so many others as well that her later works can be regarded as manuals in the art of enjoying life.

Margaret Davies. *Colette* (Grove). 1961. pp. 69–70

I remember her strong hands—serious writing is a manual labor!—
and her fine feet in sandals, perhaps larger than most, rather like the
feet of Greek goddesses. I remember her slightly frizzly hair fetched
forward almost to her eyebrows, because (as she has told her readers)
she has a square boyish or mannish forehead. I remember her delicate
nostrils and her painted thin lips.

Glenway Wescott. *Images of Truth* (Harper). 1962. p. 88

Colette has no considerable comic gift to color her measured and equ-
able fatalism; yet the effect of her major novels is not somber or
deprived. Her disbelief is only in permanence: it does not extend to
unenduring things themselves, or to the delight their exuberant diversity
provokes in a mind which has been taught to observe. Her novels are,
before anything else, tributes to the testimony of the senses. She inspires
us with the confidence of strong outlines, of inexhaustibly substantial
objects, of feelings released and defined in primary recurrent situations.
Women novelists preceding her, and since, write romances, in which
women conform, more or less, to social and sexual rôles; Colette too
writes about women mainly, but women who have lost or shaken off
their rôles, and what she sees in her women—it may not be the whole
truth, but it is what she sees—is a slow and inquisitive tidal carnality
which abolishes romance and which at the same time encourages hasty
readers to perpetuate her long-lived and still not quite moribund reputation as a sensational and suspect novelist.

Marvin Mudrick. *HdR*. Spring, 1962. p. 113

With Colette we enter a realm of literary description that has only been
touched upon by a handful of writers in all time. The bucolic poets, the
romantics, and an occasional nineteenth-century writer, such as Baudelaire, felt the need to express themselves through the medium of sharp
sensory metaphor since they were dealing with idiom the various nuances
of which could be given shape and contour in no other way. To this
extent, Colette may be said to follow in an already existing tradition.
But the similarity ends here. For Colette the senses were neither an
external called upon to explain an elusive reality, nor were they a
variety of literary greenery to be strategically placed for effect. The thing
or being observed, touched, or felt was a *raison d'être* in itself. Meaning was inherent in the perceived object, it *was* the object.

I. T. Olken. *PMLA*. March, 1962. p. 140

Colette combines a strong sense of the total otherness of plants and
animals with an equally strong assumption that they have their real

meaning in terms of a human world, thus the final cause of flowers is the art of the gardener and the florist, of rustic foods Parisian *haute cuisine*. Her intensely civilized attitude to the wild reports of sense distinguishes her clearly from Anglo-Saxon nature mystics, Wordsworth or Thoreau. . . . She is the inheritor of that great French nineteenth-century enterprise which was devoted to the confusion of nature with art. Out of it springs a delicate veneration for the cosmetic but also a grossness, the grossness of the *belle époque*. Colette has them both, is as much at home in the reeking scent factories of Grasse as in the hills. . . . Colette would have understood up to a point the New England hedonism of Wallace Stevens, his Florida with "mornings meet for the eye of a young alligator," but not the usurping metaphysics, not the poetry which says "It is not in the premise that reality is a solid."

Frank Kermode. *NYR*. Dec. 12, 1963. p. 3

See *Six Novels* (Modern Library) and *Short Novels* (Dial).

D'ANNUNZIO, GABRIELE (1863–1938)

It is a mercy that Shakespeare happened to live before the infected age of artiness! We refuse to consider what "Hamlet" would have been if Shakespeare had written it under the obsession that no one must for a single instant be allowed to forget what a terrific artist he was and what an inexpressibly deep feeling for art actuated and controlled his least utterance.

We do not wish to lay too much stress on the lesser phenomena of D'Annunzio's productions. But these dedications, these solemn asides, and a thousand other trifles in his plays and novels, do really point to the gravest defect of his individuality—namely, the tendency to magnify Art—with the majuscule—at the expense of all else, to pretend that nothing is worth aught save artistic beauty and the ability to perceive the same and finally to go about beneath a banner with the legend: "Watch me, I am an artist, not a man." The fact is, D'Annunzio is as foolishly sentimental about Art as your English novelist is about Love. He can't talk about anything else. He has got it on the brain. He is a creature of one idea.

Francis Thompson. *The Real Robert Louis Stevenson and Other Critical Essays* (University). 1959.
p. 270. Written Oct. 12, 1901

D'Annunzio, not content with the spoils that he has gathered from the arts, and discovering, naturally enough, that his own gift of word-painting serves only a decorative purpose, has met the demands of the theatre by further borrowing in a meaner quarter. He has propped his structure with two unsteady supports, the one a peculiarly gross form of theatrical sensation, the other a bastard symbolism. . . . But there is also . . . something more than words. If all the borrowed plumes can be removed, and all the moods realised with sympathy, it will be found that he is indeed a problem dramatist, not of custom or morality, but of sex itself. He lives, not in the everyday world, but in the exceptional moment. He portrays conditions of high nervous tension without the creative skill to make them develop convincingly. . . . He is meteoric, productive of much dust and little drama. But there is grace in his flight. Even the word-painting is brought, in ecstatic moments, into harmony with the conception of the play. . . . The conjurer is sometimes a magician. He has the will to illusion. Let us be grateful.

Ashley Dukes. *Modern Dramatists* (Charles H. Sergel).
1911. pp. 268, 271–2

No account of our author is complete unless we really make out what becomes of that esthetic consistency in him which . . . our own collective and cultivated effort is so earnestly attempting and yet so pathetically, if not so grotesquely, missing. We are struck, unmistakably, early in our acquaintance with [D'Annunzio's] productions, by the fact that their total beauty somehow extraordinarily fails to march with their beauty of parts, and that something is all the while at work undermining that bulwark against ugliness which it is their obvious theory of their own office to throw up. . . . We feel ourselves somehow in the presence of a singular incessant *leak* in the effect of distinction so artfully and copiously produced. . . . There is no mistaking it; the leak of distinction is produced by a positive element of the vulgar; and that the vulgar should flourish in an air so charged, intellectually speaking, with the "aristocratic" element, becomes for us straightway the greatest of oddities and at the same time, critically speaking, one of the most interesting things conceivable. . . . The vulgarity into which he so incongruously drops us is, I will not say the space he allots to love-affairs, but the weakness of his sense of "values" in depicting them. . . . The sexual passion from which he extracts such admirable detached pictures insists on remaining for him *only* the act of a moment . . . [and] from the moment it depends on itself alone for its beauty, it endangers extremely its distinction, so precarious at the best.

Henry James. Notes on Novelists (Scribner).
1914. pp. 282, 284, 292

Whatever mountebank tricks d'Annunzio may play as a human being, he has undoubtedly written some very great works. He is an intensely original artist. You may sometimes think him silly, foppish, extravagant, or even caddish. . . , but you have to admit that the English notions of what constitutes extravagance or caddishness are by no means universally held. And anyhow you have to admit that there is a man who really holds an attitude towards life, who is steeped in the sense of style, and who has a superb passion for beauty. Some of d'Annunzio's novels were a revelation, dazzling. . . . How adult, how subtle, how (in the proper signification) refined, seems the sexuality of d'Annunzio after the timid, gawky, infantile, barbaric sexuality of our "island story"!

Arnold Bennett. Books and Persons (Doran). 1917.
pp. 235–6

All fashions and schools of aesthetic and semi-philosophical thought in Europe, from the pre-Raphaelite Poets to the Russian novelists, from Ibsen to Nietzsche, from Wagner to Scriabin, are reflected in his work: through him, Italian literature (in the narrow meaning of the word, as contrasted to living, original thought) entered once more into the circle of European literature, though more passively perhaps than at any other time in the course of its history. But the high-water mark of his fortune as a writer falls between 1890 and 1905: his surviving disciples date all from those years. And his place in the general history of literature remains with the French Parnassians and Decadents, and with their cognate and derived writers abroad, the Wildes, the Yeatses, the Hofmannsthals: that is, with the last brood of irreparably "stupid Nineteenth Century" writers. After 1905, though he has never given up the pretence of being and looking "up to date," yet the novel fashions began to be introduced by younger (and often much lesser) men; and at the same time the temper of Italian culture swerved decidedly from the literary to the philosophical.

> Raffaello Piccoli. *A Dial Miscellany,* ed. by
> William Wasserstrom (Syracuse). 1963. pp. 128–9.
> Written April, 1923

Gabriele D'Annunzio is the special and peculiar product of modern Italy.

No other country, no other history, would have given birth to a genius made up of such contending and utterly opposed qualities: it is exactly as if all the small principalities that were Italy before the Risorgimento, all the amazing contradictions of stark heroics and depraved nepotism, the fanaticism and black blood and superstition, with the introspective and febrile weariness of a very old land, were bound into D'Annunzio's being.

> Joseph Hergesheimer. Introduction to *Tales of My
> Native Town* (Doubleday). 1920. p. viii

D'Annunzio has nothing to offer the sterile artists of the new illiterate literature, who are as incapable of appreciating his refined and subtle perversities as they are of admiring the beautiful form in which his full-blooded and exuberant imagination clothes his conceptions. He is an aesthete, but his aestheticism has never expressed itself in barren theory, but has always turned to life itself. He realized at the outset of his career that life is a physical thing, which we must compel to surrender all that it can offer us, which the artist must bend and shape to his own creative purposes. . . . He must be regarded as an artist of sensations, an Italian of the Renaissance set down in the middle of a drab century. He began his life by a quest for perfect physical pleasure through all the senses, and inaugurated its last phase with a gesture of military courage which was not only a retort to those who, like Croce, had called him a dilettante, but an earnest of his conviction that he was a great artist of the lineage which bred men who were simultaneously great men of action.

Ernest Boyd. Introduction to *The Child of Pleasure*
(Modern Library). 1925. pp. x–xi

D'Annunzio in his prose and poetry is a man exaltedly laboring to heave a leaden weight from his limbs. He has borne witness in a thousand forms to an indwelling death. . . . The figure of the psychically impotent artist has always haunted his imagination. . . . All his career he has searched avidly for sensation. Figured by the imagination of the general a sort of Dionysiac creature of poetic frenzies and searing lips, modern Sardanapalus of letters, artistic Vesuvius which inundates whole provinces with its outpourings and shakes Rome, Florence and Venice with the might of its travail, d'Annunzio has in truth been spending his days in the frenetic quest of a situation, a posture, a movement . . . as though secretly convinced that a certain consummation would come to pass could men but be compelled to marvel at him, and admire and applaud. . . . [But] d'Annunzio has never felt. In all the affairs of life he has been what he was to his divine mistress; the man who could not give out from his breast. For this reason, then, his poetical activity has become a form of compensation: protest of a rich and energetic nature against an inward incapacity. . . . Wellnigh each of his works contains some scene, some episode, that represents to d'Annunzio the coming of the power to feel.

Paul Rosenfeld. *Men Seen* (Dial). 1925. pp. 5–7, 11–13

The twist that the Archangel gave to the Nietzschean doctrine, or rather that "vision of my universe" which found a sympathetic atmosphere in the writings of Nietzsche, might be stated as a conception of Life which holds life to be a continual tension, a constant effort, to exalt human nature by endless aspiration.

Aspiration to what? Aspiration on the part of each to become the perfect form of himself! Aspiration to be greater than oneself! . . . He will live his life as a "superman," and the thrills of doing so will ever constitute the radiant fascination of his personality. Sublimating his vision to something beyond himself, to his country, let us say, he will make it a rallying-cry which on two occasions will have the power to gather his nation about him. To be sure, a critic may easily say that "D'Annunzio is the last of the great Romantics." Perhaps we should say that he is the only truly great Romantic!

Federico Nardelli and Arthur Livingston.
Gabriel the Archangel (Harcourt). 1931. pp. 137–8

As a novelist D'Annunzio is dated, as a poet he is eternal. His novels have his stamp of decadence, both in external form and motif, the latter being almost invariably a monotonous reiteration of the analysis of the sexual reactions of his personages. All his characters are cast in the same mould, and despite the exotic beauty of phrase and the florid imagery . . . it is very doubtful whether his novels will survive his own passing. . . . [Yet] D'Annunzio is not merely a great poet, he is a very great poet. . . . It was only in his patriotic verse that D'Annunzio raised the beautiful to the level of the ideal, which, according to Balzac, is the supreme mission of the poet. In his clarion call to his countrymen, in his militant Italian irredentism, we see the ecstasy and inspiration of the protagonist of the modern Latin Renaissance.

Gerald Griffin. *Gabriele D'Annunzio: the Warrior Bard* (John Long). 1935. pp. 272–3, 280

Few reputations I can think of have stood so high and fallen so low within a lifetime. At one period you named him along with Ibsen and Anatole France. Today he ranks with Ouida. D'Annunzio's talent consisted of a magnificent and inexhaustible gift for sensational phrase-making, and little else. This is equivalent to saying that he was not a great writer, and, in my opinion, equivalent to saying he was not even a good one. He was successful because his towering vulgarity happened to coincide with and enhance the vulgarity of his epoch. He said once, "In Leo Tolstoi, after a fierce struggle, sensibility triumphed over intelligence." In the Poet the struggle was never waged.

Having always thought that D'Annunzio's work might have been written by an excitable *parfumeur* or hairdresser, I was hardly surprised to learn . . . that at one time . . . D'Annunzio seriously considered going into partnership with Lenthéric.

Clifton Fadiman. *NY*. June 11, 1938. pp. 57–8

There are many who have wished to see in D'Annunzio a diabolic corrupter of consciences, a sort of incarnation of Lucifer—in a word, a veritable scourge of morality.

Others, on the contrary, judging him by the mystical and religious tendency of some of his work, have looked upon him, if not as an actual champion of the Faith, at least as a great sinner who has repented and been converted.

Very few, so far as I know, have come to the far simpler conclusion that D'Annunzio is, at heart, perfectly indifferent to every religious problem or religious question, and that the mystic gleams which appear here and there in his writings spring not from any warmth of religious conviction of a transitory character but from a source exclusively artistic.

This conclusion, nevertheless, is the right one. The dizzy religious heights which, in the fervour of his own creation, D'Annunzio has sometimes reached . . . only bear out this conclusion.

D'Annunzio is, in reality, the most perfect and the purest agnostic that ever lived.

Tommaso Antongini. *D'Annunzio* (Heinemann).
1938. p. 295

D'Annunzio's courage is unquestionable. He possessed both grit and dash; he could urge Italy into the War, fight in the trenches, fly over Vienna, occupy and administer Fiume against the approval of the Allies and his own Government, and he could watch his own appendix be cut out under a local anaesthetic. And his splendour—that too is incontestable, although by our standards it is often encumbered by *bric-à-brac*. He could write like music, like scents, like religion, like blood, like anything, he could sweep into the folds of his magnificent prose whatever took his fancy, and then assert it was sacred. There has been nobody like him. Fascism wisely accepted him after a little demur, and we had better do the same. We can anyhow hail him by two of the titles which he claims: poet and hero.

E. M. Forster. *Two Cheers for Democracy*
(Edward Arnold). 1951. pp. 244–5

Signor D'Annunzio's art does not either move or delight me profoundly. From his novels I have derived a pleasure which is akin to an urchin's flattening his nose against a pastry-cook's window, coupled, of course, with delight in the spectacle of a temperament deploying itself without check and having at its command to an astounding degree the means of expression precisely suited to it. Signor D'Annunzio is undoubtedly a great master of the decorative and the erotic. . . . In a moral sense Signor D'Annunzio is magnificently sincere in his interests, his admirations, his tastes, but he remains superficial. Except where the senses are concerned, he plays chiefly upon the prestige value of things. . . . His sense of the aesthetic value of things, incidents and emotions is that of a connoisseur rather than an artist.

Desmond MacCarthy. *Humanities*
(MacGibbon and Kee). 1953. pp. 86–7

It was when he visited Greece for the first time, in 1895, that [the] feeling of the Superman (and the possibilities of a *Mediterranean*

Superman) was born in the Abruzzese peasant poet. D'Annunzio no longer wanted to write poems and novels about decadents, but to create an epic in which he could express Italian ideals, like Virgil's and Dante's, only brought up to date, in a vast vision of the opening century, and Italy's imperial role in it. . . . The poem *"Maia"* which he wrote about his trip to Greece, inspired by the idea of Ulysses in these waters, is often considered his finest, and it is certainly his most patriotic, work. . . . Ulysses had long been dear to Latin literature, from Dante, and back again to the Latins before him, through Plutarch, Ovid and Virgil into the mists of the Homeric legend, where he possesses wisdom, cunning, and, above all, curiosity, or the desire to learn. D'Annunzio's vision of Ulysses is the classical one, but overlaid with Nietzsche's Superman. More than the desire for Knowledge, it is the desire for Power which drives him on; *virtute* has submerged *conoscenza* and D'Annunzio's Ulysses tends toward the Superman. There is something of this in all D'Annunzio's heroes. . . . Anyone who has lived a life more violent and powerful than that of others is to D'Annunzio a potential Ulysses, the Mediterranean Superman.

Anthony Rhodes. The Poet as Superman (Weidenfeld).
1959. pp. 50–2

Gabriele D'Annunzio . . . [made] a success of such varied careers as poet, novelist, gossip columnist, playwright, pamphleteer, fop, libertine, lover, orator, revolutionary war hero (land, sea, and air), dictator, pirate, horse thief, martyr, mystic, national hero in his old age and witch doctor to Fascism in his prime. . . . [This] multiplicity of careers had been superimposed upon a maniacal sex life. The world remembers the D'Annunzio-Eleonora Duse idyll, which lasted five years, cost the Duse a fortune, and finally broke up after the poet's dark-haired mistress found golden blonde hairpins in his bed. But Isadora Duncan also leapt after him; as did the Marchioness of Morsini, Kaiser Wilhelm's old mistress, and so many other titled ladies and tasteful tarts that no biographer could ever keep track of them.

After each major affair, D'Annunzio wrote a novel "revealing all"; and he spent what his writings brought in with glorious profligacy. . . . Growing more eccentric and withdrawn with the years, he chose his own funeral music and prepared for death by sleeping in a coffin one night every month.

Fillmore Calhoun. SR. March 19, 1960. pp. 37–8

See *The Child of Pleasure* (poetry and prose); *The Daughter of Jorio, The Dead City, Francesca da Rimini,* and *The Honeysuckle* (plays); *The Flame of Life* and *Triumph of Death* (novels); and *Tales of My Native Town* (prose).

DE AYALA, RAMÓN PÉREZ
See Pérez de Ayala, Ramón

DE BEAUVOIR, SIMONE
See Beauvoir, Simone de

DE CASTRO, JOSÉ MARIA FERREIRA
See Ferreira de Castro, José Maria

DE CESPEDES, ALBA
See Cespedes, Alba de

DE GHELDERODE, MICHEL
See Ghelderode, Michel de

DE GOURMONT, RÉMY
See Gourmont, Rémy de

DE LA SERNA, RAMÓN GÓMEZ
See Gómez de la Serna, Ramón

DEL CASTILLO, MICHEL (1933–   )

Child of Our Time is an autobiography of a child, a history of our epoch and a parable of the collapse of civilization all in one. . . . We have had many studies of modern depravity. What makes this book different is its ring of truth. The child tells his tale; there is no falsetto voice of sentiment and no moralizing. It was not without reason that Jean Cocteau in a French review wrote that after reading the book he would never dare complain of anything again.

In the line running from Céline's *Journey to the End of the Night* to Valtin's *Out of the Night* to Malaparte's *Kaputt* and thence to Michel del Castillo, we have an accelerated graph of that spiritual collapse which is the inner history of our time.

Daniel M. Friedenberg. NR. Nov. 3, 1958. pp. 17–18

A summary [of *Child of Our Time*] cannot suggest . . . the tone of the writing and the quality of del Castillo's sensibility. He has no complaint, although his life has been one of incessant suffering; no demands, although he has had nothing, and no expectations because he has seen everything. . . . Yet it is . . . unrelieved horror, we find, that has preserved his innocence. . . . But in spite of itself, *Child of Our Time* is a terrible indictment, for . . . del Castillo's life cannot be dismissed as merely the product of freakish coincidences. The locale typifies something widespread and the individuals express a whole society—composed, perhaps, largely of the well-intentioned, but too ineffectual to prevent del Castillo's tragedy and others like it, not to say to repair them. The refusal of the author to express a condemnation he has every right to pronounce, and the extraordinary poignancy of his voice, make our failure still harder to bear. We cannot live down the impact of this innocence and simplicity; but can we live up to it, either?

Jerrold Lanes. *SR*. Dec. 20, 1958. p. 23

It is very difficult to criticise, from a distance, the moral standpoint of a man whose parents, if not himself, were actually involved in the Spanish tragedy. But I am uneasy when Right and Left are equated [in *The Billsticker*] wholly because of the brutalities on both sides. No one denies them. But it still seems to me that the *primary intention* is of the utmost importance. Stalin and the trials, the labour-camps: Hitler and the gas-chambers. No difference? For me there is. One would like to make no choices, but choice is forced upon us in this world, and if we are driven back upon the intention, then that must be the touchstone. Men being as they are in war and revolution, there is little else to go on.

Pamela Hansford Johnson. *NSN*. Oct. 3, 1959. p. 449

From Dostoevsky's *The Possessed* to Arthur Koestler's *Darkness at Noon,* a Niagara of serious fiction has depicted man's outliving the mythological symbols of Christendom and his agonized groping for some new faith. In no area of contemporary life has this dilemma assumed so intense a form as in the reality of the rise and meaning of world Communism. Hitherto this dramatic Communist reality has been almost exclusively treated in the literature produced by bourgeois philosophical novelists. . . . [But] Michel del Castillo's second novel, *The Disinherited,* . . . tells the story of the making of a Communist in terms of how I saw and lived that process. I do not exclude other processes; perhaps Dostoevsky's and Koestler's mentally tormented heroes do exist, but they surely would have had no human raw material to organize and catapult into tragic action if the conditions of poverty and degradation, as so graphically depicted by Castillo, had not thrown up hordes of violently exasperated men eager to embrace any philosophy that even hinted at redemption or liberation. . . . Castillo writes with blazing fury about men thrown into conflict by forces in themselves they but dimly perceive. His is a new voice whose accent is on the wordless words of the heart.

Richard Wright. SR. April 16, 1960. pp. 21–2

Michel del Castillo . . . proves with his second book [*The Disinherited*] to be, at the age of twenty-seven, an alumnus of the school of life. Of injustice, violence and despair, and of the perilously vulnerable hopes and illusions that counterbalance them, he has nothing left to learn. Compared with his contemporaries and many of his seniors here in America, . . . Michel del Castillo is an old man. . . . He has had forced upon him the single theme of how and why men kill. . . . The author states that it was never his intention "to write a political book." Yet the whole pith, the very heart of it, is political, not only because it describes war, but because implicit from the start is its concern for the seeming impossibility of securing peace and the right of the unequal as well as of the equal to a place in the sun.

Strictly speaking, this is not a novel at all, since the disenchanted men and women who people it are archetypes rather than individuals and their fate hangs far less on what they do than on what position they occupy in the shaken and trembling social structure in which they were born. Delicate or gross, burning or blank, their faces are not so much unique as they are different aspects of the general face of man. In other words, it is not as a work of art, but as an exhortation that this book is to be read.

Virgilia Peterson. NYHT. April 17, 1960. p. 5

It seems likely that *The Disinherited* owes less to del Castillo's actual childhood memories of the war than to his more recent exposure to the debate among French intellectuals on the subject of rebellion and revolution. . . . Del Castillo's own sympathies seem to lie closest to those characters who take a religious view of life's responsibilities. . . . *The Disinherited* is . . . concerned with the problems of contemporary man as they dramatically emerged a quarter of a century ago in the context of the Spanish Civil War.

Paul Pickrel. Harper. May, 1960. p. 94

Satire is usually written from the point of view of a specially privileged witness of vice or folly, and should maintain, to be effective, the sense of an embarrassing exactitude of observation. The point of view of *Through the Hoop* is more like that of a child trying to construct a fantasy which will account for the arbitrary malevolence of the grown-ups' world, a malevolence of which he is not the witness, but the victim. Its scheming priests, grasping prelates, silly society women, vicious gossips, are constructed rather than observed, and in this sense seem to spring from the same impulse as the dressed-up dwarfs in Vigo's *Zero Conduite,* or Genet's archetypical queens, bishops, lieutenant-generals and judges. But their hollowness is not quite frightening or ludicrous enough; they seem simply stilted and overgeneralized.

There are, however, individual passages of successful comic irony in which the machinations of the characters produce results which are entirely contrary to their intentions, or in which the grotesqueness is so exaggerated as to reach heights of real comic invention.

Anita Feldman. *Com.* March 1, 1963. pp. 602–3

See *Child of Our Time, The Disinherited,* and *Through the Hoop* (novels).

DELEDDA, GRAZIA (1875–1936)

Though she is not a first-class genius, she belongs to more than just her own day. She does more than reproduce the temporary psychological condition of her period. She has a background, and she deals with something more fundamental than sophisticated feeling. She does not penetrate, as a great genius does, the very sources of human passion and motive. She stays far short of that. But what she does do is to create the passionate complex of a primitive populace. . . . Sardinia . . . [is] an island of rigid conventions, the rigid conventions of barbarians, and at the same time, the fierce violence of the instinctive passions. A savage tradition of chastity, with a savage lust of the flesh. . . . It is the human instinct still uncontaminated. . . . It is this old Sardinia, at last being brought to heel, which is the real theme of Grazia Deledda's books. . . . The old, blind life of instinct, and chiefly frustrated instinct and the rage thereof, as it is seen in the Sardinian hinterland, this is Grazia Deledda's absorption. . . . She can put us into the mood and rhythm of Sardinian life like a true artist, an artist whose work is sound and enduring.

D. H. Lawrence. Introduction to *The Mother*
(Jonathan Cape). 1922. pp. 7–13

Sardinian she is, Grazia Deledda, in every trait of her art. Her realistic observation admits of the poetic fatalism and symbolism dear to primitive people; her style has the unconventional abruptness of a rough literature, and her conception of the great principles of morality are those of her people.

She has avoided the two opposing currents in the Italian literary world, humanitarian socialism and aesthetic individualism. Ignoring all transitory social relations, she depicts that first essential, irreducible nucleus—the family. The sacredness of the family is the basis of the Sardinian code of morals, and the protection of the family the ideal of Sardinian honour.

Joseph Spencer Kennard. Italian Romance Writers
(Brentano). 1922. p. 351

[In] *The Mother, . . .* action . . . is presented with a classic simplicity that can well afford to leave to the force of clearly conceived character and situation the effect of tragedy upon the reader. . . . [The characters] are made wonderfully distinct and articulate in a few words of dialogue and description. The skill with which they are made to live is the same that makes the novel, as a whole, a masterpiece of artistic economy, and it is so fine that one begins to realize it only after the enthusiasm that the book inspires is subjected to afterthought and the dubious supererogation of analysis. . . . It is deeply moving as a familiar tragedy of common experience and it is a thoroughly expert literary performance.

Edward T. Booth. NYEP. Dec. 29, 1923. pp. 403–4

When seen in the perspective of the entire roll of [Nobel] prizewinners, Grazia Deledda's name will not appear to be so inglorious as in the isolated announcement of the fact that the Committee had again selected a writer who meant little or nothing to the average reader. To say the least of it, she is as good a novelist as Pontoppidan and Gjellerup, and, if Selma Lagerlöf had not written one masterpiece, . . . it might be argued that she and Grazia Deledda are of more or less equal standing, and rather similar in their simplicity of mood and matter. . . . Efforts to acclimatize Grazia Deledda in England and America met with the same fate as had been the lot of her master Giovanni Verga, . . . [for] not even the endorsement of D. H. Lawrence could induce much enthusiasm here for the regionalist school of which Verga was the acknowledged leader. . . . If one were to seek for an American figure of comparable importance, the name of Sarah Orne Jewett would suggest itself. Grazia Deledda is a conscientious craftswoman in a minor *genre*, at home only with her own people, an unpretentious and vivid story-teller.

Ernest Boyd. SR. Dec. 3, 1927. p. 380

She is a writer of considerable dramatic power, exact and logical in the delineation of her characters; and along with these qualities there is a third—a remarkable power of description. People, places and scenes are drawn with great clarity and skill. . . . Her prose, which has many graces, has at times a poetic ring. The Sardinian scenes are so well depicted, so faithful, that the reader is projected into the daily lives of those who dwell in one or other of the smaller towns and villages. . . . It is a life of primitive simplicity in which the very soil seems alive and imbued with a personality for good or evil. . . . Grazia Deledda has received unstinted praise for her skilful delineation of character and for the idealism which informs all her work. But it is seldom that she lets her "fancies run in soft luxuriant flow," and wit and humour are not generally to be sought for.

John Mifoud. *NSN*. Feb. 25, 1928. p. 623

Grazia Deledda was born just when the old medieval life, which lasted to within living memory in the remoter districts of Italy, was breaking down before the advance of the modern world. . . . In this transition period she passed her impressionable young days. . . . And something of the atmosphere of the popular story-teller seems to pervade her novels with their pictures of the life of a primitive people, whose passions are violent and elemental, their virtues and vices almost those of patriarchal days. . . . She has made this primitive world so completely her own, it is so much a part of herself, that for her it becomes genuine tragedy. . . . [The] rough, racy peasant humour, which Grazia Deledda has obviously caught from the life around her, is the only relief of the kind she allows herself in some of the best of her novels. The suddenness with which it flashes out is almost disconcerting in its effect. We have heard young Italians speak with dislike of the gloomy, Nordic character of her books, and she has been compared to the Russians. There is little of the brightness of the south about them. Fate seems to brood over them as does the mountain Orthohene over Nuoro. Nature too is no mere setting, but in close relation with man and his moods . . . ; and her leading characters are haunted by a dream world, which is as real to them as the world in which they live, and seems to deepen the mystery of existence.

Lacy Collison-Morley. *EdR*. April, 1928. pp. 353–6

Deledda has received unstinted praise for her skilful delineation of found faith in the forces of nature and a glowing enthusiasm for the richness and beauty of the earth. The different forces of life live in her spirit in a harmony that is never disturbed by ascetic aspirations or spiritual problems. She considers these aspirations and problems intellectual and arbitrary creations of man. Life, in its fatal unity, does not know how to separate nor isolate. Religious feeling and spirituality, however, live closely interwoven with human passions and they, too, are reduced to a form of instinct. Love, too, assumes in her a cosmic character, as the individual lives in a flux of nature; he is part of it, although rebellious to society and to any external force that may stand between him and nature.

This cosmic unity constitutes the raw material out of which Deledda fashions her novels. She sketches with a hand that is moved by the same passion for life that creates the hunger and thirst of the creatures of her fancy.

Domenico Vittorini. The Modern Italian Novel
(U. of Pennsylvania). 1930. pp. 58–9

She wielded a vigorous brush, splashing her colours upon the canvas, showing a complete mastery of the technique of chiaroscuro; for her high lights she has the delight of her characters in the world about them, a world of colour and fragrance, of brilliant sunshine, of granite-like mountain peaks and rushing mountain streams; for her shadows, storm and tempest, passion fostered by solitude, the torment of the man scarcely higher in the scale than the brute. . . . Clarity of thought and of expression distinguishes every book. . . . We are spared interminable analysis, the psychology is the psychology of action, the dialogue is crisp, the characters explain themselves. It is a strange blossoming of a remarkable talent, a veritable flower of the soil.

Mary Fraser. BkmL. Aug., 1932. pp. 239–40

[In] this last of her books . . . Cosima we read Deledda's story from her earliest years, and see the places and atmosphere in which her precocious appetite for story-telling developed. The book is alive with the immediacy of the dreams, the obstacles, the candor and the moral experiences which were the source and strength of her talent. This young Cosima, seen by herself through the veil of memories, is the last and somehow fading flower of Deledda's moving and colorful masterpieces.

Anacleta Candida Vezzetti. BA. Spring, 1940. p. 202

See The Mother, Ashes, The Ivy, and After the Divorce (novels).

DEL VALLE-INCLÁN, RAMÓN

See Valle-Inclán, Ramón del

DE MONTHERLANT, HENRY
See Montherlant, Henry de

DE OTERO, BLAS
See Otero, Blas de

DE SAINT EXUPÉRY, ANTOINE
See Saint Exupéry, Antoine de

DE SERNA, CONCHA ESPINA
See Espina de Serna, Concha

DESNOS, ROBERT (1900–1945)

Desnos seems to wallow with special predilection in the repulsive quagmire of physical erotism. There livid, slimy forms of sensual perversity, aroused from their heavy slumber, twist and turn ignominiously, releasing in their convulsive spasms an acrid and suffocating stench. The spectacle is not devoid, it must be said, of a certain awesome grandeur. In the midst of parched, scoriac landscapes, the sulpherous glow emanating from this crawling accumulation of filth irresistibly conjures up visions of those infernal haunts "where their worms dieth not and the fire is not quenched."

> Georges Lemaitre. *From Cubism to Surrealism in French Literature*
> (Harvard). 1941. p. 211

By the resonance of grief and despair, he developed a quite murderous brilliance. At seeing this almost unbelievable aspect of love, this frenzy so familiar to Robert Desnos, it is our heart that bleeds. It is a new myth too which comes gently to birth and beats within us as a tremor of fever. But this myth, what is it? Can a myth exist without a name, without a face, without any shape at all? . . . The poet has in truth invented a new means of voicing his despair. Doubtless, the principles may be allowable, but they carry the weight of endless will, of great determination: to show the true faces of revolt and Love.

> Pierre Berger. *Robert Desnos* (Editions Pierre Seghers).
> 1949. pp. 52–3. Tr. by Dorothy Nyren Curley

With Breton, Eluard and Artaud, it might well be advanced that Desnos is one of the four authentic surrealist poets.

With total honesty and passion and with more naturalness than the other surrealists, Desnos practiced automatic writing. He seemed to live within poetry, guided throughout his life by an authentic poetic inspiration. There were tragic premonitions in his life, but no pessimism. . . . Eluard . . . acknowledged this remarkable freedom of Desnos, his state of constant inspiration, his power of speaking as few poets can write.

> Wallace Fowlie. *Mid-Century French Poets* (Twayne).
> 1955. pp. 199–200

The encounter with surrealism proved to be decisive for the writer whose early taste for dreams destined him for the exploration of interior richnesses.

The basic revolution which characterized the movement led Desnos to question all the mechanisms of poetic creation. Facing up to language with the help of all the weapons that surrealism furnished: hypnotic sleep, automatic writing and speech and with the help of those which derived from his own voluble personality, such as a mathematical sensibility for the grouping of the elements of language—letters, words, rhythms—and the attraction that he felt for commonplaces, Desnos gave himself entirely to laboratory work, to alchemistic research into the possibilities of expression.

> Rosa Buchole. *L'Evolution poétique de Robert Desnos*
> (Palais des Académies Bruxelles). 1956. p. 219.
> Tr. by Dorothy Nyren Curley

None could embroider his dreams like Desnos!

He would go off in a transport, his protuberant eyes taking on a strange light, while the account of his marvelous chimeras gushed from his lips. There were the pursuers and the possessors; visions of the Apocalypse and the procession of its prophets; scenes of mythical violence filled with anguished cries; and "wizards" who now assumed the shape of "Fantômas" (as in the serial thriller of the movies) or now that of Nicholas Flamel, the thirteenth-century alchemist. How like an acrobat, with the greatest of ease, Desnos swung from one millenium to another, or from one continent to another. . . . Whereas the dream recitals of others were mostly boring, Desnos' seemed to come out of a real trance, and were narrated without clichés; they had, in fact, the quality of genius.

> Matthew Josephson. *Life Among the Surrealists*
> (Holt). 1962. pp. 216–7

Possibly the first masterpiece produced by surrealism in the theatre is *"La Place de l'Etoile"* by Robert Desnos. . . . The world of dream is allusively and delicately evoked in this fantasy having in part to do with the proliferation of starfish in Paris. Despite the subtlety of its methods, the intention of *"La Place de l'Etoile"* is as ambitious as any drama in the post-Jarry theatre: the abolition on the stage of all boundaries usually accepted for practical reasons—those lying between wakefulness and sleep, between the living and the dead, the possible and the impossible, for example. Desnos more than vaguely accomplishes the evocation of the blatantly anti-realistic world of his beliefs in his play.

> Michael Benedikt. *Modern French Theatre* (Dutton).
> 1964. p. xxxi

See a selection of his poetry in *Mid-Century French Poets,* ed. by Wallace Fowlie, and his play *"La Place de l'Etoile"* in *Modern French Theatre,* ed. by Michael Benedikt.

DE UNAMUNO, MIGUEL
See Unamuno, Miguel de

DI LAMPEDUSA, GIUSEPPE
See Lampedusa, Giuseppe di

DU GARD, ROGER MARTIN
See Martin du Gard, Roger

DUHAMEL, GEORGES (1884–   )

Georges Duhamel presents an interesting case-study of the intelligently humanitarian reaction to the harsher facts of modern life. It is peculiarly appropriate that he is, by profession, a practicing physician, and becomes a man of letters only momentarily, when he has a point of view to express. His attitude is clearly that of a bedside watcher, who speaks gently at all times, and who points out remediable ills in order that they may be cured—not, as many of his more cynical young contemporaries seem to do, merely the further to torment the sufferer.

> William A. Drake. *Contemporary European Writers*
> (John Day). 1928. p. 106

No attempt on his part to hold life at arm's length, to play with it or to photograph it. He has never been ashamed of his emotions, nor has he tried to parade as a mere onlooker in the stories he tells. . . . There was a life within life, and the novelist brought it to the surface. Life could not be learned through hearsay, nor were its secrets buried in books; life must be learned through experience, life, love, joy and grief at first hand. . . . Duhamel never reveled in the gloomy or the fantastic for its own sake, though he never renounced his sympathetic attitude toward the life which is sinister but human and fascinating.

Régis Michaud. *Modern Thought and Literature in France* (Funk). 1934. pp. 103–4

The study of man . . . in all his diversity may be said to constitute the central theme of Duhamel's works. . . . His entire literary work, whether before, during, or after the conflict of 1914-18, demonstrates the continuity of his interest in permanent human values and his anxiety concerning their survival in an age of mechanical acceleration, fantastic destruction, and epochal transformation.

Boyd G. Carter. *BA*. Winter, 1946. p. 6

Duhamel observes and records, conscious of both the sublime and ridiculous in human nature. He is a dualist in his analysis of human personalities—half biologist, half humanitarian. He is pessimistic about outward progress, but holds to an underlying faith that man can and will win through. He can see two sides to every question. Duhamel's style is subtle, but . . . always clear in the expression of his thoughts. His thoughts are free, but always reasoned, ordered. That is why he likes music. He pleads for the individual's spiritual freedom, but, like Anatole France, he can, at the same time, see the necessity for self-discipline.

L. A. Triebel. *CR*. April, 1948. p. 239

The resemblances between [Duhamel and Dickens] are indeed striking. There is a soundness and a sanity about both of them which comes, probably, from their true sense of values. Both write, not of or for an aristocratic minority or an intellectual élite, but of and for the common man. . . . Both great writers learned to understand the difficulties of the under-privileged in the school of life. This understanding has bred affection for their characters, an affection which is patently and regrettably lacking in so many present-day writers.

A. E. Ballard. *NaRL*. July, 1948. p. 78

The war books of Duhamel are composed of vignettes and short stories, with a minimum of touching up. They are told dramatically, because Duhamel's artistic sense prompted him to return to reality, through literary skill, some of the tragedy it contains. . . . Those war books are an impassioned, though restrained, indictment of war. They use satire effectively to scathe the ridiculousness of hierarchy and discipline and the vanity of otherwise intelligent men, who fondly believe that they belong to "the most intelligent people" on earth and suddenly, having donned a uniform, abdicate all critical spirit.

Henri Peyre. *The Contemporary French Novel*
(Oxford). 1955. p. 49

Georges Duhamel, despite the fading importance of his problems, remains on the stylistic level a first-class writer of the strictly logical sentence vibrating with genuine feeling. Describing the life of families of all shades he brings out the aspects, noises, and smells of a house with evocations more impressive than those of Honoré de Balzac. His imagery, never showy, is used only to bring out the psychological climate of a situation or a place.

Helmut Hatzfeld. *Trends and Styles in Twentieth Century French Literature* (Catholic U.). 1957. p. 32

For Duhamel, bread and wine—especially wine and countless cheeses and all that Nature heaps on the table of her well-loved children are very real. He is profoundly attached to life, but for all that he is constantly shattered by it. He is neither the "pacifist" nor the "humanitarian" he was believed to be. In the spiritual sense, the author of *Civilisation* is a great war casualty: he is a man who has never recovered from what he saw every day for four years. . . . The essential gift of the man who wrote *Vie des Martyres* is imagination of the heart; he had the ability to share the suffering of others, to relive it in himself.

François Mauriac. *Second Thoughts* (World). 1961.
pp. 109–10

See *The New Book of Martyrs* (sketches).

DUMITRIU, PETRU (1924–   )

His main literary merit . . . lies in his art of dramatic effects and in character portrayal, in the manner of Balzac (who is obviously his teacher). . . . *Family Jewels* is basically a novel of social passion, but it is also a record of the gradual disintegration of a class undermined by great and moral corruption. . . . Set in the conventional form of a chronicle, it makes up in its representational qualities and artistic diversity what it lacks in depth and originality. It is a highly entertaining, realistic story seasoned with exotic flashes and an amazing rendering of outdated customs.

Marc Slonim. *NYT*. Nov. 26, 1961. p. 52

With savage anger and bitterness Dumitriu writes of a social order that accepted corruption and debauchery among the rich and drove the starving poor to extremes of violence in rebellion. . . . He succeeds in painting a vivid canvas of corrupt feudal society. His strokes are bold, highly colored and frequently grotesque in pattern but they carry a strong quality of essential truth and personal conviction.

Rose Feld. *NYHT*. Dec. 31, 1961. p. 8

All of it [*Meeting at the Last Judgment*] is convincing enough, and yet as characters of a fiction, the participants in the narrative never assume separate identities, nor emerge with anything as real as the toothache that Koestler gave Rubashov. They are created "pathetic," even the villains. The best chance of all, perhaps, is missed in keeping the protagonist, who tells the story, a nameless shadow. Although he comments on the action now and then with aphoristic penetration and a sense of historical perspective, it is difficult to reconcile the concomitant sense of idealism in the man. . . . Had Dumitriu been able to establish this character as something more than thematic, the novel would have gained in strength. As it is, *Meeting at the Last Judgment* remains another interesting testament of one man's anger and despair over the abuse of political power.

William Wiegand. *NYT*. July 1, 1962. p. 18

Every time he halts his narrative to become rhetorical, Mr. Dumitriu tells us that only God can save his Rumania. The problem of such a formula is that it does not account for the minutiae of small ways in which the advanced nations have always managed to survive, to live with relative harmony within their borders, to reform themselves and replenish their resources. It was not God but the civilizing standards of behavior which Rumania has always tried hardest to avoid. One is reminded a bit of those racists who would enjoin us to change our hearts and not depend upon laws. It is all a trifle smug, but, perhaps, in Mr. Dumitriu's case it is also unavoidable. Although he had the courage to defect, he could not possibly have the resources to offer Western readers anything but an alibi for the Rumanians. A reading of his novel recalls an ancient Yiddish aphorism: "Do you seek to know the Rumanian soul? Better not!"

Richard M. Elman. *NR*. Sept. 12, 1964. p. 24

Dumitriu is neither poet nor metaphysican. The novelist he more closely resembles is the Russian Mikhail Sholokhov. Like *And Quiet Flows the Don, Incognito* gives dramatic shape to a complex, savage sweep of history. It works on a large canvas and shares Sholokhov's gruff, unyielding realism. . . . This is a big novel, in composition, in breadth of feeling. But it is not a philosophic or poetic answer to the assertion, Nietzschean or Marxist, that God has died out of man's history.

George Steiner. *NYT*. Sept. 13, 1964. p. 58

Incognito is a novel clangorous with political intrigue and ideological ritual, very much a book of and for the historical moment, quite coarse in the quality of its observation, often irritating for its didactic aggressiveness (writers who find God somewhat late in life behave as if no one had ever noticed him before). Yet, if read with primary attention to the larger rhythms of narrative, it is an interesting and, on occasion, a moving book. It is, at the very least, a novel, and not a string of prose lyrics, or a satiric vaudeville, or an allegory *à clef*.

Irving Howe. *NYR*. Sept. 24, 1964. p. 17

See *Family Jewels, The Prodigals, Meeting at the Last Judgment* and *Incognito* (novels).

DURAS, MARGUERITE (1914–   )

I admire the humility of Marguerite Duras. She carefully joins together the platitudes of the mediocre, she composes with the thread-bare, she has no need for fire in her ideas or language. However, the natural does not appear as art without a risk. An author has to study hard to speak as badly as his characters speak, Marguerite Duras is not her concierge and I remember that once in a story she had a certain Gaston sweep the streets and quote Descartes. That's where things went wrong. Neither the farmers or workmen that one hears in her books ring true. The bourgeois are best as writers when, despite themselves, they remain bourgeois.

Roger Judrin. *NRF*. Dec., 1955. p. 1160.
Tr. by Dorothy Nyren Curley

She was aiming, obviously, at a definition of existence as Western man experiences it today, in this particular moment of the mid-twentieth century. . . . The fictional world of Madame Duras is the movement of time, at once creating and isolating personality: the tilting of time toward a past which a second later is transformed into an empty nothingness. . . . These are strange lives, in which all memory of the past, all the accumulations of experience, shriveled up into the expressions uttered at that very moment. The fictional curve of temporality coils, like a planetary eclipse, around the two poles of memory and the instant, each of which defines the other.

Armand Hoog. YFS. Summer, 1959. pp. 70–2

Marguerite Duras does not describe her characters: they are before us and they talk. More or less we learn in the course of their conversation something of their physical appearance since they mention it. But they speak, as we speak, each for himself and for the others, at times indifferent and at times careful about making themselves understood. Just as with dramatists, this novelist appears not to direct the dialogue of her characters, to let them express themselves freely and that it is circumstance and not the author which links remark to remark. But the situations in which the conversations occur are hers; in the secret resemblances from book to book one finds clues to the problematical personality or, one might say, to the profound obsession of the writer.

Serge Young. RGB. April, 1960. p. 134.
Tr. by Dorothy Nyren Curley

Her novels are written to be sipped, slowly, until one really feels giddy, just as the characters themselves become intoxicated. . . . The style has the slow and repetitive obstinacy of a drunkard's comments and thoughts. And it is that very drunkenness that persuades the reader and gives the work the value of revelation. Essentially, Duras' novels are like alcohol or like a poem. Drunkenness and its truth can only be "understood" if one is drunk, just as a poem is, in the last analysis, its own explanation. . . . Each novel moves ahead with the specific unity of some systematic inebriation. There is the cognac-manzanilla "style," just as there was the Campari bitters style and, before that, the whiskey style.

Jacques Guicharnaud. YFS. Spring-Summer, 1961.
p. 112

Whether on a farm, a yacht, or a beach, the persons Mme. Duras describes play out the entire drama of human existence. They are all seeking something—meaning of life, fulfillment, or happiness—but their will is a fragile bark soon surrendering to the great currents and waves which carry them on according to plans that are not of human making. As in Simon's novels, time goes on, destinies are accomplished, and life is perhaps over before these nameless persons are fully aware of what has been happening. Their reactions have nothing of Promethean grandeur, but are feeble whinings or petty mutual brutalities.

All this is forcefully presented chiefly by means of dialogue. The novels are full of conversation—a bumbling, inexplicit flow of words that through its very incoherence and fortuity reveals the pathos of these starved lives.

Laurent Le Sage. The French New Novel
(Pennsylvania State). 1962. pp. 85–6

These words which are said in this work which nears the limit of speechlessness by men and by women foundering, with dulled senses, hypnotized, and almost paralyzed, slowly, in night, are words which traverse a space which is pale sea-green and like gelatin; they look for themselves hesitatingly in order to form sentences but they come always against an insurmountable wall. The word, with Mme. Marguerite Duras, is not communication, but solitary incantation; it fills silence like the most doomed cry for help.

Philippe Sénart. MF. June, 1962. pp. 311–2.
Tr. by Dorothy Nyren Curley

See *Moderato Cantabile, The Square,* and *10:30 on a Summer Night* (novels).

DUTOURD, JEAN (1920–   )

A Dog's Head is an excellent joke in the worst possible taste, and its author, M. Jean Dutourd, is a satirist of the first rank. . . . *A Dog's Head* is a brief *jeu d'esprit* that goes . . . to the pamphleteering tradition of the seventeenth and eighteenth centuries; it recalls Voltaire as Orwell's *Animal Farm* recalls Swift and Dutourd can bear the comparison rather better than Orwell can. To tell the truth, of the two Dutourd is, while being every bit as serious, a much funnier writer, with a lighter and gayer humor.

Anthony West. NY. Feb. 14, 1953. p. 109

One thing is certain: in a modest way the author is working in the tradition of *Candide* and *Gulliver's Travels*. The experiences of his hero [in *A Dog's Head*] enable M. Dutourd to register—lightly and divertingly—a ferocious commentary on the conduct of the human race. . . . M. Dutourd is a fine craftsman, whose work has the classic virtues of brevity, lucidity, and concentration. He has written a sardonic divertisse-ment that concerns itself with the fundamental problems of man's exis-tence—a tale that is sad-eyed, witty and often very funny.

Charles J. Rolo. NYT. Feb. 15, 1953. p. 4

His story [A Dog's Story] is a tiny masterpiece in the French classical tradition, writ small as though on a two-franc piece. It is a drama in miniature, the kind of thing that the French do superlatively well, stylish, elegant and witty, and told with an apparent light-heartedness that points rather than obscures the hero's essential tragedy. The book reminds me of those modest bog plants that shine like delicate stars in the swamp. It is only when one stoops to pluck them that one sees at the very core of the flower the rotting mess of insect life in which it grossly feeds. Edmond's story on the surface is absurd, even laugh-able: only on closer inspection does it appear, rather, a matter for tears.

P. L. Travers. NYHT. March 1, 1953. p. 7

Jean Dutourd claims to put his prejudices and sympathies to one side; he disclaims realism in his writing. We can take him at his word: he is an artist. His book is the play of wit but not the free play of irresponsible wit. The Best Butter makes a point, a very painful one. It is perhaps that in war, and particularly in the sort of civil war the French went through under the occupation, there are not the heroes on one side, the villains on the other. Conflict dirties as well as purifies. Cruelty is am-bivalent and so is selfishness. It is impossible not to agree.

Gouverneur Paulding. NYHT. March 20, 1955. p. 5

Alas! Cold reason tells us that this earth is so much old porridge, that the body is a vessel of corruption and that time destroys us all—the sooner the better, for Doucin [in Five A. M.] is bored. He is bald, he is fat, he smokes too much, he has a sore in his mouth, he overeats, he is tepid in love and he goofs at his job. And there you are—there is your story. The entire novel is nothing but Doucin. It cannot be judged unless we judge Doucin himself. And I cannot presume to say the last word about him. He is a man; he does suffer and think; he deserves to be taken seriously.

Saul Bellow. NYT. Aug. 26, 1956. p. 5

[The Taxis on the Marne] is written in the same apocalyptic style as that used by Charles Péguy and Georges Bernanos. Of course, M. Dutourd is not a prophet of the rank of Péguy or even of Bernanos, nor is he a satirist of the rank of Voltaire. Nevertheless, his book is a noteworthy tract, casting some light on France and more on the situation of our pacific, timid, comfort-loving democracies. For if the target is France, the blows fall on more than France. . . . Formally, M. Dutourd, who is the author of three satirical novels, the most recent one *Five A. M.*, is a pessimist, not only about France but about Europe.

D. W. Brogan. *NYT*. June 2, 1957. p. 4

M. Dutourd's arch foe is stupidity, which he finds as rampant today among us as in Stendhal's day, multiplied as it is by vulgarity and by the tendency of too many people to bore their fellow beings. . . . There are many . . . amusing unjust paradoxes in this disarmingly insolent book [*The Man of Sensibility*]: a professed scorn for Gide, Giraudoux and other luminaries of French literature; for the modern neurosis of hard work as praiseworthy in itself; for gastronomy. . . . The best passages, very Stendhalian in tone, denounce boredom.

Henri Peyre. *NYT*. May 28, 1961. p. 34

See *The Best Butter, A Dog's Head*, and *Five A.M.* (novels); also *The Taxis on the Marne* (autobiography) and *The Man of Sensibility* (criticism).

ECHEGARAY, JOSÉ (1832–1916)

Even in Echegaray's notable plays, strong and original as they are, there is an unmistakable ring of the past. We feel it is more a revival than a youthful outburst, with all the promise of novelty. . . . It is dominated by the modern need and its restless searching note; it must prove its mission as something more than the mere desire to divert. Not even a sermon could be more remote than this theatre from the old comedy of manners. . . . The morality and discontent that float from the meditative North have reached him in his home of sunshine and easy emotions, and his work is pervaded nobly by its spirit.

Hannah Lynch. CR. Oct., 1890. p. 576

Echegaray is apparently of the school of Schiller, Victor Hugo, and Verdi—picturesque, tragic to the death, showing us the beautiful and the heroic struggling either with blind destiny or with an implacable idealism which makes vengeance and jealousy points of honor. . . . On the whole, though I am afraid some of our critics will be . . . nauseated, . . . I suspect the Spaniards will compel us to admit that they have produced a genius of a stamp that crosses frontiers.

George Bernard Shaw. Dramatic Opinions and Essays
(Brentano). 1906. pp. 84, 89

The northern realistic drama has . . . been doomed to unsuccess in Spain. . . . The dramas of Ibsen have interested the reading classes because of the vitality, not so much passional as intellectual, of their subjects. But the harsh individualism, the intimate and subtle sentiments of self-centered men cannot be understood by the Spanish public. . . . [Of] attempts . . . to imitate Ibsen, the most notable is by Echegaray in *"El Hijo de Don Juan,"* which is a Spanish version of "Ghosts." The author states that he has been inspired by Ibsen, but if inspiration means to feel the spirit of the original, then Echegaray has signally failed. . . . There is nothing in the Spanish play which reveals any struggle between duty and moral freedom, nothing which touches on the problems of divorce, of education, or of social regeneration. There is neither dispute of ideas nor opposition of characters, nothing in fact which makes up the essential elements of Ibsen's work. Echegaray does appropriate the last incident; but it now lacks significance.

Elizabeth Wallace. At. Sept., 1908. p. 358

151

Echegaray is an old-fashioned moralizer. He is so relentless in punishing the guilty that in his plays the innocent are often punished equally with the guilty. He is a keen observer, understands human passions, and continues in the Spanish drama many of the old ideas of honor, but in the presentation of his eternal conflicts between duties he often exaggerates, and some of his plays are artificial and overdrawn as human documents. His figures are titanic, even sublime, but often they are grotesque and too exact for real life. . . . The influence of Ibsen is evident [after 1885]. The evil consequences of sin assume a pseudo-scientific character and Echegaray becomes a real modern reformer. His tendency to exaggeration, however, does not disappear, and the influence of the pseudo-realism of Ibsen is only a new weapon in his hands.

Aurelio Espinosa. Introduction to El Gran Galeoto
(Knopf). 1918. pp. ix–xi

He excels in harrowing efforts, in a certain gloomy power, in a sheer vehemence and momentum of language that carry along the worst of his plays. Quite negligible on the whole as a poet, he is scarcely more eminent as a writer of dramatic prose, yet there is a power in his phraseology, an attraction in his figurative speech, in the Oriental profusion of his bizarre conceptions, that does much to redeem his other deficiencies. There is little continental artistry in the average Echegaray production. He lacked the power of self-criticism, of technical finesse; he was a moral force rather than an artistic spirit. His fancy would penetrate a situation, his mind would supply a contention, his powerful language could easily infuse the whole, and his electric energy thus galvanized a play into existence.

Isaac Goldberg. The Drama of Transition
(Stewart Kidd). 1922. p. 66

Echegaray was old-fashioned in some respects, and new-fashioned in others. His stress upon situation, his focusing of interest upon crises in the life of a single character, his fondness for the concept of honor, remind us that he descends from Lope and Calderón. Yet, for him, as for most moderns, honor is subjective and not merely the matter of a code; fate, too, is no longer arbitrary, but rather the result of heredity and environment. He delights to portray high-strung characters, intense hysterical souls, driven by passion or idea. He shows the individual struggling with himself or against social institutions. He loves the moral, the heroic, the perfervid. He is a natural rhetorician, less poetic than theatric.

Frank W. Chandler. Modern Continental Playwrights
(Harper). 1931. p. 465

In general, he sought to revive romantic drama, to proclaim sharp conflicts in life between passion and duty. His motives were often more pronounced than his characterization; his men and women were sometimes mere mechanisms, fighting their battles for honor and truth. There was a chivalrous note in his lines where domestic fidelity formed the keynote of the emotional struggle. . . . His seriousness, combined with keen wit and insight, has been compared with similar traits of Tolstoy. Both writers have emphasized the "dignity of suffering" for the sake of spiritual freedom.

> Annie Russell Marble. *The Nobel Prize Winners in Literature, 1901-1931* (Appleton). 1932. pp. 242, 246

Reading his plays at this distance it is hard to see how some of them could have caused a furor . . . or why . . . they were awarded even half the Nobel Prize. Yet the comments of his contemporaries cannot be disregarded. Benito Pérez Galdós . . . describes "the brilliant apparition of the genius of Echegaray on the Spanish scenes." He "broke up worn-out forms and imbued the actor's art with a new strength and new resources. He electrified the general public and threw among the critics a fearful whirlwind of fervent enthusiasms struggling with the lukewarm opinions of routine." . . . Echegaray's plays erupted like "a thundering, flashing hurricane which changed discreet emotions into violent passions."

> Mildred Adams. *A History of Modern Drama*, ed. by Barrett H. Clark and George Freedley (Appleton). 1947. p. 558

See *The Great Galeoto, Mariana*, and *The Son of Don Juan* (plays).

ELUARD, PAUL (1859–1952)

Extreme verbal felicity is . . . the first and final clue to Eluard's success in a field which most of fellows invade only by violence and shock-tactics. . . . Eluard outdistances his more elementary exercising in psychic automatism when under the impulse of his intense lyric clairvoyance, and then he produces poems that require neither special elucidation nor a preliminary agreement on terms. Their exquisite sense of metaphor, and their evocation of elusive meanings compels the reader's belief in whatever logic or superiority to logic dictated them.

> Morten Dauwen Zabel. *Poetry*. Sept., 1936. pp. 348, 350

Paul Eluard's meditations gravitate spontaneously to the two opposite and yet complementary poles of solitude and love. Love is viewed by him as a mystic center of blazing forces, a fiery nucleus of passionate vibrations, diffusing energy throughout the world in ardent and pulsating waves. . . . A universe of love has as an inevitable counterpart a bleak and dismal *"univers-solitude."* With assumed outward impassibleness and yet with a perceptible throb of inward agony, Eluard has repeatedly conjured up its dripping silence, its icy glare, its crushing and boundless desolation.

> Georges Lemaitre. *From Cubism to Surrealism in French Literature* (Harvard). 1941. p. 210

Eluard rarely experimented with extremes of nonsense. He was always interested in recording a specific impression: a state of mind, the elements of emotion, ways of being—always observations from experience. . . . The Surrealists generally considered the dream as the more valid experience in itself. Eluard works the other way: he uses the dream to interpret and to unmask the world of appearances. . . . He is incapable of violence; his poetry is unclouded by the macabre. He has modified Surrealist shock into surprise.

> Carol Seeley. *WR.* Fall, 1949. pp. 31–3

Eluard is always very elegant, well-groomed, and he wears hats. He smokes enormously (too much). Even though his hands tremble a little and he is too demanding on his health, even in anger, or dogged by events, or baited (he has been a little) he has a type of slow majesty that is very remarkable. It is not at all the stiff, withdrawing, artificial majesty of someone who hoists himself up, and raises his collar (and tone) to make an impression. Eluard has the easy majesty natural to the truly great of this world: Targui chieftains, racehorses, children at play, certain fish, and grey-pink gladioli.

> Claude Roy. Introduction to *Selected Writings of Paul Eluard* (New Directions). 1951. p. viii

Eluard's virtues are apparent, and his influence, if not strong, might be importantly pervasive. His bare naturalness, existing uniquely among his contemporaries, preserves in French literature (at a time when such a delicate ingredient might be entirely lost) a *pathétique* equally as valuable as the sublimity, wit, irony, malice, and corrosive rhetorical splendors with which that literature has always been so well supplied. . . . Pathos . . . is contrary to the self-conscious, anti-sentimental, and synthetically tough spirit of the time; it is a valuable civilized and salutary element, none the less.

> Louise Bogan. *Selected Criticism* (Noonday). 1955. p. 168

Although Paul Eluard belongs to a group of poets who thought it their duty to subject their thought to the requirements of social evolution and deny an idealism which the necessities of action ordered them to sacrifice, he illustrates nevertheless in his poems the implacable movement of a dialectic which starts from the sensible world to rise to the archetypal Idea which creates that world.

> Rolland de Renéville. *From the N. R. F.*, ed. by
> Justin O'Brien (Farrar). 1958. pp. 69–70

Eluard's thought plays with the reality of love as if it were the poet's magnet. He moves toward it and then moves away. Although his amorous ecstasy is always severe and illuminated, one feels that love itself is an experience which has taken place at a great distance from the earth and beyond the limits of time, in some dark abyss. Love is the experience greater than man himself which he records and reproduces. . . . In his poetry man is no longer looking at himself for he has begun to contemplate the mysteries and has quite rightfully begun with the mystery of woman. . . . Nerval seems to have forseen what Eluard feels: the magic of all the objects of his desire, the all-encompassing realm of magic which woman represents and creates.

> Wallace Fowlie. *Age of Surrealism* (Indiana). 1960.
> pp. 146–9

Everyone who met him knows how rare it is to find such unity between an artist and his work as that found between Eluard's poetry and his personality. He was very like his poems, and his poems were always autobiographical. He was exceptionally modest and shunned fame: gentle and compassionate, he was surrounded by the love of everyone he met. He was not at all the absent-minded, ethereal poet imagined by romantically-minded adolescents: he took part in life and noticed its every detail, but he never lost sight of his great dream.

> Ilya Ehrenburg. *Chekhov, Stendhal, and Other Essays*
> (MacGibbon and Kee). 1962. p. 231

See *Selected Writings*.

ESPINA DE SERNA, CONCHA (1877–1955)

Her writings present pictures of Spanish life that are wholly unconventional, that are so close to the soil and to the labor of men and women under the traditional customs of ages, that the reader seems to be party to a ritual of Nature worship with its prayers, complaints, petitions, and songs of praise. She writes of the Spanish life that she knows through the understanding of childhood, and as she sees it . . . with the eyes of a realist. . . . Alfredo Mori, the Florentine critic, has pointed out that the realism of Concha Espina is neither brutal nor photographic, that it is tempered with idealism. . . . "She is modern; and at the same time her desire is to be classic."

Frances Douglas. *Hsp*. March, 1924. pp. 111–2, 118

One cannot doubt that [*The Red Beacon* and *Mariflor*] represent either a prevailing convention in Spanish literature, or else that they do give a veristic portrait of the peculiar conditions existent in northern Spain and the mode of life enforced upon the inhabitants. . . . The story in each case is a peasant version of the *Maiden Tribute,* of Andromeda and the Dragon, for no Perseus appears to deliver the fated heroines. Beauty and youth are remorselessly sacrificed to harsh necessity, to the racial will to survive, dignified by the name of family pride and honor. The starkness of the recital lends a touch of romantic glamor that would be dissipated by any less concentrated method of viewing these narrow and embittered toilers. . . . By generalizing the concrete fact of living into an abstract ideal, making it a test of purposeful endurance, the virtue of courage emerges shining from the bleak background. The ignorant peasant becomes a Prometheus, cherishing the vital flame in spite of the enmity of fate. . . . These novels possess . . . a melancholy and austere charm, like that of the mountains and the desert.

Isabel Paterson. *NYHT*. June 22, 1924. p. 25

As a technician she seems supremely gifted. She is unusually articulate and sensitive enough to echo the subtle moods of the earth and the sky as well as the petty sufferings of her puppets. But the conflict of truly vital and radical interests, which alone lends a tale of the moment the color of permanence, cannot be found in her. The only grace that raises her from a novelist of sentimental trash into the ranks of interesting mediocrity is a faint sense, of which she seems to be seldom conscious, that the life she describes is adumbrated by the weariness of acknowledged futility. . . . It is true that Concha Espina is "the foremost woman novelist of Spain today." . . . But . . . since the death of . . . Pardo Bazán there has appeared no woman writer capable of doing work of permanent human significance. The fact that she is the recipient of a prize from the Academy merely attests her ideologic and artistic respectability.

Eliseo Vivas. *Nation*. Aug. 13, 1924

[There is an] attraction exercised upon the Southern European mind by the reticences, the reserve, and the stoicism of a novelist whose world is the mountain region of Northern Spain, the hinterland of Santander. Her disconsolate philosophy which identifies love with pain and suffering seems to require that cold, harsh background in order to become intelligible to the easy-going children of the sun.

Ernest Boyd. *Studies from Ten Literatures* (Scribner).
1925. p. 135

Concha Espina possesses Marcel Proust's gift of calling up the impressions and feelings of childhood; and in this evocation of the past, though less clever and intellectual than Proust, she is sweeter and more natural. . . . Espina excels all the modernists in her gift of indicating that which is too vague to be expressed, analysing with a delicacy beyond the faculties of the mind. . . . She is melancholy and mystical, with a melancholy and a mysticism blending the northern and Celtic. She has a musical and pantheistic manner of seeing and feeling the spiritual unseen in all phenomena, a spiritual invisible that is really in her heart and is projected into all the sights and sounds of the landscape.

L. A. Warren. *Modern Spanish Literature* (Brentano).
1929. v. 1, pp. 304–5

The author's attitude toward her characters dates from the time when we were content to account for human action on the basis of an arbitrary category of subjective moods and emotions, such as grief, pride, love, doubt, envy and recognition. Concha Espina's psychology looms like a ghost out of the age of sensibility.

Harold Strauss. *NYT*. July 29, 1934. p. 7

Concha Espina's novel, *The Woman and the Sea* . . . belongs to the type of literature—rhetorical, sentimental and silly—which characterized and reigned supreme during Echegaray's period and up to the European War. . . . Mr. Boyd assures us [in the introduction] that Concha Espina is "an interpreter as highly to be esteemed as Pérez de Ayala, Pío Baroja and Ramón del Valle-Inclán." . . . Concha Espina sold her books because she had become a symbol, the woman writer, *la escritora,* and because, I must admit, she was liked by young girls and their pure mothers. But the serious reader and the discriminating critics respectfully kept at a distance from her sugary tracts and from those heroines of hers, beautiful she-wolves, voracious readers of

Nietzsche and Schopenhauer, whose indoor sports seem to have been the wrecking of happy homes.

Angel Flores. *NYHT*. Aug. 5, 1934. p. 7

See *The Metal of the Dead, Mariflor, The Red Beacon,* and *The Woman and the Sea* (novels).

EXUPÉRY, ANTOINE DE SAINT

See Saint Exupéry, Antoine de

FERREIRA DE CASTRO, JOSÉ MARIA
(1898–   )

To every man there comes at least once in his life an overwhelming impulse to rebel against the cruelty and inexorability of natural forces. . . . Ferreira de Castro had this experience when he was brought face to face with the power and the malignity of the jungle. . . . The hero of Ferreira's tale of the jungles . . . is caught in the grip of this vegetable world. . . . He rebels fiercely against it, but it saps his will and his resistance by its sheer tyranny and its immense monstrous vitality. Blind circumstance saves him from its clutches, but it leaves its indelible imprint on him. . . . Primitive passions ran wild . . . and [many] sank to the lowest depths of perversions. At first they appalled him—then he began to feel the same overpowering desires and temptations. . . . When [he] left the jungle he carried with him one profound conviction: "He would never be the accuser . . . after what he had seen in himself and the others." . . . It is [the] accent of sincerity, which pervades the whole book, that makes *Jungle* a remarkable human document. It can scarcely be called a novel. Every page is dominated by the author's personality and his own reactions to man's struggle against nature. All the other characters are dwarfed in comparison.

Marguerite Harrison. *NYHT*. Feb. 3, 1935. p. 3

There is no plot; the few instances of objective drama [in *Jungle*] are generally understated or permitted to trail off, as things so frequently do in real life, instead of being played up to a climax as they might easily be. . . . The real hero—or villain—of course, is the jungle itself. Not the "green hill" seen for a few days or weeks by some scribbling tripper who skips in and out simply to make a book; still less the Seabrook sort of tripe; but that appalling wilderness of the Amazon's headwaters, its vastness, isolation, impersonal cruelty, as they gradually wear down and break—swallow, so to say—the courage, pride, sense of identity, even, of the occasional white man condemned to stay there, year in and year out, and to fight for existence with his own hands against that hideously hostile natural exuberance.

The outstanding idea in his mind, the author explains. . . , "was that of humanity. It is but a short chapter of a work which one day will record the suffering of all those simple souls throughout the centuries in their search for food and justice." And he makes this plea the more effective by keeping it always implicit, never stated, as such.

Arthur Ruhl. *SR*. Feb. 16, 1935. p. 485

The Portuguese writer, Ferreira de Castro, . . . is . . . a rare example of the self-developed personality. He contradicts the old theory that the artist is a product of his race, of the environment in which he grew up, of the education he received. Very rarely, no doubt, has the vocation of fiction writer been realized so fully in the face of obstacles which seem insurmountable. This writer is an example of a self-made man at the literary level. . . . He was a country boy who spent his childhood in a mountain village and his adolescence in the back country of the virgin forest. . . . [Yet] it was Ferreira de Castro who demonstrated with his works that Portuguese letters possessed values worthy of international circulation. . . . A total independence marks the character of the writer and of the man. . . . Without precedents or tradition in his country, he was a precursor of the so-called "social novel," and . . . without a solid cultural foundation in his youth he drew from life the sum of knowledge that permitted him to produce a work that has commanded a world-wide audience.

Jaime Brasil. BA. Spring, 1957. pp. 117–21

If Nietzsche's phrase "to write with one's blood" is true of anyone, it is of Ferreira de Castro. Each of his novels is evidence of this. [*Jungle*], for example, the testimony of a man escaped from hell, is one of the most moving frescoes in contemporary literature. Yet it is utterly lacking in fine phrases, in the romanticism which the subject might seem to invite. Its simplicity is astonishing. . . . His novels are all taken direct from life, and being the bitter (though not sour) fruits of experience, they have an unmistakable authenticity. In his Portuguese and Brazilian novels his aim is to interpret the psychology of simple people, which he is supremely well qualified to do, knowing from close contact and from his own experience the whole range of human poverty and distress. . . . What one can only call his essential goodness . . . is his dominant quality. There is something of the early Christian about him. . . . He has not the least sense of property. . . . For him, life means . . . seeing and not possessing.

Henry Poulaille. LMg. Aug., 1961. pp. 80, 84

[*Emigrants*] by Ferreira de Castro . . . is the novel that won the author his justified position as Portugal's greatest novelist. . . . It is a narrative that moves with the swift inevitability of Greek tragedy toward its inexorable conclusion. Never does the reader doubt that its hero . . . is doomed but never does his interest flag as the author skillfully leads him down the slope of failure. . . . Ferreira de Castro's [novel] is almost classical in the restrained presentation of his . . . social tragedy.

Vernon Hall, Jr. NYHT. Oct. 28, 1962. p. 4

Ferreira de Castro is generally credited with having introduced a social conscience into the Portuguese novel. His pioneer work in this regard was *Emigrants,* published in 1928. . . . *Emigrants* tells the story of a Portuguese farmer . . . who sails to Brazil in quest of wealth. The author clearly intends him to symbolize the many unskilled, poorly educated wretches who have fled the poverty of their homelands only to live in poverty abroad. . . . Superficially, at least, the emphasis is sociological. The author protests against an environment that traps men like his protagonist and condemns them to poverty. . . . [However, the protagonist] is not just a victim of society: it is his own fatuity that changes a hard but decent life into one of utter defeat and humiliation. His misery is the joint product of environmental resistance and personal inadequacy, and the candor with which the author presents this inadequacy gives the book its stamp of honesty and truth. . . . Everywhere the author's compassion and indignation come through, despite the restraint that keeps them fairly free of excess and sentimentality. What gives his novel a claim to a place in world literature is less its social protest than its revelation of how a poor man's own folly may destroy him when poverty in itself cannot.

William L. Grossman. *NYT*. Nov. 18, 1962. p. 4

See *Jungle* and *Emigrants* (novels).

FOGAZZARO, ANTONIO (1842–1911)

Giovanni Verga . . . Gabriele d' Annunzio . . . [and] Antonio Fogazzaro . . . are frankly recognized as the three significant forces which, in varying degrees, will ultimately decide the form and the spirit of the Italian novel of tomorrow. . . . Fogazzaro is a mystic, an idealist, an enthusiastic dreamer, who takes fiction as he has taken everything else in life, with a tremendous seriousness, waiting until his fortieth year before giving his first novel to the public, and ardently striving to make his books not only pictures of life, but vehicles of philosophical teaching. . . . The speculative, philosophical trend of his mind would seem to be far less in accord with the impressionable, volatile, emotional Latin temperament than the poignant simplicity of Verga, the brilliant paganism of d'Annunzio.

Frederick Taber Cooper. *Bkm*. Nov., 1906. p. 261

Signor Fogazzaro . . . has the temperament, combined with the intellectual outlook of the advanced modern thinker. . . . He is not blind to any aspect of reality, but he believes the most important of realities to be those of the spirit, and this thesis he unswervingly defends. . . . He believes the Church to have been wounded in the house of its friends, to have suffered ossification in its frame, and paralysis in its vital activities. It suffers from the spirits of falsehood, and clericalism, and avarice, and immobility. It opposes science, which means that it has lost faith in itself. . . . So vibrant a voice . . . is not to be hushed by ecclesiastical condemnation.

William Morton Payne. *Dial.* Nov. 1, 1906. pp. 281–2

The novelist has become both philosopher and priest and preacher— a prime factor in our educational program. He settles—or unsettles— our morals, our religion, our social and political economy; and saves us the necessity of thinking for ourselves. Fogazzaro is the chief exponent in Italy of this theory of the Novel. . . . Fogazzaro's novels mark the turning-point dividing naturalistic from psychological fiction. He discarded the naturalistic theory of man's irresponsibility, because enslaved by biological and physiological laws and fatally controlled by environment; yet he avoids the Charybdis of psychologists who neglect the objective study of their personages.

Joseph Spencer Kennard. *Italian Romance Writers*
(Brentano). 1906. pp. 246, 248

[If we consider] the book as a work of art, meaning by art . . . that power which takes the fleeting facts of life and endows them with permanence, with deeper purports, with order and beauty . . . , [then] in this sense, Signor Fogazzaro is a great artist. He has the gift of the masters which enables him to rise without effort to the level of the tragic crises. He has also a vein of humor. . . . No realist could exceed the fidelity with which Signor Fogazzaro outlines a landscape, or fixes a passing scene; yet being an idealist through and through . . . the imagination is sovereign.

William Roscoe Thayer. Introduction to *The Saint*
(Putnam). 1907. pp. xxvii–xxviii

Fogazzaro, who finds in J. LeConte's *Evolution and Its Relation to Religious Thought* only a confirmation and expansion of doctrines which his own poetic instincts have long since made dear to him, cannot fail to be a stanch believer in the influences of heredity, . . . [and given to] relentless dissection [of his characters]. . . . [But also] marvellous descriptions of nature . . . adorn all of this author's works. . . . Fogazzaro, like St. Francis of Assisi, sees a soul in all things, in the blade of grass and in the mountain, in the rays of the sun and in the lowering storm cloud.

Mary Prichard-Agnetti. Introduction to *The Sinner*
(Putnam). 1907. pp. iii, vi

Antonio Fogazzaro reminds us of Anthony Trollope. . . . Both spare no time or trouble in the turning out of their characters—and both produce the literary equivalent of some finely, minutely painted picture of "A Dutch Interior" by Gerard Dow—each stroke finished, nothing passed over, nothing omitted. Both, too, write, as it were, of things already left, or being left, behind. Their best books are those which deal with a past rather than a present generation, and signs of labored effort and a straining to keep abreast of the most modern times becomes apparent at once when they cease to write of those things which they have passed the greater portion of their lives in living among and seeing around them. . . . Antonio Fogazzaro is Italy's Trollope.

Ruth Egerton. *NAR*. April, 1911. p. 512

The shade of Benedetto [which] appears in the volume [*The Saint,* which was condemned by the Church] . . . scarcely veils the personality of Fogazzaro. . . . He proclaims that Benedetto was not a modernist, that he himself is not a modernist; yet the first modernist personage whom he puts on the stage flutters from doubt to doubt till he almost loses himself in scepticism. . . . Certainly for the aim of the book modernism and anti-modernism are unnecessary. . . . Fogazzaro's book is a Catholic book, though there is a certain Venetian malice in giving all the ugly side to the priests who are faithful (*liga*) to tradition, and a purer and more active piety to the other party; there is a kind of subtle irony in affirming the moral purity of these priests and entangling them in actions which taste slightly of dishonesty and strangely of Jesuitism.

Renato Simoni. *EdR*. Oct., 1911. p. 291

It has been said that he imitated Dickens. It is quite possible that the great English humorist, whom he read diligently and greatly admired in his youth, may have taught him to observe men and, above all, to copy nature both in the handling of plots and of souls. . . . But Fogazzaro was original because he took all his characters from life instead of creating them artificially. Even the most eccentric are painted from life. He is, moreover, essentially Italian. In my opinion he stands as a humorist, between Goldoni and Manzoni, just as he stands between the Venetian and Lombard worlds. But the century that lay between Goldoni and Fogazzaro had given the latter what DeSanctis has called "that divine melancholy which is the idealism of the poet of comedy," and which does not allow him to approach even the most grotesque personage without a complex and psychologically delicate sense of his humanity.

Tommaso Gallarati-Scotti. *The Life of Antonio Fogazzaro* (Hodder). 1922. pp. 58–9

Fogazzaro is a novelist of character rather than of plot. Some of his leading characters are of a fine and sustained nobility; others suffer from perpetual conflicts between their weaknesses and their idealisms. His major characters are surrounded by a whole world of minor figures, creations of his own mind, but drawn on the basis of the keenest observation, and, in many cases, with a delicious humor that serves to lighten the central seriousness, a humor expressed in description, in dialogue, and in cleverly contrived incident—a humor gayer and more energetic than that of Manzoni, something like that of Dickens, but truer and more restrained. . . . Throughout Fogazzaro's work there is evidence of his preoccupation with religious problems; the sounds of music are heard frequently; and elements of the environment reflect and deepen moods, and at times become virtually participants in the action.

Ernest Hatch Wilkins. *A History of Italian Literature* (Harvard). 1954. pp. 470–1

In what measure the scant importance given to the poetry of Fogazzaro by Italian criticism has been due and still is due to the subject-matter of his poems remains a very difficult point to assess. . . . Perhaps the comparison with the three great Italian poets who were his contemporaries, Carducci, Pascoli, D'Annunzio, will always prevent a sympathetic approach to a different kind of inspiration and to one mostly alien to Italian spirit and tradition . . . [even though] the affinity of Fogazzaro's poetic ideal with that of Dante has often been described. . . . He [admired] . . . Victor Hugo . . . Heine . . . Robert and Elizabeth Browning . . . [and] Novalis . . . and perhaps from long study and from instinctive sympathy with northern poetry came his unusual use of metre and his search for a form of language and expression different from the prevailing classical perfection of diction and metre. . . . Because of . . . deliberate simplicity, because of the great variety in metre and intonation, because of the careful avoidance of any classical or literary imitation, the poetry of Fogazzaro defies the usual canons generally applied to the verse of his country.

Olga D. Bickley. *EM*. 1958. v. 9, pp. 290–3

See *The Little World of the Past, The Patriot, The Politician, The Saint, The Sinner, The Woman* and *Leila* (novels).

FOURNIER, ALAIN-
See Alain-Fournier

FRANCE, ANATOLE (1844–1924)

If by Realism we mean Truth, which alone gives value to any study of human nature, we have in Anatole France a very dainty realist;— if by Romanticism we understand that unconscious tendency of the artist to elevate truth itself beyond the range of the familiar, and into the emotional realm of aspiration, then Anatole France is at times a romantic. And, nevertheless, as a literary figure he stands alone; neither by his distinctly Parisian refinement of method, nor yet by any definite characteristic of style, can he be successfully attached to any special group of writers. . . . The charm of his art, at once so impersonal and sympathetic, is wholly his own.

> Lafcadio Hearn. Introduction to *The Crime of Sylvestre Bonnard* (Parke, Austin, and Lipscomb).
> 1890. pp. v–vi

The belief in the universal flux of things, in the absence of any ascertainable moral or intellectual order in the world, has represented the conviction of some of the serenest and finest of human intelligences. . . . M. France has put it before us once more with unrivalled clearness and beauty of expression, and with a modernity of touch that makes it move in our minds as an actual form of our own experience. The sheet lightning of his quiet irony illuminates it; and the glow of his pity suffuses it with an irresistibly attractive humanity. To have rendered thus perfectly, with so fine and conscientious an art, his personal vision of life, gives him his supreme claim on our admiration, on our intelligent sympathy.

> Algar Thorold. *Six Masters of Disillusion* (Constable).
> 1909. p. 146

Anatole France is the only living satirist. He has actually no rivals. . . . Anatole France alone upholds the ancient tradition of Voltaire, of Defoe and Swift. His satire is always effective because it is always light, always pointed and always smiling. He has none of the bitterness of Swift and therefore he is the truer cynic, for true cynicism is not fierce; it is always genial. He never labors a point; he states, presents the contrasts between, for instance, what a rich man may do as opposed to a poor one, and then passes on, laughing, Pan-like, dancing, with perhaps a tear or two in his laughter.

W. L. George. *Anatole France* (Holt). 1915. pp. 27–8

He typifies the excessive individualism of this age of democracy. Even in his conservative days he is ardently personal: he cannot keep self out of his creation. Not merely subjective, like the romanticist, from whom he differs by a greater intellectual reserve, he carries subjectivity into the things of the intellect, and to justify the dilettantism of his attitude, exalts it finally into a philosophy. Hence his skepticism, eager to show the relativity of other men's realities, rising under attack to a devotion toward philosophic nihilism which is a devotion to his own form of dialectic.

Lewis Piaget Shanks. *Anatole France* (Open Court). 1919. pp. 222–3

There is something disquieting in the seductive charm of his style. This "master of literary voluptuousness," as French critics agree in calling him, some encomiastically, some deprecatingly, lacks the force and manly vigor which would redeem a wondrously lovely grace of movement, diverse and undulating, with all the elegant sorcery of exquisite femininity, melodiously adorned with suggestive words and phrases of dubious connotation; lithe, sinuous, caressing, sensual; not infrequently rousing at the same time delight and alarmed suspicion; indescribably enticing always.

Barry Cerf. *Anatole France* (Dial). 1926. pp. 263–4

His habits, his thoughts, his opinions, and the politics he ultimately adopted, composed a complex harmony which amazed and embarrassed certain people. . . . Let us, on the contrary, admire this great capacity for contrast. Let us look with enquiring minds at this idle nature, this infinite reader engaged in the production of a vast body of work; this pleasure-loving temperament chaining itself to the tedium of a regular task; this hesitating mind groping its way through life, raising itself by movements of indecision from initial modesty to a great height; this stammerer transformed into the violent defender of the boldest thoughts; this man of wit, and of a wit so finely shaded, growing accustomed to simplicity in fame, and emitting the most crudely colored opinions; this archetype of moderation and temperance taking sides with such great and astonishing vigor in the dissensions of his time; this delicate amateur taking his place as the friend of the masses, and, what is more, doing so sincerely and with all his heart.

Paul Valéry. *Dial.* Nov., 1927. pp. 366–7

What France really best expressed was that intellectual-psychological atmosphere for which Bernard Shaw has found the best name, the "Heartbreak House" of the well-to-do cultivated people of the later phases of the capitalist era. Anatole France, who had so much to say about the pleasures of epicureanism, told one of his friends in his old age that he had never known a happy day; and what he really conveys most successfully is the experience of emotional frustration, intellectual disillusion—the abyss of neurotic despair which yawns under the tight-ropes and trapezes of a highly developed sensibility.

Edmund Wilson. NR. Sept. 7, 1932. p. 92

He wrote his books on the top of other books, that his might share in the quality of theirs; he found that by "scribbling upon the margins of books," he could restore for us some of the gentler existences out of which these other books had risen. Like an archeologist, he found a calm Atlantis, which had heaved a huge geologic sigh and sunk slowly to the bottom of the sea, where it now lay, its temples still standing, its marbles posturing, and mournful fishes peering upon these dead splendors. It is not the most "usable" attitude for today—neither is it an attitude which could be dismissed from the mind without great loss.

Kenneth Burke. NR. Dec. 7, 1932. p. 104

Perhaps France's preoccupation with the smaller units of style—the word, the phrase, the brief sentence—is as characteristic as his piecemeal way of dealing with ideas. In diction as in thought, he belongs less to the race of inventors, of profound organizers, than to that of skilled assorters. His impressions and reactions are broken up *"en mille riens"* without close co-ordination. Similarly, the *"style coupé"* often dispenses with connectives and transitions, yet without notable loss of smoothness.

Edwin Preston Dargan. Anatole France (Oxford).
1937. p. 589

Anatole France wore his laurel with a difference. Now that thirteen years have heaped a literature upon his grave, his immortality is more precarious than ever. The note of eulogy has been continually jangled by polemic and scandal. Even before his death critics and younger writers were beginning to tire of *bouquiniste* scholarship and originality that always took the form of *pastiche,* of anticlerical hagiography and skepticism that prompted a panegyric on de Lesseps. Irony and pity, when due to a lack of critical principle and an emotional instability, are reducible to dilettantism and sentimentality. What once passed for paganism looks today like a discrete blend of pedantry and pornography.

Harry Levin. *Nation.* July 10, 1937. p. 52

In spite of its great richness, France's treatment of the intellectual hero is lacking in power and scope. Partly this may be true due to certain chronic weaknesses of his art: surface grace, absence of a unifying vision, overdoses of erudite allusions, coquettish stylistic effects. France flirts with the *cultured* reader: he seeks to conquer him through charm. . . . Perhaps because nothing appeared to him as quite authentic, he was also unprepared to believe fully in his own fictional creatures. . . . France's interventions are digressions: they suggest that his characters are for him a *pretext*. Abstract discussions—on God, democracy, justice, miracles, the writing of history or the power of lies—interest him far more than individual destinies.

Victor Brombert. *The Intellectual Hero* (Lippincott).
1961. pp. 91–2

Despite his artifice, his epicureanism, his air of ripeness and skepticism, he is at heart an adolescent writer. His world . . . is the world of desire and illusion. His way is the primrose path of nostalgia, sensual pessimism and self-love. The famous irony is the artful weapon of the bookish man who never grows up, who tastes life and history. They are a gourmet's dish, sweetened by the senses, salted by horror. He observes, but does not experience; and, beginning as a dreamer, a writer of historical pastiche, a faun-like comedian of the museum and the libraries, he ends in moral nihilism. One is reminded of his own phrases about Van Dongen's portrait in his old age: "It makes me look like a Camembert that is running."

V. S. Pritchett. *The Living Novel and Later Appreciations*
(Random). 1964. pp. 359–60

See *The Crime of Sylvestre Bonnard* and *Penguin Island* (novels).

GADDA, CARLO EMILIO (1893–   )

Gadda's phonetic tricks, his mixture of barbaric Latin, sophisticated and dialectical Italian, his misspelling of foreign words, all sorts of technical devices are the despair of his translators and the delight of a limited circle of devotees. These things give a strong flavor of mannerism to all his work. He rejects, nevertheless, any reproach of artificiality and argues that the grotesque and bizarre are common traits of nature and history. . . . Gadda's followers admire his subtle art, his satirical impact, his fantasy. Those who believe that the use of regional brogue and dialects would give a new dimension to Italian neo-realism, hail him as their master. But he still remains a writer for the élite, and a slight aura of snobbism surrounds his name.

Marc Slonim. NYT. Sept. 29, 1963. p. 16

Every writer loves reality after his own fashion. There are those who can reproduce life in all its stupidity and vulgarity, without ever leaving their ivory tower, without departing by a hair's breadth from their attitude of knowledgeable uncommittedness. Writers like Gadda, on the other hand, in order to understand the vast *bêtise* we call life, this ridiculous world of barrow-boys, porters, landlords, petit bourgeois, policemen, prostitutes and pimps, have to allow it to grow inside themselves like some monstrous plant. The Berni-like burlesque that we sometimes find in Gadda, the sharp eye, the grossness, even the intentional vulgarity, the black comedy which pretends not to understand what it understands only too well, the ostentatious Lombardy practical jokes—all these, which might give offense to those of too "refined" sensibility, are really, in the last analysis, the way Gadda has chosen to educate himself in the love of the external world. . . . He has responded with the sardonic smile of the macaronic writer, the pretended philistine, to the insults, the mockery and the supidity of real life—yet he is still detached, enclosed in the sad obsessions of a psychological case. And he has succeeded in making a most extraordinarily acute awareness of reality his most noteworthy quality.

Pietro Citati. LMg. Oct., 1963. pp. 71–2

His most famous book, *Quer pasticciaccio brutto de via Merulana*, [is] a teeming canvas of Roman life, many of whose characters speak the city's expressive, but not always elegant dialect. . . . The book [is] a pastiche—as its title implies—of languages and dialects that has been compared to the work of Joyce. . . . Joyce and Gadda have this in common: a fascination with language, and a revolutionary attitude towards the use of language in fiction. . . . But *Il pasticciaccio* is not a dialect novel. Gadda uses the language of his characters to help portray them . . . , but also uses Neapolitan, Milanese, and occasional French, Latin, Greek, and Spanish expressions. . . . He exploits all the levels of Italian, spoken and written. . . . And at the same time, Gadda's vast erudition, in such disparate and recondite fields as philosophy, physics, psychology, and engineering is frequently evident—all of this is fused into a single, difficult, rich, yet flowing style.

> William Weaver. Introduction to *That Awful Mess on Via Merulana* (Braziller). 1965. pp. v, viii–ix

The title in Italian—*Quer pasticciaccio brutto de via Merulana*—might very well be exceptionally wry and intelligent, making use of the language of the Roman streets to suggest the existence of classes, of lives distorted and cramped, of the black delight in evil and disorder that human nature is prone to. . . . The language moves from high-euphuistic Latino-rhetoric through philosophico-theological jargon and gaudy Italian journalese, through . . . parodies, through a large number of dialects. . . . We are presented with a murder, the murder being that of the only character who is not outrageously comic, a woman of "classical features." I would think that she represents antique virtue—the virtue, beauty and greatness that have departed from the Peninsula—wouldn't you? Classical Virtue has her throat cut; proper in life, she is found murdered on the floor, with her skirt thrown up around her torso, and her drawers, of mid-thigh length, exposed. There is fatuity here. . . . Gadda may have been mocking all symbolic novels while writing one. Maybe he loathes Antique Virtue. . . . Gadda is self-indulgent, bitter, ironic, malicious, hateful, shrill, despairing and human, so that even while boring us he and his book achieve a species of luminescence—perhaps phosphorescence. Behind the language and the self-conscious posturing, the man is in agony. The Italian male, as so often in life, finds adult life and defeat insupportable.

> Harold Brodkey. *NYT*. Aug. 29, 1965. p. 5

One of the frightening events of our time is the emergence of the anti-hero and the anti-novel. And how about the anti-epic? I mean the poetic novel that depicts, out of thousandfold detail, not the birth of a nation but its fall. Carlo Emilio Gadda's *That Awful Mess on Via Merulana* (which Italians know as *Il pasticciaccio,* or "The Pastiche") is an anti-epic. . . . Superficially "The Pastiche" is a kind of detective story. . . . [The Detective], in his futile attempt to find out who done it, is of course Gadda vainly seeking the sources of Fascism. They both reach the same conclusion: that you can never trace a momentous event to any single cause. . . . Fascism—far from being solely the work of "Lantern Jaw"—was a kind of stench, or poisonous distillation, which dripped from a chemical compound so long in forming and so complex that no one would ever have predicted what it would lead to.

Warrington Winters. *SR*. Sept. 4, 1965. p. 25

Gadda's major work, *That Awful Mess on Via Merulana,* brings Italian fiction into the broad tradition of European literature by adding un-dreamed-of dimensions to the novel of local color and dialect that has been the richest medium of Italian realism since Verga. Indeed, as Michel Butor has remarked, it shatters this medium, inflating its rich-ness beyond either speech or the representation of reality. *Il pasticciaccio* (as it's affectionately called) is highly inventive: an ornate, slightly rank, florid murder story, crammed with classical learning, word play, parody, games in myth, dialect, anti-Fascist broadsides, and the poetry of a police detective's slow ruminations on the life of Italy. Gadda's style is most frequently compared to that of Joyce, and properly so, for it seeks to include everything in an endlessly proliferating verbosity that assumes language to be everything. It blows naturalism into a world of words.

But Gadda's ambitions are quite different from those of Joyce, and much more limited. On the one hand, *Il pasticciaccio* is a simple psycho-logical novel. . . . On the other, it is a torrential Menippean satire, in which psychology is only the pretext, or better, the prose of its poetry. . . . Gadda is not a modernist: he is directly in the tradition of Apuleius, Rabelais, Sterne and Swift.

Stephen B. Koch. *NYHT*. Sept. 5, 1965. p. 4

It is precisely this fluidity of language, this inexhaustible verbal sap that constitutes, ultimately, the gist of Gadda's book [*That Awful Mess on Via Merulana*], the juice or pith that makes his novel, perhaps, a scandal to the gentiles of art, and places it in a lineage, a descent not necessarily associated with art at all, but with an impulse located in the novel nowadays because that is the name we give our dominant literary form. . . . It is the impulse of process, the shaping of experience by a tone of voice, the definition of which is undertaken in the course of "endless" works. That gigantic and obsessive murmur which some-times rises out of literature (and perhaps justifies it), from Amiel to

Gertrude Stein, is again what we hear when we read Gadda—the sound of our own survival, the myth of our human continuity in a voice, "weaving an endless sentence," refusing to let go, to release existence until it has been recuperated by the only means in our power: the word. We hear, in short, the sound of ourselves when we seek to endure.

Richard Howard. *Nation.* Nov. 1, 1965. p. 307

Carlo Emilio Gadda's mess, piled up behind [the] messes [in *That Awful Mess on Via Merulana*], seems to be Mussolini in particular and human life in general. And his novel is a fine mess, indeed, though its impact at this moment (it was written in 1946) is somewhat lessened by the fact that the mess-novel has been with us for some time now, an extremely arty art-form which justifies itself by appealing to the natural messiness of life. . . . Gadda is a great word-boy, and [*Quer pasticciaccio brutto de via Merulana*] is a richly cunning pastiche or *olla podrida* of linguistic effects. Puns, allusions, dialects, jargons, parodies, and caricatures—perhaps not precisely God's plenty, but certainly the Italian thesaurus's. . . . Before boredom sets in, *That Awful Mess* has offered vigor, erudition and invention, some highly enjoyable set-pieces and good bawdy fun. And the author's assiduous cultivation of his private *bêtes noires* yields a fine menagerie of comic monsters. We are never far from Circe's sty. But *who* is Circe, or *what* is Circe? . . .[Most] probably, one is forced to conclude, it is human nature, all too fecund in its criminality, which turns us into swine.

D. J. Enright. *NYR.* Jan. 20, 1966. pp. 8, 10

See *That Awful Mess on Via Merulana* (novel).

GALDÓS, BENITO PÉREZ
See Pérez Galdós, Benito

GARCÍA LORCA, FEDERICO (1898–1936)

The poetry of García Lorca contains more that is truly popular than that of any of his Spanish contemporaries, but the high regard in which his work is held by a generation of poets whose poetry is preëminently intellectual is a testimony to his mastery of the pure form for which they strove. In García Lorca's case, the new poet of the people had long been the poet's poet. . . . He knew and appropriated the best of such widely different movements as surrealism and the neoclassicism of a Paul Valéry. . . . The bizarre metaphors of the one are often fused with the disciplined structure of the other; but one feels throughout the commanding presence of the poet's own individuality. Even here he showed himself the true son of the Spanish tradition. He would not break with it. Rather he sought to revive and enrich it.

William Berrien. *BA*. Spring, 1937. p. 160

Many of us may choose to regard him as a hero who died for the Republican cause, but I would rather regard him as a martyr who died because he had no cause; who, moving across the no-man's-land inhabited mainly by poets and cowards and angels, took a bullet from the side that had most guns and most murderers. . . . He is dead at the hands of a crude brute who looks upon the poem as the symptom of the paederast. . . . It is a symbolic event that tells us that the poet is the matador of the human against the creature that is not only fascism but also all principles of violence and physical domination.

George Barker. *LLT*. Oct., 1939. pp. 61–4

I begin to believe that "Blood Wedding" and "Yerma" did not spring from anything very profound and permanent in Lorca. In them he was searching, I feel, for elemental force and for passion, when his beauty lay in warmth and fantasy.

Ralph Bates. *NR*. April 24, 1944. p. 570

The impact of the mechanized civilization of New York drew from the poet the first expression of social protest. The poems he wrote during his visit are difficult, sometimes tortured, a torrent of strange figures which defy interpretation; but out of the whole there comes a denunciation of all he saw that was unjust, unnatural, mean, or vile. It is not just the cringing of a poet's soul in the presence of the ugly; it is a crying out against the degradation and defeat of human beings. . . .

There can remain no doubt that the Fascists knew what they were doing when they killed García Lorca. . . . His works could not fail to reflect his thoughts and to stir the people, who almost instinctively identified them with their cause—this in spite of the fact that he wrote much that they could but vaguely comprehend. The people were not wrong in seeing in the poet who sang of Spain without mentioning the name of Spain also a poet who sang of democracy without mentioning the word.

Helen E. Sackett. *SAQ*. Oct., 1948. pp. 484–90

Lorca's work is profoundly and revealingly Spanish and at the same time universally human. Through the shape and color of the Spanish landscape, through the earth-bound idioms, images, and emotions of the Spaniards, Federico García Lorca saw and expressed the suffering and joy, beauty and terror, love and death of mankind. . . .

Through the popular symbols of death and the loneliness of all creatures, transformed on his poetic plane, Lorca expressed the deepest human struggle such as it is fought in Spanish terms, as an anonymous myth and an individual reality. . . . The gypsies of his poems suffer from the cosmic loneliness of man.

Arturo Barea. *Lorca, the Poet and His People* (Harcourt). 1949. pp. vii, 86

Though Lorca kept aloof from partisanship with any group, his poems and plays, both during his lifetime and after his murder in August 1936 by anti-Republicans, found an audience among the unsophisticated, uneducated Spaniards who supported the Government against the symbols of feudal oppression. . . . Naturally, these poems which had deliberately re-worked folk elements could be easily recited and enjoyed by the general public. . . . Far more provocative, however, was the brilliant light which Lorca's poetry cast upon the desires and torments of the ordinary Spaniard, placing them in an emotional and realistic setting which raised them from the unconscious to a conscious level, from the particular to the general, so that the full import of those social pressures which resisted the individual's striving for self-realization was clarified with devastating impact, . . . acquainting the reader with the destructiveness of tradition and psychological confusion.

Brom Weber. *SwR.* Autumn, 1950. pp. 728–30

The writers Lorca most resembles are the Portuguese, Gil Vicente and the Spaniard, Lope de Vega. . . . In all three of them the lyric goes hand in hand with the dramatic, the traditional with the modern, the tragic with the comic, the fantastic with the realistic, the local with the universal; and although each of them is intensely personal, all manage to convey in their work what we feel is the essence of that which in Spanish.

Lorca may, then, be regarded as the most purely and essentially Spanish writer of our day and, consequently, the one hardest to translate and understand. Spanish through and through, his art resides in the words and not in the ideas; in the music, the gesture, the physical sensations and the irrational emotions, in a play of forms, rhythms and images which conceal beneath them the mystery of life and death. It demands an effort on our part to understand him as he was, and to see his work as a poetic creation of pure art in which we find anew, stripped of history, of picturesque romanticism and genre realism, a clear, profound vision of the eternal Spain.

Federico de Onís in *Writers of Our Years,* ed. by
A. M. Fiskin (Denver). 1950. p. 35

Lorca is a modern poet: his sensibility responds to all the tensions of contemporary ways of life; his language illuminates the paths of poetry with a new brilliance. But . . . he cannot be understood in his entirety unless we see him set in that tradition of the "culture of death" that he inherited from great artists of his native land, and that he has passed on to us, made richer with the proud gift of his poetic work.

Pedro Salinas. *HR.* Fall, 1951. p. 12

There has always seemed to be a doubt in the minds of Spaniards that their native meters were subtle enough, flexible enough to bear modern stresses. But Lorca, aided by the light of twentieth century thought, discovered in the old forms the very essence of today. Reality, immediacy; by the vividness of the image invoking the mind to start awake. This peculiarly modern mechanic Lorca found ready to his hand. He took up the old tradition, and in a more congenial age worked with it, as the others had not been able to do, until he forced it—without borrowing—to carry on as it had come to him, intact through the ages, warm, unencumbered by draperies of imitative derivation—the world again under our eyes.

William Carlos Williams. *Selected Essays* (Random).
1954. p. 226

Federico García Lorca is the most powerful of modern Spanish poets, and his *Gypsy Ballads (Romancero Gitano)* his most characteristic work. In these eighteen poems, with their bare, short lines, their striking images, and their colorful, changing landscape, there is Spain herself, there is a synthesis of that life, full of violence, beauty and sorrow, of passion and gloom, which only Cervantes pictured to the full. Through the Spanish gypsy, often more Spanish than the Spanish themselves, García Lorca describes, now with precise detail, again with sensuous images dazzling in their impact, the existence of the hunted outcasts of Spain, in whom the soul of the land bleeds and dies and renews itself, proud but flexible, rising in its bitter humor and ancient endurance against the oppression and cruelty of centuries.

L. R. Lind. Introduction to *The Gypsy Ballads of
García Lorca* (Indiana). 1954. p. 11

In a certain sense it can be said that Lorca was more surrealist than the surrealists. One of the differences is that Lorca never could have accepted the materialist creed and pure rational irrationality of official surrealism. He was a believer in the spirit and in human emotions, with deep, perhaps submerged, religious preoccupations. That fact and a sort of superconsciousness, rather than subconsciousness, explain the surprising unity of . . . all Lorca's work.

Angel del Rio. *NWW*. Oct., 1955. p. 186

Federico García Lorca wrote poetic drama, very much as Yeats and Eliot have taught us to understand it, yet his plays are neither cultish nor middlebrow-ersatz: they are theatre-poetry which lives naturally on the modern stage. . . . [He] achieves much that Yeats and Eliot sought with only partial success. They were both lyric poets and dramatists second; and both tended to approach poetic drama as though it were an over-grown type of lyric. . . . Lorca also was a lyric poet before he succeeded on the stage, and his lyric verse shows, like that of Yeats and Eliot, the all pervasive *symboliste* influence. He is an authentic poet, even by the exigent standards of our masters. But from the first he drew also upon the resources of the old and popular Spanish tradition of balladry. . . . And the ballad is a far more promising clue to drama than the "pure" *symboliste* lyric, precisely because it typically suggests a story. . . . The *symboliste* lyric, on the other hand, owes its purity to its source in the single feeling of the isolated poet.

Francis Fergusson. *KR*. Summer, 1955. pp. 337–43

It is true that the struggle between poetry and prose in his plays does not always lead to satisfaction, but it is a conflict which all poets have to solve for themselves in the theatre. Their fusion can only be arrived at by experiment. In these experiments Lorca was tempted by other methods, such as surrealism, which he finally discarded, and rightly so, in order to concentrate on his pure folk tragedies. For it is by these that Lorca is remembered. In them he endeavoured to introduce into the Spanish theatre the folk speech, lyricism and poetic imagination while at the same time to reduce life to an outline or skeleton of bare essentials. He wished to replace the bourgeois realism of the commercial theatre of his day, which was not specifically Spanish, with a return to the beauty of the Spanish language as spoken by the peasants who retained its purity.

Frederick Lumley. *Trends in Twentieth Century Drama*
(Essential Books). 1956. p. 105

That Lorca, one of the most narrowly regional poets of modern times, should be at the same time one of the most universally appreciated among his contemporaries, is just one more of those delightful little paradoxes which make bearable the present stereotyping, dehumanization, unification, and bureaucratic centralization of human life. This universal appreciation is the mild, humble, and corrective protest of healthy human nature against the colossus-fetishism and political elephantiasis of the herd instinct which characterizes our time. It is a protest against the sacrifice of all real and immediate values to those ridiculous Utopian abstractions invented to glut that helpless and voracious credulity which is the inevitable substitute for lost faith.

It is precisely because Lorca has roots in his native soil that he can teach us what we need in spite of having no "message"; and animate other European literatures and languages, in spite of the fact that he was ignorant of them.

Roy Campbell. *Lorca: An Appreciation of His Poetry*
(Yale). 1959. pp. 4–5

Like many another *vanguardista* of the twenties, Lorca deplored the unimaginative and hackneyed "realistic" drama that monopolized the commercial stage of those times. Through his plays he sought to reintroduce poetry and fantasy onto the Spanish stage, drawing on all the resources and potentialities of the theater to which both tradition and modernity, as well as his own poetic imagination, could lead him. At the beginning Lorca is no doubt "guilty" of a lack of poetic restraint, perhaps inevitably so, since he was a young poet trying an early hand at the drama. An over-all view of his major plays shows a steady progression from drama marked by lyrical and theatrical exuberance toward a taut, disciplined integration of poetic elements with dramatic matter. There is little doubt that Lorca consciously and with all deliberateness sought to achieve such stylistic objectivity and austerity.

Sumner Greenfield. *MR*. Summer, 1960. p. 752

Lorca's *"Llanto"* [*por Ignacio Sanchez Mejias*] is . . . an instance of the coalescence of past and present. Emerging from the rich context of centuries of elegiac verse, it speaks also in a contemporary mode which we apprehend as our own. In such a synthesis of the traditional and the actual we find the source of much of *"Llanto's"* depth and grandeur. . . . Ignacio dies in a modern, chaotic, nightmarish world, far removed from the classical pastoral setting. . . . Yet after an initial moment of surprise at the modern circumstance, I think that even an elegist like Milton would have understood what Lorca was about: . . . that in bewailing the victory of the bull over the man, he was rising up against the power that would permit such an unjust victory; . . . he was indicting a creation in which the good and the beautiful were viciously mutilated. Lorca is complaining, as the elegist has always complained, that this death was wrong, without reason, without purpose.

Calvin Cannon. HspR. July, 1963. pp. 229–31

Thematically, García Lorca's theatre revolves on a single axis: *the preservation of Honor leads to the frustration of love, hence, of life itself; this frustration, in turn, becomes a despair which leads to Death.* This is always the major theme, the premise which serves as a point of departure for many variations. Starting there, he develops richly colored situations and populates them with strong central characters, personages who live passionate lives whether their emotions find expression or are repressed. However they react, they are primarily pawns of Fate, for it is this dark force which governs the entire premise. The theme, with Fate as its primary cause, represents the nucleus of Lorca's drama.

Robert Lima. The Theatre of García Lorca
(Las Americas). 1963. p. 291

Lorca's heroines are modern versions of the warm matriarchal type found in all Spanish literature. They are magnetic fields inevitably drawing tragedy to themselves from a too ardent faith in the right of their natural instincts. Again, they are islands which the world cannot touch with its soiled and makeshift logic. Because their humanity is such an extremely procreative answer to life, they threaten to disrupt the mere man-made machinery of social law, which is, finally, a substitution for life. They are the affirmation to the question of the ultimate which man, with the beam of social exigency in his eye, is always begging. When they lose the sense of integration in life which is necessary to them, the world trembles and comes apart. Thus it is as martyrs of frustrated love, from the heroine of *"Mariana Pineda,"* who dies on the gallows, to the suicide of the youngest daughter in *"La Casa de Bernarda Alba,"* that Lorca's women uphold the insistent theme of his tragedies.

Edwin Honig. García Lorca (New Directions). 1963.
pp. 152–3

See *Selected Poems, Gypsy Ballads,* and *Poet in New York* (poetry); also *Five Plays* and *Three Tragedies.*

GARD, ROGER MARTIN DU
See Martin du Gard, Roger

GARY, ROMAIN (1914–   )

Despite the sordid substance of *The Company of Men,* it is a powerful work of bitter satire and first-rate humor. Gary is a social critic who knows how to write. The French blame the blackness of his vision on the fact that he was born in the land of Dostoevsky. However this may be, his novel, as a picture of life in newly liberated Europe, should take its rightful place beside the Italian film "Shoeshine".

Justin O'Brien. NYT. April 16, 1950. p. 5

He has been a restless traveler with a baggage of special ideas, as his new novel shows. Called *Les Racines du Ciel,* meaning those "roots of heaven" that spring from earth "in the need for justice, liberty, and love," its real concern is modern man's rapid destruction of the grandiose elements of his universal past—Nature's wild spaces and her vast remaining beasts. . . . It is a long, rich, chaotic novel of intelligent philosophical ideas, oddly jungle-thick in presentation, that could bear thinning out. It is also a novel that deals importantly with the changes going on between white races and dark all over the earth.

Genêt. NY. Dec. 15, 1956. pp. 174–5

The Roots of Heaven is often involved in its sentence structure, unshapely in construction, only half credible in its characterization. Yet it achieves dramatic power. The hero imposes himself less vividly upon the reader than the secondary characters and the spendid descriptions of equatorial scenery. The message of the novel is obvious in its allegorical form. *Moby Dick* and other allegories such as Camus' *The Plague* are called to mind. Good and evil are not clearly differentiated as in a Sunday-school story. But . . . Gary . . . asserts here his impassioned plea for the salvation of a world threatened by cruelty and injustice, of which man is a victim or an accomplice.

Henri Peyre. SR. Feb. 1, 1958. p. 16

Romain Gary's new . . . novel, *Lady L.,* is a delightful display of high spirits and wit which forms an entertaining contrast with his formidably successful best-seller, *The Roots of Heaven,* a book that was as wholly serious as this one is lighthearted, as long-winded as this one is sharp and concise, and as turgid in style as this one is lucid and direct. . . . *Lady L.* can be read as an elaborate practical joke by anyone who wishes to do so, but there is more to it than that, and it should be remembered that M. Gary is often at his intelligent and penetrating best when he appears to be writing farce as if he hadn't a care in the world.

Anthony West. NY. April 4, 1959. pp. 161–2

As writers go, Romain Gary is not a well-mannered pygmy, but a large splendid fellow whose headlong surge forms an important part of his talent. He ignores all those exquisite little frustrations whose vivisection has become novelistically fashionable. Instead his imagination feeds on ideals, Victor Hugo-sized ones, and by some Gallic alchemy (there are secret interpolations of Pascal amid the Hugo thunder) he comes up, not with old rhetoric, but with new insights.

Frederic Morton. *NYT*. March 13, 1960. p. 4

Promise at Dawn is a deliberately picaresque autobiography. To some this may seem an offense against what is presumed to be historical veracity. Yet life being so often stranger than fiction, I incline to think that only a style in keeping with the mustache-twirling flourishes and languorous, heavy-lidded gestures of the Rudolf Valentino and Lilian Gish era could do justice to these extravagant interwar events and the marvelously extravagant woman who strides invincibly through them.

The one flaw in this book is an occasional weakness for baroque over-emphasis, particularly in the reiteration of the author's sense of solitude.

Curtis Cate. *NYT*. Oct. 15, 1961. p. 40

Too often in Mr. Gary's stories the idealistic hero seems attached by too short a fuse to too small a firecracker, so that the predictable little bang comes too soon. . . . Too often Mr. Gary labels his symbols so carefully that they cannot operate freely in their own multiple possibilities. . . . And too often these symbols awaken echoes—of Tennessee Williams's glass menagerie, of Kafka's cockroach, of Ionesco's rhinoceros, to name a few. Finally, the terrain is too often horizontal. Goodness knows we get around enough in these stories. . . . As a consequence we never remain in any one port long enough to take soundings. . . . Mr. Gary would rather juggle five oranges, never six, than examine—or permit anyone else to examine—his own inner dynamic.

Warrington Winters. *SR*. March 21, 1964. p. 50

See *The Company of Men, A European Education, Lady L., The Roots of Heaven,* and *The Talent Scout* (novels); also *Promise at Dawn* (memoirs).

GASCAR, PIERRE (1916–   )

It is a world [in *Beasts and Men*] which Kafka would have understood, in which violence distorts the usual into strange, threatening, and im-probable shapes. Yet the author's powers of description and his own conviction persuade the reader that this is indeed the truth. . . . The reader must work through the dark symbolism, struggling to reach his meaning, horrified by his brutal view of the world and of Fate, unrelieved by gaiety or humour. Nevertheless, for all its unmitigated bitterness, this is a book of stature by a writer of very considerable power.

Joseph F. McCrindle. *NYHT*. July 15, 1956. p. 4

Mr. Gascar writes brilliantly, balancing details which suggest, in their precision and plausibility, literal reporting, with images and metaphors that have the unexpected, shocking rightness of poetry. . . . As Mr. Gascar develops his sidelights and subplots, new meanings keep appearing like facets of an irregular crystal, and the reader must decide for himself which, if any, is to be taken as final. One thing is decidedly clear, however, in all these fine, grim stories. The force behind them is not murky neurotic sensibility, but indomitable clearheadedness.

Phoebe Adams. *At*. Aug., 1956. p. 85

It would seem that Aymé, in reducing the entire human species to a particularly ferocious category of the animal kingdom, had carried the symbol as far as it would go. But Pierre Gascar, one of the best of the younger novelists, has used it in an entirely different kind of way. His *Les Bêtes* (*Beasts and Men*) is a book of short stories in each of which the animals, as pitiful as man himself, escape from man's control with disastrous results for man as well as for the animals. The revolt of the animals, somehow concerned with an obscure carnal part of ourselves, no doubt expresses a deep-lying anxiety. The book contains a plea for a control that would save both animal and man so much terror and blind pain.

Germaine Brée and Margaret Guiton. *An Age of Fiction* (Rutgers). 1957. p. 236

With *Les Bêtes* it is the world of Kafka born anew; strange, somber, mysterious, irrational, eternally menacing. The animals, swarming every-where, quail helplessly before the onslaughts of their human tormentors, who, in their turn, fail not only to breach the curtain of incomprehension isolating the species but also that which segregates them from their fellow creatures. And in the three most powerful stories, those directly embraced within the study, a Kafkaesque dream-like haze envelopes the impotent animals and anguished humans, overlying the world of reality and lending an air of timelessness to their tragic situation.

Chester W. Obuchowski. *FR*. Feb., 1961. pp. 327–8

Gascar has gradually achieved, in the administration of his dialectical metaphor, a structure that on the level of each work offers a perfect representation of the relations between accident and necessity, chaos and sense, which obsess him. This structure is one of reversion inscribed in the dimension of time. Like a snake swallowing its tail, the later novels at their end devour their own beginnings, so that their action is forced into an arena annulled, canceled out by the very process of the book. We get a kind of false time, outside of real life, an experimental interval in which the "meaning" happens.

Richard Howard. *Nation.* April 20, 1964. p. 401

Lambs of Fire . . . exhibits its cinematic possibilities with some insistence; like Graham Greene, Pierre Gascar seems to write with more than one eye on the screen. This, very possibly, accounts for the book's weaknesses as a novel, which might be summed up as a certain woodenness in the action and a degree of mindlessness in the supposed intellectual content. If *Lambs of Fire* were simply a thriller, there would be no great problem in assessing it, but like Greene's entertainments, it obviously aims to be more than just that. It ought to be a political thriller, but it has turned out as a political thriller minus the politics.

Bernard Bergonzi. *NYR.* March 25, 1965. p. 14

See *The Coral Barrier, The Fugitive,* and *The Seed* (novels); also *Beasts and Men* and *Women and the Sun* (short stories).

GENET, JEAN (1910–   )

Genet's great importance in the theatre is his theatricality. He does not "use" the theatre to imitate the externals of our world; he shows us that our world is as false as grease-paint itself, and that therefore the theatre can be the perfect mirror held up to the *danse macabre* which is life as Genet sees it. In other words, Genet's theatre at its best, abstract, stylised, deliberately stagy, comes closer to penetrating reality than the illusionist theatre ever did. In "The Balcony" and, to a lesser extent, in "The Maids", Genet gives back to the theatre a vital quality which it has not had since the religious drama of the Middle Ages. He gives back the quality of ritual, of ceremony. He does not do this externally, as some twentieth-century verse drama has attempted to do, but by putting on the stage the very ceremonies, be they sexual or religious, that he sees being performed in real life.

Peter Zadek. *NSN.* May 4, 1957. p. 568

Genet, as Norman Mailer said of the beatniks, is himself a "white Negro." He was, after all, a condemned but reprieved criminal and a well-known pederast; hence he writes as though he felt himself, by some trick of nature as irreversible as the colour of his skin, wholly outside society. So he piles blasphemy on blasphemy, contradiction on contradiction, in the hope of reducing the whole infuriating order of things to rubble. It is the theatre of nihilism which relies for its effect not on any depth of implication but on some stylish clowning at the very edge of sense, on the author's occasionally magnificent gift of the gab and on odd moments of sometimes surprisingly mannered wit.

A. Alvarez. NSN. Nov. 21, 1959. p. 706

Most men are able to play some kind of role in society. By feeling thus integrated with a social group, they justify their existence. Jean Genet is concerned in his two plays, as well as in all of his books, with the type of man who is alienated from society. This man has been given a role outside of society and accepts it. He can discover no justification for it. Sartre can easily find in the writing of Genet examples of a gratuitous and absurd existence. . . . But the characters in Genet know what they are doing. They know that they are counterfeiting society. They know that the actions that they invent will not justify their existence. So in reality they are always playing their own alienated selves. We are therefore always watching simultaneously two actions in the plays of Genet: the invented actions of the characters playing at being something they are not, and the fatal drama of alienation.

Wallace Fowlie. Dionysius in Paris (Meridian). 1960.
pp. 221–2

There may be . . . different interpretations of Genet's plays according to the spectator's tastes and interests. This is particularly true of "The Masks" and "The Balcony." In its meaning "The Blacks" is simpler than either of these. My own view—and it is a point I should like to emphasize—is that for all the anarchy and personal stress of Genet's dramatic work it is social and revolutionary. . . .Genet, poet and criminal, is a scourge. In the end his destructiveness is salutary, an assassin of hypocrisy, a bomb dropped on mediocrity and complacency. The contemporary French exasperation—the savagery of which we tend to underestimate as we underestimate everything that threatens—is on its moral level a signal to the world for the need of a not-too-long-to-be-delayed self-transformation.

Harold Clurman. Nation. May 20, 1961. p. 448

The core is energy, of which power is the main observable phenomenon. . . . Perhaps there is here an analogy with modern physics, which today is saying that matter is not the combination of solid elements we have supposed it to be, but rather the manifestation of intricate systems of energy. . . . Perhaps the vast quantities of psychic energy set working in us by a Genet play are the result of his having shattered the "atoms" of our normal conscious life, letting loose an energy which is the product of our ideas multiplied by the square of some great and as yet unknown factor. If so, then our attitude to Genet is as ambiguous as our attitude toward the splitting of the atom itself. We are fascinated by the potential of the newly discovered energy, but we are terrified of the results of the fallout.

Tom F. Driver. *CC*. June 14, 1961. p. 745

With this play, *"Les Nègres,"* in a manner theatrically even more persuasive than in *"Le Balcon,"* Genet gives us today a unique example of what it means to throw oneself into a scenic situation so as to draw out of it all that it can possibly give. What strikes one is the freedom and lightness of the invention, when compared to the obsessive heaviness, frightfully shut up in itself, of Genet the novelist. The theater, so it seems, is the means through which the damned Genet achieves redemption. Redemption from what? From the mire of the real, from the obsession of real experience, from the obstinacy of the outcast immured in his own biography, determined to nourish himself on the condemnation by the others, without being able to respond to this condemnation save by again and again proclaiming himself criminal and perverted, Segregated in Evil, and thus beyond the reach of the condemnation of the others. Yet by the simple act of stepping on the stage and entering the theatrical game, there appears the possibility of a judgment without condemnation—objective, since purely thought through—and, with this, imaginative freedom.

Nicola Chiaromonte. *PR*. Sept.-Nov., 1961. pp. 667–8

People say glibly that Genet lives outside society, but they do not really consider what that implies. They continue to regard him as a rebel (i.e., a kind of violent reformer) and assume that, since he has undertaken a social theme, he must be moved by some impulse of goodwill, some wish to instruct or improve. But there is not a trace of goodwill in Genet, and the question of whether society is to be integrated or segregated is to him a matter of perfect indifference. It would still be society, and he would still be outside it. . . . His plays are calculated attempts to dislodge society from its pinnings. A man alone against society does not perhaps strike one as a patently reasonable encounter; but the enemies of society almost invariably strike from within. Genet is outside, and it remains to be seen whether or not he has a lever long enough for his job.

Robert Hatch. *Horizon*. Nov., 1961. pp. 98–9

The theater of Jean Genet is a theater of revolt expressed in ceremonial terms in which death plays a predominant role, not only in the obvious use of death cells, murder, tombs, and catafalques, but in the annihilating effect of his game of mirrors in which reality is reflected back and forth until it almost reaches the point of invisibility. His revolt is not only against ordered society, it is again life itself, a life which refuses man the satisfactions of an absolute purity. Diving into the inverted world of dark and evil, Genet adopts an essentially religious attitude, attempting to reach the absolute through his inverted religion. His theater is a Mass celebrating that religion. . . . Like the Catholic Mass, like the Voodoo ceremonies of Haiti, and like the Dionysian celebrations that undoubtedly preceded the flowering of tragedy in Greece, this ritual theater speaks a language which has not been heard for many hundreds of years on the European stage.

Leonard Cabell Pronko. *Avant-Garde* (California).
1962. pp. 152–3

By holding a mirror to the world, Genet plays with it. What one reads in the mirror is inverted. Palaces and prisons, houses of parliament and brothels are not really the same, but from a special perspective, they may have something in common, something unsettlingly revelatory. One does not believe what Genet at times *appears* to be saying, perhaps he does not believe it either. But out of his dark journey to regions of human experience unknown to most of us, he has brought an angle of vision which he projects onto the stage with knowing magic. . . . For a few hours in the theatre, Genet distorts and shatters accepted perspectives, and in the sense of uncertainty he arouses may lie the seeds of a revaluation to last beyond the dimming of the lights.

Rima Drell Reck. *YFS*. Spring-Summer, 1962. p. 25

If he does not spring—with the clarity literary historians like and, not finding, create—from Pirandello, he does represent a way of getting around the problem of creating ritual among those whose beliefs are divergent, simply because he preserves what the Greeks had—a sense of theatre as ceremony—and abandons what we can no longer possess, a common outlook. Not for him is the desire to speak with his audience about consciously shared beliefs and tendencies. He will show us the semblance of such beliefs in order, by showing them to us in this indelicate overcoating, to bring us closer to his idea of reality. It is here that he advances beyond Pirandello, who, for the most part, is limited to presenting his views of the multiple levels and depths of reality by expressing this multiplicity in terms of the old and worn-out conflict between art and reality. Genet needs no such antediluvian argument, since he has moved from reality into art as the result of a process which has convinced him that art allows the only way of expressing the complexity of reality. His theatre rediscovers ritual and its power, but the faithful, expecting a ceremony of the guaranteed innocence to which they have become habituated, find more often than not, that they have been invited to assist at a Black Mass and, worse luck, that the blasphemy has been organized because it is, at the end of the day, what they wanted to assist at anyway.

Joseph H. McMahon. The Imagination of Jean Genet
(Yale). 1963. pp. 133–4

Genet is related to that family of people who are nowadays referred to by the barbaric name of *passéistes*. An accident riveted him to a childhood memory, and this memory became sacred. In his early childhood, a liturgical drama was performed, a drama of which he was the officiant: he knew paradise and lost it, he was a child and was driven from his childhood. No doubt this "break" is not easy to localize. It shifts back and forth, at the dictate of his moods and myths, between the ages of ten and fifteen. But that is unimportant. What matters is that it exists and that he believes in it. His life is divided into two heterogeneous parts: before and after the sacred drama. Indeed, it is not unusual for the memory to condense into a single mythical moment the contingencies and perpetual rebeginnings of an individual history. What matters is that Genet lives and continues to relive this period of his life as if it had lasted only an instant.

Jean-Paul Sartre. Saint Genet (Braziller). 1963. pp. 1–2

Genet's foremost achievement is his tone—an elegiac elegance, alternately muted, languorous, vituperative, tender, glamorous, bitchy, lush, mockingly feminine, "high camp," over-ripe, rigorous, exalted. It has no real counterpart in American writing to date. His scenes spur the imagination like vivid movie sequences. Dancing in the street at 5 A.M. or expounding on the methods of petty thievery or making love, Genet's characters observe themselves and others as slyly as actors in films.

Alex Szogyi. NYT. Sept. 29, 1963. p. 24

Our Lady of the Flowers may seem shamelessly immoral. It is not. It is shamelessly aesthetic. It declares itself as a deliberate sexual exercise of the imagination. The writer constitutes himself as a multiple sensory organ—seeing, tasting, touching, hearing, and smelling his characters. . . . Certainly *Our Lady of the Flowers* is in no sense a wicked book or a pornographic one. Though avowedly written out of physical pleasure, and exalting acts of terrible cruelty and the most perverse sexuality, it does not excite sexually, but spiritually. . . . I don't know whether to praise more the language of *Our Lady of the Flowers,* its daring method of construction, or the endless fertility of its ideas. Genet's reputation as one of the great stylists in the history of the French language cannot be tested by any translation. Yet, even in translation, the beauties of Genet's language are overwhelming. Genet writes a dense, intricate, highly literary prose—whose mixture of virility, intellectual refinement, and ornamental excess is something like a literary equivalent of the interiors of certain baroque churches in Munich. It is a rich prose, too rich for some tastes, perhaps. But only a handful of 20th-century writers, such as Kafka and Proust, have as important, as authoritative, as irrevocable a voice and style.

Susan Sontag. *NYHT*. Oct. 6, 1963. p. 21

No doubt most of Genet's characters are roles the author has played or wanted to play. And here we see the limits of his theater, which relies not on character as we normally understand it, but on the different roles played by persons who apart from their roles would be quite interchangeable. What distinguishes Claire from Solange in Genet's play, "The Maids"? Only the special roles they have decided to play. They even exchange names. And are not the Judge, the Bishop, and the General in "The Balcony" virtually the same? They differ only when they have put on their particular costumes and gotten up on stilts. Sometimes Genet writes as if other persons were real only when invested by him with some special authority. In fact, I think it must be very hard for him to think of anyone but himself as real.

Lionel Abel. *NYR*. Oct. 17, 1963. p. 8

As a post-Freudian writer, Genet begins at the post-Freudian beginning, not with a proud statement of principle but with a whimpered confession of fact, not with the grand program of the deliberate supermortal outlaw but with the abject confidences of the unlucky deviate, coward, outcast, and social worm. . . . And, unlike de Sade, for example, Genet begins his radical rebellion in every sense from below; he arrives at his faulted theories only laboriously, through acts. He did not *decide* to become a criminal and a pervert; he awoke one morning to find that he already *was* one, and felt obliged to explain himself. He is therefore qualified to articulate, as no genuine intellectual could, the rationale of that new and surprising phenomenon—the pure delinquent, the causeless rebel, the natural criminal who indulges in anti-social violence not out of principle or for material gain but for no discernible reason other than the sheer romance of crime. Genet has been described as a Cartesian philosopher meditating upon first principles and arriving at total negation. Nothing could be more absurd: Genet is less a modern methodologist in cerebral contact with the Devil than a conscious betrayer of the underworld, a stool pigeon, trying to render unto society an intelligible account of his Cosa Nostra, that dark underside of the social system that the French argot calls *"le Milieu."*

Renata Adler. *NY.* Nov. 9, 1963. p. 235

Genet is often accused of elevating sordidness, of making murder and sodomy glorious, of making evil seem good. In fact, he makes evil seem just like evil, and his elevation is the ridiculing of our elevation, of his own need (as one of us) to elevate. Through the smoke of his sorcery, the horror is always distinct. But through the "clear glass" of our reality, the ugly truth is enchanted away. Naturally Genet must be misunderstood and condemned. The last thing any of us want to see is the process of our hypocrisies, lies, and self-deceptions made clear to us. And our powers of self-delusion are so great that we can turn exposure into another kind of concealment. *Our Lady of the Flowers* has for example, given a new form, thus new life and justification, to a whole generation of homosexuals. Genet's savage caricatures are overlooked; his method is seized upon. What for him is burlesque, to pederasts becomes sentimental poetry. One does as one has always done, though consciously now: one decorates guilt. The naked truth of Genet's writing continues to be unbearable.

Alfred Chester. *Cmty.* April, 1964. pp. 66–7

See *Our Lady of the Flowers* (novel); also *The Balcony, The Blacks, The Maids and Deathwatch,* and *The Screens* (plays).

GHELDERODE, MICHEL DE (1898–1962)

This infernal theatre is akin, through its poetry, its audacity and its violence, to that of Marlowe, Beaumont and Fletcher, Tourneur or Ford. Like their work, his plays have a baroque flavor born of their excesses, their contrasts, their paroxysms, their love of the weird, the atrocious, their passion for movement and life. . . . Ghelderode really believes in the Devil, and even in devils like those of the Middle Ages. His familiarity with them explains how he can bring us that poetry which originates on the border between the real and the supernatural, and which, through incantation and voodoo, belongs in the realm of magic.

Suzanne Lilar. *TA*. Feb., 1951. pp. 34–5

The considerable work of Michel de Ghelderode is the result of thirty years of recreating the prodigious life of Flanders in the sixteenth century at the time of the Spanish conquest, the apogee of which was symbolized by the two great monarchs, Charles Quint and Philippe II. Ghelderode reveals to us the juxtaposition of two contradictory motivations which had related passions in common: one a religious ideal which pushed itself into a mysticism, and another a taste for revels, for conquest, war, and even more for popular celebrations.

Magdeleine E. Cluzel. *Glimpses of the Theatre and Dance* (Kamin). 1953. p. 15

The *esprit français* cannot abide Ghelderode's "unique" French language, Germanic in structure and nature, and Latin in expression. Ghelderode piles up words, throws adjectives on the straining syntax, burns up and suffocates traditional French in order to forge neologisms strong with archaic consonances. He is not satisfied with existing words—they are not vibrant enough to express the energy of life's forces.

Samuel Draper. *Com.* Oct. 28, 1960. p. 114

The surface characteristics of Ghelderode's universe are dazzling. Masqueraders, grotesque figures, living corpses, gluttonous and lustful men and women frantically move about in a décor of purple shadows, full of strong smells, and throw violent, foul, or mysterious phrases at each other in highly-colored language filled with Belgian idioms, archaisms, and shrieks. There is no rest in Ghelderode's theatre: the shock is permanent. Everything is pushed toward a paroxysm of language and spectacle —a flamboyant theatre, based on Flemish art, its culture, its puppets, its painters, its legends, its humor. . . . A joyful or macabre kermess, his theatre brings out the real meaning of the village fair.

Jacques Guicharnaud. *Modern French Theatre* (Yale). 1961. pp. 156–7

Dramatic conflict is the very essence of his plays, as it is his attitude toward life. This modern romantic with a medieval and Renaissance soul sees man in Manichean terms of dark and light, good and evil, flesh and spirit. "I have an angel on my shoulder and a devil in my pocket," he has said, and surely most of his theater bears witness to the conflict, or sometimes to the blending, of the diabolical and the mystical. As a Fleming, Ghelderode falls heir not only to the traditionally rowdy and worldly spirit of the Flemish as it is immortalized in those large and detailed festive scenes of Breughel, but he also inherits the medieval, tortured, metaphysical fantasies of a Bosch, and the mystical temperament of the Spanish invaders at the twilight of Spanish greatness.

> Leonard Cabell Pronko. *Avant-Garde* (California).
> 1962. pp. 165–6

Ghelderodian man has a sense of sin. He knows that he is guilty. He is punished because he is guilty. He is capable of every "truculence," in the Latin sense of the word, and of every extravagance of behavior because, no matter what he does, he is certain to lose. His horizon is bounded by death. Thus the sense of the tragic, in Ghelderode's case, comes from the omnipresence of death. There is a lot of dying in his plays, he declares, because there is a lot of dying in life. . . . He evolved, consequently, a kind of fetishism of death and brandished it, variously garbed, before the eyes of those eager to forget it. Western civilization, with its up-to-the-minute funeral rites and its painted and smiling corpses, has administered a tranquillizer to our feeling for death, and if ever Ghelderode set himself a mission, no doubt it was to remind men of how afraid they are—without overlooking the laugh that so often follows fear.

> Micheline Herz. *YFS*. Spring-Summer, 1962. p. 95

But what does the mask, which every character of Ghelderode's seems to be wearing, signify? It is meant neither to embellish mankind, as the impassioned words it utters might suggest, nor to execrate it, as the deeds it performs could imply. The mask is merely the face heightened out of its languid actuality into a potentiality truer than truth: it is the face of humanity exacerbated into becoming itself.

> John Simon. *TA*. Aug., 1962. p. 58

See *Seven Plays,* v. 1 and 2.

GIDE, ANDRÉ (1869–1951)

Gide is the dynamo, the generator of currents, the undefined power. He is a living Proteus: a new book, a new Gide, always delving into new depths "rich in new danger," and bringing forth new colors and new moving forms. . . . Gide is a man of extremes. . . . There is something hyperboreal about him, a mixture of St. Francis and Nietzsche. . . . But beyond this maelstrom of baffling contrasts we find in Gide a sincere precision in dissecting his strange existence and in interpreting the curious workings of our social and moral institutions.

Angel Flores. *Bkm*. Oct., 1927. p. 167

Gide's prose, as the most tangible part of his art, remains very close to real life. There is nothing theoretical or artificial about it, especially nothing conventional or ready-made. . . . The reader, watching the sentences being formed, feels that he is taking part in an exploration of reality. It is impossible after the first few words to guess even vaguely where the rest is going to lead, whether it will develop along a straight line, or turn sharply to right or left, rise or fall, or merely stop short before an obstacle. . . . There are circumlocutions, hesitations, advances and retreats, disappointments, and marvellous finds. Reading a sentence of Gide's is a miniature adventure.

Georges Lemaitre. *Four French Novelists* (Oxford).
1938. pp. 203–4

Throughout Gide's career freedom remains his *summum bonum* and the unifying principle in the unfolding of his personality and outlook. . . . In order to clear the soil for the growth of a new man within a reformed society, Gide advocates a pluralistic outlook in the realms of psychology, esthetics, religion, ethics and politics. . . . Always he is speaking for the silent, the oppressed and the disinherited, ignoring personal interests and comfort. In every realm of human activity he fights for self-reliance, heroic daring, and faith in a glorious future of man's own making which will result in a free, joyful and meaningful life.

Mischa Harry Fayer. *Gide, Freedom and Dostoevsky*
(Lane). 1946. pp. 142–5

Gide's early sense of his own peculiarity may be attributed to his being an only child, being rich and favored, being brought up a puritan. He came by it naturally. The significant thing is that he made this sense a lens through which he could see the role of the exception in science and progress; and, by contrast, the lag of culture attached to verities once eternal. His suffering from awareness of his oddity, perhaps from exaggeration of it, was compensated by optimism founded upon watching the stride of evolution from one exception to another; and feeling that man could step into the shoes of evolution to go where he would. There was nothing to hold him back but backwardness, the fear of going forward.

Van Meter Ames. *André Gide* (New Directions).
1947. pp. 250–1

His whole attitude is that of a man who tries very hard to appear placid and sedate while quivering with inner nervousness. All his gestures, even his voice and the scholarly elegance of his speech, seem to vibrate with disciplined agitation. Only some minor habits, such as frequent snuffling and his constant smoking of cigarettes, betray the tension behind this conscious and consistent self-control. There can be a sudden, disconcerting twinkle in his eyes, an uncanny flash like a warning signal from the volcanic depth of his being.

Klaus Mann. *André Gide* (Dennis Dobson). 1948. p. 22

Gide is not merely an artist, but the extreme case of the artist's sensiblity . . . one in whom sheer feeling—emotion, sensuousness, sensuality—the sense of the rich fluctuant inner world of feeling is overwhelmingly preponderant over the sense of solid eternal reality, over the plastic imagination which reflects and recreates that reality and finds satisfaction in it. As neither life with its inherent limitations, nor art—through Gide's own imaginative poverty—can satisfy this inordinate "libido sentiendi," this erotic urge, the resulting dissatisfaction itself becomes matter for doctrine, the thwarted creative instinct is analysed by an acute critical intelligence and the resulting ideas converted into an art and an ethic which is the ethic of art itself, the ethic of creativity, of individualism.

Lawrence Thomas. *André Gide* (Secker and Warburg). 1950. pp. 223–4

Gide's serious attempt, as "demoralizer," was to bring as much conflict, longing and self-delusion as possible to the level of consciousness; to get individuals and groups to explore their instinctive premises. . . . Gide's prolonged effort was to make men look into themselves, and recognize the motives for their acts and beliefs. The effort was psychiatric, maieutic. . . . As demoralizer, Gide encourages tolerance, a reasonable sympathy, suspended judgement, moral independence—all very real virtues of the critical spirit. He wants us to question our most cherished institutions, as well as our preconceptions. The only valuable demoralizer is the one who, like Gide, has much respect for the tradition he hopes to purify, and who has a strong natural impulse to order.

Albert J. Guerard. *André Gide* (Harvard). 1951. pp. 234–5

His own affection and sympathy went out to humble, pitiable and unsure beings, to those unfavoured by life. There were the beggar children of Normandy among whom he used to sit, reading them the fables of La Fontaine. They considered him their friend, running to meet him when they saw him in the distance striding along, his full pilgrim's cloak billowing in the wind. He never felt disgust though he had often, when he got home, to shake their vermin from his clothes. . . . The problem of our time as Gide sees it—the real crisis of our age—is how to reconcile the inalienable right of the individual to self-development, and the urgent necessity for the diminution of the misery of the masses.

Enid Starkie. *André Gide* (Bowes and Bowes). 1953. p. 57

We respond to Gide's luminous curiosity about himself, which is less melancholy than Montaigne's, indeed not melancholy at all, for it extends beyond what he is at a given moment to what he is becoming. He is, in fact, the trait which holds the secret of his extraordinary resilience and youthfulness. . . . Like Stendhal (another master of his) he makes us feel more intelligent, more honest than we are without him, for he brings more into the light of day. He conserves the bite and gaiety of the intelligence; all that he says, even when he is bewildered, despairing or tragic, is on the side of life, for (he conveys to us) the pride of life revives, the intellect lasts.

V. S. Pritchett. *Books in General* (Chatto and Windus).
1953. pp. 130–1

Of the many ways of saying a thing he invariably preferred the simplest. Reading Tacitus and likening him to Montesquieu, Gide contrasted the Roman's "wild austerity" with the often sugared grace of so many writers. . . . Such an attitude of mind naturally encouraged in him an innate tendency toward concentration. . . . He fled all devices of style, wanting his style to be so hidden as to be invisible. . . . On his best days . . . he wrote rapidly as if taking dictation. This seemed to him a sort of "artesian welling-up" after a long subconscious preparation. . . . Even more than the subtlety of the syntax, the deliberate archaism of the vocabulary, the new meaning conferred upon old, worn words, the unexpected juxtapositions of familiar expressions, the startlingly emphatic displacement of a word or phrase—the distinguishing mark of Gide's style is its personal rhythm.

Justin O'Brien. *Portrait of André Gide* (Knopf).
1953. pp. 347–9

"My function is to disturb," Gide was fond of saying. His influence has been profound and always a fecundating one, partly because Gide's own achievement seldom reached such greatness as would discourage emulation in others but also because he willingly sacrificed some of his potentialities to teaching others how to become more truly themselves. . . .

Gidisme, like *Beylisme* or *Renanisme,* is likely to remain as a typically French illustration of the influence of literature upon life. Like Voltaire, or rather like Goethe, to whom he prefers to be compared, Gide never summed up his very diverse gifts into one or several masterpieces that might survive independently of the author and of his life. The potentialities that one detects in him remain superior to his actual achievement. Perhaps in the preoccupation with his own problems and with the ethical and aesthetic solution he pursued for them, while it communicated a peculiar *Schaudern* to Gide's writing, prevented him from cutting the navel cord, as the French like to put it, and hampered the expansion of his inventive gifts.

Henri Peyre. *The Contemporary French Novel*
(Oxford). 1955. pp. 83–5

All [Gide's *récits*] are narratives of *disappointment.* All touch us, distress and irritate us; but intellectually they show us characters imprisoned in a formula, captives of a rule, a law, a convention or a habit, and victims of themselves. They have all *chosen* and found themselves prisoners of a choice—of a choice whose distinguishing mode is, respectively, harshness, narrowness, facility, or deception. The reader will recognize . . . the horror of choice, a sign in Gide of rigidity and ossification in an attitude, a sign of thralldom, of impoverishment, and no doubt of imbecility, of weakness, of deficiency, whether its source is the absolutism of desire, the exaltation of virtue, the seduction of the imagination, or the complacencies of conscience.

Jean Hytier. *André Gide* (Doubleday). 1962. p. 128

The success or failure of Gide's "classicism" in fiction, grafted on a symbolist conception of the hero, is not easily determined. Certainly, his characters, precisely because their motives are not plausibly rooted in the external world, lack a conviction which, despite all their subjectivism, the characters of James and Proust possess. Gide's experimentations in *Les Caves du Vatican* and *Les Faux-Monnayeurs* show his persistent attempts to come to terms with the external world and at the same time to develop forms from within a created experience that would be adequate to their tasks. But Gide's strength as a writer lies precisely in his weakness as a novelist, in the formulation of personal "inquietude" in terms of a controlling form that fashions experience into an act of aesthetic imagination.

Ralph Friedman. *The Lyrical Novel* (Princeton).
1963. p. 184

When he writes a book he is not trying to translate into its pages an inward disposition already present and perfected in him. The book is rather the cause of that disposition in that it gives what was only one of innumerable virtualities "a local habitation and a name." . . . The reality of his personality . . . is for Gide, essentially relative. At the very least none of its manifestations circumscribes and defines it; so that, where various versions of the self appear to contradict each other, none may be said to be the true version, by comparison with which the others are recognisably false.

G. W. Ireland. *Gide* (Oliver and Boyd). 1963. pp. 92, 95

Gide was peculiarly fitted for the role of moralist-poet because of his talent for dramatizing elements taken from his own personal conflicts. Although his stories are by no means simply "confessions," his characters, with all their ambiguities and tensions, were born from his own adventures, those moral situations he encountered as he shuttled Hermes fashion between the worlds of spirit and flesh. Gide is no spectator-novelist, no observer of "society." All his best work bears the unmistakable mark of having been written *from the inside.*

Joseph Gerard Brennan. *Three Philosophical Novelists* (Macmillan). 1964. p. 66
See *The Counterfeiters* and *Lafcadio's Adventures* (novels); also *The Journals.*

GINZBURG, NATALIA (1916–   )

The merit of this slender but penetrating study [*E'stato cosi*] . . . lies in the contrast between the impassioned core of the story and the simplicity of the telling which combines to advantage certain elements of Moravia's *indifferentismo* with the general sense of non-participation peculiar to the works of Camus.

Helene Cantarella. *BA*. Autumn, 1949. p. 408

The two novelettes that make up this little book [*The Road to the City*] are sicklied o'er with the Chekhovian cast of a sense of the futility of daily living. . . . Miss Ginzburg is artist enough to put her protagonists through their petty paces without attempting to enlist for them the reader's sympathy. The schoolteacher and the ignorant country girl are alike trapped in the vacuum of their empty little souls. Each, on an infinitesimal scale, is destined to torment and be tormented. Each, in her own bleak fashion, is committed to the fate inherent in her own stupidity.

Yet, perhaps because of his impatience, the American reader remains an incurable do-gooder. He feels that there must be something that will help Miss Ginzburg's heroines—a psychiatrist, a hobby, a bland diet, maybe Dorothy Dix. Certainly a sense of humor would fill some of the psychic void.

Ann F. Wolfe. *SR*. Sept. 17, 1949. pp. 37–8

[*A Light for Fools*] is written in those short sentences, loosely joined by a lot of casual commas, so beloved in Italian writing today. . . . The life it conjures, rather than describes—though youths may blow out their brains on park benches, and schoolgirls become pregnant, and people may be shot . . . —is, in fact, characterized by monotony, by the peculiar temperamental gloom, that domestic greyness and uneventfulness and general air that nothing will ever happen so pleasant for an Italian provincial fortnight, so terrible for a year. Inevitably, Chekhov comes to mind: not only because the long summer days, the endless agreeable but unrewarding chat, the whole provincial-intellectual set-up, recall him, but because the Italian charm, and volatility, and loquacity, and unselfconscious egocentricity, and inability to move out of grooves, and so on, that Miss Ginzburg so brilliantly captures, are all Chekhovian qualities. . . . She has an extraordinary gift for what you might call cumulative characterization—a method that dispenses almost entirely with description and builds up solid and memorable people by the gradual mounting up of small actions, oblique glances, other people's opinions.

Isabel Quigly. *Spec*. Aug. 24, 1956. p. 269

Natalia Ginzburg belongs to the post-war generation of Italian writers who were instrumental in the recent revival of native arts and letters. . . . She rapidly acquired the reputation of a skillful and sensitive storyteller.

A Light for Fools has all the characteristics of her genuine literary gift. . . . Vivid and often brilliant characterizations are not the only merit of this family novel. Through hints and intimations, the author succeeds in drawing a picture of Italian society between 1934 and 1944 and in revealing the hidden connection between the fate of individuals and the pressure of the times. The narrative has force and directness and there are delicate, impressionistic touches which remind us of Chekhov. Natalia Ginzburg is at her best when dealing with detail, and her descriptions of children and adolescents have a definite poetic flavor. Most of the incidents and characters are seen through the eyes of an adolescent, and the book has much of the naïveté and charm of a child's vision. This "point of view" in the Jamesian sense gives a unity of diction to the whole narrative.

Marc Slonim. *NYT*. Jan. 5, 1957. p. 5

Her themes are the solitude and anguish of life as well as the impossibility of communicating our despair to other humans. The situations depicted in her fiction are quite stark. Life is not only a wretched thing but a meaningless business. . . . Relatively little happens in her novels: Signora Ginzburg relies for her effects less on a story rich with incidents and surprises than on a subtle manner of relating a tale. . . . Whatever tension there is, is generated by the careful manner in which the author depicts the emotional or psychological state of her heroes and moves them slowly toward the climax. . . . Natalia Ginzburg's achievement is primarily a stylistic one. Her prose has a rhythm of its own and through it the author projects, with unusual simplicity, her conception of how people act, think, and behave. The texture of her style is replete with past descriptive indicative tenses; one sentence joined with another by means of the conjunctive "and." Through such deceptively simple techniques Ginzburg recaptures the rhythms of human discourse and elevates it from trifle to poetry.

Sergio Pacifici. A Guide to Contemporary Italian Literature (World). 1962. pp. 136–7, 140

Voices in the Evening is neither inspired nor competent: trying to make a virtue of its clumsiness, it reads pretentiously. For want of a personal inflection, the narrator's tone is faux naif; for want of a story, she takes us piecemeal through a Piedmontese family, recounting the fortunes of each member before, through and after the war, in a manner which may aim at the dispassionate but comes out perfunctory: the result is an academic but maladroit frieze in very low relief.

Brigid Brophy. NSN. Aug. 2, 1963. p. 147

Natalia Ginzburg is certainly one of the most competent writers of her generation in Italy. . . . Voices in the Evening is a fair example of her art. What she has to say she says economically and with a minimum of rhetoric. This book even seems at times more an outline than a final draft. . . . Signora Ginzburg's characters are, for the most part, like excellent line drawings, quite real but somehow not "filled in." Their bone structure is magnificent, but there is no flesh.

Thomas G. Bergin. SR. Sept. 21, 1963. p. 36

Miss Ginzburg has been attracting attention in the literary world of Italy —and this novel tells us why. The style of Voices in the Evening is crisp, brittle, entertaining and informative. . . . The very coolness of the style tends to defeat the subtle theme of the death of a family (and a love) through sheer lack of gumption. The brevity of the book and its semicomic treatment of a muted tragedy come to seem, not a strength but part of the general, fatal weariness. The "voices in the evening" tend to cancel each other out—succeeding only too well in presenting people who, pallid to begin with, end as mere phantoms.

Yet the heroine, her mother, the whole tone of small-town domestic concerns, have a curious, attenuated resemblance to characters in the work of Elizabeth Gaskell, or even Jane Austen. It is as if a whole set of inquietudes, hidden in these earlier women authors, had come briefly to the surface; not to be allayed by happy marriages or even by the pleasure of accurate, small observations but merely to be seen and endured.

Otis K. Burger. *NYT*. Oct. 6, 1963. p. 38

See *A Light for Fools* and *Voices in the Evening* (novels); also *The Road to the City* (two novelettes).

GIONO, JEAN (1895–   )

A self-educated man who had feasted on Homer during his adolescence Giono chose to live among the peasants in the sunny foothills of the Alps. His many novels idealizing that life are saturated with a rich poetry compounded of protracted, often charming images, a childlike naïveté and an intoxication with words.

Giono's evolution from successful novelist to ardent evangelist of Tolstoyan flavor could have been foreseen. And in his essays preaching a return to nature we find the same ultra-simple thought expressed with characteristic grandiloquence and even turgidity. His method is to drown the reader in a flood of lush prose which tends to conceal the truisms and contradictions.

Justin O'Brien. *NYT*. March 24, 1946. p. 5

He knows very well how to evoke places, the countryside, atmospheres, to establish characters, but if the novel is essentially the evolution of characters in time, he is not able to portray this evolution, or rather, for him, it does not exist. He gives himself characters and he gives them adventures, without these adventures changing them at all, such as he finds them he leaves them, not only simple but even all of a piece. More than a writer of novels, Jean Giono is a poet and a dramatist.

Maurice Nadeau. *MF*. March 1, 1952. p. 499.
Tr. by Dorothy Nyren Curley

Like our own Faulkner, Giono has created his own private terrestrial domain far closer to reality than books of history or geography. It is a region over which the stars and planets course with throbbing pulsations. It is a land in which things "happen" to men as aeons ago they happened to the gods. Pan still walks the earth. The soil is saturated with cosmic juices. Events "transpire." Miracles occur. And never does the author betray the figures, the characters, whom he has conjured out of the womb of his rich imagination. . . . In Giono's work what every sensitive, full-blooded individual ought to be able to recognize at once is "the song of the world."

Henry Miller. The Books in My Life (Peter Owen).
1952. pp. 102, 120

He has powers and aberrations in common with D. H. Lawrence, whose French equivalent he is, to a very large extent. Indeed, The Horseman on the Roof is to a certain degree what might have been the result if Lawrence had based a novel on Defoe's Journal of the Plague Year. . . . The book is a resounding and admirable statement of and argument for Voltairian humanism against the mechanistic conception of materialism. It is brutal, as all accounts of the human situation that are free from sentimental humbug are bound to be, but the brutality is balanced by Giono's extraordinarily acute sensitivity to the sensual and intellectual pleasures that make life so abundantly worth living. He is a writer who is enormously alive and continually receptive.

Anthony West. NY. Jan. 16, 1954. pp. 85, 88

His first astonishing gift is sensation. Giono plunges into the world with a freshness of perception denied to most adults. But that freshness is not the delicate sensitiveness of children, which blends the concrete and the magical. His sensations are as robust and earthy as they are intense. They do not diffuse objects in a halo of evanescent glimmering light; they accept them whole and capture their essence, concrete and spiritual. The novelist's world is a world of smells, tastes, palpable masses and shapes, caressed by the body; visual sensations account for little and the intellectual content of perceptions is sacrificed to their sensuous revelation.

Henri Peyre. The Contemporary French Novel
(Oxford). 1955. p. 145

Giono's vocabulary is very extensive not because he uses learned words or ones not currently in use, as did Huysmans and Léon Bloy, who carried around with him "a cavalry of dictionaries," but because he uses the exact and most appropriate word in each case. He avoids abstract terms, phrases from which the meaning has been worn away, in brief, all ways of speaking which have gone cold. . . . He rejoices in spoken language in which flexibility—that of life itself—models itself on our emotions.

Romée de Villeneuve. *Jean Giono, Ce Solitaire*
(Presses Universelles). 1955. pp. 241–2.
Tr. by Dorothy Nyren Curley

Poet of the grand gestures of nature, polemicist, vivacious story-teller, he has not ceased to surprise us. Giono is more than a marvelous inventor of stories, he has created a language.

The interest in his sentence is less in the form than in something which sustains and surpasses it: the unfolding with all its richness of his verbal spontaneity. If we removed the fleshing out, the syntax would appear poor, often maladroit. But this poverty does not come from lack of ability: Giono wishes to write without constraint, almost as he speaks.

Jacques Pugnet. *Jean Giono* (Editions Universitaires).
1955. p. 130. Tr. by Dorothy Nyren Curley

In a tormented world someone has the audacity to say he has come to terms with life. He smiles at the absurd, and knows how to do it without tastelessness and without frivolity. His egoism . . . does not even begin to displease because he continues—just as before—to signal us to follow him, to assure us that happiness is ours. One has to watch, eyes round and mouth open, a man who is lucid and sensible beyond the ordinary, who in 1954 says with tranquility: "For thirty or forty years I have been happy, totally, constantly, minute by minute."

Claudine Choney. *Giono par Lui-Même* (Editions du
Seuil). 1956. p. 6. Tr. by Dorothy Nyren Curley

Giono's fictional output is enormous and it shows no signs of flagging. His development as a storyteller has been continuous, but the basic conventions he uses have not changed. The Provençal landscape furnishes him with the materials of his world. But he molds it, enlarges it, detaches it from reality, empties it of its essentially civilized character, and fills it to overflowing with elements taken from his own imagination. The hills of Provence become mountains, the streamlets become rivers, the bouquets of trees turn to forests. And the wind blows, the stars shine, on the immense space of a new, unrecognizable planet made for Giono's race of men as never at any time our earth was made for us.

Germaine Brée and Margaret Guiton. *An Age of Fiction*
(Rutgers). 1957. p. 108

Giono's prestige has sagged a good deal over the past twenty years. . . . The sixty-four-year old novelist has always gone his private way, and it has been a way opposite to that of the representative literary figures of his time—opposite, for example, to that of Albert Camus. . . . [Giono's] theme has been a sort of chaste paganism, a pastoral joy in nature, the good fellowship of honest folk, and in the sheer sensation of life. . . . And all this as deliberately remote as can be from the political belligerence and the metaphysical anguish of most of his distinguished contemporaries.

R. W. B. Lewis. *SR*. May 23, 1959. p. 37

See *The Blue Boy* and *Horseman on the Roof* (novels).

GIRAUDOUX, JEAN (1882–1944)

For the reader equipped with an *Encyclopaedia Britannica*, a *Larousse*, an atlas, a mythological manual, an herbal, and a large supply of technical dictionaries, I no longer fear to recommend the incomparable Giraudoux. He prepares delightful and intricate knots, and he will not untie them for you. The cryptic allusions with which he strews his path soon reveal his intentions, and when he mentions Sakuntala, or a "dalaganpalang," he has no idea of providing further information on these subjects. He is an exacting Amphitryon at his literary feasts, and many a passage in his books will require a second reading. But in spite of every stumbling block, one never measures with impatient fingers the diminishing pages as one reads, for, in the words of Jacques Boulenger, "nothing that Giraudoux says, not the slightest little thing, has been said before."

Milton H. Stansbury. *Bkm*. March, 1933. p. 246

In my own opinion, it [*Intermezzo*] is unquestionably one of the most beautiful plays of our time and the most viable of all the works of Giraudoux. It is not, in the ordinary sense of the term, a forceful play. It is gentle and lyrical, and it comes as close to music as one can come with words. For this reason, perhaps, it has a peculiar elusiveness which to me, at least, is precious. It is, undeniably, a difficult play to do.

This is the most characteristic of the plays of Giraudoux; in a sense it is a self-portrait. It is witty, without cynicism; learned, without pedantry; it has depth, without being in the least didactic. In brief, it is civilized. But is has also the transcendent quality of imagination which is Giraudoux's special magic.

Maurice Valency. *TA*. Oct., 1950. p. 56

It is, alas, only since his death in 1943 that many of us have come to see that Giraudoux is a man to reckon with. . . . In Europe around 1950, Giraudoux confronted me wherever I went. . . . My eyes were opened to many things. I saw, for example, how I had come to overestimate the originality of "The Flies"; the mythological plays of Sartre and Anouilh are inconceivable without Giraudoux. More important, I had to grant that here was a first-rank man of letters consecrating his maturity to the theatre, finding in Louis Jouvet at once a great interpreter and a great instructor, and writing plays which constitute a claim to vast originality, plays which, if we accept them, would give to drama itself a new definition.

This definition is one towards which a great part of modern drama tends. On the technical side, it is a drama in which thought is more important than action or character and in which words are more important than thought. On the philosophical side, it is anti-materialistic, metaphysical, a drama of magic and miracle.

Eric Bentley. NR. March 8, 1954. p. 21

In Giraudoux the French theatre found a stylist with grace and nobility, of a quality with which perhaps only the language of Marivaux can be compared. Giraudoux is essentialy polite theatre, the drama of the spoken word rather than action, of conflict through thought, never through histrionics. It is the recesses of the human mind that Giraudoux seeks to explore. . . . The theatre of Giraudoux is neither realistic nor is it altogether unrealistic. Intellect and imagination walk hand in hand, for the destination is not the never-never land of Barrie. In all Giraudoux's plays one can identify situations of real life, but they have a resemblance only; they are familiar, but there is a differentiation. If, for example, some of his characters make us think of Hitler and Mussolini, we know that they are not meant to represent Hitler and Mussolini. Giraudoux was too great an artist for that. What his plays have is a moral significa-tion, and he selects those problems which have a capital importance for our time and civilization.

Frederick Lumley. Trends in Twentieth Century Drama
(Essential Books). 1956. pp. 41–2

In speaking the dialogue of Giraudoux's plays, the actors had to slow down the verbal pace and muffle the explosive consonants until the sound of the words slowly died out. By so doing, all the color and emo-tion inherent in the text stood out with sustained clarity. Jouvet spent many concentrated hours teaching the actors how to achieve these effects. They began by scanning the lines; then, giving the words their proper tonality and altering the caesuras, they would permit the words to fade. By these means Jouvet was able to achieve rhythmic effects which were as complex as human feelings themselves.

Bettina Liebowitz Knapp. *TA*. March, 1957. p. 90

The style of this writer . . . constitutes his greatest claim to what is originality for some, pedantic eccentricity for others.

The chief characteristic of this style is the continual use of metaphor and comparison, sometimes expressed, sometimes implied, extending frequently into the field of allegory; and the principal criticism directed against Giraudoux, as against all writers in all centuries who employ such a style, is that of artificiality or lack of naturalness. One comes here immediately into the field of personal preference and taste, based fairly often on nothing more solid than the necessarily limited experience and culture of the critic concerned.

Donald Inskip. *Jean Giraudoux* (Oxford). 1958. p. 38

Jean Giraudoux was no philosopher and has never exercised an influence even on his own countrymen comparable to Eliot's influence in England and America. Giraudoux was a conservative, but his work has love— a very simple kind of love for the fundamental things of life—and his love informs his best efforts with captivating brightness, color, charm. The love that we find in Giraudoux often gives his work a special creative connection with the contemporary scene. For it is Giraudoux's love that leads to a peculiar provinciality (his image of the good life is the life of his native village), a provinciality which often makes him a sharp and engaging critic of modern society. In such plays as "The Madwoman of Chaillot," for example, Paris is shown debased by money, and graciousness is made to dwell in mad exile in the subterranean passages of the city.

Harold Clurman. *Lies Like Truth* (Macmillan).
1958. p. 217

The word *précieux* has perhaps been used more often than any to describe Giraudoux and his art. Although it has meant different things to different persons, we believe there is no better word to characterize all his verbal inventiveness and the basic fastidiousness of his vision. Early critics employed it in its pejorative sense to voice their discomfort before a new and dazzling art; later ones stressed its philosophical significance —but each, whether attacking or defending the author, has thrown interesting light on his work. Today with Giraudoux's high place in the literature of the twentieth century established, we need not fear that the popular connotation of affectation and superficiality attached to the word will be prejudicial; indeed the tendency in recent years seems to be to take him overseriously. The writer once thought of as an impertinent prankster now is regarded almost solely as a tragic poet of the human condition. Actually he is both prankster and tragic poet, and to affirm the one view of him and deny the other is to substitute one partial truth for another.

Laurent Le Sage. Jean Giraudoux (Pennsylvania State).
1959. p. 198

The art of the theater is prophecy or divination, as Giraudoux calls it. It reveals to men the most surprising and the most simple truths, which they never fully realize, such as the inevitability of life, the inevitability of death, the meaning of happiness and catastrophe, the fact that life is both reality and dream. The language of the theater is liturgical both in its solemnity and its exuberance. He always pleaded for the primacy of the text in theatrical productions, and this was faithfully followed by Louis Jouvet. The purity and the importance of Giraudoux's text were such that Jouvet said that he had to teach his actors how to speak the text rather than act it. Both men always defended the literary theater at the expense of the most spectacular kind of production in which the text was sacrificed to the *mise-en-scène*.

Wallace Fowlie. Dionysius in Paris (Meridian). 1960.
pp. 62–3

We travel through his plays as through a luminous grotto, glimpsing murals of time-suspending wit and loveliness; and it would be churlish, after such a journey, to complain that the labyrinth seemed shapeless, that there were too many blind alleys, or that every picture did not tell a story. As well might one condemn the Uffizi Gallery for lacking narrative interest.

Life as Giraudoux perceived it was life as it appeared to Mr. Huxley while mescalin was tickling his cerebral cortex: cleansed, pure, alive with colour, and so transformed in the matter of dimensions that a turn of phrase was as tangible as a column of alabaster. Though he preferred what Thomas Mann called the "finer and less obvious rhythmical laws" of prose, Giraudoux was arguably the greatest theatrical poet of his time. As a prose architect he easily eclipsed Shaw in the art, now forgotten but once obligatory, of providing long speeches for crucial moments. Not for him the clipped, chopped scurry of most modern dialogue. At regular intervals Giraudoux feels a set-piece coming on, and the plot must pause while it blazes.

Kenneth Tynan. *Curtains* (Atheneum). 1961. pp. 106–7

One idea dominates his evolution: the idea that man will never live in peace because he is not alone, that God or the gods, social and psychological forces, the members of the other sex all set definitions before him which are different from his and which attract and repel him at the same time. There is no judgment on the part of Giraudoux; there are merely choices and ambiguities determined by the nature of each play. It is probably exaggerated to say with Jacques Houlet that all Giraudoux's characters "win our sympathy in some way or other." But actually in the combat that takes place on stage between man and the gods, between man and woman, between France and Germany, between Hector and Ulysses, between Lia and Jean, our sympathies are not with either side but with the struggle itself as symbolized by the combat. So that beyond more or less individual definitions or essences, dividing and wrangling over the play's universe, a radically dramatic definition of man's condition is posed.

Jacques Guicharnaud. *Modern French Theatre*
(Yale). 1961. pp. 43–4

The very similar protagonists that reappear in play after play achieve a kind of positive heroic status of their own, a status so compelling that even the gods are completely seduced by it, let alone helpless mortal males. It comes from the heroine's ability to stave off evil by refusing to recognize it as such. Imagine Eve, after her encounter with Satan, simply refusing to fall and continuing life as if nothing had happened. Such are Giraudoux's women: they manage to forget the past, which is the source of guilt, and refuse to have anything to do with the future, which is the source of anxiety; no common meeting-ground can exist between Helen and Cassandra. The plays abound in talk about innocence and purity, but of a peculiar kind. There are few virgins on Giraudoux's stage, nor does virginity seem to be particularly valued there. Whether real or imaginary, rapes turn into rather cheerful affairs. Whoever interprets this "purity" as a pre-lapsarian childlike innocence, misses the point. Much rather, it is the ability to sin gracefullly and elegantly, a feat symbolized by a love night so successful that all other considerations are blotted out for the moment. This seems to be the only genuine candor left in a world where all forms of virtue have become hollow.

Paul de Man. *NYR*. Nov. 28, 1963. p. 20
See *Four Plays* (Hill and Wang); also *Elpenor* (novel).

GIRONELLA, JOSÉ MARÍA (1917–   )

Gironella is a young Falangist and his book [*The Cypresses Believe in God*] was received with great applause in Spain two years ago. This will make many people feel that it is likely to be very biased. In fact it is remarkably objective. As a novelist the author is more interested in men than in doctrines. Behind the idea he always sees the circumstances that have produced it and his attitude to people is generous and full of understanding. . . . However, this is not simply a novelized guide to the Spanish Civil War. It is a novel about people caught in the web of politics and forced to make decisions that may lead to their death. Its subject therefore is deeply tragic.

Gerald Brenan. *NYT*. April 10, 1955. p. 5

His plan is ambitious and worth while; its execution, thus far, splendid. [*The Cypresses Believe in God*] may be the finest novel we have dealing with the Spanish Civil War. If it has not the dynamic afflatus of Malraux's *Man's Hope* or Hemingway's *For Whom the Bell Tolls,* it is unquestionably more authentic and also less "literary." . . . [He is not] writing another *War and Peace*. Despite his great talent, Gironella, lacking the magnificent fluidity and pervasiveness found in the spacious world of Tolstoy, gives the impression sometimes of imposing history upon his characters. But Gironella's style is clear and simple, and his characterizations vivid enough.

Angel Flores. *NYHT*. April 10, 1955. p. 3

Señor Gironella has written a distinguished documentary novel—no more and no less. The notable thing about [*The Cypresses Believe in God*] is that, in contrast to most novels of contemporary history, it is not a tract but a study of human nature—the nature of the Spanish people. . . . "What is characteristic," he observes, "is a tendency towards the instinctive . . . the individualistic . . . the anarchic." . . . The author's narrative power is admirably sustained throughout the novel's thousand pages. And his numerous characters—whether sketched or portrayed in detail—are drawn with vigor, humanity, and a sharp sense of individuality.

Charles J. Rolo. *At*. May, 1955. pp. 81–2

Señor Gironella has the authentic nineteenth-century megalomania, which rests on the conviction that the writer knows everything there is to know about his characters, their lives, the life around them, and indeed, the essential nature of all creation. With this conviction, he em-

barks on his program, which is to re-create the whole fabric of the
private and public life of the citizenry of Gerona from 1931 to 1936,
with the idea that this Catalonian town is Spain and that the life of the
town in those years was the life of the nation. But a Balzacian enterprise
of this order can be carried through only by a writer who has that megalomania in its pure form. . . . It becomes apparent that he is closely
engaged in the conflicts with which he is dealing. . . . *The Cypresses
Believe in God* seems to indicate the erosion of an aesthetic by partisan
passion. . . . Señor Gironella has, unhappily, given us not Spain . . . but
a Spanish novel capably expressing the ideologies of the regime in power.

Anthony West. *NY*. May 28, 1955. pp. 120–1

Even before its publication . . . [*The Cypresses Believe in God*] ignited
a controversy which seems likely to last for a considerable period.

In one rank are those who proclaim it the most important Spanish
novel in forty years, a book of strong narrative power and deep insight,
a volume which gives the best picture of Spain on the eve of its crushing
Civil War yet vouchsafed us. In the other are those who assert that it is
one-sidedly weighted in favor of Franco's rebellion against the lawful
Spanish government, that it is artistically false in being little more than
cleverly disguised propaganda, and that it is a betrayal of the economic,
social and political rights of the Spanish people.

Each of these points of view can be strongly supported. . . . [But] of
the breadth and accuracy of the human scene as painted by the author
there can be little criticism.

Joseph G. Harrison. *CSM*. July 8, 1955. p. 9

To treat a great and widely distorted subject with an impartiality that
refuses to hate only one kind of evil, or to love only one aspect of good,
is excellence enough. But Gironella is doing even more. He is attempting
to give form, not to dreams only, not to ideas, however profound and
comprehensive, but to the dirty, stubborn, irreducible facts of history.
He deserves our praise, yes; but our alert attention even more.

Thomas Curley. *NYT*. Oct. 20, 1963. p. 4

The socio-political novel, in which the characters wrestle less with
problems of their own making than with those history has thrust upon
them, seems to have died a quiet death in post-depression, post-war
America. But it remains strong elsewhere, especially in nations such as
Germany, Russia, or Spain, where the impact of recent history has been
so great that it is difficult to conceive of man outside his social setting.
In the novels of this type, the individual protagonists must share the

scene with events that shaped them . . . [as] in *Dr. Zhivago* or . . . *The Tin Drum.*

The greatness of José María Gironella lies in his ambition to join this noble tradition by rising above parties and passions to present an objective account of the tragedy of modern Spain. . . . It is so rarely that a writer tries to probe the nemesis not only of an individual man but of an entire society that even when the effort is not completely successful, his work must be placed in a minor pantheon of its own.

Edward Malefakis. *CT*. Oct. 20, 1963. p. 2

When José María Gironella published *The Cypresses Believe in God* ten years ago, it was at once evident that a new novelist of quite remarkable power had emerged. The juices flowed; there was the sense of rich and urgent life . . . ; [his] sweeping brush strokes . . . gave a sense of epic grandeur to the scene. . . . The novel was a literary event of the first magnitude. . . . *The Cypresses Believe in God* was a young man's book: there was sunlight and excitement, and the sense of the coming storm. One had the feeling that it poured out of him steadily, almost happily, even thoughtlessly, for the characters were so real that he had only to describe what he saw in his mind's eye. *One Million Dead* [its sequel] is a disappointment. There is no longer any youthfulness in the writing, and the characters no longer move at their own volition: they have become counters, shadowy emblematic creatures of the author's will. . . . The failure of *One Million Dead* has little to do with the political atmosphere in which it was written. Essentially it is a failure of nerve, which is all the more tragic because Gironella showed such astounding power in the past.

Robert Payne. *SR*. Nov. 30, 1963. pp. 33–4

See *The Cypresses Believe in God, One Million Dead,* and *Where the Soil Was Shallow* (novels).

GÓMEZ DE LA SERNA, RAMÓN (1888–1963)

His favorite form is that of the brief whimsical sketch, or aphorism. . . . It is these brief notations from life, these humorous meditations and little stories which have made their author famous. . . . Typical . . . is the title *Greguerías,* which is hard to translate, but might be rendered by *Shouts and Murmurs,* for it means a confused noise, a hubbub, the chatter of birds. . . . The shouts and murmurs which he hears are the confused cries of the sub-conscious, which suggest curious observations, unexpected parallels, and incongruous metaphors. . . . As to what the actual achievement of Gómez de la Serna is, I submit, with becoming humility, that he is simply a comedian.

Ernest Boyd. *Studies from Ten Literatures*
(Scribner). 1925. pp. 139–42

There is a moment between sleep and waking, when the mind spans an abyss between eternity and time. . . . This mysterious hinterland, Ramón Gómez de la Serna has made his realm. . . . Spain stands at this transition, between sleep and waking. Ramón is the elegist of its dissolving colors, of its shattered and luminous shapes. . . . [He] weaves the filmy spell of a dissolving world. . . . Spain stirs in this limbo: her eye peers back into the fleeting images of dream. Ramón is her eye.

Wherefore the contradictions in his work. Rich in color, it is evanescent. Affluent in imitations of form, it is formless. His books are collections of uncollectible items. His true form is chaos. He is indeed the runner of a rainbow; and should he stop one moment, he would fall through mist. His one subject is the instant of palpable inarticulation. But his world is still the dreamed Body of Spain.

Waldo Frank. *Virgin Spain* (Boni and Liveright). 1926.
pp. 278–9

There is a man in Europe whose passport bears only his first name and no photograph. He crosses the intellectual frontiers through the sheer incantation of one word "RAMÓN." . . . His prodigious creative talent . . . explodes the rusty theory about Spanish *abulia*. . . . He has discovered a new literary genre: the *greguería,* a sort of metaphoric maxim or aphorism without any moralizing or academic heaviness. The *greguerías* . . . are witty Definitions, scintillating Impressions and Comments, facetious Trivia: an ideal cocktail of haï-kaïs in prose, Sauterne, Luna Park, Chamfort, roses and peppermint. . . . RAMÓN witnesses life in midstreet with greedy, ubiquitous and clear eyes and then rushes to his . . . attic-tower. . . . Here RAMÓN performs an implacable autopsy on the things he has seen. He invertebrates them, bathes them in a piscina of vigor and grace and returns them to us crowned in a diadem of smiles. . . . RAMÓN's laughter brings out what Jaloux termed "the submarine flora of our souls" . . . and, Jaloux might have added, the soul of things.

Angel Flores. *Bkm.* June, 1928. p. 386

The progress of Spanish prose in the last thirty years or so has been little remarked outside of Spain. Yet the change . . . has been a radical one. The later writers . . . have gained in depth and complexity of thought, in power of psycholological analysis. . . . They have, as well, enlarged and enriched the Spanish vocabulary, bringing back to it words that had been almost forgotten, introducing new forms to give it flexibility.

Most revolutionary of the literary revolutionists is Ramón Gómez de la Serna. . . . "Never," says . . . [one] critic, "have such verbal frenzies, enthusiasms and intoxications been known. He is the Dionysus of words."

Perhaps Gómez de la Serna came to an early realization of the fact that truth is not static, but always receding into the past or losing itself in the future, and felt that brevity alone could express it. On the other hand, art must construct, not, as he insisted in his early youth, disintegrate; and in the immense, unrelated collection of *Greguerías* we are sometimes thrown into consternation at finding no framework.

Helen Granville-Barker. *Ftn*. Jan. 1, 1929. pp. 31, 37

Gómez de la Serna calls his *greguerías* "attempts to define the indefinable, to capture the fugitive." Although their success depends upon the instantaneousness of the impression they make, they aim at something more than wit; the best of them reveal the secret correspondences of things, employing for this a peculiar sort of poetic intuition. This kind of writing is of course surrealism, born long before that term was invented and a great deal more entertaining than any so-called surrealist writings that I have seen. It has analogies too with some things in Quevedo and in Spanish Arab poetry.

Gerald Brenan. *The Literature of the Spanish People*
(Cambridge). 1953. p. 445

The *greguerías* . . . were part of the international movement in literature and art which dissolved the rigid surface of objects and strove to express the inner connection between the fragments of life. Ramón was clearly influenced by the French forerunners of Surrealism and by echoes of Freudian theories. What he made of it was characteristically his own. In Spanish prose he was the first to convey, rather than to describe or explain, a sense of complexity and insecurity, of "things below the surface of things." He proved that literary language could be richer if it used images with the same freedom as did the symbol-studded talk of the Andalusian peasants and gypsies. In short, he extended the limits of Spanish writing. . . . Ramón's own novels were unsatisfactory attempts to apply the new form of symbolist prose. But he had started something more important than his own writings. By delayed action, his aesthetic rebellion affected the young writers of the Twenties. It set them free to use images which corresponded to their subjective experience and to the complex, uncertain, difficult world in which they lived.

Arturo Barea. *BA*. Spring, 1953. p. 125

Although in Spain Ramón Gómez de la Serna is commonly regarded as a literary school of one, a *generación unipersonal,* he is a member of that worldwide generation of writers who—aware of the disintegration of conventional concepts in science, philosophy and art—use diction and image not to conform or corroborate, but to startle and shock. . . . He has remained the *enfant terrible* of modern Spanish letters. . . . Ramón's novels, . . . his plays, . . . and his books of impressions are all marked by an outrageously unconventional and purely arbitrary vision of facts and things which have become known as *ramonismo.* . . . The free play that Ramón allows to fantasy and the subconscious identifies him with the surrealists who, in an attempt to ferret out hidden realities behind appearances, break reality up into strange angles and curves, as in a distorting mirror.

Ramón takes vast liberties in his attempt to reconcile incompatibles and to create new linguistic and poetic tensions.

> Beatrice Patt and Martin Nozick. *The Generation of 1898
> and After* (Dodd). 1960. pp. 231–2

See *Some Greguerías.*

GOURMONT, RÉMY DE (1858–1915)

As it used to be said that Meredith was the writer's writer, I might say that De Gourmont is the poet for poets. He is the great teacher of certain effects, the instructor in verbal shades. No one has studied more carefully than he the sounds of vowels and consonants. Not even from his great teacher, Mallarmé, can more be learnt. As a producer of colour in words, he cedes to no one; his knowledge of the technique of poetry is unsurpassed.

> Amy Lowell. *Six French Poets* (Houghton). 1921. p. 108

To every department of literature which Gourmont essayed, he brings his supple intelligence, lighting up his subject with a clear brilliance. Irony he used as a surgical instrument to lance the sores of society. In his study, isolated and removed from the bustle of Parisian life, he boldly dispelled the mists of ridicule and slander with which the young writers were covered. A great master, his inflence on French literature was tremendous. . . . He gives one a delicious draught of sanity; he is pure mind, unadulterated by muddy emotionalism or didacticism.

> Jack Lewis. Introduction to *Mr. Antiphon, Satyr*
> (Lieber and Lewis). 1922. pp. 23–4

He strikes us as ceaselessly hovering over hitherto uncontested facts in the passionate desire of proving them to be fallacies. The epithet "paradoxical," which is often misapplied, appears to be exactly appropriate to the method of Rémy de Gourmont, which starts by denying the truth of something which everybody has taken for granted, and then supporting the reversed position by rapid and ingenious argument. He is unable to accept any convention until he has resolutely turned it inside out, examined it in every hostile light, and so dusted and furbished it that it has ceased to be conventional. He was indefatigable in these researches, and so ingenious as to be often bewildering and occasionally tiresome.

Edmund Gosse. *Aspects and Impressions* (Cassell).
1922. pp. 218–9

Gourmont's detachment from life is in many ways a serious defect; though it does give serenity and wisdom to his writings, it renders him incapable of creating a vital character. His best work begins when the novelist is silent and the philosopher speaks. His intelligence, fine and pure as it was, seldom found its true method of expression, yet that intelligence is plain through all his earlier affectations, through even his most doubtful writing. He loved the human mind and yet he never really expressed that love. He is to be valued for his tranquil wisdom, for all the kindly or pentrating or ironic or beautiful thoughts which lie scattered through his books.

Richard Aldington. *Literary Studies and Reviews*
(Dial). 1924. p. 167

An aristocratic radical, a lover of paradox, a profound scholar, a Latinist of the first rank, his supple, smiling prose is a mask that conceals much wisdom, much irony, many disillusionments. For the man in the street he is caviar. . . . He has been variously denounced as a subtle sophist, a corrupt cynic, a hater of his kind, and a philosopher without a philosophy. He may possess a little of all these terrific attributes, but he is also something else. He is very human, very gay, very tolerant, very charming, and very erudite.

James Huneker. *The Pathos of Distance* (Scribner).
1925. pp. 303–4

His one imperative was to be venturesome. Since art, by becoming an end in itself, became a matter of the individual—or by becoming a matter of the individual, became an end in itself—he was theoretically without external obligations, at liberty to develop his medium as he preferred. And while this theoretical freedom was checked in him, as in every artist, by the desire to communicate, it did contribute to the vocabulary of his work. It is true that he ceased his stylistic development once he had reached a complete lubrication of phrase, but the nature of his books themselves is rarely the same in two successive volumes.

> Kenneth Burke. *Counter-Statement* (Harcourt). 1931.
> pp. 23–4

When we look back less than twenty years after his death, we clearly realise that Rémy de Gourmont belongs to an age that is past. That is not by any means to say that he has ceased to possess significance or that his work—his best work—is no longer worth reading. . . . For those who return to them, there are books of Gourmont's always worth reading; he deals with the essential stuff of life, and he deals with it in the medium of intellect which never dies. But it remains true that, while he appealed sympathetically to the foremost and most daring spirits of his generation, he answers no pressing questions of the generation of today.

> Havelock Ellis. *From Rousseau to Proust* (Houghton).
> 1935. pp. 316–7

In spite of limitations . . . the sceptical approach is impressive in its astringency and up to a point it constitutes a genuine intellectual discipline. Gourmont was one of the first writers who systematically attacked vague romantic appreciation and tried to make criticism not a science, but scientific in a wide sense which was not Taine's sense; and his declaration that "style is a specialisation of sensibility" is a landmark in the history of criticism. . . . Gourmont was a very stimulating and, up to a point, a very able critic; but he seems to me to fall short of greatness. He was endowed in a high degree with the Frenchman's mental alertness and his curiosity about life; but it was precisely an undisciplined curiosity coupled with a fundamental dilettantism which led him into unprofitable ways and detracted from the critical intensity of his work.

> Martin Turnell. *Critiques and Essays in Criticism*
> *1920-1948,* selected by Robert Wooster Stallman
> (Ronald). 1949. pp. 443, 446–7

You could . . . have said to Gourmont anything that came into your head; you could have sent him anything you had written with a reasonable assurance that he would have known what you were driving at. . . . Gourmont prepared our era; behind him there stretches a limitless darkness. . . . He was intensely aware of the differences of emotional timbre; and as a man's message is precisely his *façon de voir,* his modality of appreciation, this particular awareness was his "message". . . . He recognizes the right of individuals to *feel* differently. Confucian, Epicurean, a considerer and entertainer of ideas, this complicated sensuous wisdom is almost the one ubiquitous element, the "self" which keeps his superficially heterogeneous work vaguely "unified".

Ezra Pound. Literary Essays (Faber). 1954. pp. 339–41

If any part of Gourmont's literature lives into the future it will probably not be his imaginative writing. His novels, plays, and perhaps his poetry seem destined to be read only by students seeking understanding of his work as a whole, for it is only in that light that they can command attention. His essays and critiques, on the other hand, deserve present and future readers, as they remain an excellent statement of a fundamental and perennial point of view. For the historically-minded, Gourmont reflects, perhaps better than any other writer, the cross-currents of literary opinion of his period, while at the same time he gives the impressionist position in criticism its most lucid and convincing exposition.

Glenn S. Burne. Rémy de Gourmont
(Southern Illinois). 1963. p. 153

See *A Night in the Luxembourg* (novel) and *The Book of Masks* (criticism).

GOYTISOLO, JUAN (1931–   )

The young assassins . . . are a group of intellectuals . . . who have broken loose from a wealthy bourgeois background to become outcasts, or, to give them a more modern and fashionable description, "outsiders." . . . That this book should have been written and published in present-day Spain will, I think, surprise American readers who have taken for granted the intellectual barrenness of life under Franco. And, significantly, it is just this barrenness, expressed in the hedonism of the younger generation, which the author expresses without succumbing to it himself. Apparently, he is concerned with showing us how self-destructive and yet how inevitable this hedonism becomes in a society dominated by the smug and self-righteous. . . . This is Murger's Bohemia, stripped of romanticism. . . . Goytisolo, himself a member of this restless generation, is an "outsider" once removed. In this sense, *The Young Assassins* begins where the novels of a writer like Jack Kerouac leave off.

David Dempsey. SR. Feb. 14, 1959. p. 28

Apart from some awkwardness . . . and an appallingly slow start, *The Young Assassins* gives an exciting account of how a bunch of Madrid students plan to murder a politician just for the hell of it. . . . The last seventy pages, in which climax and anti-climax force maturity, self-denial, conscience and stark terror into the hermetic world of the well-heeled delinquents, are almost Dostoevskian; the characterization is steady throughout, the writing harsh and agile.

Paul West. *NSN*. April 30, 1960. p. 643

Remote from the clicking of castanets if not of prayer beads, this Spain of Goytisolo's is one in which certain men (and women and children) lead quietly desperate lives having no outlet save fantasy and yearning daydream. Some feel more keenly than others the degradation that oppresses them. Some do not consciously feel it at all. But the greyness of their life hovers over them all, and out of their plight Goytisolo has made a sad, bitter little novel like a poem. . . . The story [in *Fiestas*] does not so much end as fade out, like lingering melancholy song. You might not be too far wrong if you wagered that young Goytisolo and the hardy tradition he represents will outlive the regime that bars him.

John K. Hutchens. *NYHT*. May 17, 1960. p. 25

Fiestas is a model of harmony, sharpness, love of things and beings, originality of vision and the sense of efficacy in indirect allusion. *Fiestas* is a brilliant projection of the contrast between Spanish official and real life. . . . This mind is a mirror which does not copy . . . but which selects. . . . Goytisolo's novel is cold and precise, with a restrained passion that makes the contrasts of light and shadow more effective in the sometimes rhapsodic, sometimes satiric treatment of the Spanish realities of today, with all their esthetic, social, moral, historical nuances, their relationships and accidents. The complexity of these values implies no confusion. In spite of its wealth of tones, the novel is limpid, with fresh colors and diaphanous perspectives. . . . Juan Goytisolo . . . is without doubt the best of the young Spanish writers.

Ramón Sender. *SR*. June 11, 1960. p. 35

Consciously or not, Goytisolo uses the techniques and methods of the cinema to get many of his effects, and *Fiestas*—its way of conjuring an atmosphere, of handling people, above all its ironic, jubilant climax through which the boy hero moves, broken-hearted, a betrayer—is conceived cinematically. Physical detail is shown in close-up—a girl's hair-ribbon, a blond pigtail—then returned to under other circumstances: the dead girl's hair and ribbon, the body seen at a distance, then gradually approached until it is seen, terrifyingly over-emphasized. As in his other novels Goytisolo puts his people into a present-day situation, politically and morally explicit, but entirely without polemics, without the use of a single "political" expression. The satire is oblique, delicate: in fact the whole of "Fiesta" is a satire, the whole situation, in which people go about their daily lives preparing for an enormous religious congress, comments on the Spanish mentality today.

Isabel Quigly. MG. March 3, 1961. p. 7

Fiestas by Juan Goytisolo . . . is a very poor novel unworthy of speaking for any nation or nationality, reminiscent of the worst of the sociological novels that were written in the United States by the Upton Sinclair imitators. Why Franco Spain banned its publication is beyond me. It is a worthless book, as politically harmless as it is esthetically unrewarding.

Warren Eyster. SwR. Autumn, 1961. p. 703

What distinguishes Goytisolo from other writers in the ever-widening confraternity of young protesters is the clinical objectivity of his vision and the rigorous control he displays over his powerful, driving style.

His works—short, violent and frightening—are like pages torn out of the book of experience. . . . He limits himself to holding up a mirror which reflects the Spanish contemporary scene—one facet at a time. And he records what he sees without comment or coloring. . . . For the vigor of his talent, for his ruthless exposure of the destructive forces that are dissipating his country's inner strength, and his courage to speak out, Juan Goytisolo recalls Alberto Moravia's first book *The Time of Indifference* (1929) which in its way captured the atmosphere of moral disintegration that was poisoning Italian society during fascism. While Goytisolo's novels are in no way overtly "political," they constitute the most damning indictment to come out of Spain of a regime, which, by cutting off a proud and intelligent people from the direct management of its own affairs, has set it adrift on an empty sea of destructive self-doubt and specious values.

Helene Cantarella. NYT. March 18, 1962. pp. 5, 27

Peculiarly Spanish is the background of violence always giving way to false calm: one day burn down the churches, next day worship in them. . . .

Island of Women . . . in controlled, tight-lipped fashion . . . describes . . . people lost in darkness. . . . Not since *La Dolce Vita* have we been faced with such stony-faced frolicking: a collective life of dissolution whose rigorous leisure schedule is one of the longest and most tiring imaginable. . . . There is [a] little shade of Hemingway here in the capsule picture of a drifting generation, one lacking in romance but thereby more feverish.

Alice Mayhew. *Com.* July 27, 1962. p. 427

See *The Young Assassins, Fiestas,* and *Island of Women* (novels).

GRACQ, JULIEN (1909–   )

Few American readers will be moved by *A Dark Stranger.* The theme is old-fashioned in its labored effort at strangeness; the style, in spite of a very faithful and very adequate translation, will appear over-literary and lush. The vague characterization, the weird dreams, the conversations on Poe and Rimbaud smack too much of decadent and romantic artificiality.

Henri Peyre. *NYT.* July 2, 1950. p. 12

[*A Dark Stranger*] . . . has a promising beginning. There are some effective lines of place description and personal reflection. Even before a quote is used the likeness to the close, full style of Mauriac is apparent. But the novel never does get beyond its good beginning. There is a ponderous building up of an atmosphere which cannot account for the effects upon the character noted in the diary of the writer.

George Miles. *Com.* Sept. 22, 1950. pp. 587–8

If surrealism has made Maldoror its principle intermediary, it is because, after a half century, it finds in him its own dizziness, its cruel metaphysics. He who holds the knife, as Baudelaire had divined, is the one who receives the wound.

Seen in this perspective, the importance of Julien Gracq becomes apparent. The most talented writer of the second surrealist generation is beyond doubt the one whose work, with that of Eluard and Breton, will be recognized some years hence as the most definite contribution by the school to contemporary thought. . . . Gracq does not give realism anything which was not already there, but with lucidity not separated from inspiration he brings its tendencies to fulfillment. . . . Julien Gracq's heroes move and are slain on . . . metaphysical frontiers where the loss of the god, the sacrifice of Hercules on the pyre is constantly renewed.

Armand Hoog. *YFS.* No. 8, 1951. pp. 23–4

One might, if one were amiably disposed, meet him half-way, and, taking him at his own valuation, attack his ideas as shocking or wicked, but the truth is that they are much worse than that—they are silly. The silliness might be interesting if it could be considered evidence of a new, disturbing direction in which French culture is moving. But it is not. It is a dated, old-fashioned silliness. M. Joséphin Péladan was writing this sort of thing fifty years ago. Before that, it was Lévi, the occultist; before that, the Illuminati and the disciples of Schroeffer. . . . It has to be admitted that this same brand of guff fed and sustained W. B. Yeats in his youth, but Yeats' Rosicrucian romances seemed vapid and unrewarding when they were written, and seem even more so today.

Anthony West. *NY*. Jan. 12, 1952. p. 76

Gracq is an explorer in the childlike realms of dream. Consequently he is not easy reading: whoever continues beyond the first chapter feels like an initiate of mysteries reserved for the elect. For Gracq habitually applies the art of the lapidary to an already sumptuously complex adventure. His dazzling style is made up of long involved sentences, multiple epithets, archaisms, incantatory repetitions, and frequent use of italics for emphasis.

Justin O'Brien. *NYT*. Jan. 20, 1952. pp. 5, 18

It would be banal to underline the dreamlike character of the themes which obsess Julien Gracq, themes which are transposed in a seemingly natural way from the universe of dreams to the waking state. From this comes his curiosity about automatic writing, which seizes the daydream as it passes. From this comes his perfect understanding of Rimbaud and Lautréamont. It is revealing that Gracq recalls his own years in school to describe "that halo of abandonment" which explains so well what is essential in young Ducasse. Perhaps the only great visionaries are those who have never succeeded in freeing themselves of their childish fears.

Willy de Spens. *NRF*. Sept., 1961. pp. 529–30.
Tr. by Dorothy Nyren Curley

See *A Dark Stranger* and *The Castle of Argol* (novels).

GREEN, JULIAN (1900–   )

What is the fundamental substance of these books? They offer dream photographs mingled with evocations of reality, both expressed in pure classical language. . . . He one day assured me that he finds it impossible to use in a narrative events which he has witnessed, but that often an object or landscape he has only glanced at becomes the starting point of a lengthy work. This mingling of the real with the fictitious often results in haunting visions.

Marie Scheikévitch. *Time Past* (Houghton). 1935. p. 302

A novelist of such narrow range and limited experience, who seems to have allowed a barrier of books to stand between himself and the richness of life, cannot rank among the major authors of fiction. On reading him, we seldom, if ever, feel that continuous oscillation between opposite poles, that dynamic process of life to be found, as Ernst Cassirer has remarked, in the finest works of art. Green confines himself at one extremity, whereas a greater man would touch, or at least attempt to touch, both extremities at once. So, to many, his universe is a foreign country, almost a land of exile. And yet, because shyness and fear, even moral obliquity, above all illness, are known to every man, Mr. Green's novels never fail to reach the springs of responsive emotions in readers anxious to face, rather than ignore the anguish at life's core.

Henri A. Talon. *YFS*. No. 10, 1953. p. 42

The chronological reading of Green's work makes one increasingly conscious of his preoccupation with the purpose of life. His change of faith, his Oriental interests, and his emotional fluctuations are all indicative of a mind trying to discover its destiny, its place in the universal picture. His concern with religion naturally includes a concept of destiny which must be taken into account if we are to understand the pessimism and anguish of his work. An author of such religious sensitivity could only produce tragedy.

Samuel Stokes. *Julian Green and the Thorn of Puritanism* (Columbia). 1955. p. 80

Green uses the techniques of the thriller and, as he freely admits, plays on the ambiguous psychology of a childish fascination with terror—his own terror and ours. His heroes exhibit the helplessness of victims moving voluntarily to a violent end, as children move through horror stories. Held in someone else's power, they struggle hardly at all, so exciting is the apprehension of disaster; the giant or dragon is hidden in the shadows, and they are his promised victims. Their fearful excitement, which the reader shares, pervades the whole drama as they are carried toward their destruction. The atmosphere Green creates is somewhat akin to that of Henry James's *The Turn of the Screw*. It is moral rather than merely physical terror.

Germaine Brée and Margaret Guiton. *An Age of Fiction* (Rutgers). 1957. pp. 102–3

The Greenian canvas is liberally splashed with strokes of ebony. Now a solid mass, now a mere suggestion of an inky line, the black tone lends artistic relief to the author's message: the omnipresence of the arch-enemy—death, evil, damnation. . . . To a lesser degree, but no less conspicuous, is the presence of whiteness on the artist's palette. . . . Whiteness—vivid, stark, cold, chaste—comprises the marble mold of many a Greenian novel. Interestingly, the way tones are diversely significant, symbolizing now the purity of snow or the soft veil of a religious; now the sensual pallor of human flesh or the voluptuousness of a wax figure. It represents death—and life; body—and soul; good —and evil.

> Mother M. Gerard Cooke. *Hallucination and Death as Motifs of Escape in the Novels of Julien Green* (Catholic U.). 1966. pp. 46–9

For the public at large, *"Sud"* was first a perplexing play. But on close study, it turns out to be a remarkable composition, one of the few really successful attempts in recent years at creating the pure tone of tragedy: all the ambiguities of the characters; the richness of their inner life which is communicated; the vigor, simplicity, and directness of the writing. . . . The play is a tragedy on the theme of homosexuality. . . . In his dramaturgy, as in his novels, he passes easily from the real world to the surreal world. A supernaturally evil atmosphere surrounds many of the scenes, and yet there is intense drama in the effort of the characters to resist their fate.

> Wallace Fowlie. *Dionysius in Paris* (Meridian). 1960. pp. 191–4

He does not experiment with technique; he displays no intellectual acrobatics; he refuses to side with any school or to ride any ephemeral "new" or any more permanent wave. Unlike Aragon, or Malraux, whose exact contemporary he is, Green has consistently eschewed commitment to a political cause. His country is that of the invisible. His constant setting is the night through which tortured shades grope, seeking the light of clarity and yearning for their salvation.

> Henri Peyre. *NYT.* Dec. 10, 1961. p. 5

Others have remarked on the affinities between Green and Hawthorne or Poe. In a slightly different way he resembles Moravia and a number of the French new novelists. It is as though in each the long education of the spiritual consciousness has led only to an exaltation of a melancholy, sensitive, lonely spirituality and/or to an equally melancholy, sensitive, and lonely absorption in sexuality as something apart from the rest of life, and, because apart, evil. The result is not simply a denial of humanity, but also a paralysis that leads to the wish and need to die.

Roger Sale. *NR*. Sept. 26, 1964. p. 26

What we find in the later novels is something that belongs to a great tradition, but today is slightly out of fashion: the conflict between duty and inclination, between spirit and flesh, restated in contemporary terms. The novels are studies in violence, but there is none of the sensationalism, none of the complicity, that we meet in the work of a François Mauriac or a Graham Greene. The novelist is no longer looking for alibis or ways of escape; the issues are faced squarely and unflinchingly; the conflict is genuine and the outcome tragic.

Martin Turnell. *NYR*. Oct. 22, 1964. pp. 16–17

See *Each in His Darkness* and *The Transgressor* (novels).

GRILLET, ALAIN ROBBE-
See Robbe-Grillet, Alain

GUARESCHI, GIOVANNI (1908–   )

The Little World of Don Camillo . . . [is a] little gem in the field of clarity-amid-confusion. . . . Its humor, its charm, its simplicity, its wisdom in the guise of innocence, its masterful timing, its sense of detail, are more than sufficient to enchant any reader. . . . It won't solve the problem of Christianity versus Communism, but it will definitely, for the honest observer, reduce the size of the versus. Besides, it introduces to America a new and brilliant satirist, whose art is fully developed.

Thomas Sugrue. *SR*. Aug. 19, 1950. pp. 10–11

Giovanni Guareschi's *The Little World of Don Camillo* is . . . exquisitely wrought and . . . moving. It has a quality of which today only the Italian writers seem capable, a quality that must come from the soil and some changeless and harmonious human relationship with nature, with God, and the people whom the earth nourishes. The novel is like a legend, a tale addressed to whatever is still childlike and simple in our minds.

Harrison Smith. *SR*. Feb. 17, 1951. p. 9

If . . . only . . . the little priest and the Communist in this little Italian village had more than a merely wistful relationship to the world we live in, . . . it would only be a question of good will and time before humanity triumphed over the foolishness of men's conflict and the evil of Communism. Giovanni Guareschi is vastly persuasive that the lion and the lamb may some day lie together gazing into the landscape of the peaceful kingdom—and he is nearly credible. . . . The only trouble with Don Camillo is that he always wins. It is as if he were a priest in an American movie. It is delightful and morally satisfying that this should be the case, but it would seem evident that the cards are stacked. The reason Don Camillo always wins is that his opponent Peppone is not a real Communist; he only thinks he is one. . . . These village Communists are comic figures. Real Comunists are not. . . . They are all nice people in Don Camillo's little world and it is a pity that there is not much chance that ours can be made to resemble it.

Gouverneur Paulding. *NYHT*. Aug. 17, 1952. p. 4

The secret of Guareschi's success, of course, is the complete and irresponsible humanity of his cast. Don Camillo may be a priest, but a big-fisted, broad-chested and delightfully mercurial man all the same. And Peppone, the Communist mayor of the village and Don Camillo's chief antagonist, is equally human—a far cry from the demoniac political caricatures which seem to be rushing about everywhere. . . . Although Peppone and "his gang" mouth the usual Stalinist *clichés,* they are basically far too Italian and too Catholic to feel morally clothed without the presence of the Church. And while Don Camillo may often loose unpriestly invective on those who dare to vote Red, there is an unruffled and vocal Christ to remind him that even Communists are men.

Stanley Cooperman. *NR*. Sept. 15, 1952. pp. 22–3

All plots, as plots, are artificial and untrue to life, and moreover terribly pallid beside the miraculous richness of daily existence.

Suppose then that the writer decides to risk losing the story-avid reader by writing a book without a "story," a book about nothing— which is to say about everything, since it is about the things that are reality itself for the overwhelming majority of the human race in the overwhelming proportion of its waking moments. [Giovanni Guareschi] has taken this risk [in *The House that Nino Built*] and brought it off perfectly. . . . [His] wonderful simplicity and naturalness . . . are the same simplicity and naturalness as in the Italian films, which can succeed wonderfully with very simple things, even "corn," where Hollywood would make an unholy mess.

William Barrett. *NYT*. Oct. 25, 1953. p. 3

A sense of humor in adversity is a gift as great as it is rare. To have survived the kind of suffering which Giovanni Guareschi endured in a German prison camp in World War II, and to have written of it during and after his bitter experience with such charity of heart, bespeaks a spirit more real and more noble than that of Guareschi's famous Don Camillo himself. . . . *My Secret Diary* . . . is, of course, a work that is very much his own. His admirers will find that every page has the authentic Guareschi stamp on it, owing nothing to those who have written about war and imprisonment before him. The gentleness, the wry fantasy, the perpetual wonder at what God has wrought, good and bad together, and over it all the echo of irrepressible laughter—these are the trademarks of this writer who is so much more than a professional humorist. . . . The impression he leaves at the end is the contribution of a deeply serious artist—perhaps more priest than artist.

Ned Calmer. *SR*. July 12, 1958. p. 18

For better or for worse, the novel has become increasingly popular as a vehicle of political ideas. In some cases, fiction oversimplifies complex realities into melodramatic stereotypes. In others, it reveals the hollowness of platitudes by extending them to their ridiculous ultimate. It is to this bracing category that the novels of Giovanni Guareschi belong. . . . In a bitter postscript, Guareschi admits to feeling that his novel is out of date, done in by a contemporary Italian climate that he feels smacks of apathy and decay. . . . I differ. The wit and humanity of *Comrade Don Camillo* are universals, and they spring from a hope for the world that is more enduring than the transient excesses of *la dolce vita*.

Martin Levin. *NYT*. April 5, 1964. p. 48

See *The Little World of Don Camillo, Don Camillo and His Flock, The House That Nino Built, Don Camillo's Dilemma, Don Camillo Takes the Devil by the Tail*, and *Comrade Don Camillo* (novels); and *My Secret Diary* (biographical prose).

GUILLÉN, JORGE (1893–   )

With Señor Guillén . . . there are no bandits or bullfighters, and the verses are carefully wrought and polished. The typically Spanish is absent. Instead we find a very cultivated sensibility, influenced considerably by the great French poet, M. Paul Valéry. . . . His poems are records of momentary experience, translated through a fine and intelligent sensibility. As such the author's emotion of joy, say, or wonder, is recorded along with the phenomena described. So we often find notes of exclamation, and rather telegraphic, verbless sentences in his poems. These poems are a record of the extraordinary, and not related to our ordinary everyday experiences, or in any way a part of a picture of life as a whole. . . . In Señor Guillén we find continually praises of the present moment—the moment of the poem—in its isolation. . . . It is the experience in itself that matters, not its relation to other experiences.

Edward Meryon Wilson. *BkmL*. Sept., 1931. pp. 288-9

Juan Ramón [Jiménez] expresses an ideal conception of poetry where all elements are reduced to the pure essence that he seeks. . . . The search for the pure essence of poetry is one of the fundamental motivations in the creative existence of Jorge Guillén, but the interpretation of this term depends so much upon the individual poetic personality. The elements of restlessness, oscillation and change [in Jiménez] are entirely absent in Guillén. His poetry, on the contrary, emerges perfect, definitive, sculptural. With quiet calm mastery, Guillén constantly visualizes perfect unity without confusion. . . . Opposed to Juan Ramón's restlessness in space, his desire for flight, for transcending limits, is the serenity of Jorge Guillén's contemplation of limited units of space, his feeling for structural content, for density and outline, oriented with exactness in space.

Frances Avery Pleak. *The Poetry of Jorge Guillén*
(Princeton). 1942. pp. 22-3, 29

The poetry of Guillén does not radiate with reference to anything found outside of itself. Instead it plumbs its own depth to the springs of its poetic creation. . . . In the works of Guillén, as in all of the most exquisite contemporary lyrics, the subject matter is at a minimum; there are neither events nor external references; indeed, there is scarcely anything having reference to that world in which the reader lives. . . . His poetry . . . exhibits itself in a marvelous nudity, only protected by itself. . . . Guillén is startled by something which is neither unorganized inner experience nor clear and objective realities. His particular poetic field is something that exists in that tenuous moment between the birth of the creative élan and the actual fact of the creation. His poetic axis revolves around his surprise at living between nothingness and being, between non-existence and existence.

Americo Castro. Introduction to *The Poetry of Jorge Guillén*
by Frances Avery Pleak (Princeton). 1942. pp. xiii, xvii

Many of his poems are "moments of vision," the enthusiasm of the moment of catching sight of a thing for the first time, like Keats first looking into Chapman's Homer. . . . Like Paul Valéry, the poet watches himself emerging from sleep to wakefulness, and again like Valéry, many of his poems arose from the sudden presence of rhythms in his head. . . . Much has been made of the "influence" on Jorge Guillén of Paul Valéry. . . . Yet the influence was in the method of his poetry, rather than in the substance: his preference for classical Spanish verse and strophes. Even when he wrote a poem in lines of varying lengths, every line was a regular Spanish verse. His finish and self-discipline may [also] owe something to Valéry. . . . The fact that Guillén knew Valéry and went to his house has led critics to include him with the Abbé Bremond and the advocates of "pure poetry"—an association which Guillén himself was the first to disclaim.

J. B. Trend. Jorge Guillén (Cambridge). 1952. pp. 3-7

One seldom finds in the twentieth century a poetic <i>oeuvre</i> like Jorge Guillén's which is so exclusively a song of praise. Everything here is written in a major key, everything dances and rejoices in the sun. Here are no dissonances, no neuroses, no <i>fleurs du mal</i>. The incomprehensible high creations are as glorious as on the first day. Many readers will need at first to accustom their eyes to these cataracts of light. Here is a realm without tragedy, without bitterness, without lament. Where else in the modern lyric can one find this?

Ernst Robert Curtius. HdR. Summer, 1954. p. 223

The poetry of Jorge Guillén . . . is of clarity above all, or of the triumph of clarity: light, bright contours, tactile and visual certainty. . . . Chaos is abhorred as nothingness; only the clear outline of being is desired. . . . Delight in the moment, in pure being, is of the essence in Jorge Guillén's work. . . . His poetry combines a tight classical form with a brilliantly complex style, a metaphorical density and daring that recall not only Mallarmé but also the great baroque poet Luis de Gongora (1561-1627), yet which somehow achieve a freshness and clarity not reminiscent of either of his predecessors, in a poetry dedicated to the celebration of immediate delight, of joy in living, in being alive. . . . Guillén's celebration of the moment, of Being, of Becoming, has led some critics . . . to point out his nexus with Existentialism. . . . His is a poetry not of nothingness but of Being, of its fullness and immediacy.

Julian Palley. The Poem Itself, ed. by Stanley Burnshaw
(Holt). 1960. p. 211-3

He uses the present tense with great frequency and is even fond of exclamations without verbs. This is all part of his desire to express . . .

plenitude. . . . But why does Guillén so often use the present tense? Certainly Valéry uses it even more consistently, and his example may have been important to Guillén, but that is only a subsidiary reason. Surely the true reason is that he wishes to perpetuate the singleness of various moments of time in the artistic form of poetry, to do, in fact, something similar to what Proust does in prose. Thus Guillén's plenitude might be called a "fullness of time." His joy is that of the artist who has found his true means of expression, and what he communicates to the reader is really his own feeling of creativeness. Hence the absence of those emotions objectively expressed which are the subject of most of the lyric poetry of the past.

Charles David Ley. *Spanish Poetry Since 1939*
(Catholic U.). 1962. p. 8

See *Cántico* (poetry).

HUYSMANS, JORIS-KARL (1848–1907)

No matter what other qualities persist throughout his work pessimism is never absent, his firmament is ever clotted with black stars. He had a mediaeval monk's contempt for existence, contempt for the mangy flock of mediocrity; yet his genuis drove him to describe its crass ugliness in phrases of incomparable and enamelled prose. . . . His theme, with variations, is a strangling Ennui.

James Huneker. *NAR*. Sept., 1907. p. 41

A page of Huysmans is as a dose of opium, a glass of something exquisite and spirituous. . . . Huysmans goes to my soul like a gold ornament of Byzantine workmanship: there is in his style the yearning charm of arches, a sense of ritual, the passion of the Gothic, of the window.

George Moore. *Confessions of a Young Man* (Brentano). 1917. pp. 217–9

It is always the unpleasant aspect of things that he seizes, but the intensity of his revolt from that unpleasantness brings a touch of the sublime into the very expression of his disgust. Every sentence is an epigram, and every epigram slaughters a reputation or an idea. He speaks with an accent as of pained surprise, an amused look of contempt, so profound that it becomes almost pity, for human imbecility.

Arthur Symons. *The Symbolist Movement in Literature* (Dutton). 1919. p. 234

His face, with the sensitive, luminous eyes, reminded one of Baudelaire's portraits, the face of a resigned and benevolent Mephistopheles who has discovered the absurdity of the Divine order but has no wish to make an improper use of his discovery. He talked in low and even tones, never eagerly, without any emphasis or gesture, not addressing any special person; human imbecility was the burden of nearly all that he said, while a faint twinkle of amused wonderment lit up his eyes. And throughout all his books until almost the last *"l'eternelle bêtise de l'humanité"* is the ever-recurring refrain.

Havelock Ellis. Introduction to *Against the Grain* (Lieber and Lewis). 1922. p. vii

Against the Grain, answering some fevered need of the moment, became the breviary of the nineties in England. It is the crystallization of *fin de siècle* migraine. Certainly it remains the most consistent symbol of that languor and tired quest for whipped-up sensationalism which pervaded almost the whole of Europe at the close of the nineteenth century. It is a significant book because it voices this invalidism with insight and precision; it exhales a pallid world-weary spirit; it is beautiful and spotted just as Huysmans' soul was beautiful and spotted.

Pierre Loving. *Nation.* Jan. 10, 1923. p. 44

However limited Huysmans may be intellectually, however childish his conception of the world may appear, the style always saves his work from mediocrity. . . . Violent, loaded with material details, with sudden sarcastic outbursts, it always remains equally imaginative. One may detest it, but whoever has a taste for it will rarely find a lapse.

René Lalou. *Contemporary French Literature* (Knopf). 1924. pp. 44–5

Far from being the *Apology for the Decadent* which some critics affect to see in it *À Rebours* is a satire on the doctrines and attitudes of the younger generation of 1885. It seems necessary to put it in its proper place, not as the breviary of the Super-Esthete, but as the sarcastic analysis of his pose; not as a hymn to an existence of silken sensations, but as a *reductio ad absurdum* of such a conception of life. *À Rebours* assumed the role of an austere chaperone in the midst of the Symbolist masked ball.

G. L. Van Roosbroeck. *The Legend of the Decadents* (Columbia). 1927. p. 69

The principal merit and attraction of [his novels] lie in their autobiographical quality: they appeal to us as perhaps the most profound and candid memoirs produced by a modern writer, as an intimate record of the author's material and spiritual life. His determination to tell the truth about himself as far as he was able, and the psychological insight, the skill, and the honesty which he showed in his efforts to achieve this ambition, continue to evoke the admiration of present-day readers accustomed to twentieth-century novels of introspection.

Robert Baldick. *The Life of J.-K. Huysmans* (Oxford). 1955. p. 353

Huysmans remains essentially a figure of the late nineteenth century and he symbolizes to perfection all its varying moods. This is why *À Rebours* can never be overlooked and must be read by those who wish to understand the literary climate of the age. He does not possess the eternal essence of a Baudelaire or a Flaubert, nor their human depth and understanding. His greatest qualities lie in the beauty and variety of his literary style, so that one reads him for the manner of his saying rather than for what he says, or for the characters he creates.

Enid Starkie. *NSN*. July 23, 1955. p. 108

He was well read in Latin and French, and he frequented all types of *milieux*: slums, workshops, artistic circles, with the result that he was able to employ Parisianisms, provincialisms, scientific, archaic, classical, and foreign locutions, thus joining *"le délicat au populaire."* Huysmans seems to have looked on himself as a sort of modern Petronius, utilizing all the varied terms which the juxtaposition of cultures had poured into nineteenth-century Paris. Beginning with Romanticism, there was a mass invasion of new words into French; it enriched the vocabulary of the realists and Naturalists, but until Huysmans and even after him, it was employed with a certain timidity.

A. E. Carter. *The Idea of Decadence in French Literature* (Toronto). 1958. p. 135

Despite his famous conversion, which was undoubtedly sincere, the evidence of his work suggests that Huysmans to the end maintained an occult sensibility. He fell into the Church because the highly charged equilibrium between the two forces of naturalism and mysticism was too great for him; and short of the insanity of a Gérard de Nerval, he turned for whatever consolation he could get, to a kind of Catholicism. In embracing this kind of Church, however, he surely found the Chimera in his arms, if not the succuba herself.

John Senior. *The Way Down and Out* (Cornell). 1959. p. 126

On the grounds of sheer literary workmanship Huysmans' books are unique. His novels have certain great excellencies, and admittedly certain grave defects. Filled with art and beauty, medievalism and mysticism, decadence and diabolism, they are singular stories of the unexpected, the extraordinary, the exotic. . . . He is read by students of literature and psychology, lovers of art and music, devotees of diabolism and decadence. He had an uncanny insight into the late nineteenth-century mind, and as a child of his age, as an important representative of his time and culture, his books can serve as texts of the intellectual and spiritual of the *fin de siècle*.

George A. Cevasco. *J. K. Huysmans in England and America* (The Bibliographical Society of the U. of Virginia). 1962. pp. 2, 5

See *Against the Grain* and *The Cathedral* (novels).

IBÁÑEZ, VICENTE BLASCO
See Blasco Ibáñez, Vicente

INCLÁN, RAMÓN DEL VALLE-
See Valle-Inclán, Ramón del

IONESCO, EUGÈNE (1912–   )

One might almost say that this extreme avant-gardist has become, in a way, a classic. Such a theater, upsetting all conventions and habits and destructive of the theater itself, seems to have been expected. At any rate, it has been immediately recognized and acclaimed. This is due to the fact that Ionesco's plays, which some commentators have tried to dismiss as mere extravaganzas born of the author's dreams and anxieties, are a response to the demands of a given personal situation in history. His feelings are those of a man of his time, plunged in the agony of his century. . . . If Ionesco's works appear at first so strange and disconcerting and seem so fond of the weird and the monstrous, it is not because they are immured within the universe of dream or delirium, but precisely because they open out into our world.

> J. S. Doubrovsky. *YFS*. Summer, 1959. p. 3

Ionesco's work when well performed is a striking example of how negation can be true, almost pure, theatre. . . . The prevalence of historic imagination in his work is only one characteristic of his rampant theatricality, for which he has received much praise and blame. Ionesco is a formidable parodist, a sardonic sceptic, and an almost irrepressibly gay nihilist; he is as effective in comedy as in pathos. He is capable of challenging reflection while outraging sensibility or tickling our funny bone with his clowning, and of depressing and amusing us almost in the same breath.

> John Gassner. *Theatre at the Crossroads* (Holt).
> 1960. p. 261

Rather than trying to conceal the various artificialities and conventions of a performance (*les ficelles,* in Ionesco's language), he believed that they should go as far as possible in grotesqueness and caricature. Ionesco recalls theories of Antonin Artaud when he advocates a theater of violence where the psychological study of characters will be replaced by metaphysical themes. He does not recognize any clearly marked distinction between the comic and the tragic. He deliberately calls his plays "comic dramas" or "tragic farces." . . . These two elements of the comic and tragic are not fused; for Ionesco, they coexist. Each stands as a criticism of the other.

Wallace Fowlie. *Dionysius in Paris* (Meridian). 1960. p. 236

The richness of Ionesco's theatre—and also what makes it confusing—comes from the mixture of the domains he puts under question. All the absurdities are given equal importance, whether they be the presence of things, man's decisions, social disorder, social conventions, psychological impulses, old age, or the problems of city traffic. The world is seen simultaneously on all levels, with the result that the main problem or subject does not exclude the other levels. . . . All that can be said for this universe is that facts, events, beings, and things exist. And indeed they exist in abundance. One of the authentically dramatic dimensions of Ionesco's theatre lies in the tension between a superabundance of being and the absolute impossibility of justifying the fact of being.

Jacques Guicharnaud. *Modern French Theatre* (Yale). 1961. p. 182

His work—it has often been noted—seems dominated by a fundamental obsession, that of the commonplace. In this sense, it is attacking a clearly defined language: a language made up of clichés and ready-made formulas, which is that of an alienated society, and is ours also insofar as we belong to that society and insofar as the stupidity which it secretes, whatever our efforts to free ourselves from it, contaminates all our daily behavior. Such is the petty bourgeois language denounced by Ionesco in most of his plays. However diverse the methods he uses to make it laughable these methods all consist, in the final analysis, of creating a sort of pushing to the limit, whose purpose is never to take away the sense from a pre-existing language, but to oblige it to betray to us by itself its own absurdity.

Jean Vannier. *TDR.* Spring, 1963. pp. 182–3

A pernicious effect to Ionesco's plays is that we frequently feel that our understanding of what a human being is is beginning to fall apart. It is as if he had borrowed from that picture, yet to appear, of man when the sciences and the pseudo-sciences have completed their studies and had caused it to coalesce, meaningless and empty, in a bewildering array of malfunctioning parts. His plays seem the vanguard of that age when life will be a chemical compound, human beings will exchange thoughts via electronic instruments installed in the brain, machines will think, minds will be scientifically destroyed, and the races brought to physical perfection through the most sophisticated methods of birth control. His theatre proceeds from a society bewitched by biological, psychological, and social determinism, the unconscious, the sociological machine which stamps us out like so many gingerbread men.

Jack Murray. *YFS*. Spring-Summer, 1962. p. 86

"Les Chaises" is probably unique in dramatic literature. It draws us relentlessly into a world of the Not and when we are "dropped" we are flooded by anguish. Although styled a "tragic farce" by Ionesco, the farcical elements are soon overwhelmed; there is rarely any laughter after the middle of the play. . . . *"Les Chaises"* leads us from the false Not of bad faith to the true Not of nothingness. By scrupulously enacting the Not, the play shows us the Not within each of us; as such it transcends any purely social interpretation we may give it. The play finds its power in the exploration of that nothingness which Sartre says "lies coiled in the heart of being—like a worm."

Richard Schechner. *YFS*. Spring-Summer, 1962. p. 72

The playwright's task is to "bring forth anxieties, inner ghosts"—a repeated concern of Ionesco. . . . The only distinction of Ionesco's protagonist comes from his sensitivity to such anxieties and inner ghosts. Otherwise, he is the utterly colorless "little man," settled in the most ordinary of petty bourgeois surroundings, naive in his beliefs, and limited in his ethical concerns to conventional do-goodism. Primary forces in subverting his world are the skeletons which the bourgeois are normally able to keep in their closets. *His* inevitably escape, in conformity with the kinetic laws that impel all evil manifestations on this stage.

David I. Grossvogel. *Four Playwrights and a Postscript* (Cornell). 1962. p. 75

The world created by Ionesco is strange and nightmarish, but at the same time familiar, for it is our own little world, and the grotesque figures moving upon the stage remind us of ourselves. We have become gigantic puppets, often moving senselessly back and forth, with little apparent meaning in our words or actions. This theater recalls the Punch and Judy show, as is natural, for Ionesco had his first lessons in dramatic art at the guignol. . . . Most of Ionesco's plays are surprisingly gay, for the author wishes to underline through these tragic farces and comic dramas, not only the inseparability of the comic and the tragic, but the fundamental absurdity of the human predicament. . . . Ionesco mingles the comic and the tragic, and his audience is pulled from one to the other until it no longer knows what to think. An Ionesco audience is rarely indifferent: its members are either vehemently opposed to what they are witnessing or are just as vehemently in favor of it.

Leonard Cabell Pronko. *Avant-Garde* (California). 1962. pp. 61–3

His preferred dramatic device, excellently worked out in such pieces as "The Lesson" and "The Chairs," is a single metaphor, a dramatic conceit expanded with ingenious use of language. Words become the most powerful instrument to replace action and plot. They are used not as thoughts of the characters, but as weapons to shock and startle, to hold attention, to explore ideas, to play one against the other, to become— through manipulation—the demonstration of the absurd. . . . Above all, Ionesco uses the cliché, the platitude, and gives it startling freshness by using it out of context, twisting it to remove the dead weight of non-communication.

Allan Lewis. *The Contemporary Theatre* (Crown). 1962. p. 269

The fact is that for Ionesco, in his state of "inspiration," the spontaneous creations of his subconscious emerge as ready-made formal structures of truly classical purity.

More than that: their very spontaneity, the very freedom with which he allows characters and situations to take shape constitutes the basis and source of their purity of form: plays like "The Chairs" or "The Lesson" are above all enjoyed by their audiences as formal patterns of great simplicity and perfection. His own experience has convinced Ionesco that the spontaneous reproducton of the *structures* of the subconscious imagination is bound to emerge in the form of structurally satisfying patterns.

Martin Esslin. *TDR*. Spring, 1963. p. 174

In *Mes Pièces et Moi,* Eugène Ionesco suggests that a feeling of lightness, airiness, sometimes accompanied by the discovery of a gift of levitation restores the lost paradise of youth and innocence, whereas the proliferation of matter constitutes a concretization of man's imprisonment in the material world. Surrounded by useless objects, hemmed in by words used up by abuse, the mind feels stifled. . . . Ionesco is the poet of spectacle. He synthesizes visually the eternal grief of change, lovelessness, *"désamour."* Like Chekhov whom he admires Ionesco wishes to show that *"Nous sommes tous tués par le temps."* . . . Compounded of air or matter, Ionesco's plays never allow us to forget the tragic quality of life made bearable only by a Dionysian explosion of laughter, coupled with a deep respect for the transient, evanescent combination of mind and flesh which is our existential condition.

Rosette C. Lamont. *FR.* Jan., 1965. pp. 349, 355, 361

See *Four Plays* and *Rhinoceros and Other Plays.*

JACOB, MAX (1876–1944)

If he had so much alacrity, so much care in answering a letter (even one from a stranger), if the least scruple forced him sometimes to fill margins with ideas, with new points, with retractions, or to send ahead an answer by a second letter which contradicted an earlier letter, it is that such a correspondence had become for Max a more helpful outlet than his regular work was, whether that work was written, painted, or drawn. What had he withheld of himself in his work? Nothing at all, except the aura of his legend. But when that work risks freezing him in an attitude, like all authors of many facets such as he, letters sent out, scattered throughout a thirty year period bring him to life, take the statue from its pedestal.

> Louis Emié. *Dialogues avec Max Jacob* (Buchet-Chastel). 1954. pp. 15–16. Tr. by Dorothy Nyren Curley

His poems are never perfected works of art. They are close to being ways of producing a poetic state of awareness in the reader. Their parody intent is almost always perceptible. The music of his verse is irregular and often irritating in its eccentricities. Superficially his poetry could seem to be largely composed of commonplaces, of witticisms, of gossip about the *faits divers*. But the deeper, more total effect of his poetry is one of exceptional suppleness in verbal expression, of infinite metamorphosis. In a way, he is a poet for poets. The work of such poets as Cocteau, Maurice Fombeure and Jacques Prévert would perhaps not be exactly what it is without the example of Max Jacob.

> Wallace Fowlie. *Mid-Century French Poets* (Twayne). 1955. p. 33

Though he was never afraid of poverty and though he found in his country retreat the ideal place for meditations which sought a mystical goal, though he was conscious of inflicting a punishment on himself in leaving Paris . . . he could not bring himself to a decision to reinforce his exile by a vow of silence: to have an audience was his reason for being alive. Likewise, his thousands of letters were an integral part of a work which, whether it was poem or novel, drama or parody, confession or essay, was before all a dialogue, as one can see by his style alone (the apostrophes, the interjections, the parentheses, the dashes) and his tonality (the boasting, confidence, familiarity) toward the judgment of critics, of followers; it exacts from all at least a response and identifies itself, in all the domains that it attempts, with a missionary effort as much as with spiritual creation.

> Jean Rousselot. *Max Jacob au Sérieux* (Editions Subervie).
> 1958. pp. 175–6. Tr. by Dorothy Nyren Curley

A great mobility of spirit and sensibility manifests itself in the poems which go from argot to metaphysics, from pun to sob, from parody to hallucination. Often even in a single poem one meets all the tendencies on which, despite their contradictions, Max Jacob knew how to impose an undeniable poetic unity: far from being the toy of these diverse inclinations, he took from each of them its usefulness as a contrast: if he used a pun, he did so to provoke a sort of poetic rebounding. . . . All the work, impulsive, tender, and baffling, ingenuous and jaded, rigorous and pathetic of Max Jacob, is it not—like his faith—an act of conjuring out of anguish?

> Georges-Emmanuel Clancier. *De Rimbaud au Surréalisme*
> (Editions Pierre Seghers). 1959. pp. 258, 264.
> Tr. by Dorothy Nyren Curley

At the time of their [Jacob's and Picasso's] meeting, Jacob had thought of himself primarily as a painter, but when Picasso proclaimed, *"Tu es le seul poète de l'époque"* he all but abandoned his brushes and concentrated on a special, very personal type of dreamlike prose-poem, which he would read to friends at evening gatherings. Everyone was charmed by Jacob. He was always the life of the party, casting horoscopes, reading palms, producing one-man skits. "I have watched his imitation of the 'barefoot dancing girl' a hundred times," says Fernande Olivier, "each time with more pleasure than the last. His trousers, rolled up to his knees, showed his hairy legs; his shirt was wide open on a chest that was even hairier, a veritable curly black mattress; he was almost bald and he never took off his glasses, and he danced with airs and graces that made it impossible not to laugh and that were a perfect burlesque: his steps, his manipulations on tip-toe . . . !"

> Francis Steegmuller. *Apollinaire* (Farrar). 1963. p. 132

Some poets allow us the illusion that we understand them, that they *are* the incidents of their lives or the images of their poems, but this is not true of Max Jacob. There is always a surplus of meaning and of value which eludes us in everything that he has written or that is written about him. This surplus is the essential, the very secret that causes Max to be infinitely more mysterious, more complex, and finally, more attractive than any of his works. Max's greatness as a poet, his charm as a human being, his tenderness, his generosity, his wit and conversational genius, are articles of faith. These qualities are not specifically local, for they inhere in the totality of his life and work. . . . Max Jacob, whose indefinable charm continues to grow as the years pass, has most of the attributes of the true hero.

Neal Oxenhandler. *Max Jacob and Les Feux de Paris*
(California). 1964. p. 222
See selections in *Mid-Century French Poets*, ed. by Wallace Fowlie.

JAMMES, FRANCIS (1868–1938)

As becomes his spiritual character, M. Jammes has discarded all the vain pomp and splendor of verse, even the subtler and quieter graces of the Symbolists. His tone is conversational, almost casual; his sentences have the structure of prose. He uses rime or assonance or suddenly fails to rime at all. He seems merely bent on telling the simple and beautiful things in his heart as quietly as possible. What constitutes his eminence, his very high eminence, as an artist is the fact that his prosaic simplicity of manner, his naïve matter-of-factness, his apparently (but only apparently) slovenly technique are so used as to make for a new style in French poetry—a naturalistic style that rises constantly to a high and noble elevation of speech, and rises to that elevation, as Wordsworth sought to do, by using the simplest words in the simplest order.

Ludwig Lewisohn. *The Poets of Modern France*
(Huebsch). 1918. pp. 58–9

Francis Jammes is a Faun who has turned Franciscan Friar. As we read his early poems, his delicious rustic prose, we seem to see him prick-eared, in some green circle of the Pyrenees, with brown hands holding to his mouth a boxwood flute, from which he draws a brief, sweet music, as pure as the long-drawn note of the musical frog, as shrill as the plaintive cry of some mountain bird who feels above its nest the shadow of the falcon.

And then he met Paul Claudel and was converted. . . . Henceforth we see him, in our imagination, like Saint Francis, with a monk's hood drawn over his brow, sandals on his feet, his brown gown cinctured with a knotted cord, a couple of doves hovering over his shoulders, and, at his side, fawning and faithful, a converted wolf.

Mary Duclaux. *Twentieth Century French Writers*
(Collins). 1919. p. 98

He has been praised for a certain simplicity of style and freedom from rhetoric. Books like *Le Triomphe de la Vie* and *De l'Angélus de l'Aube à l'Angélus du Soir* were admirable as pictures of life. M. Jammes was a poet who could be realistic without being either dry or slap-dash. The "was" is significant; in recent years he has become more and more absorbed in religion; his realism tends to the vapid, his simplicity seems artificial, his emotion has slipped imperceptibly into sentimentality.

> Richard Aldington. *Poetry*. Oct., 1919. pp. 46–7

Francis Jammes is the poet of contentment, of observation, of simplicity. He is the poet of hills, and fields, and barns, not of libraries and alcoves. His poetry blows across the scented verses of the '90's like the wind from one of the snow-capped peaks of his native Pyrenees. . . . Jammes has never been moved by reason. His is an emotional nature, entirely swayed by his sentiments. Any judgement given by the intellect alone would undoubtedly seem to him cold and repellant. Francis Jammes is a charming child on one side, and a most loveable genius on the other. But a man of mature and balanced intellect he certainly is not. He loves with all his heart, and that is a most unusual and refreshing thing.

> Amy Lowell. *Six French Poets* (Houghton). 1921.
> pp. 217, 235–6

Francis Jammes deals with his ideas as delicately and firmly as the spider with his cobweb. In his poetry he throws over the subjects of his poems, small and apparently insignificant, a veil of curious softness and color, streaked with a humor so simple as to be deceptive. One does not always know whether to smile. But behind or beyond the shifting hues of his words, one is aware of the mystic who seeks to discover *"à l'extrémité de l'abîme une étoile sans nom."*

> Bernice K. Van Slyke. *Poetry*. Oct., 1922. p. 49

If Henri de Régnier's example proves what almost Parnassian reserve could survive the Symbolist revolution, Francis Jammes shows what broken barriers henceforth permitted the poet to assign as objects for his art the least romantic incidents of his daily experience. . . . Jammes tells about Jammes abundantly. Without tiring, he shows *La Naissance du poète, Un jour* (of the poet's life), *Le Poète et sa Femme, La Mort du poète, Le Poète rustique,* so that his supreme skill is probably having rendered impossible every criticism which, bearing upon his work, would seem to cast aspersions upon the Christian and family virtues of which he offers and celebrates so meritorious a model.

> René Lalou. *Contemporary French Literature* (Knopf).
> 1924. p. 133

Jammes's intense sensitiveness to every feature of pastoral life, his profound appreciation of visible Nature, his physical and spiritual perceptions, his healthy sensuousness, his deep contentment with his lot, the simplicity of all his emotional responses, and his extraordinary faculty of objective and ironical, yet sympathetic, observation, brought this more or less untutored French provincial, from his first scribblings, to an attitude of mind and spirit perfectly designed for the utterance of poetic truth. If the sentiment of love finds its most sublime utterance in poetry, every line that Jammes has written is filled with love—with the love of life, the love of every tree and flower and blade of grass, the love of every animal, the love of every man, except, perhaps the apothecaries of Orthez.

William A. Drake. *Contemporary European Writers*
(John Day). 1928. p. 244

In Jammes's verses one smells mint, marjoram and thyme, mixed with the incense of the churches; one hears the noise of the mountain streams and the cooing of the wild doves. One lives with shepherds, huntsmen and plowmen, whose lives Jammes poeticized in his *Géorgiques chrétiennes*. . . . Jammes has kept away from artistic circles and it cannot be said that any French poets have followed in his steps; yet he set the example of a quite revolutionary writing. He was systematically archaic, naive and familiar. He took the greatest liberties with versification and brought French verse very close to the vernacular.

Régis Michaud. *Modern Thought and Literature in France*
(Funk). 1934. pp. 37–8

See *Homer Had a Dog* (poetry).

JARRY, ALFRED (1873–1907)

Alfred Jarry . . . appeared to me as a personification of a river, a young river without a beard, with clothing damp as a drowned man's. His little mustache tips drooping, his cloak with its lapels swaying, a soft shirt and sport socks, all had something soft, something spongey about them and, like a demi-god still damp, he looked as though only a few hours ago he had emerged shivering from the river bed where his energies had been flowing.

Guillaume Apollinaire. *Les Pas Perdus* by André Breton
(Gallimard). 1924. p. 61. Tr. by Dorothy Nyren Curley

Jarry had a genius unique, I really think, in our literature of elevating to the literary life and to the rank of a symbol a marionette born from

the mad imagination of a disrespectful student. Just like Joseph
Prudhomme, for example, Father Ubu has come into today's vocabulary.
And what a tragic destiny: Father Ubu chases the personality of Jarry,
takes his place, finishes by killing him. Jarry was the most extravagant
of writers and men and one of the most extreme figures of a period when
the most diverse sorts of bohemians flourished. His learning was immense and he was ". . . devoured . . . by an insatiable curiosity."

> Paul Chauveau. *MF*. Nov. 1, 1926. p. 581.
> Tr. by Dorothy Nyren Curley

Although already thirty years old, he looked like an adolescent, I would
even say like an adolescent girl. To look at him one could have taken
him for a young girl in disguise. A soft felt hat shadowed his smooth and
open face down to eyes both anxious and mocking. He was dressed in
an outfit of tired black cloth on the waistcoat of which hung the rumpled
ends of an ample black necktie, twisted down from a false collar of a
dubious whiteness. . . . One must say that even if Jarry did not take
much care of his clothes, he was scrupulously clean himself. . . . He
was charming and comical and the sound of his voice, crystalline and
somewhat sharp, added to this impression of transvestitism.

> Sander Pierron. *MF*. Nov. 1, 1931. pp. 719–20.
> Tr. by Dorothy Nyren Curley

Alfred Jarry was a little squat man with a heavy torso set on bandy legs.
In a pale face with small screwed up features and a little brown mustache
appeared eyes glittering with a metallic glint. Out of short trousers
calves in long socks led down to feet shod in loafers with spongey soles.
Clad, under his jacket, in a sweater, he looked like a bicyclist or a
bankrupt newspaper boy. Solid on his feet, he appears vigorous and
supple, despite the precocious ravages of poverty and alcohol.

> Henri de Regnier. *De Mon Temps* (Mercure de France).
> 1933. p. 150. Tr. by Dorothy Nyren Curley

Jarry had a sense of the fantastic, of nightmare . . . and obtained
surprising effects by upsetting thought by use of vocabulary and rhythm,
that is to say by opposing the splendor of these to the drollery of that. He
had no need to encumber himself with the accessories dear to a magician
—spiders, owls, mummies, skeletons—the music of his words envelops
us and the charm works. . . . Jarry is a great maker of sentences. In the
magnificence of his phrases, their sonorous plenitude, and the discreet
appropriateness of his terms, he is close to Villiers de l'Isle-Adam. And

what a vocabulary is available to this scholar who mocks scholars. This scoffing luxuriousness makes one think of Rabelais.

Fernand Lot. *Alfred Jarry* (Editions de la Nouvelle Revue Critique). 1934. pp. 66–7. Tr. by Dorothy Nyren Curley

Jarry's principal interest in "Ubu-Roi" was not in the play itself as a piece of dramatic writing, nor even in the establishing of the eternal type of Ubu, but in "Ubu-Roi" as a production which was to be an experiment in a new dramatic technique. . . . As the tumult which accompanied the presentation of "Ubu-Roi" in December 1896 showed, it was not a very suitable vehicle for experiments in a new technique. The controversial character of the lines, the beginning with its celebrated *mot,* which the enemies of all innovation took as a challenge and an insult, and which the supporters of the movement took as a cue to noisy and injudicious approval, all that combined to prevent any impartial judgement as to the value of "Ubu-Roi" as an experiment. . . . Just as Jarry advocated the suppression of the conventional actor, and advocated the use of masks and puppet gestures, so [Gordon] Craig said that the actor should be replaced by a sort of *"über-marionette."* . . . In Craig's discussion of the limitations of actors, of the value of masks and the stylized acting of puppets, his reasoning followed along the same lines as that of Jarry, and he reached similar conclusions.

Henry A. Grubbs. *RR.* Oct., 1935. pp. 341–2, 344

Because he lived his poetry intensely and all through his life he had the courage to resist cowardice and all compromises; he could advance very far toward the heart of reality, for, indeed, he sought nothing else, and, if he remains a great precursor of today's poetic spirits, it is first because he was a perfect model for all those who refusing to acquiesce to the rule of stupidity have the strength to follow his example and to hurl in the face of cowards and fools, the magnificent cry of defiance which his revolted conscience has marvelously brought to life, his famous six-lettered word, the reverberating and justifiable: *"Merdre."*

Jacques-Henry Lévesque. *Alfred Jarry* (Editons Pierre Seghers). 1951. p. 103. Tr. by Dorothy Nyren Curley

"Ubu-Roi" is, in a double sense, a literary experience. First because it was dropped awkwardly into the modern dramatic repertoire by a literary impulse, French Symbolism, that was essentially un-, perhaps even anti-, theatrical. And secondly because for Jarry the figure of Ubu was not so

much a considered symbol as a neurotic obsession; and the play therefore
has more the character of an act of purgation than of creation. . . . Jarry
resembles Swift in his monstrous disgust for unalleviated flesh, his preoccupation with coprology, his sense of man as one of the cruder and more
brutal forms of animal life. But the work has nothing of Swift's brilliance
or logically controlled remorselessness.

W. M. Becker. *NR*. May 26, 1952. p. 21

It is hard to see Jarry's plays as anything beyond more or less felicitous
formalizations of the author's personality—an effort at self-projection
which he carried on throughout most of his life, according to the accounts
of his intimates. Such self-projection into the drama invalidates another
part of it, for it points to an exclusive concept of laughter—if laughter
there is indeed—limited to the single device of shock. . . . Jarry relied
too exclusively on this single trick, jeopardizing the very mirth he appears
to have sought and, incidentally, availing himself of only a handful of
the many farce modes.

David I. Grossvogel. *The Self-Conscious Stage in Modern
French Drama* (Columbia). 1958. p. 27

Alfred Jarry . . . is one of the most extraordinary and eccentric figures
among the *poètes maudits* of French literature; when he died he was
regarded as little more than one of those bizarre specimens of the Paris
Bohème who merge their lives and their poetry by turning their own
personalities into grotesque characters of their own creation that disappear when they perish, as Jarry did, from overindulgence and dissipation.
Yet Jarry left an oeuvre that has been exerting a growing influence ever
since he died and that still continues to increase.

Martin Esslin. *The Theatre of the Absurd* (Doubleday).
1961. p. 255

Jarry stands in the tradition of Jean-Paul Richter and Rimbaud and
especially Gérard de Nerval, whose professed end was to "direct his
dream." The opposition in his work between personal lyric and hor-
rendous farce dissolves before this single view of life as sustained
hallucination. . . . Jarry's writing expressed an almost unthinkable code
of conduct, which he did not shrink from applying to his own life. Dream
must invade every waking moment to become the element in which we
exist. The conscious and the unconscious fuse into a continuum which
coincides with the fusion of thought and action, art and life, childhood
and maturity.

Roger Shattuck. *The Banquet Years* (Doubleday).
1961. p. 200

The pataphysical country, the Jarry universe is more than a whirlpool of ideas, images and logical mirages. It is something which is partly toy and partly trap—a toy which could become a trap for anyone regarding it with a certain gravity, who does not know, as it were, how to play with it; a trap which could become a toy for anyone who has kept or been able to recover the spontaneity of adolescence.

Henri Thomas. *NYT*. May 16, 1965. p. 18

See *Selected Works*.

JIMÉNEZ, JUAN RAMÓN (1881–1958)

The chief Modernist poet of Spain, Don Juan Ramón Jiménez, evidently has the gift of infuriating some critics and of fascinating others. But studying his work impartially nearly ten years after the death of Rubén Darío, when modernism is seen to have been a passing craze, the critic finds that there is something to Señor Jiménez' poetry that endures. . . . This poet, who is so careless of rhyme, and sometimes of rhythm, and goes out of his way to cut a word or a phrase in twain and introduces far sought newfangled words into his verse, is very quiet and natural in the use of rhyme, when he does use it, while the rhyme helps to shape and concentrate what might tend to be the indefinite flow of his verse. He would appear to have a keener sense of sound and colour in all their shades and subtleties than of definite shape; he is the impressionist painter rather than the sculptor, and his poetry is in fact an ever-flowing though transparent stream.

Aubrey F. G. Bell. *Contemporary Spanish Literature*
(Knopf). 1925. pp. 208–10

Many critics consider this poet the chief Modernist poet in Spain today; and while this is true, he certainly is not the same type of Modernist as was Rubén Darío. There appear many of the innovations of the Modernists in his work, such as the using of strange and exotic words, and the cutting of verses in two: and yet there is a soul, a depth of feeling, a sensibility in the poetry of Juan Ramón Jiménez which even the work of Darío does not show. . . . In the matter of treatment, Juan Ramón Jiménez is very subjective. He is somewhat like the impressionist painter and is not the sculptor of verses like a Parnassian poet. He is neither Parnassian nor Symbolist, although there are some of the characteristics of each of these in his work. He is a great lyric poet. . . . Although Modernism and the influence of Darío surely have their part, the verse of Jiménez tends to become more intimate and individual, more beautiful, and more musical; in other words, more natively Spanish than the verse of many other contemporary poets. It is not the classic, formal, or rhetorical Spanish poetry, but the poetry of the New Spain, of the "Novecientos" and later.

F. M. Kercheville. UNM. Dec. 15, 1933. pp. 28–9, 34

It should be quite clear that there is nothing in Juan Ramón Jiménez of that conventional Andalusian pose called *popularismo,* so worked to death by foreign writers on Spain, and indeed important in the poetry of Villalón and García Lorca; though there it is transfigured and transformed into something deeper and more tragic, and much more fundamentally Spanish. . . . All three poets had fine, sensitive natures, sensual in the best sense; but the most sensitive is undoubtedly Juan Ramón Jiménez. . . . Jiménez, from copying or describing what he saw, or allowing its existence to be deduced from what he said, came to occupy himself not with objects but with the way light fell upon them. In this he was following the familiar road of the painters—he, too, had once thought of being a painter—who have passed from painting objects to painting light itself.

J. B. Trend. Introduction to Fifty Spanish Poems of
Juan Ramón Jiménez (Dolphin). 1950. p. 17

Juan Ramón Jiménez has never written a long-deliberated poem with an analytical catalogue of his poetic ideas and attitudes. His failure to do so reveals much of his concept of the nature of poetry. It is an interplay between the poet's soul and reality, a flash of comprehension, a moment of ecstatic oneness with some natural beauty, a wave of emotion disclosing the essence of some thing. Poems are, by the very nature of poetry, momentarily-caught butterflies; each poem is a glimpse into the realm of the poet.

Walter T. Pattison. Hsp. Feb., 1950. p. 18

Like the Imagists, Jiménez took over both the Parnassian grip on the uniquely delimited object, and the Symboliste magic, which dissolves objects into atmospheric values. These values, in his poetry, are soaked with visionary meaning. The concreteness of Parnassianism was less important for him than its precision.

Rachel Frank. Poetry. July, 1953. p. 226

Bellaza and *Poesía* (1917-1923) . . . both accentuate the essential part of the poet's work, that becomes more and more subjective and intimate with light accents of intellectualism and a constant meditation on those very words: poetry and beauty. Together, the two offer the key to

Jiménez's preoccupation. It is not a question of deciding in his works the relationship between poetry and truth, as in Goethe's case; between beauty and truth as in Keats or Emily Dickinson but between beauty and poetry which with love, woman and death form the abiding themes of his life. Death, for example, is constantly present in the poet of Moguer. . . . This theme becomes almost an obsession, and it can be seen that this preoccupation with the death of others is nothing other than the mirror of his own imagined death, almost a dialogue with it. Now, too, we can appreciate how the total work of the poet of Moguer could be —and in fact is—a triumph, not over the D'Annunzio style of death, but over death itself; the triumph of beauty and poetry; the ultimate triumph of the permanent over the temporal and perishable.

Eugenio Florit. Preface to The Selected Writings of
Juan Ramón Jiménez (Farrar). 1957. pp. xxii–xxiii

Juan Ramón's poetic creation has remained generally faithful to the *fin de siècle* climate in which it was conceived. His art, like that of the Impressionists, subordinates line to color. His world is one of haze-shrouded distances and evanescent forms, of tenuous and fleeting sensorial impressions. Its emotional foundation is a gentle sadness at the transience of things. For sheer musicality and verbal artistry Juan Ramón is without equal in Spanish poetry.

Juan Lopez-Morillas. NYHT. Aug. 11, 1957. p. 4

Platero and I is a good deal more than the children's classic it has been called for forty years. It is a very personal book, full of serene whimsy and a strongly ironic manner of straight looking at the open-air, small-town world of Moguer at the turn of the century. It is also a very objective book; the kind of realism, love, and restraint that characterizes the poet's vision has the quality of Blake's songs of innocence and experience.

Once Platero has been created as the focus of feeling, Jiménez is free to make the whole world conform to it—as, for example, the cruelty of children and adults (their "beastliness" primarily) as well as their guileless acceptance of and identification with their animals and one another.

Edwin Honig. SR. Dec. 7, 1957. p. 50

In a nation where art is often associated with a kind of willful roughness, Jiménez will be remembered always for certain exceptionally "perfect" compositions. Most typical of this perfection is a form of necessarily short poem (song, lullaby, picture, emotional moment, fleeting sense-perception, etc.) where unity resides in the sensibility, the feeling or the symbol, not in the fully developed or connected succession of lyrical comments. The peculiar quality of this writing . . . [is] that it solves a number of apparently difficult antinomies. One of these is the union of rigor and simplicity. The writer avoids rare words, does no violence to syntax, leaves out as many elements as possible and yet requires from what remains a fullness and a precision even greater than those demanded by a more elaborate or more ostentatious type of verse.

Jiménez reconciles, besides, restraint and intensity: tirelessly sincere, but never given to prattling or gesticulation, he will express moments of plentitude or of rapture while preserving a muted tone, a singular poise and weightlessness. . . . If one virtue or method may be considered characteristic of his poetry, it is that of concentration. Concentration on the indispensable effect, surrounded by silences, concentration above all on the single word, on the force and the magic of which language is capable.

Claudio Guillén. NR. Dec. 16, 1957. pp. 17–18

In his poetry, as in his life, Jiménez has tended more and more to eliminate all that is extraneous and meaningless. He mercilessly corrects his own work, always seeking to reduce things to their essence. He believes that the poem should seek to express the ineffable, that the poem should be a flower sustained in space without stalk or root, nourished by light alone—to borrow a metaphor from one of his own poems. The term "pure poetry" has sometimes been used to characterize his later works, but this is not pure poetry as Valéry and his followers understood it. From his earliest verses to his latest, the prevailing tone is one of intense subjectivity. It is present in his early elegiac works, in subsequent ones of impressionistic character, in more intellectual poems of a still later period, and finally in those of marked religious spirit. The deeply subjective awareness of nature progresses from melancholy contemplation to ardent mystic experience in a poetic trajectory of constant ascent. Once the zenith is reached, there is no route left except the one leading inward. Now the poet's ardor impels him toward the nucleus of divinity within his own being and his poetry attains the purity and radiance of a burning sapphire.

Donald L. Fogelquist. Ams. Dec., 1957. p. 11

It is now generally conceded that Jiménez . . . has had the strongest influence on Spanish poetry written in the twentieth century. . . . His first poems, published when he was eighteen, were close to the heart of a native Spanish Impressionism, what has been called the "shimmering extravagances" of his native Andalusia. Jiménez later developed a style and attitude that could accommodate direct and detailed observation of the world about him; like Yeats, he worked himself free from any device that resembled applied ornament; for him, to be modern meant to be free. . . . What seems to be most striking in Jiménez, apart from his lyric gift, is his persistence and endurance, his impulse to advance and explore. He is again comparable to Yeats in his mature insistence on examining every level and facet of his experience, of refining his expression down to essentials, of contemplating both appearance and essence. These two men, both from "backward" countries, . . . brought over into the modern, mechanized world a sense of poetry as a part of primitive ritual, and of the poet as one who is still able to touch at their source human gaiety, melancholy, and enchantment.

Louise Bogan. NY. Feb. 8, 1958. pp. 130, 132

Jiménez' world is one of roses and lilies, of golden birds, crystal streams, dark mountains, solitary paths, of colors and odors, all half-dissolved in a misty vagueness. All this poetic apparatus is employed to capture an evanescent emotion or a fleeting state of mind, to evoke a mood of gentle, languid melancholy or poignant nostalgia, agitated by an occasional gust of passion. . . . Jiménez' absorbing interest has always been his interior life, the quality of his experiences. He toiled to give form to those experiences in order to "seize the eternal", to embody eternal beauty. To this end he unflaggingly devoted his life.

Jack E. Patterson. Com. July 18, 1958. pp. 401–2

A striking feature of the poetry of Juan Ramón Jiménez is the relationship it stresses between life and death. Life is an *aprendizaje* for death; sleep is part of the learning. Life and death are concentric circles, their respective paths guided by the *conciencia amadora*. The usual feeling of anguish in confrontation with death is markedly absent in Jiménez' work. Only occasionally does he yield to what might be called normal human feeling in the face of death. . . . Life and death form equally the reality which defines mankind. . . . Through . . . painstaking care, Jiménez reiterated his idea of the closeness of life and death and of their essential compatibility. Awareness of his idea and its thoughtful presentation deepens our understanding of his poetic work.

Howard T. Young. MLN. June, 1960. pp. 502–3, 507

Tagore and Jiménez were one in sensitivity and one in lyrical expression. . . . Artistic creation became, in Jiménez as in Tagore, the prime source of delight. Like Tagore, Jiménez learned to trust his "Inner Self." He first had worshipped beauty as an outsider, and through beauty he had discovered the key to Being. . . . Although greatly indebted to the West for certain disciplines of his art, Jiménez was, nevertheless, breaking away from Western orthodoxy. . . . The European mind is generally believed to be more preoccupied with its relation to human society than with its relation to infinite Being. In this respect, Jiménez is less European and more Oriental. . . . Like Tagore, Jiménez cultivated the emotions while cultivating the intellect and the will, thus developing his nobler desires through emotions of beauty, which were voiced in his poetry. It is not strange, then, to find in the works of Tagore, a great poet of the East, and of Jiménez, a great poet of the West, so many coincidences in expression and thought.

Graciela P. Nemes. *BA*. Fall, 1961. pp. 319, 322–3

Remaining apart from reality, he places it in terms of himself, even of his own feelings. Thus he gained the reputation of being incapable of viewing the world around him objectively, of appreciating its original otherness.

How blind it is, if indeed it is not bad faith, to affix such a simple label. A single reading . . . is enough to show Juan Ramón's capacity for disinterested observation and his ability to translate reality into words tersely. What is most impressive . . . is the author's ability to discover the significant human incident, the symbolic object, and the parable. Contrary to the so-called literature of evasion, in Juan Ramón's poetry reality emerges with a fidelity and objectivity rarely achieved by *engagé* poets, whose vision is muddied by trying too hard to prove a point.

Ricardo Gullón. *Ams*. March, 1964. p. 11

See *Selected Writings* and *Three Hundred Poems;* also *Platero and I* (poetic narrative).

JORIS, FRANÇOISE MALLET-

See Mallet-Joris, Françoise

LAMPEDUSA, GIUSEPPE DI (1896–1957)

The Leopard . . . depicts, in what amounts to a series of *tableaux*, . . . the passing of an old society and the establishment of a new structure; the main pervading implication seems to be a sense of profound immutability in the ethical and physical qualities of the place, hence of a basic vanity in those historical events. . . . The author has, of course, some of the deceptive external traits of the leisurely dilettante, but, on the other hand, it was precisely his leisure, affording vast readings and a cosmopolitan experience, supported by unmistakable genius that gave him the chance to realize himself as a distinct artist. In fact, if there is anything vaguely dilettantish in him it is an occasional apparent predilection to write "artistically." His expertness is evident in the general structure of the narrative. . . . Although the book's *tableaux* are in chronological order . . . the author has received his lesson not from conventional historical novels but from a conception of narrative literature patterned on the process of evocation of things past. . . . As much as its theme implies the permanence of certain indestructible traits and of the futility of change, equally present is the sense of the ravagings of time and of physical decay and death.

P. M. Pasinetti. *SR*. April 30, 1960. pp. 14–15

If there are such things as miracles in literature, *The Leopard* comes, indeed, quite close to being one. . . . *The Leopard* is . . . written by a highly civilized man whose intelligence illuminates the pages of his novel without making them arid or spurious.

On the contrary, his art is not only intelligent, but also lively and delicate. His characters are portrayed with such colorful vividness, his scenes are so consistently full of life, that one wonders how he can maintain the significant strokes, the poetic diction, the firm craft through such a variety of pictures and situations. . . . It is true that to achieve his artistic aim Lampedusa used devices that belong more to Flaubert or Stendhal than to the modern fiction of symbolic allusions and surrealistic constructions. But its spirit of inner struggle and frustrated humanity, of social ambivalence and spiritual thirst is that of our times.

Marc Slonim. *NYT*. May 1, 1960. pp. 1, 24

Il Gattopardo . . . is an epic of worry rather than of high tragedy, and this gives it its peculiar power; serious worry; the personal and political issues are important and they can only be resolved in the night sky, by the stars. The army of unalterable law (for the stars were mistaken for that in the nineteenth century) continues invincible while kingdom and family fall, while the shield of the Leopard crumbles, while the Princely House trembles. . . . Up in his observatory . . . the Prince can endure the present and the future, and can find the greatness he would have liked to establish in his daily life. . . . The reader . . . should not forget the stars. Fixed—as they are not today—in the black Sicilian sky, they look down upon the fortunes of men, and offer to those who can look up at them not only escape but majesty.

E. M. Forster. *Spec.* May 13, 1960. p. 702

The Leopard is a taut, aristocratic work, lofty, sane, economical and austere, like a piece of jewelry from the hand of a craftsman obdurately resisting shifts in fashion while managing to infuse his creation with contemporaneity. It is also an extremely personal book, and not only in the sense that all valuable novels are personal visions, but in a testamentary way: the kind of book that an elegant subtle mind, knowing itself about to be extinguished and not yet having revealed and immortalized itself, would write. . . . A historical novel whose main theme is not history but time, *The Leopard* . . . [achieves] the serene timelessness of a highly wrought artifact, a civilized counterweight to the very principles of disintegration and loss whose action upon men's lives it mourns and records. . . . Throughout, di Lampedusa's style is elegant, urbane and aphoristic, the style of a dispassionate observer engaged in the most lucid ordering of an experience.

Richard Gilman. *Com.* Sept. 2, 1960. pp. 450–1

It is an ancient and productive literary habit to compare things as they are with things as they used to be. . . . The first requirement for such a work, on such a theme, is a dry intelligence working on real information. To be obsessed by the chosen historical moment, as a theologian might meditate the Incarnation, so that one shares it with everybody yet avoids all contamination from less worthy and less austere intelligences—that is the basic qualification. Put another way, it a power of self-criticism perhaps found only in an aristocratic, but not barbarian, sensibility. A few modern historical novelists have this quality. . . . [Lampedusa has] it to an extraordinary degree. . . . *The Leopard* is . . . a deeply meditated book, extremely original and possessing an archaic harshness of feeling. . . . If it has the brilliant intelligence of Stendhal it has also something of his superior carelessness. But only a little; it is a work entirely worthy of that master (whose admiration for Ariosto Lampedusa evidently shared) and it is also in many ways a work of this century.

Frank Kermode. Puzzles and Epiphanies (Routledge).
1962. pp. 131–2, 136–7

Three short pieces of writing [*Two Stories and a Memory*] by the author of *The Leopard* have come to light. . . . Nothing is added to Prince di Lampedusa's reputation, but the rough fragments are marked by his serene sculptural hand. Even *The Leopard* had the air of being the surviving shell of a once massive classical edifice—as if the Prince had felt, as a matter of noblesse oblige, the necessity of avoiding the ennui of great designs. . . . E. M. Forster calls *The Leopard* "one of the great lonely books," and, in the fragments, there is still the suggestion of a mind rapt in a private past that has melted away and yet is to the author as clear and strong as stone. . . . The Prince comes so marvellously close to the people and scenes he describes because he conveys, in the manner of classical artists, the hard gleam of inaccessibility that makes human beings and nature itself seem final and alone.

V. S. Pritchett. NSN. Oct. 5, 1962. pp. 455–6

Now, with the publication in the United States of Lampedusa's second posthumous book, *Two Stories and a Memory,* much of the mystery behind the Italian grandee's novel, talent and life is uncovered. . . . Here is proof, in two short stories, that Lampedusa was an artist of the highest order—a more exclusive aristocracy. . . . *Two Stories and a Memory* is a book filled with small but beautiful gems. . . . The brightest jewel in the new book is "The Professor and the Mermaid," a fantasy revealing Lampedusa's learning and powers of imagination. . . . The construction of this short story is so natural that it puts to shame all the fashionably effortless short stories. And its language . . . soars with such phrases as "the candor of the dawn sea," that are part of the spell cast by the author. . . . Even in . . . samples of travel and sociological writing, one feels in the presence of a cultured mind. . . . The Principessa di Lampedusa told me, as we sat in the library of the *Gattopardo,* that . . . she encouraged [her husband to write] . . . to lift him from the despair of seeing the rubbled Palazzo Lampedusa. The stone palaces crumble; the books survive.

Herbert Mitgang. NYT. Nov. 25, 1962. pp. 4, 60

At this stage, what looks like a rough diagram of *The Leopard's* sources can be drawn up, and it is tempting to trace some sort of pattern in the inspiration of what is in no sense a *roman à clef*. Thus, not only are the various members of the Lampedusa family of a hundred years ago mentioned in the novel by their real Christian names . . . but even the most minor characters, the most glancingly mentioned places, seem transferred from the existing originals.

What emerges more and more clearly from such investigations is that the reproduction of true detail in the book heightens the contrasting imaginative treatment of its major characters and themes. These seem partly to have acquired their extraordinary sense of actuality, of the reader's being right there, by a process of double perspective, a kind of stereoscopic view of two or more originals fused into one. Thus, the arrival of the Garibaldini in 1860 is merged with personal memories of the Allies in 1943. . . . A similar pattern of double focus was used for the main characters, taken partly from parallel originals a hundred years ago and partly from recent ones. . . . By this method is the hero . . . thrown into prismatic relief. He is not wholly historical portrait or autobiographical projection or wish-fulfillment or the result of an interior monologue, and yet is something of them all.

Archibald Colquhoun. *At.* Feb., 1963. pp. 107–8

See *The Leopard* (novel); also *Two Stories and a Memory*.

LANDOLFI, TOMMASO (1908–   )

In spite of the fact that Tommaso Landolfi first revealed his unusual gifts as a writer through two collections of short stories, his ideal medium seems now to have become a longer narrative, a type of fiction which is not the novelette, but rather a short novel. Such was the case with the best piece he ever wrote, *"La Pietra Lunare"*; and such is the case with *"Le Due Zittelle,"* where the realistic and provincial background gives place, as usual, to a fantastic tale and a half-grotesque, half-tragic climax. . . . The result, as usual with Landolfi, is a complex blend of poetic caprice and literary parody, since there is no doubt that the manifold reminiscences easily recognizable in the writings of Landolfi are rather the object than the subject of his art. . . . Italian critics have often compared Landolfi to Hoffmann and Poe; but he reminds this reviewer rather of Gogol and of a modern Anglo-Russian writer certainly unknown to him: Vladimir Nabokov.

Renato Poggioli. *Ital.* June, 1948. pp. 167–8

The first of Landolfi's whimsical and unorthodox stories appeared more than twenty years ago. The newest . . . is as far removed from realism as its predecessors. . . . The author is, as usual, not content to write a

good adventure tale, but leads his reader firmly and unsubtly into philosophical speculations. Those expressed [in *Ottavio di Saint-Vincent*],
which have to do generally with the problems of illusion versus reality
and sham versus authenticity, demonstrate that Landolfi is cognizant
both of Pirandello and of French existentialism.

Bonner Mitchell. *BA*. Spring, 1960. p. 173

By virtue of what Landolfi has produced over the past quarter century,
I would place him on the far left segment of the literary landscape, that
is to say, at the opposite extreme from authors like Moravia and Pratolini,
the neo-social realists, who work within a distinct nineteenth-century
tradition. Indeed, Landolfi occupies today the unenviable position of
"outsider" with respect to the main trends of his literature: neither a
realist nor an "angry young man," read by few and imitated by none,
he is perhaps closest to such distinguished (though more "successful")
off-beat writers as Calvino, Vittorini, Buzzati (with whose bizarre imagination Landolfi would appear to have something in common), and to the
aristocratic novelist Carlo Emilio Gadda. . . . Like Kafka, Landolfi
moves in an extraordinary, surrealist *milieu,* a restless world whose fabric
is not woven of events and action, however common or unusual, but of
fears and expectations, of anxiety that is never successfully turned into
anguish. This much his writings make clear: Landolfi's vision has neither
the depth nor the penetration of Kafka's, and he is much less haunted
by a demonic imagination. To be sure, he has a personality of his own:
he is a deft, elegant composer of frightening *scherzi,* revolving around
preposterous happenings. But, for reasons that have to do less with his
ability as a writer than with his temperament, he remains disinterested in,
or perhaps incapable of treating some of life's consequential issues.

Sergio Pacifici. *SR*. Dec. 7, 1963. pp. 62–3

From [a] story [in *Gogol's Wife and Other Stories*] . . . I should like to
borrow a sentence to introduce a brief critical comment. "It is enough to
believe that one sees to see—insofar as it is true that nothing exists."

Insofar as it is true that nothing exists, one must read all of these
nine stories in order to read one of them, for Landolfi's imagination is at
once so cohesive and various that art, in mocking nature, creates that
other country from which no traveler returns without a hole in his soul
called love; and this hole will be neither whole nor symmetrical unless
each story is related to every other, just as in music one must continue
to hear the first movement while the successive movements are being
played.

Thomas Curley. *Com*. Jan. 10, 1964. p. 439

It would be a mistake to think of Landolfi as a twentieth-century recluse devoted to writing imaginary nineteenth-century short stories. His sensibility is of an entirely modern order, intellectually playful, sardonic, and riddled with disgust. With whom might one compare him? The already semi-official tag, "the Italian Kafka," is not very apt, I think. Something of a cross between Borges and Isak Dinesen would be more accurate: Landolfi has something of the perverse ingenuity of the one, and the solemn romanticism of the other. It is likely, however, that he is a greater writer than either. For he is less claustrophobic, less febrile than Borges; and his use of irony never becomes sentimental, or merely arch, as so often happens in the work of Dinesen. . . . What, of course, makes Landolfi's stories unlike the short stories mainly being written today in England and America is not his morbid wit or his eccentric notions of disaster. It is rather the whole project of a basically neutral, reserved kind of writing. In such writing, the act of relating a story is seen primarily as an act of intelligence. To narrate is palpably to employ one's intelligence; the unity of narration, characteristic of European and Latin American fiction, is the unity of the narrator's intelligence.

Susan Sontag. *NYR*. Jan. 23, 1964. pp. 15–16

Tommaso Landolfi is alone among Italian writers for several reasons: he invents fantasies and surrealistic stories that stand off from regionalism; he shuns the limelight; and his fiction reads like classic Russian rather than modern *Cinecittá*. He would be far out in any country as a trail blazer in the art of the short story. . . . The sum of [his] fantasies and impressions is a mosaic alternately sensitive and ironic, bizarre and somehow natural. Poe, Kafka and Gogol would admire the Italian twilight zone that Landolfi has created.

Herbert Mitgang. *NYTd*. March 7, 1964. p. 21

Rien va could be defined a study in loneliness, in the form of a journal. We are invited to witness the contortions of a conscience, an idle struggle of feelings and lucidity. . . . Landolfi's prose cherishes antithesis and parenthesis, sudden suspensions and returns as a means of introspection. Such devices, though, seem to break too often the line of development of the text. Paraphrasing a statement by the author about pity, the reader might be tempted to say that such a suborn self-searching is almost a shameful vice.

Angela M. Jeannet. *BA*. Summer, 1964. p. 304

See *Gogol's Wife and Other Stories*.

LA SERNA, RAMÓN GÓMEZ DE
See Gómez de la Serna, Ramón

LEVI, CARLO (1902–   )

Christ Stopped at Eboli is one of the few books we have had out of the new Italy; there could be no better testimony to the kind of democratic and creative mind that was buried so long under Fascism. . . . It has analogies to Dostoevsky's *The House of the Dead*, to Peter Kropotkin's memoirs of Siberian life and to . . . James Agee's *Let Us Now Praise Famous Men*. Here again is the story of the intellectual voyaging into the darkest land of his own people, seeking his true relation to them, and converting what might have been a sterile exile into a recovery of human solidarity. There is something in the very nature of Levi's observations that suggests the anthropologist studying primitive cultures. But his attitude toward the peasants lifts a descriptive memoir into a realization of universal problems. . . . It is . . . striking that this book, one of the first open counterstatements to twenty-three years of Fascist bombast, should be written out of such deep feeling for rejected human beings and with such hatred for power and insincerity. In the discipline of this writing, as in the purity of its opinions, can be felt the reaction of the new Risorgimento against the whole spirit of Fascism.

Alfred Kazin. *NYHT*. April 20, 1947. pp. 1–2

There will be inevitable comparisons between Levi and Silone, and already a number of Italian intellectuals hold Levi to be the superior writer. The comparison is unfair. Silone's work is symbolic fiction, which by its very nature narrows its scope while it defines it. Levi, as an autobiographical observer, is limited to observation, but he is free to comment without the intervention of the conventions of fiction. . . . Levi [appears to be] . . . a great prose stylist, as well as a brilliant observer of human life and a wise and patient diagnostician of our condition.

George Mayberry. *NR*. April 21, 1947. p. 32

Overtly, *Christ Stopped at Eboli* is merely sensitive reporting. . . . The silent plot of the book, however, resides in the attempt of "history" or "Christian civilization" or "consciousness"—in the person of Mr. Levi—to *see,* or establish continuity with, something that is very much not itself. The product of this attempt is a new kind of modern lyricism: the book is a well-wrought, lyrical vase.

There are two very striking features of this new lyricism: one is its great objectivity—the calm, almost total submission to the reality of the Other; the second is the silent, pervading dream quality which is created by this admission of an alien but genuine reality. . . . Essentially, I think, Mr. Levi was fulfilled by a thrilling awareness of the peasant sense of timelessness and death. . . . He had cleaned out of him enough of the Christian world to be able to perceive the basic meanings that that world attempts—so successfully—to deny.

David T. Bazelon. *Nation.* May 24, 1947. pp. 635–6

It is fear that created the gods; the gods *are* our fear of them; Carlo Levi is in perfect agreement with eighteenth-century thought—which he probably despises. . . . So the children of darkness are not simply the animals, and the primitives, and the subhuman characters in Faulkner's nightmares; they are the enemies of freedom, for freedom is the eternal quest. And this, to the timid souls who cuirass themselves with theologies, ideologies, doctrines, and other mass allegiances, is the greatest panic fear of all, *Paura della Liberta,* the dread of liberty, as in the original title [of Levi's *Of Fear and Freedom*]. They seek, not the truth that will make us free, but the system that will bind both the gods and ourselves. This to Levi is sin. . . . To the powers of darkness that rule through fear Levi opposes the "Muses," the arts, including the art of thought, which freely play with symbols and are never the slaves of their own imaginations.

Albert Guerard. *Nation.* Feb. 18, 1950. p. 158

Carlo Levi . . . makes a strong distinction between two civilizations— that of the country and that of the city. The former he regards as pre-Christian, the latter as a civilization no longer Christian. . . . Mr. Levi's ideas . . . on the problems of myth, sin, slavery, symbols, love, art, and politics . . . help explain the "pre-Christian" country civilization with its tendency toward religious expression, and the "no longer Christian" city civilization with its political emphasis. Freedom resides within neither and must still be sought out. . . . Fond of startling paradoxes, contrasts, and statements whose opposites imply equal, or equally questionable, truths . . . Carlo Levi has the gift of baring psychological motives clearly and of summarizing neatly a wealth of experiences.

Siegfried Mandel. *SR.* Feb. 25, 1950. p. 30

[*The Watch*] isn't a novel, as the jacket and its blurb would have you believe. It would be a mistake to expect Levi to construct, out of historical incident and personal experience, a technically acceptable work of fiction. . . . It is, instead, a prolonged meditation upon one moment in recent history. Levi's work has always had to do with man in relation to the historical moment, and the present book gives it continuity and cumulative force. He is a writer animated by a clinical interest in his fellow-man, but unlike many clinicians, he has also great love for his fellows. . . . The duality between real and false, between sincere and conventionally bland and faceless . . . is the prime element in the book. . . . It is a healthy experience to come on a subjective and personal work so teeming with awareness of the world about one, an "I" book so human, so honestly thought through, and so vast.

Frances Keene. Nation. July 21, 1951. pp. 54–5

Like George Orwell, Carlo Levi . . . was an "angry young man" long before the petulant and ineffectual contemporary breed knew what the world was about. . . . That a Piedmontese like Levi should have become Italy's most fervent champion and interpreter of the peasant, primitive, almost pagan masses of the Mezzogiorno is an irony of history. The average northerner in Italy is as much a foreigner to the southerner as if he came from another country.

The special quality that gives Levi such insight lies in the fact that he is a painter first and a writer by derivation. He thinks and writes in terms of painting. . . . He philosophizes, moralizes, and puts his whole heart into the moment of time and the little, remote place where he happens to be. Such an approach is subjective, sometimes excessively so. . . . But the descriptions of what he sees have the complete authenticity of an artist's vision. He sees vividly, with a close attention to detail. . . . Levi can always write much about little, and still make it significant.

Herbert L. Matthews. NYT. Oct. 5, 1958. p. 18

For Levi politics means the "eternal" moment of popular enthusiasm, and only such moments. When I talked to him shortly after the War, while the Resistance was still in power, he was impatient with questions concerning capitalism, Bolshevik organizational techniques, loans, relations of production. How could these determine the future? The new energies in the Italian people would transform everything. Politics consisted of hoping for the prolongation of the dance.

Perhaps the conversation was pointless on both sides. If the "historical elements" I referred to were going to dominate the situation, why should we, interested in human time and dancing, concern ourselves with it? On the other hand, if the future was to be a completely creative novelty —as Levi expected—nothing could be said in advance.

Harold Rosenberg. The Tradition of the New
(Horizon). 1959. p. 205

Levi is a kind of writer found more often in Europe than in America. Basically he is a journalist and his material is factual, but he treats it in a novelistic style and he has a novelist's insight and flair for character.

With this combination of qualities he manages to be both objective and personally involved in his material at the same time. . . . As an anti-Fascist he associates himself with the peasant attitude, and since this is confused and ambivalent his own feeling about the facts he is describing is ambiguous. . . . If the journalist Levi is objective, the novelist Levi is still an Italian. In spite of his Jewishness and his Turin urbanity, the peasants of Gagliano are his people and the soil of Lucania is his soil.

Donald Heiney. America in Modern Italian Literature
(Rutgers). 1964. pp. 130–1

He talked as charmingly as he wrote. He noticed everything, was amused by everything, and his insatiable curiosity reminded me of Giacometti; even death seemed to him an interesting experiment; he described people or things without ever using general ideas but, in the Italian manner, by the use of brief and well-chosen anecdotes. . . . Amid the motley accumulation of papers, books, and canvases cluttering his apartment, he was carefully preserving some dried-up roses. "Anywhere else, they would have fallen to bits long ago," he said. "My presence is beneficent." And he believed his influence was quite as decisive on men as it was on flowers. . . . Although so convinced of his own importance, he was not the least bit vain about it. He attributed it less to his own merits than to an aura, bestowed upon him in the cradle by some lucky chance and always surrounding him; this atmosphere was a protection against all misfortunes. His optimism amounted practically to a superstition.

Simone de Beauvoir. Force of Circumstance (Putnam).
1965. p. 99

See *Christ Stopped at Eboli, Words Are Stones,* and *The Linden Trees* (social narratives); also *Of Fear and Freedom* (essays) and *The Watch* (novel).

LORCA, FEDERICO GARCÍA

See García Lorca, Federico

MACHADO, ANTONIO (1875–1939)

His theme is the robust and brutal world in which the *pícaro* careered.
. . . This world of four centuries past . . . lives on, evaporated and
refined, in the subconscious tone of Spain. Machado captures the old
splendor by imaging its reverberations. His prosody is a canon of
echoes. The echo is the shell of the shout. So the rounded and mellow
music of Machado suggests the hollow form of an heroic life. The
graphic density of life in heroic Spain has left this pattern. If the hard
bodies of the Spanish soil were bubbles holding a void as hollow as the
Spanish sky, they would be the poems of Machado. He harks back to
Velásquez: the supreme graphic master reappears in words, diminished,
lyrical, plaintive. The voice of the stark past of Spain comes muffled in
this sleep.

> Waldo Frank. *Virgin Spain* (Boni and Liveright).
> 1926. p. 277

Antonio Machado is about half-way between the Modernism introduced
by Rubén Darío and what some critics call "the Castilian reaction."
Although he takes advantage of the new freedom gained by the Modernists in choice of subject matter and verse form, he most certainly
leans toward the Spanish traditions and is truly Spanish. His inspiration
comes largely from Spanish sources and especially from the bare and
baked plains of Castile, from her people and their customs. . . .
Machado's poetry is always at its best, is always most musical, most
sincere, and most deeply penetrated with his own spirit when he is
writing of the soul and spirit of Castile as reflected in her lands
and people.

> F. M. Kercheville. *UNM*. Dec. 15, 1933. pp. 37–8

No writer belonging to that Generation [of 1898] has quite so successfully
isolated the elements which make up its individuality, or expressed its
clamant ideas with more clarity, emphasis, or courage. He himself described the signs of his times as *"inquietud, angustia, temores, resignación,
esperanza."* Give each of these substantives its full value and you have
the elements of the spirit of the '98 Generation—and the qualities,
reflected in his austere, introspective, concentrated writing, by virtue of
which he belonged to it. . . . But it would not be too much to say that
he synthesizes in his work the spirit of the '98 Generation, the most

valuable part of the technique of Spanish modernism, the reactionary inspiration of that post-modernist phase sometimes called *novecentismo* and the guiding principle of the *literatura de vanguardia*.

E. Allison Peers. *Antonio Machado* (Oxford). 1940.
pp. 28–9, 38

A true poet, opposed to a mere versifier, must have a philosophy and expound it. Antonio Machado was no exception. His philosophy . . . was mainly concerned with not-being and the various forms of *nada,* which (he considered) was the one creation of God. . . . To a philosopher of today, to a logical positivist for instance, Machado's peculiar doctrine of nega-tion may seem to be founded on . . . a curious conjuring trick: the illusion of treating the word "nothing" as if it were "something." The emotional attitude, the appeal, and their cumulative effect are in a way poetic; though taken in isolation, cut off from the current of rhythmical language, the statements about Nothing may seem unintelligible or even nonsense. It is a poetry of nihilism, perhaps, the expression of an irrationalist outlook on the world; but it reflects the tendency of our times, a tendency which Antonio Machado, the poet, foresaw forty years ago.

J. B. Trend. *Antonio Machado* (Dolphin). 1953.
pp. 39, 43

Even as a child, Antonio Machado sought death, the dead, and decay in every recess of his soul and body. He always held within himself as much of death as of life, halves fused together by ingenuous artistry. When I met him early in the morning, I had the impression that he had just arisen from the grave. He smelled from far away of metamorphosis. A pit of worms did not disturb him, he was so familiar with it. I think he felt more repelled by smooth flesh than by bony carrion, and butterflies in the open air seemed to him almost as enchantingly sensual as houseflies or flies of the tomb and train, inescapable gluttons. A poet of death, Antonio Machado spent hour after hour meditating upon, perceiving, and pre-paring for death; I have never known anyone else who so balanced these levels, equal in height or depth, as he did, and who by his living-dying overcame the gaps between these existences.

Juan Ramón Jiménez. Reminiscence in *Eighty Poems of Antonio Machado* (Las Americas). 1959. p. 5

On hearing Henri Bergson lecture with the charm and insight that were his, the Spaniard began to ponder on what he termed "poetry in time." . . . Man had known before that movement does not measure true time;

the traveling of a hand over the face of a clock, the slant of the earth toward the sun, have little to do with time as it is experienced. Bergson made this an important tenet of his philosophy. Time as the center of experience was therefore of great importance to Antonio Machado; it followed that poetry written "outside time" was valueless. "The true poet sings" he wrote, "time, time and I!" . . . Machado strove to convey in his poetry a sense of the past contained in the present, the future born of both and destined to become the past so that all is continuance.

Alice Jane McVan. Antonio Machado (Hispanic Society).
1959. p. 35

On one occasion he said that for him "the poetic element" was not "the word for its phonic value, nor color, nor line, nor a complex of sensations, but a deep palpitation of the spirit." On another occasion he defined poetry as "the essential word in time," and again as "the dialogue of a man with his time." If we add one more element of prime importance in his poetic theory, intuition, we can attempt a definition of the poet as Machado would have him: a man whose inner being is in contact with the world of his time, deriving inspiration from the deepest experience of life, and who *intuitively* rises above his temporality by means of the word; that is, by means of the verbal expression he gives to his spiritual experience.

Paul Rogers. The Poem Itself, ed. by Stanley Burnshaw
(Holt). 1960. pp. 172–3

The spare and rock-ribbed landscape of Spain continues to give birth to the spiritual grandsons of St. John of the Cross and El Greco. . . . And although both Dos Passos and Jiménez emphasize Machado's complete acceptance of death, his poems convince me that his acceptance was only the recoil of one to whom the sights and sounds of life were unbearably sweet. He turned his back on Millay's "World, world, I cannot hold thee close enough," and limned the other side of that shield with phosphorescence. . . . The younger poets today, in their reaction to the compressions of Pound or Eliot, are trying perhaps to attain Machado's simplicity too soon, for it is a simplicity that does not belong to youth, but to the distillation of a complex maturity. Youth is *not* wasted on the young; extravagance belongs to the young who in their abundance rift their ore with gold; what Machado attained is worthy of such extravagance.

Kimon Friar. SR. Feb. 6, 1960. p. 20

In spite of his acquaintance with the French and Spanish poets, Machado did not follow their styles to any appreciable degree. His poetry lacks the *fin de siècle* quality of much of that of his contemporaries and tends to be bare and straightforward. He was preoccupied with time and the search for the inner core of his own being. The verse is not sensuous nor sensational and tends to be melancholy without indulging in self-pity. He seems to listen to the language of the soul speaking for itself through the natural symbols which abound in his verse—rocks, trees, roads, and especially water.

> J. Robert Feynn. *NMQ*. Spring, 1960. p. 104

Although his life was disorderly, unsuccessful, even romantic, Cervantes wrote with the happy confidence of one who knew his side is bound to win. With the debacle of the end of the nineteenth century, the men of Machado's generation knew that the humanism for which they stood was very likely to lose forever. This constant awareness of doom gave them all a classic nobility, like the heroes of Plutarch. Machado never lost this grandeur. . . . Dying in exile, everything that he valued in Spain reduced to slavery and ruins, his poetry retained its old calmness and order, the kind of formal magnanimity spread abroad by the shattered Parthenon. . . . Clarity, objectivity, humanity—these were Machado's virtues to a most eminent degree. . . . Machado is the poet of a way of life which has changed little and only grown each millennium more humane since the end of the Stone Age—the Mediterranean way of life which is all some people think our race of man has to show for six thousand years in Western Europe.

> Kenneth Rexroth. *Assays* (New Directions). 1961.
> pp. 229–30

Machado, when defining his aesthetics, has said that poetry is: "the essential word in time." . . . Machado's assertion means that poetry should not revert to an eternity, which is abstract, impassive, devoid of human feeling, but that it should be a living force of our own age, and its passion should be set aflame by feelings of the men, who live around us. Temporal signifies alive in the technical language of Machado. Poetry should find its inspiration in life, not in the more external aspects, but in the deeper essential meaning of life. True poetry must be living and made up of essentials, that is to say, it must be vital and profound. Such is the signification of the definition put forward by Machado on poetry, as being "the essential word in time."

> José Antonio Balbontin. *Three Spanish Poets*
> (Alvin Redman). 1961. p. 121

He was able to fuse personal tragedy with a landscape. By contemplating an austere scene . . . he could bring to expression the sense of irremediable loss. His own feeling is inscribed on the terrain. . . . It is a perfect correspondence; Castile and Antonio Machado are made one. . . . The eminence of Antonio Machado, a mind erect in its solitude, comes from character—his own, and that of the severe and practical language that never fails him. Beauty of tone animates his plainest verses, rectitude of design controls them, brevity and reticence are their guardians. He is the master of unobtrusive grace and of quiet finality. Knowing his compass, and keeping only what matters to him in view, he has won the most difficult of attainments in this age: self-possession.

Henry Gifford. HdR. Summer, 1962. pp. 212, 216

Modernismo disclosed to him how Spanish poetry might be revitalized. Either through Darío or independently, he discovered Verlaine. . . . [But] he ultimately responded to what Unamuno called the "deep native note," founded upon the pressing imperative of Spanish reality and intrinsically different from the princesses and myths of the *modernistas*. . . . His own life was a running battle between an overwhelming inclination towards aesthetic introspection and a guilty desire to reach a broader understanding of the surrounding world and mankind. The latter concepts he lumped together under the term "objectivity," and constantly tried to find a place for them in his poetry. Of one thing he was certain— sentiments were stronger than ideas and poems were made with emotions first and words second. Here too the influence of Unamuno was decisive.

Howard T. Young. The Victorious Expression
(Wisconsin). 1964. pp. 36–7

Machado is one of the three major figures in twentieth-century Spanish poetry, born Andalusian, the most Castilian, the most difficult, a philosophical poet who begins the poem in agony where his powers begin to fail him, in a place almost without objects,—the *nulle* of Pascal, the *nulla* of Ungaretti, in the non-being of Heidegger, in the bone-marrow of self-knowledge of the last poems of Roethke. . . . Machado found in Castile's landscape and people the perfect illustration of the Heideggerian principle. . . . He worked toward positions taken by Valéry in 1889. Gone the "disheveled madman," we have "the poem of concentration carefully *composed* . . . the cool scientist in service of the subtle dreamer." . . . Machado stood opposed to the Spanish *modernismo*, and its splendor. He was after the bone.

Stanley Moss. Poetry. Dec., 1964. pp. 198–9

See *Eighty Poems* and *Castilian Ilexes* (poetry); also *Juan de Mairena: Memoirs of an Apocryphal Professor* (prose).

MAETERLINCK, MAURICE (1862–1949)

Maeterlinck first saw his drama as music. . . . As in music there are ebb and flow, rhythmic pulse, so his little landscapes unroll themselves with iteration to the accompaniment of mournful voices. No dramatist, ancient or modern, so depends upon vocal *timbre* to embody his dreams as this one. In reality his characters are voice or nothing. From the deeps of haunted gardens come these muffled voices, voices suffocated by sorrow, poignant voices and sinister. . . . He pushes much farther than Ibsen and Wagner the rhythmic correspondences of man and his artistic environment. But the voice dominates his drama, the human voice with all its varied intonations, its wealth of subtle *nuance*.

James Huneker. *Iconoclasts* (Scribner). 1905. pp. 385–6

The one real struggle in modern life is the struggle between the man like Maeterlinck, who sees the inside as the truth, and the man like Zola, who sees the outside as the truth. . . . He brings, not something which is more poetic than realism, not something which is more spiritual than realism, not something which is more right than realism, but something which is more real than realism. He discovers the one indestructible thing. . . . It matters not one atom how often the lulls of materialism and scepticism occur; they are always broken by the reappearance of a fanatic. They have come in our time: they have been broken by Maeterlinck.

G. K. Chesterton. *Varied Types* (Dodd). 1909.
pp. 212, 214

Maeterlinck's idea of woman is perhaps more quiescent than these modern times care for. Her chastity, in his eyes, is largely due to her negative qualities, to her inertness; for does he not say she is "a tissue of vices quiescent?" . . . Maeterlinck's interest in women . . . is from an angle totally different from that of Ibsen; it is all instinct and the exercise of certain mystic powers that characterize them. And if he deals with them under the impetus of passion, he transmutes that passion into a chastity which is pure and strong. His knowledge of sex takes on a nobleness, a poetic ecstasy which Ibsen failed to realize. Yet Ibsen's feminism is more impelling.

Montrose J. Moses. *Maurice Maeterlinck* (Duffield).
1911. pp. 210–11, 214

M. Maeterlinck's representative figures are like the bees, they are unconsciously under the domination of the spirit of the race, of the destiny of humanity, of the wisdom of life. The feeling leads them to strange acts, it is true, but it does lead them. Maeterlinck presents them to us and that in a form in which we may sympathise with them. That is his work as a dramatist. It is not his business to preach either by symbol or by sermon. He is content . . . to present the essential things of life as he recognises them. He presents them in forms in which, as nearly as may be, those things which cannot be spoken can be made evident.

Edward Everett Hale, Jr. *Dramatists of Today* (Holt).
1911. p. 202

Maeterlinck is . . . not anti-scientific or pseudo-scientific, but rather sub-scientific. He speaks of delicately felt and subtle influences and aspects of reality that lie beneath the surface of our lives, of forces and shadows that cannot be measured quantitatively or turned into philosophical categories. . . . His influence in our time is so great because we believe that he is a seer, a man with knowledge of things hidden from our eyes. We go to him as to a spiritual clairvoyant,—to have him tell us where to find the things our souls have lost.

Randolph S. Bourne. *Youth and Life* (Houghton).
1913. pp. 209–10

Maeterlinck is often called a mystic, and himself uses the word so freely that you might well think it the title he chiefly covets. . . . Only an unheeding acceptance of impressive words will lead one to accept Maeterlinck as a mystic. He writes mysteriously, but there is nothing mysterious in mysticism. To be vague is not to be mystical, for mysticism often presents things and visions with intolerable sharpness. Nor is a mystic necessarily uncertain, abstract, inconsequent, unintelligibly impressive, eloquently bewildered. . . . In truth, I note in his work very little that points to the spiritual profundity which is thus inadequately named. . . . He sees the world as a vast perplexity, beauty at odds with misery, life with destiny, and eternity cloud-like enfolding all. . . . In this, where is there a touch of mysticism?

John Freeman. *The Moderns* (Robert Scott). 1916.
pp. 213–4

Maeterlinck's predilection for scenic effects suggestive of weirdness and superstitious fear become apparent in the recurrent choice of sombre scenic motifs: oppressive nocturnal silence,—a stagnant sheet of water, —moonlight filtered through green windows, etc. The diction, too, through the incessant use of terms like *morne, las, pâle, désire, ennui, tiède, indolent, malade,* exhales as it were a lazy resignation. . . . Most of his plays depend to a considerable degree for their dark and heavy nimbus of unreality upon a studied combination of paraphernalia in themselves neither numerous nor far-sought.

Otto Heller. Prophets of Dissent (Knopf). 1918. pp. 31, 40

Maeterlinck's dramas, so deliciously unreal, are deeply alive and true; his characters, with the appearance of phantoms, are steeped with life, like those seemingly inert balls, which, when charged with electricity, grow fulgent at the contact of a point; they are not abstractions but syntheses; they are states of soul or, better still, states of humanity, moments, minutes which shall be eternal. In short, they are real, by dint of their unreality. . . . Others doubtless have or have had a richer language, a more fertile imagination, a clearer gift of observation, more fancy, faculties better fitted to trumpet the music of words. Granted; but . . . Maeterlinck works at books and booklets that have a certain originality, a novelty so truly new that it will long disconcert.

Rémy de Gourmont. The Book of Masks (John W. Luce). 1921. pp. 23, 31

Maeterlinck has always realized, better than anyone else, the significance, in life and art, of mystery. He has realized how unsearchable is the darkness out of which we have but just stepped, and the darkness into which we are about to pass. And he has realized how the thought and sense of that twofold darkness invade the little space of light in which, for a moment, we move; the depth to which they shadow our steps, even in that moment's partial escape. But in some of his plays he would seem to have apprehended this mystery as a thing merely or mainly terrifying. . . . Fear shivers through these plays, creeping across our nerves like a damp mist coiling up out of a valley.

Arthur Symons. Dramatis Personae (Bobbs). 1923. pp. 42–3

Surely this fellow, with his darkling mood and his ornate, sententious simplicity, is little more than one who calculates carefully each flutter in the bosom of the Ladies' Wednesday Afternoon Literary and Chitchat Club in every Gopher Prairie in the world. . . . But then all this is saying in many words what was perfectly said in one sentence in the most felicitous criticism of Maeterlinck ever recorded. The author, oddly enough, was the fair Tallulah Bankhead. After watching in rebellious silence for two acts of the perfumed posturing of "Aglyvaine and Selysette," she turned and whispered: "There is less in this than meets the eye."

Alexander Woollcott. Enchanted Aisles (Putnam). 1924. pp. 224, 226

As to Maeterlinck's fame, we have to confess no more and no less than that his work, the dramatic as well as the lyric, verses and prose are a lovely, charming, childish-precocious, delightful and touching symphony of harmonies in which we become conscious of the most intimate connection with nature, of the primitive fear of the finite and the infinite, of the compassion with suffering and with suffering people, and of a resignation that is more passive than proud.

O. Forst de Battaglia. *CR*. Feb., 1940. p. 218

The most abiding impression one is left with after a study of his life and work is the sense of mystery. The mysterious may be clad in forms of mysticism, or of the occult and the unknown, or of mere mystification. All these are present in Mateterlinck's work, sometimes simultaneously. . . . The mystification is all the trappings of charlatanism that invest much so-called occultism. Maeterlinck may have advanced the boundaries of knowledge, but it was in reality the concept of the unknown that fascinated him more than the love of truth. This unknown he magnified, poeticized, and, on occasions, debased.

W. D. Halls. *Maurice Maeterlinck* (Oxford). 1960. p. 169
See *Blue Bird*, *Pélleas and Melisande*, and *Monna Vanna* (plays).

MALAPARTE, CURZIO (1898–1957)

Those who dread the "overthrow of our government" are generally too busy thinking of the horrid results to ask by what means that engineering operation might be performed. But it is to just this fascinating subject that Signor Malaparte, with all the cocksureness and all that Machiavellian amorality in which Fascist political thought appears to glory, addresses himself [in *Coup d'Etat, the Technique of Revolution*]. . . . Signor Malaparte . . . advances in the novel (and entertaining) role of a connoisseur of violence; he writes as the dispassionate critic of *coups d'état*; he reviews revolution. . . . He distinguishes between the "parliamentary" and the "modern" style of seditious uprising with all the nicety of a Spanish *aficionado* appraising a killing by Belmonte.

Walter Millis. *NYHT*. June 19, 1932. p. 1

Curzio Malaparte . . . saw much of Europe at a time when a black curtain shrouded nearly everything from us. He is one of the first eye-witnesses to bear witness against the brutality and debauchery, the decay and degradation that nazism and fascism visited on the Continent. . . . He

intimates he was a victim of fascism and tells of suffering and imprisonment . . . [but he] finds it convenient not to mention some facts about
himself that can be found in newspaper clippings of years ago: that he
took an active part in the seizure of Florence and accompanied Mussolini
on the march to Rome; that he was advertised for a long time as the
"strongest pen" of the Fascist party; that when the Allies took Capri in
1943 he was living there in a luxurious villa bought and furnished with
his earnings from Fascist journalism.

Howard Taubman. *NYT*. Nov. 3, 1946. p. 5

The official *enfant terrible* of the Italian Fascist party has produced a
personal account of his war experiences which exerts a horrid fascination. Malaparte has culture and talent: indeed he was the only real talent
produced by Fascism. . . . Malaparte's talent is remarkable, and this, of
course, distinguishes his work from the scribblings of Ciano. . . .
[*Kaputt*] is not told in ordinary chronological order or with an ordinary
journalistic equipment. It is conceived and executed like a work of art,
which indeed it is. From the professional point of view the technique surpasses anything I have seen lately in the same category. The author
wishes to exhibit the ruin of Europe by contrapuntal developments and
contrasts, and to do this he frames his picture of horror inside conversations which evoke the peace, humility and culture of other days. . . . The
horror pictures make us think of El Greco at times, more often of
Magnasco or Chirico. . . . The style is a little ornate for American taste—
the Italian language tolerates a great deal more decoration than we are
used to—but is the panoply of a genuine gift.

Vincent Sheean. *NYHT*. Nov. 17, 1946. p. 6

Malaparte has brilliant literary gifts of a theatrical order. He has a flair
for the atrociously bizarre, and he depicts it with a bravura which makes
some of his pages unforgettable.

His dual theme in *The Skin* is the abasement and suffering of the
Neapolitans, and the failure of the well-meaning but naïve liberators to
understand that war has left these people with nothing to live for but
their skin. The book is a succession of episodes in which . . . the accent
is on the sordid and the fantastic. . . . Malaparte's emotional tone is
consistently inflated. And all in all, it might be said that he has a genius
for creating disbelief. But while one can seldom accept his reporting as
literal truth, it is often highly arresting in a nightmarish way and it makes
one original and worthwhile contribution. Malaparte's is surrealistic
reportage which projects the extreme awfulness of certain wartime hor-

rors and abnormalities with a greater graphic intensity than could be achieved, I think, by strictly factual documentation.

Charles J. Rolo. *At*. Jan., 1952. p. 109

Malaparte's anti-Americanism is a sick man's petulance, and one realizes that what inspires it is the invalid's hatred for those who offer him the burden of renewed hope, the prospect of prolonging a struggle he is ready to give up, when all he wishes is to be left in his exhaustion to wait for the ease and comfort of darkness and silence. D. H. Lawrence diagnosed this disease . . . when he visited Germany immediately after the First World War. He detected in the exhausted and embittered German people . . . a cold longing for the gloom of the primeval German forests and . . . [a] turning toward the bleak, Icelandic cradle of the Saga culture in search of a Nihilistic creed. . . . Malaparte testifies to the virulence of the sickness, and to the Fascists' success in spreading it. They may have lost all their territories and all their power over men's bodies, but they have planted their cult of death and Nihilism deep in their real victims' minds, and hold them more securely in the cage of hopelessness than they were ever held in party organizations or behind wire.

Anthony West. *NY*. Nov. 1, 1952. p. 28

Malaparte's truly memorably works—*Kaputt,* for example, or *La Pelle*— were basically dependent on externals. Essentially a journalist (and a highly readable one) he could take an event or a pattern of circumstance and shape from it an exciting if not always truthful account. But within himself there was little; he was a shrewd, sharp-minded man but essentially a shallow one. And . . . where there is no dark chronicle of man's vileness or nature's violence to relate . . . the shallowness is apparent. . . . Of course Malaparte "writes well" as they say in Italy. His Tuscan is authentic, his rhetoric sleek. The trouble is he has really nothing to say.

Thomas G. Bergin. *BA*. Summer, 1962. p. 314

See *Kaputt* and *The Skin* (novels); also *Coup d'Etat, the Technique of Revolution.*

MALLARMÉ, STÉPHANE (1842–1898)

To Mallarmé, poetry was first of all not a vehicle for conveying a definitely elaborated thought. Mere lucidity meant nothing. . . . He appeals to the senses rather than to the intellect; he charms the ear with a hundred harmonies, with the most exquisite cadences, with rhythmical movements that linger in the memory and haunt it and ravish it; and he calls up a host of undefined delicious half-sensations that one may be quite incapable of understanding or of analysing, and yet that for this very reason are often all the more delightful.

Harry Thurston Peck. Bkm. Nov., 1898. p. 228

One of the best talkers of our time, he was, unlike most other fine talkers, harmonious with his own theories in giving no monologues, in allowing every liberty to his guests, to the conversation; in his perfect readiness to follow the slightest indication, to embroider upon any frame, with any material presented to him. There would have been something almost of the challenge of the *improvisatore* in this easily moved alertness of mental attitude, had it not been for the singular gentleness with which Mallarmé's intelligence moved, in these considerable feats, with the half-apologetic negligence of the perfect acrobat.

Arthur Symons. The Symbolist Movement in Literature
(Dutton). 1919. pp. 184–5

Stéphane Mallarmé did not disclose the many traces that might help his reader in interpreting the content of a poem; he left only the isolated and absolute pattern; he relied upon the poetic nature of his reader to imagine all that had been cleansed from the poem, all the words and phrases that had either been entirely omitted or else substituted by a single word, more vague in its meaning; or else he even substituted an entire sentence by a mark of punctuation, a dash, a broken line, even an omitted period. Wagner had called music the bond between a present and an abstract emotion; Mallarmé, when he conceived that the end of poetry was music, seems to have believed that the task of poetry was to create the bond.

Hasye Cooperman. The Aesthetics of Stephane Mallarmé
(Koffern Press). 1933. p. 104

He would wish to be left undisturbed, in the exclusive purity of his poetic self, on what he finely calls the "furtive threshold" of his kingdom. Even the vibrating verse in which he conveys his Ideas and his Absences must be so delicate, so fragile in its constitution, that it almost seems to disappear. As nearly as possible, "the immortal word" itself must be "tacit"— it must be the projection of a Silence in which is embodied an Absence.

Randolph Hughes. NC. July, 1934. p. 118

Mallarmé . . . believed that words devitalized by their everyday use could again be made living by giving them an unusual place in the sentence;

prepositions, conjunctions and words which marked the transitions, or gave a too commonplace clarity, should be thrown out altogether; punctuation and other marks, like capital letters, which are a logical or a conventional imposition on the line, should be rejected. The poet's business was not to trim his ideas into a logical order; it was the business of the reader to give them such an order. He held that a poem was a mystery, the key to which the reader or hearer had to search for.

> Mary M. Colum. *From These Roots* (Columbia).
> 1937. p. 331

The strangeness of Mallarmé's metaphors is, in a sense, due to his belief that those who wish to comprehend unusual thoughts should be prepared to think in an unusual way. He sought with words, in his prose, as well as in his verse, to give utterance to thoughts which lie too deep for ordinary verbal expression. The poet, he believed, should go on, as it were, from where the musician left off. . . . To these reasons for the obscurity of Mallarmé's works might be added that of his tendency to abbreviate and condense. He was extremely impatient with banal prose and what he termed the "journalistic manner" of writing. . . . His whole theory of poetic expression was based on the conviction that condensation and abbreviation are absolutely necessary for a truly artistic method.

> Grange Wooley. *Stéphane Mallarmé* (Drew U.). 1942. p. 8

Mallarmé continued and deepened principally one of the aspects of modern poetry founded in France by Poe and Baudelaire. It is concerned with the practice and the mastery of the means of poetry, in the belief that the subject of a poem is important only as a means of expression which should exist within the poem as an integral part of its texture. The unique power of poetry's language and hence the sacredness of the poet who speaks this language and finds himself almost subconsciously its source, are two lessons of Poe which Mallarmé made significantly his own.

> Wallace Fowlie. *Mallarmé* (Chicago). 1953. p. 253

The lack of correspondence between Mallarmé's poetry and the external world is his weakest point. The attempt to create something perfect in itself has led to self-containment and then to isolation from both material and spiritual values. This isolation can be attributed to too high a conception of the poet's function rather than the reverse. . . . His work demands to be admired for the beauty of its own complex patterns rather than to be related to any kind of lived experience. It illustrates both the triumph of "pure poetry" and its limitations.

> Geoffrey Brereton. *An Introduction to the French Poets*
> (Methuen). 1956. p. 216

Martyr to an absolute and mystic to a beauty which were perhaps no more than the extraordinary abstractive power of his own thought (this was his tragedy), Stéphane Mallarmé endures in the chaste and harrowing image of the poet met at midnight with his demon and tempted toward the re-creation of his universe: met—like the most reverent and aware victims of the Word—with prescience of defeat which, nonetheless, he sometimes overcame and so composed a perfect poem. . . . For all its outward obscurities, Mallarmé's work has become one of the most beautiful and arresting evocations of purity that literature has ever had. This mind born to silence, rarity, and impeccable structure—all perfectly absorptive of our passions—was eminently Mozartean.

> Bradford Cook. Introduction to *Selected Prose, Poems,*
> *Essays and Letters by Stéphane Mallarmé*
> (Johns Hopkins). 1956. pp. xiii, xxi–xxii

The Faun is disturbingly human: like man as Pascal saw him, he is *ni ange ni bête,* and yet is both. His sensuality is quite animal, but he is capable of exquisite notations and sublimations. The artist in him, painter and musician, lifts him out of his animality and sublimates his hot dreams into music and into pictures alternately.

He is to some extent Mallarmé himself. The latter had in him a strong fund of sensuality. Yet in it there was always a certain indifference, the dreamy aloofness of the artist. This frequently, in his poems, sublimates the pleasures of the senses into something like the Faun's *"sonore, vaine et monotone ligne."*

> Alan Rowland Chisholm. *Mallarmé's L'Après-Midi d'un*
> *Faune* (Melbourne). 1958. pp. 30–1

Up to Mallarmé, for a whole century since Balzac, literature had subsisted on inventories and descriptions. . . . Mallarmé is the first man to take his stance before the eternal object, not as before a spectacle, or a subject for composition in French, but as before a text, with this question: *What does that mean?*

A question which for him, furthermore, required not a response, not an explanation, but an authentication by means of that magical mode of abbreviation that is Poetry. . . . Poetry for Mallarmé was the means *par excellence* by which reality was made to pass from the domain of sensation to that of intelligibility.

Paul Claudel. From the N. R. F., ed. by Justin O'Brien
(Farrar). 1958. p. 149

Mallarmé defined literature as the antithesis of journalism. Literature, for him, is never a piece of report, never an account of a *chose vue*—a thing seen in the external world or even a thing seen, with any degree of precision, by the inner eye. Both classes of seen things are too concretely real for poetry and must be avoided. Heredity and a visual environment conspired to make of Mallarmé a Manichean Platonist, for whom the world of appearances was nothing or worse than nothing and the Ideal World everything.

Aldous Huxley. Collected Essays (Harper). 1959.
pp. 131–2

According to Mallarmé's theory of pure poetry, the poet, in the act of manipulating correspondences, must disappear along with all other points of departure. . . . By a suicide of the personality, the author is resurrected as pure spirit. Death, if we detach it from its purely negative implications, is the true condition of existence, as silence is of speech. But the pure existence of death is more pregnant even than the pure existence before birth, because it contains the womb, the life, and the tomb—all three—and transcends them. If we may understand a poet by his obsessions, Mallarmé may be understood by the countless recurrent symbols for this state of being, white, virgin, pure, and by its opposite, Chance, the condition of time and space. His life and work are a single dedication to the abolition of Chance.

John Senior. The Way Down and Out (Cornell). 1959.
p. 139

I believe firmly that Mallarmé's work will endure almost intact. . . . For Mallarmé literature was the aim, yes, the very end of life; here one felt it to be authentic and real. In order to sacrifice everything to it as he did, one had to believe in it to the exclusion of all else. I do not think that, in all our literary history, there is an example of a more intransigent conviction. . . . In an age when we needed to admire, Mallarmé alone inspired a legitimate admiration; how could it have been other than violent and impassioned?

André Gide. Pretexts (Meridian). 1959. pp. 129–34

Social man satisfies instinct or submits to censorship: Mallarmé rejects such brutality. The great concern of the new art must be—at once following and opposing the example of music—to play with revelation: to amass mystery, and then tear it apart or dissolve it. Thus ambivalence is still present, but the emotional ambiguity which the conscious would deem turbid, the oscillating between shadow and light, here becomes the supreme aesthetic game. For us, these more or less torn or lifted veils have a long filiation, which runs from snow to the white page, passing through shrouds or batiste lifted with the finger, riddled dresses of dancing gypsies, funeral draperies starred with holes or tears, the clown's wall of cloth, windows, eyes, the devil's purple, tatters, clouds, banners full of holes, and so on.

> Charles Mauron. *Introduction to the Psychoanalysis of
> Mallarmé* (California). 1963. pp. 240–1
> See *Poems* (New Directions).

MALLET-JORIS, FRANÇOISE (1930–   )

The Illusionist . . . centers on a relationship that must generally be considered unnatural. . . . Françoise Mallet writes about it with a directness and simplicity that few, I think, will find offensive and many, moving and enlightening. . . . *The Illusionist* deals with experience that fortunately is, at least at this extreme, off the beaten track, but the sincerity of the young author and the effectiveness of her narrative give her theme general interest and importance.

> Mary Ross. *NYHT*. Sept. 7, 1952. p. 12

This author, now 27, is a writer of scope and force. Her third book [*House of Lies*] is solid, interesting throughout, at times brilliant. And its strong grasp of human motivation, its understanding of the essential isolation of man (to the point where he cannot believe even in another's disinterestedness if it cost him his life) are truly profound. The author's work, stemming from the vital tradition of Belgian woman novelists, is worthy of such splendid predecessors as Marguerite van de Wiele and, more recently, Julia Frezin. Françoise Mallet-Joris is, I believe, the only young woman writing in French today who deserves the title of novelist.

> Frances Keene. *NYT*. Nov. 10, 1957. p. 39

With the appearance of these two novels [*The Illusionist* and *The Red Room*] Francoise Mallet-Joris, still in her twenties, was hailed as a modern successor to the Marquis de Sade and Laclos. Combining a striking command of novelistic technique with scandalous subject matter, Mme. Mallet-Joris revealed a preoccupation with the politics of conflicting wills which could not fail to recall these masters of the eighteenth century. The publication of two subsequent novels and a collection of short stories, however, has seen the eroticism of constraint take second place to an elaboration of the anatomy of will. Closer to the classical seventeenth century in its analysis of motives and illusions, this inquiry into the will is almost geometrical in form and moralistic in intent.

Rima Drell Reck. *YFS*. Summer, 1959. p. 74

The award of the Prix Femina to this novel [*Café Céleste*] was a recognition of the broad sweep of her talent, since here all the dimensions of life are present. Her technique which owes a great deal to the realists and naturalists of the nineteenth-century, perhaps the most to Zola, successfully creates a believable world. Beyond the technique, however, is that feeling of involvement with all mankind which is her legacy from Tolstoy and Dostoevsky. . . . This excellent novel . . . is one of the best that France has sent us recently.

Vernon Hall, Jr. *NYHT*. Jan. 10, 1960. p. 6

Although each novel involves a different set of events, we feel an underlying unity in the world of Françoise Mallet-Joris because it rests upon a fear that is intrinsic to each human being, and because it receives its light from a merciless look, the symbol of which could well be the "single eye" which has obsessed Stéphane, the pitiable hero of *L'empire céleste*, dominated since his childhood by a one-eyed grandfather. How well has the author transmitted her objectivity to the characters! We see them all engaged in a veiled war with each other, armed only with their look, spying upon one another, ready to seize the minute of weakness which will permit them to freeze the enemy into an attitude forever repulsive to himself.

Genevieve Delattre. *YFS*. Spring-Summer, 1961. p. 122

A Letter to Myself is as persuasive as the best of novels, and it is more than a novel. Free from any theorizing or dogma, fuss or posturing, it describes an experience in which living and writing are bound closely together, one substantiating the other. The book may well be a turning point in the present orientation of the French novel.

To compare one woman writer to another, just because they are women, is a pointless game. But if the mantle of Colette is to fall on another woman writer in France, Françoise Mallet-Joris, different though she be, is certainly at the moment, the most likely heir. Her earlier novels had testified to her unusual acuity of vision, her rich sense of the concrete, and her undeniable ability to create character. *A Letter to Myself* reveals the scope of her imagination and sensibility.

Germaine Brée. *SR*. May 23, 1964. p. 42

See *Café Céleste, The Favorite, The House of Lies, The Illusionist,* and *The Red Room* (novels); also *Letter to Myself* (autobiography).

MALRAUX, ANDRÉ (1901–   )

Malraux seemed formerly to think that the impure sources of lust and cruelty were directly connected with a sort of underground lake beyond which nothing at all existed. . . . These times of ours have led Malraux to repudiate that fatal attraction which teaches that only evil and only death are inexhaustible. Life is more inexhaustible than death, and still more primitive than death, life with all it promises of joy and discipline and brotherhood; and inexhaustible too are the works of man building upward toward a sky, a heaven against which the powers of Hell shall not prevail. . . . Everything falls into its proper rank, and Satan himself takes his proper rank, in a broader universe, a universe which is more ample than the other and more true, which is completely infused with the essential sap of life. Such has been Malraux's experience and such . . . is the central meaning of his most recent testimony.

Roger Caillois. *Com*. Feb. 2, 1945. p. 393

When an intellectual writes novels, the presence of ideas in the fiction constantly incites the critic to extract the idea from its context, and to ascribe it directly to the author. Malraux's way of constructing characters also lends itself to the same treatment; they are motivated by inner obsessive drives, and what most frequently obsesses them is an idea. A given character acts as he is forced to by his attitude toward death, sex, human dignity, power, liberty, or something similar. He appears at once as an individual and as the incarnation of his special drive. . . . But looking in Malraux's novels for *clear* lessons is as fruitless as asking them to be conventional novels, and extracting theses from them is like extracting theses from Shakespeare. . . . They are excellent documents on how he *felt*—which is to say that his work should be treated primarily as the work of a poet.

W. M. Frohock. *André Malraux* (Stanford). 1952. pp. xi–xii

Malraux's themes are universal; his tone is one of metaphysical anguish, which has become the *mal du siècle* of our neo-romantics; the stress of an intense personal suffering underlies his stories of violence. Malraux is obviously not an Anatole France smiling with detachment at man's insoluble contradictions nor a jesting Pilate amused by the diverse follies of human puppets under exotic skies. He is engaged in the struggle that he depicts. He has, in Pascal's terms, gambled his whole life on the causes for which he successively fought. But he never failed to do justice to his adversaries, and his novels have the artistic irony that envisages the two opposite sides as impelled by noble and metaphysical motives.

Henri Peyre. *The Contemporary French Novel* (Oxford). 1955. p. 183

He is difficult to assess, because of the magnetic qualities of his personality and of his writing; he has a glamour that is more than style. In his writing, he uses words and thoughts that seem to mean even more than they state. This special margin between what the reader does and does not understand is accepted as another dimension of Malraux himself. He conveys something profound in what is already difficult and indefinite. His writing has a triple potential: first, in his ideas, which are always intelligent; second, in his use of them, which gives them the echoing effect of poetry; and third, in the fact that they perfectly support his personality. What early conferred upon him his high *classement littéraire* was his real need for physical action that risked and tried to prove all, coupled with his equally real necessity for writing, for the self-expression of the artist on the written page.

Janet Flanner. *Men and Monuments* (Harper). 1957. p. 20

There are at least two Malraux: the one who gives himself irrevocably to some historical momentum and, almost always for too long a time, does not stop to wonder whether it has been deflected from its original or proclaimed purpose, and the other who knows that in all historical action blood will be shed without good reason, without recompense or possibility of recompense. Neither of these figures is interesting in himself, only through the unity of their struggle does Malraux become a significant writer. All too often, however, his infatuation with action leads him to exalt the will at the expense of the mind, thereby betraying him into a dubious adventurism. Starting with the valid, or at least defensible, assumption that in modern times inertia is a form of self-betrayal, he proceeds to the dangerous conclusion that one must follow through to the desperate end an action in which one no longer retains faith.

Irving Howe. *Politics and the Novel* (Horizon). 1947. pp. 212–3

[Malraux] has been greatly admired by the existentialists. . . . Malraux's interest in exploring the meaning of the human, the metaphysical possibilities of man as a species, is indicated by the title of one of his books— *The Human Condition* [*La Condition Humaine*]. In the truest sense his characters in choosing themselves choose for all mankind. Yet at the same time Malraux does not forget Man for men. In his novels human possibilities are revealed in the course of the very real and disillusioning struggles against oppression in Spain and in China. He is interested in re-evaluating both what might be called the metaphysical facts of man's situation and the specific possibilities which are offered him in the twentieth century.

Hazel E. Barnes. *The Literature of Possibility*
(Nebraska). 1959. p. 376

The new and "as yet indefinable humanism" toward which Malraux seeks to guide his disinherited age in *The Voices of Silence* after having, in the novels, led his heroes out of despair to manhood and to a glimpse of a "mystery" become accessible once again, is not a prophecy. It is less and much more: not a philosopher's exultant assertion claiming for man a divine power and autonomy, but a poet's deeply realized intuition that the artist's power of response which has never failed men in times of anguish will not fail now if he does not surrender to the voices of death.

The nature of this response as he has evolved it in image and exposition lies halfway between total freedom and total servitude, for man is neither fatally delivered to the power of death nor ever free from its menace.

Gerda Blumenthal. *André Malraux* (Johns Hopkins).
1960. p. 153

In Malraux's novels it is less the particular act which is problematic (should a or b or c be done? . . .) than the man himself, who harbours a deep reserve on the effectiveness of human action in general. . . . Malraux does not disdain psychology in creating his characters but explores a relatively new domain: the psychology of men confronted by the will to inaction in themselves or in others. Axioms flow from him or his characters as if an unexplored geometry of action were being revealed. It is not by chance that his first three novels deal with an Asia where jungle, opium and even art deck a deep-seated distrust of the efficacy of Man's act.

Geoffrey H. Hartman. *André Malraux* (Bowes and Bowes).
1960. pp. 18–19

Malraux's novels . . . represent simultaneously an action and a commentary on that action; a sequence of tragic events and a meditation on tragedy. But the intellectual is not merely the commentator, he is also the victim. There is sometimes pathos in this sense of victimhood, in the meek acceptance of one's condemnation. . . . Yet there is also a hard lucidity (the very kind of lucidity which impels the tragic hero to stare into the unadorned face of his destiny): the lucid inventory of despair. And there is also the more resilient feeling of justification which comes from the awareness that thought means suffering . . . and from the Pascalian pride in this ability of man to *comprehend* and consequently to rise above the forces that crush him: the victory of being "the only animal who knows that he must die."

Victor Brombert. The Intellectual Hero (Lippincott).
1961. p. 177

Perhaps the greatest single element of unity in the works of André Malraux is their fundamentally ethical conception, a unity stemming from the fact that man's inhumanity to man is, for him, simply one aspect of a destiny that moves to reduce man to absurdity, dependence, and death. Like any humanist worthy of the name, he must try to give dignity and stature to man; but when man is as comically insignificant as Malraux interprets him to be, the problem of finding a minimum on which to base ethics is extremely difficult. Since the reduction of any individual detracts by that much from all mankind, Malraux has reached the conclusion that the minimum must be based on the value of the individual. . . . His ethical aim is an existence in which no man's dignity is violated.

Charles D. Blend. André Malraux (Ohio State). 1963. p. 77

The impossibility of communication through intelligence, love, or death is expressed by Malraux's novelistic technique in both the manipulation of episodes and his style. . . . Juxtaposed disconnected affirmations are held together by no logic, no syntax, but by the rhetoric of periods and paragraphs, just as his novels set up characters beside and in front of one another (often too, at least in conclusion, one against the other) each of whom is a unique existence, imprisoned at times unwittingly in the separateness that makes him fundamentally incapable of living harmoniously with others.

Claude-Edmonde Magny. Malraux, ed. by
R. W. B. Lewis (Prentice-Hall). 1964. pp. 120–1

A universe of debate, of torment, which remains the universe of the individual consciousness. Here the conflict is not between inner truth and its surrounding world. However different his characters may be, Malraux inhabits them all, and it is himself he confronts. In each one of them, he expresses either the part he momentarily prefers, or a part painfully sacrificed; his choices, his temptations, his regrets. Like Goethe before the final choice . . . Malraux never ceases questioning and answering himself by means of those intense and feverish dialogues whose secret he possesses. . . . All of these diverse voices unite in the one who animates their dialogue. All of these enemies are brothers.

> Gaëtan Picon. *Malraux,* ed. by R. W. B. Lewis
> (Prentice-Hall). 1964. p. 167

More than simply a duality of interest, all of Malraux's work presents an essential play between an action and its perspective, between the present and the eternal, between the loss of oneself in the moment and the recognition of oneself in terms of one's whole destiny. And this duality endures however violent the changes in ostensible subject matter or in genre. Or one might put it that the underlying subject matter itself never changes, and in his first works as in his last the same issues dominate: there is an obsessive and consistent investigation of the place of the private individual in historical time, the place of the individual passion in the overwhelming and unintelligent rush of events. And beyond the historical query lies a metaphysical one, distinguished not by its intellectual form but by its felt presence and insistence, a dramatization of the human demand to know something of its place in the pattern of things beyond itself, to relate the very course of human history to some intelligible feature of the structure of things.

> William Righter. *The Rhetorical Hero* (Chilmark).
> 1964. pp. 4–5

See *The Conquerors, Days of Wrath, Man's Fate,* and *Man's Hope* (novels); also *The Voices of Silence* (criticism).

MARAINI, DACIA (1936–   )

[*La vacanza*] is a sensitive, gripping story told with a control and clarity of style which more than attests to the seriousness and maturity of its young author. Its greatest merit lies perhaps—as Moravia states . . . —in the delineation of the character of the protagonist. The fourteen year old, convent-bred Anna can be placed, without apology or fear of the comparison, beside Moravia's own Agostino and Luca and Elsa Morante's Arturo, among the more successful characterizations of the adolescent in Italian literature. . . . The events of [a] brief period spent

in a decaying, corrupt world in which the only morality is self-survival
. . . are narrated by Anna simply, matter-of-factly, without comment or
reflection. . . . Her passivity and indifference temper the pathos of a
childhood of anonymous neglect, the depravity of sexual perversion, the
fearful horror of war, and save the novel from sentimentality and sensationalism.

Zina Tilone. BA. Summer, 1962. p. 311

The Age of Malaise provides you with comfort and chic, for it isn't new,
it is merely *à la page*. And what is more *à la page* these days than
malaise? The world and the emotions of this novel have become familiar
to us, in various ways, through . . . Camus and Françoise Sagan . . . and
Fellini. Miss Maraini's influences are evident, but since she is clearly
in possession of them rather than they of her, *The Age of Malaise* does
not seem unoriginal. It seems original, though in a very definite vogue
out of which it never manages to climb. It never becomes itself deeply. . . .
It seems to me that Miss Maraini's intention is to debunk the Age of
Malaise, to reveal it as the veneer coating all the traditional vices and
vanities. . . . It is the work of a very gifted young writer.

Alfred Chester. NYHT. May 5, 1963. pp. 5, 11

Its naturalism, less intellectually contrived than Moravia's, belongs rather
to the Italian cinema. . . . Light, warmish Roman rain seems to drizzle
throughout the book. . . . The publishers mention *"La Dolce Vita,"* but
there is not a touch of Fellini's histrionic spuriousness. Signorina
Maraini's vision is sincere, direct, pure as rain.

There is missing [from *The Age of Malaise*] only the last thrust, the
last initiative, of imagination. Christianity has long ago been washed
away from this Italy, leaving only compassion; and in a sense Signorina
Maraini's characters are more compassionated than imagined. Failing to
apply the last ruthlessness of artistic intelligence, she stops the book short
of tragedy and never penetrates to the actual structure of the loneliness
which surrounds her people even in the dreadful sociability of Italian
manners.

Brigid Brophy. NSN. May 10, 1963. p. 717

As presented by the author, Enrica is certainly representative of a generation that is unable to find meaning in life or new values in a world
robbed of its dignity and humanity by too many blunders, too many
wars, too many betrayals. The evidence presented in [*The Age of
Malaise*] speaks eloquently to this point: we have become incapable of
enjoying even the rawest physical pleasure; we are unable to find a sense

of purpose in the futile struggle of everyday living; finally, we have allowed ourselves to be turned into neurotic automatons. In that sense, the novel's characters reveal the sickness of our condition. . . . It is easy to see why the novel should have attracted the sympathy of Alberto Moravia. It is his own early novel, *The Time of Indifference,* that has considerably influenced Miss Maraini's sensibility, and it is Moravia's cold, semiclinical, grayish style that the young author has made her own, ably using it to depict the monotony of her sordid, hopeless world.

Sergio Pacifici. *SR.* May 11, 1963. p. 74

The title of Dacia Maraini's novel [*The Age of Malaise*] is, perhaps intentionally, ambiguous. Does it refer to Our Times, or to the period of adolescence? This may seem a minor point, but the titles of novels nowadays can imply a sociological generalization which may not necessarily be warranted by the text.

Miss Maraini's seventeen-year-old heroine . . . tells her own story in a laconic style with no emotional comment—her malaise, it seems to me, is quite insufficient. Miss Maraini is trying to suggest the unformed and bewildered heart which has as yet no imaginative content, and she relies on objective correlatives—what is going on in the physical environment —to suggest, or replace, feeling. . . . Miss Maraini has talent and skill, but she may have set herself an impossible task. It is difficult to be interesting about total emptiness, very difficult indeed in the first person, lacking the maturity of self-satire. This is a clever picture of total negation. I find the attempt impressive. But I am asking myself if the negation does not extend far beyond the book.

Kathleen Nott. *NYT.* May 26, 1963. p. 5

While economists tell us Italy is in the midst of a boom unparalleled in its history, Italian films and novels go on declaring that emptiness and desolation lurk beneath all the glittering prosperity. *The Age of Malaise* by Dacia Maraini could be a scenario for one of the earlier and more modest films in the "realistic" style of De Sica, with the same flat, bleak story of humble people carrying on with a forlorn stoicism under oppressive circumstances. Neither its material nor its mood is appealing, but the spare and unrelieved veracity of its telling establishes Miss Maraini as one of the younger Italian writers worth watching. . . . For [the novel's heroine], her sexual encounters are as meaningless as all the other prospects life holds before her. All values, except that of survival, have disappeared from her world.

William Barrett. *At.* July, 1963. p. 132

Rosamond Lehmann wrote a more stylish English version of this story before Dacia Maraini was born; Françoise Sagan more recently a French version with ritzier props, but no greater passion. [*The Age of Malaise*] deals with an authentic tedium in an authentic fashion. This is the Italian style, a class up from Pasolini's sub-proletariat. The writing is laconic, but never flabby. The detail, from furnishings to cars, from clothes to food, has the Fleming touch, without the advertising. . . . This may be a book about trivialities, but it is not a trivial book. It is calculated and detached, with a nervous tautness of narrative. Only a real writer could have brought it off.

Alan Ross. *LMg*. Aug., 1963. p. 88

See *The Age of Malaise* (novel).

MARTIN DU GARD, ROGER (1881–1958)

As for Roger Martin du Gard, he resembles none of the French masters past or present. Moreover, he seems at first glance to have no strongly marked character of his own. There is little color in his prose, which is classical in syntax and sometimes rather slipshod in its choice of words. The technique is simply that of the realistic tradition: it includes none of the innovations that were made by the Symbolists with the aim of suggesting new overtones or revealing new depths of emotion. Everything is reasonable, purely objective, and the author does not intrude his personal judgements—it is as if he effaced himself from his own novel with the same modesty he has shown in literary society. At most his personality reveals itself in the form of a scrupulous and almost passionate fairness toward all his characters.

Malcolm Cowley. *NR*. Jan. 5, 1938. p. 260

Some of the volumes in *Les Thibault* have been linked with the French naturalists. . . . The author's latent view of man cherishing the pursuit of truth, spurning many of the solaces of traditional religion, and stressing clear-headedness and the senseless inhumanity of war and of fanaticism has reminded some of the positivism of the earlier French naturalists. The analogy is superficial. Unlike the naturalists, Martin du Gard derives no joy from exploring the lower side of man or from exposing the selfish meanness of the bourgeois class. His novel or volume of sketches on peasant life, *La Vieille France,* is doubtless somewhat reminiscent of Zola in its satirical onslaught on the agrarian myth. Sentimental idyls are not to the taste of that clear-sighted observer. But if such a great name is not too overpowering, Tolstoy is the writer with whom Martin du Gard has most in common.

Henri Peyre. *The Contemporary French Novel*
(Oxford). 1955. p. 40

Granted Martin du Gard's inclination to make a point for the position of the non-believer this *roman à thèse* [*Jean Barois*] is moderate and dignified. One-sided in its almost exclusively intellectual discussions, it offers an unusual structure, consisting of scraps of conversation, situations, unlinked impressions, with so few and so economically used elements that its clever prose sometimes seems to consist rather of dramatic dialogues with some stage directions.

Helmut Hatzfeld. *Trends and Styles in Twentieth Century
French Literature* (Catholic U.). 1957. pp. 30–1

Gide had few friends as close to him as was Roger Martin du Gard. The deep sympathy they had for one another could serve to illustrate the fundamental compatibility between what is best in the rationalist tradition, and what in Gide's thought will perhaps one day come to be called pre-existentialist. . . . The questions posed by Antoine Thibault are those with which Gide was all his life preoccupied. . . . We read in Gide's *Journal*: Faced with any question whatever of psychology (even—or rather especially—in his capacity as a novelist) Roger readily drops anything to do with the exceptional, even with the minority. What he is continually asking himself is—what, in these particular circumstances, most usually happens?

Everett W. Knight. *Literature Considered as Philosophy*
(Routledge). 1957. pp. 101–2

It is their continuous search for values, in itself an act of faith, that makes Martin du Gard's characters so human and endearing. Their search recalls the attitudes of Corneille's characters, though these, to be sure, are less deeply baffled. But the stubborness and stoicism with which Antoine and Jacques [in *Les Thibault*] find their human way in an inhuman situation, drawing their values and their dignity only from themselves, is reminiscent of their seventeenth century predecessors.

Germaine Brée and Margaret Guiton. *An Age of Fiction*
(Rutgers). 1957. p. 83

In du Gard there is minute and exact description. Every detail of the environment, every physical and moral aspect of the characters is evoked with scrupulous care. This preoccupation with setting and form is no doubt "old-fashioned." But the themes of *Les Thibault* are astonishingly modern; the characters of *Les Thibault* are committed, even more so than most of the moderns, because they have more to lose. What we conclude in retrospect from the modern novel we see in operation in *Les Thibault.* . . . For *Les Thibault* is a novel of refusal, not of acceptance. *Le Rouge et le Noir,* a century before, sounded the death-knell of the old aristocracy; *Le Mort du père,* volume VI of *Les Thibault,* marks the end of the massive, comfortable, self-righteous bourgeoisie.

> John S. Wood. *FS.* April, 1960. p. 134

Martin du Gard's ever-present scepticism brought both rewards and penalties: it prevented him from committing the naive intellectual errors of so many of his nineteenth-century predecessors, but at the same time, it deprived his work of that infectious enthusiasm which, in the novels of Balzac or Dickens or Tolstoy or Zola, the majority of readers find a more than adequate compensation. There is no poetry, no gusto and scarcely any humour in Martin du Gard's major works, and as realistic studies of the whole range of human experience, therefore, they cannot fail to seem deficient when set beside *War and Peace* or *A la Recherche du Temps Perdu.*

> Robert Gibson. *Roger Martin du Gard*
> (Bowes and Bowes). 1961. p. 116

It is difficult to assess Martin du Gard's chances of survival as a novelist. It is certain, however, that since the last war his reputation has been in decline, outshone by younger writers whose works seem to have more relevance to the present generation. . . . Yet basically Martin du Gard's themes are very similar to those of Malraux, Sartre, or Camus. . . . The theme of the relationship of the individual and the collectivity and the search for a satisfactory replacement for religion is common to both Malraux and Martin du Gard. . . . There is even a parallel between *Barois* and *Les Mandarins*: in both novels we find the same arid intellectual atmosphere, the same preoccupation with ideas and with their propagation, the same involvement with practical politics. The greatest difference between Martin du Gard and these later writers (apart from his greater pessimism) lies in the vehicle chosen, which in their case is more striking and more immediately relevant to the present historical context.

> Denis Boak. *Roger Martin du Gard* (Oxford). 1963.
> p. 212

See *Jean Barois* and *The World of the Thibaults* (novels).

MARTÍNEZ RUIZ, JOSÉ
See Azorín

MARTÍNEZ SIERRA, GREGORIO (1881–1947)

Martínez Sierra is an inspired poet and always writes with deep feeling and sincerity. To his poetic gifts he adds faith in humanity and in himself and a sympathetic feeling toward all existing things. He is often a mystic and a symbolist. In his pantheism he resembles Walt Whitman, and in his symbolism we see the influence of Maurice Maeterlinck. . . . His lyricism, deep feeling, love of nature, optimism, sincerity, almost rustic simplicity, and his style, clear and easy, although often symbolic, delight and inspire. . . . He is in a sense a neo-romanticist who loves everything and enjoys everything. For him Spain is a country where sin is still considered a sin, and where virtue in women and the veneration of womanhood continue as traditional ideals. He finds Spanish womanhood worthy of idealization, and he has made the depiction of its virtues the cardinal feature of his dramatic art.

> Aurelio Espinosa. Introduction to *Teatro de Ensueño*
> (World). 1917. pp. xiii–xvii

The chief fault to be found with Martínez Sierra's dramas is that he has only thought of the heroine and has forgotten the hero. . . . It seems as if Martínez Sierra started off with Ibsen's deterministic ideas and worked straight ahead. Like Ibsen, he makes all his heroines carry on a dialogue between their two egos—the momentary ego that they are and the ideal one toward which they strive. . . . Perhaps one of the greatest virtues of Martínez Sierra is that he abolished that ideal of renunciation in drama which had lasted into the twentieth century, and had cast its pall over literature. His heroines do not, as many of the Benaventian heroines do, sacrifice themselves in order that others may be happy. Ever since the days of Senta and the Flying Dutchman there has been too much renunciation in literature. The heroines of Martínez Sierra . . . devote themselves to sane, healthy life, not to death. And it is perhaps this splendid optimism and belief in life that makes the theatre of Martínez Sierra one of the durable edifices in this storm-tossed twentieth century.

> Walter Starkie. *CR*. Feb., 1924. p. 205

Doña Maria Martínez Sierra, who has helped her husband through a series of collaborations, . . . has always insisted that their joint productions shall bear the signature G. Martínez Sierra. This combination of masculine and feminine qualities is regarded by Spanish critics as the essential characteristic of the work of Martínez Sierra. . . . The qualities which Spanish criticism attributes to the dual personality implied by the signature of Martínez Sierra . . . cannot fail to strike the reader of these plays. Sentimentality is their common feature and their outstanding virtue, or defect, as one prefers. He began by writing symbolical and mystical playlets in the manner of Maeterlinck . . . he soon, however, found the vein of sentimental comedy which has produced the greater number of his characteristic works.

Ernest Boyd. *Studies From Ten Literatures* (Scribner). 1925. pp. 114–6

Of all the countries of Europe, Spain must be the one which modern ideas have touched the least. . . . Realism, rationalism, and disillusion remained to Spain fundamentally incomprehensible. The bleakness of mere intelligence is not for her temperament, and in spite of all efforts in a contrary direction she cannot help seeing life in terms of melodrama, romance, and sentiment. . . . That we are capable of feeling a certain charm in Sierra's work the unexpectedly great success of "The Cradle Song" . . . is enough to prove, but that charm is of something quaintly exotic, it has nothing to do with the moods or the aspirations which are potent for us, and it leaves nothing except a faintly pleasant memory.

Joseph Wood Krutch. *Nation.* May 25, 1927. pp. 590–1

[Martínez Sierra is] a medievalist viewing the world as a vale of tears and seeing salvation only in religion and morality. . . . Sierra's drama of the life and consecration and sacrifice [*The Kingdom of God*], is one of the rare, beautiful things of the theatre. We modernists are little likely to accept his attitude or bow to his conclusions. We challenge life rather than accept it as the will of God; we reform society rather than minister to it. Nevertheless, watching this play we are caught up in his alien philosophy. . . . Nothing since the Tchekov productions has conveyed the loneliness, the detachment, the meaningless futility of individual lives; this play, so entirely dissimilar in its technique and ideas, has some curious affinity with them.

Horace Shipp. *ER.* Dec., 1927. pp. 728–9

It is in the works of Gregorio Martínez Sierra, more than in those of any other Spaniard, that we find the clearest impress of [Ibsen's] "A Doll's House." . . . [But] though a realist, Martínez Sierra does not believe in reducing literature to the position of a mere handmaiden to cold, objective analysis. In translating the realism of existence into words he strives to make it glow with all the feeling that his powers of expression are able to evoke; even if one is not always entirely convinced of its lasting quality, the sheen of optimism which characterizes his dramatic fabric cannot fail to give pleasure.

Halfdan Gregersen. *Ibsen and Spain* (Harvard). 1936. p. 163

In the kind of modern plays we know best, plays Northern or Nordic in their quality and mind, such a story of a woman as this in "The Kingdom of God" would turn more on her inward state, her changes of mind, her development and growth through her experience. But in this Latin piece it is the background itself that carries the drama along. . . . The theme of her is not inward, introspective, psychological in our familiar sense, but is set against the whole idea of woman the mother, the bosom of life, the love that mediates between harsh law and human needs, which the world of the Mediterranean understands so easily. . . . The play is foreign, too, is Latin, in the way the characters are put in, their strong outlining, the typicality of their self-revelation, and their habit of generalizing and running off into philosophical statement anywhere and everywhere. And most of all it is Latin in . . . the manner in which subtlety is achieved by a certain *combination* of single simple things instead of by some single complexity.

Stark Young. *Immortal Shadows* (Scribner). 1948. pp. 103–4

See *Cradle Song and Other Plays* and *The Kingdom of God and Other Plays*.

MATUTE, ANA MARÍA (1926–   )

Tres y un sueño . . . is a book which combines fantasy worthy of Lewis Carroll with satire comparable to that of Rubén Darío's *"El rey burgués"* and picaresque cruelty unsurpassed even in some of Camilo José Cela's darkest pages. It is marked by an intensity of feeling and a style which is occasionally lyrical, usually somber and terse. . . . The case for the existence of a transcendental reality in the world of fantasy is persuasively presented.

Daniel S. Keller. *BA*. Winter, 1962. pp. 61–2

The literary talent of Ana María Matute seems to be the most powerful among recent novelists. [In *Historias de la Artámila*] the author reaches the full maturity of her inspiration. In previous, very valuable works, Ana María Matute often ran the risk of being too *précieuse* not only in language but also in the mental subtleties expressed; now her language becomes direct and wonderfully simple without ceasing to be tremendously creative and poetic, and the types of feeling that are depicted are uncomplicated and fundamental. . . . There is a Chekhovian quality in this beautiful book, an emphasis on the intense lyrical and emotional impact of little things and apparently insignificant happenings. . . . Ana María Matute combines this appreciation of little things with a sensitive and realistic presentation, through the memory of personal experience, of the present tragedy of the Spanish people. This is a book of protest, subtle and lyrical but nonetheless strong and brave.

Rafael Bosch. *BA*. Summer, 1962. p. 303

The theme of children caught in an adult world which they do not understand, and reacting to it with innocent craft and cruelty, made an English novel so famous in the 1920's that it continues as a paperback classic. Ana María Matute has spun the development of very different lives in her Spanish story [*School of the Sun*], but the plot, while developed with less complexity, recalls *High Wind in Jamaica,* and is good enough to stand comparison with Richard Hughes' earlier book. . . . This is a slighter book than *High Wind in Jamaica,* but its brooding sense of the tragedy of innocence in evil is as true, and its telling is skillful. . . . Ana María Matute has produced one of the more competent of the novels which have come from the younger generation of Spanish writers.

Mildred Adams. *NYT*. April 21, 1963. pp. 4, 30

The impression [*The Lost Children*] makes is not one of bitterness and horror, but of the strength of life and the unfailing resurgence of the human spirit. The explicit pessimism of Miss Matute's novel is somehow illuminated from within by a celebration of the power and vitality of mankind. . . . Miss Matute [has an] exact observation which sees so deep into an ordinary situation that it becomes fresh [and she] clothes this story in clear light as uncompromising at it is unsentimental. Like *Ship of Fools*, . . . *The Lost Children* reveals the understructure of the world, the beams and girders that sustain society as it is; or, if you prefer a more dynamic metaphor, it shows us the lines of force binding people together and holding them apart. . . . This book . . . has a classic power expressed in brilliant prose.

Elizabeth Janeway. *CSM*. May 20, 1965. p. 7

Her mode—her choice—is what in the axiological language of form we call the trivial. Her method is to combine the stammering, mind-refusing world of childhood with the almost idiot, brute world of the senses. . . . The . . . stubborn, stuttering, mindless refusal to know the world beyond the senses, beyond the preoccupation with immediate, unreflected experience . . . makes [*The Lost Children*] no more—and no less, for it is remarkably written—than a lyric cry, a long cortical spasm.

Miss Matute retreat[s] from history—from the notion that not only do things happen, but that their happening has meaning, that a set of values can be assigned to them—her preference [is] for unmeditated Experience. . . . The lobotomy-by-childhood, the anesthesia-by-intensity which *The Lost Children* so insistently evokes gives us, as no ideological intervention could do, the measure of the . . . terror and the surrender to which the Spanish writers have been, and are still, subject.

Richard Howard. *NL*. July 5, 1965. pp. 19–20

Ana María Matute . . . sees the world through the eyes of childhood. It is this quality of mystery, of magic, of fairy tale, combined in a unique mixture with the harsh and bitter realities of life, that gives the distinctive stamp to all of her work. Many of her most characteristic images assume a child's point of view. . . . In Matute there is always the hint that behind the surface realities of the everyday world hovers another existence, strange and secret. Her fiction rests on a solid substratum of realistic and concrete detail, but Matute's special talent lies in extracting the invisible interior reality from the visible reality of the external world. . . . The Matutean world has virtually nothing in common with the Spain of the tourist. . . . Her pages are vibrant with passion and tragedy, but bull-fighters and gypsy dancers are nowhere mentioned. . . . She is more concerned with the recurring seasons, the anguished eroticism and frustrations of adolescence, the disappointments of age, relations between the rich and the poor, the tensions between the past and the present, than she is in current events and fashions.

George Wythe. *BA*. Winter, 1966. pp. 18–20

See *School of the Sun* and *The Lost Children* (novels).

MAURIAC, CLAUDE (1910–   )

M. Mauriac said in his critical work, *The New Literature,* that the future would perhaps "reconcile in the same novel the discoveries of Proust and those of Joyce"; this is undoubtedly what he has aimed at in [*The Dinner Party*] and what he has succeeded to a remarkable degree in achieving. One finds his book exciting for the psychological revelations he makes available to the reader through a counterpoint of social situation and stream-of-consciousness narration. The basic theme, returned to again and again, is mortality, the brevity of life, and the transitoriness of our abilities, accomplishments, and passions.

Dorothy Nyren Curley. *LJ*. April 1, 1960. pp. 1473–4

The Dinner Party moves simultaneously on two levels, both fragmentary, which the reader must complete, combine, and connect: the sophisticated conversational level of well-to-do Parisians; the inner consciousness of each isolated individual with his private obsessions, concerns, memories, and anxieties. As the conventional conversational patterns form and move from character to character they reach into each private world, eliciting moods which, even in so guarded a group, erupt to the surface, deflecting the conversation, causing sudden mute exchanges, tender, hostile, happy, or sad, abrupt flashes of understanding. From time to time a gust of emotion breaks through, blending the dinner party into a whole as it releases in all the characters preoccupations common to them all: love, time in the form of age, and death.

Germaine Brée. *SR*. May 7, 1960. pp. 20, 66

The Marquise Went Out at Five is a truly modern work. Even its models are all new. It is like a highly intelligent film made by a mobile camera and then edited, with many flashbacks and much crosscutting, by a poetic producer. It is like an on-the-spot tape recording; indeed, it could well be made into a play for radio, with dozens of different voices rising and fading against the busy music background of a city. . . . Like other practitioners of "the new novel" in France . . . Mauriac has given up the concept of a single thread of plot called "the story"; and like them, he brings the reader into direct and intimate confrontation with his characters.

Gilbert Highet. *Horizon*. May, 1962. p. 115

Mauriac is trying to put imagined actuality—people themselves talking and thinking, and not a novelist writing about people talking and thinking —on the printed page. . . . Actual thought is rarely elevated into words and sentences at all but like a subterranean mumble or music, pours along just below the level of language. Joyce, coining words by the pound, transposed this sub-language into print, and the results are closer to music than prose. Since Mauriac depends on conventional words, which reveal their meaning in their own sweet way, his books tend to settle into a slow-motion approximation of reality.

Whitney Balliett. *NY*. Sept. 15, 1962. p. 174

Curiously Anglo-Saxon in his literary allegiance, Mauriac writes as if *Ulysses, Mrs. Dalloway* and *Nightwood* were more familiar to him than any of the works of Proust or of his own illustrious father. . . . Yet the world of *The Marquise Went Out at Five* is pure French. . . . Again and again in Mauriac's strangely esthetic if not always poetic rigamarole of a novel, we are thus reminded of the underlying scandal and horror of *La Torture* and *La Gangrène* in contemporary French life—and indeed in contemporary life in general. It is the basic honesty and humanity of Claude Mauriac, who seems to have inherited these traits from his often wrong-headed but right-hearted father, that saves him as a writer.

Edouard Roditi. *NL.* Oct. 15, 1962. pp. 24–5

Like the "Wandering Rocks" section of *Ulysses, The Marquise* has a pattern which hardly depends on individual identities. The title of Mauriac's novel comes from a phrase of Valéry's, expressing impatience with the machinery of nineteenth century verisimilitude. The novelist has gained very little if he has escaped from this machinery only to leave his reader obsessed with its absence.

What, then, are Mauriac's achievements? A view of one spot in depth, as an overscribbled palimpset of history; a sense of individual action as random, incoherent, fantasy-ridden, convulsively incomplete; a definition of a world which is sensual, witty, corrupt, alive. What he cannot or does not choose to present is the experience of intimacy. . . . Whether this is a consequence of Mauriac's method or a quality of his vision, one cannot tell; it certainly contributes to the sense of his book as a hard hollow shell, murmuring the impersonal music of time.

Robert Martin Adams. *HdR.* Autumn, 1962. p. 430

The same characters appear and reappear in all of his novels, but they do not change, that is, they bear perpetually the same relationship to each other. At the bottom of all this lies a personal obsession about the inevitability of solitude and the mystery of communion (thus, the "interior" nature of the "dialogue"). One Mauriac personage affects another, if he does, principally by being a constant reminder that each is entirely replaceable for the other, that all men are interchangeable, all women are fatal, that each encounter is a reminder of our habitual aridity. Conversation is to be understood as simultaneous monologue.

Alice Mayhew. *Com.* Sept. 25, 1964. p. 20

This eldest son . . . of François Mauriac is, to employ Yeats's phrase, "a crow who has followed many ploughs." In his journalism and his ten volumes of literary and film criticism, he has written about a number of novelists. . . . In his tetralogy . . . he has imitated several other novelists. None the less, not merely his fourth novel [*L'Agrandissement*] but the series itself can be described as unique. By sheer dint of writing, he has worked his way out of the derivative and the slick into a personal style and an individuality whose existence he himself might paradoxically deny. . . . The career to date of Claude Mauriac seems to me all the justification that technical experiment in the novel will ever need. . . . Mauriac has learned a great deal from his experiments, not only about how to write novels, but also, I believe, about life and about himself.

Vivian Mercier. *Nation*. Feb. 1, 1965. p. 121

See *All Women Are Fatal, The Dinner Party,* and *The Marquise Went Out at Five* (novels); also *The New Literature* (criticism).

MAURIAC, FRANÇOIS (1885–   )

Let us admit frankly that Mauriac is drawn to the "things of this world" for the same reasons that so much affect the post-war generation—the charm of all that is sensual, color and symmetry and youthful flesh. He can caress these things with as much zest as the Renaissance poet's, perhaps; but he can also phrase his renouncement of them in terms not of pure spiritual sacrifice, but in the language of a man who has discerned the absence of satisfaction in them, the penalty which beauty exacts, the lassitude of desire fulfilled. When Mauriac's theme is lust his men and women are no healthy animals, brotheling like pagans, but creatures tormented even as were Paolo and Francesca in the inferno of their discontent, seeking sweetness under the blows of a scourge. He can set before you the mysterious throes of adolescence curious of passion, but he cannot imagine them akin to happiness. One's chief regret is that happiness does not exist in Mauriac's world. Joy—even the most legitimate joy—is always discounted because of the high tariff exacted for it.

George N. Shuster. *Bkm*. Jan., 1931. pp. 470–1

His men and women avid for profit always end by making some slight gesture of denial with their stubborn faces. Then Mauriac's novel stops: he has found one of God's creatures beneath the Pharisee girded with selfishness and wealth. This individual is no longer a criminal, but a sinner. He is aware of his abjectness. He is a human "person."

Mauriac's theology does not go much further than that. "At the age when the blood awakens," he confesses in *God and Mammon*, "everything crystallizes around notions of purity, sin, and the state of grace."

Since then the creative artist has grown; his vision, sharpened by rancor and hate, has penetrated further and more deeply. But his metaphysics remains that of a choir boy.

Roger Garaudy. *Literature of the Graveyard* (International). 1948. p. 20

Those pages from Mauriac's *Journal* in the June *N.R.F.* no longer find any echo in my heart. I no longer even understand *what is concerned here.* "Even in the state of grace," he writes, "my creatures are born of the murkiest part of me; they are formed of what subsists in me in spite of myself." What a confession! This amounts to saying that if he were a perfect Christian, he would cease to have any material of which to make his novels. Is this not precisely what I told him?

How anguished he is! And how I like him thus! But what is the use of this anguish? May a time come for him when it will seem to him as vain and fanciful, as monstrous as it seems to me today.

André Gide. *The Journals* (Knopf). 1949. v. 3, pp. 162–3

M. Mauriac knows how to tell a story. In fact, I can think of no other living novelist whose sheer narrative power is at all comparable with his. Impossible to stop reading any of his novels. . . . His method is traditional and presents no difficulties or obliquities such as we find in writers like Bernanos or Elizabeth Bowen (to take two very dissimilar examples). Reserving all complexity for the analysis of character and interplay of shadowy moral forces, M. Mauriac's prose has the close, economical texture, the hard definition and the smooth serenity of Racine's verse. And because he never flinches before the worst, he is an entirely unsentimental writer.

Edward Sackville-West. *Inclinations* (Scribner). 1949. pp. 236–7

Mauriac's most widely acknowledged achievement consists in his style. And we do not mean by that, of course, that he merely has certain purple passages to his credit, but that his writing does normally do its work so well. It may be an exaggeration to say, as M. Gaéton Bernoville does, that he is, "along with Montherlant, the greatest living prose-writer in the French language," but the distinction of his style cannot be denied. Even in novels that as a whole are failures we find the characteristic and effective Mauriac periods occurring.

Martin Jarrett-Kerr. *François Mauriac* (Yale). 1954. p. 53

Mauriac's fiction has been charged with monotony. It moves in a world that indeed is, geographically and socially, narrowly limited. It revolves around the same perennial obsessions with money, property, the entice-ments of the flesh, and the wages of sin. Within these confines, however, it explores in depth. What is more, it conjures up that diseased and haunted world, and gains in vivid intensity what is sacrificed in diver-sity. In contrast with several experimenters among contemporary nov-elists, Mauriac stands as the upholder of the traditional virtues of the French novel. He is fully aware of the new complexity that Stendhal, Dostoevsky, and Proust have led us to expect from fiction. But his purpose is not to experiment with new fictional forms or to explore recesses of the unconscious with awe, or with the naïveté of one who has lately discovered the jargon of clinical psychology. He writes because he must rid himself of the obsession of his characters and endow with shapes and sounds the desolate world that he carries within his imagination.

> Henri Peyre. *The Contemporary French Novel*
> (Oxford). 1955. p. 103

It is plain . . . that M. Mauriac has no liking for time, no fondness for the Bergsonian necessity of waiting "for the sugar to melt." To him, his creature's time is a dream, an all-too-human illusion; he gets rid of it and resolutely sets himself up within the eternal. But this alone, to my way of thinking, should have deterred him from writing novels. The real novelist is stirred by things that offer resistance; he is excited by doors because they must be opened, by envelopes because they must be unsealed.

In Hemingway's admirable *Farewell to Arms,* objects are time-traps; they fill the narrative with innumerable tiny, obstinate resistances which the hero must break down one after the other. But M. Mauriac detests these lowly barriers that deter him from his purpose; he speaks of them as little as possible. . . .

La Fin de la Nuit is not a novel. How can anyone call this angular, glacial book, with its analyses, theatrical passages and poetic medita-tions, a "novel"? How can anyone confuse these bursts of speed and violent jamming of the brakes, these abrupt starts and breakdowns, with the majestic flow of fictional time? How can anyone be taken in by this motionless narrative, which betrays its intellectual framework from the very start, in which the mute faces of heroes are inscribed like angels in a circle?

> Jean-Paul Sartre. *Literary and Philosophical Essays*
> (Criterion). 1955. pp. 19–23

When the reader recalls a work of Mauriac . . . it is the characters, more particularly their states of soul, that come to mind rather than their

situations or the plots in which they are involved. . . . The reason is to
be found in Mauriac's . . . conception of the responsibility of the man
of letters as essentially moral. The novelist and the dramatist are for him
the interpreter of man to himself, the revealer of the secrets of the
human heart. Without their efforts few men would have the courage to
see themselves as they really are. The artist whose activities are suspect
to many Christians really deserves well of his fellow-men, he insists, in
so far as he is profoundly imbued with the conviction of the "sanctity of
truth." To lay bare man's weaknesses without flattery, connivance, or
complacency is to direct him to the only progress which Barrès called the
education of the soul.

> Michael F. Moloney. *Francois Mauriac* (Alan Swallow).
> 1958. p. 152

Mauriac's Catholic sensibility is in the sometimes visible and sometimes
invisible background of his plays. Even when they do not refer to Him,
God exists for his characters as a reproach or a source of exaltation. It
has been said, with some degree of justice, that Mauriac's heroes are less
free and more directed and controlled than are the heroes of other contemporary French writers. This seems to come from the fact that in
Mauriac's universe sin is a presence, and evil is someone. The playwright-
novelist fully realizes his intermediate position of not pleasing the world
and of displeasing the saints. Montherlant has recalled that each century
of French literature has had to deal with one great Catholic novelist.
This may well be Mauriac's position.

> Wallace Fowlie. *Dionysius in Paris* (Meridian). 1960.
> p. 155

Sartre's opinion notwithstanding, Mauriac is undoubtedly an artist. . . .
Admittedly, his range is limited: he has compared himself to a man
continuously plowing the same small field over and over again. But from
that field he has harvested extraordinary fruit—bitter though they may
have been to many a complacent reader. Tearing away the mask of
Catholic, bourgeois respectability from his outwardly very proper,
socially responsible characters, he has revealed torrents of hatred and
greed boiling beneath the surface and occasionally bursting out in the
open like ruptured sewers.

> Leon S. Roudiez. *SR*. Feb. 25, 1961. p. 27

M. Mauriac always sees one thing in terms of something that it is not,
and in particular sees all that arises from the necessity of man's physical
being through the Mauriac veil of abstract ideas about some creature

finer than man—all spirit and no flesh. He consequently tends to view all human situations that involve actions as disgusting betrayals and descents into the slime. Sex especially upsets him. He is blind to the innocence, and to the fundamental decency, of most relationships based on sexual attraction. He can regard them, drained of all that gives them meaning, only as failures to reach something higher.

Anthony West. NY. Nov. 4, 1961. p. 219

Two atmospheres blanket all, a summer and a winter atmosphere, an atmosphere of siesta and scorching vineyards and an atmosphere of shuttered houses in which landlords brood greedily and destroy each other to a nocturnal accompaniment of murmuring pines. . . . There is to many minds a natural affinity between hot weather and sexual desire. . . . Mauriac's skill in conveying the sensations of torridity has led many critics to regard his novels . . . as characterised by their sensuality. I do not find them sensual, merely hot. The characters themselves I think frigid. They are possessed by greed, but seem to me never to exhibit desire which is specifically and properly sexual (so different from Colette, where desire stirs unmistakably even on cold days). In the same way, despite the bright light outside the shutters, I find Mauriac's world gloomy, his religion bleak. His trend as a Christian apologist is to show that the world without God is intolerable. Therefore God must exist.

Rayner Heppenstall. The Fourfold Tradition
(New Directions). 1961. pp. 167–9

See The Lamb and Thérèse (novels); also Mémoires Interieurs (essays).

MICHAUX, HENRI (1899–   )

Put him next to Rabelais and his extraordinary men and animals seem in place; put him next to Swift and his voyages, his uninhibited exposures, his angers almost have a tradition. His saeva indignatio, it is true, is usually concealed, and he is less explicit than Swift or Voltaire in what men ought to be. . . . But his standards are, like theirs, medicinal; good and evil fall into place. The mind's inner workings are exposed in a way that is modern but compatible with tradition. . . . Unawed by form or fashion in society or literature, he has waged his battle not against social or literary values, but with a new tone and from a new perspective, against the tyranny of conventional experience.

Richard Ellmann. KR. Spring, 1949. p. 198

A great deal has been made of Michaux's originality. But where is he in the tradition of French writing? Not too far from Valéry and Gide. Like them driven by the demon of possibility. Michaux's notion of *self*, for instance, and Valéry's. Michaux feels himself a victim of hostile forces, dependent, and helpless except for the resources of ruse and blind attack. There is a certain will in him, but hardly conscious enough to be identified at its source with self. Will operates for Michaux only as a vague motive to get out of some predicament, as "exorcism," to clear up a painful situation, as a ruse of the imagination, to outwit the world in "self" defense.

Jackson Mathews. Poetry. Nov., 1949. p. 101

His is a work which discourages commentators, because they don't know how to get hold of these strange books which are at the same time intimate diaries, journalism, narratives, tales, and poems, and sometimes all at the same time; where one passes, without a signal, from the most pointed humor to a lyricism most naked and most distressing; from the wildest fantasy to the most brutal realism; from the description of imaginary countries to that of completely real countries (and one does not know which of the two sorts is most real); from the metaphysical tone to that of interior monologue and from a proverb to an epic poem— without any regard for genres.

René Bertelé. Henri Michaux (Editions Pierre Seghers).
1953. p. 13. Tr. by Dorothy Nyren Curley

The twelve sections of *Face aux verrous* offer a varied sampling of Henri Michaux's verbal gifts, of his iconoclastic humor, of that strain of violence and often a delight in cruelty which characterizes much Surrealist writing. Striking as his images are, the total effect is not quite convincing. The revolt sounds a little too deliberate—a sort of programmatic spontaneity very different from Gide's fresh invitation to open the door and go out, a few decades back. Michaux's invectives, his anger, and fantasies of destruction seem arbitrary and occasionally a shade shrill.

Albert Roland. BA. Spring, 1955. p. 173

Michaux is a magician-creator, watching, almost terrified, the world that has come into being through his mind and his art. The objects and bodies he conjures up become obsessions and often give the impression of turning against their creator. The power to perform metamorphoses carries with it a very particular kind of panic which is the poet's. Michaux is the man who questions the universe and ends by being questioned himself. This is the poet's condition, his ambivalence, the two extremities between which he moves, where a triumph is never reached without a defeat at the same time.

Wallace Fowlie. *Mid-Century French Poets* (Twayne). 1955. pp. 233–4

His explorations in the world of drugs were, over and over again, explorations of himself; they tended toward extension of experience, to a growing pursuit. Given up to invisible, all-powerful and bizarre masters, he tried to recover possession of himself again, to stand still, and, in observing the drug, to spy upon himself; to track down his own image (and, through it, the laws of the spirit) in the magic mirrors which made him grimace. And, inversely, the experience of traveling in such a drifting fashion, of abandoning himself to a devastating passivity, prodigiously full of phantoms, beyond all interventions of the "great demolishers of the spirit" was for a long time a commonplace for him. "Knowledge through the depths," such was always his method.

Pierre Robin. *MF*. June, 1963. p. 322. Tr. by Dorothy Nyren Curley

Henri Michaux shares with Audiberti the surrealist appeal to violent imagery, his sense for the magic force of words, as well as his poetic shrewdness, which aims at the neutralization of inner tensions by the very energy of imaginary outbursts. (Michaux calls this function of his poetry *exorcisme*.) Yet in Michaux's poetry—verse and poetic prose alike—these outbursts are under the strict control of a profoundly rebellious, skeptical and ironic mind, which sharpens and stylizes them into distinctly perceived clusters of turbulence.

Alexander Aspel. *Contemporary French Poetry* (Michigan). 1965. pp. 7–8

See *Selected Writings*.

MIRÓ, GABRIEL (1879–1930)

The realism of Miró's treatment of the crucifixion itself, his descriptions of Christ, have been called repellant. . . . The New Testament does not withhold such realistic details as justify the elaborations of such imaginative reconstruction as that which Miró has essayed. . . . [To recoil from such realism] is to recoil from a fundamental thing in Spanish art, its streak of crude brutality. . . . *Figures of the Passion of Our Lord* must be taken for what it is, an expression of a Spanish artist's imagination. Gabriel Miró is essentially an artist in words, a poet; he is not a propagandist with a thesis or a message. He is a master of prose unequaled in his country, endowed with a prodigious verbal wealth and gift of original style, whose gamut is full of lovely tones, sonorous and strong, tender and delicate. He can render not only the form and color of things, but their interior emotion. His landscapes can be seen and touched; their smell rises to the nostrils; the reader becomes part of them.

Ernest Boyd. *Ind.* April 4, 1925. p. 384

Gabriel Miró's *Figures of the Passion of Our Lord* . . . belongs in spirit to the period of fervently aesthetic interpretation. [It is] more impressive as a work of creative imagination than as a tribute of piety. . . . Its author is of Jesuit upbringing, enamored of landscape and mountain scenery, and temperamentally enriched with the aesthetic melancholy of the later romanticists. His imagination is passionate, colorful, sensuous, with a touch of Latin *morbidezza.*

In painting the scenes and telling the stories of the Passion, he seizes, like Flaubert, in his Carthaginian picture, upon all its exotic possibilites, its luxury, its cruelty—like the merciless painters of the early Renaissance, he counts the blood drops under the lash. He revels in the Herodian pomp and the sumptuous softness of the Roman procurator's palace and the subtle degeneration of his mind. Not in isolation and little companies does he see the protagonist moving toward his doom, but with his pitiful broken humanity poignant against the riotous springtime, drenched in odors of tropical fruits, wending toward Calvary amidst the buzz and brilliance of Oriental bazaars, and all the scent and hum and murmur of the Roman East.

Stuart P. Sherman. *NYHT.* April 12, 1925. p. 2

His style is modelled upon Azorín. It is cool, clear, light and objective; he makes great use of the descriptive present; has no rhetorical gorgeousness or sonorous pomp, none of Zola's power or heaviness. He describes the things he sees, he endeavors without much success to give an aesthetic impression of fine, sharp, subtle sensations and achieves dullness. . . . He lacks imagination, is no creator or describer of character, cannot tell a story; and, therefore, is wanting in the essential qualities of a novelist.

L. A. Warren. *Modern Spanish Literature* (Brentano).
1929. v. 1, p. 283

Señor Miró, although undoubtedly a Symbolist in style, need not be too accurately placed in relation to other writers. He is Miró, with a strong individuality of his own. His style, with its wealth of strange, artificial but indigenous, carefully chosen words, its concentration, its accumulation of brief co-ordinative clauses, its syncopated metaphors, is striking and original. Somehow it resembles the work of a goldsmith striving to achieve an artistic pattern, but the material beneath his hand is too rich and the lines become blurred. . . . Señor Miró is saved by his clearness of vision and by his love of Nature, his almost fascinated love of Nature in its beauty and its cruelty. When his rich style, the choice words, the symbols and images, are applied to things of the imagination or to the reconstruction of history, the result may be too heavy and cloying. On the other hand, when it describes the simple things of everyday life, the style can, by its careful vocabulary and artistic insight, bring out and heighten the reality without spoiling its simplicity.

Aubrey F. G. Bell. Contemporary Spanish Literature
(Knopf). 1933. pp. 141–2

For sheer beauty of expression in prose Gabriel Miró occupies a unique position in Spanish literature. Unamuno once lamented the fact that this beauty had not been recorded in poetic form. Although he did not employ the poetical devices of rhyme and meter, Gabriel Miró possessed a poet's soul, as sensitive and impressionable as that of any man who ever wrote exquisite verse. Imagist, symbolist, impressionist, call him what you like: he was pure artist.. His art has one controlling purpose: to paint a picture, to transfer a striking impression in no less striking word combinations and figures.

Albert Brent. Hsp. Nov., 1951. p. 369

Miró represents with extraordinary intensity the type of man destined to the concrete world: Miró, or Concrete Man. From that superb speci-men of the human animal, spirit emanated as a luminous irradiation from matter. And that combination of matter and spirit was marvelously organized for examining, suffering, feeling the world. In him sensations, emotions, passions developed continuously in constant gradation. Miró walks along the street, and the street is a new world to him, discovered for the very first time. He appears before us as a barbarian, bringing new materials. Quite the opposite of an intellectual, and even less of a rhetorician, even though rhetoric may appear in a subordinate posi-tion. For this man—an unusual barbarian, possessing great knowledge—everything turns into landscape: the earth and its inhabitants, space and time; for Miró sees landscape with his eyes and with his memory. Hence the importance of recollection. Miró, in his attitude toward Nature, is sensitive and enthusiastic; in his attitude toward society, he is sensitive and mocking. Hence the importance of irony. This, then, is Gabriel Miró: sensitivity chaneled through recollection and irony—and expression.

Jorge Guillén. *Language and Poetry* (Harvard).
1961. pp. 196–7

See *Our Father San Daniel* (novel); also *Figures of the Passion of Our Lord.*

MISTRAL, FRÉDÉRIC (1830–1914)

He produced the most original poem (*Mirèio*) of modern times,— a poem rustic in theme, unconventional in treatment, full of the sunshine and the untaught grace of out-door life, yet stamped with the inalienable dignity of high literary descent. M. Mistral seldom reminds us of any other author. When he does, it is of the greatest. Vincen and Mirèio occasionally recall Romeo and Juliet; but only, it may be, through their youth, their abandon, their southern precocity, and their similar misfortunes, while their passion has far more of childlike innocence than that of the immortal lovers of Verona.

Harriet W. Preston. Preface to *Mirèio* (Roberts). 1874.
pp. xi–xii

His thought is ever pure and high; his lessons are lessons of love, of noble aims, of energy and enthusiasm. He is full of love for the best in the past, love of his native soil, love of his native landscape, love of the men about him, love of his country. He is a poet of the *Gai Saber,* joyous and healthy, he has never felt a trace of the bitterness, the disenchantment, the gloom and the pain of a Byron or a Leopardi. He is eminently representative of the race he seeks to glorify in its own eyes and in the world's, himself a type of that race at its very best, with all its exuberance and energy, with its need of outward manifestation, life and movement.

Charles Alfred Downer. *Frédéric Mistral* (Columbia).
1901. p. 250

He is not only a poet of Provence. He is Provence incarnate, and apart from the noble quality of his work, his position as the foremost representative of his compatriots is romantically unique. No other country today, pointing to its greatest man, would point out—a poet; whereas Mistral, were he not as unspoiled as he is laurelled, might, with literal truth, say: *"Provence—c'est moi!"*

Richard Le Gallienne. *Vanishing Roads* (Putnam).
1915. p. 307

Mistral is, like Vergil, irreproachable in his choice of words, in the clearness and simplicity of his figures of speech, and in the crystalline limpidity of his language, so transparent that at first it seems to have no depth, yet so full of meaning that, after long consideraion, one hardly sees the bottom of it. And what measure, what tact, what truth in his magnificent idyllic pictures! What sustained harmony! What faultless purity! In French letters only Racine and Fénelon have this marvellous limpidity; but the Provençal tongue, like the Latin, has in addition, some taste of the sun that is lacking in our less coloured and less concrete tongue.

> Jean Carrère. *Degeneration in the Great French Masters*
> (Brentano). 1922. p. 241

Mistral is primitive in his traditional convictions which all his culture has not uprooted, his attachment to the land, to the patriarchal customs of his ancestors, and in the essential frankness and realism of his art, a realism foreign to that of his French contemporaries, for whom realism meant a reaction against sophistication, an attempt to return to something lost, whereas for Mistral it was the expression of something that had never ceased to exist. . . . It is the primitive character that justifies the comparison so often made between him and Homer. Alone among all modern poets, he gives that impression of a fresh and youthful world which we receive from Homer.

> C. M. Girdlestone. *Dreamer and Striver* (Methuen).
> 1937. p. 259

From its first appearance this poem (*Mirèio*) had an astonishing success; for it made no concessions to the spirit of the times. Its triumph in Provence was to be expected, but in Paris it was acclaimed by Adolphe Dumas, who likened its author to Virgil, and by Lamartine, who compared him with Homer. Its beauty and freshness have never faded: on the contrary, its popularity has constantly grown. Since its first triumph it has been translated into more than a dozen languages. And Mirèio herself has become a part of our civilized consciousness; another Antigone, another Beatrice, another Juliet; only *"un chato de Prouvenço,"* but a country maiden, for all that, of an unsurpassed purity, beauty, and heroism, who is, and must forever be, the shining symbol of the country in which she was conceived.

> Rob Lyle. *Mistral* (Bowes and Bowes). 1953. p. 20

Mistral *was* somebody. What is far more to the point, Mistral still *is* somebody, still inspires and influences the grandchildren of his contemporaries and great-grandchildren of his contemporaries to an extent which no other writer of his time has achieved. He is to Provence what Marx is to the intellectual underworld and the materialist under-dogs; and it is because Mistral stands for the values Marxism destroys that his memory and his writings are to be loved and revered.

> Richard Aldington. *Introduction to Mistral*
> (Heinemann). 1956. p. 1

If the Provençal poets lacked the unity and coherent history and culture that produces a living traditional epic such as Adam Mickiewicz's *Pan Tadeusz,* Mistral by the skillful portrayal of life in a rustic community, from firsthand experience, achieved at least the semblance of such unity and coherence. There is indeed a deal of affinity between Mickiewicz and Mistral, for both wrote poetic pictures of country life, and both wrote to express their proud but wounded patriotism and their political hopes. . . . A man of many facets, if he was an inspired dreamer he was also an inspired thinker and a national leader. "A synthesis of local forces," he not only recreated a language and made a large slice of France vocal, but he also made the civilized world aware of its heritage and of the blight which threatened it.

> Tudor Edwards. *The Lion of Arles* (Fordham). 1964. pp. 72, 204

See *Mirèio* (poem).

MONTALE, EUGENIO (1896–   )

No other Italian poet of our century has created so concrete a language, so continuous a stream of powerful and daring images. Montale's lines are original, austere, and possess a tense hidden melody. He has expressed the drama of modern man who cannot mold his life but is helplessly led through days and years by external factors and circumstances. Yet Montale knows the power of dreams and illusions. He feels the profound interrelation between things and human existence: His poems are full of objects which provide the substance of human dreams, help "to exist," and therefore are the constant symbols of life. The result is a kind of dynamic despair which circulates within all the manifestations of life and has its primary origin in the invariable rhythm of time. Man becomes the prisoner of ignorance about his own destiny. Montale is pessimistic, but of a strong pessimism, without futile rebellion or querulous sentimentality. From this point of view, he can be considered the Leopardi of our century.

> Giovanni Cecchetti. *BA*. Summer, 1957. p. 260

Normally Montale's language has a vertebrate compactness going back to Dante's; fighting shy of the all-too-obvious music into which the Italian lyrical tradition had come to melt, it lowers its tone to become an intimate conversation averse to epic peals, high-strung melody or set cadences. Montale came thus to disjoint verse and freely treat the eleven-syllable line, shrinking discourse into a sequence of intense hard passages . . . ; he transposed sound onto an inner level, varying rhyme with dissonance, shifting it into the body of the line, where it will exercise a more secret charm, and often seeking in alliteration a sound-unity for the context—a unity to be reconstructed from within, by valuing syllables and consonants to the extent of making them the verte-brae of a poetical organism.

> Glauco Cambon. SwR. Winter, 1958. p. 5

[It is the] task of every modern Italian poet . . . to resurrect or to bury the cadaver of literary Italian. . . . Montale . . . buried—or ignored—the cadaver. With an expansive verbal fantasy, he ransacked prose for poetry, and with an agonizingly minute graphic precision, he fashioned, of myriad visual epiphanies, the various hell that is his world. Montale's mainspring is the restless horror of any immobility, a vision of nothing but vacuous repetition in the permanent.

> Allen Mandelbaum. Introduction to *Life of a Man* by
> Giuseppe Ungaretti (New Directions). 1958. p. xi

Diffusion by its nature is a principle of composition; it must be so in its function of putting parts of a poem together (and apart). For this reason it has to do with the unity of a poem, and this is very close to what a poem is finally about. . . . Eugenio Montale, in a poem so pulsing with its moment that it is given no name, stresses the furtive union between his personal self and nature by presenting the diffuse images of a few moments by the sea. The poem [*Avartice s'abbatte,* etc.] comes from a section entitled *"Mediterraneo,"* the name of a sea whose root implication places it at the land's center . . . and the title of the book is *Ossi di Seppia,* cuttlefish bones. The cuttlefish is of such softness in his drift through the sea that we think of it as having no bones, just as these drifting poems, ejecting like cuttlefish their brown ink over a small diffuse area of a sea of images, do without a rational spine. . . . The self is defined by what it is not: the poet's feeling is buried in the landscape that rejoins him . . . in the form of surf, a momentary whiteness of waters.

> Albert Cook. *KR.* Spring, 1959. pp. 202, 212, 214

That Montale's poetry originates from a negative position, from a belief in non-existence or from a non-gnosis, has been known for some time now. But to write poetry is always a gnosis or way of becoming conscious; a way of learning about oneself and the world which surrounds one, one's own drama in relation to the self as well as in relation to external realities. To arrive at such a consciousness Montale looks inside himself with a searching and pitiless glance until he feels or even sees a terrible anguish from which there is no hope of escape: he sees the evil of life itself. For him, all of nature suffers. And each thing suffers in accordance with its capacity to suffer, in its own particular way. . . . In man this suffering becomes intellectual, metaphysical. His doom consists of aspiring for a happiness which is pure illusion; in aspiring for it and at the same time being fully aware that it is an illusion; in searching for a truth which continually escapes him, a truth which is always beyond his grasp. . . . Montale asks . . . the "why" of this suffering, only to conclude that it is a suffering without reason and without purpose.

Maria Sampoli-Simonelli. IQ. Summer, 1959. pp. 43–5

The chief stylistic characteristics of Montale's poetry [are]: on the one hand, his full utilization of poetic naturalism in definition, coloring, detailing of landscape—all the more lifelike and concrete as it is exemplary and symbolic; on the other, his constant tendency to resolve the elements of static description in the running temporal line of song. In his music there is a polarity between discursive expansion, marked by ample refrains and curvatures, and a melodic contraction characterized by stressed and violent rhythms bristling with internal rhymes, assonances and consonances.

Sergio Solmi. QRL. No. 4, 1962. p. 225

Montale is basically a negative spirit. The themes of his poetry revolve around the concept that man is alone and that the world is futile and meaningless. He is a man conscious of his crisis, who lives his crisis from moment to moment, from day to day, to its last bitter instant, without ever being able to overcome it or to leave it behind. It is the crisis of the intellectual and already bears the mark of the later existentialist. In the period between the two world wars, Montale reflects the moral discomfort of a generation that is on its way to utter tragedy and is powerless before it. In poetry the spiritual wasteland of Montale is translated into a detailed depiction of nature—an unfriendly, harsh nature, in which even the spectacle of beauty, of joy, is quickly obscured by the undercurrent of futility that cold reason introduces. Montale's poetry . . . possesses a tension, an evocative power, and such novel musical and rhythmical resolutions that it remains unsurpassed in modern Italian literature.

Carlo L. Golino. Contemporary Italian Poetry
(California). 1962. pp. xvii–xviii

Struck by divine indifference and by the nothingness of life, Montale sees in nature an appropriate symbol of man's condition. True, nature does resist time and man does not—yet both are exposed, so to speak, to gradual erosion and are ultimately condemned to be the victims of a constant, never-ending process of consumption, decay, and eventual disintegration. It is in this personal vision of the world that Montale drastically differs from his contemporaries, whose sensibility is closer to the French Romantics and Symbolists, while his is more akin to that of the English poet, T. S. Eliot, whose poems Montale introduced to the Italian audience in 1929, in his own brilliant translations and whose "objective correlative" has found in the Genoese a successful practitioner. . . . Like Eliot, he made of the reality surrounding him, and in particular of the rugged Ligurian region, living poetic symbols of a vision devastatingly devoid of sentimentality and emotionalism.

Sergio Pacifici. A Guide to Contemporary Italian
Literature (World). 1962. pp. 181–2

See *Poems.*

MONTHERLANT, HENRY DE (1896–   )

Montherlant's Spain is a gorgeously colored canvas where blue skies, yellow buttercups, and shimmering fountains give brilliant relief to the sinister blacks and reds of the bulls and bleeding horses. He has painted haunting pictures of the World War—notably, the impenetrable nights and even more desolate dawns of No Man's Land. In his unusual way Montherlant was also a psychologist, and his admirable analysis of emotion, whether it be the athlete's anguish in the drama of the race, or the matador's cold fear before the ordeal in the ring, revealed him, if not an intellectual giant, at least as an artist whose virile originality deserves recognition.

Milton H. Stansbury. French Novelists of Today
(U. of Pennsylvania). 1935. p. 170

Montherlant has been, I understand, accused of indecency on a rather subtle plane. He gets nearer the nerve of the matter—in fact, "our women"—than people, even in France, like. . . . He is likely to displease women, to unnerve men. He has a ruthless touch on a good many illusions. But his drive, his clarity, his magnetic style are unlikely to be forgotten. Above all, he arouses intellectual amazement.

Elizabeth Bowen. *NSN*. Oct. 30, 1937. p. 688

For all his high spirits and predilection for the punning epigram, M. de Montherlant is a very serious writer whose novels are a subtle and penetrating analysis of the relation between men and women. [His] contentions are three: that marriage ruins the artist; that women are by nature base, being oriented on man as man is on the universe; and that men's pity for women, the demon of good, is in the end the greatest harm and cruelty to both parties. . . . If one inclines to discuss M. de Montherlant as a philosopher, it in no way implies any deficiency as a novelist. . . . M. de Montherlant is one of the best living novelists, and may, when his work is seen as a whole, be rated higher even than that.

John Mair. *NSN*. April 13, 1940. p. 500

Male and female, according to Montherlant's view, are forever at odds, with masculinity constantly threatened by the seductions and corruptions of femininity. His successful heroes are men who realize the satisfactions of carnal love to the limit, while eluding the tentacles of romantic love, which can only debilitate and destroy its victims. There was a time when the Church refused to admit that women had souls: Montherlant goes the misogynic Fathers one better by refusing to admit women into the category of human beings. Their only excuse for their inferior existence is that they are essential to what he likes to call The Act.

Ben Ray Redman. *SR*. Oct. 12, 1940. p. 15

An ironist, an egotist, a Byronic *poseur,* Montherlant aims to shock. And he succeeds in shocking with his ideas, his situations and his vocabulary. But the directness, the biting irony, the assurance in analysis and the rich style suffice to prove him a born writer, *un écrivain de race,* one can say without any hidden reference to his title of Count or to the antiquity of his Catalan-French family, who writes racily. A French critic once described him as a dandy with a grain of jovial brutality and another of systematic insolence.

Justin O'Brien. *NYT*. Oct. 20, 1940. p. 5

By refusing to give an objective meaning to the words which he handles so adeptly—greatness, sanctity, heroism—Montherlant turns them into hiccups. He was frightened to test his superiority among men and to get drunk on the wine of exaltation he retreated to the clouds: the unique is always superior. He shuts himself up in a roomful of mirrors: to infinity they will reflect his image and he thinks that he alone is enough to populate the earth; but he is only a recluse, his own prisoner. He thinks himself free but he makes over his liberty to the benefit of his ego. . . . Montherlant's liberty is an attitude, not a reality, and since without an aim action is impossible for him, he consoles himself with gestures: he is a mimer.

Simone de Beauvoir. *HorizonL*. Nov., 1949. pp. 304–5

It is unlikely that Montherlant's plays will ever be performed on Broadway. . . . They deride with haughty sarcasm not only the materialistic values of money and success, but also the religious delusions, the democratic consolations, the effeminacy of the modern world. The author is contemptuous of the decadence of his country and, indeed, of all our modern civilization. The theatre served him well because he could set his proud and lonely heroes in Renaissance Italy, in sixteenth century Portugal and Spain. And, while his personality is ever present in these dramas and occasionally obtrudes in the long speeches of his disillusioned and cruel moralists, Monsieur de Soi-Même de Montherlant, as he has been called, succeeds in keeping his inflated ego in the background.

Henri Peyre. *SR*. Sept. 29, 1951. p. 29

M. de Montherlant seems to me to be a man who, out of a romantic exaggeration of the importance of his own aristocratic origins, loathes and despises the rest of us to a fanatical degree. His strength as a writer is derived from the lengths to which he is prepared to go in insulting his women and blackening his men. Sympathy is the last thing that he wants to evoke for any of his characters. If we identify ourselves with them, it is not with our generosity or our affection or our pity, but with that part of us which wants to fly out at human nature and kick it in the teeth and stamp it into the ground.

T. C. Worsley. *NSN*. March 2, 1957. p. 275

By background and inclination a conformist, a believer in traditional virtues, he has, in a series of novels, essays and plays over a period of thirty-five years, constantly and vehemently assailed the twin standpoints of conformity and belief in traditional virtues. Instinctively religious he has rejected religion; instinctively a fighter he has asserted that there is no cause worth fighting for; instinctively associated with his class and its creed he has become both classless and creedless.

Derek Lindsay. Spec. June 21, 1957. p. 818

A celebrant of violence, action, and bull-fighting? I dare say, though "celebrant" would need qualifying, and he is not (though we might expect it from such cross-channel winds of reputation as have reached us) another bullying oaf with a monotonous charm over words, a bullock escaped from his own bull-ring with little red-edged eyes and a mystique of flowering rifles. . . . He has exulted . . . in the game of violence between equals, not (for instance, in Algeria) in the bellicosity of violence against the weak. He exalts sensuality, not the indulgent hoggishness of a Norman Douglas, but sensuality with tenderness, inseparable from intelligence and generosity. . . . No mysticism. The self is a haven, not a Class, a God, or a Sex God.

Geoffrey Grigson. Spec. Nov. 18, 1960. p. 788

Since the Second World War, Montherlant has emerged as a fine playwright. His novels seem less important. His attitude towards life is interesting now only as it contributes to his wonderful descriptive power. Montherlant's descriptions are drained of personal excess and present a scene as if it were the residue left when dozens of conflicting eyes and minds have moved away from it. There is one novel which, because it lies outside his usual belligerence, begins to look like lasting. This is *The Bachelors*. . . . It is one of those carefully framed, precise and acid studies on a small canvas in which French writers again and again excel. The small becomes vast. Cosiness vanishes from cosy corners. Eccentricity is seen to be tragic.

V. S. Pritchett. NSN. Nov. 19, 1960. p. 797

The trouble with Montherlant is his exasperating lucidity. He is an aristocrat who has seen through the prejudices and hollow pretensions of his caste; a Catholic who was soon convinced of the absurdity of Christian myths; a Frenchman who was aware of the decadence of the Third Republic and of its colonial abuses; a male who has torn down the romantic image of woman that other males have built up for their own satisfaction; a member of society who, in politics, can be neither with the exploiting right nor with the demagogical left; finally a human being who might well have made his the words of Ecclesiastes: "Vanity of vanities, all is vanity." One does not care to hear such words too often repeated.

Leon S. Roudiez. SR. Aug. 26, 1961. pp. 21, 28

See *The Bachelors* (novel) and *The Master of Santiago and Four Other Plays*.

MORANTE, ELSA (1916–   )

Elsa Morante is the wife of novelist Alberto Moravia. Her work, however, does not betray the slightest trace of conjugal affinity or influence. She is not interested in psychological realism, nor in the conflicts of urban life. She is a visionary teller, who writes, an Italian critic has observed, "as if contemporary literature did not exist"; and Robert Penn Warren has called what she is after "the real fictional magic."

Paolo Milano. *NYT*. Oct. 7, 1951

Elsa Morante . . . reveals in this first novel [*House of Liars*], a concern for that theme which has attracted and preoccupied almost every major novelist of our times, the problem of personal disintegration and paralysis of action. . . . At first glance the novel would appear to be a belated realistic novel of the late nineteenth century. But it does not require much reading to become aware that the psychology which motivates the characters is completely, darkly modern, and that in using a somewhat dated setting and technique, the author has achieved a horror effect, like that sometimes provoked by a surrealist painting in which a familiar everyday object is placed in an utterly incongruous position.

Serge Hughes. *SR*. Oct. 20, 1951. p. 19

Miss Morante is writing out of her epoch [in *House of Liars*]. She is giving us, in too extended form, a cross between a Gothic tale and a picaresque novel. . . . The writer is an observant, stick-to-itive young woman: nothing escapes her. And she recreates the Palermo of two hundred years ago . . . with painful exactitude. Her splendid vignettes of the particular insular culture she seeks to explore are full of smoky fire. . . . Miss Morante writes about what she knows, and she seeks fictional pegs simplified to suit her literary purpose. By projecting the Sicilian world against a screen she will at times silhouette and exaggerate certain details; at other times by putting a light behind a slide she will seem to diminish other views, making them appear as perfect and as unreal as detailed miniatures.

Frances Keene. *Nation*. Oct. 27, 1951. p. 357

[Elsa Morante is] a woman . . . whose work has masculine imaginative power. . . . [She] has continued slowly to deepen and explore her own particular vein . . . ; her rich style is one that many of her contemporaries might envy, and sensitivity tends to save her from mere intellectual exercise. She offers escape and fascination; she is not just a painter of the scene and time into which she was born.

Frances Frenaye. *BA*. Winter, 1958. pp. 27–8

Elsa Morante's *Arturo's Island* does well what many novels do badly, or rather what they often cannot—however much they may pretend—do at all. It is hard for any writer of our time to persuade us convincingly that men grow out of soil instead of cement, and of all falsities a spurious earthiness can be among the worst. . . . This novel is different. It really does strike roots in the thin and painful soul of reality. . . . The shifts of the plot, and with them the moods of the book, change like a darkening or clearing sky.

Norman Shrapnel. *MG*. May 15, 1959. p. 6

[*Arturo's Island*] is a poetic story, with all the charm the improbable has when it is told in the tone of probability. It is beautifully managed; the child's eye view is never lost for a minute, the impersonation never falters. Elsa Morante has that kind of stern, firm, factual imagination which such a book as this needs, if the reader is not to suspect that he is being slid into a fantasy or a dream. The theme of the book is remoteness; the remoteness of the island from the world of politics and war, the remoteness of the child from the parent, the remoteness of homosexual desire from marriage, from birth, from all the domestic symbols. It is extraordinarily clever of the writer to have set her lost world within touching distance of the real one; Naples is no more than a short boat trip away, but it might be a million light years. *Arturo's Island* . . . has the mesmeric, lingering quality which inhibits immediate assessment.

Pamela Hansford Johnson. *NSN*. May 23, 1959. p. 734

Although it would be a mistake to push the comparison too hard, the hero of . . . *Arturo's Island* bears a certain resemblance to Huck Finn . . . and in the early part of the novel there are passages as idyllic as anything in *Huckleberry Finn*. . . . *Arturo's Island* [however] . . . is a study of disillusionment in a sense that *Huckleberry Finn* . . . is not. Both boys are exposed to evil in varied and terrible forms, but Arturo is profoundly changed, whereas Huck isn't.

The novels also differ in the way evil is experienced. . . . The innocent Arturo . . . encounters evil . . . not in strangers but in himself and those close to him. . . . *Arturo's Island* is a psychological novel as *Huckleberry Finn* is not, and Miss Morante's great strength lies in her ability to render Arturo's emotional states. . . . It is on the poetry, on the ingeniously-wrought figures of speech that Miss Morante relies for her crucial effects. . . . *Huckleberry Finn,* as everyone remembers, peters out; at the end, as Ernest Hemingway said, Mark Twain cheated. *Arturo's Island* rises to an overwhelming climax. That is not to say that it is a better book than *Huckleberry Finn* but merely to call attention to the fact that it is in a tradition of more conscious craftsmanship.

> Granville Hicks. *SR*. Aug. 15, 1959. p. 16

Both [*House of Liars* and *Arturo's Island*] . . . have an impressionistic rather than a dramatic style, as well as a theme dealing with the fraying-away of human ties. But *Arturo's Island* is a much more successful creation. Perhaps Miss Morante's style was too efflorescent, too cluttered with tiny virtuosities, for the narrative pace of her earlier, more realistically framed tale. Now she has chosen a milieu that luxuriates in the oblique, the opalescent, the delicately enchanted—just the sort of thing she can do best. . . . Miss Morante possesses the Italian gift of distilling universality out of the primitive. But she has also a fine feminine instinct for the singing detail.

> Frederic Morton. *NYT*. Aug. 16, 1959. pp. 4–5

See *Arturo's Island* and *House of Liars* (novels).

MORAVIA, ALBERTO (1907–   )

Outside of sexual passion these people have no life whatever, and even their passion is little better than a decayed wisdom-tooth. In a similar confrontation, Mr. Aldous Huxley supports himself—however wearily—by the Anglo-Saxon heritage of humor and a borrowed shred of Gallic wit. Such props are denied Moravia. Instead he has a ferocious authenticity which Mr. Huxley lacks, and a style which for morbid delicacy and the bite and thrust of words can scarcely be matched among his contemporaries.

> Vincent Sheean. *NYHT*. Aug. 7, 1932. p. 3

To Moravia the one indisputable and reliable virtue is self-honesty. It has often been said that he is a moralist without faith in a moral order, but it would be more exact to say that he is a moralist whose theme is the danger of moral ambition. His fiction contains an unobtrusive but distinct didactic undertone, which tells us that we are never as bad as we think we are, and that we can never be as good as we think we can be—two notions which the Anglo-Saxon, imbued with moralism and meliorism, is apt to look upon as indulgent and defeatist. Moravia does not intimate that clear-eyed self-acceptance will unlock the gateway to

Paradise, but simply that it enables us to make the best of Purgatory. . . . In Moravia's Purgatory, the sun also rises and the sea brings refreshment. Its creator has a straightforward and engaging appreciation of the good material things of life—fine clothing, comfortable homes, a pastry, and a glass of vermouth. Although in Moravia the wages of fleshly love are usually unhappiness, the flesh itself remains a perennial wonder—a thing of strange, tormenting beauty.

Charles J. Rolo. At. Feb., 1955. p. 74

Can it be true that most of life's big issues (growing up, self-confidence, peace of mind, romantic love, worldly success) must pivot wildly upon the Freudian by-products of erotic encounters? Putting it directly, is sex really this intricate and is the author dealing with truth or the consequences of not telling it? Although Philip Rahv, in his brief introduction to the present volume [*Bitter Honeymoon*], compares the author to titillating tale tellers of the fourteenth century, some readers will decide that Signor Moravia's preoccupation with the human body compares more closely with that of the late Bernarr Macfadden than to Boccaccio.

James Kelly. SR. Aug. 11, 1956. p. 17

On the technical side, Moravia's skill is admirable. His phrases and images are stimulating by their aptness, and his sentences have some of the rhythmical movement and ease of the old masters. His descriptions of nature, which are frequent, coalesce with and heighten the action. Moravia's depiction of moods and of momentary states of mind is perhaps his strongest quality. He is skilled in making much out of the seemingly trivial. The movement of his stories is vigorous without being at all nervous. Moravia writes like a man sure of himself and this confidence carries over easily to the reader. The only question is whether his themes are worth the effort.

C. S. Kilby. NYHT. Aug. 26, 1956. p. 2

The . . . stories . . . are about love, or rather about situations between men and women which require some pretense of or attempt at love. A dour irony underlies all of them. Nothing is quite what Moravia's bemused heroes suppose it to be; or if they see a situation clearly, their vision comes after the opportunity to profit by it has passed. Love is represented as a melancholy joke on humanity, offering the irresistible bait of companionship which turns out, when it is swallowed, to be merely another form of isolation. For all the wealth of solid setting and intimate action in these stories, the protagonists are enclosed in little worlds of their own, like ice cubes, and Mr. Moravia uses them to illustrate various aspects of the modern preoccupation with the remoteness of individual being.

Phoebe Adams. *At*. Sept., 1956. p. 85

The typical Moravia manner . . . may be described as the employment of vigorous, dispassionate prose for the report of some brutal deed or the delineation of some unsavory character, not without an underlying stony irony. . . . In all the tales the action takes place in Rome or its immediate environs and all the characters are drawn from Roman life. In recent years, Moravia has succumbed to the growing cult of Rome (not limited to Italians, either) and has taken to pinpointing his plots, fixing them on the Via dell'Anima or in the Trastevere or near the Acqua Acetosa, as the case may be. This gives the reader who knows Rome a kind of topographical *frisson* but in truth the characters themselves do not seem particularly Roman either in motivation or reaction. Greed, egocentricity, sensual material are not necessarily limited to the inhabitants of the Eternal City.

Thomas G. Bergin. *SR*. Sept. 21, 1957. p. 18

To say merely that Moravia's fiction is erotic is a truism that can stifle rather than enlarge our sense of his achievement: like saying, with a final simplicity, that Dante's poetry is religious. For Moravia's fiction provides a major treatment of a minor but honorable and suggestive view of things: the sexual view, the view of human relations and of everything that arises in or impinges upon human relations as beginning and ending in the sexual encounter. Everything other than sex is, in the satires of Moravia, an extension of sex; or perhaps better, everything other than sex is sooner or later converted into it. Moravia, in fact, is a minor master of the strategy of conversion in literature: that is, of *artistic* conversion, of the transformation of one set of values into another. The typical Moravian narrative shows us, not the precise and detailed movement of the sexual encounter . . . but the full amount of life that culminates in the sexual encounter or in observable deflections from it.

R. W. B. Lewis. *The Picaresque Saint* (Lippincott). 1959. p. 37

Those who understood Moravia could not doubt that he saw dictatorship as the crowning example of everything hateful and false in Italy. Moravia could not write a line which did not exude his admirable hatred of the world as it was. However, the moralizing and the general thinking of the anti-Fascist movement did not impress him. He thought the opposition amounted to little more than honest sighs, and he reached the sorrowful conclusion that from now on the world belonged to the violent. Why should he have hidden his conviction? Why should he have made believe he was Cato, when he was drawn to the world of Petronius and Apuleius?

Nicola Chiaromonte. *PR*. Fall, 1959. p. 644

Indeed, despite the fact that he is the Italian novelist with the greatest world-wide reputation, Alberto Moravia is not an Italian writer at all; he is a French writer writing in Italian. The existentialist void in which his characters move, the deadly self-conscious solemnity with which they brush their teeth or go to bed with each other, the clinical precision with which a sense of incommunicability is communicated (like the philosopher Bergson analytically demonstrating the limitations of analysis), the device of the first-person *récit*—all these qualities belong rather in the camp of Sartre, Camus, Jouhandeau, and Gide than with Brancati, Pratolini, Calvino, or Pirandello. Italians as a people smile easily. But Moravian characters never smile.

Sidney Alexander. *Reporter*. Nov. 23, 1961. p. 55

Moravia's world, like Svevo's, is sick. But unlike Svevo, Moravia does not treat it ironically. His art is hard and metallic. He does not take refuge in pretense or escape, because he does not believe in them, or in pity either. He sees no refuge for man except in vice, and for this reason his picture of society is a deformed one. He is not negative, but he is completely pessimistic. Having his cultural roots in post-Romantic decadence, he is attracted by the violently erotic contortions of the Marquis de Sade, rather than by the healthy lustiness of the characters, such as Moll Flanders, created by Daniel Defoe.

Goise Rimanelli. *Perspectives: Recent Literature of Russia, China, Italy, and Spain* (U.S. Library of Congress). 1961. pp. 36–7

He began his career in 1929 with a novel that dramatized "indifference" that soon became synonymous with absurdity. Through the following years, he proceeded by way of several stages aptly dubbed "mistaken ambitions," "disobedience," "conformism," "contempt," to give us a disconcerting tableau of the decay of the bourgeoisie. Recently, he has reached the extreme, but valid accusation that the cancerous disease corroding the fiber of a complacent, affluent, over-mechanized society is *"la noia"—tedium vitae*. . . . The predicament in which Moravia's heroes invariably find themselves is rooted in their incapacity to find something that may replace a long lost love of life, and an involvement with the human tragedy (or comedy), without which no reality can have any meaning.

Sergio Pacifici. *BA*. Summer, 1962. pp. 259–60

As all of Moravia's readers know, his moral passions do not include the sexual *mystique*. I do not know many contemporary novelists who give that mystique a rougher ride, and I don't know quite how a rougher ride could be arranged. Henry Miller is tougher but not rougher; and perhaps some of the toughness is still entangled with the magic—both incantational and avertive—of the taboo sexual language. In Moravia's fiction the magic is altogether dispelled; but in *The Empty Canvas* the sexual performance is not by any means written off as mere copulation: it is expressed rather as the futile efforts of dead souls to reach some kind, any kind, of external reality; and must therefore be understood as being metaphysically much nearer Augustine than Freud. I do not mean that his latest novel shows the author to be on the Road to Rome or any other religious capital. I mean only that in this novel it is the essential human being who struggles with evil, with nothingness, with death. The spirit is not the disease of the flesh nor the flesh the medium of spirit's corruption.

J. N. Hartt. *YR*. Winter, 1962. p. 302

See *Bitter Honeymoon* and *Roman Tales* (short stories) and *The Empty Canvas* (novel).

ORTEGA Y GASSET, JOSÉ (1883–1955)

What Professor Ortega denounces most violently . . . is precisely the idea upon which the whole science and art of republicanism has always been based, to wit, the idea that there is some mystical virtue, and what is more, some mystical wisdom, in men and in the mass—that what everyone believes is somehow likely to be true. . . . The liberation of the masses, he believes, has done Europe a lot of harm. . . . Mere quantity is substituted for quality, and all the high aspirations and emprises of superior men sink into desuetude.

Señor Ortega's thesis is here clear enough, but it cannot be said that he maintains it with an unfailing consistency. It is hard to follow an argument which begins with an eloquent plea for aristocracy, and ends with the conclusion that "liberal democracy based on technical knowledge is the highest type of public life hitherto known." Nor is it easy to agree, on the one hand, that the stupidities of the mob engulf and smother *homo sapiens,* and on the other hand that his "vital tone" which "consists in his feeling himself possessed of greater potentiality than ever before," is now at its historic maximum.

H. L. Mencken. Nation. Sept. 2, 1932. p. 260

Señor Ortega . . . argues that what we call "scientific method" cannot be applied successfully to the study of man; that the "idealistic" philosophical reaction to "materialistic" science is equally ineffective in the study of man, since the concept of "spirit" is a disguised naturalism, static and purely intellectualised; and finally that man is only what has happened to him, that history is the only possible ontology. . . . He would seem to share with Whitehead, Bergson, and many other moderns a distrust of the intellectualist traditions of Western philosophy. . . . He also distrusts natural science, but only when it goes beyond what he thinks its necessary limits, that is, study of "nature." For what science has done and can do he has the highest respect, and he never voices romantic dislike for science and scientists. He will have no maunderings over *Geist.* . . . But science (*la razón física*), a revelation to Galileo, is no longer such.

Crane Brinton. SR. April 15, 1941. p. 5

For those who see in history brute forces and sinister interests which no amount of enlightenment will of itself remove, Ortega y Gasset . . .

is an impossible political and social philosopher. . . . The basic idea in Ortega's equipment is this: "The convulsive situation in Europe at the present moment is due to the fact that the average Englishman, the average Frenchman, the average German are *uncultured.*" As if it were lack of culture and not its cause that we should attack! As if lack of culture actually were cause and not symptom!

Ortega's entirely justified dissatisfaction with the ordinary man grows into something entirely unjustified when he comes, as nearly all such thinkers do, to stake everything upon the extraordinary man and when, looking for him today in vain, he assumes his existence in some past era, which is thereby sentimentalized. . . . A return to which period in history? Ortega hedges. . . . A man whose philosophy has so shaky a foundation as this is surely not to be taken very seriously.

Eric Bentley. *SR*. Dec. 23, 1944. p. 8

A generation whose rallying cry is engagement rather than detachment will not apply to him for its philosophy of history. Yet the intellectuality that chills, whenever he condescends to discuss the masses, illuminates his vivid interpretations of the cerebral life. His German training blends with his Latin temperament to produce a zest for ideas which is never dogmatic, a flair for epigrams which is never verbalistic. And since Anglo-American criticism tends toward evaluation rather than formulation, we stand in particular need of the clear-cut distinctions that continental writers and thinkers have sharpened.

Harry Levin. *NYT*. June 6, 1948. p. 4

Ortega's esthetic ideas are a particular application of a broadly-encompassing concept of the nature of culture which, in turn, involves a general theory of reality. . . . His ideas constitute a search for a new monistic solution to the schismatic thinking of our times, an attempt to correlate all aspects of human knowledge and to bridge the gap between man and the universe. Applied to the question of art, this theory may be summed up in the form of a syllogism: reality is existence, culture the perception of existence; the perception of existence is a distortion of reality, with which it is not to be confused; of all the forms of culture the most imaginative, that is, unreal, is art: art is unreality. . . . All the aspects in which art may be examined in Ortega's system—perspectivism, ratiovitalism, historic reason—are complementary, and all serve to confirm for Ortega the basic tenet of his esthetics: the unreality of art.

Leon Livingstone. *PMLA*. Sept., 1952. pp. 609–10, 654

Less obsessed with the Spanish past than his elders, he resolutely plunged into the currents of European ideas. . . . He championed the "European" solution versus Unamuno's Spanish gospel. The remedy he proposed for the ills of Spain was to make her an integral part of liberal, humanist Europe "at the height of the times." He did his successful best to open doors of communication through his work as educator, writer and editor. Yet his liberalism was based on an élite theory and therefore predestined to clash with the popular democratic movements. He saw mankind divided into those with truly cultured standards, qualified to be an "eminent minority," and "mass men." These categories did not coincide with social classes; among the mass men unfit to lead Ortega included the rulers and servers of the monarchy. It made him a Republican *sui generis,* and an ouspoken adversary of the dictatorship, even though his ideal Republic (in whose service he formed a "league" of intellectuals) had little in common with the social democracy for which the mass of Spaniards were pressing.

Arturo Barea. *BA.* Spring, 1953. pp. 123–4

Ortega impresses and infuriates. He was determined to turn philosophy and history into belles lettres. Half of him was prophet and rather smug on that account. He sought in prose for a Paterian radiance, and appeared to think metaphor and repetition essential to the expression of sincere thought. Most of his works—*The Revolt of the Masses* excluded —support a tribal dance of ideas, some of them huge and seminal. But his vatic repetition too often becomes erratic variation, and we have to read him with a potato-peeler. He puts nothing plainly until he's baffled us with adumbration. He is a self-celebrated writer and at his best only when he isn't trying too hard. This forefather of Malraux has much in common with Arnold Toynbee and the Algerian in Camus. Their ways of self-conception are his, and so are most of their ideas.

Paul West. *TC.* Oct., 1959. p. 241

Ortega proposed what he conceived to be a new direction in philosophy. The self and the world, he argues, cannot be placed in independent categories; neither is definable or intelligible without the other. . . . Philosophy itself is to be understood as the activity of the self at its most intense. . . . It is pure contemplation, thinking cut loose from all practical interests and partial concerns; and so it is a form of disinterestedness so complete that it is the most complete form of immersion in the world. . . . There are affinities between many of Ortega's ideas and ideas that have emerged independently in philosophical climates as different as existentialism, pragmatism and Oxford analysis. Ortega, however, does not so much argue his ideas as allude to them, and frequently one can only guess at what he means. . . . His strength lay in his *aperçus*, in his vitality as a moralist, in his passionate and unrepentant individualism.

Charles Frankel. *NYT*. July 30, 1961. p. 6

See *The Modern Theme, Revolt of the Masses*, and *Man and Crisis* (essays).

OTERO, BLAS DE (1916–   )

With [Blas de Otero] social interests are bound up with religious, and the prevailing influence is . . . that of the tough and questioning Miguel de Unamuno. Like Unamuno, Otero finds it impossible to fit his thoughts exactly to his lines. His aim is to speak to the "great majority," but . . . he is at the same time conscious of man's isolation in his relationship with God. Like Unamuno, he wrestles with his Maker for a faith that never comes easily to him, and when he thinks of his audience it is of a multitude of individuals engaged in the same secret struggle. . . . While many of Otero's poems call broadly for peace and the freedom to speak, for a reconciliation between man and man, and between man and God, others are preoccupied with . . . the question of Spain itself and of the country's isolation. . . . Otero uses the compound term *españahogándose* (drowning oneself in Spain) to describe this state of preoccupation, in mingled love and horror, with a land which has been nourished with so much of the blood of its own sons.

J. M. Cohen. *Enc.* Feb., 1959. pp. 48–9

Blas de Otero is outwardly a quiet, slow man, from the North of Spain. His poems are filled with passion and sensuality that one would hardly expect from this intense man with a distracted air. . . . In his earlier work words exploded with savage passion in love poems to a withdrawn God and in poems about death. . . . The poet is possessed by an Unamunesque preoccupation with himself, with God—if such a being exists—and eternal peace. . . . The violence that follows out of wasted love for God in his earlier poetry gives way to a more mature calmness in his later work. Driven out of himself to a more human kind of poetry by a hard historical circumstance, from the sadness and desperation of private concern to a deep interest in his fellowmen, the poet's anger becomes less concentrated and more compassion comes into his words. There is also hope. . . . Otero listens to the unusual logic of his imagination and there is a thread of irrationality in many of his poems that attracts us like the dark fierce moments in Blake or Rimbaud.

. . . His poetry has a sort of baroque interior . . . in contrast to the baroque exterior of Lorca and some of his generation.

> Hardie St. Martin. Introduction to *Twenty Poems* by
> Blas de Otero (The Sixties Press). 1964. pp. 7–10

Otero speaks as one who has seen the shaking of the foundations and has discovered that the traditional patterns of belief have lost their sustaining power. His is a generation uprooted with no greater destiny than that of shoring up the ruins. . . . Otero is able to rise above the ruins to a firm and unyielding conviction that, in spite of everything, man and his life are in themselves sufficient centers of worth and dignity. Out of the depths of his awful knowledge of the human condition, Blas de Otero stands to assert an heroic and modern humanism in which man not only survives, but prevails. . . . Otero demands that poetry participate in the world's immediacy and that it be a positive force for the salvation of these difficult moments of human time. Poetry is thus no longer a luxury or a simple object of beauty, but an instrument— hammer and scythe as he says in one of his poems—in man's contemporary fight for justice.

> Calvin Cannon. *Modern Spanish Poems* (Macmillan).
> 1965. pp. 84–5

The international style in poetry flourishes most attractively in the literature of the European marches. In countries where modernism is unable, for various reasons, to exploit a native mode—in Russia, in Spain, in Greece—poets like Mayakovsky, Otero, and Seferis have produced, without of course abandoning their specifically national character . . . a poetry of a particular kind: a *European* poetry whose identifying quality is a deliberate incoherence necessarily conjugated with political disorder. It is remarkable, indeed, that so many of Otero's poems have been permitted to appear in Spain today. . . . As chronicles of political injustice and the endurance of abused soil, as litanies of martial *anomie,* protests against the outrages of tyranny and the excesses of the Church Militant, Otero's public voice has gained its peculiar authority from his private declension of surrealism, that eminently international program for dealing, as no other has dared, with the heart's reasons and those of State together.

> Richard Howard. *Poetry*. Feb., 1966. pp. 339–40

See *Twenty Poems.*

PALACIO VALDÉS, ARMANDO (1853–1938)

Señor Valdés is a realist, but a realist according to his own conception of realism; and he has some words of just censure for the French naturalists. . . . He sees the wide difference that passes between this naturalism and the realism of the English and Spanish. . . . Beauty, Señor Valdés explains, exists in the human spirit, and is the beautiful effect which it receives from the true meaning of things; it does not matter what the things are, and it is the function of the artist who feels this effect to impart it to others. . . . The reflection of exterior nature in the individual spirit, Señor Valdés believes to be the fundamental of art.

W. D. Howells. *Criticism and Fiction*
(Osgood, McIlvaine). 1891. pp. 59–62

Realist as he is, he nevertheless holds that to live cradled in a gentle ideality is the best for the artist . . . [that] the first obligation of the artist is, not exactness, but to make felt the beautiful. . . . He proposes to banish from his productions every false and unreal element; his endeavor being to produce an effect, not violent, but deep. . . . [He] seeks the simplest form for his work, with the purpose of giving verisimilitude to the picture; avoiding the idea that what is presented is a phantasmagory; striving to make it appear, on the contrary, that it is an integral part of the truth, something that has been experienced. . . . To be guided by nature, not to do violence to her, is his principle.

Sylvester Baxter. *At.* April, 1900. pp. 555–6

Valdés's art at its best recalls the qualities that M. Henri Lechat attributes to Attic art—measure, simplicity, distinction without effort, precision without hardness. . . . A certain slightness [is] felt in some of Valdés's works. This may be what is meant by the assertion sometimes made that he is inferior to Galdós as a psychologist; or perhaps we should invoke another useful word, and say he lacks intensity. Yet I hesitate to say this. Measure, in the twentieth century, must pay the penalty of being misunderstood. Measure means calm and serenity, virtues not wholly appreciated in an age when virtue means to shout and to run and to come to grips with much purpling of face and starting of eyes. . . . The depths of Valdés are calm depths, but they are depths. . . . For keenness of observation, for the artist's instinct in selection, for truth to nature and freedom from the improbable, for measure in every one of its literary manifestations, it is not too much to say that no novelist in Spain or anywhere else has written a half dozen novels that surpass the half dozen best from his pen.

Grant Showerman. *SwR*. Oct., 1914. pp. 402–4

He has been severely criticised for following the Naturalistic school, but . . . . he is really natural rather than Naturalist. . . . The great difference between Señor Palacio Valdés and the Naturalists is that they as a rule go out of their way to describe impersonally a slice of what they call life, arbitrarily cut off from its surroundings, whereas he found his inspiration in the ordinary life around him, the life which he had himself lived and felt. He is thus more human and natural and presents a truer picture of reality than the one-sided determinist school. He is more of a poet than a scientist, a fact to which his work owes its broader, more personal interest. . . . All his books, varying as they do in interest and merit, bear the stamp of his genius. Its essential traits are insight into feminine character, a sense of humour, a certain savour of the soil, tolerant sympathy and extreme naturalness and ease, both of form and substance.

Aubrey F. G. Bell. *Contemporary Spanish Literature*
(Knopf). 1925. pp. 70–2

Except in the art of the Goncourts, the Naturalistic method has never been applied to the novel with so much purity and logic, and at the same time, with such an uncompromising submission to the principles of literary art, as in the fictions of Armando Palacio Valdés. . . . By rationalizing Naturalism, by lending it kindliness and infusing it with the authentic spirit of art, what Palacio Valdés really has done is create a type of the psychological novel. . . . He cannot, by any exuberance of appreciation, be accounted great. He loves the earth too well to soar high above it; but his art is the better for the soil which bears it down.

William A. Drake. *Contemporary European Writers*
(John Day). 1928. pp. 212–3

He is a light, gay, spontaneous writer with no settled attitude to life, but plenty of talent. His characteristic vein is comedy of manners, set in a small circle of rich, upper middle-class people who have no serious problems to contend with. He specialized in light drawing-room conversations and courtships, related in a half-frivolous tone. For this reason, perhaps, even his early novels make such a modern impression that one has difficulty in believing that they did not come out in the 1920's.

However, most of his books are too casually written and too unorientated to be classed as literature: all one can say is that they make pleasant books for a railway journey, easy to read, with some clever scenes and descriptions.

Gerald Brenan. *The Literature of the Spanish People*
(Cambridge). 1953. p. 410

During [his] earlier period, when realism was the norm of the novel . . . his approach and his procedures were realistic; . . . none of the authors of his day was more faithful to reality. . . . Nevertheless, Palacio Valdés viewed and interpreted reality in a manner which differed radically from the methods of realism. . . . His own personal traits, his nobility of soul, his tenderness, his humor, color the reality he depicts and give his novels their enduring charm.

With the triumph of "modernism," . . . he had only to intensify the personal element, which had always been present in his work, and his ideological and religious preoccupations, in order to meet the new canons of literature. . . . The great critic Azorín has said of him: "In his literary art he achieved the supreme art: unpretentiousness, simplicity of expression, the evocation of a delicate, ineffable, ideal reality which is above the violent and vulgar reality which is apparent to all eyes."

Harriet de Onís. Introduction to *José* by Palacio Valdés
(Barron). 1961. pp. vii–xi
See *The Joy of Captain Ribot, The Marquis of Peñalta,* and *Sister Saint Sulpice* (novels).

PALAZZESCHI, ALDO (1885–   )

The impish Aldo Palazzeschi, who had it gravely appear that his cat had published his first book of verse, began as a futurist, that most solemn of literary rebels, and here [in *Perelà: The Man of Smoke*] appears as a biting and intelligible satirist, in what amounts to an Italian version of Gulliver standing on its head. Palazzeschi has been characterized by the French critic Benjamin Crémieux as *"L'enfant moderne, très malicieux goguenard,"* and it is the jeerer, the rakish clown who cannot resist a dig at literary stuffed shirts in his most placid scenes, who is prominent here. As a writer of fantasy Palazzeschi recalls the nineteenth century idealists who worked on a purely human scale, rather than the metaphysical Pirandello; Palazzeschi's ribbing is reserved for man as a social animal, not for the mechanism of his thought or the structure of his manners, though some of the more delicious passages in this volume are devoted to the fact that the subconscious doth make fools of us all.

Alfred Kazin. *NYT*. May 31, 1936. p. 8

To describe Palazzeschi's writing as mellow, however, is not to suggest delicately any dullness of perception. His psychologizing is as labyrinthian as that of any good modern writer. There is simply a welcome absence of the tortured, anguished motivation, a knowing, unaccented spoofing of a whole genre of the novel, the novel of motivations, which has taken itself so solemnly. . . . One had almost forgotten that the Italians are not too good at striking the modern, all too easy tragic pose. In the best of Italian writing there is an abundance of ironic compassion and gentle detachment which has been lost sight of in recent years.

Serge Hughes. *SR*. July 18, 1953. pp. 14–15

Palazzeschi is for many reasons a special author: first a poet and wit, always a student (without pedantry) of the mores of his Tuscan world, he turned to straight fiction only after he had achieved distinction in other forms. Florentine by birth, he is so too, one might say, by profession, for his humorous, at times mordant, touch stems from attitudes accepted as characteristic of that city. It is in the search for the very flavor of its household smells, the beat of its pulse, that Palazzeschi excels. . . . It should be said that a younger author like Pratolini can scarcely be understood as a literary phenomenon without recognizing that Palazzeschi came first.

Frances Keene. *NYT*. July 12, 1953. p. 4

Materassi Sisters is a very curious novel. . . . The theme is a serious, even a painful one and begs to be treated as such. The longing of starved old age for youth and gaiety and love, the blithe indifference to it of the young, require the utmost gentleness of handling. Signor Palazzeschi's style is portentous enough, almost indeed Germanic in its reiteration and constant rammings-home, but his point of view is wholly frivolous and Latin. The snigger of the complacent Italian male sounds all the way through the book.

Honor Tracy. *NSN*. July 25, 1953. p. 111

Two discernible paths wander off from the realistic mainstream of the postwar Italian novel. Silone's virile proletarianism affected the young writers of the forties, to the extent that a romantic discontent pervaded their work, but minus the active impetus toward revolution. . . . A second offshoot recognized the limiting effects of subject-matter chosen strictly on class lines and developed the Italian version of the Proustian novel—introspective, in love with the physical accoutrements of the past, and enjoying a leisurely dalliance with all the possibilities of spiritual decay through the agency of great bodily beauty. Palazzeschi must be a major representative of this group. . . . His primary concern is with character, both dominant and recessive. Like Proust he submits good to evil and microscopically examines the results. And like Proust again, the struggle between the two is unevenly weighted because eccentricities of character and personality outbalance the strength of moral decision.

Doris Grumbach. *Com.* July 31, 1953. p. 425

The Sisters Materassi, by Aldo Palazzeschi . . . was written nearly twenty years ago—which means that it is a European novel and not, like so many later Italian books, an imitation of an American novel by a European. . . . *The Sisters Materassi* is a brilliant examination of . . . the symbiosis of emotional relationships. . . . The double-entry of emotional bookkeeping makes the balance sheet almost inscrutable.

The moral insight in Mr. Palazzeschi's book does not result from the fact that he writes of a society rich in moral insight. His stodgy, unintrospective, provincial characters are moral enough . . . ; but they would never understand the compassionate, sophisticated, humorous breadth of view he brings to bear upon their situation. *The Sisters Materassi* derives its stature from its author.

Paul Pickrel. *YR.* Autumn, 1953. pp. xiv, xvi

The Sisters Materassi . . . lingers throughout on the details of the dailiest kind of life and out of them creates an entire little world, all wonderfully alive, for Signor Palazzeschi knows exactly what he is about and is sure of his power. . . . Signor Palazzeschi, though he never loses sight of the spiritual and moral idiocy which animates the self-sacrifice of his victims, sees their folly as conferring on them a perverse minor triumph. . . . As a study of the material destruction of those ripe for destruction the novel is first rate.

Technically it is remarkable for the way in which, on occasion, the careful realism is deliberately violated by the introduction of passages of grotesquerie which point up in comic horror the monstrousness of the victor and his victims. The wedding scene . . . is a brilliant example of pure Expressionist fiction. What one had thought of—*Caligari* and a few other films excepted—as a method which had come to very little, can be astonishingly powerful in the hands of an accomplished writer.

Ernest Jones. *PR.* Nov.-Dec., 1953. pp. 712, 714

Palazzeschi, as a complete artist and mature prose stylist, creates his world with absolute sincerity, . . . that is to say, he becomes the intimate chronicler of our times—for the purpose of establishing some parallels, Balzac, or better still, Flaubert, were in this sense chroniclers. Palazzeschi reveals to us the most hidden aspirations of men, the most intimate and secret facets of the human heart. He sheds light on feelings that men barely communicate to each other even while their actions suggest and favor the desire for such comunication.

Vasco Pratolini. *MLN*. Jan., 1964. p. 34

See *The Sisters Materassi, Perelà: The Man of Smoke,* and *Roma* (novels).

PARDO BAZÁN, EMILIA (1852–1921)

[Her earliest work reflects] the formative influences that developed the author: an innate tendency to direct and faithful artistic interpretation, a substantial foundation of the best literary traditions of Spain, and an ephemeral ingredient of romanticism, destined to speedy dissipation in the powerful solvent of the author's true nature. The remarkable erudition of Señora Pardo Bazán, her well grounded knowledge of science and philosophy, was manifest . . . in her first novel. . . . She comprehended more and more the tendency of the modern novel, its leading place in contemporary letters, its obligation to reflect nature and society in their vitality, without juggling the truth to give place to literary fictions more or less beautiful. She concluded that every country must cultivate its own literary traditions, particularly when they were so illustrious as those of Spain, but must do this without prejudice against the acceptance of modern methods. . . . With these ideas fresh in mind, [she provided] one of the first echoes in Spain of French Naturalism, with which she contrasted, and gave preference to, a national realism.

Sylvester Baxter. *Csmp*. June, 1893. p. 232

Although credited by some writers with having founded the realist school in Spain, the authoress herself always denied it, affirming that Pereda had been before her. However that may be, there is no doubt that her novels, and still more her polemical writings, in which she showed herself a fearless champion of the New School, had a great and permanent influence on the literature of her country. It is the position taken up by this intrepid woman writer at a critical stage of literature, as well as her gallant struggle against sex disabilities, more marked in Spain than in other lands, that make her story so interesting. Regardless of criticism, she deliberately threw herself across the strong current of contemporary national production, taking what she required from French sources—from Daudet rather than from Zola—and grafting it on to the sturdy tree of the old Spanish tradition, started that series of novels that have since made her famous.

Beatrice Erskine. *CR*. Aug., 1921. p. 241

Doña Emilia discreetly calls those books that aspire to reform while they divert hybrids, and she considers it less evil not to pay attention to morals than to falsify morals, and she regards as deadly and pernicious almost all novels that sustain theses or theories, granted that they are taken seriously. . . . After affirming such things . . . , for this lady to persist in telling us that she is a naturalist is as if, after expounding the Christian doctrine in as Catholic a fashion as Father Ripalda, she should say to us that she is a Quaker or an Anabaptist. . . . When Zola learned that there was in Spain a militant Catholic woman who defended his system he hardy believed it; he was astonished. . . . It is evident that Spanish naturalism is of another sort and not Zola's. . . . Doña Emilia strives to reform naturalism in order that she and other Spanish authors may be comfortably embraced in the movement.

Juan Valera. *UTB*. July 1, 1926. p. 14

For her contemporaries, Pardo Bazán was a writer of surprisingly virile temperament. She was considered very much as the next generation regarded Unamuno, as an aggressive polemicist brought up in the stale odor of tradition yet inwardly craving for life-giving breezes from distant horizons. . . . This polemical activity, incompatible with traditional domesticity of Spanish womanhood, seemed most unusual to critics; they adopted the practice of referring to the "masculinity" of Pardo Bazán. . . . What Pardo Bazán lacked in originality was offset by her understanding and breadth of vision. No side of human activity failed to awaken vibrations in her mind, and in every sphere of knowledge she displayed an understanding superior to that of, say, Unamuno. . . . These qualities make her much more typical of her period than Unamuno. . . . [She is] the most enlightened, if not the most illustrious representative of her age.

Ronald Hilton. *BA*. Autumn, 1952. pp. 345, 347

Doña Emilia was essentially a truth-worshipper. This is what undoubtedly first attracted her to Zola's naturalism. It was a school that made of the novel a study, something more than a mere piece of entertainment. And she has a gift for seeing the truth. . . . A firm equilibrium and a clear penetration are her two outstanding qualities. . . . She could appreciate Zola's epic genius and lyricism, although in attempting to imitate them she was unsuccessful. Her pictures always came out as clear and real as her own matter-of-fact way of seeing the world around her. And this is the inevitable realism of her temperament that gives unity to her work.

The influence of Zola upon Pardo Bazán was great, long-continued, and entirely beneficial. Under it she wrote her best novels. Ostensibly regional many of them, yet they have a cosmopolitan, modern spirit which will make them last and which makes them intensely readable.

> Donald Fowler Brown. *The Catholic Naturalism of Pardo Bazán* (N. Carolina). 1957. pp. 154–5

Pardo Bazán was similar to Zola in her sensitivity to the momentary effects of light on objects and to the varying nuances of color. . . . In the novels which best represent her modified Naturalism . . . Pardo Bazán has recourse to Impressionist techniques in her descriptions of landscapes and characters, and examples of these techniques occur often enough to affirm that they were the result of a conscious effort to effect Impressionist verbal imagery. . . . Like the Impressionist artist who seeks to capture the everchanging colors of the landscape, Pardo Bazán, through vigorous expressions of shades and colors, endeavors to convey the kaleidoscopical nature of the landscape. . . . [After a period of] near disregard for Impressionist techniques . . . she [then] reverts to those methods impelled by a new interest, awakened by the influence of Modernism, in the procedures of the painters of the Impressionist school.

> Mary E. Giles. *HspR.* Oct., 1962. pp. 306–15

See *Swan of Vilamoreta, Midsummer and Madness,* and *Mystery of the Lost Dauphin* (novels); also *Russia: Its People and Its Literature* (criticism).

PASINETTI, PIER MARIA (1913–   )

[The] two family groups [in *Venetian Red*] can also be seen as symbols of the two dimensions of the novel; the moralistic taste for contemplation and intellectual definition of the human condition; and the sense of movement and action, the transformation of morality into events. It is precisely these two aspects which make Pasinetti's novel so rich and interesting—so easy to read, because of its figurative visualization, and at the same time so subtle. The psychological penetration serves to give vitality to the many characters in the novel, to separate their personalities from the plot, from the richness of events and the amplitude of the landscape, and at the same time to transform the book from a novel of character to one of atmosphere.

Dante Della Terza. *IQ*. Winter, 1960. p. 82

It is not often that a writer appears of sufficient linguistic adaptability to write in two languages. When one does it is likely to be an Italian: one thinks of Casanova, Goldoni and more recently D'Annunzio, equally at home in French and Italian. Since English is not a Latin sister to Italian, P. M. Pasinetti's performance is still more remarkable; he offers us [in *Venetian Red*] his own English version of his novel published in Italian. . . . It is a novel concerned primarily with subtle relations between people: it has a touch of political commentary, more than a touch of allegory, but more than anything else it is an analysis of inter-personal relations between individuals who are sensitive, intuitive and articulate. . . . *Venetian Red* is a novel of real but unobtrusive sophisti-cation. Pasinetti . . . has written a significant and beautiful book.

Thomas G. Bergin. *NYHT*. May 8, 1960. p. 4

Among many other things, P. M. Pasinetti's first novel very admirably undercuts a certain depressing theory about the relation between fiction and the modern mind. The theory is this: that because of contemporary habits of perception, it is no longer possible to write effectively a "traditional" novel, with ample plot, numbers of highly diversified and recognizable characters, in a solidly realistic setting and at a distinct moment in history. *Venetian Red,* however, presents a highly traditional chronicle of two interlocking Italian families during the critical years 1938-1941, and moves with ease among the fortunes and passions and idiosyncracies of about two dozen quite memorable characters; and at the same time it reflects the peculiar emphases and the ways of seeing experience of the contemporary mind. Less lyrically than the not too unlike work of Lawrence Durrell, but not less substantially, *Venetian Red* suggests how the novel can still offer a meaningful and thoroughly engrossing form for life, even in our present moment of dislocated sensibility.

R. W. B. Lewis. *SR*. May 28, 1960. p. 30

Presumably the relations between the two families [in *Venetian Red*], though perfectly "realistic" in presentation, may be read as an account of the conflict in the human spirit between creativity and destruction, between the impulse to realize a more abundant life of the senses and emotions and mind on the one hand, and the will to power on the other. . . . But all this is to allegorize too rigorously a book whose virtue

lies less in its grand plan than in its incidental observation and detail. . . .
Venetian Red is an old-fashioned Continental novel, something like
Thomas Mann's *Buddenbrooks* in its emphasis on family relationships
and traditions, on the place of the artist in society, on houses and furniture and old aunts. . . . The book . . . is unmistakably the product of a
distinguished mind, broad sympathy, and uncommon perception.

Paul Pickrel. *Harper*. June, 1960. pp. 98–9

P. M. Pasinetti . . . has spent his life in college. . . . Not surprisingly,
Venetian Red, which has been ten years in the making, has its professorial airs. But it is a fascinating book. In content and form, it is a
nineteenth-century novel in which opposing classes (the declining and
the rising), moralities, and intelligences grapple ponderously and intri-
cately for five hundred pages, and with a most gratifying outcome.
Never out of step with its subject matter, the book moves like thick
cream. . . . Now and then, the narrative steps aside for spacious flashbacks, which, however, do not flash but glimmer softly, like candles.
The characters talk at length, in a slow, circling, ambling-on-the-lawn
pace. Venice . . . infuses nearly every page. . . . After a time, one falls
easily into [the] venerable poetic flow, and it becomes a struggle to pay
attention to the island of moral conflict in its midst.

Whitney Balliett. *NY*. Aug. 27, 1960. pp. 100–101

In the end, it hardly matters what a novel is about, or what techniques
the writer uses. What does matter, always, is the quality of his mind,
present in every sentence, in every character and situation. An interesting
mind will have the humour, the passion, the tenderness, the wisdom, in
brief the right tone, at its disposal, simply by being what it is. . . .
Signor P. M. Pasinetti has such a mind. *Venetian Red* . . . is formally
old-fashioned, and within the form the author makes some elementary
mistakes . . . , [but] none of these things matter because they get
absorbed into the author's successful grappling with themes larger than
his characters, larger than himself—war and peace, the meaning of
patriotism . . . , the meaning of family ties, the functioning of the
liberal imagination . . . , as against the functioning of accepted forms
in life, love, politics, death. . . . The whole is shot through with a
quiet humour.

Christine Brooke-Rose. *LMg*. Sept., 1961. pp. 79–80

This second novel by P. M. Pasinetti [*The Smile on the Face of the
Lion*] is linked to his first—*Venetian Red*—by a world that is basically
the same. Here again the writer takes us into a milieu that he knows

firsthand and, at the same time, demonstrates his skill in using the latest narrative techniques—even though his work is, structurally speaking, traditional—to define what he regards as the central problems of contemporary existence: the general collapse of human values, the decay of the meaning of personal relationships, and man's loss of the sense of reality. . . . Superficially original and "free" in their actions, Pasinetti's characters (an Italian version of the "jet set") are ultimately conformists *sui generis,* for they too must obey the conventions and rules that govern any social group or clan. What does emerge out of the confusion that surrounds them all is an absorbing tableau of automatons, of puppets who talk but do not communicate, exist but do not live, make love without loving. The confusion Pasinetti so frequently mentions in his book is, in the last analysis, a confusion of human values and of human relations. And without resolving it, there cannot, alas, be anything but alienation.

Sergio Pacifici. SR. Feb. 13, 1965. p. 39

P. M. Pasinetti's second novel [*The Smile on the Face of the Lion*] is concerned with that segment of society which *Vogue* has dubbed "the beautiful people." Rich, handsome, urbane, socially desirable and, above all, unfettered by the bonds that keep less fortunate mortals lashed to the humdrum business of everyday life, they form a sort of supranational élite whose febrile but invariably glamorous activities are in fashionable magazines.

Although many of the characters of the present work have already appeared in *Venetian Red,* each of the two novels stands as a literary entity. Combined, they provide a panoramic picture of upper middle-class Venetian society from 1940 to our day. . . . It is in essence a paean of praise for the enduring strength and indestructible spirit of Venice and its women . . . [whose] fiber . . . matches that of the strong city of hard stone rising in deceptively fragile beauty out of the sparkling waters and the opalescent haze in which it bathes. . . . Under its sophisticated veneer and behind the intellectualized abstraction of its protagonists, this is a frankly romantic novel vibrant with . . . Protean life.

Helene Cantarella. NYT. Feb. 14, 1965. p. 4

Why shouldn't the first serious bilingual novels about the international high life of post-war Italy be written by a Venetian aristocrat teaching comparative literature at U.C.L.A.? It seems eminently reasonable. Italophilia of recent decades has had an endearingly promiscuous quality —owing in various degrees to the glamor of international chic, the lingering post-fascist euphoria, to the extreme dullness of the old Italian aristocracy, composed as it is of bits and pieces of England, France, and now America—so that gifted aristocrats like P. M. Pasinetti are obliged to make their careers from the ground up. . . . In one of his warmest apostrophes to his native city, he calls Venice "uninhabitable" . . . because of the unbearable restlessness the international *bel mondo* creates in Venice for anyone who accidentally belongs there. As a professor of World Literature in California, Pasinetti can now safely confront this fashionable world which, in its heights and depths, he is convinced, is terrified of mere fashion, as devoted to simple ideas of pure goodness as any monk in the *Fioretti* of St. Francis.

R. W. Flint. *NYR*. April 22, 1965. p. 24

See *Venetian Red* and *The Smile on the Face of the Lion* (novels).

PAVESE, CESARE (1908–1950)

Between 1943 and 1945, Pavese took to the woods as so many thousands of Italians did. On the hills of Nazi-occupied Piedmont, he lived close to those partisan bands around which the best part of the Italian people gathered to fight the foreign occupants and to work for future justice. These proved to be decisive years for Pavese. He felt he had personally discovered that the modern writer, if he is to escape isolation and despair, must align himself with those who are oppressed, and his work must reflect the social struggle. No doubt Pavese's convictions were deeply sincere; but they were also peculiarly naïve. Further, the writer's task as he now conceived it was at odds with his lyrical and elegaic temperament. Yet this contradiction is the mainspring of Pavese's art.

Paolo Milano. *NR*. May 4, 1953. p. 18

Like other Italian writers of the present day Pavese was something of an experimentalist; he was, like Vittorini, much influenced by the Americans; he has, like Buzzati or Brancati, a kind of myth-making tendency (which does not prevent some critics from classifying him as a "neo-realist"); he had to grope . . . through the residue of the D'Annunzian and regional traditions and under the restrictions of Fascism, for his own artistic personality. And in fact it is probably only in *The Moon and the Bonfire* that he succeeded in finding it.

Thomas G. Bergin. *NYHT*. May 24, 1953. p. 7

The real unity which is discoverable in Pavese's work under its superficial shifts from realism to regionalism, from the political to the archetypal, is his preoccupation with the meanings of America. . . . In rhythm and movement, and in a conviction, an understanding of art that underlie both, Pavese's art, profoundly Italian as it is, is rooted in our literature and could not have existed without it. . . . Pavese's impulse as an artist was toward a dimension he liked to call "mythic," a dimension he found in Melville and not in Flaubert. It is primarily through the author of *Moby Dick* that Pavese approaches American literature, and it is through him that he finds in our books an identity of word and thing that goes beyond mere anti-rhetorical immediacy to a special sort of symbolism: not the aristocratic *symbolisme* of the French . . . but a democratic faith that a "colloquy with the masses" might be opened on the level of myth, whose unity underlies the diversity of our acquired cultures.

Just as American literature had found a third way between the European poles of naturalism and *symbolisme,* so Pavese felt we had found an escape from the dilemma of classicizing traditionalism and romantic rebellion, between academicism and futurism. The American artist, Pavese believed, had discovered how to reject conformism without becoming "a rebel in short pants," how to be at once free and mature.

Leslie Fiedler. *KR.* Autumn, 1954. pp. 539–42

He sometimes came to see us in the evening. He would sit with his scarf round his neck, looking pale, and begin turning his hair or crumpling a piece of paper in his hand. All evening he would say nothing. He would answer none of our questions. Then, quite suddenly, he would put on his overcoat and go. . . . Talking to him was never easy, even when he appeared gay. But a conversation with him could brace and stimulate one like nothing else. In his presence we became much more intelligent. We felt driven to express only what was best and most serious in us. We discarded commonplaces, vague thoughts, and inconsistencies.

Natalia Ginzburg. Introduction to Pavese's *The Burning Brand: Diaries 1935–1950* (Walker). 1961. p. 14

When Cesare Pavese died [by suicide] . . . there was a quick moment's revulsion that a man so insistently vibrant with inner life had denied it for himself. . . . But what if "someone had known"? Would this solitary man have been talked round to a tolerance of life, if not of optimism? . . . The fact is that everyone who knew Pavese and his work "knew." The intense preoccupation with death (*"sei la terra e la morte"*) runs through all his work. . . . The months preceding Pavese's death included an emotional experience with a young American woman who epitomized for him the several attempts at a lasting relationship. The writer's chief experiences had ended in bitterness and failure, frequently in self-castigation, inevitably in depression. . . . But can this, if it be accepted as the immediate cause, be then blamed as ultimate cause? Surely not. For his awareness of death as a concomitant of life is in some form present in each of the novels, and in the poems to an obsessive degree. Pavese was on intimate terms with death from his early stories. Even in his lifelong interest in American letters, he reflected the pull of this lode: it is Melville who, above all, fascinates and moves him.

> Frances Keene. Introduction to Pavese's *The Burning Brand: Diaries 1935–1950* (Walker). 1961. pp. 11–13

[*The Burning Brand: Diaries 1935-1950*] is a document of a strange, harrowing pathos. That it was written without intent to publish is confirmed by internal evidence. The always spontaneous, sometimes cryptic and occasionally valueless entries are those of a note-book. But the notes are by a considerable poet and thinker: he is talking to himself, literally—addressing himself very often in the second person singular. And this dialogue is characteristic of his peculiar mentality, which is of a phenomenal objectivity, a detachment that is almost (although actually not at all) schizophrenic, and of a condition of such tragic isolation that he can write of spending "a whole evening sitting before a mirror to keep myself company."

> Philip Mairet. *NSN*. July 14, 1961. p. 59

Cesare Pavese, who took his life at the peak of his career in 1950, can still be considered today as the most elusively complex Italian writer of his generation. . . . For Cesare Pavese introspection was the way of life, it led not to escape through fantasy but to an intensification and "purification" of experience through an anguished search for the truth about himself and the world in which he lived. Intense, paradoxical, tormented by self-destructive fears and doubts, humble in the face of the gifts he knew were his, he poured forth [in his diaries] . . . without trace of self-consciousness, his innermost thoughts on whatever troubled or interested him.

> Helene Cantarella. *NYT*. Dec. 10, 1961. p. 4

In his native Italy the late Cesare Pavese is recognized as one of the country's very best recent novelists. . . . In his diaries Pavese explores what, in addressing himself, he calls "your own tendency . . . to wallow in your own unhappiness, to touch bottom," thus shedding considerable light on his suicide in 1950. Unquestionably a profoundly melancholy, lonely man, Pavese was especially bitter during the years when he had to face Fascism in government, neglect in his literary life, and disappointment in love. . . . The "literary" pages of the diaries deserve every conventional compliment. They contain the intelligent observations of a dedicated, thoughtful, extremely learned man of letters. But to read the lines in which Pavese records his private sorrows is to share the unique experience of his tortuous life, to see his blood staining the printed page.

Henry Popkin. SR. Dec. 23, 1961. p. 23

Pavese's work has the dual theme of city and country. The country was a reservoir of recollections, the hills among which he grew up, the mythical age of childhood; the city was a symbol of crowded streets and intellectual development. This theme is like that of Sherwood Anderson, to whom the whole modern world lies in the contrast between country and city, between innocence and empty vanity, between the grandeur of nature and the pettiness of man. In the virile loneliness in which all of his characters are enveloped, Pavese entered into the world of myth.

Giose Rimanelli. Perspectives: Recent Literature of
Russia, China, Italy, and Spain (U. S. Library of Congress).
1961. p. 38

The . . . verse of this great novelist shows Pavese's gifts—his extraordinary psychological acumen, his close-grained realism, his universal compassion. . . . The early Pavese prefers the loose line, the poignant human destiny or incident, to tight personal lyricism; in some respects close to E. A. Robinson, his talent runs primarily to ballad and narrative, shot through with nostalgia, which lends an unforgettable aroma to his compositions. . . . Only in the final series of poems . . . written during the poet's last years, do we find the complete translucency and economy of great lyric verse.

Francis Golffing. BA. Summer, 1963. p. 329

For the modern consciousness, the artist (replacing the saint) is the exemplary sufferer. . . . The unity of Pavese's diaries is to be found in his reflections on how to use, how to act on, his suffering. . . . Apart from writing, there are two prospects to which Pavese continually recurs. One is the prospect of suicide, . . . the other is the prospect of romantic love and erotic failure. . . . The two themes are intimately connected, as Pavese himself experienced. . . . The modern view of love is an extension of the spirit of Christianity. . . . The cult of love in the West is an aspect of the cult of suffering—suffering as the supreme token of seriousness (the paradigm of the Cross). . . . The sensibility we have inherited identifies spirituality and seriousness with turbulence, suffering, passion. . . . The modern contribution to this Christian sensibility has been to discover the making of works of art and the venture of sexual love as the two most exquisite sources of suffering. It is this that we look for in a writer's diary, and which Pavese provides in disquieting abundance.

Susan Sontag. Against Interpretation (Farrar). 1966.
pp. 42, 44, 47-8

See The Moon and the Bonfire, Among Women Only, and The House on the Hill (novels); The Political Prisoner (two short novels); Festival Night and Other Stories; The Burning Brand: Diaries 1935–1950; and Dialogues with Luecò (poetic meditations).

PÉGUY, CHARLES PIERRE (1873–1914)

Literature as such never interested him. All he ever wrote came to him as a spontaneous creation. Once he had surrendered to the call of the voice within himself, he could not stop, and we had his endless litanies, hymns, soliloquies and prayers. Words went marching in battle array at his command like so many waves in the World War offensives. Péguy plowed slowly and painstakingly in the field of words and sentences. He wove patiently and obstinately what he called his tapestries, and there could be seen hanging on the walls the archaic figures of Saint Genevieve, Saint Joant of Arc, and Our Lady of Chartres whom he worshipped as a medieval pilgrim.

Régis Michaud. Modern Thought and Literature in
France (Funk). 1934. p. 25

The idealism he championed, the sporting, free action in the constant presence of the eternal good, Péguy called mysticism. The enemy was politics, lust for power; politics and its offspring, the exploitative, unfaithful, all-prostituting modern world. Péguy attacked its representatives with unremitting vehemence. . . . Romain Rolland and Henri Bergson were among his masters, and Bergson's philosophy thrilled him and made him lifelong a fervent Bergsonite. This was not fortuitous. Péguy was immensely sanguine by nature: in all his despairs and disillusionments constantly in touch with some ground of happy expectations; convinced that what he desired was obtainable.

Paul Rosenfeld. Nation. Feb. 20, 1943. p. 276

Péguy was surely one of the world's innocents. His writing radiates a comprehensive and simple rapport with mankind, a goodwill which was the wellspring of his socialism. It will not even do to call him a humanitarian; the word is too conscious, too studied to designate his artless essence. He was, quite simply, an articulate peasant. And it is inapt to speak of the craft of his poetry, which amounts to an art without artifice, and served beautifully for the communication of a faith that transcends dogma.

Peter De Vries. Poetry. July, 1943. p. 209

It is perhaps significant that the three most eminent Catholic writers of modern France, Léon Bloy, Péguy and Claudel are the least amenable to any selective process. Each of their works is long, and of one piece, incapable of being cut into smaller parts. Their work is one of persistence and explanation, composed in a period when their faith had to be carefully and laboriously defended. . . . The temporal and the eternal and their commingling—that is the temporal in the eternal— is the problem which pervades most of the long works of Péguy. . . . Every line recommences the debate on eternity.

Wallace Fowlie. Poetry. April, 1945. pp. 43, 45

Péguy was a great man—perhaps a very great man—but he was not a good writer. In fact, he could not write; he talked in print. His talk is often very good, even when he talks in verse, which he does for amazingly long periods. . . . His great fault is repetition. He will not only say the same things, but repeats the same words over and over again, as though he were a teacher addressing a class of half-deaf children. Nevertheless he often hits. His intellectual honesty is amazing, his power of expression is sometimes of the highest order.

Denis Saurat. Modern French Literature (Putnam).
1946. p. 93

By his poetry, his canticle of Hope, Péguy was to assume his richest significance—a poetry movingly lovely in its profusion of image and its intensity of emotion; close to earth by its human simplicity; close to heaven by its liturgical inspiration and its meditative depth. This poetry became the uninterrupted prayer of a man who was conscious of his vulnerability and limitations but who had achieved an attitude of complete trust and ineffable love, since salvation had become an invincible certitude.

Yvonne Servais. Charles Péguy (Newman). 1953. p. 390

He had said so many things, and he had said them so vehemently, that it was easy to pull him wildly in all directions. . . . The patriots were pleased by Péguy's great love for France, and by his insistence on the need to be prepared for the coming war with Germany. The nationalists were pleased by Péguy's attacks on the existing order of things which he found rotting and corrupt, and by his attacks on old Dreyfusist comrades, like Jaurès and Herr, whom he conceived as deserters. The Catholics were cheered by his very clear movement towards them, a movement marked by the great poetic works published between 1910 and 1914 and attested by the friendship of Maritain. All these things were sufficient to make of Péguy a hero of that almost-revolutionary Right which appeared in France about 1885—part-chauvinist, part-royalist, part-catholic—and of which the *Action Française* was to become the clearest (though not the only) expression.

Eugen Weber. FR. April, 1954. pp. 340–1

The relationship between tradition and freedom is one of the central themes of Péguy's work. . . . Péguy was . . . plunged into the violent debates of the Dreyfus Affair and began using words in a new sense and, moreover, in a sense which was to lead him in a direction which at first he did not understand. His thought, in fact, was coloured by his conception of poetry long before that conception became clear to him. . . . It is not his quick temper which explains his quarrels, but his difficulties of language which made them inevitable. . . . He refused to be lumped with the traditionalists or the progressives. He wanted the best of both worlds and in his poetry tried to express it.

Alexander Dru. Péguy (Harvill). 1956. p. 6

The metaphors [in his poems] are concrete and earthy. The image is chanted over and over again, slightly qualified and altered with each repetition, as in the patterns of dreams and night thoughts. In the long stanzas, specific images are modified until they blur in the mind like the outer ripples of a stone dropped in a pool. Gide likened the vast, monotonous litanies to the music of an Arab flute. The style can be exceedingly tedious, but it carries the reader into the dim kingdom of the instinctive and the unconscious.

Joseph Featherstone. NR. April 16, 1966. p. 25

See *Basic Verities* (prose and poetry).

PÉREZ DE AYALA, RAMÓN (1881–1962)

The youthful Asturian poet already revealed in . . . his early work . . . an earnestness in which it was possible to detect two wholly different moods: one dominated by a philosophical, almost religious preoccupation with the idea of destiny: the other, marked by an aesthetic instinct towards truth and restrained expression. . . . The typical qualities of Ayala's style can already be detected: his rich vocabulary, his sense of the value and the music of words, his precision, his clear vision and the neatness of his expression. . . . His main weakness lies perhaps in a tendency to sink into mere criticism. . . . The critic in Ayala often pulls down the poet. His poetry then falls into the anecdotical, the didactical, or merely the jocular. This feature, curiously enough, is not so prominent in his early as in his later work.

Salvador de Madariaga. The Genius of Spain (Oxford).
1923. pp. 77–9

Some critics have maintained that Don Ramón Pérez de Ayala is chiefly a poet and that he should have continued to write poetry. . . , in which . . . he combined imitation of the Modernists and French Symbolists with thought and style of his own and achieved not perfect art but occasional beauty, lovely flowers glowing in a surrounding harshness, in an intermittently successful groping towards the light. . . . But the work of the author during the last ten years has triumphantly demonstrated his power as a writer of novels. . . . With a strong gift for description, his real study has always been man, his interest in psychology. . . . He belongs to the realistic school, but to Spanish realism, which gives to the strange and fantastic a clear and concrete expression, binding it definitely within the limits of the visible and living and, in dislike of vagueness, fitting the ideal into the real.

Aubrey F. G. Bell. Contemporary Spanish Literature
(Knopf). 1925. pp. 135–6, 139

Ayala . . . is his epoch's most cultivated novelist and most fanciful poet. This man who in Política y Toros has written the profoundest apologia of the bullfight and the subtlest satire on Spain's political abulia, beneath his disguise of timeliness is an archaicizer also: one who dwells . . . deep . . . within Spain's narcissistic adoration. . . . Ayala is a musing man: a man of satiric, wistful fancy rather than of imagination. His style progenitors are those amazing mystics of sixteenth century Spain who managed to endow ecstasy with Horatian polish. The sedulous, synthetic texts of Ayala are a panoply of dream: Spain dreaming of her cathedrals and her schools, Spain blowing lovely and seductive patterns—two volumes upon the Names of Christ —from the effluvia of medieval culture. The modern in Ayala is the ironic salt of intellectual awareness.

Waldo Frank. Virgin Spain (Boni and Liveright). 1926.
p. 278

Ayala's poetry is modernistic; free in its form, it has usually no great beauty of language; often it is trivial, has nothing to say, is moved by no great emotion. There is in it a strain of pagan sensuousness. . . . Ayalà's poetry usually, however, is sombre, serious, and melancholy; it has no grand waves and rolling forms, no dancing gaiety, no stormy turbulence, it is broken and subdued both in form and substance. Slight, wanting body and substance, it is vague; but Ayala has an aesthetic sensibility of extreme delicacy and expresses the vagueness of the unseen felt in the soul. Like all modernistic poetry, his verse consists of a number of detached pieces concerned with delicate shades and tints of ideas, of feelings, of flitting impressions in his own mind; and these states of mind arise from delicate sensations received from scenery and are reflected back again into a tinted and etherealized landscape.

L. A. Warren. *Modern Spanish Literature* (Brentano). 1929. v. 1, p. 293

Death is accepted by all Spaniards with an almost Oriental resignation as the inevitable conclusion to life's vicissitudes . . . and perhaps the eternal popularity of the bullfight itself is partially explained by its symbolism, representing life's fleeting dance with death.

In each of Ayala's three "Poetic Novels"—*Prometheus, Sunday Sunlight,* and *The Fall of the House of Limón*—the tale concludes with a tragic death. . . . The innocence of Spring, the unconscious happiness of youth, are invariably followed by the blighting tragedy of autumn.

There is about Ayala's writings, both in style and in matter, a refreshing virility, nervous and youthful, which reflects life from a peculiar, almost spiritual angle. Youth and its ideals, the shattering effect on them by time, and their replacement by yet new ideas—these are the keys on which Ayala plays his graceful melodies.

Peter Trentham. *BkmL.* Aug., 1931. pp. 250–1

When Russian novels first appeared in this country, the world they described must have seemed odd in the extreme. We have absorbed them now, and the samovar, the ascetic, the philosophical sensualists and the endless discussions about God are more familiar than the world of His Excellency Señor Ramón Pérez de Ayala. No Karamazov talked more than these provincial Spaniards, whose minds still move in circles round the sixteenth century conception of "the point of honour." . . . They have a strange, acrid vitality, they smell of wine and dung, they cannot sit down to cards without falling into the attitudes of tragic farce. . . . And though this exciting, difficult book [*Tiger Juan*] begins and ends in talk on the same "point of honour" which Calderon wrote about four hundred years ago, the modern world has crept into the corners of the market at Pilares.

Graham Greene. Spec. Feb. 10, 1933. p. 196

Plot has never interested Ayala. His capital virtues have been the depiction of character and atmosphere, and his style. . . . Despite his familiarity with European literature, especially with English, he has remained untranslatable. . . . Not merely because of linguistic impossibilities—his Castilian has an autochthonous raciness which simply cannot be transferred into another tongue—but because of his local humor, of his ideology and spirit. Ayala thinks and feels like a rancid Spaniard; his books contain an exclusively Spanish flavor; Cassou has called it "an oily flavor of the kitchen and the sacristy."

Angel Flores. NYHT. Sept. 24, 1933. p. 12

Pérez de Ayala, as is evident, makes no effort to hold the reader by a mere story. Analysis and observation revealing the heart and kernel of Castilian Spain are of the essence of his work. His characters, for all the external realism and quaint humor of their description, hold one by their disputations and arguments. Dr. Starkie declares that it is the Celt in him which accounts for the bitter humor in Ayala, and that may well be the reason, too, why there is a fund of talk in all his novels which reminds an Irishman of his own literature.

Ernest Boyd. SR. Sept. 30, 1933. pp. 141, 146

The *Quijote* not only blends the dual worlds of reality and imagination but reproduces the totalitarian function of reality in the multiple nature of the genre, which is an amalgamation of all the then known forms of the novel: the pastoral, the sentimental, the picaresque, the chivalrous, and so on. It is particularly noteworthy that Ayala, the author most acutely aware of the problematic nature of the form of the novel, should have expressed this awareness in what is probably the finest modern example of the *Quijote*-type novel (*Belarmino y Apolonio*) as well as in novels that he himself considered "poematic."

Leon Livingstone. PMLA. April, 1958. pp. 394–5

See *Tiger Juan* and *The Fox's Paw* (novels); also *Prometheus: The Fall of the House of Limón: Sunday Sunlight* (a trilogy of "poetic novels").

PÉREZ GALDÓS, BENITO (1843–1920)

He not only voices the aspirations of religious liberalism and social progress, but is at the same time the exponent of the national and patriotic spirit of his country. . . . "Electra" is the symbol of progress and of revolt against clericalism and Jesuitism. . . . It certainly cannot be said that Galdós has initiated a literary or dramatic revolution. He is neither a Victor Hugo nor an Ibsen. "Electra" is an interesting and well-written play, but its methods are a little old fashioned. . . . Its importance lies solely in the fact that it has given expression to the latent progressive and anti-clerical feelings throughout a country which has hitherto been regarded as of all the chief European countries the least progressive and most hopelessly bound to the Church.

> Havelock Ellis. *LA*. Oct. 26, 1901. pp. 236–7

The vigorous modernity of Galdós's genius was a compelling force in the orientation of Spanish art. . . . All his plays . . . deal with the things of today and with problems peculiarly if not exclusively Spanish. It is the fierce duel between the old spirit and the new. It is society, petrified in its traditions, decrepit and stubborn, defending itself with the whole dead weight of the past against the new force that is pushing its way to the light. That may well be considered the general subject of his dramatic work, subdivided so as to present with each play a peculiar phase of the struggle.

> R. W. Waldeck. *Critic*. Nov., 1904. pp. 448–9

Galdós' plays . . . develop from a core of passion that is the play itself. They reveal a healthy disregard for the conventions of stage technique. They do not yield readily to the arrogant confines of the proscenium and tend to overflow the banks of the accepted form. But in so doing they exercise a liberating influence; they rebel. . . . Surely he was not in revolt against life, but just as surely he was a rebel against the conventions and traditions that impede its freer play. He did not create for the stage a form fully adequate to the artistic illumination of that spiritual rebellion, perhaps because he did not see fully into its deeper implications. At any rate, his form impresses one as intermediate; he fought evils rather than illuminated a new day. He was held back by the very past that he opposed. He was himself too deeply rooted in the soil out of which he sought to rise. This . . . explains his shortcomings as a dramatist.

> Isaac Goldberg. *The Drama of Transition*
> (Stewart Kidd). 1922. pp. 83, 92

There is little of the human underworld which he did not fathom and express with Wordsworthian penetration and felicity, and, in a sense, the whole of his work may be interpreted as the drama of impulse lurking under the comedy of action.

This central idea explains several of the most prominent features of his art, and particularly his frequent recourse to dreams and apparitions. With Galdós, dreams are not mere tricks for melodramatic effect. They ... act as small explosions from the subconscious. . . . . Another aspect of Galdós's "impulsological" manner is his tendency to picture those revulsions of character which take place when a natural group of tendencies has been repressed by education, environment, or self-deception and is suddenly released by a shock of fact giving back in one second all the energy locked up for years in the under-soul. Such dramatic reversions to type occur in practically every book of Galdós.

Salvador de Madariaga. *The Genius of Spain*
(Oxford). 1923. p. 54

He regarded the novel as a means of propaganda; and all his novels are, in a sense, thesis novels. . . . It is no exaggeration to state that Galdós is the greatest master of the novel of tendency in Spain. He purged it of its most objectionable characteristics and incorporated it into the novel of manners—which, in his view, must always have a "purpose." What, in Galdós' case, was that purpose?

It was, in the first instance, we venture to suggest, the diagnosing of the spiritual malady from which he conceived Spain to be suffering. . . . Galdós may justly be regarded as the founder of the new school of writers, which grew to maturity after the disaster of 1898. . . . His revolt against what was evil in the existing order . . . prepared the way for an attack upon that order itself. He cannot be relieved of a certain responsibility for much that was thought, said and written by the "generation of '98," and almost all the great figures in contemporary Spanish fiction must look to him as their master.

L. B. Walton. *Pérez Galdós and the Spanish Novel of the*
Nineteenth Century (Dutton). 1927. pp. 221–9

Perhaps the only assertion that is safe to make is that from first to last Galdós' dramatic career was a struggle against forces hostile to his concept of drama, which aimed to induct the public into the limitless spaces of spiritual speculation and psychological analysis, in quest of that inner wisdom which alone gives meaning and direction to human behavior. His concrete accomplishment? Artistically, the creation of an atmosphere propitious to further experimentation by the rising generation of dramatists; philosophically, dissemination of the gospel that however baffling life may seem, one can discover its meaning if he will only carry out the dictates of his conscience with sincerity and tolerance.

H. C. Berkowitz. *Pérez Galdós: Spanish Liberal*
Crusader (Wisconsin). 1948. p. 263

We may call Galdós a novelist of the school of Balzac. He wrote soberly and objectively about the world as he saw it and did not associate himself with any of his characters. But to the Frenchman's rather colorless narrative he adds the warmth, humor and melodramatic sense of Dickens and the ironic wit and detachment of Cervantes. Further he is one of the great psychological novelists, endlessly curious about the varieties of human conduct and character. His books abound in abnormal types, religious maniacs and people on the border line of insanity. . . . He shows an intuitive understanding of their case histories, which one can only compare with that shown by Dostoevsky, though his approach is far more objective and clinical.

> Gerald Brenan. Introduction to *The Spendthrifts*
> (Farrar). 1952. pp. 9–10

As a social study of aristocratic parasitism and bureaucracy, *The Spendthrifts* is admirable for its precision and dramatic impact, but it is nevertheless a secondary work. It suffers from the same superficialities and stock typologies (the stingy, ugly husband, the clothes-mad spendthrift wife, the heartless usurer) which so frequently marred the work of many of his contemporaries. . . . Its angular psychology often suggests sheer melodrama. . . . [A] kind of tendentiousness represents the perishable aspect of his work.

> Angel Flores. *NYHT*. Aug. 24, 1952. p. 10

The Spendthrifts . . . [and] *Torment* reveal the qualities of the best Galdós: intensity in describing the physical world, harmony of composition, and an interpretative gift more kind than sharp. . . . In his interpretation of persons and things he displays once again the generosity of a Cervantine spirit. . . . Galdós' weaknesses are those of the period he lived in: garrulousness, verbosity and polemical eloquence, sanctified under the banner of populism. . . . The anti-heroes of Galdós have renounced many things. They are often vanquished by money, conventional morality, or simple adversity. Yet behind the bitterness of each experience a new faith is being born. . . . They are like the humble and tenacious ants that begin all over again when their ant hill has been trampled underfoot.

> Ramón Sender. *NYT*. Aug. 2, 1953. pp. 4, 11

Galdós is deep in Spanish egoism. But he was sufficiently a European to explore that; he wrote at the time of intellectual revival; he is free from that "typical" regionalism which travels so freely in literature. He has the certainty, sharpness and power of the novelist who is saturated in his subject. If, as they say, everything in Spain is personal, then Galdós is the novelist of this kind of society which destroys every idea and issue by the thickly involved personal concern.

V. S. Pritchett. *Books in General* (Harcourt). 1953. p. 36

Galdós is frequently referred to as a psychological novelist. It is more exact to call him a socio-psychological novelist or a literary social psychologist, for he is interested more in the formative influence of social relations, as regards the individual, than he is in the intricate workings of the mind. His technique is often more descriptive of outward manifestations than interpretive of deep-lying motives. Nevertheless, he visualizes personality in its broad functional aspects and records his interpretation in one comprehensive treatment. In an important respect it is proper to call his portrayal dynamic.

Sherman H. Eoff. *The Novels of Pérez Galdós*
(Washington). 1954. p. 3

At the time Galdós wrote *Gloria* and *Marianela,* he thought of himself as a realist as always. . . . Yet his notion of realism at this time did not include the idea of slavish copying from reality. He felt that elements from reality could and should be rearranged to enhance the interest, picturesqueness, and beauty of the thing described. . . . Galdós was still partly influenced by the so called idealistic novel whose slogan was "Art intensifies nature."

The same procedure is applied to most of the characters: they are composites. But as compared to earlier characters, such as those of *Doña Perfecta,* they represent a long step toward realism. No longer are they so obviously incarnated moral forces.

Walter T. Pattison. *Benito Pérez Galdós and the Creative
Process* (Minnesota). 1954. pp. 137–8

Galdós's earlier efforts, which he called *Episodios Nacionales* . . . were, indeed, tendencious, if I may anglicize a very necessary word from the Spanish *tendencioso.* That is, they dealt with very obvious problems, and had very distinct and poignant significations, at least in the case of *Doña Perfecta, Leon Roch,* and *Gloria.* . . . For me, *Doña Perfecta* is not realistic enough—realistic as it is; for realism at its best is not tendencious. It does not seek to grapple with human problems, but is richly content with portraying human experiences. . . . I have called, or half-called, this book tendencious; but in a certain larger sense it is not so. It is the eternal interest of passion working upon passion, not the temporary interest of condition agonizing condition, which renders *Doña Perfecta* so poignantly interesting, and which makes its tragedy immense.

William Dean Howells. *Criticism and Fiction, and Other Essays* (N.Y.U.). 1959. pp. 134–8

It is rather paradoxical that an artist endowed with the fanciful imagination of Galdós should be presented as a prime example of "Realism" by critics whose vision of realist practice includes a veneration of the photographic, that is, very definite restriction placed upon the unusual, the bizarre, the contrived image. With the introduction of dreams into his novels, Galdós found a way to give free rein to his imaginative powers within the framework of true realism—for even in the most prosaic life the dream is imaginative, strange, almost poetic in its extraordinariness.

Joseph Schraibman. *Dreams in the Novels of Galdós* (Hispanic Institute). 1960. pp. 184–5

See *Doña Perfecta, Marianela,* and *The Spendthrifts* (novels); also *Electra* and *The Grandfather* (plays).

PERSE, ST.-JOHN (1889–   )

[The poems of Perse] have their own rank and place: they are remarkable for a rhythm new in French and European poetry; for the gift of conveying the essential of landscapes, destinies, visions; for their richness of metaphor, their density, the boldness of their ellipses. And they take command of the full resources of the French language, so rarely summoned up.

Herbert Steiner. *YR.* Sept., 1944. p. 181

The poetry of Perse, with its presentness of time, its odor of eternity, its vast image of life like a landscape without trees, is a poetry written not out of action but against it or behind it. . . . I believe the poetry of Perse, which has been a powerful influence in the minds of many men who could not remember what it was that so deeply moved them but only that they were moved as a man might be moved by a fragrance he could not remember—that this poetry, like all true poetry, will take its place outside literature and all doctrine, in the desert sunlight where the stone survives.

Archibald MacLeish. Introduction to *Éloges* (Norton). 1944. pp. 11, 14

In this magnificent poem ("Rains") which is at once a kind of litany, or litany of litanies, and an allegorical history of mankind, a history in terms of metaphor, the poet drives his tandem of methods with complete mastery. The *whole meaning,* the history of man in terms of rain, or the interpretation of him in terms of rain—rain as the fertilizer, rain as the purifier, even as the principle itself of life and change—gives a majestic centripetal design to the poem, and a tremendous sense of controlled richness, but it is also of such a nature . . . as to make the utmost possible use of incidental, but directed, improvisation. . . . It isn't *about,* it becomes and is, our sad rich dreadful glorious disastrous foul and beautiful history.

Conrad Aiken. NR. April 16, 1945. pp. 512–4

His chief work in poetry has been marked by a kind of racial or planetary character, in keeping with his experience of East and West and his feeling for the most ancient memories and legacies of man. . . . The poems are written in a kind of Dionysiac free verse, difficult because of its shifting level of meaning and its rare terms, often resistant to translation. They have, however, extraordinary visionary power which both retains realistic objectivity and opens up the creative levels of spiritual life.

Amos N. Wilder. Modern Poetry and the Christian
Tradition (Scribner). 1952. pp. 104–5

In its essence, in spite of great superficial sophistication and all it may owe to Pindar or Xenophon, this is primitive poetry, in the sense in which Whitman, Conrad, and D. H. Lawrence are primitive. In Saint-John Perse, exoticism is not a sophistication, but an innocence, a memory of childhood. I know of no other poet who has surveyed civilization at its greatest complexity with eyes that have first understood the substrata upon which human societies form so thin a layer of the crust of time. Only in India could one find a comparable range of barbarity and culture existing simultaneously, and by the same vital impulse.

Kathleen Raine. NR. April 20, 1953. p. 17

Perse has taken his place beside the four or five major poets of modern France: Baudelaire, Mallarmé, Rimbaud, Valéry, Claudel. Like theirs, his work defies any facile nomenclature of romantic or classical. . . . The official attitude of the symbolists was aloofness. The official attitude of the surrealists was aggressiveness. St.-John Perse represents a more traditional, more central attitude of the poet. The precise word is difficult to choose, because on the whole this attitude is seldom felt today, but it would be perhaps solemnity or sacredness. It would be a word powerful enough to contain and harmonize the contradictions of man's fate as it appears to us within the limits of time and space.

Wallace Fowlie. *Poetry*. Sept., 1953. pp. 347, 350

Movement, progress, action. Saint-John Perse's crowds and heroes, worthy of praise or blame, belong to the epic poems to the extent that they are never at rest. Each one devotes himself to an act of conquest by means of physically taking possession or through knowledge. These men do not represent static moods; they change, consume, and travel through the world, they come and go; if they stop, it is to praise their acts or to express their demands. They might be said to be a positive sign. They exercise powers.

Jacques Guicharnaud. *YFS*. Spring-Summer, 1958. p. 75

One of the first characteristics of his world is the complete absence of proper names. Landscapes are vividly described but no indication is given of where they are situated. As befits a modern world in which historical knowledge has made all past present, the events which occur in St.-John Perse's poems could be taking place in any historical epoch. Its inhabitants have neither names nor genealogies; they have functions.

There is suffering and death in this world, but not tragedy. What the poet celebrates, that is to say, is not the refusal of the noble individual to live at any price, but the inexhaustible power of life to renew itself and triumph over every disaster, natural or human. What he looks for and tries to express in every one of his poems is the sacredness of being.

W. H. Auden. *NYT*. July 27, 1958. p. 1

Perse's poetry should be read as an exercise in spiritual intrepidity. His poems offer a man no shelter from the night and bad weather; they are themselves an encampment under the open sky. No roots here: wings. His theme is singular and plural: time, the times. History minus any characters, because the only real character in history is a nameless and faceless being, half flesh and half dream: the man all we other men are and aren't. . . . Perse's theme is time, our very substance. The poetry of time, which buries and banishes us. Insofar as we are men, we are a metaphor of time. A migrant image.

Octavio Paz. *Nation*. June 17, 1961. pp. 522–3

See *Anabasis, Chroniques, Éloges, Exile, Seamarks,* and *Winds* (poetry).

PIRANDELLO, LUIGI (1867–1936)

Pirandello has neither faith nor philosophy, with the result that we are driven to reject his sorry masquerade of humanity as ingenious but unreal. . . . The life whch he presents whirls passionately round, but without a principle, even of evil, to give it significance; and the emotions he would evoke lose their edge because they too, on his showing, are part of a senseless flux. . . . By excluding every element of permanence from his conception of human life, Pirandello, with all his attractive gifts, his ingenuity and his dramatic sense, has banished the quality of greatness from his art.

Orlo Williams. *Corn.* Sept., 1923. pp. 274–5

Pirandello, it seems, is a cunning, and possibly inspired, play-boy of the psychological world, who delights to use all the tools in the sophists' outfit in order to shake our senses of security in values, to dethrone reason, and to confuse all common beliefs in the nature of reality. He is so much a sceptic that he is sceptical of the very instrument of his scepticism, the human mind. He appears to regard all efforts at the rational guidance of self and society on common-sense lines as futile interferences with an impersonal, ungovernable stream of life. His drama, in short, is a flow of impulse and a feast of unreason.

Ivor Brown. *SR.* April 18, 1925. p. 410

The author [of *Six Characters in Search of an Author*] has completely achieved the desired illusion that the characters are *always* acting; that by their very nature they can be doing nothing else. . . . That is the significance of the characters—they were born for one thing only, to play this sordid tragedy of theirs; in it is all of their life, their birth, their eternity; they simply do not exist save within its compass. . . .

The conception of the characters is, I think, Pirandello's greatest achievement. . . . His phantoms serve him perfectly as illustrations of his philosophy. They are appearances who are at the same time real, and are able to cast a doubt on the reality of folk who judge only by appearances.

Milton Waldeman. *LM.* Aug., 1925. pp. 399–400

The essence of Pirandello's art lies in the idea that nothing is, but thinking makes it so. Yet to regard his plays merely as studies in the accidents and incidents of psychology is to consider the surface and the machinery and miss their psychic movement. Tragedy and comedy, the deep pity and significant fervour and the cleansing laughter of life are born of these, and it is to these more important matters that the mind-dramas of Pirandello point the way.

Horace Shipp. *Eng.* Sept., 1925. p. 439

With Pirandello it is not so much the words and actions of his characters but the implication we draw from them that is significant. He deals with the unexpressed. His men and women seek to extend the limitations of human personality and to discover who and what they really are. They live with illusions and ideals and ignore the destructive commonplace. . . .

Questioning the veracity of the mental and physical accidents of every-day life, Pirandello looks behind them for a deeper reality. He interrogates the passionate spiritual significance of personality and confronts us with riddles.

Joseph Spencer Kennard. *The Italian Theater From the Close of the Seventeenth Century* (Wm. Edwin Rudge). 1932. pp. 303–6

In a thousand ways he insists that the quest of our own personalities is bafffling, if not fruitless, because as we strip off our outer selves in order to reach a core upon which we may create our structure in the world, we can keep on stripping as if we were removing the skin of an onion. In the end there is no core. Which layer, then, is really we? Up to the very last whatever is left is we, and after that nothing.

E. C. Knowlton. *SAQ.* Jan., 1935. p. 54

All modern philosophy is based on a profound intuition of the dualism which exists between Life which is absolute spontaneity, creative activity, and the forms which tend to restrict and enclose Life. The Life Force, like an inexorable tide, dashes up against those forms created by man; it breaks down barriers which impede its triumphal progress. It is from this point of view that we must start off to criticise Pirandello. With him it ceases to be an abstract philosophical theory and becomes dramatic— dramatic because it appeals to him with such intensity and assumes such moral semblance that it causes him to suffer. To him the struggle between the Life Force and the masks with which men try to cover it becomes the material for tragic drama.

Walter Starkie. *Luigi Pirandello* (Dutton). 1937. pp. 43–4

The most fertile property of Pirandello's dramaturgy is his use of the stage itself. By so boldly accepting it for what it is, he freed it from the demand which modern realism had made of it, that it be a literal copy of scenes offstage, and also from the exorbitant Wagnerian demand, that it be an absolutely obedient instrument of hypnosis in the power of the artist. Thus he brought to light once more the wonderful property which the stage *does* have: of defining the primitive and subtle medium of the dramatic art. "After Pirandello"—to take him symbolically rather than chronologically—the way was open for Yeats and Lorca, Cocteau and Eliot. The search could start once more for a modern poetry of the theater, and even perhaps for an Idea of the Theater comparable to that of the Greeks yet tenable in the modern world.

Francis Fergusson. *PR*. June, 1949. p. 603

Pirandello's main concern is with the (basically insoluble) problem of personal identity in its relation to individual personality, and the questions of reality and insanity as they touch on this problem. The typical Pirandellian situation is paradoxical, and involves the dissolution of apparently firm "reality" into a series of only apparent "truths," differing from one person to the next, and without any possibility of ever arriving at an objective or absolute grasp of the facts. Pirandello goes beyond psychology, to a quasi-philosophical approach in which the study of human character becomes subordinate to the analysis of cognition and existence. In his best novels and plays, he strikes a happy balance between the dynamic forces of dramatic conflict, and the static nature of intellectual reflection, though this latter comes in Pirandello's work to have a rather more overt expression and effect than is normal in modern Italian life. On occasion, however, Pirandello's work loses its effectiveness because of the essentially untheatrical nature of his subject matter, and his philosophizing becomes obstruseness, his paradox becomes obfuscation.

Robert A. Hall, Jr. *A Short History of Italian Literature* (Linguistica). 1951. p. 396

Italian decadentism is a complex phenomenon. Resulting . . . from the breakdown of scientific determinism on the one hand and the accepted ethical and artistic categories on the other. . . . If there is no reason, there is no plan, no consistency in life or personality, we have no control over ourselves or our destiny and men are creatures of Chance.

Intellectual and pseudointellectual circles in Italy were infected with this black pessimism and the great feat of Luigi Pirandello is to have put it into dramatic form, to have translated it into human emotional situations, to have shown what happens to an average, fairly intelligent person when ethical and philosophical props are pulled from under him and he is left floating in a sea of doubt; turning introspectively inward he rends not only himself but those with whom he comes in contact. The resultant suffering is the subject matter of the theatre of Pirandello.

Lander MacClintock. *The Age of Pirandello*
(Indiana). 1951. p. 175

Pirandello carries on an attack against our animal faith and seems determined to persuade us not merely that we cannot make value judgements, not merely that we cannot distinguish appearance from reality, but that the whole concept of reality as opposed to appearance is inadmissible.

Moreover and in the process, the "I" itself, the thing which perceives appearances and becomes the victim of illusions, disintegrates—if, at least, one means by the "I" any continuous, persisting, relatively stable thing. Every "I" is not merely all the things which at various times it seems to itself to be or all the things which at various times it seems to various people to be. It is also all the different things which at different times it has been. There are the "I's" of yesterday, today, and tomorrow, as well as what every observer has taken each of them to be.

Joseph Wood Krutch. *"Modernism" in Modern Drama*
(Cornell). 1953. p. 82

Pirandellian man is isolated not only from his fellows, but also from himself at other times. Farther than this, isolation cannot go. This is a "nihilistic vision," and no mistake.

Perhaps it would nowadays be called an existentialist vision: life is absurd; it fills us with dread and anguish; yet, without knowing why, . . . we fight back, . . . and because all living, all life, is improvisation, we improvise some values. Their Form will last until Living destroys them and we have to improvise some more.

Pirandello's plays grew from his own torment, . . . but through his genius they came to speak for all the tormented, potentially *to* all the tormented—that is, to all men.

Eric Bentley. *In Search of Theater* (Knopf). 1953.
pp. 313–4

Pirandello is a dominant pessimist; everything is purely transitory, reality only exists at a given moment of time, the flash of a camera or a gun. Nothing will stem the tide of physical destruction, the heart beats slowly a funeral march which makes our hopes of tomorrow the lost chances of yesterday. Again and again Pirandello expounds the motivation for his pessimism in his plays, until the drama of action becomes a scientific investigation of the human mind, or cerebral-theatre. The audience is asked to give attention to the complexities of inner contradiction. . . . Pirandello . . . is one of the few modern writers whose pessimism does convince; his pessimism, however, does not spring from a surfeit of hate, or from the fact that this is the worst of possible worlds; it is because his eyes sadden at seeing so much that is beautiful and yet so irrelevant to the human façade with its bruises and scars.

> Frederick Lumley. *Trends in Twentieth Century Drama*
> (Essential Books). 1956. pp. 19–20

A character is not *real* simply because it is modeled on a man actually existing, actually known and studied in the world close at hand. If art is the product of fancy, Pirandello felt, a complete definition of aesthetics should embrace not only the use of Greek myths (classicism), not only historical material (romanticism), not only material observed in the society and environment in which the artist lives (naturalism), but also whatever dreams and enchanted or awesome places the artist evokes from his imagination (contemporary art). *Reality* resides not in the material used, but in the life that the magic power of imagination can awaken in it.

> Domenico Vittorini. *High Points in the History of*
> *Italian Literature* (McKay). 1958. p. 270

One of Pirandello's basic themes is the eternal opposition of life and form, the latter unchanging and eternal, the former vital and continuously fluctuating. The pursuit of life, not the search for form, must be the human endeavor, since the basic condition of human existence is one of vitality and change. The two principles are mutually exclusive: form tends to encroach on and stifle life, while life, by sometimes imposing itself on form, changes it from inert to living matter.

> Thomas Bishop. *Pirandello and the French Theater*
> (N.Y.U.). 1960. p. 42

Pirandello's plays are tragic precisely because they are so resolutely cast in the naturalistic mode; that is, a theatrical convention which assumes the prime "reality" of the "outside world," the world of money, family obligations and human relations. It is out of this world that we construct ourselves and its violence, its inadequacies, its lies doom all our attempts at transcendence. These plays turn on domestic conflicts or incest or obsessional violence in bourgeois settings; the very theatrical convention assumed by the plays dooms the characters to failure. The esthetic strategy here is the way in which Pirandello brings these two urgencies together and, through the manipulation of action and point of view, strives to wrest some kind of transient or partial victory from the brute facts of a naturalistically conceived environment.

Neal Oxenhandler. *IQ.* Winter, 1961. pp. 57–8

See *Naked Masks: Five Plays* and *Short Stories.*

PONGE, FRANCIS (1899–   )

In painting, the still life is completely accepted; it has been a long time since it was a discovery to see an unfathomable world in some apples placed on a tablecloth by Cézanne. In poetry, it is otherwise. Language, which, more than anything else, is used for dealing with the most common things, feels a certain fear at using poetic forms for banal subjects. Now that is precisely what Ponge does, and that is enough to give his work a provocative, revolutionary look.

Gerda Zeltner-Neukomm. *NRF.* Sept., 1956. pp. 422–3.
Tr. by Dorothy Nyren Curley

One notices that Ponge's method, to be more exact, what his method attempts to be, is far from photographic; quite the contrary; anyone might experience the same difficulty in recognizing at first glance the objects, plants, shells, cigarettes, etc., described by Ponge as in accepting the images of his personal world as they are reflected in Picasso's art. For Ponge, despite the astonishing virtuosity of his palette, is not particularly interested in color and form; what has an imperious fascination for him is the essence of the interior life of the plant or shell, so that we feel in reading him almost as though it were the plant which spoke to express miraculously, without human intervention, its personality which until then, except for occasional rare flashes of intuition, had remained completely inaccessible to the most persistent observer.

Betty Miller. *NRF.* Sept., 1956. pp. 415–6.
Tr. by Dorothy Nyren Curley

Ponge is determined not to let us feel secure in *any* single point of view very long, because he is the poet of man's real insecurity in the universe. Basically, he is saying two things; 1) Man *has* indeed a point of view, his own, from which he can never escape, and 2) Man being imperfect, his point of view is contestable every second, at every turn. . . . Ponge's extraordinarily playful use of language is not merely a magnificent side-show but an essential element in his poetry—perhaps, indeed, *the* essential element of his contribution. By an implicit metaphor he makes of the poet's native tongue . . . a symbol for the particularity and limitedness of human existence, forever separate from the world of things with their utterly alien existence that perpetually haunts man but which he can only vaguely sense, never accurately translate in terms of his own.

Blossom Margaret Douthat. *YFS.* Spring-Summer, 1958.
pp. 80–1

Poetry appears here in the high place which Francis Ponge judges appropriate for his project, in an air of carefully defined freedom which he has chosen for himself. In so far as he exceeds his plans, he is transformed and more fully realized. This work gives us finally access to the universal and brilliant singularity of the world. . . . In the abyss where the sun is shown us, we recognize the space which is created by a free and truthful word, which, far from limiting our own freedom, rouses it, reveals it.

Jean-Pierre Burgart. *MF.* July, 1960. p. 433.
Tr. by Dorothy Nyren Curley

This double movement, from enthusiasm and lucidity, from attention, from passionate attachment, to detachment at the last moment, bears at once on two worlds: that of language and that of things (and it is essential, I think, to realize that with Francis Ponge one never deals with language alone); it is in this perhaps that we find the singularity of the author. And I see him brought to the highest point of freedom, warmth, daring in the work of the last fifteen years.

Philippe Jaccottet. *NRF.* April, 1962. p. 694.
Tr. by Dorothy Nyren Curley

Francis Ponge has adopted the method of a meticulous and objective observer of things in the outside world, which he describes not by the elliptic technique of a visionary witness, as did Reverdy, but in the exact terms of a rational yet lyrical observer. Each thing described is seen as a world in itself, divorced from the human world. We recognize in these things the working of our own fundamental needs, desires, and fears, but a cool distance reduces the current of empathy to the sheer awareness that such phenomena are present. . . . The art that conveys this world of isolated yet radiant things has a tone of lucid discretion and the dry grace of perfect drawing.

Alexander Aspel. *Contemporary French Poetry*
(Michigan). 1965. pp. 6–7

See seven prose poems in *New Directions in Prose and Poetry 17.*

PRATOLINI, VASCO (1913–   )

Pratolini began his career with childhood reminiscences that showed a delicate and very subjective talent but which hardly foreshadowed the popular novelist that he has since become. He is oriented toward communism, apparently from motives of emotional bitterness rather than from any considerable political conviction. In his hands the social themes of life among the poor become picturesque and pathetic; he embroiders them with a twilight grace that displays little true feeling for humanity. . . . In Pratolini you can see traces of the influence of American fiction.

Elena Craveri Croce. *NR*. May 10, 1948. p. 25

Mr. Pratolini belongs to the new, realistic school of Italian writers, with which we have become familiar through the work of Ignazio Silone and Carlo Levi, and his novel [*A Tale of Poor Lovers*] is one of the best things that have come out of that particular development in modern Italian literature. . . . It has a quiet, gentle, completely unsentimental compassion that lifts it high above the rather dehumanized plane that realistic and naturalistic writing in this country so often rests upon.

An Italian critic . . . praised it for making use of the myth ("tradition" is an equally good word for it) that is inherent in the living of day-to-day life. I know of no better way of pointing out the book's special accomplishment. . . . [For] the poor have a tradition. . . . If the only people who are not afraid of being poor are the poor themselves . . . , it is because they find in their heritage of long-suffering and patience a source of strength, fortitude, and even nobility. Unlike most of his American colleagues, from Dreiser on down to James Farrell and Richard Wright, Mr. Pratolini seems fully to understand this tradition.

Hamilton Basso. *NY*. July 2, 1949. p. 57

Most Italian novelists are provincial (so are all Italians) and Rome has no unifying influence in the way that Paris or London have. Pratolini is a Florentine, and a slum street near Santa Croce is all the world he needs. It is world described with complete realism, in the sense that Rossellini gives reality in his films, and not merely the illusion of reality. . . . Pratolini . . . keeps his camera (the word is appropriate) continually on the move, . . . on and on the camera goes, cutting and panning, obviously fascinated by the sordid, yet full of pity and compassion. Moravia has the same fascination for the sordid, but he approaches it as a rather commercialised Dostoievskyan, whereas Pratolini is probably the most "unliterary" novelist in Europe today. Form, character, development, plot, moral significance he knows not, and has no wish to know. He breaks all the rules, recreates life with all its rough corners and no polishing done. "Clumsy Life at her stupid work," Henry James once exclaimed, and Pratolini would agree with the remark, but call it a virtue to imitate the clumsiness and the stupidity. And how magnificently he succeeds. . . . Pratolini, with Berto, [is] among the leaders of the *écrivains engagés*.

Michael Swan. *NSN*. Oct. 29, 1949. p. 492

Considering the field of fiction, we find that some of the useful analogies and contrasts with the films relate to the problem of language. . . . Here, according to some people, Italian fiction writers found themselves hampered by the conventions of that prose tradition which for the sake of simplicity we may call humanistic. Writers like . . . Pratolini . . . split with that tradition, as it were, by splitting first of all the well-reasoned out phrase and the more objective kind of exposition; and while doing so they profited also by the local experience of lyrical intensity of language which characterized the literary atmosphere in which they grew. Pratolini is supposed to have read certain French authors with profit (Charles Louis Philippe, the author of *Babu de Montparnasse*). The narrative results . . . are by no means expressions of "spoken" and "natural" language. Rather in the same way as the language of . . . Giovanni Verga, with its use of a Sicilian tone, it is a sort of very personal idealization. It is an intellectual and literary product. In fact I think that in trying to understand and describe such developments one must practically reverse the face-value assumptions: rather than "returns to nature" they are elaborate exercises in style.

P. M. Pasinetti. *KR*. Autumn, 1950. pp. 683–4

Nihilism . . . is familiar . . . in Vasco Pratolini's [works]. . . . Pratolini's hero [in *A Hero of Our Time*] is a young lout of sixteen who . . . is, in short, a psychopath, one of those unpleasant human beings who are indifferent to the consequences of their actions. . . . Pratolini says that [this is] because he was enrolled in the Fascist junior militia and felt betrayed when Fascism collapsed, and that he is a natural hero, bold, courageous, and true, who was tricked by fate into an ignoble role. It seems, rather, that confused times provided him with an excuse for doing shabby things toward which he had an inclination. . . . The statement that he is a hero of his time involves an intolerable perversion of values. . . . Pratolini's writing is incisive and readable, and if storytelling were all, this would be a good book, but the ideas that are its backbone are sentimental and destructive, the debris of the disintegration of Fascism.

Anthony West. *NY*. Dec. 15, 1951. pp. 150, 153–4

[*The Naked Streets*] is another novel in the neo-realist vein which has become the favorite vehicle of the Italian literary revival. . . . Mr. Pratolini creates in crude but often true strokes a mood picture of Italy between the two great wars. . . . Mr. Pratolini's forte is not the projection of single personalities. His figures talk, drink and love more or less alike. What he does achieve, with an almost blunt simplicity, is something else: the evocation of the togetherness shared by all the folk in Santa Croce as they support one another against the burden of their days. These people, one senses, will endure. And their endurance is a masterpiece of mutual loyalty. The primitive lyricism with which Mr. Pratolini celebrates such fellow feeling lends the book its power.

Frederic Morton. *NYHT*. Nov. 6, 1952. p. 10

Two Brothers . . . is probably factual; but through its uncluttered lyricism of tone and feelings and its steady sense of the tears in things, the pathos of sheer mortality, it rises toward that broader significance that mere fact can only suggest. . . . What one can perceive, though faintly, is a parable of environment and its effect upon character and especially upon the would-be communion between persons—a theme Pratolini, here as elsewhere, handles with delicate insistence and great comprehension.

R. W. B. Lewis. *SR*. Dec. 8, 1962. pp. 25–6

Pratolini was . . . inspired by Fascism's often proclaimed intention of building the kind of just social order that, he felt, could not be achieved by bourgeois liberalism, Socialism, or Communism. For Pratolini, as for so many of his contemporaries, Fascism was the equivalent of state Socialism, but of a Socialism with nerve and muscle. The ideal that inspired him was the utopian vision of a nation of workers and intellectuals bound together in indestructible unity. He was convinced that Fascism was an essentially equalitarian movement whose principal aims were the elimination of capitalism and the establishment of a just social order. Fascism, he believed, had closed the gap dividing manual and intellectual labor. . . . But Fascism had not repudiated capitalism, and Pratolini began to have certain apprehensions about the direction in which the Italian government was moving after the Ethiopian campaign. . . . In the summer of 1936, Pratolini was introduced to Elio Vittorini. . . . Vittorini was among the first in Florentine intellectual circles to make a decisive break with Fascism, and he was responsible for accelerating Pratolini's disengagement from Fascism in 1936.

Frank Rosengarten. *MLN*. Jan., 1964. pp. 37, 39

Circling the sternly elegant core of Florence runs a broad peripheral zone teeming with an intelligent, urbane, critical and politically sophisticated left-wing proletariat that plays a vital part in that city's complex creative life. Just as the French miners have had their Zola, Sicily's fishermen their Verga and Gibbsville, U.S.A. it's O'Hara, so this very special world has its chronicler. He is Vasco Pratolini. Born in 1913, he has been working on two widely divergent yet subtly connected levels: the historical, in his great but still uncompleted trilogy, *"Una Storia Italiana,"* . . . and the contemporaneous, to which belongs [*Bruno Santini*]. . . . Pratolini has given us in Bruno Santini another "hero of our times," but this is a positive one who finds his true measure not so much in alienation as in a deeply-felt sense of human and class solidarity and in an awareness of its strength.

This is no facile idyll to be swallowed down at one gulp. It is a work of human and class solidarity, and one which requires what might be called creative writing. But this reviewer knows of no other recent novel that gives a clearer insight into the socio-political reasons which prompt this "aristocracy of the Italian working class" to lend its continued support to what has become Europe's largest Communist party outside Russia.

Helene Cantarella. NYT. Feb. 28, 1965. p. 4

In Vasco Pratolini's naturalistic novels . . . (*A Tale of Poor Lovers, A Hero of Our Time, The Naked Streets*) he has evidenced a steady growth, which now culminates in *Bruno Santini*. Rooted in the painful dynamic of the author's own life, his own family, and his own class, his sturdy proletariat pushes always stubbornly upward, through the infected atmosphere of the tenements of his native Florence toward the agonizing realization that the poor can achieve maturity only through the tragedy of compromise. We must forget, then, the socialism of a Silone, the poetic existentialism of a Pavese, the grim cynicism of a Moravia. Pratolini's is a more affirmative world. . . . We have read about death in the miasma of many great cities: Moravia's Rome, Mann's Venice, Genet's Paris, Montherlant's Madrid, even Rechy's Forty-second Street. But death in Pratolini's Florence gives way to a bigger life. Pratolini is a big man and a healthy one.

Warrington Winters. SR. March 6, 1965. pp. 28–9

Once, novels were really novel. The form emphasized the characters' total freedom, their emancipation from the prearranged order of neo-classical art. . . . Parallel with this freedom of behavior there went, from Richardson onward, an ever-increasing flexibility and subtlety in the formal devices open to the novelist. . . . Both kinds of freedom, of physical or psychological action and of formal expressiveness, culminated in the work of Proust and Joyce, which in many ways brought the free development of the novel to a halt. . . . For most practitioners since then . . . the choice has been, at best, consolidation, at worst, imitation. . . . Zola described working class life better than Signor Pratolini, and the central situation of his novel . . . takes one straight back to *Sons and Lovers*. . . . *Bruno Santini* [is] a fundamentally worthy book. . . . The book is worthy because of Signor Pratolini's positive feelings about humanity; but the writing is so drab and unselective, the naturalistic detail so pointlessly piled up, that I found it a grinding bore to read.

Bernard Bergonzi. NYR. March 25, 1965. p. 14

Since the background of time and place [in *Bruno Santini*] . . . are part of the author's own experience, the novel as a realistic creation has vigor and authority.

But what does it mean—what of the allegory? Here, I think, the Italian title supplies the clue. In the original the work was called *La costanza della ragione* ("The Constancy of Reason")—a phrase taken from Dante's *Vita Nuova,* used to describe the poet's fidelity to the dead Beatrice. . . . Although it would be fanciful . . . to see young Bruno as a neo-realistic Dante, yet the "constancy of reason" is a refuge as appropriate for Bruno as it was for the poet of old.

Bruno will write no *Divine Comedy,* but through love, grief and self-questioning, he has arrived at a stage of maturity, a sense of purpose, proper to his condition and his times. . . . Illusion and betrayals will trouble him no more; in the constancy of reason lie compassion for others and understanding of oneself. Pratolini has given us a fine novel, "tender and true" in the old phrase—true for the sharp and sometimes even sordid naturalistic detail, tender for its evocation of full-dimensioned, warm-hearted humanity.

Thomas G. Bergin. NYHT. March 28, 1965. p. 17

Many Italian novels are . . . dedicated to the problems, habits and psychology of the workers, but few writers manage to sound authoritative. Pratolini does. He is the best of them.

Consider his use of language: Italian has been for centuries a musty and bookish Mandarin. People spoke it seldom and only on formal occasion. At home and with their friends, they preferred the local patois which vividly expressed their feelings and best described their familiar world. (It is still almost impossible to write witty comedy dialogue in

Italian or translate it from French or English.) Contemporary authors feel caged within these dead literary forms, and are trying to escape. They experiment with new words; graft expressions borrowed from provincial dialects and street talk of the common people into the literary language. Pratolini . . . has a natural advantage over his competitors. He not only belongs to the people but his native *Fiorentino* is the wittiest and richest of all patois. He uses it as skillfully as a jeweler making a finely chiseled *oeuvre d'art* from base metal.

Luigi Barzini. *Nation.* May 3, 1965. p. 482

Bruno Santini [*La costanza della ragione*] is the familiar story of the education of a young man, an account of what he has to forget, and the suffering, sordidness, and disgust that attends the rites of passage into maturity. I can already hear the cries that would go up from my classroom if I were to read it with my students, for the rites of passage have nothing to do with them; this is not Samoa, for Christ's sake! From their embattled visceral position within our parochial moral superciliousness, they would call Bruno, at the end of the book, a rat fink, at least, for he reaches the conclusion that "the desecration of our feelings introduces us to maturity." It is, of course, an outrage to have one's feeling desecrated. Is nothing sacred? Yes, but not one's feelings, one's desires. The knowledge of reality is sacred. It is earned with too much agony to be any less than that. The knowledge that one's life is lived in either acknowledged or unacknowledged complicity with others —regardless of what one's own heart's desires in the matter may be— that is the "constancy of reason." "Constant" because it is always there, silently judging our vanities.

Wayne Carver. *CM.* Fall, 1965. pp. 98–9

See *A Hero of Our Time, The Naked Streets, A Tale of Poor Lovers, Two Brothers,* and *Bruno Santini* (novels).

PROUST, MARCEL (1871–1922)

He will never be read by the large class of novel readers who create the market demand for novels of action and plot; nor will he appeal to that hardly less numerous class—chiefly women—who find the emotional novel palatable food. However, those who, like the writer, cannot push themselves by struggling through a detective story and by whom the most skillfully constructed plot can be endured only if the harassment which it causes is counterbalanced by the charm of its literary style or its interpretation of the personality of the author reacting to conditions more or less common to all mankind, may find in M. Proust a novelist whom they can ill afford to ignore. And no writer of fact or fiction today would be just to himself were he to proceed with his art without making the acquaintance of this master artificer and psychologist. Proust will be remembered as a pioneer who explored the jungle of the unconscious memory and a marvelous interpreter of the laws governing associated memories. I doubt not his name will be as inseparably connected with the novel of the future as that of de Maupassant or Poe has been with the short story of the last few decades, even while his wares will still find scant sale, save to writers, dilettantes, professional students of letters, of form and of psychology.

> Joseph Collins. *The Doctor Looks at Literature*
> (Doran). 1923. pp. 116–7

It is significant that the majority of his images are botanical. He assimilates the human to the vegetal. He is conscious of humanity as flora, never as fauna. (There are no black cats and faithful hounds in Proust.) .... This preoccupation accompanies very naturally his complete indifference to moral values and human justices. Flower and plant have no conscious will. They are shameless, exposing their genitals. And so in a sense are Proust's men and women, whose will is blind and hard, but never self-conscious, never abolished in the pure perception of a pure subject. They are victims of their volition, active with grotesque predetermined activity, within the narrow limits of an impure world. But shameless.

> Samuel Beckett. *Proust* (Grove). 1931. pp. 68–9

Whether narrating a series of events, describing a scene, or cataloguing the contents of the mind of a character at any moment, he is certain to select incidents, to set down particulars, and to list details which most would have omitted in favor of certain others now in their turn passed over by Proust. The result is the creation of a strange new world. Perhaps we recognize its elements even though we have not ever been consciously aware of their existence; but the whole which they compose is new. We enter the pages of *Remembrance of Things Past* as we might enter a realm totally unfamiliar, and before we are aware of the fact we have closed the door behind us, forgetting the standards and the conventions of familiar life as completely as we forget its personages. For the world which the novel reveals is more than merely strange; it is also so consistent, so self-sustaining, and so logically complete that we are never by any reference led back to the other world of our ordinary concerns.

> Joseph Wood Krutch. Introduction to *Remembrance*
> *of Things Past* (Random). 1934. p. xiii

The beauty of Proust's masterpiece is that while it hits off with such exquisite malice all the fine shades of middle-class snobbishness and upper-class arrogance, and discloses with such subtle sympathy all the humorous refinements of old-family-retainers, its *real theme,* its inmost essence, has to do with the most evasive element in our secret personal life, namely with those obscure feelings of delicious ecstasy which are as hard to arrest or analyse in their swift passage as it is hard to explain why such small, slight, trivial, and casual chances are the cause of their rising up out of the depths.

These rare individual ecstasies are to Proust—or at least to that prophetic soul in Proust embodied in his hero—precisely what the same experiences were to Wordsworth, that it to say, authentic "intimations of immortality"; and it is impossible to think of any great novel that proves this daring proposition, and this very definite proposition, so effectively as Proust does. Neither Goethe in *Wilhelm Meister* nor Romain Rolland in *Jean Christophe* conveys to us such a clear-cut unmistakable "mesage" as to the nature of the human soul and its relation to the Eternal as Proust does in *A la Recherche du temps perdu.*

John Cowper Powys. Enjoyment of Literature
(Simon). 1938. pp. 481–2

Basically his difficulties sprang from his temperament. The sensitivity of his emotional side gave him insights and aspirations which the weakness of his active nature prevented him from realizing, while the acuity of his intelligence precluded the narcotic of self-deception. He had a tendency to asthma and to homosexuality; he rationalized both, but he was unable to avoid the conviction that both were in a sense his own fault. He was not responsible for the original respiratory sensitivity, but he believed that with a steady adherence to a sound régime of diet, exercise, work, and rest, and with a little self-control, a little willingness to face discomfort without recourse to drugs, he could conquer asthma. This effort he could not make, and his incessant lamentations about his health were his excuse to himself as much as to his correspondents, for his failure. Similarly, with homosexuality: he was not to blame for the predisposition, but he felt that he should and could conquer his inclination. . . . The hope that he had lost for himself he put increasingly into his work. If he had failed as a man, he could at least find consolation in his art.

Harold March. The Two Worlds of Marcel Proust
(U. of Pennsylvania). 1948. pp. 250–1

It is a fact of importance that in all the greatest works of fiction, there is almost always a monster, and sometimes more than one. The characters thus designated are at once superhuman and inhuman, and they dominate the works in which they appear, giving them unity in a way that nothing else could do. This is true of Balzac's Vautrin, and it is true of Proust's Charlus. The monster opens windows on to mysterious depths just because it is beyond our power to understand him completely. He passes beyond our range of vision, if only by the horror he inspires: but he does, nevertheless, contain elements of a kind that are in us as well. Had the circumstances been different, we might have become what he is, and this thought at once terrifies and fascinates us. Monsters provide the story with unexplored and secret depths which reveal the sublime.

Before Proust, Shakespeare alone had succeeded in orchestrating the magic dissonances amidst which these monsters move. The humor which expresses itself in lovely lines, the earthbound bodies which can loose spirits on the world, the allegories and the ravishing images which end in horseplay, the flicker of fairy lights, all these things bring the world of Shakespeare to our minds. Proust, like Shakespeare, had plumbed the extremes of human misery, but, like Shakespeare, found in humor a saving grace, and, again like Shakespeare, serenity in Time Regained.

André Maurois. *Proust: Portrait of a Genius* (Harper).
1950. p. 246

The greatest virtue that Proust possesses can probably be best represented by one word—depth. Where others would have passed by, content with rendering the world of appearances, Proust dislocates, assimilates the shattered fragments, and reconstructs them. Like his hero Elstir, he spares no effort to "dissolve that aggregate of reasonings that we call vision." His own vision has the newness and the same quality of wonder as that of a child. But it is supplemented by memory, by knowledge of other artists who have already penetrated into the secrets of reality, by an intense concentration of the attention and by knowledge. Proust probably appreciated the impressionists most among the painters of his age, but Cézanne, and before him Chardin, are those to whom he stands closest. His treatment of concrete objects . . . has all the solidity and the multidimensional quality of a post-impressionist painting. And it retains motion or the potentiality of motion, grace, and elusiveness as well.

Henri Peyre. *The Contemporary French Novel*
(Oxford). 1955. pp. 82–3

A la Recherche de Temps Perdu is a homeopathic treatment against death. In contradistinction to a writer like Thomas Mann, who, in *The*

Magic Mountain, maintains that since the act of dying is the one and only act about which nobody has ever been able to speak, it cannot in any way be an object of knowledge, Proust exerts himself to the utmost to detect the presence of nothingness in being, to see all human beings as creatures granted a reprieve from death, and to consider himself as one of them. ". . . for I understood"—he says—that "dying was nothing new, but that, on the contrary, I had since my childhood, died many times."

Georges Piroué. Proust's Way (Essential Books). 1957. p. 139

The intellect has a curious history in Proust's novel. Generally in the earlier volumes, and even in *Le Temps retrouvé,* it is represented as an inferior function of the mind, one that falsifies and distorts. It is almost invariably contrasted with sensibility, which alone reveals the real world. But now, in discussing his novel, Proust suddenly remarks that the intellect is not after all contemptible. The truths that it draws from reality may at least supplement, may, as it were, "enchase in a grosser substance," the impressions of sensibility or memory. But as he goes on, Proust indicates that these truths of the intellect are far more than a supplement: they are the very substance of a work of art. For the novelist is a man who instinctively, from his earliest years, has trained himself to see the general in the particular and to ignore everything that is not general. . . . There is no suggestion, at this point, that his memory is arbitrary or mystical, or that its exercise is always accompanied by unearthly happiness. In fact, the sense of relief that the novelist feels comes from his intellect, which enables him to understand his suffering, to represent it in its most general form, and thus, in some measure at least, to escape its strangling grip.

Richard H. Barker. Marcel Proust (Criterion). 1958.
pp. 311–2

Most novels that deal with society take on some of the meretricious gaudiness that it is their avowed purpose to deplore. Their authors become guilty of the snobbishness and triviality of which they accuse their characters. . . . Proust comes closest to escaping the contamination of his subject matter because he does not set society apart from the rest of mankind. To him the differences between class and class are superficial. Snobbishness reigns on all levels, so why does it matter which level one selects to study? Why not, indeed, pick the highest level, particularly if one's own snobbishness is thus gratified? Society in Proust parades before us, having to represent not a segment of mankind, but something closer to mankind itself. It is the very boldness of

Proust's assumption that his universe is *the* universe, like the boldness of his assumption that all love is jealousy and all men homosexuals, that gives to his distorted picture a certain universal validity. It is his faith that a sufficiently careful study of each part will reveal the whole, that the analysis of a dinner party can be as illuminating as an analysis of a war. It is his glory that he very nearly convinces us.

Louis Auchincloss. *PR*. Fall, 1960. p. 701

Remembrance of Things Past is the story of how a little boy becomes a writer. That is the first—and last—simple statement that can be made about it. A truer definition is impossibly complicated: it is the biography of a novelist written by its subject, who has decided to write a novel instead of an autobiography, and whose only novel is the biography he is writing. A book in which real people, natural objects, and institutions appear, yet resorting, like a fairy tale, to deception to reach the truth, *Remembrance of Things Past* is a house of mirrors. Scenes are mapped out and actions take place. Resembling a novel, it is not what the French would call a "roman" or what we would call a "story," and it uniquely combines the qualities of the epic and the lyric. Though its characters end up as heroes, it is completely metaphorical. It is the first epic ever written whose battles are mostly internal; yet those battles are merely the minor actions in a gigantic poem.

Howard Moss. *SwR*. Summer, 1962. pp. 451–2

If Proust's work (even *Jean Santeuil*, imperfect and unsatisfactory and unintegrated as it may be) retains a perennial charm for us it is not because of its story or people or ideas but because of its lyricism and poetry. Auden once wrote: "Poetry makes nothing happen"—an observation that is especially applicable to this book by Proust which contains such large tracts of stationary idylls. No one is capable of refreshing our vision of the beauties of nature more effectively than Proust in parts of *Jean Santeuil* and in the whole Combray section of *Swann's Way*— not even the Romantic poets or Rousseau.

Milton Hindus. *A Reader's Guide to Marcel Proust*
(Farrar). 1962. p. 220

The revelation Marcel receives in *Le temps retrouvé* which shows him the unity of his entire past enables him to recount this life in such a manner that it contains this revealed unity. Thus the novel not only sets forth the revelation; it is also a demonstration of it. In the writing of the novel in accordance with the principles of the revelation a synthesis is performed between seeming irreconcilables—between sleeping and waking, day and night, consciousness and unconsciousness, objectivity and subjectivity, past and present. The unity of all aspects of an individual life can only be demonstrated in a work of art, since it can never be fully apprehended by observing life as it is lived in time and space. Only the creation of a work of art operating, like the dream, outside of time and space is capable of revealing such a unity.

William Stewart Bell. *Proust's Nocturnal Muse*
(Columbia). 1962. pp. 268–9

The Proustian experience is often labeled Platonic because memory plays a great role in it and because the word *idea* is used repeatedly in *The Past Recaptured*. Platonism, however, revokes the notion of a serene and unbroken ascent toward the Ideal, bearing little resemblance to what happens in *Remembrance of Things Past*. Almost to the end, the dynamic element of the novel is amour-propre, which leads outward and downward from the relatively high starting point of Combray. This direction is reversed only in extremis, and the change cannot be logically explained. All we can say—and this remains an impression rather than a demonstrable fact—is that the downward movement had to be pursued in extremis before it could mysteriously reverse itself. Similarly, Dante went down to the bottom of his Inferno and, as he kept descending upon Satan's own body without ever turning around, suddenly found himself climbing toward Purgatory and Paradise.

René Girard. *Proust* (Prentice-Hall). 1962. p. 11

Proust has made us focus our attention on the process of memory iself, not the meaning of it for the characterization of the first-person narrator. We thus become so conscious of the personality who is manipulating the first-person narrator, for whom the narrator is speaking, that the autobiographical relationship is set up. In other words, from the outset we must read *Remembrance of Things Past* not only for what is happening in the action (a first-person narrator talking about himself as a child) but for its relationship to the authorial personality. And, as he often does, he actually tells us, in an oblique fashion, what he is doing, for he says of the book the child had been reading that "my thoughts had run into a channel of their own, until I myself seemed actually to have become the subject of my book . . ." (note, however, the word *seemed!*). The dimension of memory is involved; again, not the first-person narrator's memory alone, but that of the authorial personality as he describes the narrator remembering. There are thus three different *times* involved: the childhood of Marcel, the adulthood of the remembering narrator, and the time at which the authorial personality is remembering and creating.

Louis D. Rubin, Jr. KR. Summer, 1963. p. 402

The book's central metaphor, which arches over the entire action, interior and exterior, is contained in the *deux côtés,* a division of the environs of Combray and of the universe into two parts later reconciled and recognized as one. Yet it has never been pointed out that the *deux côtés* represent most basically the action of metaphor itself—different elements folding into one. Proust-Marcel lives a palpable metaphor that implants in the story itself "the links essential for good style" and that suggest by geography the gradual commingling of contrasting areas of consciousness. . . . The action which dominates all of *A la recherche,* then, is the action of metaphor: the reconciliation of a duality or, in more complex cases, of a multiplicity. It encompasses all aspects of the book, from the aspects of personality to the division of society itself to the stereoscopic assembling of past and present. Marcel finally understands that he has himself produced this great fusion by growing up, by coming to terms with himself, by living his own life as no one else could live it for him, and by heeding the vocation of literature.

Roger Shattuck. Proust's Binoculars (Random). 1963.
pp. 123, 126

Marcel retells his dreams and fantasies, but he remains essentially an insomniac, who stays wide awake while others sleep. Among the various optical instruments with which he metaphorically supplements the naked eye, he suggests that his book could be used as a sort of magnifying glass for studying ourselves—scanning the fine print, no doubt, and reading between the lines. Elsewhere, apropos of *Sesame and Lilies,* he remarks of books in general what seems to be particularly true of *A la recherche du temps perdu*: "reading is our guide whose magic keys open the doors of dwellings we could not have entered within the depths of ourselves." Not so much for the modelling of his characters as for the training of our perceptions, for our enhanced awareness of the way things happen to happen, of how human beings respond or do not respond to one another, we may talk of keys in connection with Proust. That is why the serious reader, completing the final page of the many-volumed novel, is not the same person who opened the first volume some time ago.

Harry Levin. The Gates of Horn (Oxford). 1963. p. 444

Within the space of a mere quarter of a century, Proust has come to represent a new classicism in the history of French letters. He is a classical writer at least in the sense that he is an established writer, one whose name has become synonymous with a certain style and with a certain philosophy concerning the nature of reality. A work of such dimension, accompanied by such success in establishing a place for itself in a long tradition of letters, must inevitably come from a tradition which it summarizes. More and more the work of Proust is looked upon as the supreme inventory of romanticism and symbolism. It recaptures, in its extreme introspectiveness, in its meditations on nature, and in its analyses of the artistic creations of man, the experiences both conscious and subconscious which we associate with the romantic and symbolist movements.

Wallace Fowlie. *SwR.* Autumn, 1963. pp. 580–1

See *Remembrance of Things Past* (multivolume novel).

QUASIMODO, SALVATORE (1901–   )

Considered at first as the most typical and extreme representative of *poesia ermetica,* Quasimodo has steadfastly progressed toward a clearer statement, a more lucid style, a chaster feeling. . . . The man has purified and the poet renewed himself through the trial of war, invasion and defeat. Almost all . . . [his later] poems evoke, with classical restraint but with moving sincerity, the tragedy of destruction, hatred and bloodshed. The poet complains that it is impossible to sing "with the stranger's foot upon one's heart," yet he sings: he sings "day by day," not the tragic pageant of history, but the chronicle of life under the pressure of world shattering events. And while he sings, it seems to us that we see new flowers growing again on the soil of an Italy eternally ancient and eternally young.

Renato Poggioli. Ital. March, 1948. pp. 55–6

Salvatore Quasimodo certainly has an important place in the contemporary Italian Pleiad, even if some of his recent work seems disappointing; and to be sure, careful reservations on his ultimate validity as a poet, at least in his post-war phase, have come from some critical quarters. His relative position in the hierarchy culminating in Ungaretti and Montale is still a matter of debate; yet when Spagnoletti resents the "literary" quality of his diction (De Robertis would say "Parnassian"), it has to be added in all fairness that this is also a plausible part of his Southern heritage—the rich feeling for words as intrinsic melody. . . . In Quasimodo's case we should consider the additional factor of Sicily's insular mentality—not as an excuse, but as a characterization. Likewise, his translation of the Greek lyrical poets before the last war was somehow a return to the Mothers—to the deepest available layer of his culture.

Glauco Cambon. IQ. Fall, 1959. pp. 16–17

His earliest poems were published in 1930 . . . [and] by 1938 Quasimodo had become a recognized exponent of the "hermetic" school of poetry. . . . Critics almost unanimously acknowledged the mastery of Quasimodo and the modernity of his verse, whose "verbal and rhythmic sensitivity, at times exquisite," was well evidenced by many of his youthful poems. Although he had begun writing under the partial influence of Carducci, Pascoli, D'Annunzio, and of his contemporaries Ungaretti and Montale,

Quasimodo soon found a style of his own through which he could sing, with both passion and detachment, his loneliness and anguish. . . . His gradual maturing coincided with his particularly fortunate "encounter" with the Greek lyrical poets, and with his "discovery" of his native soil. . . . A poet of the highest integrity, supremely conscious of our condition, Quasimodo has never despaired. Not an optimist in any sense of the word, he has an indestructible faith in the written word. He has sought, with words, and with all the intellectual resources at his disposal, to illuminate for himself and for us the meaning of life and man's condition in the universe.

Sergio Pacifici. *SR*. Nov. 7, 1959. pp. 20, 42

He has dared, to a degree unusual in this tradition-ridden society, to employ his limpid, sensitive, classical idiom to confront "social" themes: the anguish of contemporary man, and to affirm a new humanism. . . . What worries . . . objective critics is whether Quasimodo's more recent work has not lost force and beauty precisely to the degree that he has committed himself to a too narrowly conceived "engagement." The earlier work . . . is the poignant lyricism of a humanist who has drunk deeply of Greek and Latin springs, and, in the blaze of Mediterranean light, projects a luminous grief-stricken image of modern man. . . . [His] translations, especially from Greek and Latin, are fresh limpid re-creations, not transcriptions, and, in the judgement of many, represent Quasimodo's highest achievement.

Sidney Alexander. *Reporter*. Dec. 10, 1959. p. 38

I arrived in Rome for a short visit on an unfortunate day. The Nobel Prize had just been awarded to the Sicilian poet Salvatore Quasimodo and this seemed to turn literary circles upside down. I must say I shared in the consternation when we thought of the possible claimants from Ezra Pound to Malraux. If I had played guessing games and had set down the first twelve likely Italians, my list would not necessarily have included Quasimodo. . . . Even if the list were confined to Italian poets —excluding novelists and other writers—the mystery remains unsolved. In Italy for years there have been three poets whom nearly everybody considers more highly than Quasimodo. They are Giuseppe Ungaretti . . . Eugenio Montale . . . and . . . Umberto Saba.

Bernard Wall. *TC*. Dec., 1959. p. 486

His voice is not only unique in contemporary European poetry, but it is a voice of rarest distinction: absolutely free of rhetorical influence, at once generous and fastidious . . . the formal perfection of his verse is matched by both solidity and urgency of matter. . . . Italian critics have made much of Quasimodo's changes of style, of his evolution . . . but what strikes the reader most forcibly is the continuity of Quasimodo's work, not its discontinuity. . . . From first to last Quasimodo is an extraordinarily subtle but rather simple poet, compared with such writers as Montale, Eliot, Yeats. His poetic extensions have been lateral rather than in (intellectual) depth; his gains have been gains in technical mastery, made possible by the influx of fresh subject matter. . . . Quasimodo triumphs in the abolition of both facile dualism and mystical vagueness, in the resolute allegiance to what *is,* and, since it can be, *will* be. Not only is the past on his side, but the future as well.

Francis Golffing. BA. Winter, 1960. p. 17

While a number of the earlier poems may have seemed derivative, with echoes of D'Annunzio and Pascoli and certain attitudes of despair reminiscent of Ungaretti or Montale, it was also evident that Quasimodo had fused these elements in the alchemy of a personal style. The sensual music of his verse was not audible in any of his contemporaries, who were perhaps wary of the facile musicality of too much Italian poetry. Compared to the harsher line of Montale, for instance, the lush cadences of many of Quasimodo's earlier poems make him sound less "contemporary." To find the equal of his rich melody one must go as far back as Tasso. . . . In Quasimodo's poems of the Thirties one finds phrases whose music, while more subdued, is hardly less striking. . . . But despite his musicality, Quasimodo shared with Ungaretti a sparse phrase reduced to the bare essentials of discourse, yet rich in suggestive power. Like Montale, his poems encompassed a vast and changing landscape over which moved the elemental forces of winds, tides and rivers, and he filled it with the sounds of nature and with things that stand as mute witnesses to the solitude of man. And like his contemporaries, but more than they, he discovered in this world stripped of illusion the presence of mystic signs.

Louis R. Rossi. ChR. Spring, 1960. p. 4

Even if Quasimodo would never utilize the rich and earthy Sicilian speech, as did Pirandello, he remains admittedly a Sicilian Greek (*greco siculo*) endowed with the one gift bestowed by that stark, picturesque island: a tremendous flair for words and communication. . . . Although . . . [he] abandoned his homeland . . . his greatest poetry sings of that island. . . . Quasimodo composes in free verse and without rhyme, and his stylistic tricks are simple enough (suppression of articles and conjunctions, for example). . . . The greatness of Quasimodo is in his traditional power of nature description, classical expression, and concern with the eternal themes of death, love, solitude, campanilism, and reminiscence. . . . Quasimodo the paysagist is of the impressionist school. The word-paintings in his earlier and latest poems are sheer delight. The cumulative effect of his nature elements is powerful.

Robert J. Clements. *SR*. June 11, 1960. p. 14

Quasimodo goes more easily into English than many other poets, for two reasons. First, he relies for much of his effect on his strikingly concrete and vivid imagery, which gives its own message just because it is so firmly conceived. His keen, observing eye is always at work. Secondly, he avoids rhyme and uses a regular rhythm in his verse which is akin to much that we use ourselves. . . . [There is] an unusual charge of emotion which Quasimodo puts into his restrained and almost classical verse. . . . His latest poems show how he can face a situation in all its reality and in all his passionate response to it. For this he was indeed well trained by his "Hermetic" period, when, under the influence of Giuseppe Ungaretti, he made every word do its full task and pruned his poetry of anything that smacked of padding or rhetoric. . . . What counts for us with Quasimodo is that he combines this self-control with powerful emotions drawn from the agony of the modern world and the special tribulations of Italy. More than any living European poet he speaks for the whole of Europe, and is not afraid of attempting themes of profound and common concern.

C. M. Bowra. *NYT*. July 3, 1960. p. 4

His verse does show an independent development which no other major Italian poet can rival. For Quasimodo began as a member (some would say the founder) of the "hermetic" school and is now a proponent of something very close to "social oriented" verse. The "hermetics" dominated Italian poetry for most of the Fascist period; "hermeticism" in a broader sense has characterized much post-Eliot poetry in the countries of the West (with perhaps the exception of Spain). Its roots are in the French symbolists; its distinguishing features are a highly personalized imagery, the cult of the word, and an austere intellectualism, often cryptic and obscure. By no means derivative, the poets of Italy made of hermeticism a vehicle for expression of private anguish, nostalgia and even affirmation. And such in fact are the themes of Quasimodo.

Thomas G. Bergin. *NYHT*. July 10, 1960. p. 8

The poetry of Salvatore Quasimodo . . . hermetic in its earliest phases and given to what the critic Anceschi called "a metaphysic of aridity," did something of an about-face during the bitter experiences of the Second World War. The German occupation of northern Italy in particular did much to shock Quasimodo out of his poetic seclusion: in grief and protest he began to write poetry of wider appeal, its avowed purpose to *rifare l'uomo,* to "remake man," a task for which many of Quasimodo's critics considered his literary talents inadequate. . . . But few would question the grace of phrasing and rhythm . . . and the vividness and power of the imagery in such a poem as *"Dalla rocca di Bergamo alta."* . . . Like many of Quasimodo's poems, this one is addressed to an impersonal "you." Perhaps for the same reason that the other poems were: the device breaks the circle of the poet's loneliness and establishes communication with someone, if only an ideal reader.

Wallace Fowlie. *The Poem Itself,* ed. by
Stanley Burnshaw (Holt). 1960. p. 326

The immediate impression, if one compares Quasimodo's work before and after the war, is that what has happened is . . . a passage from poetry of the private world, closed in upon itself, to poetry of more open communication. . . . The poetry of exclusion, whose logical end is the brief cry or, indeed, silence itself has been transformed into the poetry of affirmation. Quasimodo's struggle against silence is significant. . . . Silence, often the silence of the night, is an image that occurs frequently in Quasimodo's pre-war poetry. It is a silence which envelops all things, which deadens. . . . It is a silence that invites breaking, yet the breaking can only be of the moment, a brief cry . . . an instant of anguish. Here is the very pattern of Quasimodo's early poetry, the poetry of the isolated word, of the carefully protected image, of the voice that dare hardly speak. . . . With the coming of the war this all-enclosing, impalpable silence acquired new substance. . . . The cry in the silence became one of horror and protest, not of impotence, and that cry reached out to his fellow men who were fellows in suffering.

C. A. McCormick. *Mjn.* Sept., 1961. pp. 269–72
See *Selected Writings;* also *The Poet and the Politician* (essays).

QUENEAU, RAYMOND (1903–   )

If a situation or a remark contains a germ of a certain style or tone, Queneau immediately seizes upon it to create an exuberant parody. In the expansion of the idea, the epic is always present, but it is often complemented by a parody on detective novels, or journalistic, analytic, neo-realistic, and philosophical styles. This gives an effect not unlike a distortion of the way the so-called serious authors might treat the same themes. Queneau goes much farther than Marcel Aymé. Although both authors bring the realm of the marvelous into the commonplace, Queneau, less fantastic and less concerned with satire of what is immediately contemporary, evades realism to a greater degree, distorts with greater ingenuity, and never offers a slice of life he has not first completely transformed by stylistic procedures.

Jacques Guicharnaud. *YFS.* No. 8, 1951. p. 44

Raymond Queneau is perhaps not a great novelist but he is a great writer and an incomparable virtuoso of style. His chief concern seems to be re-creating language through effective use of colloquial speech, of slang and of many of the devices of rhetoric, entertainingly used. But he owes as much to Charlie Chaplin as he does to James Joyce. . . . The stumbling blocks for Queneau are probably his immense store of knowledge, rivaling that of Joyce and occasionally intruding into the tale as pedantry, his total disregard of the structure of his novels, hence some monotony in the "flat" comic characters, and an ending usually unequal to a brilliant beginning.

Henri Peyre. *The Contemporary French Novel*
(Oxford). 1955. p. 328

A poet as well as a novelist, Queneau has written one novel, *Chêne et Chien* (The Oak and the Dog), in verse form and has also incorporated verse passages into his prose novels. More important than this, however, is his extension of certain poetic conventions to the novel form itself; not, as with the surrealists, the convention of metaphor, which he uses sparingly, but that of repetition. . . . A sentence, perhaps a single word, recurs insistently. Characters alone or in groups of two or three (Queneau is especially fond of the conventional fairy tale trilogy) advance and retreat at regular intervals and mirror each other's words and gestures. Our final impression is that of a dance, at times stately, at times wildly orgiastic, but always ceremonial in nature.

Germaine Brée and Margaret Guiton. *An Age of Fiction*
(Rutgers). 1957. p. 171

Great is the need of something to laugh at, and one of the present successes, *Zazie dans le Métro,* is a funny book. . . . *On se moque de tout*—the younger generation, law and order, tourists, even the French language. The author catches exactly the voice of the Paris populo, and his use of argot and his linguistic gymnastics add a certain savour. . . .

Queneau keeps his story going with his high spirits and ironic wit, but there is hardly any plot, and the characters are made of papier-mâché.

Len Ortzen. *TC*. Dec., 1959. pp. 463–4

Intellectually Queneau is a formidable proposition. . . . He has said that his hobby is mathematics, but it is less known that he is one of the two greatest French experts in Hegelian philosophy, although the Hegelian concept of man's relationship to history does permeate his work, accounts for much of the mental processes of his heroes and finds full expression in that admirable novel, *Le Dimanche de la Vie*. But with the mental equipment of *un grand penseur* Queneau wrote his personal novels and his personal poems. One could say that the characteristic stamp of his work is timidity: a profound timidity and hesitancy which is expressed in the sadness of his poetry, the helplessness of his heroes, the wistfulness of the desires and hopes of his characters, and his humour expresses this too. He is undoubtedly the funniest writer the French have had for a long time; but his vision is not that of a humorist like Gogol. It is of the essential sadness of human life.

Sonia Pitt-Rivers. *LMg*. Nov., 1960. p. 76

With *Zazie* Queneau, in many ways the most refined and esoteric of French writers, became a best-seller. If, in reaching this consummation, he did not aim at, or achieve, his own highest standards, the success of the book was nevertheless a great vindication: for, if he was right in campaigning for a literature in the language actually spoken by the common man, he had to demonstrate the common man's response to hearing—and above all *reading*—his own everyday speech. In *Zazie* as in some of his *chansons* Queneau has triumphantly bridged that most dangerous gulf of our culture, the gulf between the artist, the intellectual, the highbrow on the one hand and the common man on the other.

Martin Esslin. *The Novelist as Philosopher*, ed. by
John Cruickshank (Oxford). 1962. p. 96

In many respects Queneau was one of the first novelists of the absurd; often he preceded other writers who a little later took up in a serious or dramatic way themes which he had treated playfully and stripped of their tragic character. . . . Skeptical, without presuppositions and false illusions, he was led to turn from a world of appearances, from a world denuded of significance to consecrate himself to the only justification for existence—amusement. Quite often critics, seeing only the result, have judged his work superficially and have refused to take seriously a writer who plays with serious ideas, as if, in all logic, it were not natural to treat the absurd absurdly.

Andrée Bergens. *Raymond Queneau* (Librarie Droz). 1963. p. 223. Tr. by Dorothy Nyren Curley

See *Pierrot, The Skin of Dreams,* and *Zazie* (novels).

QUINTERO, JOAQUÍN ÁLVAREZ
See Álvarez Quintero, Joaquín

QUINTERO, SERAFÍN ÁLVAREZ
See Álvarez Quintero, Serafín

RADIGUET, RAYMOND (1903–1923)

The Devil in the Flesh is like an expert dry-point; there is the same economy without any fashionable "starkness," the same intimacy of work done with speed that comes from decision rather than slovenly haste, and the same quickening of the imagination. It is that decision, the complete lack of adolescent groping, which is the chiefest of Radiguet's talents; and, though the sureness of his strokes is aided by the cruelty of adolescent egoism, it is to his credit that he progresses beyond this partial insensitivity and never uses it to obtain a *frisson nouveau.*

> Geoffrey Stone. *Bkm.* April, 1932. p. 112

Both *The Devil in the Flesh* and *The Count's Ball* are amplifications and adaptations of the legend of Nero's behavior at the burning of Rome, except that Radiguet added another touch by making his characters seriously and morally concerned over relatively inconsequential affairs, rather than perversely frivolous at the spectacle of disaster. They live as they would live in normal times, chiefly disturbed at their relationships with other people, and it is the reader who establishes the contrast between their absorption in their small matters, in their trivial jealousies and vague disappointments, and the great collective death struggles going on off-stage.

> Robert Cantwell. *NR.* April 6, 1932. pp. 214–5

Raymond Radiguet appeared. He was fifteen and claimed to be eighteen, which confuses his biographers. He never had his hair cut. He was near-sighted, almost blind and rarely opened his mouth. The first time he came to see me, sent by Max Jacob, I was told "In the waiting room, there is a child with a cane. . . ." As he lived at Saint-Maur Park, along the Marne, we called him the miracle of the Marne. He seldom went home, slept anywhere at all, on the ground, on tables, with the painters of Montparnasse and Montmartre. Sometimes he pulled out of his pocket a dirty torn piece of paper. The scrap was passed around and they read a poem as fresh as a seashell or a bunch of currants.

> Jean Cocteau. *Men I Hold Great* by François Mauriac
> (Philosophical Library). 1951. p. 122

Radiguet shows us, through a glass, the working of hearts entirely engaged in deceiving themselves. "This is what they think they are discovering in themselves. This is what is really going on," he seems to tell us. All his art as a novelist is based on that formula. Perhaps he is too much the master of his creatures; they never drag him along; they follow in a straight line, from which we sometimes wish they would deviate. . . . Passion, to a certain degree, mechanizes us. This is what was very well seen by Radiguet who would quickly have acquired more suppleness. Such as it is, his work is enough for us, his elders; the cause is clear, that child was a master.

> François Mauriac. *Men I Hold Great* (Philosophical
> Library). 1951. p. 123

One should insist that he was a poet, in one of the major French ways of being one, by raising rational lucidity to a high intensity. . . . His sentences seem to have been conceived in alexandrines, in that specific tensility, pointed, balanced, and final, but then in mere graciousness allowed to come out in prose. He said that he aimed at a negligent style as the height of elegance; and his prose is in fact the highest pitched poetry taking itself lightly. Radiguet died at twenty, and there is the emotional edge of that age under the only relatively loose style of the prose to keep it from ever going either soft or vulgar.

> Donald Sutherland. *NR*. April 13, 1953. pp. 19–20

Radiguet describes states of mind as if they were campaigns. He does not use the stream-of-consciousness technique or attempt to draw the reader into his imaginary world and make him participate in the feelings of the inhabitants. Instead he displays the imaginary world in such a blaze of clarity that it fills the eye and obliterates all other considerations.

> Phoebe Adams. *At.* June, 1953. p. 80

At a time of the greatest confusion, when young writers, right after the First World War, abandoned themselves to disorder or took refuge in more or less ephemeral attempts at escape, he, on the contrary, knew how to be self-possessed. Breaking with all the influences of his generation, he rejoined his elders of the preceding generation and reinforced the powerful neo-classical current which toward 1923 skirted the mad enterprises through which an epoch in the throes of anxiety sought to defend itself. If one can speak of a "new classicism" . . . Raymond Radiguet was one of its precursors.

> Keith Goesch, *Raymond Radiguet* (La Palatine).
> 1955. pp. 67–8. Tr. by Dorothy Nyren Curley

The astonishing thing about Radiguet was that barely had the whole avant-garde movement got into its stride, than Radiguet, still practically a schoolboy, started a reaction to all the conflicting isms of the moment. His attitude was that of a mature man who saw through it all. He frequently repeated to Cocteau and the other writers he met, *"il faut faire des romans comme toute le monde,"* "you must write novels like everyone else." Although he admired Apollinaire's work and the music of *Les Six* he had the perspicacity to see, at nineteen, that a total break with tradition in form was not necessarily of any use at all and he himself was content to use the old forms, modelling himself on the classical novels which he had only just finished reading at school.

Margaret Crosland. *Jean Cocteau* (Peter Nevill). 1955.
p. 63

The value of Radiguet's work does not lie least in the fact that it shows that the method of the classic novelists is still a perfectly adequate instrument for exploring the intricacies of contemporary psychology. It shows, too, that "normal feelings" are not an exhausted theme and that the study of them is by no means incompatible with the sort of psychological discovery which is always so highly esteemed in France. Finally, it suggests that the sacrifices which were certainly made when the inner monologue and other technical innovations were introduced may not all have been really necessary.

Martin Turnell. *Com.* July 15, 1955. p. 379
See *The Devil in the Flesh* and *Count d'Orgel Opens the Ball* (novels).

RAMUZ, CHARLES FERDINAND (1878–1947)

What is of most interest in the work of C. F. Ramuz is its analysis of the French Protestant mind, and the expression in literature of an element whose absence from the literature of France must always seem a loss to English readers. . . . M. Ramuz has admirably preserved the Protestant note which, coupled with the familiar idiom of the country people in which he writes, lends a piquant contrast to his novels as compared with the very different atmosphere of French fiction. . . . The puritan suspicion of joy pervades the communities of town and country of which M. Ramuz has made himself the interpreter. The rhythm of folk-speech alternates with that of the Bible.

Ernest Boyd. *Studies from Ten Literatures* (Scribner).
1927. pp. 225–6

Ramuz is a man who writes and who, each time that he writes, recreates the world. To his eye, for his understanding, each event is new and surprising. This minute attention, this manner of spelling things out, of saying names clearly, such is the character of his art as it must be. . . . Here are objects, here is a lake, mountains, a countryside. Things are as they are given, what is necessary is to describe their lasting features, to tell of their inner being.

> Emmanuel Buenzod. *C. F. Ramuz* (Lettres de Lausanne). 1928. pp. 9–10. Tr. by Dorothy Nyren Curley

Ramuz has a true love of the real, and because of this he does not struggle against inner sadness, before which men professionally attached to the intellect or even to the soul find themselves retreating. His passion for the country of his birth, his lake, his hills, his peasant friends, is so authentic and goes so deeply that it discovers there the most generous and most modest care for both the universal and the human.

> Jacques Maritain. *Hommage à C. F. Ramuz* (Porchet). 1938. p. 27. Tr. by Dorothy Nyren Curley

He deliberately rejected the "classical" style—which he admired—believing that a new and genuine classic could only be achieved by the rejection, that is by a return to the tradition from which it first arose.

He departed, too, from the classical rules (the period and so forth); from the normal shape of the *roman*. . . . He adopted a spoken language. . . . His *goût de l'élémentaire* was, he discovered, very closely related to the *goût de l'universel*: far from his adoption of a particular language and place leading to isolation, to the impossibility of communication with those of other traditions, he found that it was an emancipation and a widening of his understanding.

> Martin Jarrett-Kerr. *NC*. Sept., 1947. p. 135

When the Mountain Fell is a novel which has the rather strange effect of calling to mind both Knut Hamsen's *Growth of the Soil* and John Hersey's *Hiroshima*. . . . Its quiet heroism does somehow achieve a kind of nobility which makes it an unpretentious story of human endurance. It is not a work of remarkable stature; it is not deeply stirring or extraordinarily dramatic. Despite the wild outburst of nature it describes, it is always quiet and in a minor key. It is, in truth, as modest a work of art as its central figure is a modest hero.

> Richard Watts, Jr. *NR*. Oct. 20, 1947, pp. 31–2

When the Mountain Fell . . . is being hailed by reviewers as a classic and a masterpiece. I do not agree with this judgment. . . . We should not be surprised at the fact that the same opinion which supposes that the truth of modern life is conveyed in such books as *The Hucksters* or *The Story of Mrs. Murphy* now thinks that the ideality of modern life is conveyed by M. Ramuz's pious and banal little fable. . . . Its style is the crooning Biblical prose long sanctified as the proper way to write about peasants, idiots, and other of God's innocent children—the kind that swells the heart with virtue while it lulls the mind to rest. . . . The insidious thing, of course, about a book of this sort is that although it is a straight religious document and a profoundly anti-intellectual one, it takes no open theological or anti-rational position: so that even people who might be stopped by a formulated faith are available to its seductions. Its appeal to non-reason is entirely implicit in its nostalgic exaltation of the primitive.

Diana Trilling. Nation. Nov. 15, 1947. p. 533

See *When the Mountain Fell* (novel).

REVERDY, PIERRE (1889-1960)

Pierre Reverdy was especially influenced by the particular trend, within Cubism, which emphasized the value of the spiritual atmosphere in which objects and facts are steeped. Indeed, for him, objects and facts are often merely accessories whose surface here and there catches reflections of a transcendental cosmic effulgence. So he devoted himself to a subtle notation of the impalpable qualities of the universe revealing themselves in the most elemental spectacles of nature. For him the stars glittering against a dark velvet sky, the limitless expanse of the ocean, or the silent epic of the crimson-stained clouds under the setting sun are authentic fragments of a sublime, heavenly entity or, as he himself calls them in his suggestive title, genuine *Epaves du ciel*.

Georges Lemaitre. From Cubism to Surrealism (Harvard).
1941. pp. 144–5

The final impression of this poetry is that of complete economy in words. The inner thought of the poet, with connecting ideas weeded out, emerges startling and at first glance too brutally naked. Qualifying adjectives, save those of emotional value, are eliminated; and adverbs play little part in this direct language of the essential. The resultant style, with its powerful and evocative verbs, is vibrant and moving. This is all part of a carefully conceived plan, in which the poet has chosen only the simple, constant things and has refrained from any amplifying description.

W. Kenneth Cornell. *Essays in Honor of Albert Feuillerat,*
ed. by Henri Peyre (Yale). 1943. p. 274

Animated, not able to stay more than five minutes in a chair, eagerly talkative and argumentative, with a voice by turn thundering and coaxing, hands always moving, flashing eye but also sometimes moist, Mediterranean from top to toe, small in stature, harsh accent, hair black and vigorous, skin swarthy and clean shaven, white teeth, constant agitation of the nerves and heart, a childish laugh following sarcasm, sweetness after thunder . . . one scarely was able to welcome him, to dare a few questions, before he was running off to the station "with a gloomy gladness," anxious to go back to Solesmes, to return to his own place.

Jean Rousselot. *Pierre Reverdy* (Editions Pierre Seghers).
1951. pp. 29–30. Tr. by Dorothy Nyren Curley

Reverdy is a mystic in the sense that he can disentangle from the object which captures his attention its spiritual qualities which express themselves plastically and which, according to the esoteric view, convey the abstract through the concrete. What counts—and it is one of the imperatives of poetry—is not the celestial material, but the use that one makes of it, what it becomes when it has passed through the heart of man, put again in an emotional context which brings it to birth as a discovery.

Michel Manoll. In *Pierre Reverdy* by Jean Rousselot
(Editions Pierre Seghers). 1951. p. 62.
Tr. by Dorothy Nyren Curley

This devotion to clean shapes, this essential lineation of prosaic objects that discards sentiment for a palpable texture, transposes into poetry the plastic ideals of cubism: the innermost poet assumes the tangible shape of objects; the poem which is self is matter in the same way as the cubist painting renders material the inner vision of the painter. Such creation is in fact disciplined re-creation. Where Claudel's catholicity conjoined all things through divine grammar and thus reinstated the simile (discarded by Rimbaud), the cubist world of Reverdy is an artistic unity that eliminates simile and metaphor because it exists as an inter-refraction of planes determined solely by the nature and structure of the artifact.

David I. Grossvogel. *YFS.* Spring-Summer, 1958. p. 101

Like Benn, [William Carlos] Williams, and Montale, Reverdy makes his rhythms up as he goes along. . . . He gets a feeling almost of dream into the rhythms by omitting all punctuation. Even more than in Mallarmé and Apollinaire, from whom he borrows this practice, we cannot establish in Reverdy the points of sentences. Lines are sentences and at the same time appositional clauses rephrasing each other. Each of the diffuse images comes to the same thing, or is a different flicker, a *lueur,* of the same meaning.

Albert Cook. *KR.* Spring, 1959. p. 215

He accepts the fact that death is the greatest enemy of man and the invincible one. But this fact creates in him neither a sense of defeat nor of cynical disdain. Disdain of death would be accompanied by disdain of life, and although he admits the tragic basis of life he refuses to disdain living. The alternative is to transmute life within our limited number of years. How to transmute it becomes the preoccupation of his life and work. . . . With the simplest words in the French language, the universal words and the earthy ones, and some of the translucent ones interspersed, he has labeled the most common forms and beings with a mystic significance not because he spurns the world as it is, but to leave on it the imprint of his love of life. For life is to him not the antithesis of death, not a passage, but an absolute condition.

Anna Balakian. *Surrealism* (Noonday). 1959. p. 73, 88

He is not a prophet, though he puts the questions that a prophet answers. And since there are no answers in Reverdy, his poetry harmonizes with this empirical age after all! All those questions of agonizing import, about the nature of death, fate, God, eternity, "Real reality," and so forth, to which traditional religion or traditional idealism answered with stupendous (and to us incredible) positives, and whose very meaning is denied by modern linguistic philosophers are asked, in Reverdy, *for the sake of their question marks,* because it is natural for human beings, caught as we are between past and future, to ask them. . . . The absence of an answer, the bewilderment, are part of this poetry's atmosphere and of its meaning.

Martin Daniel. *MLR.* April, 1963. p. 189

Surrealist poetic revolt was intended to change life; the function of poetry for Reverdy was, on the contrary, to live the given life at its utmost point of authenticity, at the sharp edge between dream and reality, trying to catch the fleeting instants where reality could meet the absolute. Reverdy assumed entirely in his poetry the misery of man's fate, he laid it bare in hard and short sentences and direct images that have an ominous ring because they are separated from any comforting human context and devoid of any reference to personal existence.

Alexander Aspel. *Contemporary French Poetry*
(Michigan). 1965. p. 5
See selection of poems in *Chicago Review*, No. 4, 1965.

RIBEIRO, AQUILINO (1885–1963)

When his novel was published in Portugal he was arrested and charged with attempting to discredit Portugal in the eyes of the world, inciting action against the security of the state and insulting the magistrate and the secret police. I am not surprised: *When the Wolves Howl* is an all-out attack on the Portuguese dictatorship. . . . Aquilino Ribeiro is clearly a considerable writer. . . ; but his novel invokes comparisons it cannot stand up to. In essence, it is a Portuguese *Fontamara,* but though Ribeiro has something of Silone's passion he has nothing like his art. . . . Ribeiro is deficient in narrative skill and, of a possible three or four novels, never seems to have decided which one he wants to write. . . . The book strikes one . . . not as a composed whole so much as a heap of discrete material. All the same, it deserves to be read.

Walter Allen. *NSN*. May 17, 1963. p. 754

One of Portugal's contemporary grand old men of letters, Aquilino Ribeiro, candidate for the Noble Prize, . . . at seventy-five continues to be a major voice of political opposition to the authoritarian Salazar regime. Because of his outspoken democratic views, Ribeiro has been twice exiled from Portugal. . . . *When the Wolves Howl* is set in the mountain country that has always been the author's *milieu* [and is] told in the best tradition of European realism. . . . Ribeiro's description of the trial of . . . a man who is against violence yet seems to be continually surrounded by it . . . and the other villagers charged with rebellion is a masterly exposé of the tragic-farcical turnings of the wheels of justice in Portugal today for those who, like the author himself, oppose the regime. His portraits of the highland villagers, a rude, hardy, colorful people, are rich and vivid—particularly that of [an] incredible old man . . . who stops at nothing in his fierce resolve to maintain a life of freedom and dignity in his beloved highlands.

Abel Penn. *NYT*. Oct. 13, 1963. p. 46

Theoretically, censorship and oppression choke off literary talents. In fact, they seem sometimes to inspire novelists with a passion that results in a deeper commitment to their craft than they might have in a freer society. . . . Aquilino Ribeiro, a strong opponent of the "New State" in Portugal, uses the novel form to indict his country's regime. However, he is far from being a crude propagandist; he remains an artist even when his personal emotions are most involved. Even those few readers to whom the rights of political freedom are irrelevant will be caught up by the skill of this story-teller. Ribeiro has the old-fashioned ability —scorned by so many new novelists—of forcing the reader to identify himself with the characters. . . . His style [is] a mixture of the realistic and the ironic.

Vernon Hall, Jr. NYHT. Nov. 3, 1963. pp. 18–19

Aquilino Ribeiro was in his seventies when he wrote *When the Wolves Howl,* but he had not lost the combination of vigorous prose, and heroic, earthy Portuguesism that makes his fiction memorable and important. . . . With little sacrifice of narrative interest the author shows the folly of an attempt to impose "progress" on a backward region by piecemeal, external measures in conflict with the local mores and with the region's entire complex of educational and economic inadequacies. . . . It is not surprising that the book aroused resentment in official circles. But this was nothing new to Aquilino Ribeiro, and it never induced him to change his course. How well he maintained his integrity as both man of letters and citizen is suggested by this surprising tribute from the dictator Salazar himself: "He is an enemy of my regime. He will give you a most unfavorable report of me. But no matter: he is a great writer."

William L. Grossman. SR. Nov. 9, 1963. p. 48

A characteristic word in [his] vocabulary was the complex adjective *fero,* implying at one and the same time the fierce, sturdy, and rural qualities of the Portuguese mountain folk. More than any other word, it expressed the exaltation of a pagan appetite for living, within a rustic Portuguese setting, which was Aquilino's gospel to his city readers. With this lusty earthiness, he transformed the country novel in Portugal. . . . The rural roots show in the larger part of Aquilino's fiction. . . . Another side of Aquilino's character [is] the satirist in him, who castigated Portuguese society. Before his mind he kept the ideal of a future self-governing, just, and more rational society. . . . Cutting the famous and the powerful down to human proportions was another constant trait of Aquilino's mentality. He was a skeptic, in the manner of the country-people who are afraid to be taken in by city slickers. . . . Two other facets were related to Aquilino as an irreverent, realistic biographer. One was the historian in him, who felt drawn to other nonconformists in the national past . . . [and] the other was the journalist, who reported as precisely as he could what he had seen in other countries. . . . There is an erudite side to his work also. . . . [But] his rural stories are the core of his work. For them he will be remembered, and for the affirmation of life which they express.

Gerald M. Moser. *Hsp.* May, 1964. pp. 341–2

See *When the Wolves Howl* (novel).

RIMBAUD, ARTHUR (1854–1891)

The rascal adroitly passed himself off as a political sniper in trouble and inspired the fine gesture of a collection in his behalf. Quite thin in any case and besides, as was appropriate, in the worst disarray, violently ravaged by literature, by long studious hours on benches, in libraries, at this time master of a certain premature expression, intense, excited by unheard of subjects,—in search also of "new sensations, ones yet to be discovered," he insisted and he took pleasure in the thought that he would find them in the city's bazaars of illusion; vulgar, but one who was given up to an adolescent demon, one night to grandiose and prolonged artificial visions, the next to drunkenness only.

Stéphane Mallarmé. *Oeuvres Complètes* (Pléiade). 1945. p. 514. Written in April, 1896. Tr. by Dorothy Nyren Curley

Went to see Paul Claudel yesterday at his sister's. . . . As I chide him for having, in his study, glossed over the ferocious side of Rimbaud's character, he says he wanted to depict only the Rimbaud of the *Saison en enfer,* in whom the author of *Les Illuminations* was to *result.* Led, for a moment, to speak of his relations with Verlaine, Claudel, with an absent look, touches a rosary in a bowl on the mantel.

André Gide. *The Journals* (Knopf). 1947. v. 1, pp. 334–5. Written in *Journal* on Nov. 19, 1912

He was a demon, that is, nothing either bad or good, but a spirit or metaphysical hypothesis, above the laws of men and below the power of divinity. And this condition was induced in him, I think, by the precocity of his intellectual maturity, the habit of slave-driving his intellect which his mother taught him, and the poverty of his early emotional life. His mind outstripped his experience, and so built out of abstract words the idea of absolute satisfaction which lured his boyish genius into the abyss of disgust. Could he have accepted some small corner of life as material for his art on whatever terms, I do not see his peer in the century. But then he would not have been Rimbaud, who based his genius on this refusal.

Edgell Rickword. Rimbaud (Knopf). 1924. pp. 194–5

The Cybele-idea is . . . one of the guiding principles of Rimbaud's poetic existence. This love of the earth and the teeming forms of life . . . is to be found . . . throughout his work. The immensity of life haunts him, and his pages swarm with the multitudinous movements of life: birds, animals, plants. . . . He condemns Christ as a destroyer of energies and an enemy of liberty. That being so, his hostility must be lasting, for energy and liberty are the very breath and substance of his being. . . . His spiritual energy during his poetic period is as immense as his physical energy during his "Arabo-Ethiopian" days. . . . And liberty is such an instinctive craving with him that certain harmless things which happen to symbolise restriction of liberty are rarely mentioned without his unconsciously attaching to them an unpleasant epithet or association.

A. R. Chisholm. The Art of Arthur Rimbaud
(Melbourne). 1930. pp. 53, 56–7

He had launched himself into his amazing adventure like a madman, daring everything, overturning everything, destroying everything. He opposed his own gifts and acted in violence to his own inclinations. . . . His poetry, like his life, is a tremendous transposition, a pathetic disguise. He experienced a satanic pleasure in exalting himself and destroying himself at the same time. He was the victim of his Lucifer-like pride, of his spirit of contradiction and revolt.

Jean-Marie Carré. A Season in Hell (Macauley).
1931. pp. 153–4

Rimbaud's life has a typical significance: it moves us, it seems to put before us an acute phase of the human predicament, as if it were a great play. The other poets of whom I have been writing [the Symbolists] were as little at home in their nineteenth-century world as Rimbaud, and they were mostly as disillusioned with its enthusiasms; but they had remained in it and managed to hold their places in it by excreting, like patient molluscs, irridescent shells of literature—whereas Rimbaud, with genius equal to any's, with genius perhaps superior to any's, had rejected Europe altogether—not merely its society and ideas, but even the kind of sensibility which one cultivated when one tried to live at odds with it and the kind of literature this sensibility supplied—getting away to a life of pure action and a more primitive civilization.

And if actions can be compared with writings, Rimbaud's life seems more satisfactory than the works of his Symbolist contemporaries. . . . His career, with its violence, its moral interest, and its tragic complete-ness, leaves us feeling that we have watched the human spirit, strained to its most resolute sincerity and in possession of its highest faculties, breaking itself in the effort to escape, first from humiliating compromise, and then from chaos equally humiliating.

Edmund Wilson. Axel's Castle (Scribner). 1931. pp. 282–3

He was one of the first to employ distortions and dissociations system-atically. He used verbs, instead of adjectives, to lend violence to his page; he used adjectives chiefly to summon up precise color; he sought a great variety of meters: ranging from that of the quick, nervous lyric to that of pompous oration; and where Hugo had freed the Alexandrine from the *caesura,* he broke from regular meter to experiment with free verse. . . . He would use now the tones of direct vulgar speech, or now drawing upon technical language, similes suggestive of laboratories, even of the magnifying motion picture, which of course did not exist in his time. And significantly he would use repetition or "recapitulation," of phrases or images, in the way of a sonata or a symphony, scorning the sequence of common-sense, informative literature, as no one had dared before him.

Matthew Josephson in The New Republic Anthology
1915–1935, ed. by Groff Conklin (Dodge). 1936.
pp. 401–2

The lesson to be learnt from Rimbaud is that, after him, romanticism can go no farther, a reaction is necessary, inevitable. Rimbaud himself knew this. . . . Surrealist poetry ignores the conclusions which Rimbaud drew from this theory and in consequence it has not produced anything to equal him. However much Rimbaud raided the subconscious and the world of dreams, it must be remembered that he was a first-rate intellect and a ruthlessly conscious artist. . . . What must remain supreme in Rimbaud is the fusion of romantic imagination, militant thought and verbal mastery into, in his best passages, a precision of inspiration.

Cyril Connolly. The Condemned Playground
(Routledge). 1945. pp. 74–5

On the one hand, as a Romantic, he adhered to the doctrine of self-expression which, by assimilating the utterances of art to those of life or nature, tends to lead the artist in the final analysis, to reject all the devices or pretences of art because he can obviously express himself more directly and freely in immediate speech or action. On the other hand, as a disciple of Baudelaire and Poe, Rimbaud believed also in the thaumaturgic nature of art and, whether as mystic or as mystifier, tried to project hallucinations or illusions onto his readers. . . . Between the poetics of Wordworth's "Prelude" and those of "The Raven," as extreme examples of these two views, Rimbaud was constantly tossed and never able to choose; and the very nature of his art thus varied from poem to poem, or from one part of a poem to another.

Edouard Roditi. *Poetry*. Feb., 1946. pp. 279–80

Rimbaud . . . was the child who dreams awake, who believes all things are possible (as they are to the child-mind), and who refuses to go further (in art, in this instance) when he discovers the rules of the game are quite other than he has understood them to be. The adult "adjusts himself"; Rimbaud refused to play any more, dropped his toys, and went off in a rage. For this reason, our admiration of the *voyou* must be tempered, although that is no bar to our intensity of amazement at his achievement as poet and visionary.

Gerard Previn Meyer. *SR*. Dec. 7, 1946. p. 72

After all the physical and real flights, Rimbaud undertook his real poet's flight which was his flight before the ordinary locutions of the language, before all familiar words, and even before the memory of language. He was the "voyant," and at the same time the mystic, the messiah of the new poetic alchemy. . . . The poet not only sought a poetic language worthy of bearing his experience, he explored the universe of his heart for the transcendental language for the poetry which would celebrate the silent and untranslatable message of his heart. The attempt was not pursued for very long. It has been recommenced in our day by James Joyce who, perhaps because he didn't feel the same torture of the absolute that Rimbaud did, was successful in creating a new language.

Wallace Fowlie. *The Clown's Grail* (Alan Swallow). 1948. p. 88

What I want to suggest is that much of Rimbaud's value as a poet lies precisely in the use of the method of discontinuity. It is a form of shock tactics which continually compels a fresh effort of attention on the part of the reader, makes him look at the world in which he finds himself from a fresh angle or in a new way. It is closely connected with his emphasis on violence, with the glimpses he gives us of the disintegration of material reality and with his liking for buildings and machines of an impossible size which sometimes suggests the films of Fritz Lang. . . . What these images do, or are intended to do, is to undermine our confidence in the stability and finality of the world of common perception.

Martin Turnell. *TC*. Aug., 1953. pp. 152–3

His was the most terrible deception I know of. He asked for more than any man dared and he received infinitely less than he deserved. Corroded by his own bitterness and despair, his dreams turned to rust. But for us they remain as pure and untarnished as the day they were born. Of the corruption he passed through not a single ulcer adheres. All is white, glistening, tremulous and dynamic, purified by the flames. More than any poet he lodges himself in that vulnerable place called the heart. In all that is broken—a thought, a gesture, a deed, a life—we find the proud Prince of the Ardennes. May his soul rest in peace.

Henry Miller. *The Time of the Assassins*
(New Directions). 1956. p. 158

Rimbaud [was] a sort of magician of the sensibility, of that specifically modern sensibility invented by Blake and Holderlin and Baudelaire, and an innovator in syntax, the first thoroughly radical revealer of the poetic metalogic which is the universal characteristic of twentieth century verse. . . . He applied to literature, and to littérateurs, the minute he laid eyes on them, the devastating methods of total exploitation so graphically described in the *Communist Manifesto*. . . . He "ran" the vowels as he later ran guns to the Abyssinians. . . . He did things to literature that had never been done to it before, and they were things which literature badly needed done to it.

Kenneth Rexroth. *Nation*. Oct. 12, 1957. p. 248

In some ways, Rimbaud's work (like that of Baudelaire, too) is "dated." It is rooted in a fundamentally Romantic conception of the poet and his role which, as poets writing in a different and rapidly changing social context are finding, is no longer valid or appropriate. . . . But if time, social change, and new literary doctrines are modifying some aspects of Rimbaud's work, they will leave untouched, and further reveal, its deep and underlying theme: a child's belief in his omnipotence. That, from the first poems to the last letters, is the unifying theme of Rimbaud's work. . . . The striking fact is that Rimbaud's fierce lyricism, which appeals not to our reason but to the tumultuous and undisciplined emotions of our childhood, continues to provoke extreme reactions. . . . It is perhaps only in so far as we can develop beyond our own immaturity, and are unafraid to recall the ecstasies and the terrors of a time when we too were omnipotent children, that we shall really be able to *see* and to understand Rimbaud's work.

C. A. Hackett. *Rimbaud* (Bowes and Bowes). 1957. pp. 93–4

In *Illuminations* is found expressed, as nowhere else, except perhaps in the poems of Saint John of the Cross—man's eternal longing for spiritual satisfaction and beauty. *Une Saison en Enfer* is the hell of doubt which is always with us, the age-long struggle between the angel and the beast, and few writers have expressed in so poignant and moving a manner, the bitterness of the cry that bursts from us; while in *"Le Bateau Ivre,"* we find all the nostalgic longing of human nature, its aspirations and its passionate desire to escape from outworn values and to sail toward new hope. *"Le Bateau Ivre"* is freighted with the suffering of a stricken world, with its infinite weariness with all that surrounds it; it carries on board the world's ardent longing for escape to the open sea from the stifling stench of the port, there to wash itself clean from all that has soiled and defiled it and to find a newer and cleaner self.

Enid Starkie. *Arthur Rimbaud* (New Directions). 1961.
pp. 445–6

Nothing could be more natural than that our time should have made Rimbaud one of its special heroes. We have been aware of ourselves as living in—perhaps living through—an age of anxiety, and identified him as typically anxious. The heroes of our fiction have been alienated figures, and we know that Rimbaud's alienation was deep. We have honored, above all, those who have shown themselves capable of pronouncing a total refusal of the world in which we have no choice but to live, and written down Rimbaud as one of the most exemplary of such *révoltés.* . . . Even if closer inspection reveals that Rimbaud fell rather short of being the model he has been said to be, his example made it considerably easier for the latter-day stereotype of the *révolté* to come into existence.

W. M. Frohock. *Rimbaud's Poetic Practice* (Harvard).
1963. pp. 201–2

See *Illuminations* and *A Season in Hell* (poetry).

ROBBE-GRILLET, ALAIN (1922–   )

His gives us in his novels objects in their simple crudity as the eye sees them, lighted as they are at 9 A.M. or 5 P.M., and without any symbolic overtones. If the eye of a man who has just committed a particularly horrible crime calmly notes a flattened frog in the roadway and his brain wonders at length whether the stiffened leatherish object was a frog or toad, this may reveal something of his psychology, but the implications and conclusions are ours and not the author's. . . . With such an original technique—which may well owe more to the films than its creator is aware—he can weave a spider web whose meshes of apparent anti-logic eventually catch us in a demonstration as convincing as if we ourselves had produced every thread.

Justin O'Brien. *NYT*. Oct. 12, 1958. p. 4

What about character? Character is out. The writer must not cheat by pretending to split himself among his creations. There must be a central personage who sees, but nobody who knows. What, after all this, is left? Nothing is left but the auctioneer's catalogue, the mindless eyes. Has tragedy thereby been avoided? Yes: and so has anything else of the smallest intellectual interest. . . . In *The Voyeur* M. Robbe-Grillet adds nothing to the novel, but goes as far as anyone can go in taking things away from it.

Pamela Hansford Johnson. *NSN*. March, 1959. p. 341–2

Robbe-Grillet has indeed a system, and a coherent one, more readily discoverable in his fiction than in his theoretical pronouncements. In it each pole shuttles us to the opposite, while the pattern itself remains fragmentary and self-enclosed. Thus his novels demonstrate the impossibility of reflecting the world in any way except via its debris, each fragment being molecular in structure and perfectly formed but neither constituting a whole nor having the capacity to do so. Robbe-Grillet has created significant parts which, while evoking no global significance, make it impossible, and so refer us to the impossibility of signifying, which in itself is highly significant.

Bernard Dort. *YFS*. Summer, 1959. p. 28

The originality of Robbe-Grillet's technique in *Jalousie* consists in limiting his medium of expression and exploiting to the full certain of the techniques used by some surrealist painters: the meticulously precise, detailed presentation of certain places or objects—solid objects—seen, to be sure, as refracted by an observant eye, but an eye charged with an intense emotion. . . . How far really have we moved from the novel of psychological analysis? The recurrent pattern of images, though it may not be "symbolical," a word Robbe-Grillet eschews, is nonetheless primarily significant psychologically.

Germaine Brée. *YFS*. Summer, 1959. p. 89

What is new in Robbe-Grillet (or rather what would be new without the precedent of Francis Ponge), is the concrete character of the images, whether they are caught by a glance or seen in the darkroom of the mind. He deliberately uses in his novels the revealing difference mentioned by him between reality and its cinematographic representation. It is then not only his heroes but their creator himself who makes movies —avant-garde movies and novels. No doubt Robbe-Grillet is a pioneer. It is possible that he has found a way out of the impasse which the most advanced literature had reached—so that it was no longer advancing. . . . By grasping objects visually without judging them, being satisfied to take them without wanting to understand, Alain Robbe-Grillet escapes perhaps, and perhaps makes literature escape inanity.

Claude Mauriac. The New Literature (Braziller).
1959. pp. 233–4

Now why does M. Robbe-Grillet deplore "the story" so much? Because the writer who wants the story, *invents* it—it isn't *true.* And "the enlightened reader," who reads the story, discovers this and—horrors! "he fears he has been led into a trap." What, may one ask, did the enlightened reader think he was in for in the first place? . . . M. Robbe-Grillet's view seems to me extraordinarily naif, in fact positively quaint. But the quaintest thing out is his recording with approval the enlightened reader's turning from "the sham of fiction" to "the real-life story—the personal document or 'testament'." M. Robbe-Grillet seems to think that in real-life stories and testaments, the authors are out to tell the truth and nothing but the truth—*and* succeed. Good gracious me.

William Cooper. International Literary Annual No. 2,
ed. by John Wain (John Calder). 1959. pp. 34–5

View is what matters. M. Robbe-Grillet isn't the first and won't be the last writer to be troubled by the falsity or conventionality of our viewing. . . . As a novelist Wyndham Lewis declared himself for outsides as the only firm, focused way of rendering the insides, in the interest of the pure consciousness of action. As another novelist and liberator, Robbe-Grillet declares himself again for the accurate outsides, for vision restricted as far as possible to contours, in the interest of defining the essential in men and women. . . . He wants to destroy the "soul-bridge" between ourselves and things, to deliver the mountain from the moral characteristic which follows when we call it "majestic." . . . Man is man, things are things. Things when cleaned are definers. Things left dirty and contaminated with our feelings are confusers and slave-makers.

Geoffrey Grigson. Spec. Dec. 16, 1960. p. 993

Robbe-Grillet has accomplished the difficult feat of using language to negate the implications of verbal, personalizing symbology. We have finally a construct in which the human elements are eliminated by their very imprecision, banality, and meaninglessness. André Gide has worried, but not resolved, the problem of writing the *"pur récit,"* of forestalling the reader's proclivity to mythologize and elaborate—to achieve an "élan" on the springboard of the novelists' fiction. Robbe-Grillet dissolves the human elements or restricts them to mere focus: man is apparatus, not subject. Thus we have a work that may be likened to a cubistic or geometric painting.

Seymour S. Weiner. MLQ. Sept., 1962. pp. 223–4

Robbe-Grillet's unorthodox narrative structure, his violation of chronology, and his repetition (with variation) of anecdote, are apt to disconcert the reader expecting a story forthrightly told. It makes sense, however, if we think of the protagonist's consciousness as being the field of the narrative. There events that are taking place mingle with those which already have taken place. Memory and imagination function as importantly as immediate perception, and reality is spread over the three. Such a technique sets the mind of the protagonist directly before the reader, revealing it more dramatically than author explanation or other conventional means.

Laurent Le Sage. The French New Novel
(Pennsylvania State). 1962. p. 116

Dans le Labyrinthe, more than any other novel by Robbe-Grillet, is a work which creates itself while it is being written, and the "secret tracks to result in an eventual pattern" are inherent in the work itself. To call this work an allegory of literary creation would be to commit an error as serious as to make from Robbe-Grillet's objects symbols in the proper sense of the word. It is itself creation: the novel creates itself as we watch.

Bruce Morrissette. Les Romans de Robbe-Grillet
(Editions de Minuit). 1963. p. 180.
Tr. by Dorothy Nyren Curley

These novels are effective because they deal always with a self-enclosed microcosm, and we are persuaded that once the individual is caught in the web of fury (*Jalousie*), search (*Labyrinthe*), or sex (*Voyeur*), he can only buzz erratically around like an angry fly trapped in a small box. We are dealing in Robbe-Grillet's novels, with a queer aspect of personality, which might be termed a reciprocating or reverberating mind, in which an idea, once seized, dominates the mind like a ritual or superstition.

Peter Cortland. Cq. Winter, 1963–4. p. 91

Robbe-Grillet's novels, though they may seem antipodal to Sarraute's, also reveal an extreme fascination and preoccupation with the workings of the mind. Whereas Sarraute's inner monologue is an extension of Joyce or Proust, Robbe-Grillet's "objectivity" descends in direct line from Flaubert. But Robbe-Grillet carries the technique of minute and detailed visual description of objects beyond anything envisioned by any other writer. Even though superficially this technique of the visual (*l'école du regard* or *chosisme*) would seem to negate any concern with depth pyschology (as the hasty pronouncements of some critics indicated), it does in fact project the subconsciousness onto these objects.

> Ben F. Stoltzfus. *Alain Robbe-Grillet and the New French Novel* (Southern Illinois). 1964. p. 10

A geometrical, non-metaphorical description of an object does not exactly reduce that object to its mere *être-là,* or, in fashionable French critical vocabulary, "reify" the human world. Though the object may allude to nothing beyond its own physical presence and shock us by its apparent irrelevance to what surrounds it in the novel, it also acquires a rare open-endedness, thus becomes peculiarly *available* to meaning. The meaningless object is ready to be flooded with meaning, and in Robbe-Grillet the profusion of fantasy and the deliberately unimaginative description are perhaps really two ways of expressing a single interest. There is both an ascetic refusal to novelize about the world (ascetic because this refusal means, of course, the denial of a spontaneous impulse) and a temptation to go on novelizing endlessly. Both procedures constitute an attack on the novelist's usual willingness to mythologize reality by organizing it into specific meaning, and to *exclude* many other meanings in order to protect his created significance from the assaults of uncontrollable conjecture.

> Leo Bersani. *PR.* Spring, 1965. p. 307

See *The Erasers, In the Labyrinth, Jealousy,* and *The Voyeur* (novels).

ROLLAND, ROMAIN (1866–1944)

Romain Rolland is intellectually a worshipper of power: at times we might be tempted to say: even of brute force. It is hard for the idealist to live in these days of Anglo-Saxon supremacy and Pan-Germanism, and not be contaminated. But he worships strength all the more because strength is not in him. His soul and his art are gentle and subtle, rich in half-tints, fine shades and scruples. When he describes strength, when he attempts to blow the heroic trumpet, he reminds us of the late imitations of Michael-Angelo, with the muscles of their athletes bulging to monstrous proportions—well-padded lay figures rather than living men. In passages of delicate melancholy, on the contrary, he is supreme.

Albert Leon Guérard. *Five Masters of French Romance*
(Scribner). 1916. pp. 286–7

Jean Christophe is perhaps the most remarkable work of contemporary fiction: a singular moral fervour, rare imagination, an unequalled sensibility, a torrent of sarcasm, rancour, revolt, tenderness, stream from its disconcerting pages. . . . Romain Rolland sacrifices every grace of measure and composition to his abundance, to his enthusiasm for life. He has no sense of style. His endless files of short, breathless sentences succeed each other interminably, with no variation, till we experience at last the sensation of a drop falling at regular intervals on the crown of our head!

Mary Duclaux. *Twentieth Century French Writers*
(Collins). 1919. pp. 47–8

He desires to be just to every epoch as to every individual. He never wishes to display a chance section, but would fain exhibit the entire cycle of happenings. . . . He aims at presenting, not only the central force of an era, but likewise the manifold counterforces; not the action alone, but the reaction as well. For Rolland, breadth of scope is a moral necessity rather than an artistic. . . . It is this ethical demand for justice to the small no less than to the great which makes spacious forms essential to Rolland. . . . The circle, the cycle, which unrestingly environs all its wealth of content, wherein discords are harmoniously resolved—to Rolland, ever the musician, this symbol of sensory justice is the favorite and wellnigh exclusive form.

Stefan Zweig. *Romain Rolland* (Seltzer). 1921. pp. 68–9

Romain Rolland is something different from, something more than, the artist in words who wrote *Jean-Christophe* and the conscience that produced *Au-dessus de la mêlée*. He is a man, a synthesis, and therein lies the secret of his strength. He is beyond the confines of parties; he cannot be pigeon-holed. He is something different from that which fanatical admirers worship and from that which his enemies revile. There is that in him which laughs at them all, eludes them. . . . There may be minds endowed with a more savage power, but there can hardly be a mind that is richer and more lucid. Morever, he knows how to be clear without forfeiting strength, how to be intelligent without the loss of creative fire, how to be splendidly Apollonian and yet at the same time Dionysian —harmonious after the manner of a Greek tragedy.

Charles Baudouin. *Contemporary Studies*
(Allen and Unwin). 1924. p. 69

His own country never adopted Rolland wholeheartedly. . . . This was due not only to his pacificism but to his sublime naïveté, his sentimental attitude in art and his surrendering too easily to his emotions under cover of music. In a time when the French élite discarded Wagner for Debussy and the new music of Ravel and his contemporaries, Rolland kept his enthusiasm for the great romantic masters. . . . André Gide declared that Rolland would be, among all the French writers, the one who would have least to lose from the war, since his French would be neither more nor less French if he were translated into German.

Régis Michaud. *Modern Thought and Literature in
France* (Funk). 1934. p. 26

The English reader of *Jean Christophe* is struck not so much by new material and a new technique as by a new intensity. Rolland's vivid treatment lighted up the years of infancy. The reader's attention is focused upon the painful family situation, the early discouragment and hate. . . . And then he witnesses the treatment of adolescent love, fumbling liaisons and passion—presented with an unconventional detail of half-satisfactions so lacking in the English novel. . . . Without the intense spaciousness of *Jean Christophe* to serve as an example, English writers would not have permitted themselves a slow inquiry into the stages of formative experience. . . . The book signified to English writers that a new day had dawned, and that fiction might be poetry, autobiography, a discussion of ideas, or anything else so long as it was honest and interesting.

William C. Frierson. *The English Novel in Transition*
(Oklahoma). 1942. pp. 190–2

An ancient pantheism of the people is the true religion of mountaineers, and Romain Rolland strove throughout his life to make it clear—a pantheism that is always on the move toward polytheism and deism and never reaches Christianity proper. From this came Pascal: a desperate attempt to be a Christian and destroy all possible arguments against Christianity. Three hundred years later the problem for Romain Rolland is different: How is one to link up the ancient intuitions of the French with the feelings of the world at large? From *Jean Christophe* to *Vivekananda* Rolland carries on that effort.

Denis Saurat. *Modern French Literature* (Putnam).
1946. pp. 80–1

While presenting the complexity of observed reality in works of epic length and temper, Romain Rolland also sought to demonstrate the harmony behind this apparent multiplicity. . . . Rolland was particularly helped in his task by his love for, and understanding of, music. . . . His longer novels and play-cycles resemble symphonic compositions in which certain original themes are stated, developed, elaborated according to the rules of counterpoint, and finally recapitulated.

John Cruickshank. *MLR.* July, 1951. p. 386

I don't think [*Jean Christophe*] will live like another French panorama-novel of the period—the novel of Proust. It is too episodic and diffuse, the conception sags, the satire is often journalistic and the style flat. But Romain Rolland was a far bigger person than Proust from the social and moral point of view; he cared about other people and tried to help them, he fought for a better world constantly and passionately, and he moved across frontiers towards internationalism as surely as the Rhine moves through Germany to the universal sea. He may be forgotten today, but insight and sincerity such as his will return to a world which needs them badly, and through other lips he will inspire youth once more and clarify its hopes.

E. M. Forster. *Two Cheers for Democracy*
(Edward Arnold). 1951. p. 241

What kind of man do we find? A religious socialist, an anti-clerical mystic, a revolutionary idealist; a Christian who rejected the dogma of the Christian religions, and a socialist who disliked the socialists for their economic materialism. He insisted on international cooperation, condemned violence and hatred, and felt the keenest anxiety over the fate of his invaded country while refusing to admit the national state as a rational, true, and necessary entity. There seemed to exist in him a series of dichotomies. . . . His sense of a multiple personality was highly developed and he consciously and purposefully availed himself of this faculty at times to live an even fuller life. At other times, when he was oppressed by the war, by his anxiety over the fate he saw in store for Europe and possibly for Occidental civilization, it was a means of evasion.

William T. Starr. *Romain Rolland and a World at War*
(Northwestern). 1956. p. 12
See *Jean Christophe* (novel).

ROMAINS, JULES (1885–   )

The subject of the highly original poems and novels which have compelled lovers of literature to study him is . . . human personality dwelling not in the understanding, but in a necessarily vague region, our sub-liminal self, and even in the masses around us. And in this way he appeals to a feeling which is older than man himself. He hymns the aggrandizement of human personality and consequently of all those tempestuous actions which bear our souls on into an unknown region. . . . So that this *Unanimisme* in Jules Romains is really the worship of the superman as he realizes himself in those nameless forces which everyone feels in an enthusiastic public meeting, or any great public demonstration.

G. Turquet-Milnes. *Some Modern French Writers* (McBride). 1921. p. 189

One could speak of the general "composition" of the works of Romains, for the same method, the same qualities appear indeed in his novels, his plays and poems. . . .

What strikes one particularly, when one considers the works from a little distance in order better to observe their composition, is an undeni-able and quite curious sense of the whole which is a dominant charac-teristic of Romains. He thinks and he composes in masses; whether it is a question of sound or of form, the entire work is laid out by a grand plan. It is amusing to notice in this respect that a little after his literary beginnings analogous compositions by the cubist painters began to appear.

Madeleine Israël. *Jules Romains* (Kra). 1931. pp. 173–4. Tr. by Dorothy Nyren Curley

The balance in favor of Unanimism is important. It can be credited with making a revolution in poetry, the drama and the novel, with the inven-tion of a new lyricism and a new style, with a suggestive exploration of the modern myth, what the French call *"le merveilleux moderne."* Modern it is, especially in its attitude toward mechanical inventions and machines, in its attempt to appropriate the moving-picture process of presentation and even to steal from radio broadcasting some devices to solve the problem of time and space in his dramatizations. The Un-animist psychology also inaugurates new means of approach to study human contacts while doing away with hackneyed plots and love stories.

Régis Michaud. *Modern Thought and Literature in France* (Funk). 1934. p. 120

The object of unanimist literature coincides with the object matter of the sociology of Durkheim: it is group life on the level of consciousness. By a common emphasis upon the hyperspiritual nature of social life;

upon the psychic energy of collective thought; upon society as the origin of knowledge and ethics; upon the apotheosis of the group, but a group conscious of itself and of its responsibility; upon the real existence of a collective consciousness which has no single organic substratum, but which is exclusively a creative synthesis and, as such, a psychic continuum, the unanimism of Jules Romains and the sociology of Emile Durkheim mutually support each other and bear witness to the unanimist nature of collectivity today.

Mildred Rubin Minter. SSR. July-Aug., 1941. p. 547

Victor Hugo and his disciple Jules Romains have made their creatures indistinct one from another in their meditation before the collective force of the city and the collective beauty of its murmur and its color. Their creatures are subdued and live mechanically as under the direction and spell of a very mysterious but omnipotent power. In both Hugo and Romains, the theme may shift from that of the city to that of humanity but the total effect is the same. The vastness of the power admits an unlimited flow of expression. The poem (or the novel) grows and grows, almost rapidly, without ever striking against an obstacle, without ever seeing a living person.

Wallace Fowlie. Clowns and Angels (Sheed and Ward).
1943. pp. 64–5

What one admires . . . in this work, is its total encylopedic character, the infinite variety of knowledge and experience which is revealed in it. From philosophy to business, passing through polite society, literature, politics, the police, little stores, le faubourg Saint-Germain, L'École Normale, journalism, revolutionary ferment, all appear before our eyes with the hallucinatory intensity of what has been not only seen, but lived and gone through, and all these the artist has been able to recreate by an internal and almost unconscious operation. I do not hesitate to say, and I will hold to it steadfastly, that since Balzac no novelist has performed a like miracle in observation and objectivity.

André Billy. Hommage à Jules Romains (Flammarion).
1945. p. 22. Tr. by Dorothy Nyren Curley

For nearly fifteen years Jules Romains has been engaged in a leisurely but thorough fashion, upon a monumental project, a history of contemporary France in fiction form. . . . This is truly a philosophic novel in the sense that all its interests are translated in terms of ideas. . . . Yet none of this is pompous, pretentious, or ponderous. Jules Romains has the gift of translating ideas into the language of spirited, idiomatic, and pointed talk. . . . Several men of our time have attempted to write series of novels which dramatize the great movements and impulses of whole societies. . . . Only Jules Romains has had the intellectual hardihood to give real dignity and spaciousness to his tremendous project.

James Gray. *On Second Thought* (Minnesota). 1946.
pp. 231, 233–4

Is *Men of Good Will* a novel? In many ways it is an epic poem; in others one might say that it constitutes an essay on twenty-five years of European history. . . . Romains has shown better than anyone the efforts and hopes of the small team of men of good will who thought for a long time that they could rebuild Europe. . . . Great novelist, greater essayist and poet, he has written an epic that, however pessimistic in its facts, remains inspiring in its love of freedom and in its deep sympathy for the adventure of the human race.

André Maurois. *NYT*. Nov. 24, 1946. pp. 7, 42

Like many moderns who do not subscribe to Christian faith but try to find substitutes for religious experience in poetical experience, like Rimbaud and Proust, among others, Romains has secularized mysticism. Repeatedly, in his early works, even in some of his farces, then in several volumes of *Les Hommes de bonne volonté,* he has depicted the action of a few individuals giving a soul to a group or controlling their own bodies, even the mechanism of their breathing or the beating of their hearts. And he has described their hallucinations. He is a mystic, not only without God (not an uncommon occurrence after all) but with more rationality than sensibility and with an unflagging practical sense. . . . He had the good fortune to coin a word for his intuition, which soon became a reasoned and consistent view of men—"unanimism." . . . Romains aimed at being the magician unleashing and controlling spiritual forces latent in groups. He always contended that he was not an analyst of social phenomena but a captor of magnetic currents passing through and electrifying crowds and transfiguring them into conscious, dynamic organisms with a collective soul.

Henri Peyre. *The Contemporary French Novel*
(Oxford). 1955. p. 54

Les Hommes de bonne volonté partially fails as a novel in the same way that Romains' conception of man's fate fails to meet the test of history. His conception of an individual existence, like his conception of history, raises to the status of an abstract system what was at best an excellent novelistic point of view. This point of view is rich in such literary possibilities as inventiveness and humor and gives Romains' farces and less ambitious novels their special savor. But it is unable to sustain his more ambitious project of showing how modern man moves, thinks, feels and acts, still less of revealing "the shape of things to come."

Germaine Brée and Margaret Guiton. *An Age of Fiction*
(Rutgers). 1957. p. 75

Unanimism is original because, in the first place, no author before Jules Romains had devoted almost the whole of his work to the study of human groups. . . . Nor had any author attempted with such persistence and such success to explore this collective theme so deeply, to reveal so many of its aspects. Romains is most profoundly original in developing the psychological aspects of his artistic study of groups, striving both by intellectual and by intuitive methods to discover and to give the fullest possible expression to the mysterious personalities and forces that arise when two or more people meet.

P. J. Norrish. *Drama of the Group* (Cambridge).
1958. p. 157

The merit of Romains and Chennevière . . . is to have developed a poetic and quasi-religious language to express the evolving consciousness of the collective life of groups and the city. Romains chose to express this new awareness in terms of a Christianity which he transposed from a theistic to a humanistic level for the purposes of unanimism. He invented a new terminology with a modern emphasis to illuminate old concepts. . . . *"L'unanime"* was a spiritual reality, similar to the state of religious experience William James had described. . . . Unanimism was to be the poetry of the social, intellectual, and artistic evolution of man.

Ben F. Stoltzfus. *MLQ*. Sept., 1960. pp. 243–5
See *Death of a Nobody, Men of Good Will,* and *Seventh of October* (novels); also *Knock* (play).

ROSTAND, EDMOND (1868–1918)

Cyrano is in fact a type—a type of the largest class of people in the world (for it includes every one), namely those who do not get what they know they deserve, who find no chance to do what they know they could do, who are so much greater to themselves than to the cold world. . . And so Cyrano takes our sympathy. We are even as he. With him it is a nose, with us fortunately a something else, that prevents our standing forth to the world for all we are worth. This . . . is the thing that unconsciously touches all.

Yet, because M. Rostand is not Shakespeare or some one like him, we do not have everything. Some would say because he is a Frenchman, decadent, pessimist, morbid, he has nothing more to say than just that. Here is a man who was fine, strong, brave, good, and never got his due. What of it? Well, the rest is silence, or nearly so.

Edward Everett Hale, Jr. *Dramatists of To-day*
(Holt). 1905. pp. 28–9

"Cyrano de Bergerac" is the supreme dramatic achievement of Rostand.
. . . The Romantic elements of "Cyrano" are unmistakable. In it Rostand conforms to practically all the theory of the Romanticists— but he also excels most of them in practice. . . . The connection of Rostand's drama with Hugo's is too obvious to need comment, but there is one fundamental difference between these two authors: Rostand is a dramatist and Hugo is not. . . . It is doubtful if anything in Hugo can be found as perfect and sustained dramatically, without the false notes of melodrama, as the final act of "Cyrano."

Hugh Allison Smith. *Main Currents of Modern French
Drama* (Holt). 1925. pp. 93, 94, 100

M. Rostand is not a great original genius. . . . He comes to us with no marvelous revelation, but he is a gifted, adroit artist, who does with freshness and force things that have been done before; and he is, at least, a monstrous fine fellow. . . . Personally, I like the Byzantine manner in literature better than any other, and M. Rostand is nothing if not Byzantine: his lines are loaded and encrusted with elaborate phrases and curious conceits which are most fascinating to any one who, like me, cares for such things. Yet, strange as it seems, none of these lines is amiss in the theatre. All the speeches blow in gusts of rhetoric straight over the footlights into the very lungs of the audience. Indeed, there is this unusual feature in M. Rostand's talent, that he combines with all the verbal preciosity of extreme youth, the romantic ardor and technical accomplishment of middle-age.

Max Beerbohm. *Around Theatres* (Knopf). 1930. pp. 8–9

We can see how far the great mantle of Victor Hugo has, all these years, trailed, and how, out of a mere corner of it, the cleverest of his grand-sons can cut a complete suit. The form of M. Rostand's style, is it not, broadly speaking, Victor Hugo's style brought down to date, attuned to the age of the interview, the automobile, and the decennial exhibition, the age of the American campaign and Madame Sarah Bernhardt? I say it not in mockery, nor even in familiarity, for M. Rostand will always dazzle me; but is it not practically a fair account of his use of his magnificent master to assert that he has done with him what we do with everything nowadays—has reduced him to the terms of contemporary journalism? . . . Happy an age, certainly, in which the vulgarisers are of M. Rostand's pattern.

Henry James. The Scenic Art (Rutgers). 1948. pp. 312–3

"Cyrano" did not turn out to be the beginning of a revolution, not even in France. The play is a vigorous and faithful revival of the great heroic drama of the French classical and romantic periods; it is in no sense a new creation. . . . The play is like a rich brocade which on close examination is found to contain crudities of colour and gems which are not real, but this is less disturbing because it contains an undertone of burlesque. Less easy to forgive are the hackneyed situations of the Scribe type which occasionally occur in it.

Martin Lamm. Modern Drama (Blackwell). 1952.
pp. 172–4

Edmond Rostand is not a major writer, yet somehow he is an important one. His importance lies in the fact that he is not only a kind of reaction to symbolist poetry, but a combination of two strains—idealism and realism—which at the end of the nineteenth century were contending for pre-eminence, and also the representative of a great tradition in French poetry, the tradition of rhetorical poetry. Rostand's romanticism is counteracted by his rationalism and trust in reality, and these two contending tendencies assume, in turn, the mastery of his creative mind, or blend harmoniously in order to produce his best writings.

Joseph Chiari. The Contemporary French Theatre
(Rockliff). 1958. p. 32

La dernière comédie de Don Rostand—I allude, obviously enough, to "La Dernière Nuit de Don Juan," a play profoundly born, profoundly wise, and profoundly beautiful. Three times in nine months I have read it, and three times, intoxicated by its beauty, I have found myself periodically raising my eyes from the manuscript and pausing to address to myself a glowing critical soliloquy. For here are the laughter and tears of genius woven into a great, gay ache—a super-Schnitzlerian tapestry shot through with the brilliant threads of fancy, poetry, and sardonic pathos. For here are literature and drama inextricably intertwined; a masterpiece of the modern theatre.

George Jean Nathan. Magic Mirror (Knopf). 1960.
pp. 177–8

"L'Aiglon." Yes, it's another world, but, every moment, it moves me. Rostand forbids nothing, and he profits by this. He uses all the strings, but he ties down all the birds with them, eagles as well as goldfinches.

You may be full of horror for war: Victor Hugo and Rostand almost succeed in making you accept the butcheries of Napoleon.

All this crushes me. And all that movement makes me want to write plays with people *sitting down.*

Jules Renard. *Journals* (Braziller). 1964. p. 150

See *Cyrano de Bergerac* (play).

SABA, UMBERTO (1883–1957)

The effect of this poetical monument [*Il canzóniere*] is imposing; the impact of its sincerity, freshness and unity of inspiration, overpowering. The blend of naïveté and wisdom, the economy and appropriateness of the technical and artistic devices, a lyricism which has not descended to prose, as one critic has declared, but is subdued by a wonderful chastity of feeling and a classical restraint almost unique among contemporary poets in Italy or elsewhere; all of these qualities make this book a poetic achievement and a human document of rare significance.

Renato Poggioli. *BA*. Spring, 1947. p. 232

Disillusioned with the external world, [Saba] was forced in upon himself, upon the mysterious fact of his own essence and personality. . . . Nostalgia . . . is, indeed, his essential attitude to life. The older he grows, the more he is inclined to celebrate (in what is perhaps the most exquisite lyrical verse to come out of Italy in half a century) the phenomenon of youth. He has ceased to believe in anything except the fact of life, which for him is a constant falling away from original perfection, a gradual decay and disillusionment. It is almost a Wordsworthian conception, but with a full acceptance of the implications and consequences. Romantic in sensibility, he works exclusively in classical forms, with remarkable restraint and economy. His poems are direct, deceptively simple, frequently dramatic, and always intensely personal. He reminds one somewhat of Housman, but his ear is more sophisticated. He is in the tradition of Tasso (*via* Metastasio) and Leopardi.

Oliver Evans. *Voices*. May-Aug., 1951. pp. 35–6

Saba's style . . . seems not to be there at all: no screen is interposed before the experience recounted. Stylistic critics have labored strenuously and in vain to account for this style. It can be shown to contain rags and tags of Petrarch, Tasso, Leopardi, and other classics, stuck between expressions borrowed from dialect; it combines the unfolded and singing rhythm of the traditional lyric, openly expressive of clearly defined states of mind, with the sinuous progression and ambiguous, hesitating tones of the decadents, and the allusive technique of the *trobar clus* analogists. By rights it should be a hodge-podge, but the various elements are not so much reconciled as dissolved in a fresh flow of language which calls no attention to the absorbed components during the reading process and yields them up only to conscious analysis.

Edward Williamson. *Poetry*. Jan., 1952. p. 233

He began to sing—no other word can so well describe his gift—at the age of seventeen, and the music never ceased for over half a century. . . . He was unfashionable under Mussolini, persecuted for singing often of Trieste, but never in the required, portentous, triumphant way. . . . He loved his city from the first moment. . . . Love poems fill the years until the first war, varied, tender, imperative but gently so. . . . As the first war begins to threaten, Umberto Saba becomes more and more Leopardian in his poems. They are always brief, and they become elegiac. . . . The Fascist dictatorship only proved that peace . . . might be signed, ships might again sail the seas freely, but there was no peace in the hearts of men. The landscape of Saba's poems becomes more restricted: the small things which give pleasure and the many which bring melancholy are all sung, the undertones are still serene. . . . In that Italy between Abyssinia and the 1940 entry into the war, there was hardly an educated Italian who was not fearfully concerned about the course of events, only there were so few educated Italians. To be educated then meant being self-educated, for the régime's education could provide no enlightenment. Saba had spent a lifetime educating himself, cherishing his gift for looking and listening. . . . I think he was one of the truest poets Italy has had.

Sylvia Sprigge. *LMg*. April, 1958. pp. 45–7, 50

A native not of one of the traditional centers of Italian culture but of the bustling port of Trieste across the Adriatic, where to be born in 1883, he says, was like being born anywhere else a generation earlier, Saba felt himself both *arretrato,* behind the times, and *periferico,* on the periphery of Italian letters. In some ways this was an advantage: he was protected from the hurlyburly of churning values in the Italy of his day and confirmed in his devotion to traditional rhythms, particularly of the hendeca-syllable, the standard eleven-syllable line of Italian poetry. He describes himself, a bit tongue-in-cheek, as the least revolutionary of poets, but adds in the next breath that his lines are so individual that one knows at a glance they are not by anyone else. Saba has been far from an isolated poet. Many would agree with G. Titta Rosa, who says that his poetry "has accompanied our generation like a friendly voice: we would even say, the dearest."

Jonathan Levy. *The Poem Itself,* ed. by
Stanley Burnshaw (Holt). 1960. p. 300

Although he was one of the most influential figures of Italian twentieth-century poetry, Saba occupied an isolated position throughout his life. Born and raised in Trieste, before the city was reunited to Italy . . . , Saba differed in background and development from his contemporaries in Italy. He remained at the edge of Italian culture and his activity seemed always tangential. His poetry issued entirely from his own personality; and his insistence on self-examination gives his work as a whole the appearance of an autobiographical obsession. He foreshadows the hermetics' closed, personal world, and although his language is seldom obscure, he gives certain words an emphatic importance—a habit that suggests the hermetics' technique. The world of Saba recalls the unpretentiousness of the crepuscolari, but there is no resigned meekness in him; indeed, the commonplace world seems brightened by his faith in it.

Carlo L. Golino. Contemporary Italian Poetry
(California). 1962. p. xiv

His uniqueness consisted not in revolutionizing the genre by resorting to a new vocabulary or new metrical schemes, but, on the contrary, by making use of the most ordinary language and of those schemes provided by the examples of his predecessors, from Petrarch to Leopardi. . . . As a craftsman he lacked the severity of such contemporaries as Ungaretti and Montale or the *engagement* of a Quasimodo. He was perhaps too frequently prone to be uncritical about his verse simply because it responded to a deep urge to give form to a particular moment of his life. But even in those moments when Saba does not reach the stylistic perfection of an artist, we know that without the weaknesses inherent in his poetry, the *Canzóniere* [his collected works] would not be what it is. When set side by side with Petrarch's lofty, and perhaps over-labored and therefore unspontaneous, perfection, the *Canzóniere,* with its ingenuity and occasional naïveté is the more moving and the more human document.

Sergio Pacifici. A Guide to Contemporary Italian
Literature (World). 1962. pp. 162, 164–5

See poems in *Contemporary Italian Poetry,* ed. by Carlo L. Golino.

SAGAN, FRANÇOISE (1935–   )

The French language, by English standards, is inflexible—although the French don't think of it that way—and the more literate are constantly aware of separate, if overlapping sets of vocabulary. This makes for a somewhat different and more acute audience appreciation of not only the *mot,* but the style *juste,* than a writer in English could expect. Sagan's handling of literary French is classic and formal, and for a Frenchman, the conventions of tense and syntax used in a perfect academic fashion, have an expressiveness and charm quite apart from the ideas they help to convey. In the view of an academician like the respected critic of *La Monde,* Emile Henriot (who has praised Sagan to the skies), such a demonstration of pure diction is doubtless, all by itself, a sign of major talent.

> Robert Parris. *NR.* Aug. 20, 1956. p. 19

The novels written by Françoise Sagan have shown obviously and increasingly the sexual anarchy in which some adults and consequently many young people live. . . . Françoise Sagan has written about people she has met on the Côte d'Azur, at the University, and in the milieu of journalism, the theatre, and literature. Whatever may be the limits of her experience, it appears that she has put her finger on an illness of our period and the patient has flinched at her touch.

> Georges Hourdin. *Le Cas Françoise Sagan*
> (Editions du Cerf). 1958. pp. 73–4.
> Tr. by Dorothy Nyren Curley

What she has that is new is a rhythm. Whence her love of music and the musical allusions which appear so often. The common denominator of an air by Mozart and of a well-worn story is rhythm—more physical, more overpowering than melody. It pervades the very air we breathe, it changes systems of currents, and by almost physiological elements, it subjugates the reader. This is perhaps one of the factors of the prodigious success of [her] work.

> Gérard Mourgue. *Françoise Sagan* (Editions
> Universitaires). 1958. pp. 117–8.
> Tr. by Dorothy Nyren Curley

In order to write about people who do nothing, think nothing and bear no particular distinguishing mark, one has to be an observer—an angry one or a well-disposed one, but an observer. But one constantly has the feeling that Françoise Sagan is incapable of judging the people she talks about, for the reason that they are the very people she has lived among since the day she was born, whom she has seen every day of her life, and still does. Being unable to make her characters act in any significant way —to her everything they do is commonplace because their behavior is part and parcel of her own life—she determines to attempt to define them. . . . Her characters remain silhouettes; and what is worse, nothing ever happens to them.

Jean Bloch-Michel. PR. Winter, 1958. pp. 118–9

That *lucidité* which Sagan's characters never abandon for a second tells them that the absurdity of life and one's loneliness can only be escaped through love, but that theirs is no lasting flame (the leitmotiv of time's destruction, *dans un mois dans un an* occurs over and over again in these novels). . . . In Sagan's first two novels one could already suspect that, behind the rage to live that seemed to possess her characters, there lay a craving for an inaccessible ideal. The quest unremittingly goes on in *Aimez-vous Brahms?* . . . This . . . novel's poignant description of *la condition humaine* confirms, if it were necessary, Françoise Sagan's unusual literary gifts.

Michel Guggenheim. YFS. Summer, 1959. p. 95

This deliberate limitation of her role to depicting the life of the bourgeois society she was born and brought up in is without doubt one of the keys to Sagan's popularity. She has described the vapid emptiness of this world without embellishment, and in doing so she has come to be recognized as one of the figures that best symbolize the bourgeois membership of France's first post-war generation. . . . In Sagan's hands the tortured philosophizings of Sartre have been turned into easily digestible clichés; the classic *roman d'amour* has been streamlined into the *roman déma-quillé*—the novel without make-up. Its popularity goes hand in hand with the steadily expanding vogue for simplicity in everything: speech, gesture, dress.

Curtis Cate. At. March, 1960. p. 94

The elements of Françoise Sagan's plays are in a way her own property —or at least are not instinctively used, or even borrowed, by other writers for the French theatre. For her, as a romantic, love is the fine flower of life—the most important gift you get or give—and it fades. As a modern intelligence, she perceives that between lovers the practice of ideas usually destroys emotions, that personal liberty is a dangerous necessity, that most human beings suffer from and give off ennui, and that fantasy is a final refuge from reality, especially for the French. This inventory she used in such perfect proportion in her *"Chateau en Suède"* that the play will likely be regarded for its delights as a personal period piece, and will be revived over time, like a minor theatre classic.

Genêt. NY. Jan. 26, 1963. pp. 107–8

See *Aimez-vous Brahms?, Bonjour Tristesse,* and *A Certain Smile* (novels).

SAINT EXUPÉRY, ANTOINE DE (1900–1944)

Saint Exupéry in all he tells us speaks as one who has "been through it." His personal contact with ever-recurrent danger seasons his book with an authentic and inimitable tang. We have had many stories of the War or of imaginary adventures which, if they showed the author as a man of nimble wit, brought smiles to the faces of such old soldiers or genuine adventurers as read them. I admire this work not only on its literary merits but for its value as a record of realities, and it is the unlikely combination of these two qualities which gives *Night Flight* its quite exceptional importance.

André Gide. Preface to *Night Flight* (Century). 1932.
p. xi

He knows better than any writer that the hardships of life in one of the vanguard services bind men together in a feeling that goes farther around the world and across the years than any emotion of the Deathless Odes. . . . He is making the grave poetry of an unknown and difficult craft, but underneath he is talking about the poetry of all the crafts men have worked at. . . . [*Wind, Sand and Stars*] brings out the thing men really live by, or rather among; for men live by and in their work only when their work becomes a passion that is understandable to and shared by their fellows.

Otis Ferguson. *NR*. July 5, 1939. p. 256

In the world today the articulate airmen can be numbered on the fingers of one hand. Plenty of people write about flying; some have thrills to write about, some war careers, some long-distance records, some hothouse descriptions; but the real thing, though it is sometimes compounded of such ingredients, is stamped with a special quality. It is a mixture of technical accomplishment and poetic imagination, a blend which can see an instrument board as an array of jewels or an isobar map as a coil of serpents: a rare combination. M. Antoine de Saint Exupéry has it.

Cecil Lewis. *Spec*. Oct. 6, 1939. p. 478

One could take chapter by chapter [of *Wind, Sand and Stars*], passage by passage, and quote and analyze the texture of the writing. There is the quality of flight itself, of imperceptibly gliding from the ground, which has somehow been put into the words, the rhythm, and the style. There is the dream quality of the fairy tale in the oasis, as haunting, as suggestive as the misty scent of heliotrope in a garden at night. And there is that song of praise to water, refound and recovered, which seems to hold some of the clear austere quality of Gregorian chants, or of those pure morning hymns of St. Francis—as pure, as clear, as liquid, as water itself, gushing from a mountain spring. What a chameleon touch that can write of flying and create flying—that can write of water and create water!

Anne Morrow Lindbergh. *Essay Annual*
(Scott, Foresman). 1940. p. 3

The writing of Antoine de Saint Exupéry resembles that of André Malraux in one respect: it is marked by the special kind of frenzy which results when passion is joined to technique. Such writing reminds me of the performance of a ballet dancer whose wonderful freedom of movement rises from and is released by a technical control of the body in motion strict in the extreme but so complete that it has been "forgotten" by the performer and is invisible to the observer, and it yields the same keen pleasure.

Margaret Marshall. *Nation*. March 7, 1942. p. 286

Saint Exupéry has one fit companion, but only one that I can happily envisage. In Malraux's *Days of Hope* war in the air rose to the same high level of articulation [as in *Flight to Arras*], and was infused with the same peculiar spiritual significance. Both writers build on the foundation of technical knowledge, using the immensely powerful medium of technical terms to achieve a strange aerial construction of technical sensation. . . . Saint Exupéry is a rare combination of technician, man of action and gifted introvert. In all the fields covered by these abilities he is a consummate descriptive writer.

Philip Toynbee. *NSN*. Oct. 10, 1942. p. 245

Saint Exupéry, who was six feet tall, had the head of a bird. His skull was round and his hair was beginning to recede, his nose was tilted and rather pointed, his chin (like Bedell Smith's) was stubborn, but not prominent, and his eyes, which were protuberant, seemed almost to be set sideways. This bird's head, meanwhile, was mounted on the body of a Negro prize-fighter: the neck and shoulders of a bull, a great barrel chest, a fine slim waist, thin knock-kneed shanks that ended in long flat feet on which, when he was in a hurry, he shuffled rather than ran. Not very flattering, you say, and yet his bearing was noble, the dignity, the intelligence, and the open fearlessness of his countenance were so endearing, that he was actually one of the most attractive of men.

Lewis Galantière. *At*. April, 1947. p. 138

No one has surpassed him in suggesting poetically the exciting, intensely happy or tragic moments in the life of a growing boy. His understanding of boyish dreams and aspirations, his feeling for the fairyland of a *"domaine mystérieux,"* have caused him to be compared to Alain-Fournier, but there is this distinction that he never turned to childhood as an escape; for him the past was not another world but was still alive as part of his present. . . . He refused to turn into a "grown-up." Between the boy and the man there was no cleavage, no metamorphosis; he matured as a plant does, depending on its roots for nourishment.

Philip A. Wadsworth. MLQ. March, 1951. pp. 101–2

He never indulged in writing merely to retain the attention of the public or because of tempting contracts offered by publishers. He patiently waited until he had matured inwardly what he had to say and had mastered the form that would say it most adequately. Saint Exupéry's books are usually brief, almost to a fault; there is no redundance in them, few irrelevant digressions, no trace of superfluous fat, as it were. In his rare moments of confiding in his readers, he would compare himself to a diamond cutter or to a sculptor, chiseling away from the first drafts of his writings all extraneous substance; or, better still, to a baker kneading his dough over and over again until it developed enough resistance for him to fight successfully against its plastic matter.

Henri Peyre. The Contemporary French Novel
(Oxford). 1955. pp. 165–6

Malraux, the revolutionist, has come to typify the twentieth-century adventurer; but Saint Exupéry, the air pilot, is more of a knight-errant. His life, as we see it in his writings, seems to have consisted of a series of quests. And a quest, as distinguished from an adventure, is a search for something that remains elusive but that is known to be of great value. . . . The true purpose of the quest is not merely a search for new horizons, new antagonists, new metaphors and new sensations—intriguing as these may be. Saint Exupéry is seeking a new aspect of the self, a spiritual power that will enable him to pierce through the shell of outward appearance.

Germaine Brée and Margaret Guiton. An Age of Fiction
(Rutgers). 1957. p. 194

There is something instinctive and sensual about people's response to the desert: it is either hated utterly—when it is, indeed, fearful—or passionately loved. Saint Exupéry not only succumbed at first sight, but exulted in the solitude, feeling "a sort of appeasement" and giving himself up to a world of dreams. . . . He fell under its spell but he did not choose the desert. It was his destiny, surely, to live there, for we can no more imagine him apart from the desert than we can think of him apart from the airplane. Both favored his meditations and satisfied a strange combination of needs, providing him with long hours of solitude while still offering adventure and contact with the lives of men.

Marcel Migeo. Saint Exupéry (McGraw-Hill). 1960. pp. 89–90

He did not wish to write anything which his life did not substantiate or that he had not had occasion to verify on his own. It is because of this that the strictly literary world remained suspect since it may trick the reader, transporting him to a world facile and false. Saint Exupéry remained one of those men constrained by exactitude, for whom imagination could add to reality, but not take its place; for reality absorbs them completely and sternly.

Roger Caillois. Preface to Oeuvres de Saint Exupéry
(Bibliothèque de la Pléiade). 1961. p. xiv.
Tr. by Dorothy Nyren Curley

From the first book [<i>Southern Mail</i>] in which some awkwardness is noticeable, a style developed which, soon liberated from the uses of the novel, achieved amplitude and beauty. The characters which appeared in it already showed a need for concreteness, a need for combining matter and spirit. . . . This need to give body to an impression, to an idea, to loan it thickness, a palpable reality, gave the style of Saint Exupéry a substantial character, a weight (in the best sense of the word) which distinguished it from all others.

Pierre Gascar. In Saint Exupéry by René Marill Albérès
and others (Hachette). 1963. p. 134.
Tr. by Dorothy Nyren Curley

See <i>Night Fall</i> (novel); also <i>Wind, Sand and Stars</i> and <i>Wisdom of the Sands</i> (prose).

SALINAS, PEDRO (1891–1951)

Señor Salinas' qualms at offering . . . [his] poems to the American public are due to our "insane desire for utility and efficiency." How will such a public accept his poetry? . . . Its strength is to be found in its luxury and its being a useless thing.

His range of inspiration is broad. Sometimes it is external nature— the soil, the ocean, the seashore, a bird, a sea breeze, landscape, mountain, trees, snow, the setting sun. Seldom, however, is he content to consider these elements objectively; more often than not they are the means of expressing his emotion. Interesting are his verses of yearning—yearning for the unattainable. Juxtaposed with the mystical side of our poet is the sensual. A lively appeal is made to each sense, especially to those of touch and sight.

On the mechanical side, rhyme or assonance is merely accidental. There is no regular stanzaic arrangement. To add to the mechanical confusion, many groups punctuated as sentences are paratactic. . . . [He writes] verses of airy illusion, sensuality, fantastic emotion, and fresh images.

A. E. LeVey. *BA*. Spring, 1939. p. 239

Pedro Salinas does not dabble with poetry as an avocation. He was born a poet and he would be unable to write anything but poetry—subtle, striving, and uncompromising poetry which doubtless baffles the man in the street and which probably demands knitting of the most capacious brows. The author has labeled *La bomba increíble* a *"fabulación."* In form it is a quasi-scientific novel, in substance it is a noble arraignment of the arrogant and presumptuous pseudo-science which is dessicating our world and threatening the very existence of the race. It is devastating satire, rich and roguish fancy, generous emotion, and exquisite poetry. . . . It is a titanic achievement. . . . Pedro Salinas is first of all a poet, and a poet is a preacher. . . . The scientists need not answer him. He is not attacking science, he is reminding us of its *raison d'être*.

Roy Temple House. *BA*. Winter, 1952. p. 41

His books of verse composed in Spain, from *Presagios* through *Razón de amor,* were concerned with universal, rather than contemporary problems: love, death and the sense of nothingness. The Spanish Civil War and the years spent in America awakened him brutally to the realities of the technological forces which are most significant for our life in the twentieth century. The amatory, two-dimensional dialogues ended with *Razón de amor;* and human love is generally absent from the works that follow. *Todo más claro* is the most anguished of his books. It is the poet, the pure and limpid thinker and artist that was Pedro Salinas, face to face with the horrors and the promise of the technological revolution which is everywhere and inescapably occurring. As his residence was in our industrial East, he could not fail to be impressed by the bleakness and the crushing of the spirit which technology often effects in that region. In this book the sense of nothingness, which runs as a threat to Being and love, as an agnostic undercurrent, through most of his work, is carried to its most anguished conclusion.

Julian Palley. *Hsp*. Sept., 1959. p. 336

Razón de amor (Love's reason) and *La Voz a ti debida* (The Voice due you) are the heart of Salinas' poetry. The latter is his great poem of love, and one of the most important love poems in contemporary European literature; the former incorporates some of the most intensely lyric of his poems; and together the two books compose a hymn to love, a liturgical Sequence, as it were. This is poetry of a wholesome love, healthy and sound; a love that is affirmative, happily innocent of complications and deviations. Or let us say that such complications as arise are of the metaphysical order, springing from Salinas' preoccupation with the reduction of sensation to idea, with the transformation of real time into an ideal abstraction of time. The problems are difficult, but the solution is inevitably poetical.

Eugenio Florit. *The Poem Itself*, ed. by
Stanley Burnshaw (Holt). 1960. p. 207

Salinas' contempt for visual impressions is one aspect of a literary pose already assumed at the beginning of his career and faithfully maintained thereafter: that of the poet who distils and wholly re-fashions his contacts with reality. In one of the early poems in *Presagios* he catches sight of a fruit hanging from a tree, and immediately blames his eyes for their superficiality in seeing only its exterior; closing them, he transforms his hand into a *mano de ciego,* aspiring to bypass that exterior in quest of the invisible, untouchable essence of the fruit. . . . Ignoring the evidence of his eyes, Salinas puts his trust in the light generated through his fingertips; they are his beacons in a world he has chosen to make dark and colorless.

C. B. Morris. *BHS*. Jan., 1961. pp. 103, 106

Pedro Salinas inherited the influence of Juan Ramón Jiménez but soon developed his own style. He has been called at various times a pure poet, full of classic images, Gongoristic, Calderonian. His poetry, often subtle and intellectual, was less dry and bare than that of Unamuno and more spiritual than that of Jiménez. He used his words very carefully to convey their conceptual values. He also strove for quiet contemplation, however, and was especially concerned with the interior reality of the poet. . . . Since his verses are refined, subtle, cultured, and intelligent, the casual reader might suspect Salinas' poetic world were limited in its search for a hidden reality and apparent rejection of human elements. Indeed, Cernuda insists that all of Salinas' work is a game, and his human pose, affectation. Yet Salinas is a human poet. . . . His yearnings, often anguished and feverish, are those of humanity. . . . Salinas suffered from nostalgia, was preoccupied with modern man's anguished problems, worried about a loveless world, and hoped for one in which someday the restoration of ideas and idealism would be a possibility.

> Richard E. Chandler and Kessel Schwartz. *A New History of Spanish Literature* (Louisiana). 1961. pp. 381–3

See *Lost Angel and Other Poems, Truth of Two and Other Poems, Zero,* and *Sea of San Juan* (poetry); also *Reality and the Poet in Spanish Poetry* (criticism).

SARRAUTE, NATHALIE (1902–   )

The best thing about Nathalie Sarraute is her stumbling, groping style, with its honesty and numerous misgivings, a style that approaches the object with reverent precautions, withdraws from it suddenly out of a sense of modesty, or through timidity before its complexity, then, when all is said and done, suddenly presents us with the drooling monster, almost without having touched it, through the magic of an image. Is this psychology? Perhaps Nathalie Sarraute, who is a great admirer of Dostoievsky, would like to have us believe that it is. For my part, I believe that by allowing us to sense an intangible authenticity, by showing us the constant coming and going from the particular to the general, by tenaciously depicting the reassuring, dreary world of the inauthentic, she has achieved a technique which makes it possible to attain, over and beyond the psychological, human reality in its very *existence.*

> Jean-Paul Sartre. Preface to *Portrait of a Man Unknown* by Nathalie Sarraute (Braziller). 1958. p. xiv

Nathalie Sarraute does not offer a rational description of [the] interior universe whose swarming activity, instability and disconcerting logic many critics have already analyzed. She explores it with intelligence, with relentless lucidity and determination not to be fooled by the *trompe-l'oeil* of appearances; she also looks at it with an eye at times childish. Yet the task to which she has set herself and which gives her works both a new content and a personal style, is precisely to shun the temptation of making hasty clarifications, to avoid limiting herself to the exclusive use of rational analysis.

> Anne Minor. *YFS.* Summer, 1959. pp. 96–7

In *The Era of Suspicion,* a brilliant essay on the novel, Mme. Sarraute staked out her domain: the hidden, emotional life of the depths in constant flux, with its subtle interchanges, its infinitesimal variations in pressure, which reveal, way beneath the rational social patterns of behavior, the watchful, hunted human hunter, peering like some small

ferocious shell-fish fearfully out of his shell. What is most curious perhaps . . . is that she manages so intensely to suggest not the modes of
a solitary individual life, but patterns emerging from a common human
substance, that of the "species," organically a whole, our ultimate
reality.

Germaine Brée. *NYT*. Nov. 1, 1959. pp. 4, 43

She insists that the reader spend his time with nerve-racking, irritating
people whose problems are either banal or factitious. Yet Mme. Sarraute is not boring at all. The risk is run but failure is avoided. She
is fascinating because, while she seems to be entirely concerned with
little truths about small personalities, she has a firm grip on a very large
truth—the accepted description of man as a "social animal" means
not that he loves his fellows but only that he can't do without them.

The thoroughness with which Mme. Sarraute pursues this single
theme, delineating the constant fluctuations of feeling in a small group
in close emotional quarters is compelling. To some readers it may seem
almost cruel.

Naomi Bliven. *NY*. March 26, 1960. p. 152

Few contemporary novelists have been so successful at portraying sensitive and frail beings at odds with a dark, hostile world in which perfidy
and conventionality regularly triumph. Nathalie Sarraute, who has
criticized Virginia Woolf, is not unlike her. She directs her microscope
at the apparently insignificant and endows it with poetry and with tragic
implications. She implicitly protests against all that is insincere in men
and delves into a deeper authenticity, buried in our lower depths.

Henri Peyre. *NYT*. May 15, 1960. p. 46

The center of Mme. Sarraute's nondescript universe is occupied neither
by the author nor by a proxy hero. Through many eyes and more than
one consciousness we encounter the characters, not in repose but as
they gravitate toward or away from each other. . . . Mme. Sarraute does
not lead her reader by the hand into the subconscious strata of her
characters, but instead projects their self-awareness into the exterior
world, where they may be observed. She does not pass judgement on their
moral worth with intricate analyses of their actions. She does not break
down personality to arrive at its comprehension; she aspires, instead, to
its synthesis.

Anna Balakian. *SR*. June 11, 1960. pp. 35–6

Steadily, at the rate of one novel every sixth year, Nathalie Sarraute
has been forcing upon her readers a new awareness of their sub-surface

selves. An inner world of gelatinous beings thus stands revealed under a pallid light; all anxiously groping for identical satisfactions, these pseudo-human creatures alternately experience pleasure and pain as tumor-like feelers either mingled with similar excrescences or become bruised by hostile reactions and are forced back into their own transparency and nakedness.

Leon S. Roudiez. YFS. Spring-Summer, 1961. p. 90

For Madame Sarraute, the reader is the enemy; he is there to be ambushed, demoralised, ultimately brainwashed. But the reader . . . is sometimes tempted to resist his fate. He snarls and starts looking for a bolt-hole. If only, somehow, out of this faceless nightmare, he could create a sane, familiar world, he might perhaps escape. If he could see these monsters, suddenly as *characters* well-classified, related to a solid social setting, then he might climb above them, criticise them, drive them off. Facelessness and anonymity are the essential materials from which Madame Sarraute constructs her particular Inferno. But suppose the reader will not have this? Suppose in desperation he should restore faces to the flayed and bleeding heads, and thus, out of mere pronouns, start creating *people*? At once, of course, the hallucinatory power of the novel is lost.

That this *can* happen is the evident weakness of Nathalie Sarraute the novelist.

Richard N. Coe. TT. March 29, 1962

What is the point of this multiplication of realities? . . . When [the writer] comes to the literary marketplace bearing his jar of tiny and as yet uncatalogued marine specimens, are we to welcome him in the name of science? (The writer as marine biologist.) Of sport? (The writer as deep sea diver.) Why does he deserve an audience? How many fragments of reality will readers of novels tolerate? How many do they need?

It really is science, or better yet sport, that Sarraute has in mind. Hence her revulsion against the beautiful and the pleasurable as such. . . . Thus Sarraute summons the novel to take its belated place in the anti-hedonistic revolution that has already conquered painting and music—to renounce pleasure and beauty, because these are attached to "familiar appearances." It is a stern appeal and may find a willing audience.

Susan Sontag. PR. Summer, 1963. p. 267

It is hard not to sound like a Philistine in bringing opposition to Mme. Sarraute, because she walls her position around with all the traditional bricks of the avant-garde. She grabs off the right to be boring; she promises herself recognition by posterity; she speaks of art as though it were a vow of celibacy; she keeps distinguishing between the modern and the old-fashioned—the modern always being hers. . . . She would rather be right than true, and one way of seeming right is by making all others appear wrong—very irritating in someone posing all the time as a relativist who is conscious of the eclectic nature of our period.

Alfred Chester. *AS.* Summer, 1963. p. 490

See *The Age of Suspicion* (essays); also *The Golden Fruits, Martereau, The Planetarium,* and *Portrait of a Man Unknown* (novels).

SARTRE, JEAN-PAUL (1905–   )

It is Sartre's great strength in his time that he has managed to remain quite uninfected by the Cocteau-esque Parisian chichi of the interval between the wars. If Existentialism has become, like surrealism, something of a *mouvement à exporter,* no one has probed so shrewdly as Sartre . . . the recent attempts of the French to distract the attention of the world from their political and military discredit by exploiting the glory of their writers, or pointed out so boldly the abuses to which this practice may lead. If he sometimes has the air of pontificating, it is probably almost impossible for a French literary man whose influence is being felt to refrain from playing the role of *chef d'école.* And Sartre, bourgeois and provincial, has succeeded in preserving for the French qualities which they very much need and which it is cheering to see still flourish: an industry, an outspokenness and a common sense which are the virtues of a prosaic intelligence and a canny and practical character.

Edmund Wilson. *Classics and Commercials* (Farrar).
1950. pp. 402–3

He is a thinker who stands full in the way of three post-Hegelian movements of thought: the Marxist, the existentialist and the phenomenological. He has felt the impact of each and has brought to each his own modifications. He uses the analytical tools of the Marxists and shares their urgent passion for action, but without accepting a theological view of the Dialectic. He remains at heart a liberal social democrat. He takes from Kierkegaard the picture of man as a lonely anguished being in an ambiguous world, but he rejects the hidden Kierkegaardian God. He uses the methods and the terminology of Husserl but lacks Husserl's dogmatism and his Platonic aspirations. . . . Sartre's great inexact equations, like those of his master Hegel, inspire us to reflect. His passion both to possess a big theoretical machine and to gear it on to the details of practical activity compares favorably with the indifference of those who are complacently content to let history get on without them. His inability to write a great novel is a tragic symptom of a situation which afflicts us all. We know that the real lesson to be taught is that the human person is precious and unique; but we seem unable to set it forth except in terms of ideology and abstraction.

Iris Murdoch. *Sartre* (Yale). 1953. pp. vii, 114

He is one of those people of whom solemn persons say, just because they are amusing, "Do you think he can be sincere?" He can make the ideas dance to his piping, and he has let loose the Maenads in the academic grove; we should not grumble overmuch, at so lavish a feast of reason, if unreason has also its place. There is a fool in Sartre who, in a less logical climate and a less austere time, would be a happy fool; being a Frenchman who (in more than the usual sense) *a vu le loup,* he wears a red cap and builds a guillotine for "Values." Even in his grittiest chapters (and my stomach in these matters is as an old maid's), the general effect is one of mental exhilaration. He has given back to literature a density, a frame of reference, which it lacked between the two wars; he has restored to things their outside and their skin, even if it was with loathing—and the loathing was partly at least ironical. He is a fighter who can lay about him from sheer lustiness, without counting on whose heads the blows may fall; no Totalitaria, certainly, will ever regiment him—no capitalism will buy him.

Arland Ussher. *Journey through Dread* (Devin-Adair).
1955. p. 146

The flashes of poetry in prose, which illuminate the novels of Malraux and of Giono, are absent from Sartrean fiction. Metaphors are scarce, but they are precise, convincing, and sharply delineated. Sheer adornments are spurned by him, as well as the music of prose. . . . Above all, Sartre's mastery is conspicuous in some of his dialogues, in an interior monologue purified of much of the irrelevancy and insignificance of much of the genre, and in his unorthodox use of the spoken language. With less artificiality than Céline or than Queneau, Sartre has successfully broken with the romantic illusion that interposes a pretty screen of words between the reader and the scene represented. His language welcomes slang, profanity, and obscenity. It catches up with the least conventional spoken language, as written words had not done for a whole century.

Henri Peyre. *The Contemporary French Novel*
(Oxford). 1955. pp. 233–4

M. Sartre offers a decidedly systematic work and peoples his book [*Being and Nothingness*] with many abstract entities whose existences are very real for him. In fact he seems addicted to transforming descriptive generalizations into substantive entities. This, however, may be largely a matter of style. Existentialists prefer to write ambiguously and enigmatically, and Sartre is no exception. Hegel allegedly murdered philosophical style, but whatever he left alive is being snuffed out by the kind of philosophical semantics employed by Sartre. If he wants to talk about people other than oneself, he must refer to them as the "other." If he wishes to discuss the distinction between consciousness and the world of things, he must use such language as "for itself" and "in itself." And when he uses such a term as "being" he is not clear whether "being" is a descriptive term covering the empirical world of what there is, or a substantive entity "Being" which supports or overlays it. It is often said that existence precedes essence in Sartre, but in this work, the nominal becomes real, the adjectival becomes ontological and, in traditional language, process becomes substance.

Harold Weisberg. *NR*. July 30, 1956. p. 19

In this work [*Being and Nothingness*] Sartre has defended a more radical form of human freedom than any which has so far appeared in our intellectual history. Many readers will probably feel that this position is too one-sided and fails to do justice to natural obstacles and limitations. But whatever their views may be they can hardly fail to be impressed by Sartre's cogent argument that human consciousness is no objective *thing* with a fixed essence from which life develops, as a screen display is developed from a roll of film. . . . In any case he has shed a genuine light on the problems of personal freedom and the kind of struggle that must now be carried on by lonely individuals if it is to survive here and there amongst the ever expanding apparatus of technology.

John Wild. *SR*. Oct. 6, 1956. p. 45

The book we've just finished is Sartre's novel translated, called *The Age of Reason*! You *ought* to read it—it's a peach!—a lovely soft rotten *peach*! whose juice keeps running down your chin as if down Aaron's beard! and you have the lovely liquorish taste long after it's done and down.

John Cowper Powys. *Letters to Louis Wilkinson*
(MacDonald). 1958. p. 232

Jean-Paul Sartre possesses that gift that enables a writer who is not really an artist (except as a critic-essayist) to turn out respectable and significant work in media—such as the short story, the novel and, particularly, the drama—to which his approach is chiefly intellectual. In other words, though Sartre is not truly a dramatist, he knows how to make a play which will serve the contemporary theatre better than some of his more highly endowed colleagues.

Sartre's plays are philosophic melodramas. He knows the value of action in the theatre: a forceful story line which makes use of either familiar or topically exciting material. . . . Sartre knows how to profit by the unstable moral condition of his audience—its potential hysteria— so that a number of symptoms can be passed off as psychological types, as in "No Exit." In any case, Sartre's characters and situations are so shrewdly selected that they strike the theatre public as acceptable realism or as understandably poetic drama, though in fact they are only tight frameworks constructed to convey a critical perception, a thesis or an attitude which by force of skill and literary agility might be called a philosophy.

Harold Clurman. Lies Like Truth (Macmillan). 1958.
p. 211

There are two aspects of Sartre the thinker and the rational connection between them is still to be made. . . . On the one hand he appears as an inward-looking, almost insanely subjectivist or solipsistic thinker, intellectualising the imaginative writer who conveys to us *la nausée* and the "glueyness" of existence. On the other hand, he appears as a progressive, melioristic intellectual with utilitarian leanings, avowedly confident at the prospect of Man's freedom to shape his destiny (the same prospect of limitless possibilities that seemed to frighten the author of *The Diary of Antoine Roquentin*). . . . The "tension and ambiguity" . . . that results from this duality may be a grave fault in an abstract thinker; it is perhaps impossible for a philosopher to incorporate both the spirit of Fichte and the spirit of Bentham. But it is reasonable to suppose that from the conflicts and revulsions the imaginative writer and above all the dramatist may benefit.

W. W. Robson. *Spec.* Sept. 23, 1960. p. 455

He blames himself for having sought to follow a middle road, for having yielded even if only for a moment, even if only as in a dream, even if only on a few rare occasions, to the appeal of compromise with the social order. He blames himself also for growing old. Never has a man, who after all is not yet an old man, scorned with such cold fury the decrepitude of those who have outlived their youth. . . . It seems as if Sartre desperately regrets, as one regrets a lost love, that he did not die before rounding the fatal cape of forty, that he did not simply clear out, as Nizan did at thirty-five, in a gesture of haughty disdain, saying "No" to the last. . . . He is obsessed with growing old, and the jealousy an aging idealist feels toward those who are taking his place in the front ranks is perhaps the most acute of jealousies. No longer can Sartre speak for the young. And he has been quicker than they to recognize the fact.

Madeleine Chapsal. *Reporter*. Sept. 29, 1960. p. 46

Of course, Sartre's France is not at all the *douce France* of our Sunday reviewers. It is a France altogether more sinister and disagreeable: the anguished, anarchic France of Villon, Pascal, Rousseau, de Sade, Rimbaud—above all, Pascal. One feels that Sartre's God, if he had one, would be the God of Isaac and Jacob, *pas des philosophes*. And— need one say?—Sartre too is haunted by the silence of the infinite spaces. At point after point, it is to Pascal that one turns for an analogy in French tradition. Yet again, like Pascal the Jansenist, how unFrench Sartre is! How exceedingly German, for example! Tortured, compulsive, overbearing, long-winded: worrying at truth like a dog at a bone: utterly absorbed, though a sworn enemy of systems, in the perfection of his own system.

John Mander. *NSN*. Oct. 8, 1960. p. 531

The overwhelming facility of Sartre and his disarming intelligence are almost impediments in his more purely literary works and especially in his plays. One feels that the writing of his dialogue has been accomplished without effort because it is dominated by the very clarity of the subject matter as he sees it. But this dialogue, in its freshness, spontaneity, liveliness, is dramatic in itself, and because of these very qualities. One follows so many ideas, as they multiply rapidly in scene after scene, that they hold our full attention and we end by not missing, in any serious sense, the psychological hesitations and subtleties, and the dramatic insights of poetic metaphor that are pervasively present in such playwrights as Shakespeare, Pirandello, and Claudel. So substantial is the intellectual nourishment of a Sartre play, that we forget what it lacks.

Wallace Fowlie. *Dionysius in Paris* (Meridian). 1960.
pp. 169–70

In his insistence that man must always be responsible for what he becomes, and that he can never legitimately claim to be better than his acts, Sartre is laying the foundation for an extremely healthy approach to personal morality. He does away with all alibis and excuses, and makes each person look his own failure straight in the eye. His arguments depend, it is true, on an assertion that free will exists rather than on a convincing refutation of the arguments for determinism, but like all "libertarian" approaches it is a very healthy one. The nihilism which it fails to transcend is perhaps the inevitable darker side of a theory which also does away with all fixed values and shows man his complete and terrifying freedom. The challenge to try to go beyond this nihilism is in itself perhaps the most stimulating part of Sartre's moral philosophy.

On a literary plane Sartre must first of all be given credit for having expressed these moral and philosophical ideas in an immediately accessible form.

Philip Thody. *Jean-Paul Sartre* (Macmillan). 1960. p. 236

There is much truth in the assertion that each of us, in coming into the world, makes his choice. This choice may never be verbally declared: our being may emerge silently into the world (in which case it will be our acts which will betray us); or the choice may be formulated into a doctrine, and this doctrine will express our choice systematically.

This last is the choice that Sartre has made, and his qualities are manifest: sharp dialectic; an entirely new approach to the problem of Nothingness; a penetrating analysis of bad faith, anguish, and desire; an original statement of the possibles; and a defense of freedom which, although extreme, is impressive. He has, furthermore, the merit of reminding us of some points—such as the inanity of existence and the fragility of happiness—which we had decided not to examine any longer. For anyone who considers not only the immediate and pragmatical result, but has the audacity to view the totality of the real, it may appear that Sartre has something to say. The technician and the pragmatist glue us to the visible world. The Existentialist, on the contrary, takes to himself all those things which others want to frustrate in us: experience of existence, experience of freedom and of its absurdity.

Wilfred Desan. *The Tragic Finale* (Harper). 1960. p. 185

He has nothing very new to say about the meaning of existentialism, yet by identifying that Janus-like word with his own thought he has done far more than profounder existentialists to create an interest in the mental processes that it covers. At a time when exhaustion and satiety had marked European civilization almost equally, Sartre was one of those who issued an effective recall to order. He formulated the kind of message that can usefully be conveyed to a world which has lost interest in theology, in humanism, in liberal values; which evaluates all systems in terms of the power at their disposal; which prefers privilege to respon-

sibility. A pessimist himself, he is anything but supine. . . . It may turn
out in the end that his creation of *Les Temps Modernes,* the independent
left-wing journal that is run largely to promote his ideas and those of
M. Merleau-Ponty as a running commentary on contemporary history,
will prove his most valuable contribution to the life of his time.

Alan Pryce-Jones. *SR.* June 10, 1961. p. 39

What is unique in his works is the fact that they somehow ought not to
exist at all, that they arise on a place which should have made them
impossible. They are not *natural* works; behind them we sense a
motive-power of great violence bringing them into being, the mere feeling of the uniqueness of a personal world pushed and extended until it
becomes work, until it generates out of itself the narratives through
which it can come to expression. This will to create is, it seems to me,
characterized by the turning of description into prescription, the straining at a fixed "set of conditions" until it yields a temporal expression of
itself, the transformation, by fiat, of a static dilemma into fable and
action. . . . Action, both in the subject matter of the works, and in the
work itself of elaborating it, is resolutely undertaken in a situation which
seemed to make it impossible; and the very imperfections of the works
are merely another face, the negative dimension, of their vastness.

Frederic Jameson. *Sartre* (Yale). 1961. pp. 202–4

It would be churlish to say that Sartre's nerve has failed; if nothing else,
his recent works show the same kind of courage in probing his interests,
despite outside protests, that was characteristic of his first important
essays. It might, however, be more pertinent to say that his original
intention has wavered and then been deflected from its honesty into
the dishonesty which must necessarily rear its unpleasant hypotheses
when a man who had opposed all systems, because of their distortion of
reality, begins to define a system of his own. Looking back, we can
trace the process and see how it grows out of an agile mind which
becomes submerged in its own dexterity and begins to confuse the products of skill with the more authoritative results of observation. And
we can begin to feel that Sartre has left us the better part of his contribution as he wanders off into a never-never land we must shun precisely
because he has taught us so well that Utopia is nowhere. The greatest
irony in what has happened is that we are now able to criticize Sartre
with the tools we have taken from him.

Joseph H. McMahon. *YFS.* No. 30, 1963. pp. 103–4

See *Existential Psychoanalysis* and *Literary and Philosophical Essays;* also
Saint Genet (literary criticism), *The Age of Reason* and *Nausea* (novels),
and *No Exit* and *The Flies* (plays).

SENDER, RAMÓN (1901–   )

Ramón J. Sender's *Dark Wedding* is . . . an allegory of ignorant men caught in a world of war. . . . Parallel with the action runs the deeper tragedy of men's souls sometimes fighting against and sometimes fighting for something greater than themselves. . . . "Life is an ideal in process." It is that process, painful and faltering at times, that is the real heart of Señor Sender's book. . . . *Dark Wedding,* then, is the story of a whirlpool where many souls circle in the constant rush of circumstance and reach their hands toward green branches that they hardly understand. It is another proof of the excellence of Señor Ramón Sender.

                              Herbert Gorman. *NYT.* March 28, 1943. pp. 10, 12

Sender belongs to that small company of left-wing moralists, like Silone, Malraux and Koestler, who have learned from the disasters of the last decade to study more closely the springs of evil in men and the human itch for authority. Where the left-wing novel was once a naturalistic photograph, or a list of grievances, it can now be, in certain hands, an almost poetic instrument of interpretation—poetic not in the sense of "poetic" texture, but in the desire to go down into the crevices of reality and to light up their darks through the use of symbol and myth. And Sender, like Silone, is also a radical *religieux* . . .; he is the heir, whatever his own syndicalist leanings, of a Latin church culture in which the concept of original sin and the use of a formal religious vocabulary of grace, sanctity and aspiration are bred in men from their birth.

                              Alfred Kazin. *NR.* April 5, 1943. p. 451

In *Dark Wedding* Ramón Sender does not succeed in solving the problem of how to deal with misery and the brutalization that results from it, but at least he makes a considerable and admirable effort. He has chosen the method of fantasy and symbolism. . . . There are many elements in *Dark Wedding* which brought "King Lear" to my mind. Both works are concerned to show man as naked as possible; both have a plethora of madness, by which they achieve their largest effects; both are pervaded by the themes of justice and both involve justice with sexuality; in both there is a dominant sense of the horror of nature (of creeping, crawling, and decaying things) as well as of the terror of nature, and both constantly question whether nature is good or bad; in both love in its perfection . . . is true salvation, in its perversion . . . the source of evil.

                              Lionel Trilling. *Nation.* April 24, 1943. pp. 603–4

[As] the average American reader passes from the world of his daily living into . . . the world of Ramón J. Sender's *Dark Wedding* . . . he becomes aware of grotesque and fantastic deviations from normality, from reality as he knows it. Patterns of life and character are warped and distorted; the air is not the air he is used to breathing; the farcical and the macabre are strangely mingled; here a detail is gross with exaggeration, there a feature is drawn with the gruesome expertness of a Hieronymus Bosch. A sense of nightmare grows. The reader looks round him, and, borrowing a phrase from Sender, sees that everything is as ugly as a monkey's armpit.

Then, gradually, the presence and use of symbolism make themselves known. . . . We may be sure that the island is the jungle world of men and women, where "life is peopled by monsters, but with a little path between the monsters. For everybody, no matter whom, some little path."

Ben Ray Redman. SR. May 15, 1943. p. 13

Malraux and Sender are very different writers. Two years ago I would have said that the Frenchman was the man of greater imaginative force, for the Spaniard had not yet learned to express his sensations wholly in images and concrete experiences. Malraux had grasped that necessity and carried it out with quivering intensity. Sender has now [in *Chronicle of Dawn*] accomplished this also. The point is, however, that both have used their almost hallucinatory force to analyze the single duty of contemporary man, of becoming a man.

Ralph Bates. SR. April 15, 1944. p. 27

Sender's life and work are bisected by the Civil War. In his first period, he shared the struggles and illusions of the Spanish working class as no other professional writer has done, and expressed them in his novels. . . . His earlier novels . . . were based on his personal observations in the war, in prison and in Anarchist circles, and had the grim reality of things seen. But . . . they were not realistic novels, unless it is permitted to speak of a symbolist realism. Their underlying theme was compassion for helpless, inarticulate human beings whose dreams of goodness and freedom lead them into violent action. Sender's search for what he called the "truth of living humanity" made him keenly aware of the social struggles and of their distorting affect on all their victims. He was, indeed, the first Spanish novelist who attempted to describe the new workers' movements from within, through the mind of individuals, and probably the first to understand the character of the social changes which were alien to the comprehension of the "realist" Pío Baroja. The style which Sender used to describe these violent problems was . . .

bizarre, harsh, full of images, and lit by flashes of poetry. If he stressed the "anti-intellectual" and anti-literary character of his art, it was because the existing aesthetic cliques were barred to the outsider who jumped to fame.

Arturo Barea. *BA*. Spring, 1953. pp. 125–6

Ramón Sender's three-part novel, *Before Noon,* is . . . laid out as what, at first, appears to be a linked series of leisurely anecdotes of childhood. . . . But this frame . . . [is] a novelist's device to intensify belief, and at the same time to define a symbol for the life of the exile. . . . It is . . . written in a style which . . . opens onto the depths of positivity in the human character as it builds its major symbols.

I should say at this point that Mr. Sender is possibly the only other realistic novelist Spain has produced aside from Pío Baroja. . . . And Baroja's realism restricts itself mainly to surface action, where Sender moves much more deeply and satisfactorily into the people he portrays.

Paul Blackburn. *Nation*. April 19, 1958. p. 346

His progress, obviously, has been from the social protest to the metaphysical quest. His method has become increasingly surrealistic but at the same time more abstract and theoretical. . . . Sender, in exile, is retracing his steps, becoming more and more mystical as he goes. The struggle upwards (of man in general) and the individual effort to attain a self-definition (sometimes through a Cause, a revolt or a passionate defence) are Sender's themes. . . . But Sender, like Malraux, reaches a vision of plenitude and peace only through increased inattention to the immediate contemporary scene. The compassionate, deep, brave, active man of the world is still there, but he has to be inferred from beneath the veils of mystagogy.

Paul West. *The Modern Novel* (Hutchinson). 1963. p. 416

The central figure of Ramón Sender's *The Affable Hangman* is a kind of latter-day Candide. . . . This Spanish wanderer in search of a philosophy . . . sees with the grim lucidity of the completely alienated man that human experience is doomed to be simultaneously beautiful and ugly. His persistent impulse is to avoid participation in the chaos of betrayal and of ever more appalling degradation that he takes the pattern of man's fate to be. He represents, in Sender's withering denunciation of our twentieth century brand of corruption, the escapist who stands by, with a cynicism no less criminal for being consistently passive, and watches civilization destroy itself with the meanest and most vulgar of all possible kinds of perversity. . . . Sender delivers his uncompromising judgement upon the decadence of man's spirit, alienated from all positive impulse, slack in its uncomprehending surrender to evil.

James Gray. *SR*. Sept. 7, 1963. p. 22

His *Affable Hangman* is a fascinating technical achievement, a curious amalgam of harsh realism and dream fantasy, of the allegorical and the picaresque (a novelistic form that Spain has given us, named for us, and which Spanish novelists still cherish and use to advantage). Since Sender is dealing with Spanish realities, the real is often more fantastic than the dreams. . . . The dream, on the other hand, has the quality of myth and is written in prose of the highest order. . . . There is a quality of madness in this novel which is the highest form of sanity. . . . Those who believe that the tragedy of the Spanish civil war purged Sender of politics have not read this novel, or have not read it carefully.

Warren Miller. *NYHT*. Sept. 29, 1963. p. 6

See *Dark Wedding, Chronicle of Dawn, Before Noon,* and *The Affable Hangman* (novels).

SERNA, CONCHA ESPINA DE
See Espina de Serna, Concha

SERNA, RAMÓN GÓMEZ DE LA
See Gómez de la Serna, Ramón

SIERRA, GREGORIO MARTÍNEZ
See Martínez Sierra, Gregorio

SILONE, IGNAZIO (1900–   )

He is a standing menace to Caesar, this sad-eyed little editor who has become the whole of Italian literature to thousands beyond the Fascist garrisons, a walking arsenal of the world's contempt for the brass Molochs, and one of the most honest democrats alive. An exile, . . . he has refused to fight Fascism on the level of its own culture, and has so purified his own philosophy of society that he finds himself alone amidst the factions who are only too eager to claim his warm humanism for their own. There is a modern tragedy in that, and an immemorial lesson. Silone has moved up slowly to a point where nothing the liberal and radical enemies of Fascism may offer will satisfy him. He personifies the profound disillusionment that has come with the disintegration of the nineteenth-century philosophies of hope, and he has dismissed the twentieth-century answers one by one.

Alfred Kazin. *NYHT*. Dec. 25, 1938. p. 2

One of the important accomplishments of Silone's fiction is that of revealing to us the fate of the individual in a fascist society. In other words, he presents us concrete pictures of how human destinies unfold under the regime of Mussolini. We know that a fascist dictatorship is horrible in its oppressiveness. But living under these regimes, there are men and women who must go on and live out their lives, minute by minute, and day by day. What happens to these people? What happens to their very selves? What happens to change the very content of their consciousness? One of the most significant features of Silone's writings is that in the terms of literary art of a high order, he answers these questions. . . . His characterizations show us society creating the *self*. . . . His books shine among the relatively few contemporary works that give promise to live in any future world of intelligence and liberty. They are brilliant, bitter, and above all, *human*.

James T. Farrell. *SoR*. Spring, 1939. pp. 775–6, 783

What happy kindergarten lives, single-hearted and single-minded, were those of the unflinching apostles of the nineteenth century, a Mazzini, a Bakunin, even a Lenin. The man who has lived the tragedy of society in our days must needs have died many deaths, and of this, the fundamental spiritual process that is taking place, we have only the first documents in men like Koestler and Silone. The unfolding of the thought of Ignazio Silone presents one of the most important stories of modern times. His is the only voice that represents dozens of unknown millions in fascist countries.

George de Santillana. *At*. Oct., 1942. p. 131

Silone has grasped boldly . . . the central problem of the present time: the justification of a human morality at this moment when the religions are losing their authority and man finds himself alone on the earth. The situation of the German Nazis was precisely . . . why worry about moral principles if you are never to be called to account? . . . Silone himself, in the face of this problem, has reverted to the Christian religion in a special non-ecclesiastical version, a version which one may find it easier to sympathize with than the formal and official version of some of the recent Protestant converts to Catholicism. His point of view is a curious one. He makes one of his characters speak of "the new idea of good and evil" of "those who do not believe in a death and resurrection of Jesus but do believe in his agony." . . . Yet certainly the life of Jesus has still for him a mystical meaning.

Edmund Wilson. *NY*. Sept. 8, 1945. pp. 84–5

In the period between the two great wars, absolute, particularly Marxist, principles exerted a tremendous appeal. However, the shifts in Marxian political tactics . . . led many to [reject] . . . their late allegiance. . . . Yet it is questionable whether any major persuasion can be completely nullified. . . . In many writers one may note an element of "guilt" . . . and uneasiness. . . . In André Gide doubt assumes a high level of general circumspection. In Ignazio Silone . . . it is transposed into a more concrete political character centering in the relation between individual apartness and communal alignment. Gide's interest in the social field came relatively late, and from its beginnings his work is wary of assent and attachments. Silone's formative years, on the other hand, fall into the period when fascism was beginning to exert its compulsions. Hence the works of the younger writer show a more direct preoccupation with the problems of society. And where Gide long confined himself to mere counterposition, Silone began replacing the rejected authorities by a new Father-principle—the people.

Harry Slochower. *No Voice Is Wholly Lost*
(Creative Age). 1945. pp. 56–7, 62

As [Silone] has stated, . . . Christianity is a heritage for the revolutionist to draw upon. But as Silone's development as an imaginative artist indicates, Christianity is not so much an ethical heritage for him as a living tradition, the symbolism and literal meaning of which are becoming the basic sources of his work. This, I am sure, must present a difficulty to all his old admirers. The world from which Silone comes as a radical, and whose conscience he now represents more clearly and more personally than any other living writer, insists, as a matter of its own tradition and its own inner necessity, upon a natural morality, and conceives its struggle as neither sacred nor secular but entirely self-sustaining, a drama in which man is the sufficient character. And yet Silone's examination of natural morality and the questions he has put to the revolutionary conscience, asking it precisely how far it has come and how far it is going, remain the most searching that any man has posed in our time.

Isaac Rosenfeld. *Nation*. June 22, 1946. p. 760

A riddle that baffles foreigners [is] the failure of Silone to become popular in Italy. . . . Silone, despite the prestige that he personally merits and enjoys, is not a great writer in Italian. His books do not come alive in our language; they necessitate laborious deciphering. And this difficulty arises not from any technical inadequacies of his style, but because he lacks expressive power.

Elena Craveri Croce. *NR*. May 10, 1948. p. 24

Silone has seen, as few of his generation have been able to, that though man is by nature a political animal, as Aristotle contended, his full stature cannot be defined in terms of political categories alone, that consequently no purely political statement of man's destiny can do justice to the subtleties of the human situation, for when the political order seeks to embrace the whole of the natural community it obstructs our natural proclivities, thereby finally exhausting and destroying itself. Such a false politic has, of course, been the bane of contemporary history and has presented us with the present occasion that demands, in Silone's view, a reorientation of the political task in the light of Christian principles. Politics thus reoriented will proceed from the basic presupposition of the ontological duality of man, a duality consisting in the natural and supernatural dimensions of his being, . . . [recognizing] loyalties beyond those of a citizen.

Nathan A. Scott, Jr. *Rehearsals of Discomposure*
(Columbia). 1952. pp. 110–1

If the term "socialist realism" made any sense Ignazio Silone would be the only contemporary writer to whom it could be applied. For Silone is a "realist" through his exclusive attachment to the . . . *cafoni* (peasants). . . . "Realist," too, is the simplicity of his narration, good-natured and sardonic in the peasant style, seeking its effects by allusions and sudden silences rather than by subtleties. . . . As for Silone's "socialism" it consists entirely of his recollection of the intricate reality of peasant life, which contains, as an integral and daily part, the need for justice and the hope that the reign of superior force will some day cease. . . . But . . . Silone's realism is essentially ironic and his socialism staunchly religious, if by religion we understand a quest and a passion for the enduring—for something beyond appearances and "changes." . . . The truth of the *cafoni* is rustic and inarticulate. But they remain and everything else changes. . . . Their truth . . . is . . . expressible only through irony. And it is this irony that Silone explains and develops in the form of novels.

Nicola Chiaromonte. *PR*. May-June, 1954. pp. 307–8

Silone has never been on the side of those who sneer at stumbling truth. He belongs, like Tolstoy and the Shakespeare of "Troilus," with those who have a deep respect for the naïve. His new novel [*The Secret of Luca*] has a theme central to this feeling: the pursuit of truth for the sake of love. . . . We realize that there is a kind of truth which does not defend itself, but simply exists. Its purity lies in its defenselessness. . . . At times it seems that Silone is approaching an almost Hindu position in his objection to the idea of necessity, his admiration of the idea of passive resistance. . . . One is left wondering whether Silone is on the verge of condemning altogether that compromise with the world of means, legalities and forms which is action. . . . *The Secret of Luca* . . . has an extraordinary richness of dream-like tone. The whole book seems bathed in a Giorgionesque golden light. . . . One feels that, for Silone, gentleness is all.

Stephen Spender. NYT. Aug. 24 ,1958. p. 5

Silone's desire to locate the ethic of an unspoiled primitive Christianity in the insulted and injured of our time is an act of intellectual desperation. Abstractly, it is hard to defend. He himself must surely know this better than anyone else, for nowhere in his work is his desire presented in the language of fanaticism or even self-assurance. There shines through all of his writing a tone of modesty, the tone of a man who knows it is his fate to expend himself so thoroughly on a question that the very idea of an answer fades into inconsequence.

For Silone the socialist and Silone the novelist, the only miracle of Christianity is Christ, a man whose sufferings have burdened humanity with an *intolerable* example. . . . His whole effort, after *Fontamara,* has been to reduce—perhaps the verb should be, to exalt—Christ to the level of a secular participant, a fellow sufferer and thereby a sustaining example, in the misery of our time. . . . He has tried to bring to life an image of the lonely and forsaken Christ, so as to reclaim the moral possibility of socialism, though not of socialism alone.

Irving Howe. NR. Sept. 22, 1958. p. 18

Silone's trustfulness is Christian and it is grounded in love; but it is very human and extremely modest. He cannot, as he admits, use a stronger word. What he professes is not quite a faith, and definitely not Faith. In Catholic Italy, Silone is endowed with a singularly Protestant mentality; he has a hearty disregard for hierarchies and dogmas, and it might be said that he sees life as justified by faith rather than by reason or by the observed actions of mankind. But in fact, Silone is less a Protestant Christian than a primitive Christian. He resembles most of all some member of the earliest Christian community—during the earliest years, indeed during the earliest days of Christianity, before the shock of the Crucifixion had worn off or the meaning of the Resurrection had sunk in.

R. W. B. Lewis. *The Picaresque Saint* (Lippincott). 1959. p. 110

[Like] *The Grapes of Wrath* . . . *Fontamara* is also a legend of families dispossessed from the soil, but one that belongs to a different tradition. What the novel suggests—or rather what it suggested in the original version— is the group of medieval fables that deal with peasants and the Devil. The peasants are always preposterously stupid and ignorant, but shrewd in their own fashion. The Devil is full of artifice, and sometimes he is helped by a priest, but he is sure to be defeated in the end. *Fontamara* couldn't have that happy ending because it was written in 1930 . . . however, there was the hint of the apocalypse to come. . . . Among those few lasting novels of a revolutionary era, *Fontamara* is the only one to have been revised after the Second World War. . . . We still have the sense of hearing a medieval legend, rough-hewn and angular, reduced to its essential outlines as if by generations of storytellers in the village marketplace, but it is no longer a *fabliau* about peasants and the Devil. Instead it becomes a golden legend about Christ reborn, tempted in the wilderness, and crucified in Jerusalem—or is Berardo rather John Baptist, who prophecies the coming of the Solitary Stranger? . . . Losing some of its humor, the new version gains in somber intensity, being stripped of everything inessential so as to reveal the permanent themes of poverty, brotherly love, and sacrifice.

Malcolm Cowley. Foreword to *Fontamara* (Atheneum). 1960. pp. v–viii

Fontamara may not, I concede, surprise today's reader as it did in the Thirties. Few people now would lend much faith to the worn legend of the Italian South as a land of music, sunshine, heady wines, and sensual passions. A whole spate of novelists and newspapermen . . . have written with candor and compassion about the *Mezzogiorno,* its squalor, its hopelessness, its vast problems. Yet, despite the three decades that have elapsed since the original edition, *Fontamara* has lost little of its power and certainly none of its relevance. Indeed, in the revised form . . . it is less the socio-political document it was than a profoundly human story about people and their immense capacity for suffering.

This, it seems to me, is the point of the book. Although *Fontamara* tells one main story and several incidental ones, it has hardly a plot in the traditional sense. The effect and poetic quality of the novel are in the stark simplicity with which Silone depicts his *cafoni* (peasants, with a distinct derogatory connotation), raising them to symbols of mankind in a state of perpetual suffering.

Sergio Pacifici. SR. July 23, 1960. pp. 18–19

In an epoch of lies and propaganda, when words have lost their authenticity and art too often is turned into a political tool, a writer who speaks the language of sincerity and humanness is a powerfully attractive figure. Such a writer is Ignazio Silone. A kind of natural wisdom irradiates from the unassuming pages of his novels. . . . His moral quest propels him toward simple aims which are the hardest to attain: companionship, brotherhood of men, honesty with one's self and with others, and obedience to the eternal rhythms, to the natural breath of life. . . . Perhaps the main reason Silone is more widely read in New York than in Rome is that he is a moralist—and Italians have never liked moralists, though they admire and revere them. . . . Besides, he is such an enemy of rhetoric (the national disease) and so carefully avoids all theatricals (the main national entertainment), that many of his fellow countrymen look upon him with surprise mixed with awe.

Marc Slonim. NYT. May 28, 1961. pp. 1, 33

Silone's body of work is at once highly representative and highly individual. Like many European intellectuals, he made a deep commitment to, and a searing withdrawal from, the Communist Party. But in contrast to a Koestler or a Malraux, Silone grew up in a "medieval world"—a village in the *Abruzzo,* whose only culture was a primitive Christianity. And although Silone himself was not a believing Christian, it was a religious impulse rather than Marxist ideology which made him a revolutionary; he became convinced that, since formal religion had lost its authority, political action was the only channel through which the love of man could be made effective.

After his departure from Communism in 1931, Silone pursued a course similar to that later chosen by Albert Camus. He has shown that the abstractions of ideology inevitably lead to inhumanity and nihilism, and he has asserted that the brotherhood of man is a human truth; Camus finds it rooted in the universality of man's revolt against his fate, Silone in the universality of suffering.

Charles J. Rolo. At. June, 1961. pp. 104–5

In title-conscious Italy, Silone has no title, but something all his own: an international reputation greater abroad than at home, a moral position that is respected by the neo-right and the neo-left, though he is out of the current literary swim, an anti-Fascist past in exile preceding the partisan underground experience that is the common bond of so many Italian novelists, and a body of work that—curiously—is being revised. . . . A figure of former crises in a country that for the first time in decades was without any . . . he seemed solid, assured, with neither inner torment nor enthusiasm for lost causes. He looked more dignified and less embittered than expected—as if he, too, had undergone revisions in his nature. . . . His penetrating dark eyes seemed at once quizzical and melancholy, but, from time to time, the corners of his mouth lifted into a sweet smile, himself surprised.

Herbert Mitgang. *NYT.* Oct. 21, 1962. p. 4

Silone . . . is preoccupied by the will to shape a just and harmonious social order. This preoccupation dates from the time Silone, in 1925, joined the Communist Party. . . . Adopting communism in an act he has described as a "conversion, a complete dedication," he sought to advance its cause as the best means to accomplish his lifelong ideal: the establishment of a humane community to replace the inhumane aristocratic one. When that god failed . . . he left the Party.

This shift of politics . . . is an act typical both of Silone's life and of his art. Despite a general diminution of faith in the idea of Utopia, Silone has remained steadfast in commitment to a single belief: men possess resources of moral energy which society can either channel or divert. This energy is constant; it cannot be depleted. Forestalled here, it is diverted there, ever quick to adopt diverse means in order to achieve its ends.

Each of Silone's heroes . . . exhibits this kind of constancy and this kind of resourcefulness. . . . Under whatever stress, however isolated, they choose to resist, they remain intransigent.

William Wasserstrom. *The Modern Short Novel*
(Holt). 1965. p. 293

See *Bread and Wine, Fontamara, The Fox and the Camellias, A Handful of Blackberries, The Secret of Luca,* and *The Seed Beneath the Snow* (novels); also *The School for Dictators* (satire) and *And He Hid Himself* (play).

SIMENON, GEORGES (1903–   )

Simenon begins by reminding us, both in his gifts and his limitations, of Maupassant. When he tells a story, it is done with a conscious skill and at the same time it seems to have been prompted by some inner compulsion, as though to tell stories were a necessary activity of his being. His characters have until recently been created like those of Maupassant from outside; but they belong not to a France which has just known the Franco-Russian War, but to a France between two wars, between a defeat of the Germans and a defeat by the Germans. And the air they breathe is alive with an immense disquietude, which increases as Simenon goes on, until . . . the atmosphere is heavy with helplessness and tense with dread.

John Peale Bishop. NR. March 10, 1941. pp. 345–6

His wonderful book (*Act of Passion*) is so spare as to be hardly more than a skeleton. His people are not very likable, and their effect on each other is detestable, but what Simenon knows, and has the genius to impart, is that their need for each other is fatal. . . . It would be useless to describe the disturbing quality of Simenon's work, because his writing changes color and meaning according to the heart, the memory, the age, and the sex of the person who is reading. To some readers the story may seem simple and straightforward. Others will find it irresistibly complex. It is mean and ugly, or tragically beautiful, depending on each one's own experience of life, and there may even be some who will see nothing at all in it, but there can hardly be anyone who will deny its strength.

Maeve Brennan. NY. Nov. 8, 1952. pp. 161, 165

The time has . . . come, Simenon believes, to try to write what he calls "*le roman pur*"—the quintessential novel—which should do for our time what was done by the tragedies of ancient Greece. Starting at the moment of decisive crisis, it should pose the problem of man's destiny; should give an accounting of a man's life. Simenon was attracted to the murder mystery because it offers a convenient way of doing just this in terms of the murderer, the detective serving as an explanatory prop akin to the Chorus in Greek tragedy.

In working his way toward the *roman pur* via detective fiction, Simenon brought a crucial innovation to the whodunit. He made it an exploration of personality—a quest whose goal is not so much punishment of the crime as understanding of the criminal; a mystery whose solution unravels not so much a tangled skein of events as a tangled skein of motives.

Charles J. Rolo. Mass Culture, ed. by
Bernard Rosenberg and David M. White
(Free Press). 1957. p. 172

Simenon brings before us in a seemingly endless procession living beings high and low, rich and poor—but mainly low and poor—who may not always be profoundly realized, but on the surface level, and some way below the surface, are brilliantly observed. His pre-war novels, with their almost stifling evocation of an atmosphere of apathy, cynicism and despair, should have prepared us for the virtual inevitability of the fall of France. . . . Simenon is not just a camera, in Christopher Isherwood's misleading phrase—no novelist ever is—but at times he reminds us of a photographer, brilliantly composing his pictures, giving us without distortion "exposures" of life as it really is.

Luke Parsons. *CR*. Jan., 1960. pp. 56–8

It is not too much to say that Simenon is one of the great revolutionists of the detective story, one of the first to turn away from the well-shaped plot and the devious gimmick (though he could be very good at these when he chose) to lay stress on the ambience and milieu of the crime and on the ambivalent duel (in the mainstream-novel tradition of Valjean-Javert and Raskolnikov-Porfiry) between the murderer and Maigret. . . . Estheticians . . . should be led from [*The Bells of Bicêtre*] back to the entire corpus of Simenon's work, where they will find (and not least in the cases of Maigret) the same delicate and precise probing into human character and interplay, the same compelling calling up of the spirit of a place or a mood—in short, the same combination of insight and skill that stamps (whatever the genre) the true novelist.

Anthony Boucher. *NYT*. April 5, 1964. p. 1

If Simenon's serious works have not been taken seriously enough by the general public, one reason must be that so many of them revolve around acts of violence—a circumstance that in no way diminishes the stature of a Shakespeare or a Dostoevski but is bound to work against a writer whose first reputation was built on the *roman policier*. For Simenon, violence provides the most direct access to several themes he regularly turns to in his novels. One of these is the irrevocable act whereby a man cuts himself off completely from everything his life has been. . . . A second is the condition summarized in another connection by Simone de Beauvoir: "a guilty man is, first of all, a man accused." . . . Another is the impossibility of human communication.

Jay Jacobs. *Reporter*. Jan. 14, 1965. p. 40

See *The Accomplices, Act of Passion, The Bells of Bicêtre, Blind Path, The Blue Room,* and *Pedigree* (novels).

SIMON, CLAUDE (1913–   )

Scraps of dialogue, frequently disrupted in the middle of words, bits of interior monologue, pungent images, abrupt shifts in time and place—these bits and pieces create a bewildering collage, that is at first tantalizingly disoriented and then increasingly significant. M. Simon attempts to reproduce his view of reality by constructing a surrealistic chaos in which the exterior and interior intermingle. The fragmented impressions he presents eventually fuse into a total picture that is curiously haunting.

Martin Levin. NYT. March 29, 1959. p. 30

What Simon finally tries to do is to render living experience *present* to the reader. The constantly moving *presence* of motion-picture images (to which he makes numerous illusions) would seem to have had a strong influence on his style. Malraux used a motion-picture technique of composition in *La Condition Humaine* but only in his cutting and sequences. Simon uses the very essence of the motion picture: the presence of an unpredictable continuum (adding to it the possibility, given by the written word, of a permanent simultaneity of the inner and outer worlds). His style in *L'Herbe* is one possible solution to the problem originally stated by Sartre in *La Nausée* and a constant concern to French novelists ever since; that of recapturing the *here and now* of a story. In fact it is the subject of his novel.

Jacques Guicharnaud. YFS. Summer, 1959. p. 107

Claude Simon combines the realist concern for detailed description of sensation with the current French interest in the complexity of the moment, that is, in the layers of contingent sensations from the past that adhere to the present moment. . . . His plots are nonexistent, his situations merely junction points at which one glimpses birth and death impinging on the individual. . . . There is no development, no change, but the reader's understanding of the characters and of humanity's dilemmas deepens as he follows M. Simon through his labyrinth of Faulknerian paragraphs and palimpset-conversations.

Dorothy Nyren Curley. LJ. Feb. 1, 1960. p. 680

The most Faulknerian of a whole generation of French writers inspired by American novelists, Simon has created a universe as dominated by fatality as Faulkner's Yoknapatawpha County and has adopted most of the devices used by his model. However great is his debt to Faulkner, he gives the appearance, at least, of indebtedness to Camus as well. . . . His heroes are outsiders like Meursault, and all his characters testify to the author's strong penchant toward the philosophy of the absurd. Their common enemy is Time, as invincible as it is incomprehensible, for man is moved by forces and for reasons that he cannot understand. By means of a heavily sensuous imagery that makes his style unique among the new novels, Simon creates a cosmic atmosphere of doom and bewilderment to enshroud mankind. Man's ultimate defeat is a sort of victory, however, since it is release and liberation whereas nature must go on without rest or end.

Laurent Le Sage. The French New Novel
(Pennsylvania State). 1962. p. 137

The Palace displays again the literary qualities which made The Flanders Road such a remarkable book: an opulent, sinuous prose; an exuberant but thoroughly accurate vision; an uncanny ability to make words adhere to forms and movement. Time and decay are once more the steady flow of life which leads to death, but in a series of slow motion tableaux. The experience communicated lies half way between the hypnotic precision of a film and the vagueness and redundancy of nightmares.

Victor Brombert. NYT. Sept. 22, 1963. p. 5

If <i>The Wind</i> borrows from the traditional novel some of its elements: intrigue, an interesting human adventure which governs the movement of the book, it also offers more than a little glimpse of the "new novel." The author adopts the well-known method of using a narrator, but it is to create the opposite of an escape: an incarnation of the author at work. He reveals tendencies which grow from work to work: the wish to respect the creative process, the affirmation of the primacy of the senses, the need to give an intense presence to things, and a taste for a type of evocativeness which substitutes for the unrolling in a plot of a predestined composition.

Jean-Luc Seylaz. RLM. No. 3, 1964. p. 228.
Tr. by Dorothy Nyren Curley

See <i>The Flanders Road, The Grass, The Palace,</i> and <i>The Wind</i> (novels).

SOLDATI, MARIO (1906–   )

He proves a virtuoso of the quick, telling trait, of the *coup de scène* deftly contrived, a fictional "etcher" of outstanding gifts. The technique of cinema, instead of corrupting, seems to have intensified and concentrated his talent. Soldati is a master of suspense . . . [with] Conan-Doylish ability.

Elio Gianturco. *BA*. Autumn, 1951. p. 383

Mr. Soldati . . . is a master of the art of telling a story.

The three tales which make up this volume [*Dinner with the Commendatore*] are decidedly different in mood and style from the dominant trends in post-war Italian letters as represented by, say, Moravia or Berto or Pratolini. With their smooth flow, their urbane tone and concentration on the quirks of character, these three tales are somewhat reminiscent of Somerset Maugham. And while Soldati's plots are not, perhaps, as arresting as Maugham's, he deals more subtly with the mysteries of the human heart and mind. . . . In each of these stories, a baffling mystery of character is swiftly and tantalizingly presented and unraveled with surprising twists, flashes of insight which throw out clues without disclosing the final answer, and an engrossed fascination with the complexities of human nature. At the conclusion, the incidents that decisively affect a life have been deftly uncovered and a human being has been—not analyzed but understood. This is storytelling in the great tradition.

Charles J. Rolo. *NYT*. Oct. 18, 1953. pp. 5, 52

Mario Soldati's new novel [*The Capri Letters*] combines that taste for ambiguous emotions, tortured psychological finesse, and directness in narrative technique which distinguishes that section of contemporary Italian writing which has not fallen under the spell of neo-Realism. Not without reason is the whole book a confession, containing within the framework of the principal confession . . . a secondary and parallel one. . . . The confession gives the story its tone and makes possible the almost merciless prying into the many aspects of love, taken both as a personal and a social experience.

Olga Ragusa. *BA*. Spring, 1955. p. 176

You might say that the theme of *The Capri Letters* is the inestimable boon of the contemporary Italian form, both male and female, to the hitherto inhibited Anglo-Saxon; but it would be an incomplete description. For despite an overtone of sustained, humourless, engine-whistle hysteria, that reminds me of D'Annunzio on the eve of a thunderstorm, there is plenty of depth in Signor Soldati's little tragedy. Motivation is mixed; there are religious as well as sexual urges, Roman Catholic ideology, several kinds of guilt. . . . If it came right off, it would be a shattering masterpiece, but something is wrong somewhere. Signor Soldati's narrative, always in the first person, flows on with nineteenth-century eloquence and facility but the characters and their motivations are not convincing. . . . I get the feeling that he has sketched [them] in . . . to fit a framework of ideas, preconceived, perhaps, from the Kinsey reports, with the religion strung on to provide a third dimension.

Maurice Richardson. *NSN*. Aug. 6, 1955. p. 169

Mario Soldati's *The Capri Letters* . . . is not funny at all, unless you laugh it off as another proof that impressionable Anglo-Saxons should not go to Italy; which would waste a remarkable book. . . . The crux of the book is not in people but in bodies, a passionate insight into the joys and rapt evils of sex. Appreciation of it will depend on whether you think better or worse, impatiently or indulgently, of intelligent people mastered by their bodies; but nothing should gainsay the force of its vision, the sense of its argument . . . and the uncomfortable turns of its perception. It is an uncommon achievement.

Anne Duchene. *MG*. Aug. 9, 1955. p. 4

[In *The Real Silvestri*] the old Pirandellian problem looms up again: . . . where indeed, outside the context of a man's relationship with others, resides the true personality? In a traditional Pirandellian way the question is left a little in the air, but not before the reader has had a chance to savor the taste of the pungent Soldati brew in which irony, sharp observations and a gentle tolerance for the weaknesses of humanity are cunningly intermingled.

This is a mature and perceptive account of human relations; . . . a parable, at once contemporary and eternal, of the mystery of person-ality: . . . and it is of course written with the deftness and grace charac-teristic of the author.

Thomas G. Bergin. *NYHT*. Jan. 22, 1961. p. 34

Versatility and virtuosity are Mario Soldati's stock in trade. In the good, old humanistic tradition, he can do an astonishing variety of things and does them all superlatively well. A first-rate motion-picture director, lin-guist, radio lecturer and writer on art, he is also a sensitive poet and an ingenious novelist. As arresting and complex a personage in his own right as the characters he creates, the "true," "untrammeled" Soldati expresses himself through his novels, whereas the film maker represents merely "a collective product" that subsidizes the novelist. . . .

The Real Silvestri, . . . [an] incisive study of adult personalities, with its skillful insights into the complexities and bitter ironies of adult emotional life, is the work of a mature mind. In its unusual amalgam of wry, sophisticated humor, bitter analysis and elementary human compassion, it is Soldati at his best. And that is very good indeed.

Helene Cantarella. NYT. Jan. 22, 1961. pp. 4–5

Even in translation, The Real Silvestri has . . . elegance of means. . . . Like many story-tellers in the classic Italian vein, Mario Soldati prefers the brief narrative enclosing in sharp limits a small group of characters. . . . Doubt gnaws with its fine mocking tooth. It is all very much in the manner of Pirandello, but deftly executed.

George Steiner. YR. March, 1961. p. 424

Mario Soldati is a skilled movie director in Italy, as well as an author of note, and everything about his work suggests the trained, methodical, quick-clever eye of the cinema artist. He sights the color, the shape, and the visual mood of the scenes in which he is going to set his players playing. . . . His style is naturalistic: the camera-narrator moves listlessly about among the characters. He has a point of view, naturally, but so does the lens. And like the latter, though he can focus true, he can only pick up the surface effects. He depends, as does the cameraman, on catching his subjects at on and off moments, exposed under a bright glare that makes deception difficult, involved in small thoughtless actions. . . . Through a series of artful subterfuges, the narrator passively submits to the points of view of the participants who must be in conflict. . . . Like all story tellers of innate common sense, Soldati does not inhibit or dissipate his drama by pausing to ask if truth exists, for there could be no drama if it did not. He understands this, even though he takes a cautious position on men's ability to recognize the truth in themselves, and in each other.

Alice Mayhew. Com. April 28, 1961. p. 131

The real confrontation of Italy with American culture begins, strangely enough, toward the end of the first decade of Fascist rule, in 1930. The story of the encounter . . . has its own cast of "villains" and "heroes." [One of] the chief protagonists of the first group . . . [was] Mario Soldati . . . [for whom] America was a barbaric country without a culture. . . . Mario Soldati's sentimental journey to the American shores represented the author's attempt to abandon, physically and intellectually, his beloved European continent and the traditions of his native country—only to discover how hopelessly European, and how deeply rooted in his land, he was. Appropriately enough, Soldati's work bore the title America primo amore (America, first love), a love which, being perhaps too adolescent, was bound to fail in its attempt to formulate a new synthesis of a strange land.

Sergio Pacifici. *A Guide to Contemporary Italian Literature* (World). 1962. pp. 298, 300

See *The Real Silvestri, The Capri Letters,* and *The Confession* (novels); also *Dinner with the Commendatore* (short novels).

SOUPAULT, PHILIPPE (1897–   )

The author of *Bon Apôtre,* what a good disciple he is! If André Gide was right to write that "those who fear influences and get rid of them tacitly admit the poverty of their own soul," M. Philippe Soupault shows us here his unbelievable spiritual richness. Certainly, it would be enough to hold our attention for *Le Bon Apôtre* to teach us the literary preferences of its author, one of the most unusual poets among the newcomers. But the marvel of it all is that this first novel of M. Philippe Soupault is the last work of M. Philippe Dada. That is what has so much excited some critics: one of the leaders of dadaism is finally letting them see his true nature! However all Dada is not Philippe Soupault. Each initiate of a doctrine tailors from it a suit to fit himself.

François Mauriac. *NRF.* Nov., 1923. p. 610.
Tr. by Dorothy Nyren Curley

On this side of Dada, Soupault's *Le Bon Apôtre* may well be taken for the Bible of the young revoltés. A most classic penman, a cold-blooded and deft analyst, Soupault has left to posterity in this book the most self-revealing portrait of those restless youths who had just graduated from Rimbaud's, Lautréamont's, and Bergson's courses. . . . Philippe Soupault has for a long time been parted from the movement, but his nimble and crystalline poems, short and long, sad and gay, must not be forgotten here.

Régis Michaud. *Modern Thought and Literature in France* (Funk). 1934. pp. 78, 193

Philippe Soupault shows in several of his *Poésies complètes* a subtle and graceful ease recalling the manner of Guillaume Apollinaire. Here a wondrous rainbow-tinted light, softened by a vague opalescent mist, suffuses the clear outline of a delicate and subtle filigree. In this enigmatical twilight, an Elysian peace seems to float over a prodigious efflorescence of inextricably intertwined festoons, blending their innumerable variegated arabesques into a chaste and subdued harmony.

Georges Lemaitre. *From Cubism to Surrealism in French Literature* (Harvard). 1941. p. 212

Philippe Soupault's *Age of Assassins* is a minor but thoughtful addition to the contemporary literature of incarceration. . . . Its theme is disgust rather than terror. But, as Soupault writes, "an experience of half a year in jail seems short, especially to those who have never been in jail." One advantage of the short term is that sensations are not dulled; and Soupault's record has the precision and immediacy of one who never became fully accustomed to the life. . . . His book is an honest and sensitive account which, if neither very powerful nor very profound, yet supplies sympathetic insights into a predicament which the war against the Axis has not solved. In an age in which the dominant question is getting to be whether you believe in the police state or not, we should all know at least what we are being asked to accept.

Arthur M. Schlesinger, Jr. SR. May 4, 1946. p. 13

I think of this elusive man who passes lightly like a breeze, a man limpid and secretive, amiable and cruel, courteous and insolent, buoyant and profound. I think of this traveler without luggage who has experienced so many countries, so many stories, so many books. I think of the friend faithful, available, always open to all, attentive to what stirred him, marvelously at ease in the climate of youth because insatiably young himself. I think of the poet unconstrained and sincere, droll and pathetic, he who proclaims anguished grey hours and who snorts with laughter at the storms of Love and Liberty.

Henry-Jacques Dupuy. Philippe Soupault
(Editions Pierre Seghers). 1957. pp. 103–4.
Tr. by Dorothy Nyren Curley

The one who was the true soul of Dadaism . . . was the poet Philippe Soupault. . . . He was often called "the heir of Apollinaire," whose particular style certainly influenced Soupault's own finely cadenced *vers libre*. . . . Soupault's verse was deceptively simple, often gossamer light, like the smoke of his perpetual cigarettes, yet composed of sharp images and dashes of strong color. Like Apollinaire, he wrote at great speed, under the impulse of the moment, a direct, terse, unfeigned poetry. . . . His breathless rush (like his legendary "seven mistresses," no doubt) was the manifestation of his being *"alive"* he explained to us. . . . Soupault's fast pace was also related, no doubt, to his having adopted what he regarded as the "American tempo," reflected in early Edison films that used to show everyone hopping about madly because of the slow-timed motion-picture cameras.

Matthew Josephson. Life Among the Surrealists (Holt).
1962. pp. 121–3

See *Age of Assassins* (essay); also, in French, *Le Bon Apôtre* (novel) and *Poésies complètes*.

SVEVO, ITALO (1861–1928)

Svevo is a born novelist. He has only to name a character for it to come to life. There are very few descriptive passages, little imagery, no rhetoric, no romantic glamour, and though there are plenty of fantastic situations, they do not motivize the action but spring from vagaries of character. No one was ever less sensational; even a suicide is the quietest and least flamboyant of full-stops.

Beryl de Zoete. NationL. Jan. 12, 1929. pp. 521–2

Svevo's art is deeply psychological and introspective. In each of . . . [his] novels, one finds the author's analysis of essentially the same type of man. . . . They are men who show a tragic moral misery but who find a source of solace in the lucidity of mind with which they analyze themselves. . . . Thomas Hardy's characters readily present themselves to one's mind by way of association. Svevo's characters are suspended between a formalized world of ideals and the actual world of activity, in which new conditions have arisen, which he, like all transitional writers, refuses to accept.

Domenico Vittorini. The Modern Italian Novel
(U. of Pennsylvania). 1930. pp. 155–6

Exactly because he does not judge the bourgeois spirit, Svevo amuses himself, tremendously and naively, by looking at it. A perfect bourgeois as a man, as a writer he is almost alone in not looking like one. Instead of descending or condescending to the bourgeois spirit within his own soul, he raises and uplifts it along with himself to the sphere of imagination, to a world of fancy and dream, which is at the same time the world of reality itself. . . . A kind of innocent wisdom was the real source of his greatness and originality. He was with everybody, including himself, a man of the world. This makes him . . . a kind of contemporary Henry James, without the latter's snobbism or narcissism.

Renato Poggioli. Introduction to Confessions of Zeno
(New Directions). 1930. p. 8

Italo Svevo never fully realized his art; he was very consciously and very scrupulously an amateur; he was subject to obscure prohibitions. Whether because of sophistication or naïveté or the blending together of both, there is about Svevo's writings a certain *veulerie,* a going-nowhere. His heroes, whom he follows very closely, all suffer from a failure of the nerve; behind them and never clearly visualized is a chorus forever laughing softly and persistently. . . . Fundamentally good

—full of compassion and warmth, and an odd combination of innocence and awareness—the heroes tell in a dramatic monologue their own stories, compounds of evidence and experience which never become distilled into knowledge.

Austryn Wainhouse. *WR*. Winter, 1950. pp. 148–50

Self-improvement is the obsession of his unlucky heroes, and, as Svevo's life went on, they do improve. Their anxious analysing of motives, their eagerness for illusion, their inevitable failures, and their anxiety to understand and to arrive at a sane attitude to life gives them the pathetic air of miming clowns: they talk so much that it creates by a paradox, the pathos of dumbness. But they become as wise, gentle, and restful in their indetermination as the Chinese and walk with the fullness of the super-annuated. It has been their curious fate to learn the lesson of life backwards, becoming younger and more apt for life as they grow older; so that if they were to look back upon their youth, and even their middle age, these would seem to them like a puzzling sleep from which, little by little, they have been permitted to awake.

V. S. Pritchett. *Books in General* (Chatto and Windus).
1953. p. 26

One does not think of reading him for novel architecture, any more than one really reads him for the evocation of the background of Trieste, effective in a subdued fashion though that is. . . . His special gift is something different again. It is something like an absolute candour. In a certain range of emotional experience, no one could be more unselfsparingly honest. It is that special kind of truth-telling which makes him so funny and so sad. An unavailing young man finding that he is expected to marry the wrong girl—a respectable elderly man taking a mistress who is too much for him—in all the situations where self-respect is at its most precarious, Svevo tells the truth in a manner fluid, straightforward, naked to life.

C. P. Snow. *In* English Association's *Essays and Studies*
(Murray). 1961. p. 15

This congenital inability to keep in step with the surrounding world (and what intelligent or good man, intent upon eternity, can feel at home in our evil and foolish age?), is the cause of all the unhappiness of Svevo's heroes and precludes the success of all conscious action in their lives. It makes them bungle everything that they ever attempt, so that they are pleasantly surprised if chance or unconscious action bring success. Relegated to the margin of social and economic activity, instead of acting, they generally dream, analyse and comment on the action of others or on the workings of chance.

Edouard Roditi. Introduction to *Confessions of Zeno* (Secker and Warburg). 1962. p. 17

There are few novelists of Svevo's stature who are equally entertaining, poignant and profound at the same time, few writers who can sustain the delicate balancing act on the narrow ridge between the tragic and the comic. . . . Svevo's irony places him apart from the mainstream of the Italian tradition which glories in the grand heroic gesture. Italian critics have pointed out that his very language in its dryness eschews the sonorities, the rhetorical flights to which the beauty and resonance of the Italian language irresistibly draw most Italian writers.

Martin Esslin. *Spec.* March 30, 1962. p. 409

In the first place Svevo is honest. . . . He excels at depicting the maladroit and the fumbler, uncomplex affection and the reprisals which (in their minds only) functionaries enact against bosses. In other words, Svevo masters the unheroic. . . . It is hardly surprising that the attempt to portray hapless, baffled people fumbling in a haphazard world should have given rise to the prose of inconsequence, of no surface glitter and small dignity: for such purposes it is the perfect prose and, in Svevo's hands, becomes also a satisfactory vehicle for interior monologue by characters who verge on the Dostoevskian when not having a snigger at the silly mystery of it all.

Paul West. *The Modern Novel* (Hutchinson). 1963.
pp. 361–2

We were familiar with illness as a weapon against bourgeois complacency and well-being or as a perverse form of Prometheanism, we had been steeped in malaise as the proper subject of contemporary writing. But what Svevo had done in *The Confessions* went beyond what Proust, or Mann, or Strindberg or Eliot had accomplished or intended; it seemed entirely new, even though there was an atmospheric resemblance to Kafka. He had taken illness as the condition of existence itself, making uprootedness, alienation, moral uncertaintly and social weakness—as opposed to unseeing robustness and coerced integrity—into agencies of wily enduring and liberating instruments of self-knowledge.

Richard Gilman. *NR.* Nov. 2, 1963. p. 19

Svevo . . . builds upon Nietzsche's vision of the European sanitarium, but also expands it. . . . Thanks to his social awareness, Svevo gave his "victim-heroes" the compassion which Nietzsche could not. Besides, Svevo's misfits are in some sense the wave of the future, prototypes of pathetic modern men whose habitual introspection gives them the power of prophecy but not the gift of life. . . . In this perspective Svevo's protagonists—the Chaplinesque Zeno above all—tend to become images of man-in-mutation; hideously deformed or impoverished from the viewpoint of the heroic tradition, they are nonetheless the transitional prototypes of future man's enormous consciousness.

William Arrowsmith. *NYR*. Feb. 6, 1964. p. 9

See *A Life, As a Man Grows Older,* and *Confessions of Zeno* (novels).

UNAMUNO, MIGUEL DE (1864–1936)

This astute and exquisitely analytical philosopher cannot separate himself from the mysticism of St. Teresa and St. John of the Cross; and his deification of Don Quixote is the result of that mysticism which is not only part of his tradition, but an essential part of his very being. He raises a cant of joy at the thought of Christian revelation, of the Incarnation, the Eucharist, the Resurrection; and yet he accepts, with Kierkegaard, while admitting that Christianity is the only religion which can be accepted by Europeans in the twentieth century, that it is a "desperate sortie," a sortie which can be successful only through the martyrdom of faith. . . . We must all believe in the other life, though this belief "comes through the foolishness of the cross." . . . The madness of Don Quixote is the exultation of a saint; and Don Quixote, the mystic, the chivalric Catholic, is De Unamuno's Spanish Christ!

Maurice Francis Egan. *NYT*. March 19, 1922. p. 3

Unamuno fights because he knows there is not a chance in the world to win. He has tasted the glory of absurdity. He has decided to hope what he cannot believe. He has discovered ground for faith in the very fact that there are no grounds. . . . The tragic sense of life is nothing more or less than a sense of disparity between what we know we can be and what we can think of being, between the limitations Nature has imposed upon us and the limits of our imagination; or, as Unamuno puts it, between the necessities of reason and the necessities of life. Both reason and life are necessary, but they slay each other, and the spectacle of the double death is tragic. . . . We begin to live, says Unamuno, as soon as we become aware of our limitations. . . . Above all, there is none of the nonsense in him of "reconciliation" between knowledge and belief. Supremely intelligent, he never believes; religiously alive, he hopes.

Mark Van Doren. *Nation*. May 17, 1922. p. 600

Unamuno is . . . a profoundly serious man, utterly devoid of a sense of humor. In the few instances in which one is able to find humor in his essays and stories, that humor is expressed in a manner which is repugnant, because its source is pathological; it is born of some deep spring of agony and pained frustration in his soul; it is savage, ferocious, intent, not light and detached. It is a grimace of despair rather than humor. He

454

has, furthermore, no conception of the meaning or true function of skepticism. Though he pretends to establish his spiritual life upon conflict, there is in him, if one cares to go deeply enough into his thought, a need for resting upon the comfortable foundations of faith. He is, therefore, completely incapable of any sympathy for doubt.

Eliseo Vivas. *NYHT*. Dec. 4, 1927. p. 18

Unamuno sees in man not the creature who must live merely through a fulfilment of the body. He sees the man who cannot fully live in body or mind until, discarding the objections of Reason, he discovers faith in his personal immortality. The cult of death has often been noted in the sombre Spanish nature. Like a Spanish Tolstoy, Unamuno is asking in all his books, "What does Truth matter if a man dies?" It is the characteristic and gnawing problem for the out and out individualist, for individualism without faith is reduced to futility and eccentricity. . . . Against western European rationalism, and its great culture, particularly as it is expressed in France, Unamuno puts the mysticism of Spain. . . . Against a religion of happiness, is placed the stoical argument that a true philosophy teaches men the value of suffering, how to live by preparing them for death.

V. S. Pritchett. *Spec*. Feb. 28, 1936. p. 350

If doubt were merely the point of departure for Unamuno's thought, he would not differ radically from most other philosophers who embark on their search for answers with the specific aim of overcoming perplexity. But doubt does not serve him merely as a springboard; it remains an organic, integral part, the warp and woof of his schemata. It has been the traditional objective of the philosopher to offer solutions; he has always tended to use the dialectic of reconciling opposites into a congruent, conclusive synthesis. Unamuno, on the contrary, does not bring to his reader the finality which comes from harmonizing discords. Because . . . he is not concerned with establishing truth; he is concerned with understanding living man, and man is a discord, a creature of reason and intuition, mind and heart, knowledge and hope, resignation and yearning. In the unappeased war of these opposites he finds his peculiar peace. . . . Life exists by virtue of its dynamism; it creates itself out of its opposites, nothingness and death, just as immunity is acquired through the introduction of the virus of disease into the bloodstream.

Martin Nozick. *SAQ*. July, 1950. pp. 334–5

The Christ of Velasquez purports to be a series of religious meditations in verse. It is an excellent example of what Toynbee calls archaism, the deliberate adoption of the vesture of baroque mysticism to clothe a diseased and irreligious sensationalism. Unamuno has written on the tragic sense. Yet these poems show no tragic insight but only a worship of pain and death as ends in themselves.

In essence, these poems are not just anti-secular, they are anti-religious, not only anti-humanistic but anti-human and murderous. Such poetry, however depraved, might have some literary interest if it were well done. Unamuno's Spanish is characterized by a false elegance, at once tortured and vulgar—Huysmans without the dirty words.

Kenneth Rexroth. NYT. June 17, 1951. p. 5

It was an obsession of Unamuno that he incarnated the soul of his people. He was the Don Quixote of modern Spain. . . . The truth is that no one can understand the Spanish soul who does not study the personality and writings of Unamuno. A member of the generation of '98—the generation of young Spanish writers who were stabbed awake by the Spanish-American War to rethink the problem and significance of their country—Unamuno is undoubtedly the greatest interpreter of the Spanish race. It was his view that the true, the eternal Spain, was found in the Spanish mystics of the sixteenth century and in Cervantes' *Don Quijote*. What Spain needed, so he wrote in an early essay, in order to awake— to be herself, to make her contribution to the world, was to open all the doors and windows of the Pyrenees, and let the breezes in that blew from the rest of Europe. . . . The prince of individualists, he possessed the universalism which is part of the glory of the Spanish genius. . . . Miguel de Unamuno had a sense of the tragic when writers in general were romantic optimists. He has been well called the Dostoevski of Spain. . . . Unamuno will speak again, and within him and through him, Spain.

John A. Mackay. Foreword to Poems by
Miguel de Unamuno (Johns Hopkins). 1952. pp. viii–ix

Unamuno had an ardent wish to be recognized as a great poet in verse and prose. . . . His rough-tongued poems with their blend of fervor and contemplation brought indeed a new note into Spanish lyrical poetry at the turn of the century, but their poetic form was never strong enough to absorb the sentiments and thoughts that inspired them. . . . And yet Unamuno was not wrong when he called himself a poet: he was a poet who had to create a world in his image so as to assure himself of his self. Taken in this sense, Unamuno's true poetic creation was the personality he projected into all his work; his "agony," his ceaseless struggle with himself and the universe, was the core of every one of his novels and stories, poems and essays. . . . And in the end it is always the complete unity of the man and his work, the man and his life, which emerges with overwhelming force. . . . If in the present generation his agony and incurable inner schism touch us all, he has also left us a legacy of moral courage and integrity. A thinker who teaches how to turn conflict, contradiction and despair into a source of strength has something to give men of this age.

Arturo Barea. *Unamuno* (Yale). 1952. pp. 37, 58

There was nothing of the exquisite or the literary *recherché* in Unamuno. His poetry is the direct, often crude loud thinking of a passionate man, and, perhaps because of this, terrifyingly sincere and pervasive. He is, in short, a philosopher meditating poetically rather than a poet philosophizing.

Angel Flores. *NYHT*. Feb. 15, 1953. p. 7

Implicit in Unamuno's metaphors there is a kind of mysticism of the flesh, an unformulated belief or hope that death cannot quench a desire to live so deeply rooted in the flesh and so powerfully felt. . . . The most pervasive function of fleshly images in Unamuno's writing is to express his passionate longing for immortality. . . . They express and sustain his revolt against mortality, for Unamuno was a rebellious spirit more given to struggle than to longing. . . . Unamuno wrote as though he were straining every fiber of his animal being not to fall into the cold abyss which reason foretold would finally extinguish his flaming spirit forever.

R. L. Predmore. *PMLA*. Sept., 1955. pp. 604–5

Ortega was our Turgenev, and Unamuno was our Dostoevsky. Ortega would Europeanize Spain, while Unamuno would Hispanify Europe. . . . By "Europeanizing" Spain Ortega meant making it objective; while for Unamuno, to "Hispanify" Europe amounted to making it subjective. Ortega wanted order, science, technology, and more social service and social spirit—a movement forward. Unamuno longed for character, experience, self-expression, individual freedom, and creativeness—a yearning upward. Ortega stressed social morality; Unamuno, individual faith. . . . Spain meant for Unamuno that particular way of reaching universality which yearns upward and not forward. . . . He was so subjective that everything he saw and touched became Unamuno. His egotism made him concentrate all the world in his own self. One feels . . . in all Unamuno's works, that his real aim is to prove that God exists, not so much for the sake of God or of the world, but because if God exists, Unamuno will live forever, while if God does not exist, Unamuno's hope of surviving his own death on earth all but vanishes. "All but" because even then Unamuno would be sure to fight for it.

Salvador de Madariaga. *At.* Jan., 1961. pp. 95–7

When he spoke of intensifying contact with Europe he actually meant bringing fully to bear upon the Western mind the tremendous impact of the Spanish sixteenth century. When it came to Spain receiving the full impact of modern rationalism, he was anti-European. . . . By rejecting Cartesian doubt and all that came of it, Unamuno pitted himself against the modern world. He could do this and live—live magnificently —because for him the question was never one of *being* but of believing: hence that *Cogito ergo sum* struck him as absurd and *Sum ergo cogito* as self-evident. Hence, too, that his foremost obsession was with immortality; an obsession inconceivable in one concerned with "knowing," such as the rationalist, and not with "being." But such consciousness as Unamuno possessed of the reality of being is precisely what alienates the religious from the modern rationalist mind. No amount of praise given to the Spanish sixteenth century contemplatives can therefore cause them to substantially affect modern thought.

Amalia Elguera. *Com.* March 31, 1961. pp. 14–15

To leave everything unfinished, whether a literary work or life itself, was one of Unamuno's constant aims. Small wonder that his works impress us as being a kind of continuous creation, a sort of "interminable poem." . . . He rejected that "mere perfection" of verse and prose whose hallmark is completeness. . . . In the essentially unfinished character of Unamuno's works we encounter once again that impulse to overturn, to pour out, to overflow . . . which so faithfully represents Unamuno's temperament, his aims. Such an impulse is present even when, as in poetic forms fixed by tradition—like the sonnet—all would seem to end with the final verse. But if the last line of any of Unamuno's sonnets is a formal conclusion, it is also a new beginning; the poet has ceased to move his pen, but he keeps his spirit—and the spirit of his readers— mobile.

José Ferrater Mora. *Unamuno* (California). 1962. pp. 95–6

The basic contradictions of Unamuno's thinking and his struggle to express them in metaphors inevitably produced poetry, metaphysical poetry of an intimate lyrical nature wherein thought and feeling are

mingled in a contrapuntal imaginative style which externalized the evolution of his own soul and hence *was,* and *is,* Unamuno. . . .

In poetry the metaphor, in prose the paradox, both products of his
fertile imagination, relieve what might otherwise be a monotonous repetition of a few basic ideas, and characterize his intimate style of writing
and talking. But Unamuno's style is marked by another quality which
makes it peculiarly his own. He had a special knack for concretizing
the abstract. This habit of fusing the spiritual with the material lends
clarity and vividness to his thoughts.

Margaret T. Rudd. *The Lone Heretic* (Texas). 1963.
pp. 199–200

See *Poems* and *The Christ of Velasquez* (poetry); also *The Tragic Sense of
Life* (essay); and *Three Exemplary Novels.*

UNGARETTI, GIUSEPPE (1888–   )

The epigraph for all of Giuseppe Ungaretti's work is the poem . . .
"Between one flower gathered and the other given/the inexpressible
Null." The given word: the moment of "unmerited" poetic Grace, the
word that waits not on will, but on humble expectation. The gathered
word: the word wrested, won from silence or from the inertia of dying
forms. . . . Ungaretti was the first to face unequivocally the problematic,
terrible task of every modern Italian poet, the task that takes its toll in
silence: to resurrect or to bury the cadaver of literary Italian. Ungaretti
resurrected. But so drastic were his means—sweeping away the clam-
orous inconsequences of D'Annunzio, the tenuous meanderings of the
Crepuscolari (the Twilight School), and almost all after Leopardi—that
resurrection was revolution. Ungaretti purged the language of all that
was but ornament, of all that was too approximate for the precise tension
of his line. Through force of tone and sentiment, a syntax stripped to
its essential sinews, he compelled words to their primal power.

Allen Mandelbaum. Introduction to *Life of a Man*
(New Directions). 1958. p. xi

A painstaking writer who paid great attention to style, Ungaretti fits into
the century-old current of interchange between Italian and French authors. A friend of French poets of the time, he writes about life in Paris
and refers repeatedly to poets of the Symbolist movement, in particular to
Baudelaire. Ungaretti's poems are similar to his French predecessor's
in subject matter, portraying painful moods of dejection by means of
symbols and recollections from the vague past. Like Baudelaire he
describes the jagged misfortunes of death against a foreboding back-

ground of nocturnal silence and solitude. Ungaretti's poems also recall those of Baudelaire in form since they are marked by fairly complicated syntax. His art, like that of Baudelaire, is enhanced by his masterful selection of vague images and subtle inner harmonies.

Patricia M. Gathercole. *Ital.* March, 1958. p. 8

More abstruse, constricted, and elliptical than Ungaretti's earlier work, his *Sentimento del tempo* created a furore in the world of Italian letters. Magazines were founded with the express purpose of attacking Ungaretti, who was accused of being a "hermetic" poet and the leader of the "hermetic school." Flung at Ungaretti by the famous critic Francesco Flora in 1936, "hermetic" (*arcane, mysterious,* or, in modern usage, *airtight*) implied that for the uninitiated reader there was no way into this terse, cryptic, densely written poetry, in which so much of the meaning lay not only in the far-ranging metaphors, but even in the arrangement of the lines and in the blank spaces between. Defenders did not hesitate to point out that this kind of poetry was merely a logical consequence of the process of exfoliating the nineteenth-century incrustations of politics, philosophy, oratorical eloquence, etc.—all that heritage of a gaudy romanticism—to get at the *essenzialità* of poetry, and that the conditions of the difficult and bitter '20's, in which so many of the traditional values seemed to have peeled and crumbled, made necessary a speech that would have, in order to be honest, the wry, crabbed, complex tone of the age.

John F. Nims. *The Poem Itself,* ed. by
Stanley Burnshaw (Holt). 1960. p. 308

Ungaretti, after a Parisian start which acquainted him with Guillaume Apollinaire and with the direct heritage of Baudelaire and Mallarmé, was initiated into the mysteries of carnage in the Carso trenches. . . . The exhilaration of a lucidly faced despair prevented him from accepting the heroic myth in which d'Annunzio, that belated Renaissance adventurer, strove to drape the skeleton War. . . . To face daily death was to sense one's precariousness as a creature and to return to the elements, to the only form of existence safe from corruption and entropy: stone, water, sun. . . . D'Annunzio's baroque Pegasus reared toward the stars in a loud gesture; Ungaretti's Muse became a terse confession of entropy in the soul. . . . The poet is not the beautifier of a hopeless reality, but a thorough confessor. Whatever the success or failure in each poem, this wholesale refusal to become a mouthpiece of public wishful thinking recommends him to our gratitude as an example of artistic honesty for all times.

Glauco Cambon. *Ital.* Dec., 1960. pp. 231–3

Ungaretti, we might say, was attempting to create a poetry "in progress" in which every word would be restored to its virgin meaning (historically speaking), untainted by the accretions of centuries of conventions, and would thus evoke an immediate, candid image. Upon this premise he began to build his "poetics," enriching it as he went along with a profound emotive content, in which human sorrow allied itself with religious fervor in a language of primitive desperation. There remained the problems of rhythm, of meter, of versification: elements that had reached such a state of chaos that the *rondisti* had flatly declared that strict verse was dead and buried. Ungaretti, however, remained firm in his faith that Italian poetry could be written with a newly balanced technique; after years of painstaking effort he proved that it could be done. From the earlier works in which the versification seemed almost external to the poetry itself and in which punctuation is almost completely discarded, Ungaretti sought to reconstruct the rhythm of the Italian language by recasting into new form the traditional hendecasyllable. All subsequent Italian poetry felt the impact of this reform.

Carlo L. Golino. *Contemporary Italian Poetry*
(California). 1962. pp. xvi–xvii

Ungaretti's long poetic itinerary points to the fact that his conquest is not a mere linguistic one. He has constantly moved from one stage to the next, from a poetry of innocence to one of memory to a supreme co-penetration of the two with a mythical poetry. . . . No one in our times has felt as Ungaretti has the gravity of the poet's task and has so fervently and brilliantly dedicated himself to making his readers conscious of the beauty of the written word. But he has also created, with a style probably unmatched in contemporary Italy for its sheer melody, a vast landscape of dreams, of feelings, and, in spite of its pain and sorrow, peace. His is, indeed, the promised land toward which we may all aspire, here and now, to retrieve that part of us only poetry can recapture.

Sergio Pacifici. *A Guide to Contemporary Italian
Literature* (World). 1962. pp. 176–7

See *Life of a Man* (poetry).

VALDÉS, ARMANDO PALACIO

See Palacio Valdés, Armando

VALÉRY, PAUL (1871–1945)

One is confronted by a pure intellect that has achieved integrity through a tortuous sequence of distinctions and relationships. One is filled with the need to penetrate and to participate in its austere isolation.

The intellect resists this invasion, by every subterfuge of abstraction. Then, one by one, the antagonist captures the keys to its high place. And when one has traversed a certain distance, the other doors open of themselves, and one beholds, in the writings of Paul Valéry, a miraculously calm and assured awareness of those hidden motives of the modern mind which others have lacked the hardihood to interrogate.

William A. Drake. *Contemporary European Writers*
(John Day). 1928. pp. 230–1

Mallarmé is always a painter, usually a water-colorist . . . whereas Valéry's genius is sculptural rather: these mythological poems have a density of cloud-shapes heavily massed—if they were not clouds, we should call them marmoreal. He gives us figures and groups half disengaged—and he runs to effects less of color than of light: the silvery, the sombre, the sunny, the translucent, the crystalline. And his verses carry off with the emphasis of an heroic resounding diction reminiscent of Alfred de Vigny the fluid waverings, the coy ambiguities and the delicately caught nuances which he has learned from Mallarmé. . . . Valéry is, indeed, a sort of masculine of an art of which Mallarmé is the feminine.

Edmund Wilson. *Axel's Castle* (Scribner). 1931. pp. 71–2

Life, instincts and the vital impulse grope their way toward consciousness and thought through Valéry's symbols. The Tree (*"La Platane"*), The Snake (*"Ebauche d'un Serpent"*), the Woman (*"La Jeune Parque"*), as they do in Bergson's philosophy. But Valéry is no pantheist; he believes in matter, time and space. Evolution, if there is any such thing, tends to thought, and nothing is worth while unless it takes a form. Obscurity must be brought into light and consciousness into contact with the visible world; dreams must take lines, shapes and colors; a soul cannot exist without a body. A shell is more human than the sea, a palm tree than the desert, a column than the cosmos.

Régis Michaud. *Modern Thought and Literature in France* (Funk). 1934. p. 208

Valéry . . . chose the intellectual side. His ambition resembled that of T. S. Eliot's early days: he was obsessed by the idea of always moving through and "going beyond." Each poem could be translated into a problem capable of solution, capable of supplying a principle which could then be applied to the writing of other poems. . . . Always he was driven further, to attack new problems, discover new principles. And, at a certain point in the process, it became evident that literature itself was a problem capable of solution, and was therefore only an intermediate goal, a stage to be passed through and left behind. The poet was free to abandon poetry.

Malcolm Cowley. *NR*. Jan. 3, 1934. p. 219

His poetry, he has said, has for him been a set of "exercises." He disparages the element of chance, "inspiration," and insists on the function of the will in art. He has swallowed without a tremor Poe's rationalizations of instinctive creative workings. He has peppered his writings with italics, as though he were constantly bearing down on their essential "thought." Beneath all this underscoring his style flows on fluidly, often with rhetorical magnificence. He is a writer, all his protestations to the contrary, endowed with a natural feeling for sonorous language, operating under the force of a highly refined and subtle intuition. Gifts of this kind cannot be concealed and cannot be forged. The fact that Valéry continually denies them lends to his work as a whole a faint, continual tone of sophistry.

Louise Bogan. *Nation*. Jan. 7, 1939. p. 38

In *Le Cimetière Marin,* and indeed in most of *Charmes,* Valéry has moved far from Mallarmé. He may use some of the same symbols . . . but the intention and the effect are different. The mystical view of poetry has been replaced by the acceptance of it as a fact like other facts. The special place of the poet in society is not mentioned. . . . The poet has found his relation to life, but on the whole he lives in a rare and special atmosphere. He writes for the few. . . . Above all it is the poetry of an extremely intelligent man, who knows what things are and is not afraid to see them in their true nature.

C. M. Bowra. *The Heritage of Symbolism* (Macmillan). 1943. pp. 54–5

Paul Valéry turned figures into gold in the noble fire of his soul. He was an alchemist and a goldsmith; a cabinetmaker and a spiritualist, the man who puts the table together and the man who forces it to speak.

No one knew so many secrets; no one more effectually brought order into disorder and turned order into disorder; no one laid a more prudent and more imprudent hand on the cunning explosives of poetry.

Jean Cocteau. *NYT*. May 7, 1950. p. 6

He was at ease with us (probably with everyone), generally gay, always spontaneous and natural, never caring to hide his humours, giving way unaffectedly to his fancies and absurdities. If one asked him a question, he answered readily, and one felt he answered the truth without disguise and with no other motive than sheer love of truth—swayed neither by self-interest nor self-respect, nor indeed by any sort of respect, whether for persons or opinions, impelled by his whole nature, in small things and great, to look truth unflinchingly in the face, to follow it wherever it might lead, with a courage that to most men seems almost superhuman.

Dorothy Bussy. In *The Golden Horizon*, ed. by Cyril Connolly (Weidenfeld). 1953. p. 355

His poetry, in agreement with his theories, relies on sensations for its primary contact with the reader—the aural sensation of the sound of the verse, the evocation of physical sensations through imagery—while revealing on examination the existence of an intellectual process running through, or behind, the physical texture. This is precisely the manner and order in which a live human being presents himself to us: the physical presence first, and afterwards the intellectual or spiritual *persona*. It distinguishes Valéry from his master, Mallarmé, who strikes us as an intelligence without an adequate, or with a contrived physical presence.

Geoffrey Brereton. *An Introduction to the French Poets* (Methuen). 1956. pp. 260–1

Valéry spent the whole of his life brooding over the problem of how to live, as Mallarmé spent his meditating on "The Great Work" which he never managed to write. The outcome is that all Valéry's finest poems are studies in "method," "exercise," experiment rather than an expression of the human condition. It is precisely this kind of interest in "method," which he shared with Flaubert, Mallarmé and Joyce, that stamps a writer as a mandarin. It must be said of him, as it must be said of his master, that he was the author of great lines rather than great poems, that he had hit on a form of poetry which leads in the end to the disappearance of poetry.

Martin Turnell. *Com.* Aug. 30, 1957. p. 547

There is, in the mind and work of Valéry, a curious paradox. He presents himself to the reader, not only as a tireless explorer of the labyrinths of philosophic speculation, but also under the aegis of Leonardo da Vinci, as a man of scientific temper, fascinated by the problems of method; a ranging and restless mind; a dilettante of science but a specialist in a science of his own invention—the science of poetry. Yet, when we peruse the list of titles of his essays, we find a remarkably limited subject matter, with no evidence of omniverous reading, or of the varied interests of a Coleridge or a Goethe. He returns perpetually to the same insoluble problems. It would almost seem that the one object of his curiosity was—himself. He reminds us of Narcissus gazing into the pool, and partakes of the attraction and the mystery of Narcissus, the aloofness and frigidity of that spiritual celibate.

T. S. Eliot. Introduction to *The Art of Poetry*
by Paul Valéry (Pantheon). 1958. pp. xxii–xxiii

Valéry was small, about my own height in fact, which for some reason surprised me. He was quick, quiet (he spoke in rapid, *sotto voce* mumbles), and extremely gentle. He seemed a terrible dandy at first sight because of his monocle and boutonniere, but that impression dissolved as soon as he began to talk. Wit and intelligence were in everything he said, though not merely in what he said but in emanation from his whole person. This was to be expected of Valéry, of course; what I did not expect, however, but was delighted to discover in him that first day was a truly joyful sense of humor.

Igor Stravinsky. Memoir in *Plays* by Paul Valéry
(Pantheon). 1960. p. xx

Nothing could be more different than our two natures, nothing more contrary than the bent of our two minds. Mine "naturally inclined to veneration," as Goethe said of his own, as much as Valéry's was bent on impiety, antagonistic to all accepted and unverified beliefs, resolutely skeptical (at once doubting and seeking), regardless of agreement, approval, or sympathy and apparently free from all human weaknesses, vain curiosities, adventitious preoccupations, procrastinations, sentimental dallyings. To everything likely to distract him from his quest, he said "No!" . . . One thing was clear to me, of which I never doubted—that he was always right. His scorn occasionally hurt me, at least at some points, but I acknowledged he had the right to be scornful—a right he had won in hard-fought battle. His stark, iconoclastic hammer spared nothing.

> André Gide. *The Creative Vision*, ed. by
> Haskell M. Block and Herman Salinger (Grove).
> 1960. p. 65

If Victor Hugo might be fancied as the Beethoven of French literature, Paul Valéry would be its Mozart. . . . Nothing clearer, simpler, more diaphanous than Mozart's music, Valéry's poetry or prose; but what a difficult simplicity! Here, no volume, no show of power, though power is there, hidden under the terse skin of apparent ease; no roaring of the crowds; no outcry of the passions; no developments, no eloquence, no violent contrasts. Line, melody, clarity, and a curious purity due perhaps to a distance from the grosser forms of human life.

> Salvador de Madariaga. Introduction to *History and
> Politics* by Paul Valéry (Pantheon). 1962. p. xxi

See *Selected Writings* and *The Art of Poetry*.

VALLE-INCLÁN, RAMÓN DEL (1866–1936)

The main quality of Valle-Inclán, that which gives formal excellence and emotional music to his art, is the purity of his aesthetic attitude. He turns his soul on nature like a mirror, the limpidity of which is untarnished by any moral or philosophical preoccupation. . . . It is here, to my mind, that the flaw in the art of Don Ramón María del Valle-Inclán is to be found. His aesthetic attitude is not merely the natural one of an artist intent on creation. It arises from a real indifference towards the higher philosophic and moral issues. . . . Hence that jarring note of insincerity throughout his work. . . . It explains the indifference with which man's most sacred passions are handled without leaving the slightest tremor in the hands of the artist. . . . It stimulates the search for the merely weird and picturesque, for the horrible and the morbid.

> Salvador de Madariaga. *The Genius of Spain* (Oxford).
> 1923. pp. 145–7

His profound originality consists in his rhythmical prose. In the minute attention given to the musical cadence of his sentences, he is, superficially at least, a Symbolist. In his cult of the senses he pays more heed to sound and shape and scent than to colour. He is, as it were, a sculptor of miniatures. . . . [But] if Señor Valle-Inclán is in a limited sense a Symbolist, he also has a touch of that petulant audacity which marked the Romantics and sometimes takes our breath away in Victor Hugo.

The magic of his style is partly derived from a variety of contrasts. In his modernist prose he writes of ancient things and he describes the artistic and luxurious with unfailing sobriety. With delicate fingers he draws scenes of horror and barbaric savagery. . . . He has a passion for the minute, the refined and exquisite, but he does not lack vigour, and is in fact a very energetic decadent.

Aubrey F. G. Bell. Contemporary Spanish Literature
(Knopf). 1923. pp. 128–9

This perennially ironic race has distilled the love of failure from its too great success. . . . Despair is voluptuous. Incompetence is a cult. And votaries of this narcissistic trance are among Spain's finest writers.

Chief of them all perhaps is Don Ramón María del Valle-Inclán. . . . The volumnear body of Valle-Inclán's prose serves to mass a death: his drama is one of furious rhetoric. All the more glorious ghosts of Spain stalk in his books. The Church with its "charity of the sword," chivalry mildewed and broken from its long passage southward, clanwarfare, mystic fealty and love are personified in the were-wolf bombast of his scenes. But though these shapes be ghosts, they have no charnel odor: the salt of modern irony—the perennial Spanish irony—is on them. There puissance is not to be challenged. The dark firm candor of this prose is so enchanting that one accepts the nightmarish or sentimental dumb-show: this gesturing pageantry of Dream which is the Dream of Spain.

Waldo Frank. Virgin Spain (Boni and Liveright). 1926.
pp. 275–6

Valle-Inclán is limited, in his artistic achievement, by a singular incapacity for any moral feeling, which places the seal of sterility upon the exquisite vessel of his art, distorts it with the lust of cruelty. . . . Herein lies the limitation of Valle-Inclán as a creator . . . because he is inhuman, because there is a senseless and wanton quality in his perpetual cruelty that has no human answer, because he writes as if in an infernal void, with black hate, not in his heart, for there it might serve as a powerful creative force, but with the door of his heart closed and with black hate in his brain. Great artist as he is, he cannot create magnificently, because he cannot feel; because he cannot experience through any medium except his meticulously wrought style and his too subtle, sarcastic intellect. And the intellect is not enough.

William A. Drake. Contemporary European Writers
(John Day). 1928. pp. 136–7

Don Ramón is the last member of that mythical family which came so near its termination with the death of Oscar Wilde and Paul Verlaine. His imagination is always at work. His beautiful lies come to us wrapped in a gorgeous, lyric garb. . . . He is fond of the bizarre, the supernatural and the archaic. His works seem to have been exquisitely wrought by a gongorized Benvenuto Cellini inspired by a Barbey d'Aurevilly. In his *Sonatas* (translated . . . as *The Pleasant Memoirs of the Marquis de Bradomín*) the "Catholic, sentimental and ugly" Marquis carries on his Casanova existence in the polychromic and baroque setting of a D'Annunzio, whose *Figlia di Jorio* especially helped Don Ramón to create his *comedias bárbaras,* and later a new genre, the *esperpentos,* a cross between the sublime and the ridiculous. The *esperpentos* are really literary abortions. In them grotesqueness mixes with charm, slang with symbolic language, chaos with distilled lights. Since Alfred Jarry's *Ubu Roi* literature had never seen such hybrid nightmares.

Angel Flores. *NYHT*. Oct. 20, 1929. p. 23

He enters into the houses of stone and into the huts of the village. On the pretext of resting and slaking his thirst, he listens to what passes in them. He knows equally well the story of the beggar and of the wealthy colonial who marries a young girl and was killed by a secret poison.

The late afternoons of great panoramas rule in his work, and one sees there how on his return home, he slackens his steps a bit to marvel. In his work are seen vast beaches in the sands of which remain, when the tide recedes, only the print of his feet.

Don Ramón, in the midst of great nature, is the astrologist of flowers, of echoes of things, which pass by very far off; and no one knows whether they are phantoms or an overwhelming reality.

Ramón Gómez de la Serna. *Bkm.* Nov., 1930. p. 262

Above all, the poetry of Valle-Inclán is not superficial. Behind every evocation, something is hid. The words do not exhaust the sensation. No one will stop merely with the image the poet conjures up, because this image brings with it an ineffable train, a complex of suggestions. This, and his tendency to unite in one verse many qualities derived from the other arts, modulating it, modeling it, giving it tonal depth, converts him at once into one of the subtlest representatives of symbolism, even more than Rubén Darío himself, for Valle-Inclán is more consistent. Symbolism, with him, does not confine itself to the nostalgia of mysticism, but at times reveals a play of humor, as in a Gothic

cathedral, where beneath the spiritual uplifted spires pointing heaven-
wards, appears, of a sudden, the laughter of a gargoyle.

Enrique Diez Canedo. Bkm. Nov., 1930. pp. 261–2

The "Generation of '98" . . . looks to [Ramón del Valle-Inclán], the
Galician counterpart of D'Annunzio, for supreme guidance in the
composition of the most rhythmic and musical prose that has ever come
from the pen of a Spaniard.

Valle-Inclán has done for Spanish prose what the Nicaraguan, Rubén
Darío, did for Spanish verse. He has set himself a standard of supreme
artistry—that of "bringing together two words for the first time." Like
Darío the poet, Valle-Inclán is keenly alive to the musical and even
the metallic and almost gaseous significance of words.

Charles K. Colhoun. BkmL. July, 1932. p. 196

Valle-Inclán specializes in talk and keeps analysis and portrayal to a
minimum. He is readable now only because his dialogue is jerky and
harsh enough to keep us from surrendering completely to the anodyne
of his mannered, cadenced prose. . . . He cannot stay with a theme:
he deals in cuts, explosions of emotional energy, lunges at irrelevant
notions and acerb reversals of tone. . . . For him, only the deformed is
eloquent and he himself seems like some cavorting Goya of prose.
Swaggering, reckless, impulsive, self-obsessed, ever suspicious of formal
literary purpose, he is essentially the stylist, the effects-man, looking
forwards to the anti-novel . . . and looking back to the generation of '98.

Paul West. The Modern Novel (Hutchinson). 1963. p. 413

See The Pleasant Memoirs of the Marquis de Bradomín, The Dragon's Head,
and The Tyrant (novels).

VERCORS (1902–   )

One of the most fascinating and dramatic stories of the literary resistance
is the origin of the cachet Editions de Minuit. Until the day of liberation
the close associates of Jean Desvignes [a pseudonym used by Vercors]
knew him only as a moving spirit in the publication of Underground
books of a high literary order. Even Mme. Desvignes, a publishing
partner, had been unaware that he was the author of the internationally
successful war novel Le Silence de la Mer. To throw the hounding
Gestapo off the track he had set up a secret one-man press and published
his novel behind the brave new front of the Editions de Minuit.

Henry C. Wolfe. SR. Oct. 14, 1944. p. 12

M. Vercors is a man with a mission. What is the nature of man? M. Vercors is not only concerned to arrive at a definition himself: he is deeply disturbed by the frivolity embedded in this nature of ours which seems to prevent the rest of us from being very much interested in the question. His last novel, *You Shall Know Them,* approached the problem from the biological angle. . . . In *The Insurgents* he approaches the same question "the fundamental notion of what we call human," on two fronts, the physiological and the social. . . . No one can deny that M. Vercors makes his thesis clear and proves to his own satisfaction that man is not only a social being—to which we would all surely agree—but that he is *exclusively* a social being. If he proves anything else, it is that an idée fixe is a singularly poor foundation for the construction of a novel.

Elizabeth Janeway. *NYT*. Oct. 28, 1956. p. 7

The Insurgents is a work of existentialist science fiction, and it was at first difficult to see what I saw in it. . . . I was surprised that in spite of Vercors' philosophical speculation, which was sometimes dull, I enjoyed this new novel very much. It may be that although Vercors' ideas are neither profound nor original, his characterization and his style, and more than either of these, his emotional intensity—for it is a great pleasure these days to read a prose writer who feels deeply, to whom people and ideas *matter*—move and involve the reader.

Dachine Rainer. *Nation*. Dec. 22, 1956. p. 544

Vercors . . . won sudden fame during the war as a leader of intellectual resistance and as the author of *The Silence of the Sea*. . . . Vercors has since written political tracts, reports of his travel in Red China, an allegorical novel, *You Shall Know Them,* and contributed to moral debates between Christian and Marxist scientists. He is primarily a moralist calling for more ethics and more spirituality in politics. His attitude is very close to that of Albert Camus; but his imagination is less vivid and his style, concise, swift, a trifle dry and colorless, lacks the vibration which makes every sentence of Camus tingle.

Henri Peyre. *NYT*. Feb. 19, 1961. p. 5

Jean Bruller—Vercors is a pseudonym—is not a man to settle down in any one mental groove, nor is he inclined to lose the humor which once made him an amazing cartoonist. Since World War II, and his contribution to Resistance literature with the clandestine publishing house Les Editions de Minuit, he has given a good deal of thought to what goes into the making of a human being, where the line can be drawn between the animal and the human. He has moved steadily away from Marxism toward a point comparable to Teilhard de Chardin's in its emphasis upon the unique nature of the human mind. But Vercors overburdens his tales with philosophical disquisition. In fact he enjoys poking fun at his own speculations and, on the way, at such popular fads as psychoanalysis.

Germaine Brée. *NYT*. Jan. 7, 1962. p. 5

Someone called Vercors an unfortunate affectation that blights French literature. Unfair. He's a dependable nineteenth-century liberal, intelligent company, and good clean fun. For two evenings, no more.

Webster Schott. *NYT*. March 13, 1966. p. 4

See *Paths of Love, Quota*, and *Sylva* (novels).

VERGA, GIOVANNI (1840–1922)

When we talk of the great modern movement towards reality we speak without the documents if we leave this book out of the count, for I can think of no other novel in which the facts have been more faithfully reproduced, or with a profounder regard for the poetry that resides in facts and resides nowhere else. . . . The effect [in *The House by the Medlar Tree*] is precisely that which the author aimed at. . . . He meant to let the people show themselves with the least possible explanation or comment from him. The transaction of the story is in the highest degree dramatic; but events follow one another with the even sequence of hours on the clock. You are not prepared to value them beforehand; they are not advertised to tempt your curiosity like feats performed at the circus, in the fashion of the feebler novels; often it is in the retrospect that you recognize their importance and perceive their full significance. In this most subtly artistic management of his material the author is most a master.

W. D. Howells. Introduction to *The House by the Medlar Tree* (Harper). 1890. pp. iii–vi

Verga's atmosphere is naturally in good measure that of his native scene, where life is lived amidst a ferocious intensity of passions and a powerful belief in fate. His so-called impersonality should not mislead his readers, however. "It is not to satisfy a Flaubertian esthetics," writes Luigi Russo. . . , "that the author of '*Cavalleria Rusticana*' tries not to intervene in his tale; it is because his model, the Sicilian peasant, is convinced that he himself does not intervene in the conduct of his own life."

Isaac Goldberg. *Plays of the Italian Theatre* (John W. Luce). 1921. pp. 2–3

If he disregards what one considers the laws of aesthetics, if he does not strive for unity, if he is careless of what one has been taught is the technique of the short story, he does so because laws and rules and a predetermined technique are the crutches of mediocrity. . . . In Verga beauty as aesthetic perfection loses its importance and one is face to face with something which moves more deeply: the tragedy of men on whom fate has feasted itself pitilessly. . . . This is not to imply that Verga philosophizes about human misery. He is too great an artist to be didactic. Whatever attitude toward life the reader may find in his work he must contribute to it through his own imaginative sensibility.

Eliseo Vivas. *NYHT*. April 19, 1925. p. 15

This is the tragedy of tragedies in all time, but particularly in our epoch: the killing off of the naïve innocent life in all of us, by which alone we can continue to live, and the ugly triumph of the sophisticated greedy. It may be urged that Verga commits the Tolstoyan fallacy, of repudiating the educated world and exalting the peasant. . . . But Verga by no means exalts the peasants as a class: nor does he believe in their poverty and humility. Verga's peasants are certainly not Christ-like, whatever else they are. They are most normally ugly and low, the bulk of them. . . . Verga turned to the peasants to find, *in individuals,* the vivid spontaneity of sensitive passionate life, non-moral and non-didactic. He found it always *defeated.* He found the vulgar and the greedy always destroying the sensitive and the passionate. The vulgar and the greedy are themselves usually peasants: Verga was far too sane to put an aureole round the whole class. . . . The greedy and the vulgar win all the time: which, alas, is only too true, in Sicily as everywhere else.

D. H. Lawrence. Preface to *Cavalleria Rusticana and Other Stories* (Jonathan Cape). 1928. pp. 18–21

He reproduced the speech he heard about him. . . . But if he merely reproduced exactly he would be writing Sicilian and not Italian. Some enthusiastic regionalists thought he would have done better if he had used the dialect. But it was Verga's idea to reproduce the sense of the dialect, to give the impression of dialect and at the same time to write his tales in good standard Italian. It will be seen that it was a very delicate task; much more so than simply telling the story in dialect or using a few words of *argot* for local color. His method is to arrange good Tuscan words in Sicilian word order and to make the reader aware of the rhythm of dialect under the Italian sentence. Outside of a few titles . . . and a few nicknames . . . and a very occasional quotation of a proverb in the original, there are no words in his Sicilian stories which cannot be found in any standard Italian dictionary. But the arrangement of the words, the loose order of the sentence, and a certain rhythm in his prose: in brief, the style—these things are very far from Tuscan.

Thomas G. Bergin. Giovanni Verga (Yale). 1931. p. 107

Verga conceived himself as a naturalist. He would have liked his two great novels to provide the first parts of a vast cycle *à la* Zola, about "the Defeated" in the social struggle. Happily, he gave us, in fact, something less programmatic and more precious: a stoic picture of human endurance and squalor. Thus, an Italian critic, thinking of Verga's themes, could praise him as "the only plebeian novelist of our time," while D. H. Lawrence, with an eye to his style, felt that he is "too aristocratic a writer for the casual reader." The truth is that Verga is merciless: he reports the village gossip as implacably as he describes a storm at sea; and the quality of his language never exceeds the story he has to tell. . . . Verga is a virile writer. He does not ask obsessively "What does the world *mean*?," because he is busy *representing* it.

Paolo Milano. NYT. April 26, 1953. p. 33

It is at least an apparent irony that Verga's two tragic novels should be founded on a theory of progress; but the irony evaporates when we understand that his novels—and he projected five at various social levels —were to be concerned with the *victims* of progress, the conquered, and that the whole series was to appear under the collective title, *I vinti*.

Human society is a river that begins with low, denying springs and ends in a great, fulfilling torrent. At every point in this stream, some individuals feel that it would be desirable to be farther upstream, and the friction of their efforts to get there causes the whole to swell. The incessant wave that the total effort creates drowns many of the individuals who are making it, and they are tossed lifeless—*i vinti*—on the shore. . . . It is a mark of Verga's modernity that, while he was still charmed by the idea of progress, he wishes to write of it as *"Il cammino fatale,"* and it is surely a part of his greatness that, while he wished merely to observe, he made true tragedies out of this fatal modern idea.

Mark Schorer. NR. Jan. 11, 1954. p. 18

Giovanni Verga is the most modern of the old Italian novelists. . . . His art holds a strong appeal to the contemporary reader. . . . Verga was the leader of *verismo,* which is an Italian version of French naturalism, but he displayed strong national and personal traits which, some years later, endèared him to the Italian neo-realists of the post-Mussolini period. His literary manner presents surprising parallels to modern American prose. A direct approach to reality, a throbbing vitality mitigated by irony and insight, a perfect control of realistic details combined with the art of understatement and, above all, a warm feeling of humanity— these features of Verga's insure his permanent value as a writer. They also explain how his followers in the twentieth century were prepared to feel close kinship to American story-tellers.

Marc Slonim. NYT. Sept. 11, 1955. p. 4

What Verga actually wanted to do was to interpret his Sicilian world not in literary terms but in terms that were ideally those of that world itself. For this purpose he adopted a very limited vocabulary, which consisted of words that were popular in quality, or would sound so in a given context. He condensed the narration as much as possible, eliminating everything except what seemed absolutely indispensable and could not be suggested between the lines. His syntax became linear, and kept some traces of the syntax of Sicilian dialect—the language most of his characters would have spoken in real life. His sentences acquired certain peculiarities of everyday speech. The conjunction *"e"* ("and") was employed repeatedly to connect coördinate clauses and sentences, as in common popular narration.

Most of all—and this may be the primary source of all the characteristics of Verga's style—he had his people "narrate themselves," without apparent intrusions on his part.

Giovanni Cecchetti. Introduction to The She-Wolf and
Other Stories (California). 1958. pp. xiv–xv

He has a rich range of mood, a pungency of metaphor; something in him is equal to the clamor of the heart; he has a comprehensive grasp of scene; and without being naturalistic he seems to be able to pull up people by the roots straight out of nature and put them, rife as they are, upon the page. They come out with such vocal, physical emphasis that at first one is stunned and deafened. Verga depends on the crackle of his dialogue and on an allusive atmosphere which each sentence creates. You have to watch that and keep your senses keen or you will miss his transitions. . . . Verga is not a regional novelist in the provincial sense of the word. . . . No, Verga is European and modern. His visual power, which is heightened by his constant use of peasant metaphor and his identification with the peasant mind, is very modern. . . . The intensity of Verga is achieved by dense detail. He is totally without rhetoric.

V. S. Pritchett. *The Living Novel and Later Appreciations* (Random). 1964. pp. 323–5

The realistic tendency which had become more and more prominent in Italy in the course of the nineteenth century culminated in the work of Giovanni Verga. . . . When *verismo* coincides with great art it has the power of resisting the years; it is always contemporary; such is the *verismo* of Giovanni Verga. . . . Verga had imbibed the lesson of French realists; the objectivity of the artist, the scrupulous reproduction of human data, the so-called *tranche de vie,* etc., were canons in which he believed, and these canons formed the programme of Flaubert, the Goncourts and Zola. . . . There was, in him, . . . a sense of wonder, which was developed by his sojourn on the Continent, at the discovery of the virgin, almost mythical, world of Sicilian peasants.

Striking away from the aureate tradition of Italian prose, Verga made the Sicilian shepherds talk their own language: it was, at the end of the nineteenth century, in Italy, a repetition of Wordsworth's discovery of the virgin world of peasants and humble people, unadulterated by the sophistications and conventions of society. . . . One cannot talk of Italian neo-realism, both in fiction and in the cinema, without recognizing its antecedents in Verga's art.

Mario Praz. *The Literary Reputation of Hemingway in Europe,* ed. by Roger Asselineau (Lettres Modernes). 1965. pp. 106–7

See *Mastro-don Gesualdo* and *The House by the Medlar Tree* [trans. by Eric Mosbacher] (novels); also *Cavalleria Rusticana and Other Stories, Little Novels of Sicily,* and *The She-Wolf and Other Stories.*

VERHAEREN, EMILE (1855–1916)

As certainly as Maeterlinck is the representative dramatist of his country at the close of this nineteenth century, so is Verhaeren the representative lyric poet. It is impossible to avoid bringing the two names into constant juxtaposition. Both men are the product of one and the same literary movement and both are characteristic of their age and their country. Verhaeren, though today only in his forty-fourth year, has been in turn materialist and symbolist, the poet of blind revolt and the poet of mystical faith, the passionate lover of beauty and the morbid delineator of life in its most ludicrous aspects. But throughout the ever-varying emotions of an intense and poetic temperament, capable of appreciating at one moment the purest and most ecstatic joys and at another of wallowing in the blackest and most unrelenting misery, we can trace the strong and lasting influences of his early surroundings and his Flemish birthright.

Virginia M. Crawford. *Studies in Foreign Literature*
(Duckworth). 1899. pp. 110–1

I do not know whether any one has pointed out the similarity between Crabbe and the Belgian poet of our day. It is, however, very striking when we once come to think of it, and it embraces subject-matter, attitude to life and art, and even such closer matters as diction and versification. . . . If Byron were now alive, he might call Verhaeren a Victor Hugo in worsted stockings. There is the same sardonic delineation of a bleak and sandy sea-coast country, Suffolk or Zeeland as the case may be, the same determination to find poetic material in the perfectly truthful study of raw peasantry, of narrow provincial towns, of rough and cheerless seafaring existences. In each of these poets—and scarcely in any other European writers of verse—we find the same saline flavour, the same odour of iodine, the same tenacious attachment to the strength and violence and formidable simplicity of nature.

Edmund Gosse. *French Profiles* (Heinemann). 1913.
p. 326

Verhaeren is a man of the North, of wild cries and mystic raptures, of boundless exaltations and agonies. There is a touch of fever in his visions both of his Flemish country-side and of the turbulent modern cities that he loved. He sought finally to release his tortured soul from the bondage of self by sinking it, merging it—not like the Germanic mystics of old in God or nature, but in that vast brotherhood of pain and effort that bears the burden and the heat of an industrial civilization. . . . The liberating experience, since he could find peace in no form of personal idealism, religious or philosophic, came to him about 1892 through his identification with the socialist movement.

Ludwig Lewisohn. *The Poets of Modern France*
(Huebsch). 1918. pp. 29, 33

The whole atmosphere of our times seems compressed in the organ music of his work; and whether he touches the bright keys or the dark, whether he rolls out a lofty diapason or strikes a gentle concord, it is always the onward-rushing force of our time that vibrates in his poems.

While other poets have grown ever more lifeless and languid, ever more secluded and disheartened, Verhaeren's voice has grown ever more resonant and vigorous, like an organ indeed, full of reverence and the mystical power of sublime prayer.

Stefan Zweig. *Emile Verhaeren* (Constable). 1915. p. 12

What Verhaeren has done for poetry is this. He has made it realize the modern world. He has shown the grandeur of everyday life, and made us understand that science and art are never at variance. He has shown that civic consciousness is not necessarily dry and sterile, but can be as romantic as an individual and he has done all this without once saying it directly, by force of the greatest and most complete art.

Amy Lowell. *Six French Poets* (Houghton). 1921. p. 47

Of all the poets of today, narcissi along the river, Verhaeren is the least obliging in allowing himself to be admired. He is rude, violent, unskillful. Busied for twenty years in forging a strange and magical tool, he remains in a mountain cavern, hammering the reddened irons, radiant in the fire's reflection, haloed with sparks. . . . With Verhaeren, beauty is made of novelty and strength. This poet is a strong man, and since those *Villes tentaculaires* which surged with the violence of a telluric upheaval, no one dares to deny him the state and glory of a great poet.

Rémy de Gourmont. *The Book of Masks* (John W. Luce).
1921. pp. 35, 37

The contribution that Verhaeren has made consists of an enriched vocabulary, a more flexible verse-form, a sincerity of self-revelation, a personification of modern man, powerful symbolism drawn from modern conditions, a belief in the primacy of thought, and a message of courage for the present and of faith in the future. Verhaeren was a pioneer in the use of modern civilization, its tendencies and complexities as a source of symbols to express the longings, passions, and sensations of the modern man. By means of this symbolism to embody the new rhythm of life, Verhaeren became the poetic mouth-piece for our age, expressing modern man more completely than has any other French poet up to the present.

Alice F. Corell. *The Contribution of Verhaeren to Modern
French Lyric Poetry* (Buffalo). 1927. p. 72

Verhaeren was no metaphysical; yet like some of our prominent metaphysicians he could not have placed essence before existence. If to be an

existentialist means to believe in life and to enjoy it, then he would
be the greatest existential poet. But he is merely a great singer of
existence, and so for the moment his message is effaced by a type of
philosophy which recommends life with a grimace of courage, as if it
were largely repulsive. His insistence on *orgueil* (self-reliance) and
freedom has all the force which the Existentialists attach to these words
—without the desperation.

> P. Mansell Jones. *Verhaeren* (Bowes and Bowes).
> 1957. p. 54

See *The Plays of Emile Verhaeren* and *The Poems of Emile Verhaeren.*

VERLAINE, PAUL (1844–1896)

With Verlaine, that is, in the work that is truly *Verlainien* and not, as
occasionally, a wistful dallying with the spent wave of classical or
romantic impulse, there was no fixing of the stage, no bunting on a
processional route, no reliance on stock sentiment, no "curtains." It
was not his purpose to give us subjects of sensational or emotional
appeal, but rather to show us, as his brothers of the brush were also
doing, the results of sensation or emotion, set down as a musical effect,
without betraying any predisposition of moral principle towards the
thing expressed. His predispositions were those of taste and not of
mind.

> Wilfred Thorley. *Paul Verlaine* (Houghton). 1914. p. 86

With his careless, slovenly dress he would have passed unremarked in
any street crowd, French or English. He seemed, indeed, to wish to avoid
notice: there was something timid and shy, a shrinking even, in his
manner, due to constitutional nervousness rather than to reserve. With
friends Verlaine gave himself as freely and simply in talk as he did in
his writings. I have never known any human being with such childlike,
perfect frankness, such transparent sincerity in thought and being. . . .
Of course it was the absence of malice in Verlaine, the absence of all
spite, envy and hatred, the lovingkindness of the man which was so
engaging, and a touch of gay ironic humour lent an ineffable fascination
to his childlike good nature.

> Frank Harris. *Contemporary Portraits: First Series*
> (Mitchell Kennerley). 1915. pp. 270–1

The note of Verlaine's poetry is new in French verse; his form is new.
For the first time the French language has become capable of all the

delicate songfulness of the English language; those stiff impracticable lines which Victor Hugo bent, Verlaine has broken. His verse is as lyrical as Shelley's, as fluid, as magical—though the magic is a new one. It is a twilight art, full of reticence, of perfumed shadows, of hushed melodies. It suggests, it gives impressions, with a subtle avoidance of any too definite or precise effect of line or colour. . . . The impressions are as remote and fleeting as a melody evoked from the piano by a frail hand in the darkness of a scented room.

> Arthur Symons. *Colour Studies in Paris* (Dutton). 1918.
> pp. 199–200

With the frankness of a child babbling to some stranger of its toys and its relations, Verlaine is convinced that the most trivial events of his experience are tremendously interesting, are of almost cosmic significance. . . . For him the value of an emotion is not its depth, not even its intensity, but its truth. He knew full well that his peculiar poetic quality was not attuned to the grandiose, he knew that the deeper emotions would always elude him, and he perferred, therefore, to deal with the more incidental sensations, and to reflect in them the passions and tragedies in which his life was involved. In this he was abundantly right: the minor key can convey its message only by the indirect method.

> Harold Nicolson. *Paul Verlaine* (Houghton). 1921.
> p. 242

He is childish, but never simple; not childish, of course, in the way in which some contemporary poets are childish, clumsy rhymers of false naiveties. Verlaine's technique, for one thing, is of an extreme originality and refinement. Verlaine is childish in a positive, if not wholly a good sense. He is, in the main, a mere vehicle for emotions. They pass through him, he knows not why or whence; they leave him and they leave nothing behind them, not so much as a particle made immune or resistant. . . . The great poet grows from strength to strength. Verlaine did not. All that finally remained of his emotions was a vague memory, sufficient only to blunt their keen edge when they came to him again. Instead of having conviction added to them, their freshness was taken away.

> J. Middleton Murry. *NationL*. April 9, 1921. p. 64

With rhymes obtained from verb tenses, sometimes even from long adverbs preceded by a monosyllable from which they fell as from a rock into a heavy cascade of water, his verses, divided by improbable caesuras, often became strangely obscure with their audacious ellipses and strange inaccuracies which none the less did not lack grace.

With his unrivalled ability to handle metre, he had sought to rejuvenate the fixed poetic forms. He turned the tail of the sonnet into the air, like those Japanese fish of polychrome clay which rest on stands, their heads straight down, their tails on top.

Joris-Karl Huysmans. *Against the Grain* (Lieber and Lewis). 1922. pp. 277–8

To see him you would think he was a village sorcerer. With his bald head, bronzed and battered like an old pot, his small, glittering, slanting eyes, his flat face and inflated nostrils, he looks with his short, sparse, harsh beard, like a Socrates without philosophy, and lacking in self command.

His appearance surprises and shocks. His air is at once wild and wheedling, savage and familiar. A natural Socrates, or better still, a faun or satyr, a being half beast and half god, which alarms one like some natural force unsubmissive to any known law.

Anatole France. *On Life and Letters: Third Series* (John Lane). 1922. p. 295

In all genius there is the child; Verlaine was a child on a colossal scale, with the child's eternal freshness, and the full endowment of those less innocent instincts which in some degree psychologists find to mark even the healthy normal child. A mass of living sensitive protoplasm open to every influence of Nature and humanity, he remained unconfined by that tough restricting hide which gives to most of us adults a certain stolid rigidity, a factitious indifference to our environment. He stood at the furthest remove from the pachyderms, more like those primitive molluscous creatures of the sea which zoologists have shown to be permeated all through by as yet undifferentiated and unprotected senses.

Havelock Ellis. *From Rousseau to Proust* (Houghton). 1935, p. 268

How many times have I seen him passing my door, furious, laughing, swearing, striking the ground with the thick stick of an invalid or menacing vagabond. How could one imagine that this tramp—at times so brutal in looks and speech, sordid, at once so disquieting and pathetic— might be the author of the most delicate poetic music, of the newest and most touching verbal melodies in our language? Every conceivable vice had respected, and perhaps sown, or developed in him, this power of suave invention, this expression of sweetness, of fervor, of tender meditation, that nobody else has been able to dissimulate or to cast the resources of a consummate art, skilled in all the subtleties of the most skillful poets, in works simple of appearance, naïve in tone, almost infantile.

Paul Valéry. *Variety: Second Series* (Harcourt). 1938.
pp. 26–7

To write poetry like English poetry in a language like French, which had been developed logically with the avowed intention of becoming an instrument of expression of the greatest clarity, was immensely difficult. To express under-tones and over-tones, hidden meanings, to attain the half-said thing, to make an appeal directly from one sensibility to an-other, was, in the language and in the existent metres, if not exactly an impossibility, at least a perplexing task. Consequently Verlaine's "Art of Poetry" . . . was accepted as a liberation; Verlaine, following Poe and Baudelaire, demanded in poetry *de la musique avant toute chose*—music above all—and he marched haughtily past the great French sign-posts demanding the *mot juste*.

Mary M. Colum. *From These Roots* (Columbia). 1944.
p. 324

Where he differed from other men was in the completeness of his sur-renders. No arrow grazed him. They all went to the heart. But none deadened him or quieted his suffering or, until very near the end, dulled his genius. Other men distinguish among the arrows, avoiding some, raising a shield against others. Verlaine did not distinguish because, as an artist, he desired intuitively to be struck again and again. As a man who desired peace, he ran away again and again. This was the relevance of his life to his art, and the tension between them.

Charles Morgan. *Reflections in a Mirror: Second Series*
(Macmillan). 1946. p. 163

Verlaine is entirely a natural poet, to be sure a very refined and complex one, knowing how to profit by influences, but spontaneous and immediate, profoundly original, and drawing his force from life itself. . . . He was born to bring to its perfection the intimate and sentimental lyricism founded by Marceline Desbordes-Valmore and Lamartine, and to dis-cover that tone of spoken poetry which belongs exclusively to him, suitable both for the unaffected prayer and for the whispered con-fidence, for the expression of harsh desire or tender effusion, a tone in which a certain "outline of subtle voice" always dies down in the end like a fleeting arabesque in a sonorous halo. With unequalled in-tensity this poetry evokes the music of everyday joys and sorrows, the sense of life, naked physiological life, in which thought is only a dream of the blood that sustains the flesh.

Marcel Raymond. *From Baudelaire to Surrealism* (Wittenborn). 1949. p. 22

The fact is that he has always had a special appeal for the English. Like Villon and Baudelaire, those other two bad boys, he seems to be immediately accessible. He is the perfect example of the toad with a jewel in its forehead. He can be thought of with comforting pity, because he was an ugly, bald little man whose private life was entirely disastrous; and his genius does not intimidate, being of a non-intellectual, almost childlike, spontaneity.

J. G. Weightman. *NSN*. Oct. 5, 1957. p. 438

He is not to be criticized for the fact that he is relatively superficial. It was part of a valid conception of poetry which he evolved to harmonize with his own temperament. He aimed at other effects than the effect in depth. His work marks the beginning of Symbolism, and if he is now more usually classed as an impressionist, in this instance the one led to the other. In any case, in spite of his openly personal and "intimate" style, he marks very clearly the end of Romanticism as poets from Lamartine to Hugo had conceived it. The *moi* in Verlaine no longer performs the same function as in them. It is more like the "I" in Marot, or even in La Fontaine.

Geoffrey Brereton. *An Introduction to the French Poets* (Essential Books). 1957. p. 174

Personal detachment from the statements and situations of the poems appears to us characteristic of at least part of Verlaine's many-toned poetic creation. . . . Verlaine's humor and irony serve to alienate him from the emotional situations of his poetry; this statement is especially true, in *Fêtes Galantes,* of love. By treating amorous relationships humorously, Verlaine dissociates himself from them, implying that he, too, is remote and unmoved. Humor stems from incongruous situations, often suggested by the comic possibilities of the *commedia dell' arte.*

Philip Stephan. *RR*. Oct., 1961. pp. 196, 199–200

Verlaine's interest in an objective beauty was fundamentally antiromantic. A full aesthetic dedication to the object of beauty implied a sacrifice of the self, for, no matter how completely or imperfectly one enjoyed beauty, it remained independent of one's faculties. To give

poetic form to such beauty meant to recognize this autonomy, and only
then, if one wished, could its relationship to personal faculties be investigated. The poet's first activity was a symbolic transformation of
plastic beauty into language by means of poetic image. If following this
came the implementation of beauty for the indulgence of the poet's
senses, this was only made possible by a prior establishment of beauty's
independence.

Paul Ilie. *CL*. Summer, 1962. p. 264

See *Selected Poems* and *The Sky Above the Roof* (poetry).

VITTORINI, ELIO (1908–1966)

Although *Conversation in Sicily* is written in the first person, it does not
strike one in the least as subjective. It is interesting to ask why Vittorini's hero. . . , sensitive to every change of light and shade, extremely
observant, and thus so different from the common run of humanity,
does not strike the reader in the least as a sensitive, a "Stephen Dae-
dalus," a "Herr Ishgroo" (of Isherwood's Berlin stories), a "Mrs.
Dalloway," or even as a Hemingway hero, so self-conscious of being
an ordinary guy.

The answer, I think, is that the whole of Vittorini's sensibility is
directed away from himself. His hero . . . is a very sensitive instrument,
combination of microphone and microscope. . . . Vittorini's . . . protest
against Fascism is to lay his magnifying instrument against the chest
of the victim of these times and show that the heart is still beating. Yes,
you gentlemen at Rome, you inventors of the atom bomb, you makers
of peace treaties, the victim for whom you are preparing these graves
is still alive. Listen to his heart. It is still beating. Indeed, the pulsation
is a roar, it is loud as a drum, universal as a Niagara fall, filling the Universe, the whole of humanity.

Stephen Spender. Introduction to Vittorini's *Conversation
in Sicily* (Lindsay Drummond). 1948. pp. 7–8

Elio Vittorini is one of the very best of the new Italian writers. . . . He
is not a regional writer, for Italy is certainly not a region, and Vittorini
. . . learned his Italy in the same way American boys who ran away from
home learned their own country.

The Italy he learned has little to do with the Academic Italy . . . that
periodically attacks all writing like a dust storm and is always, until
everything shall be completely dry, dispersed by rain. . . . I care nothing
about Vittorini's politics . . . but I care very much about his ability to

bring rain with him when he comes if the earth is dry and that is what you need.

Ernest Hemingway. Introduction to Vittorini's
In Sicily (New Directions). 1949. pp. 7–9

As for Mr. Vittorini's style, it is all tricks and devices, fanciness or fancy over-simplicity, ponderous whimsy, half-formulated statement, false poeticism. Inevitably we recognize the Saroyan-Steinbeck taint, and decide that here is merely an Italian version of our own all-too-current sentimentality about the superior virtue and sensibility of the poor and simple-minded.

But in a last chapter [of *In Sicily*] . . . Mr. Vittorini's novel is revealed to us in a wholly new light. A soft research into humanitarianism is transformed into a statement of firm biological faith such as the author of *In Sicily* might have learned, not from Saroyan or Steinbeck, but from D. H. Lawrence. . . . Apparently what [Ernest Hemingway] admires in Mr. Vittorini's performance is not its firm idea—of this he makes no mention [in his introduction]—but its ostensible distance from the life of intellection. . . . We refer Mr. Hemingway . . . to what is really the "rain" in Mr. Vittorini's novel—its deeply felt *idea*—and reject Mr. Hemingway's effort to assimilate *In Sicily* into the ranks of the irresponsibles.

Diana Trilling. *NYT*. Nov. 27, 1949. pp. 1, 37

It has sometimes been said that Vittorini is excessively influenced by American writing, especially by Hemingway and Steinbeck . . . and it is true that his dialogue now and then shows traces of the Hemingway manner, and much of his fiction is concerned with very simple people who are treated with a blend of humor and seriousness that for some readers may suggest Steinbeck's attitude in, for example, *Tortilla Flat*. But Vittorini's use of the Hemingway manner is only incidental, and his general style owes nothing to Hemingway. . . . And as for Steinbeck's influence, I can find no trace of it; certainly Vittorini's characters are not presented with the sentimental condescension that so often taints Steinbeck's work. All in all, whatever Vittorini has derived from his study of American literature he has quite fully absorbed and made a part of his own highly personal work.

Robert Penn Warren. *Nation*. Dec. 3, 1949. p. 548

One of the functions of the difficult or "hermetic" poetry and prose in the "dark years" in Italy was that of defense of language, of style, against the demagogical degradation to which it was officially exposed, a degradation which reflected the corresponding state of moral values. The more exclusive forms of literature, though accused of obscurity and emptiness, created a certain atmosphere of artistic integrity and also trained the literary practitioners in certain directions (restraint, intensity, and some sort of "illuminative imagination") which proved fruitful. . . . In some . . . writers such tendencies were increasingly combined with the influence of certain types of American writing. Vittorini's prose, perhaps most intensely in some of his short stories, is one of the prominent results of that alliance.

P. M. Pasinetti. *KR*. Autumn, 1950. p. 678

Among the "new" Italian writers Vittorini seems to have made the most determined effort to estimate the Fascist experience. Though not strictly allegorical, his novels tend toward allegory; and reveal a political mind of shrewdness and warmth, though of little experience or generalizing power. Neither tender like Berto nor sensual like Moravia, he creates ambiguous paradigms about life in an imaginary Italy which, like the real Italy, has been undermined by nihilism.

Irving Howe. *NR*. Aug. 4, 1952. p. 19

He is avant-garde in the true sense of the word; he is not a member of the avant-garde school or of any other school. He writes in an experimental idiom not because he seeks to startle, to shock, or to impress his readers but because he is driven by a profound necessity to find that kind of writing that is uniquely "his own." He is not, in the narrow sense of the word, an intellectual. He is the kind of writer frequently encountered in America but as yet rare in Europe: a writer who comes from the heart of the people and is totally independent of the academic literary tradition. . . . He wrote because he felt he had to, not because he moved in a literary society. Here the best comparison is perhaps with Faulkner; both are indifferent toward the academic tradition, and both are genuinely and spontaneously experimental in technique. . . . Vittorini is a writer with a deep sense of the seriousness of his métier, and he cannot write anything, even a personal letter, without committing himself to it totally.

Donald Heiney. *WHR*. Summer, 1955. pp. 197–8

Vittorini has . . . what Henry James called the imagination of disaster: a sensibility which, like a peculiarly delicate seismograph, can register the strirring of some human earthquake at enormous distances. . . .

Reality . . . in Vittorini's view . . . is a twofold affair. And it is perceived in its totality only when the immediate and historical reality becomes transformed or enlarged—through its vital relinking with the past—into what Vittorini calls "the greater reality."

Reality . . . is a key word for Vittorini and probably the crucial one for an approach to his fiction. It is by reality that his special sensitivity is so agitated; or, more accurately, it is the loss of reality which his psychic seismograph habitually registers—the loss of that higher reality as a result of erratic disturbances on the lower or historical level. To say so, obviously, is to modify rather sharply the usual characterization of his primary impulses in essentially political terms. . . . But the fact is that, like Silone, Vittorini is jolted less by politico-economic upheavals than by their effect upon—by the lesion they produce in—the sense of the real. And to heal that lesion, Vittorini believes (it is a belief he shares with André Malraux and Albert Camus), is a defining function of art: in his case, of the art of the novel.

R. W. B. Lewis. IQ. Fall, 1960. pp. 55–7

Fostered to distinguish the real from the sham, and to grow daily in an understanding of those truths man must grapple with if he is to stay free, he drew on what he knew of his own literature only insofar as it seemed to him strictly relevant to the problems of the present. He cut out those sinuous meanderings which, from Manzoni through D'Annunzio, had found varying ways to stifle fiction in a coil of words. Stripped to bedrock, his style strove for one thing: appropriateness for his time. . . . [For] Vittorini . . . the American moderns, Faulkner, Sherwood Anderson, Hemingway, Steinbeck . . . were the writers who belong to "the bloodline of those whom life will not tame, who will not adapt themselves." Here were the stylists Vittorini had been looking for.

Out of first reading, then . . . translating "the Americans," Vittorini began to forge his own Italian style.

Frances Keene. Introduction to The Dark and the Light
(New Directions). 1960. pp. vi–viii

Vittorini sought to form his own prose style on the model of Hemingway and other Americans he admired. During the Thirties, he "discovered" our literature, saw in it a means of renewing conventional Italian literary language. He translated many texts, published a comprehensive anthology (Americana), which did much to create an "American mythology" for young Italians. . . . He was instrumental in starting in Italy that vogue for our literature which at first was the clandestine passion of an avant-garde, but which, since the war, has become an accepted academic discipline.

John L. Brown. *NYT*. June 4, 1961. p. 5

The controlled rhythm of its prose, the agile pace of the whole narrative, and the beauty of the descriptions should persuade the reader that with Vittorini the novel, in Italy at least, has been brought back to poetry. . . . Like [his previous novels] . . . *"La Garibaldina"* [from *The Dark and the Light*] can hardly be called a conventional novel on thematic, stylistic, or structural counts. . . . What gives the tale its uniqueness is the manner in which the author turns into a symbolic tableau of the human condition a number of seemingly fantastic and preposterous "encounters" (where historical events are superimposed and chronology magically evaporates). Precisely because the events are sparse and relatively unimportant we grasp the fact that Vittorini's purpose is less to dramatize psychological or social situations as such than to give us a feeling of a great drama being enacted on the stage of twentieth-century history. . . . It is that of a society moving toward and desperately searching for universal fellowship and a life of dignity, peace, and work. . . . Vittorini has been true to what he considers the task of literature, that "of making visible the human motives of a revolution." He has also demonstrated, in his own brilliant way, how novelists, and not politicians, are the true barometers of their age.

Sergio Pacifici. *SR*. Aug. 19, 1961. p. 17

Hemingway's technique, devised to carry the impression of actual life by reproducing word by word a dialogue of short sentences, becomes in Vittorini a mannerism, because he is not such an impassive onlooker and listener as Hemingway, but invests everything with a lyrical mood, or merely with a rhetorical emphasis. The effect is very curious. Starting from Hemingway, Vittorini comes near certain effects of Charles Péguy, whose exasperating repetitions give the impression of a person seized with the symptoms of general paralysis. Péguy had caught the rhythm of peasants' talk, and tried to couch it in an artistic pattern; Vittorini does the same with the talk of the man in the street. But Hemingway never tries to impose a pattern on his dialogues: hence their impression of freshness, even in monotony. Thus the lesson of simplicity and directness of Hemingway has been lost on a writer hopelessly predisposed to mannerism.

Mario Praz. *The Literary Reputation of Hemingway in Europe*, ed. by Roger Asselineau (Lettres Modernes). 1965. pp. 116–7

See *In Sicily, The Red Carnation,* and *The Twilight of the Elephant* (novels); also *The Dark and the Light* (two short novels).

VOLPONI, PAOLO (1924–   )

Paolo Volponi's beautifully written novel . . . is one of the finest and most important books to have appeared in Italy over the past decade. Seemingly a novel of protest, *My Troubles Began* may be read in various ways: as a pathetic account of a workingman's grievances against an economic order that has enslaved him to a robotlike existence, as a poetic dramatization of the malaise of our technological society that psychologists call alienation, or as a hauntingly accurate portrayal of a paranoid mind. . . . "Mother Factory," in whom the hero had placed his hopes for a tranquil and meaningful existence, thinking that she possessed the instruments to resolve the problems of the human predicament, fails [him]. . . . The factory where he had sought order, harmony, and security, reveals itself to be a source of disorder, disharmony, and insecurity—an apt symbol of the chaos of human relations and of the absurdity of life.

Sergio Pacifici. *SR*. Jan. 9, 1965. p. 54

This young Italian poet's first novel seems calculated to irritate more readers than it will attract by its rarefied atmosphere, flimsy narrative, and eccentric narrator. The same thing could, of course, be said about *Notes from Underground* and *The Voyeur,* and the reader who is put off by such warnings is depriving himself of an uncommon literary experience. . . . *My Troubles Began* is not another soul-as-assembly-line protest. Patently paranoiac, the narrator chillingly readjusts our view of social assistance, medical-care programs, and industrial paternalism. Only Dostoyevsky and Poe have transposed the audience so convincingly and so terrifying into an unbalanced mind or made antilogy so persuasive. Everything is in character, even the corrosively personal poems that end the book. . . . This is an amazing novel with no resolution but hopelessness and a glazed, inescapable stare.

James Frakes. *NYHT*. Jan. 17, 1965. p. 18

Deprivation [of love] makes this almost the pure novel of "love or death"—not love as sexual freedom, nor as Christian charity, but love as it confirms the bond of blood that binds brother to brother. . . . There is as little overt Freudianism in Volponi as there is in Simone Weil, a comparison Claude Mauriac drew when he reviewed the French edition of this book. Moravia, who led the chorus of critical praise for *Memoriale* [*My Troubles Began*] in Italy, found its qualities best communicated by reference to the young Dostoevsky. That true compassion flows only from insights that are love's special attributes, and that to be without love is to be separated from all that can keep a man sane, is not an unusual theme. But to have its retelling from Volponi, whose position [administering an industrial social assistance program] gives him command of a stage on which the tragedy . . . may be enacted, is to have it with the force of a confession that may be the author's catharsis. . . . The disciplines learned in creating poetry are clearly at work here: the images from which the reader draws his own symbols, the accretion of metaphor that builds feeling, the fugue-like progress of the tensions that mount slowly to their signalled climax, and the unity, as in a poem, of a single voice. . . . It is with the poet's craft, and with his own personal feeling of universal guilt, that Volponi has made . . . [this] story into literature.

Merlyn S. Pitzele. PR. Spring, 1965. pp. 311–2

Paolo Volponi's <i>Memoriale</i> [<i>My Troubles Began</i>] was welcomed enthusiastically by the more disaffected Italian novelist-critics. . . . Impressive as it certainly is, a major text in modern Italian industrial psychology and sociology, written with a dark, systematic economy so alien to most of our fictional prejudices that even at its modern best, in Kafka, it is likely to win more respect than affection over here. Volponi is considerably more a naturalist than Kafka, but only because he has so well absorbed the Kafkaesque spirit and used it as a modern Italian Kafka would and should, to attack the new north-Italian phenomenon of <i>neocapitalismo</i> (welfare industrialism) that is fantastic enough in itself not to need much additional fantasy from a good novelist. . . . This is strong dark stuff, brewed from the pure essences of Piedmontese gloom. . . . Volponi's [hero] is . . . a particularly gifted and stubborn spokesman for the old European humanistic mind, hurling against the raw new industrialism every humane and poetic objection that Svevo leveled against the bourgeois dullness of Trieste.

R. W. Flint. NYR. April 22, 1965. p. 25

See <i>My Troubles Began</i> (novel).

WEIL, SIMONE (1909–1943)

One thinks finally of Don Quixote, of Melville's Pierre, of the tragic buffoons who can never keep our time because they are set by the eternal chronometer of the Holy Fool, whose wisdom is an unforeseen power of what we call stupidity, the ridiculous raised to the level of the ultimate, divine, absurd. . . . The absurdity, the absolutism, the incandescence of the prophets survive in Simone Weil, and for all her blemishes, their terrible purity.

Leslie Fiedler. Cmty. Jan., 1951. pp. 39, 46

What makes us in the end unwilling to accept her claims? What is it that more often than not distorts her genuine love of truth? . . . She claims too much (St. Joan heard rightly when she was told to tell no one of her visions), and sometimes too stridently. She talks of suffering "atrocious pain" for others, "those who are indifferent or unknown to me. . . ," and it is almost as if a comic character from Dickens were speaking. We want to say, "Don't go so far so quickly. Suffer first for someone you know and love," but love in these pages is only a universal love.

Graham Greene. NSN. Oct. 6, 1951. p. 374

When she reviews and interprets the modern political history of France, or when she lists the needs of the soul of man, needs which must be taken into account in any social planning, what she has to say is of immense importance and should be studied with care, for it is beautifully penetrating and balanced. Her specific recommendations are not by any means always so, however.

Nor is the over-all impression to be gained of her mind, for all her brilliance, one of balance. Her thinking is sometimes idiosyncratic in the extreme, displaying a lack of objectivity that seems almost willful, and some of her outbursts are so emotional as to be almost altogether untrustworthy.

S. M. Fitzgerald. NR. Aug. 18, 1952. p. 18

I cannot conceive of anybody's agreeing with all her views, or of not disagreeing violently with some of them. But agreement and rejection are secondary: what matters is to make contact with a great soul.

490

Simone Weil is one who might have become a saint. Like some who have achieved this state, she had greater obstacles to overcome as well as greater strength for overcoming them, than the rest of us. A potential saint can be a very difficult person: I suspect that Simone Weil could be at times insupportable. One is struck, here and there, by a contrast between an almost superhuman humility and what appears to be an almost outrageous arrogance.

T. S. Eliot. Preface to *The Need for Roots* (Routledge).
1952. p. iv

The personality which emerges from these writings is not always attractive, but it compels respect. She is sometimes unbalanced and scarcely accurate. . . . She seems at times almost too ready to embrace evil and to love God as its author; many find a repellant and self-destructive quality in her austerity. . . . Yet the other side of this is the sense of a profoundly disciplined life behind her writings: the union of a passionate search for truth with a simplicity and austerity of personal living, which gives to what she writes an authority which cannot be imitated. She is one who, like Kierkegaard's "subjective thinker," does not simply convey information, but is most properly to be understood as an example.

Iris Murdoch. *Spec*. Nov. 2, 1956. p. 614

The hair's breadth which separates Simone Weil's philosophy from vulgar determinism is the mysterious factor, among all the others which acted upon her, which compelled her to face . . . ultimate tests and to challenge the stony-hearted egoism which she perceived everywhere, and in herself, so much more clearly than most of us dare to do. This is the mysterious factor which compels the fool to persist in his folly until he becomes wise and makes it true that he who endures to the end shall be saved. It is strange, but it is a fact, that Simone Weil, for all her unrelenting realism, was martyrised by compassion not only for the suffering in the world around her but even for the sufferings of slaves in the distant past. It is surely no exaggeration to say that her place is with the heroes and geniuses who incarnate the conscience of the human race.

Richard Rees. *Brave Men* (Gollancz). 1958. pp. 209–10

She was a fantastically dedicated participant in the most crucial experiences of our time, who tried to live them directly in contact with the supernatural. Her real interest for us lies less in what she said than in the direction of her work, in the particular vision she tried to reach by the whole manner of her life. What she sought more than anything else was a loving attentiveness to all the living world that would lift man above the natural loneliness of existence. . . . When a French apprentice who is new on a job complains that the work hurts him, the older men usually say that "the trade is entering his body." This saying, which Simone Weil picked up in the Renault factory, had a special pathos for her. It expressed her belief that there is a particular closeness we can reach with the world, that the truth is always something to be lived.

> Alfred Kazin. *The Inmost Leaf* (Noonday). 1959.
> pp. 211–3

In her last years Simone Weil seems to have sought enlightenment by a systematic cultivation of maximum hypertension. Her thought proceeded by no other way than paradox. This is not new. . . . But there is a tension of life and a tension of death. Simone Weil was a dying girl. Hers was a spastic, moribund, intellectual, and spiritual agony. We can sympathize with it, be moved to tears by it, much as we are by the last awful lunacies of Antonin Artaud, but we imitate it, allow it to infect us, at our peril. This is a Kierkegaard who refuses to leap. *Angst* for *angst*'s sake. Anguish is not enough. When it is made an end in itself it takes on a holy, or unholy folly.

> Kenneth Rexroth. *Assays* (New Directions). 1961. p. 199

What else can we do, however uneasy or inferior we feel, but admire her passionate, sometimes maladroit devotion to the working class, her intense and unsectarian religious zeal, her capacity for self-denial, her attempt to convert pain into something wholly fruitful, her brilliant disruptive mind and painstakingly trenchant prose, her audacity in teaching the young, her almost peasant simplicity in aphorism, her refusal to defer to evil wherever she found it, her will, her guts, her crabbed truthfulness? We admire, but with a hunch that much of it amounts to a frenetic displacement of womanhood. Something crackpot emerges alongside what is her evident genius and her almost pernicious goodness.

> Paul West. *Nation.* April 19, 1965. p. 422

See *Need for Roots, Notebooks,* and *Selected Essays (1934–1943).*

INDEX TO CRITICS